# A Glossary of Literary Terms

## NINTH EDITION

**M. H. ABRAMS**
*Cornell University*

**Geoffrey Galt Harpham**
*National Humanities Center*

WADSWORTH
CENGAGE Learning

Australia • Brazil • Japan • Korea • Mexico • Singapore • Spain
United Kingdom • United States

**WADSWORTH**
CENGAGE Learning

**A Glossary of Literary Terms,
Ninth Edition**
M. H. Abrams, Geoffrey
Galt Harpham

Publisher: Michael Rosenberg

Managing Development Editor:
Karen Judd

Senior Editorial Assistant:
Megan Garvey

Content Project Manager:
Jessica Rasile

Production Technology Analyst:
Jamison MacLachlan

Senior Art Director:
Cate Rickard Barr

Senior Print Buyer: Betsy Donaghey

Text Permissions Editor: Margaret
Chamberlain-Gaston

Production Service/Compositor:
Newgen

Cover Design: Ross Carron Design

For product information and technology
assistance, contact us at
**Cengage Learning Academic Resource Center,
1-800-423-0563**

For permission to use material from this text or
product, submit all requests online at
**www.cengage.com/permissions**.
Further permissions questions can be
e-mailed to
**permissionrequest@cengage.com**.

Library of Congress Control Number: 2008924505

ISBN-13: 978-1-4130-3390-8

ISBN-10: 1-4130-3390-3

**Wadsworth Cengage Learning**
25 Thomson Place
Boston, MA 02210
USA

Cengage Learning products are represented in
Canada by Nelson Education, Ltd.

For your course and learning solutions, visit
**academic.cengage.com**.

Purchase any of our products at your local college
store or at our preferred online store
**www.ichapters.com**.

Printed in Canada
1  2  3  4  5  6  7  12  11  10  09  08

*To Ruth*

# About the Authors

**M. H. Abrams,** Class of 1916 Professor of English at Cornell University, Emeritus, is a distinguished scholar who has written prize-winning books on eighteenth- and nineteenth-century literature, literary theory and criticism, European Romanticism, and Western intellectual history. His *A Glossary of Literary Terms* is a series of succinct essays on the chief terms and concepts used in discussing literature, literary history and movements, and literary criticism. Since first published in 1957, the *Glossary* has become an indispensable handbook for all students of English and other literatures.

**Geoffrey Galt Harpham** is president and director of the National Humanities Center in North Carolina. He has written extensively in the fields of intellectual history and critical theory, and on the work of Joseph Conrad. Among his books are *The Character of Criticism, Shadows of Ethics: Criticism and the Just Society*, and *Language Alone: The Critical Fetish of Modernity*.

# Contents

# Preface

This book defines and discusses terms, critical theories, and points of view that are commonly applied in classifying, analyzing, interpreting, and writing the history of works of literature. The component entries, together with the guides to further reading included in most of them, are oriented especially toward undergraduate students of English, American, and other literatures. Over the decades, however, the book has proved to be a useful and popular work of reference for advanced students, as well as for the general reader with literary interests.

*A Glossary of Literary Terms* consists of succinct essays in the alphabetic order of the title word or phrase. Terms that are related but subsidiary, or that designate subclasses, are discussed under the title heading of the primary or generic term; in addition, words that are often used in conjunction, or as mutually defining contraries, are discussed in the same essay. The alternative organization of a literary handbook as a dictionary of terms, defined singly, makes dull reading and requires excessive repetition and cross-indexing. It may also be misleading, because the application of many terms becomes clear only in the context of other terms and concepts to which they are related, subordinated, or opposed. The essay form also makes it feasible to supplement the definition of a literary term with indications of its changes in meaning over time, and of its diversity of meanings in current usage, in order to help readers steer their way through the shifting references and submerged ambiguities of its varied applications. In addition, the discursive treatment of literary terms provides an opportunity to write entries that are not only informative, but pleasurable to read. In each entry, **boldface** identifies terms for which the entry provides the principal discussion, and *italics* indicate terms that are discussed more fully elsewhere in the *Glossary*.

The purpose of this new edition is to keep the entries current with innovations in critical views and methods, to take into account important new publications in literature, criticism, and scholarship, and also to take advantage of suggestions for improvements and additions, some solicited by the publisher and others volunteered by users of the *Glossary*. All the entries have been reviewed, and most of them have been revised in order to clarify or add verve to the exposition, but above all, to bring the entries up to date in their substance, their references, and their lists of suggested readings. Books originally published in languages other than English are listed in their English translation.

Mainly in response to requests by readers, 24 terms have been added in this edition of the *Glossary*. Especially notable are substantial new essays on the *book, book history studies, Darwinian literary studies*, and the concept of the *fine arts*. The book now encompasses discussions of more than 1,150 literary terms.

The aim of this new version of the *Glossary* remains the one announced by its author in the first edition: to produce the kind of handbook he would have found most valuable when, as an undergraduate, he was an eager but sometimes bewildered student of literature and literary criticism.

# Acknowledgments

This edition, like preceding ones, has profited greatly from the suggestions of both teachers and students who proposed changes and additions that would enhance the usefulness of the *Glossary* to the broad range of courses in American, English, and other literatures. The following teachers, at the request of the publisher, made many useful proposals for improvements:

Michael Sharp, *Binghamton University*
Roxanne Eberle, *The University of Georgia*
Richard Frost, *State University College, Oneonta, NY*
Norbert Schürer, *California State University, Long Beach*
John H. O'Neill, *Hamilton College*
Jonathan Gross, *DePaul University*
J. Caitlin Finlayson, *University of Texas at Dallas*
Dr. Kim Stone, *Illinois State University*
Kerry L. Johnson, *Merrimack College*

As in many earlier editions, Dianne Ferriss has been indispensable in preparing, correcting, and recording the text of the *Glossary*. Michael Rosenberg, Publisher at Cengage Learning, continues to be an enthusiastic supporter of each new edition. Karen Judd has helped tremendously in her role as Managing Development Editor, Jessica Rasile ensured that the production process went smoothly, and Sharon Grant performed her usual professional job of copyediting the manuscript.

# How to Use This Glossary

To expedite reference to a literary term, this edition has merged the former *Index of Terms* with the entries that make up the text of the book. The reader will now find, in a single alphabetic listing, all the terms discussed in the *Glossary*. Each term that is not itself the subject of the entry it identifies is followed, in **boldface**, by the number of the page in which it is defined and discussed. This is followed by the page numbers, in *italics*, of the occurrences of the term in other entries, in contexts that clarify its significance and illustrate how it is used in critical discourse; in the text of these entries, the term itself is italicized.

Some of the listed terms are supplemented by references to a number of closely related terms. These references expedite for a student the fuller exploration of a literary topic, and make it easier for a teacher to locate entries that serve the needs of a particular subject of study. For example, supplementary references list entries that identify the various types and movements of literary *criticism*, the terms most relevant to the analysis of *style*, the entries that define and exemplify the various literary *genres*, and the many entries that deal with the forms, component features, history, and critical discussions of the *drama*, *lyric*, and *novel*.

Those terms, mainly of foreign origin, that are most likely to be mispronounced by a student are followed (in parentheses) by a simplified guide to pronunciation. The following vowel markings are used:

|   |   |   |   |
|---|---|---|---|
| ā | (fate) | ĭ | (pin) |
| ă | (pat) | ō | (rope) |
| ä | (father) | ŏ | (pot) |
| ē | (meet) | oo | (food) |
| ĕ | (get) | ŭ | (cut) |
| ī | (pine) | | |

Authors and their works that are discussed in the *Glossary* are listed in an *Index of Authors* at the end of this volume. To make it easy to locate, the outer edges of the *Index* are colored gray.

# A Glossary of Literary Terms

# Literary Terms

**abstract** (language): **54**.

**absurd, literature of the:** The term is applied to a number of works in drama and prose fiction which have in common the view that the human condition is essentially absurd, and that this condition can be adequately represented only in works of literature that are themselves absurd. Both the mood and dramaturgy of absurdity were anticipated as early as 1896 in Alfred Jarry's French play *Ubu roi* (*Ubu the King*). The literature has its roots also in the movements of *expressionism* and *surrealism*, as well as in the fiction, written in the 1920s, of Franz Kafka (*The Trial, Metamorphosis*). The current movement, however, emerged in France after the horrors of World War II (1939–45) as a rebellion against basic beliefs and values in traditional culture and literature. This tradition had included the assumptions that human beings are fairly rational creatures who live in an at least partially intelligible universe, that they are part of an ordered social structure, and that they may be capable of heroism and dignity even in defeat. After the 1940s, however, there was a widespread tendency, especially prominent in the *existential philosophy* of men of letters such as Jean-Paul Sartre and Albert Camus, to view a human being as an isolated existent who is cast into an alien universe; to conceive the human world as possessing no inherent truth, value, or meaning; and to represent human life—in its fruitless search for purpose and significance, as it moves from the nothingness whence it came toward the nothingness where it must end—as an existence which is both anguished and absurd. As Camus said in *The Myth of Sisyphus* (1942),

> In a universe that is suddenly deprived of illusions and of light, man feels a stranger. His is an irremediable exile. . . . This divorce between man and his life, the actor and his setting, truly constitutes the feeling of Absurdity.

Or as Eugène Ionesco, French author of *The Bald Soprano* (1949), *The Lesson* (1951), and other plays in the **theater of the absurd**, has put it: "Cut off from his religious, metaphysical, and transcendental roots, man is lost; all his actions become senseless, absurd, useless." Ionesco also said, in commenting on the mixture of moods in the literature of the absurd: "People drowning in meaninglessness can only be grotesque, their sufferings can only appear tragic by derision."

Samuel Beckett (1906–89), the most eminent and influential writer in this mode, both in drama and in prose fiction, was an Irishman living in Paris who often wrote in French and then translated his works into English. His plays, such as *Waiting for Godot* (1954) and *Endgame* (1958), project the irrationalism, helplessness, and absurdity of life in dramatic forms that reject realistic settings, logical reasoning, or a coherently evolving plot. *Waiting for Godot* presents two tramps in a waste place, fruitlessly and all but hopelessly waiting for an unidentified person, Godot, who may or may not exist and with whom they sometimes think they remember that they may have an appointment; as one of them remarks, "Nothing happens, nobody comes, nobody goes, it's awful." Like most works in this mode, the play is absurd in the double sense that it is grotesquely comic and also irrational and nonconsequential; it is a parody not only of the traditional assumptions of Western culture, but of the conventions and generic forms of traditional drama, and even of its own inescapable participation in the dramatic medium. The lucid but eddying and pointless dialogue is often funny, and pratfalls and other modes of slapstick are used to give a comic cast to the alienation and anguish of human existence. Beckett's prose fiction, such as *Malone Dies* (1958) and *The Unnamable* (1960), presents an *antihero* who plays out the absurd moves of the end game of civilization in a nonwork which tends to undermine the coherence of its medium, language itself. But typically Beckett's characters carry on, even if in a life without purpose, trying to make sense of the senseless and to communicate the uncommunicable.

Another French playwright of the absurd was Jean Genet (who combined absurdism and diabolism); some of the early dramatic works of the Englishman Harold Pinter and the American Edward Albee are written in a similar mode. The early plays of Tom Stoppard, such as *Rosencrantz and Guildenstern Are Dead* (1966) and *Travesties* (1974), exploit the devices of absurdist theater more for comic than philosophical ends. There are also affinities with this movement in the numerous recent works which exploit **black comedy** or **black humor**: baleful, naive, or inept characters in a fantastic or nightmarish modern world play out their roles in what Ionesco called a "tragic farce," in which the events are often simultaneously comic, horrifying, and absurd. Examples are Joseph Heller's *Catch-22* (1961), Thomas Pynchon's *V* (1963), John Irving's *The World According to Garp* (1978), and some of the novels by the German Günter Grass and the Americans Kurt Vonnegut, Jr., and John Barth. Stanley Kubrick's *Dr. Strangelove* (1964) is an example of black comedy in the cinema. Some playwrights living in totalitarian regimes used absurdist techniques to register social and political protest. See, for example, *Largo Desolato* (1987) by the Czech Vaclav Havel and *The Island* (1973), a collaboration by the South African writers Athol Fugard, John Kani, and Winston Ntshona.

See also *wit, humor, and the comic,* and refer to: Martin Esslin, *The Theatre of the Absurd* (rev. 1968); David Grossvogel, *The Blasphemers: The Theatre of Brecht,*

*Ionesco, Beckett, Genet* (1965); Arnold P. Hinchliffe, *The Absurd* (1969); Max F. Schultz, *Black Humor Fiction of the Sixties* (1980); and Enoch Brater and Ruby Cohn, eds., *Around the Absurd: Essays on Modern and Postmodern Drama* (1990).

For references to the *literature of the absurd* in other entries, see pages *14, 44, 166, 203.*

**absurd, theater of the:** **1**; *373.*

**accent** (in meter): **194**.

**accentual meter: 194**.

**accentual-syllabic meter: 194**.

**accentual verse: 198**.

**accidie** (ak′ sidē): **330**.

**act and scene:** An **act** is a major division in the action of a *play*. In England this division was introduced by Elizabethan dramatists, who imitated ancient Roman plays by structuring the action into five acts. Late in the nineteenth century a number of writers followed the example of Chekhov and Ibsen by constructing plays in four acts. In the twentieth century the most common form for traditional nonmusical dramas has been three acts.

Acts are often subdivided into **scenes**, which in modern plays usually consist of units of action in which there is no change of place or break in the continuity of time. (Some recent plays dispense with the division into acts and are structured as a sequence of scenes, or episodes.) In the conventional theater with a **proscenium arch** that frames the front of the stage, the end of a scene is usually indicated by a dropped curtain or a dimming of the lights, and the end of an act by a dropped curtain and an intermission.

**action: 42**.

**adversarius** (adversär′ īus): **320**.

**aesthetic distance: 83**; *210.* See also *empathy and sympathy.*

**Aesthetic ideology:** Aesthetic ideology was a term applied by the *deconstructive* theorist Paul de Man, in his later writings, to describe the "seductive" appeal of *aesthetic* experience, in which, he claimed, form and meaning, perception and understanding, and cognition and desire are misleadingly, and sometimes dangerously, conflated. Such a conflation, he held, is manifested in some formulations of Nazi politics as an artful remaking of the state. In de Man's view, the concept of the aesthetic came to stand for all *organicist* approaches not only to art, but to politics and culture as well. The experience of literature, he argued, minimizes the temptation of aesthetic ideology to confuse sensory experience with understanding, since literature represents the world in such a way that neither meaning nor sense-experience is directly perceptible. (See Marc Redfield, *Phantom Formations: Aesthetic Ideology and the Bildungsroman,* 1996.)

In *The Ideology of the Aesthetic* (1990), the *Marxist* theorist Terry Eagleton presented a history and *critique* of "the aesthetic," noting the many "ideological" perversions and distortions of the concept. Originally articulated in terms of freedom and pleasure, and therefore possessing an "emancipatory" potential for humankind, the aesthetic has often been appropriated by the political right so as to represent the essence of a reactionary ideology, which works most efficiently when it seems not to be working at all. (See *ideology* under *Marxist criticism*, and for essays on this subject, refer to George Levine, ed., *Aesthetics and Ideology*, 1994.)

**aesthetic movement: 4**.

**Aestheticism:** In his Latin treatise entitled *Aesthetica* (1750), the German philosopher Alexander Baumgarten applied the term "aesthetica" to the arts, of which "the aesthetic end is the perfection of sensuous cognition, as such; this is beauty." In present usage, **aesthetics** (from the Greek, "pertaining to sense perception") designates the systematic study of all the *fine arts*, as well as of the nature of beauty in any object, whether natural or artificial.

**Aestheticism**, or alternatively the **aesthetic movement**, was a European phenomenon during the latter part of the nineteenth century that had its chief headquarters in France. In opposition to the dominance of scientific thinking, and in defiance of the widespread indifference or hostility of the middle-class society of their time to any art that was not useful or did not teach moral values, French writers developed the view that a work of art is the supreme value among human products precisely because it is self-sufficient and has no use or moral aim outside its own being. The end of a work of art is simply to exist in its formal perfection; that is, to be beautiful and to be contemplated as an end in itself. A rallying cry of Aestheticism became the phrase "l'art pour l'art"—**art for art's sake**.

The historical roots of Aestheticism are in the views proposed by the German philosopher Immanuel Kant in his *Critique of Judgment* (1790), that the "pure" aesthetic experience consists of a "disinterested" contemplation of an object that "pleases for its own sake," without reference to reality or to the "external" ends of utility or morality. As a self-conscious movement, however, French Aestheticism is often said to date from Théophile Gautier's witty defense of his assertion that art is useless (preface to *Mademoiselle de Maupin*, 1835). Aestheticism was developed by Baudelaire, who was greatly influenced by Edgar Allan Poe's claim (in "The Poetic Principle," 1850) that the supreme work is a "poem *per se*," a "poem written solely for the poem's sake"; it was later taken up by Flaubert, Mallarmé, and many other writers. In its extreme form, the aesthetic doctrine of art for art's sake veered into the moral and quasi-religious doctrine of life for art's sake, or of life conducted as a work of art, with the artist represented as a priest who renounces the practical concerns of worldly existence in the service of what Flaubert and others called "the religion of beauty."

The views of French Aestheticism were introduced into Victorian England by Walter Pater, with his emphasis on high artifice and stylistic subtlety, his recommendation to crowd one's life with exquisite sensations, and his advocacy of the supreme value of beauty and of "the love of art for its own sake." (See his Conclusion to *The Renaissance*, 1873.) The artistic and moral views of Aestheticism were also expressed by Algernon Charles Swinburne and by English writers of the 1890s such as Oscar Wilde, Arthur Symons, and Lionel Johnson, as well as by the artists J. M. Whistler and Aubrey Beardsley. The influence of ideas stressed in Aestheticism—especially the view of the "autonomy" (self-sufficiency) of a work of art, the emphasis on craft and artistry, and the concept of a poem or novel as an end in itself, or as invested with "intrinsic" values—has been important in the writings of prominent twentieth-century authors such as W. B. Yeats, T. E. Hulme, and T. S. Eliot, as well as in the literary theory of the *New Critics*.

For related developments, see *aesthetic ideology, decadence, fine arts,* and *ivory tower.* Refer to: William Gaunt, *The Aesthetic Adventure* (1945, reprinted 1975); Frank Kermode, *Romantic Image* (1957); Enid Starkie, *From Gautier to Eliot* (1960); R. V. Johnson, *Aestheticism* (1969). For the intellectual and social conditions during the eighteenth century that fostered the theory, derived from theology, that a work of art is an end in itself, see M. H. Abrams, "Art-as-Such: The Sociology of Modern Aesthetics," in *Doing Things with Texts: Essays in Criticism and Critical Theory* (1989). Useful collections of writings in the Aesthetic Movement are Eric Warner and Graham Hough, eds., *Strangeness and Beauty: An Anthology of Aesthetic Criticism 1848–1910* (2 vols., 1983); Sally Ledger and Roger Luckhurst, eds., *The Fin de Siècle: A Reader in Cultural History, c. 1880–1900* (2000). A useful descriptive guide to books on the subject is Linda C. Dowling, *Aestheticism and Decadence: A Selective Annotated Bibliography* (1977). In recent years, the concepts of the aesthetic and of beauty have been revisited, often in a spirit of renewed appreciation, by philosophers and literary critics alike. See George Levine, ed., *Aesthetics and Ideology* (1994); Elaine Scarry, *On Beauty and Being Just* (1999); Arthur C. Danto, *The Abuse of Beauty: Aesthetics and the Concept of Art* (2003); Jonathan Loesberg, *A Return to Aesthetics: Autonomy, Indifference, and Postmodernism* (2005); Denis Donoghue, *Speaking of Beauty* (2003); John Armstrong, *The Secret Power of Beauty* (2004); and Susan Stewart, *The Open Studio: Essays on Art and Aesthetics* (2005). Berys Gaut and Dominic McIver Lopes, eds., *The Routledge Companion to Aesthetics* (2d ed., 2005) is a useful collection of historical and descriptive essays on the aesthetic. A comprehensive reference work is Michael Kelly, ed., *Encyclopedia of Aesthetics*, 4 vols. (1998).

For references to *Aestheticism* in other entries, see pages *68, 83, 123, 169, 183.*

**aesthetics: 4;** *83.*

**affective fallacy:** In an essay published in 1946, W. K. Wimsatt and Monroe C. Beardsley defined the affective fallacy as the error of evaluating a poem by its effects—especially its emotional effects—upon the reader. As a result of this fallacy "the poem itself, as an object of specifically critical judgment, tends to disappear," so that criticism "ends in impressionism and relativism." The two critics wrote in direct reaction to the view of I. A. Richards, in his influential *Principles of Literary Criticism* (1923), that the value of a poem can be measured by the psychological responses it incites in its readers. Beardsley later modified the earlier claim by the admission that "it does not appear that critical evaluation can be done at all except in relation to certain types of effect that aesthetic objects have upon their perceivers." So altered, the doctrine becomes a claim for *objective criticism*, in which the critic, instead of describing the effects of a work, focuses on the features, devices, and form of the work by which such effects are achieved. An extreme reaction against the doctrine of the affective fallacy was manifested during the 1970s in the development of *reader-response criticism*.

Refer to: Wimsatt and Beardsley, "The Affective Fallacy," reprinted in W. K. Wimsatt, *The Verbal Icon* (1954); and Monroe C. Beardsley, *Aesthetics: Problems in the Philosophy of Criticism* (1958), p. 491 and chapter 11. See also Wimsatt and Beardsley's related concept of the *intentional fallacy*.

**affective stylistics: 301**.

**African–American writers: 246**; *27, 223, 247, 250*. See *Black Arts Movement; Harlem Renaissance; performance poetry; slave narratives; spirituals*.

**Age of Johnson: 254**.

**Age of Sensibility: 254**.

**Age of Transcendentalism: 246**.

**Agrarians: 249**.

**agroikos** (ăgroi′ kŏs): **343**.

**alazon** (ăl′ ăzŏn): **343**; *165*.

**Alexandrine** (alexan′ drīn): **196**; *342*.

**alienation effect:** In his *epic theater* of the 1920s and later, the German dramatist Bertolt Brecht adapted the *Russian formalist* concept of "defamiliarization" into what he called the "alienation effect" (*Verfremdungseffekt*). The German term is also translated as **estrangement effect** or **distancing effect**; the last is closest to Brecht's notion, in that it avoids the negative connotations of jadedness, incapacity to feel, and social apathy that the word "alienation" has acquired in English. This effect, Brecht said, is used by the dramatist to make familiar aspects of the present social reality seem strange, so as to prevent the emotional identification or involvement of the audience with the characters and their actions in a play. His aim was instead to evoke a critical distance and attitude in the spectators, in order to arouse them to take action against, rather than simply to accept, the state of society and behavior represented on the stage.

On Brecht, refer to *Marxist criticism*; for a related aesthetic concept, see *distance and involvement*.

**allegorical imagery: 7**.

**allegorical interpretation** (of the Bible): **163**.

**allegory:** An allegory is a narrative, whether in prose or verse, in which the agents and actions, and sometimes the setting as well, are contrived by the author to make coherent sense on the "literal," or primary, level of signification, and at the same time to communicate a second, correlated order of signification.

We can distinguish two main types: (1) Historical and political allegory, in which the characters and actions that are signified literally in their turn represent, or "allegorize," historical personages and events. So in John Dryden's *Absalom and Achitophel* (1681), the biblical King David represents Charles II of England, Absalom represents his natural son the Duke of Monmouth, and the biblical story of Absalom's rebellion against his father (2 Samuel 13–18) allegorizes the rebellion of Monmouth against King Charles. (2) The allegory of ideas, in which the literal characters represent concepts and the plot allegorizes an abstract doctrine or thesis. Both types of allegory may either be sustained throughout a work, as in *Absalom and Achitophel* and John Bunyan's *The Pilgrim's Progress* (1678), or else serve merely as an episode in a nonallegorical work. A famed example of episodic allegory is the encounter of Satan with his daughter Sin, as well as with Death—who is represented allegorically as the son born of their incestuous relationship—in John Milton's *Paradise Lost*, Book II (1667).

In the second type, the sustained allegory of ideas, the central device is the *personification* of abstract entities such as virtues, vices, states of mind, modes of life, and types of character. In explicit allegories, such reference is specified by the names given to characters and places. Thus Bunyan's *The Pilgrim's Progress* allegorizes the Christian doctrine of salvation by telling how the character named Christian, warned by Evangelist, flees the City of Destruction and makes his way laboriously to the Celestial City; en route he encounters characters with names like Faithful, Hopeful, and the Giant Despair, and passes through places like the Slough of Despond, the Valley of the Shadow of Death, and Vanity Fair. A passage from this work indicates the nature of an explicit allegorical narrative:

> Now as Christian was walking solitary by himself, he espied one afar
> off come crossing over the field to meet him; and their hap was to
> meet just as they were crossing the way of each other. The
> Gentleman's name was Mr. Worldly-Wiseman; he dwelt in the Town
> of Carnal-Policy, a very great Town, and also hard by from whence
> Christian came.

Works which are primarily nonallegorical may introduce **allegorical imagery** (the personification of abstract entities who perform a brief allegorical action) in short passages. Familiar instances are the opening lines of Milton's *L'Allegro* and *Il Penseroso* (1645). This device was exploited especially in the *poetic diction* of authors in the mid-eighteenth century. An example—so brief that it presents an allegoric tableau rather than an action—is the passage in Thomas Gray's "Elegy Written in a Country Churchyard" (1751):

> Can Honour's voice provoke the silent dust,
> Or Flatt'ry soothe the dull cold ear of Death?

Allegory is a narrative strategy which may be employed in any literary form or genre. The early sixteenth-century *Everyman* is an allegory in the form of a *morality play*. *The Pilgrim's Progress* is a moral and religious allegory in a prose narrative; Edmund Spenser's *The Faerie Queene* (1590–96) fuses moral, religious, historical, and political allegory in a verse *romance*; the third book of Jonathan Swift's *Gulliver's Travels*, the voyage to Laputa and Lagado (1726), is an allegorical *satire* directed mainly against philosophical and scientific pedantry; and William Collins' "Ode on the Poetical Character" (1747) is a *lyric* poem which allegorizes a topic in literary criticism—the nature, sources, and power of the poet's creative imagination. John Keats makes a subtle use of allegory throughout his ode "To Autumn" (1820), most explicitly in the second stanza, which personifies the autumnal season as a female figure amid the scenes and activities of the harvest.

Sustained allegory was a favorite form in the Middle Ages, when it produced masterpieces, especially in the verse-narrative mode of the *dream vision*, in which the narrator falls asleep and experiences an allegoric dream; this mode includes, in the fourteenth century, Dante's *Divine Comedy*, the French *Roman de la Rose*, Chaucer's *House of Fame*, and William Langland's *Piers Plowman*. But sustained allegory has been written in all literary periods, and is the form of such major nineteenth-century dramas in verse as Goethe's *Faust, Part II*; Shelley's *Prometheus Unbound*; and Thomas Hardy's *The Dynasts*. In the twentieth century, the stories and novels of Franz Kafka can be considered instances of implicit allegory.

Allegory was on the whole devalued during the twentieth century, but has been reinvested with positive values by some recent theorists. The Marxist critic Fredric Jameson uses the term to signify the relation of a literary text to its historical subtext, its "political unconscious." (See Jameson, under *Marxist criticism*.) And Paul de Man elevates allegory, because it candidly manifests its artifice, over what he calls the more "mystified" concept of the *symbol*, which seems to promise, falsely, a unity of form and content, thought and expression. (See de Man, under *deconstruction*.)

A variety of literary *genres* may be classified as species of allegory in that they all narrate one coherent set of circumstances which are intended to signify a second order of correlated meanings:

A **fable** (also called an **apologue**) is a short narrative, in prose or verse, that exemplifies an abstract moral thesis or principle of human behavior; usually, at its conclusion, either the narrator or one of the characters states the moral in the form of an *epigram*. Most common is the **beast fable**, in which animals talk and act like the human types they represent. In the familiar fable of the fox and the grapes, the fox—after exerting all his wiles to get the grapes hanging beyond his reach, but in vain—concludes that they are probably sour anyway: the express moral is that human beings belittle what they cannot get. (The modern expression "sour grapes" derives from this fable.) The beast fable is a very ancient form that existed in Egypt, India, and Greece. The fables in Western cultures derive mainly from the stories that were, probably mistakenly, attributed to Aesop, a Greek slave of the sixth century BC. In the seventeenth century a Frenchman, Jean de la Fontaine, wrote a set of witty fables in verse which are the classics of this literary kind. Chaucer's "The Nun's Priest's Tale," the story of the cock and the fox, is a beast fable. The American Joel Chandler Harris wrote many Uncle Remus stories that are beast fables, told in southern African-American dialect, whose origins have been traced to *folktales* in the oral literature of West Africa that feature a trickster like Uncle Remus' Brer Rabbit. (A **trickster** is a character in a story who persistently uses his wiliness, and gift of gab, to achieve his ends by outmaneuvering or outwitting other characters.) A counterpart in many Native American cultures are the beast fables that feature Coyote as the central trickster. James Thurber's *Fables for Our Time* (1940) is a recent set of short fables; and in *Animal Farm* (1945) George Orwell expanded the beast fable into a sustained satire on Russian totalitarianism under Stalin in the mid-twentieth century.

A **parable** is a very short narrative about human beings presented so as to stress the tacit analogy, or parallel, with a general thesis or lesson that the narrator is trying to bring home to his audience. The parable was one of Jesus' favorite devices as a teacher; examples are his parables of the good Samaritan and of the prodigal son. Here is his terse parable of the fig tree, Luke 13:6–9:

> He spake also this parable: A certain man had a fig tree planted in his
> vineyard; and he came and sought fruit thereon, and found none.
> Then said he unto the dresser of his vineyard, "Behold, these three
> years I come seeking fruit on this fig tree, and find none: cut it down;
> why cumbereth it the ground?" And he answering said unto him,
> "Lord, let it alone this year also, till I shall dig about it, and dung it.
> And if it bears fruit, well: and if not, then after that thou shalt cut it
> down."

Mark Turner, in a greatly extended use, employs "parable" to signify any "projection of one story onto another," or onto many others, whether the projection is intentional or not. He proposes that, in this extended sense, parable is not merely a literary or *didactic* device, but "a basic cognitive principle" that comes into play in interpreting "every level of our experience" and that "shows up everywhere, from simple actions like telling time to complex literary creations like Proust's *A la recherche du temps perdu*." (Mark Turner, *The Literary Mind*, New York, 1996.)

An **exemplum** is a story told as a particular instance of the general theme in a religious sermon. The device was popular in the Middle Ages, when extensive collections of exempla, some historical and some legendary, were prepared for use by preachers. In Chaucer's "The Pardoner's Tale," the Pardoner, preaching on the theme, "Greed is the root of all evil," incorporates as an exemplum the tale of the three drunken revelers who set out to find and defy Death and find a heap of gold instead, only to find Death after all, when they kill one another in the attempt to gain sole possession of the treasure. By extension the term "exemplum" is also applied to tales used in a formal, though nonreligious, exhortation. Thus Chaucer's Chanticleer, in "The Nun's Priest's Tale," borrows the preacher's technique in the ten exempla he tells in a vain effort to persuade his skeptical wife, Dame Pertelote the hen, that bad dreams forebode disaster. See G. R. Owst, *Literature and the Pulpit in Medieval England* (2d ed., 1961, chapter 4).

Many **proverbs** (short, pithy statements of widely accepted truths about everyday life) are allegorical in that the explicit statement is meant to have, by analogy or by extended reference, a general application: "a stitch in time saves nine"; "people in glass houses should not throw stones." Refer to *The Oxford Dictionary of English Proverbs*, ed. W. G. Smith and F. P. Wilson (1970).

See *didactic, symbol* (for the distinction between allegory and symbol), and (on the fourfold allegorical interpretation of the Bible) *interpretation: typological and allegorical*. On allegory in general, consult C. S. Lewis, *The Allegory of Love* (1936), chapter 2; Edwin Honig, *Dark Conceit: The Making of Allegory* (1959); Angus Fletcher, *Allegory: The Theory of a Symbolic Mode* (1964); Rosemund Tuve, *Allegorical Imagery* (1966); Michael Murrin, *The Veil of Allegory* (1969); Maureen Quilligan, *The Language of Allegory* (1979).

For references to *allegory* in other entries, see pages *80, 86, 186, 201.*

**alliteration:** Alliteration is the repetition of a speech sound in a sequence of nearby words. Usually the term is applied only to consonants, and only when the recurrent sound is made emphatic because it begins a word or a stressed syllable within a word. In Old English **alliterative meter**, alliteration is the principal organizing device of the verse line: the verse is unrhymed; each line is divided into two half-lines of two strong stresses by a decisive pause, or *caesura*; and at least one, and usually both, of the two stressed syllables in the first half-line alliterate with the first stressed syllable of the second half-line. (In this type of versification a vowel was considered to alliterate with any other vowel.) A number of Middle English poems, such as William Langland's *Piers Plowman* and the romance *Sir Gawain and the Green Knight*, both written in the fourteenth century, continued to use and play variations upon the old alliterative meter. (See *strong-stress meters.*) In the opening line of *Piers Plowman*, for example, all four of the stressed syllables alliterate:

> In a *s*ómer *s*éson, when *s*óft was the *s*ónne. . . .

In later English versification, however, alliteration is used only for special stylistic effects, such as to reinforce the meaning, to link related words, or to provide tone color and enhance the palpability of enunciating the words. An example is the repetition of the *s, th,* and *w* consonants in Shakespeare's Sonnet 30:

> When to the *s*essions of *s*weet *s*ilent *th*ought
> I *s*ummon up remembrance of *th*ings past,
> I *s*igh the lack of many a *th*ing I *s*ought
> And *w*ith old *w*oes new *w*ail my dear time's *w*aste. . . .

Various other repetitions of speech sounds are identified by special terms:

**Consonance** is the repetition of a sequence of two or more consonants, but with a change in the intervening vowel: live-love, lean-alone, pitter-patter. W. H. Auden's poem of the 1930s, "'O where are you going?' said reader to rider," makes prominent use of this device; the last stanza reads:

> "Out of this house"—said *r*ide*r* to *r*eade*r*,
> "Yours never will"—said *f*are*r* to *f*eare*r*,

"They're looking for you"—said *hearer* to *horror*,
As he left them there, as he left them there.[1]

**Assonance** is the repetition of identical or similar vowels—especially in stressed syllables—in a sequence of nearby words. Note the recurrent long *i* in the opening lines of Keats' "Ode on a Grecian Urn" (1820):

Thou still unravished br*i*de of qu*i*etness,
Thou foster ch*i*ld of s*i*lence and slow t*i*me. . . .

The richly assonantal effect at the beginning of William Collins' "Ode to Evening" (1747) is achieved by a patterned sequence of changing vowels:

If aught of oaten stop or pastoral song,
May hope, chaste Eve, to soothe thy pensive ear. . . .

For a special case of the repetition of vowels and consonants in combination, see *rhyme*. For references to *alliteration* in other entries, see pages *106, 127, 198.*

**alliterative meter: 10**; *198, 252.*

**allusion:** Allusion is a passing reference, without explicit identification, to a literary or historical person, place, or event, or to another literary work or passage. In the Elizabethan Thomas Nashe's "Litany in Time of Plague,"

Brightness falls from the air,
Queens have died young and fair,
Dust hath closed Helen's eye,

the unidentified "Helen" in the last line alludes to Helen of Troy. Most allusions serve to illustrate or expand upon or enhance a subject, but some are used in order to undercut it ironically by the discrepancy between the subject and the allusion. In the lines from T. S. Eliot's *The Waste Land* (1922) describing a woman at her modern dressing table,

The Chair she sat in, like a burnished throne,
Glowed on the marble,[2]

the *ironic* allusion, achieved by echoing Shakespeare's phrasing, is to the description of Cleopatra's magnificent barge in *Antony and Cleopatra* (II. ii. 196ff.):

The barge she sat in, like a burnish'd throne,
Burn'd on the water.

---

[1]Lines from "O where are you going?" from *W. H. Auden: Collected Poems 1927–1957* by W. H. Auden, ed. by Edward Mendelson. Copyright © 1934 and renewed 1962 by W. H. Auden. Reprinted by permission of Random House, Inc., and Faber & Faber Ltd.

[2]Lines from "The Waste Land" from *Collected Poems 1909–1962* by T. S. Eliot. Copyright © 1964, 1963 by T. S. Eliot. Reprinted by permission of Faber & Faber Ltd.

For discussion of a poet who makes persistent and complex use of this device, see Reuben A. Brower, *Alexander Pope: The Poetry of Allusion* (1959); see also John Hollander, *The Figure of Echo: A Mode of Allusion in Milton and After* (1981); Edwin Stein, *Wordsworth's Art of Allusion* (1988); Christopher Ricks, *Allusion to the Poets* (2002).

Since allusions are not explicitly identified, they imply a fund of knowledge that is shared by an author and the audience for whom the author writes. Most literary allusions are intended to be recognized by the generally educated readers of the author's time, but some are aimed at a special coterie. For example, in *Astrophel and Stella*, the Elizabethan *sonnet sequence*, Sir Philip Sidney's punning allusions to Lord Robert Rich, who had married the Stella of the sonnets, were identifiable only by intimates of the people concerned. (See Sonnets 24 and 37.) Some modern authors, including Joyce, Pound, and Eliot, include allusions that are very specialized, or else drawn from the author's private reading and experience, in the awareness that few if any readers will recognize them prior to the detective work of scholarly annotators. The current term *intertextuality* includes literary echoes and allusions as one of the many ways in which any text is interwoven with other texts. See Joseph Pucci, *The Full-Knowing Reader: Allusion and the Power of the Reader in Western Literary Tradition* (1998); and Gregory Machacek, "Allusion," *PMLA*, Vol. 122 (2007).

**ambiance:** (ăm′ bē̈äns), **18**.

**ambiguity:** In ordinary usage "ambiguity" is applied to a fault in style; that is, the use of a vague or equivocal expression when what is wanted is precision and particularity of reference. Since William Empson published *Seven Types of Ambiguity* (1930), however, the term has been widely used in criticism to identify a deliberate poetic device: the use of a single word or expression to signify two or more distinct references, or to express two or more diverse attitudes or feelings. **Multiple meaning** and **plurisignation** are alternative terms for this use of language; they have the advantage of avoiding the pejorative association with the word "ambiguity."

When Shakespeare's Cleopatra, exciting the asp to a frenzy, says (*Antony and Cleopatra*, V. ii. 306ff.),

> Come, thou mortal wretch,
> With thy sharp teeth this knot intrinsicate
> Of life at once untie. Poor venomous fool,
> Be angry, and dispatch,

her speech is richly multiple in significance. For example, "mortal" means "fatal" or "death-dealing," and at the same time may signify that the asp is itself mortal, or subject to death. "Wretch" in this context serves to express both contempt and pity (Cleopatra goes on to refer to the asp as "my baby at my breast, / That sucks the nurse asleep"). And the two meanings of "dispatch"—"make haste" and "kill"—are equally relevant.

A special type of multiple meaning is conveyed by the **portmanteau word**. "Portmanteau" designates a large suitcase that opens into two equal compartments, and was introduced into literary criticism by Humpty Dumpty, the expert on semantics in Lewis Carroll's *Through the Looking Glass* (1871). He is explicating to Alice the meaning of the opening lines of "Jabberwocky":

> 'Twas brillig, and the slithy toves
> Did gyre and gimble in the wabe.

"Slithy," Humpty Dumpty explained, "means 'lithe and slimy'. . . . You see it's like a portmanteau—there are two meanings packed up into one word." James Joyce exploited this device—the fusion of two or more existing words—in order to sustain the multiple levels of meaning throughout his long dream narrative *Finnegans Wake* (1939). An example is his comment on girls who are "yung and easily freudened"; "freudened" combines "frightened" and "Freud," while "yung" combines "young" and Sigmund Freud's rival in depth psychology, Carl Jung. (Compare *pun*.) "Différance," a key analytic term of the philosopher of language Jacques Derrida, is a portmanteau noun which he describes as combining two diverse meanings of the French verb "différer": "to differ" and "to defer." (See *deconstruction*.)

By his analysis of ambiguity, William Empson helped make current a mode of *explication* developed especially by exponents of the *New Criticism*, which greatly expanded awareness of the complexity and richness of poetic language. The risk is that the quest for ambiguities will result in **over-reading**: ingenious, over-drawn, and sometimes contradictory explications of a literary word or passage.

For related terms see *connotation and denotation* and *pun*. For critiques of Empson's theory and practice, refer to Elder Olson, "William Empson, Contemporary Criticism and Poetic Diction," in *Critics and Criticism*, ed. R. S. Crane (1952). For references to *ambiguity* in other entries, see page *71*.

**anthropocentric: 88**.

**anticlimax: 24**.

**antifoundationalism: 279**.

**antihero:** The chief person in a modern novel or play whose character is widely discrepant from that of the traditional protagonist, or *hero*, of a serious literary work. Instead of manifesting largeness, dignity, power, or heroism, the antihero is petty, ignominious, passive, clownish, or dishonest. The use of nonheroic protagonists occurs as early as the *picaresque* novel of the sixteenth century, and the heroine of Defoe's *Moll Flanders* (1722) is a thief and a prostitute. The term "antihero," however, is usually applied to writings in the period of disillusion after the Second World War, beginning with such lowly protagonists as we find in John Wain's *Hurry on Down* (1953) and Kingsley Amis' *Lucky Jim* (1954). Notable later instances in the novel are Yossarian in Joseph Heller's *Catch-22* (1961), Humbert Humbert in Vladimir Nabokov's *Lolita* (1955), and Tyrone Slothrop in Thomas Pynchon's *Gravity's Rainbow* (1973). The antihero is especially conspicuous in dramatic tragedy, in which the traditional protagonist had usually been of high estate, possessing dignity and courage (see *tragedy*). Extreme instances are the characters who people a world stripped of certainties, values, or even meaning in Samuel Beckett's dramas—the tramps Vladimir and Estragon in *Waiting for Godot* (1952) or the blind and paralyzed old man, Hamm, who is the protagonist in *Endgame* (1958).

See literature of the *absurd* and *black comedy*, and refer to Ihab Hassan, "The Antihero in Modern British and American Fiction," in *Rumors of Change* (1995).

**antimasque: 188**.

**antinovel: 231**; *268*.

**antipathy: 95**.

**antistrophe** (antīs′ trŏf e): **235**.

**antithesis:** Antithesis is a contrast or opposition in the meanings of contiguous phrases or clauses that manifest **parallelism**—that is, a similar word order and structure—in their *syntax*. An example is Alexander Pope's description of Atticus in his *Epistle to Dr. Arbuthnot* (1735), "Willing to wound, and yet afraid to strike." In the antithesis in the second line of Pope's description of the Baron's designs against Belinda, in *The Rape of the Lock* (1714), the parallelism in the syntax is made prominent by *alliteration* in the antithetic nouns:

> Resolved to win, he meditates the way,
> By *f*orce to ravish, or by *f*raud betray.

In a sentence from Samuel Johnson's prose fiction *Rasselas* (1759), chapter 26, the antithesis is similarly heightened by alliteration in the contrasted nouns: "Marriage has many *p*ains, but celibacy has no *p*leasures."

For references to *antithesis* in other entries, see page *142*.

**antithetical criticism: 156**.

**antitype: 162**.

**anxiety of influence: 155**; *113, 293, 301*.

**aphorism** (ăf′ ŏrism): **101**.

**apocrypha** (ăpŏk′ rĭfa): **38**.

**apologue: 8**.

**aporia** (ăpŏ′ rēa): **72**; *239*.

**apostrophe** (apŏs′ trŏf ē): **313**.

**apothegm** (ăp′ othĕm): **101**.

**applied criticism: 62**.

**appropriation** (in reading): **222**.

**Arcadia** (arkā′ dia): **240**.

**archaism:** The literary use of words and expressions that have become obsolete in the common speech of an era. Spenser in *The Faerie Queene* (1590–96) deliberately employed archaisms (many of them derived from Chaucer's medieval English) in order to achieve a poetic style appropriate to his revival of the medieval *chivalric romance*. The translators of the King James Version of the Bible (1611) gave weight, dignity, and sonority to their prose by a sustained use of archaic revivals. Both Spenser and the King James Bible have in their turn been major sources of archaisms for Milton and many later authors. When Keats, for example, in his ode (1820) described the Grecian urn as "with *brede* / Of marble men and maidens *overwrought,*" he used archaic words for "braid" and "worked [that is, ornamented] all over." Abraham Lincoln achieved a ritual solemnity by biblical archaisms in his "Gettysburg Address," which begins, "Fourscore and seven years ago."

Archaism has been a standard resort for *poetic diction*. Through the nineteenth century, for example, many poets continued to use "I ween," "methought," "steed," "taper" (for candle), and "morn," but only in their verses, not their everyday speech.

**archetypal criticism:** In literary criticism the term **archetype** denotes recurrent narrative designs, patterns of action, character types, themes, and images which are identifiable in a wide variety of works of literature, as well as in myths, dreams, and even social rituals. Such recurrent items are usually held to be the result of elemental and universal patterns in the human psyche, whose effective embodiment in a literary work evokes a profound response from the attentive reader, because he or she shares the psychic archetypes expressed by the author. An important antecedent of the literary theory of the archetype was the treatment of myth by a group of comparative anthropologists at Cambridge University, especially

James G. Frazer, whose *The Golden Bough* (1890–1915) identified elemental patterns of myth and ritual that, he claimed, recur in the legends and ceremonials of diverse and far-flung cultures and religions. An even more important antecedent was the depth psychology of Carl G. Jung (1875–1961), who applied the term "archetype" to what he called "primordial images," the "psychic residue" of repeated patterns of experience in our very ancient ancestors which, he maintained, survive in the "collective unconscious" of the human race and are expressed in myths, religion, dreams, and private fantasies, as well as in works of literature. See *Jungian criticism*, under *psychoanalytic criticism*.

Archetypal literary criticism was given impetus by Maud Bodkin's *Archetypal Patterns in Poetry* (1934) and flourished especially during the 1950s and 1960s. Some archetypal critics dropped Jung's theory of the collective unconscious as the deep source of these patterns; in the words of Northrop Frye, this theory is "an unnecessary hypothesis," and the recurrent archetypes are simply there, "however they got there."

Among the prominent practitioners of various modes of **archetypal criticism**, in addition to Maud Bodkin, were G. Wilson Knight, Robert Graves, Philip Wheelwright, Richard Chase, Leslie Fiedler, and Joseph Campbell. These critics tended to emphasize the persistence of mythical patterns in literature, on the assumption that myths are closer to the elemental archetype than the artful manipulations of sophisticated writers (see *myth critics*). The death/rebirth theme was often said to be the archetype of archetypes, and was held to be grounded in the cycle of the seasons and the organic cycle of human life; this archetype, it was claimed, occurs in primitive rituals of the king who is annually sacrificed, in widespread myths of gods who die to be reborn, and in a multitude of diverse texts, including the Bible, Dante's *Divine Comedy* in the early fourteenth century, and Samuel Taylor Coleridge's "Rime of the Ancient Mariner" in 1798. Among the other archetypal themes, images, and characters frequently traced in literature were the journey underground, the heavenly ascent, the search for the father, the Paradise/Hades dichotomy, the Promethean rebel-hero, the scapegoat, the earth goddess, and the fatal woman.

In his remarkable and influential book *Anatomy of Criticism* (1957), Northrop Frye developed the archetypal approach—which he combined with the *typological interpretation* of the Bible and the conception of the imagination in the writings of the poet and painter William Blake (1757–1827)—into a radical and comprehensive revision of traditional grounds in both the theory of literature and the practice of literary criticism. Frye proposed that the totality of literary works constitute a "self-contained literary universe" which has been created over the ages by the human imagination so as to assimilate the alien and indifferent world of nature into archetypal forms that satisfy enduring human desires and needs. In this literary universe, four radical **mythoi** (that is, plot forms, or organizing structural principles), correspondent to the four seasons in the cycle of the natural world, are incorporated in the four major *genres* of comedy (spring), romance (summer), tragedy (autumn), and satire (winter). Within the archetypal mythos of each of these genres, individual works of literature also play variations upon a number of more limited archetypes—that is, conventional patterns and types that literature shares with social rituals as well as with theology, history, law, and, in fact, all "discursive verbal structures." Viewed archetypally, Frye asserted, literature turns out to play an essential role in refashioning the impersonal material universe into an alternative verbal universe that is humanly intelligible and viable, because it is adapted to universal human needs and concerns. Frye continued, in a long series of later writings, to expand his archetypal theory, to make a place in its overall scope and on different levels for including many traditional critical concepts and procedures, and to apply the theory both to everyday social practices and to the elucidation of writings ranging from the Bible to contemporary poets and novelists. See A. C. Hamilton, *Northrop Frye: Anatomy of His Criticism* (1990).

In addition to the works mentioned above, consult: C. G. Jung, "On the Relation of Analytical Psychology to Poetic Art" (1922), in *Contributions to Analytical Psychology* (1928), and "Psychology and Literature," in *Modern Man in Search of a Soul* (1933); G. Wilson Knight, *The Starlit Dome* (1941); Robert Graves, *The White Goddess* (rev. 1961); Richard Chase, *The Quest for Myth* (1949); Francis Fergusson, *The Idea of a Theater* (1949); Philip Wheelwright, *The Burning Fountain* (rev. 1968); Northrop Frye, "The Archetypes of Literature," in *Fables of Identity* (1963); Joseph Campbell, *The Hero with a Thousand Faces* (2d ed., 1968). In the 1980s, *feminist critics* developed forms of archetypal criticism that revised the male bases and biases of Jung and other archetypists. See Annis Pratt, *Archetypal Patterns in Woman's Fiction* (1981), and Estella Lauter and Carol Schreier Rupprecht, *Feminist Archetypal Theory: Interdisciplinary Re-Visions of Jungian Thought* (1985).

For discussions and critiques of archetypal theory and practice, see Murray Krieger, ed., *Northrop Frye in Modern Criticism* (1966); Robert Denham, *Northrop Frye and Critical Method* (1978); Frank Lentricchia, *After the New Criticism* (1980), chapter 1. For references to *archetypal criticism* in other entries, see pages *49, 205, 207, 268, 293*.

**archetype** (ar′ kĕtīp): **15**; *126, 135, 209, 345*.

**argument** (in narrative forms): **98**.

**art for art's sake: 4**; *63*.

**article: 103**.

**aside, the: 335**; *58*.

**assonance** (ă sōnăns): **11**; *106*.

**atmosphere:** Atmosphere is the emotional tone pervading a section or the whole of a literary work, which fosters in the reader expectations as to the course of events, whether happy or (more commonly) terrifying or disastrous. Shakespeare establishes the tense and fearful atmosphere at the beginning of *Hamlet* by the terse and nervous dialogue of the sentinels as they anticipate a reappearance of the ghost; Coleridge engenders a compound of religious and superstitious terror by his description of the initial scene in the narrative poem *Christabel* (1816); and Hardy in his novel *The Return of the Native* (1878) makes Egdon Heath a brooding presence that reduces to pettiness and futility the human struggle for happiness for which it is the setting. Alternative terms frequently used for atmosphere are **mood** and the French word **ambiance**.

For references to *atmosphere* in other entries, see pages *137, 152, 330.*

**aubade** (ō bäd′): **205**.

**Augustan Age** (awgŭs′ tan): **254**.

**author and authorship:** The conception of an author in ordinary literary discourse might be summarized as follows: **Authors** are individuals who, by their intellectual and imaginative powers, purposefully create from their experience and reading a literary work which is distinctively their own. The work itself, as distinguished from the written or printed texts that instantiate the work, remains a product accredited to the author as its originator, even if he or she turns over the rights to publish and profit from the texts to someone else. And insofar as the literary work turns out to be great and original, the author who has composed that work is deservedly accorded high cultural status and achieves lasting fame.

Since the 1960s this way of conceiving an author has been put to radical question by a number of structural and poststructural theorists, who posit the human *subject* not as an originator and shaper of a work, but as a "space" in which conventions, codes, and circulating locutions precipitate into a particular text, or else as a "site" wherein there converge, and are recorded, the cultural constructs, discursive formations, and configurations of power prevalent in a given cultural era. The author is said to be the product rather than the producer of a text, or is redescribed as an "effect" or "function" engendered by the internal play of textual language. Famously, in 1968 Roland Barthes proclaimed and celebrated "The Death of the Author," whom he described as a figure invented by critical discourse in order to set limits to the inherent free play of the meanings in reading a literary text. (See under *structuralist criticism* and *poststructuralism*.)

In an influential essay "What Is an Author?" written in 1969, Michel Foucault raised the question of the historical "coming into being of the notion of 'author'"—that is, of the emergence and evolution of the "author function" within the discourse of our culture. The investigation would include such inquiries as "how the author became individualized," "what status he has been given," what "system of valorization" involves the author, and how the fundamental category of "'the-man-and-his-work criticism' began." Foucault's essay and example gave impetus to a number of studies which reject the notion that the prevailing concept of **authorship** (the set of attributes possessed by an author) is either natural or necessitated by the way things are. Instead, historicists conceive authorship to be a *cultural construct* that emerged and changed, in accordance with changing economic conditions, social circumstances, and institutional arrangements for the writing and distribution of books, over many centuries in the Western world. (See *new historicism*.)

Cultural historians have emphasized the important role, in constructing and reconstructing the concept of an author, of such historical developments as:

1. The shift from an oral to a literate culture. In the former, the identity of an author presumably was not inquired after, since the individual bard or minstrel improvised by reference to inherited subject matter, forms, and literary formulae. (See *oral poetry*.) In a culture where at least a substantial segment of the population can read, the production of enduring texts in the form of written scrolls and manuscripts generated increasing interest in the individual responsible for producing the work that was thus recorded. Many works in manuscript, however, circulated freely, and were often altered in transcriptions, with little regard to the intentions or formulations of the originator of the work.

2. The shift, in the course of the fifteenth and sixteenth centuries, from a primarily manuscript culture to a primarily print culture. (See *book*.) The invention of printing greatly expedited the manufacture and dissemination of printed texts, and so multiplied the number of producers of literary works, and made financially important the specification of the identity and ability of an individual writer, in order to invite support for that individual by the contemporary system of aristocratic and noble patronage. Foucault, in addition, proposed the importance of a punitive function in fostering the concept of an author's responsibility in originating a work, which served the interests of the state in affixing on a particular individual the blame for transgressive or subversive ideas.

3. The emphasis in recent research on the difficulties in establishing, in various periods, just who was the originator of what parts of an existing literary text, which was often, in effect, the product of multiple collaborators, censors, editors, printers, and publishers, as well as of successive revisions by the reputed author. See *multiple authorship* under *textual criticism*.

4. The proliferation of middle-class readers in the late seventeenth and eighteenth centuries, and the attendant explosion in the number of literary titles printed, and in the number of writers required to supply this market. Both Foucault and Barthes, in the essays cited above, emphasized that the modern figure of an author as an individual who is the intellectual owner of his or her literary product was the result of the *ideology* engendered by the emerging capitalist economy in this era. Other scholars have stressed the importance of the shift during the eighteenth century, first in England and then in other European countries, from a reliance by writers on literary patrons to that of support by payments from publishers and booksellers. A result of the booming literary market was the increasingly successful appeal by writers for copyright laws that would invest them, instead of the publisher, with the ownership of the works that they composed for public sale. These conditions of the literary marketplace fostered the claims by writers that they possessed originality, creativity, and genius, and so were able to produce literary works that were entirely new. They made such claims in order to establish their legal rights, as authors, to ownership of such productions as their "intellectual property," in addition to their rights (which they could sell to others) to the printed texts of their works as "material property." Historians of authorship point out that the most emphatic claims

about the genius, creativity, and originality of authors, which occurred in the *Romantic Period*, coincided with, and was interactive with, the success of authors in achieving some form of copyright protection of an author's proprietary rights to the literary work as the unique product of his or her native powers. (See Mark Rose, *Authors and Owners: The Invention of Copyright*, 1993; Martha Woodmansee, *The Author, Art, and the Market: Rereading the History of Aesthetics*, 1994; and the essays by various scholars in *The Construction of Authorship: Textual Appropriation in Law and Literature*, ed. Martha Woodmansee and Peter Jaszi, 1994.)

Historicist scholars of authorship have succeeded in demonstrating that there has been a sustained interplay between the economic circumstances and institutional arrangements for producing and marketing literary texts and details in the conception of authorship, or in ideas associated with authorship. The radical further claim, however, that the modern figure and functions assigned to an author are in their essentials a recent formation, resulting from the distinctive conditions of the literary marketplace after the seventeenth century, does not jibe with historical evidence. Some two thousand years ago, for example, the Roman poet Horace wrote his verse-epistle, the *Ars Poetica*, at a time when books consisted of texts copied by hand in rolls of papyrus. (See the entry *book*.) Horace adverts to a number of individuals from Homer to his friend Virgil who, he makes clear, as individuals who conceived and brought their works into being, are responsible for having achieved their content, form, and quality. A competent literary author —Horace refers to him variously as *scriptor* (writer), *poeta* (maker), and *carminis auctor* (originator of a poem)—must possess a natural talent or genius *(ingenium)* as well as an acquired art, and purposefully designs and orders his *poema* in such a way as to evoke the emotions of his audience. The bookseller, Horace indicates, advertises his commodities locally and also ships them abroad. And if a published work succeeds in instructing and giving pleasure to a great many readers, it is a book that not only "makes money for the bookseller," but also "crosses the sea and spreads to a distant age the fame of its author." Clearly, Horace distinguishes between material and authorial, or intellectual, ownership, in that the author, even if he has no proprietary interest in a published book, retains the sole responsibility and credit for having accomplished the work that the text incorporates. (See M. H. Abrams, "What Is a Humanistic Criticism?" in *The Emperor Redressed: Critiquing Critical Theory*, ed. Dwight Eddins, 1995.)

Another revealing instance is provided by the publication of the First Folio of Shakespeare's plays in 1623. As writings intended for the commercial theater, Shakespeare's plays were a collaborative enterprise in which textual changes and insertions could be made by various hands at all stages of production; the resulting products were not Shakespeare's property, but that of his theatrical company. Furthermore, as Stephen Greenblatt remarks in the Introduction to *The Norton Shakespeare* (1997), there is no evidence that Shakespeare himself wanted to have his plays printed, or that he took any "interest in asserting authorial rights over a script," or that he had any legal standing from which to claim such rights. Nonetheless, as Greenblatt points out, seven years after Shakespeare's death his friends and fellow actors Heminges and Condell were confident that they could sell their expensive *folio* collection of his plays by virtue of the fact, as they claimed in a preface, that their printed texts were exactly "as he conceived them" and re-presented what he himself had "thought" and "uttered." The identity of the con-ceiver of the plays, serving to attest to the authenticity of the printed versions, is graphically represented by an engraved portrait of Shakespeare by Martin Droeshout in the front matter. The First Folio also included a poem by Ben Jonson, Shakespeare's friend and dramatic rival, "To the Memory of My Beloved, The Author Mr. William Shakespeare." In it Jonson appraised Shakespeare as the equal of the Greek tragic dramatists Aeschylus, Euripides, and Sophocles; lauded him as not only "The applause! delight! the wonder of our stage!" but also as an individual who, by the products of his innate abilities ("nature") even more than his "art," was "not of an age, but for all time!"; and asserted that his "well-turned" lines reflect the "mind, and manners" of the poet who had fathered them. It would seem that, in broad outline, the figure and func-tions of Horace's "auctor" and of Jonson's "author" were essentially what they are at the present time, in ordinary critical discourse.

See the entry *sociology of literature.* In addition to the items listed above, refer to Frederick G. Kenyon, *Books and Readers in Ancient Rome* (1951); A. J. Minnis, *Medieval Theory of Authorship* (1984); Wendy Wall, *The Imprint of Gender: Authorship and Publication in the English Renaissance* (1993). Roger Chartier, in "Figures of the Author," *The Order of Books* (1994), describes the diverse functions assigned to an individual author, from the late Middle Ages through the eigh-teenth century. For references to *author and authorship* in other entries, see pages *221, 281, 348.*

**authoritative** (narration): **272**.

**authorship: 18**.

**autobiography: 26**.

**automatic writing: 202**; *357.*

**avant-garde** (ăʹ vŏn-gardʺ): **203**.

**ballad:** A short definition of the **popular ballad** (also called the **folk ballad** or **tra-ditional ballad**) is that it is a song, transmitted orally, which tells a story. Ballads are thus the narrative species of *folk songs,* which originate, and are communicated orally, among illiterate or only partly literate people. In all probability the initial version of a ballad was composed by a single author, but he or she is unknown; and since each singer who learns and repeats an oral ballad is apt to introduce changes in both the text and the tune, it exists in many variant forms. Typically, the popular ballad is dramatic, condensed, and impersonal: the narrator begins with the climactic episode, tells the story tersely in action and dialogue (sometimes by means of dialogue alone), and tells it without self-reference or the expression of personal attitudes or feelings.

The most common stanza form—called the **ballad stanza**—is a *quatrain* in alternate four- and three-stress lines; usually only the second and fourth lines rhyme. This is the form of "Sir Patrick Spens"; the first stanza also exemplifies the abrupt opening of the typical ballad, and the manner of proceeding by third-person narration, curtly sketched setting and action, sharp transition, and spare dialogue:

> The king sits in Dumferling towne,
> Drinking the blude-red wine:
> "O whar will I get a guid sailor,
> To sail this schip of mine?"

Many ballads employ set formulas (which helped the singer remember the course of the song) including (1) stock descriptive phrases like "blood-red wine" and "milk-white steed," (2) a *refrain* in each stanza ("Edward," "Lord Randall"), and (3) **incremental repetition**, in which a line or stanza is repeated, but with an addition that advances the story ("Lord Randall," "Child Waters"). See *oral poetry*.

Although many traditional ballads probably originated in the later Middle Ages, they were not collected and printed until the eighteenth century, first in England, then in Germany. In 1765 Thomas Percy published his *Reliques of Ancient English Poetry* which, although most of the contents had been revised in the style of Percy's era, did much to inaugurate widespread interest in folk literature. The basic modern collection is Francis J. Child's *English and Scottish Popular Ballads* (1882–98), which includes 305 ballads, many of them in variant versions. Bertrand H. Bronson has edited *The Traditional Tunes of the Child Ballads* (4 vols., 1959–72). Popular ballads are still being sung—and collected, now with the help of a tape recorder—in the British Isles and remote rural areas of America. To the songs that early settlers brought with them from Great Britain, America has added native forms of the ballad, such as those sung by lumberjacks, cowboys, laborers, and social protesters. A number of recent folk singers, including Woody Guthrie, Bob Dylan, and Joan Baez, themselves compose ballads; most of these, however, such as "The Ballad of Bonnie and Clyde" (about a notorious gangster and his moll), are closer to the journalistic "broadside ballad" than to the archaic and heroic mode of the popular ballads in the Child collection.

A **broadside ballad** is a ballad that was printed on one side of a single sheet (called a "broadside"), dealt with a current event or person or issue, and was sung to a well-known tune. Beginning with the sixteenth century, these broadsides were hawked in the streets or at country fairs in Great Britain.

The traditional ballad has greatly influenced the form and style of lyric poetry in general. It has also engendered the **literary ballad**, which is a narrative poem written in deliberate imitation of the form, language, and spirit of the traditional ballad. In Germany, some major literary ballads were composed in the latter eighteenth century, including G. A. Bürger's very popular "Lenore" (1774)—which soon became widely read and influential in an English translation—and Goethe's "Erlkönig" (1782). In England, some of the best literary ballads were composed in the *Romantic Period:* Coleridge's "Rime of the Ancient Mariner" (which, however, is much longer and has a much more elaborate plot than the folk ballad),

Walter Scott's "Proud Maisie," and Keats' "La Belle Dame sans Merci." In his *Lyrical Ballads* of 1798, Wordsworth begins "We Are Seven" by introducing a narrator as an agent and first-person teller of the story—"I met a little cottage girl"— which is probably one reason he called the collection "*lyrical* ballads." Coleridge's "Ancient Mariner," on the other hand, of which the first version also appeared in *Lyrical Ballads*, opens with the abrupt and impersonal third-person narration of the traditional ballad:

> It is an ancient Mariner
> And he stoppeth one of three. . . .

See W. J. Entwistle, *European Balladry* (rev. ed., 1951); M. J. C. Hodgart, *The Ballads* (2d ed., 1962); John A. and Alan Lomax, *American Ballads and Folk Songs* (1934); D. C. Fowler, *A Literary History of the Popular Ballad* (1968). For the broadside ballad see *The Common Muse*, eds. V. de Sola Pinto and Allan E. Rodway (1957).

**ballad stanza: 22**; *341.*

**baroque:** Baroque is a term applied by art historians (at first derogatorily, but now merely descriptively) to a style of architecture, sculpture, and painting that emerged in Italy at the beginning of the seventeenth century and then spread to Germany and other countries in Europe. The style employs the classical forms of the *Renaissance*, but breaks them up and intermingles them to achieve elaborate, grandiose, energetic, and highly dramatic effects. Major examples of baroque art are the sculptures of Bernini and the architecture of St. Peter's cathedral in Rome.

The term has been adopted with reference to literature, with a variety of applications. It may signify any elaborately formal and magniloquent style in verse or prose—for example, some verse passages in Milton's *Paradise Lost* (1667) and Thomas De Quincey's prose descriptions of his dreams in *Confessions of an English Opium Eater* (1822) have both been called baroque. Occasionally—though oftener on the Continent than in England—it serves as a period term for post-Renaissance literature in the seventeenth century. More frequently it is applied specifically to the elaborate verses and extravagant conceits of the late-sixteenth- and early-seventeenth-century poets Giambattista Marino in Italy and Luis de Góngora in Spain. In English literature the metaphysical poems of John Donne are sometimes described as baroque; but the term is more often, and more appropriately, applied to the elaborate style, fantastic conceits, and extreme religious emotionalism of the poet Richard Crashaw, 1612–49; see under *metaphysical conceit*. Refer to René Wellek, "The Concept of Baroque in Literary Scholarship," in *Concepts of Criticism* (1963).

The term "baroque" is derived from the Spanish and Portuguese name for a pearl that is rough and irregular in shape.

**bathos and anticlimax: Bathos** is Greek for "depth," and it has been an indispensable term to critics since Alexander Pope, *parodying* the Greek Longinus' famous essay *On the Sublime* (that is, "loftiness"), wrote in 1727 an essay *On*

*Bathos: Of the Art of Sinking in Poetry*. With mock solemnity Pope assures his readers that he undertakes "to lead them as it were by the hand . . . the gentle downhill way to Bathos; the bottom, the end, the central point, the *non plus ultra*, of true Modern Poesy!" The word ever since has been used for an unintentional descent in literature when, straining to be pathetic or passionate or elevated, the writer overshoots the mark and drops into the trivial or the ridiculous. Among his examples Pope cites "the modest request of two absent lovers" in a contemporary poem:

> Ye Gods! annihilate but Space and Time,
> And make two lovers happy.

The slogan "For God, for Country, and for Yale!" is bathetic because it moves to intended **climax** (that is, an ascending sequence of importance) in its rhetorical order, but to unintended descent in its reference—at least for someone who is not a Yale graduate. Even major poets sometimes fall unwittingly into the same rhetorical figure. In the early version of *The Prelude* (1805; Book IX), William Wordsworth, after recounting at length the tale of the star-crossed lovers Vaudracour and Julia, tells how Julia died, leaving Vaudracour to raise their infant son:

> It consoled him here
> To attend upon the Orphan and perform
> The office of a Nurse to his young Child
> Which after a short time by some mistake
> Or indiscretion of the Father, died.

*The Stuffed Owl: An Anthology of Bad Verse*, ed. D. B. Wyndham Lewis and Charles Lee (rev. 1948), is a rich mine of unintended bathos.

   **Anticlimax** is sometimes employed as an equivalent of bathos; but in a more useful application, "anticlimax" is non-derogatory, and denotes a writer's deliberate drop from the serious and elevated to the trivial and lowly in order to achieve a comic or satiric effect. Thus Thomas Gray in his *mock-heroic* "Ode on the Death of a Favorite Cat" (1748)—the cat had drowned when she tried to catch a goldfish—gravely inserts this moral observation:

> What female heart can gold despise?
> What cat's averse to fish?

And in *Don Juan* (1819–24; I. ix.) Byron uses anticlimax to deflate the would-be gallantry of Juan's father:

> A better cavalier ne'er mounted horse,
> Or, being mounted, e'er got down again.

**battle rapping: 243.**

**beast fable: 8.**

**Beat writers:** Beat writers identifies a loose-knit group of poets and novelists, in the second half of the 1950s and early 1960s, who shared a set of social attitudes—antiestablishment, antipolitical, anti-intellectual, opposed to the prevailing cultural, literary, and moral values, and in favor of unfettered self-realization and self-expression. The Beat writers often performed in coffeehouses and other public places, to the accompaniment of drums or jazz music. (See *performance poetry*.) "Beat" was used to signify both "beaten down" (that is, by the oppressive culture of the time) and "beatific" (many of the Beat writers cultivated ecstatic states by way of Buddhism, Jewish and Christian mysticism, and/or drugs that induced visionary experiences). The group included such diverse figures as the poets Allen Ginsberg, Gregory Corso, and Lawrence Ferlinghetti and the novelists William Burroughs and Jack Kerouac. Ginsberg's *Howl* (1956) is a central Beat achievement in its breathless, chanted celebration of the down-and-out and the subculture of drug users, social misfits, and compulsive wanderers, as well as in representing the derangement of the intellect and the senses effected by sexual abandon, drugged hallucinations, and religious ecstasies. (Compare the vogue of *decadence* in the late nineteenth century.) A representative and influential novel of the movement is Jack Kerouac's *On the Road* (1958). While the Beat movement was short-lived, it left its imprint on the subjects and forms of many writers of the 1960s and 1970s; see *counterculture*, under *Periods of American Literature*.

Refer to Lawrence Lipton, *The Holy Barbarians* (1959); Seymour Krim, ed., *The Beats* (1960); Ann Charters, ed., *The Portable Beat Reader* (1992). Brenda Knight, ed., *Women of the Beat Generation: The Writers, Artists and Muses at the Heart of a Revolution* (1996); Jonah Raskin, *American Scream: Allen Ginsberg's "Howl" and the Making of the Beat Generation* (2004). Holly George-Warren has edited a collection of essays, reviews, memoirs, and interviews: *Rolling Stone Book of the Beats: The Beat Generation and American Culture* (1999).

For references to *Beat Writers* in other entries, see pages *69, 249, 287.*

**beginning** (of a plot): **267**.

**beliefs** (in reading literature): **118**.

**bibliography: 30.**

**Bildungsroman** (bĭld″ ungsrōmän′): **229**.

**binary opposition: 71**; *88, 118.*

**biography:** Late in the seventeenth century, John Dryden defined biography neatly as "the history of particular men's lives." The name now connotes a relatively full account of a particular person's life, involving the attempt to set forth character, temperament, and milieu, as well as the subject's activities and experiences.

Both the ancient Greeks and Romans produced short, formal lives of individuals. The most famed surviving example is the *Parallel Lives* of Greek and Roman notables by the Greek writer Plutarch, c. AD 46–120; in the translation by Sir Thomas North in 1579, it was the source of Shakespeare's plays on Roman subjects. Medieval authors wrote generalized chronicles of the deeds of a king, as well as **hagiographies**: the stylized lives of Christian saints, often based more on pious legends than on fact. In England, the fairly detailed secular biography appeared in

the seventeenth century; the most distinguished instance is Izaak Walton's *Lives* (including short biographies of the poets John Donne and George Herbert), written between 1640 and 1678.

The eighteenth century in England is the age of the emergence of the full-scale biography, and also of the theory of biography as a special literary *genre*. It was the century of Samuel Johnson's *Lives of the English Poets* (1779–81) and of the best known of all English biographies, James Boswell's *Life of Samuel Johnson* (1791). In our own time, biographies of notable women and men have become one of the most popular of literary forms, and usually there is at least one biographical title high on the bestseller list.

**Autobiography** is a biography written by the subject about himself or herself. It is to be distinguished from the **memoir**, in which the emphasis is not on the author's developing self but on the people and events that the author has known or witnessed, and also from the private **diary** or **journal**, which is a day-to-day record of the events in one's life, written for personal use and satisfaction, with little or no thought of publication. Examples of the latter type are the seventeenth-century diaries of Samuel Pepys and John Evelyn, the eighteenth-century journals of James Boswell and Fanny Burney, and Dorothy Wordsworth's remarkable *Journals*, written 1798–1828, but not published until long after her death. The first fully developed autobiography is also the most influential: the *Confessions* of St. Augustine, written in the fourth century. The design of this profound and subtle **spiritual autobiography** centers on what became the crucial experience in Christian autobiography: the author's anguished mental crisis, and a recovery and **conversion** in which he discovers his Christian identity and religious vocation.

Michel de Montaigne's *Essays*, published in 1580 and in later expansions, constitute in their sum the first great instance of autobiographical self-revelation that is presented for its inherent interest, rather than for religious or didactic purposes. Among later distinguished achievements in secular autobiography are Rousseau's *Confessions* (written 1764–70), Goethe's *Dichtung und Wahrheit* ("Poetry and Truth," written 1810–31), the autobiographies of Benjamin Franklin, Henry Adams, Sean O'Casey, Lillian Hellman, and Gertrude Stein (published in 1933 under the title *The Autobiography of Alice B. Toklas*), and *The Autobiography of Malcolm X* (1964). Many spiritual histories of the self, however, like John Bunyan's *Grace Abounding to the Chief of Sinners* (1666), followed Augustine's example of religious self-revelation centering on a crisis and conversion. An important offshoot of this type are secular autobiographies that represent a spiritual crisis which is resolved by the author's discovery of his identity and vocation, not as a Christian, but as a poet or artist; examples are Wordsworth's autobiography in verse, *The Prelude* (completed 1805, published in revised form 1850), or the partly autobiographical works of prose fiction such as Marcel Proust's *À la recherche du temps perdu* (1913–27), James Joyce's *Portrait of the Artist as a Young Man* (1915), and Ralph Ellison's *Invisible Man* (1965). In recent years, the distinction between autobiography and fiction has become more and more blurred, as authors include themselves under their own names in novels, or write autobiographies in the asserted mode of fiction, or (as in Maxine Hong Kingston's *The*

*Woman Warrior,* 1975) mingle fiction and personal experience as a way to get at one's essential life story (see the entry *novel*).

On biography: Donald A. Stauffer, *English Biography before 1700* (1930) and *The Art of Biography in Eighteenth-Century England* (1941); Leon Edel, *Literary Biography* (1957); Richard D. Altick, *Lives and Letters: A History of Literary Biography in England and America* (1965); David Novarr, *The Lines of Life: Theories of Biography, 1880–1970* (1986); Linda Wagner-Martin, *Telling Women's Lives: The New Biography* (1994). Catherine N. Parke, *Biography: Writing Lives* (1996), includes a chapter on "Minority Biography." On autobiography: Roy Pascal, *Design and Truth in Autobiography* (1960); Estelle C. Jelinek, ed., *Women's Autobiography: Essays in Criticism* (1980); and *The Tradition of Women's Autobiography from Antiquity to the Present* (1986). For an extended discussion of Augustine, Rousseau, and Beckett, see James Olney, *Memory and Narrative: The Weave of Life-Writing* (2001). John N. Morris, in *Versions of the Self: Studies in English Autobiography from John Bunyan to John Stuart Mill* (1966), deals both with religious and secular spiritual autobiographies. M. H. Abrams, in *Natural Supernaturalism* (1971), describes the wide ramifications of spiritual autobiography in historical and philosophical as well as literary forms. Paul John Eakin's *How Our Lives Become Stories: Making Selves* (2001) is an account of autobiography that draws on cognitive science, memory studies, and developmental psychology.

**Black Aesthetic: 27**.

**Black Arts Movement:** The Black Arts Movement designates a number of *African-American* writers whose work was shaped by the social and political turbulence of the 1960s—the decade of massive protests against the Vietnam War, demands for the rights of blacks that led to repeated and sometimes violent confrontations, and the riots and burnings in Los Angeles, Detroit, New York, Newark, and other major cities. The literary movement was associated with the Black Power movement in politics, whose spokesmen, including Stokely Carmichael and Malcolm X, opposed the proponents of integration, and instead advocated black separatism, black pride, and black solidarity. Representatives of the Black Arts put their literary writings at the service of these social and political aims. As Larry Neal put it in his essay "The Black Arts Movement" (1968): "Black Art is the aesthetic and spiritual sister of the Black Power Concept. As such it envisions an art that speaks directly to the needs and aspirations of Black America" and "to the Afro-American desire for self-determination and nationhood."

The **Black Aesthetic** that was voiced or supported by writers in the movement rejected, as aspects of domination by white culture, the "high art" and modernist forms advocated by Ralph Ellison and other African-American writers in the 1950s. Instead, the black aesthetic called for the exploitation of the energy and freshness of the black vernacular, in rhythms and moods emulating jazz and the blues, dealing especially with the lives and concerns of lower-class blacks, and addressed to a black mass audience. The most notable and influential practitioner of the Black Arts was Imamu Amiri Baraka (born LeRoi Jones) who, after an early period in Greenwich Village as an associate of Allen Ginsberg and other

*Beat* writers, moved to Harlem, where he founded the Black Arts Repertory Theater/School in 1965. Baraka was distinguished as a poet, a dramatist (his play *Dutchman* is often considered an exemplary product of the Black Arts achievement), a political essayist, and a critic both of literature and of jazz music. Among other writers of the movement were the poets Etheredge Knight, Sonia Sanchez, Haki Madhubuti, and Nikki Giovanni; the authors of prose fiction John Alfred Williams, Eldridge Cleaver, and James Alan McPherson; and the playwrights Paul Carter Harrison and Ed Bullins.

The revolutionary impetus of the Black Arts Movement had diminished by the 1970s, and some of its pronouncements and achievements now seem undisciplined and crudely propagandistic. But its best writings survive, and their critical rationale and subject matter have served as models not only to later African-American writers, but also to Native American, Latino, Asian, and other *ethnic* writers in America. For a later emergence, on the popular level, of antiestablishment poetry by African-Americans, see *rap* under *performance poetry*.

*The Black Aesthetic*, ed. Addison Gayle (1971), includes essays that were important in establishing this mode of criticism by Ron Karenga, Don L. Lee, and Larry Neal, as well as by Gayle himself. See also Imamu Amiri Baraka, *Home: Social Essays* (1966), and editor with Larry Neal of *Black Fire: An Anthology of Afro-American Writing* (1968); Stephen Henderson, *Understanding the New Black Poetry* (1973); and the text, biographies, and bibliographies for "The Black Arts Movement: 1960–1970" in *The Norton Anthology of African American Literature*, ed. H. L. Gates, Nellie Y. McKay, and others, 1997.

**black comedy: 2**; *373*.

**black humor: 2**; *322, 382*.

**Black Mountain poets: 249**.

**Black writers: 246**. See also *African-American writers*.

**blank verse:** Blank verse consists of lines of *iambic pentameter* (five-stress iambic verse) which are unrhymed—hence the term "blank." Of all English metrical forms it is closest to the natural rhythms of English speech, yet flexible and adaptive to diverse levels of discourse; as a result it has been more frequently and variously used than any other form of versification. Soon after blank verse was introduced by the Earl of Surrey in his translations of Books 2 and 4 of Virgil's *The Aeneid* (about 1540), it became the standard meter for Elizabethan and later poetic drama; a free form of blank verse remained the medium in such twentieth-century verse plays as those by Maxwell Anderson and T. S. Eliot. John Milton used blank verse for his epic *Paradise Lost* (1667), James Thomson for his descriptive and philosophical *Seasons* (1726–30), William Wordsworth for his autobiographical *Prelude* (1805), Alfred, Lord Tennyson for the narrative *Idylls of the King* (1891), Robert Browning for *The Ring and the Book* (1868–69) and many dramatic monologues, and T. S. Eliot for much of *The Waste Land* (1922). A large number of meditative lyrics, from the *Romantic Period* to the present, have also been written in blank verse, including Coleridge's "Frost at Midnight," Wordsworth's "Tintern Abbey," Tennyson's "Tears, Idle Tears" (in which the blank verse is divided into five-line stanzas), and Wallace Stevens' "Sunday Morning."

Divisions in blank verse poems, used to set off a sustained passage, are called **verse paragraphs**. See, for example, the great verse paragraph of twenty-six lines which initiates Milton's *Paradise Lost*, beginning with "Of man's first disobedience" and ending with "And justify the ways of God to men"; also, the opening verse paragraph of twenty-two lines in Wordsworth's "Tintern Abbey" (1798), which begins:

> Five years have past; five summers, with the length
> Of five long winters! and again I hear
> These waters, rolling from their mountain-springs
> With a soft inland murmur.

See *meter*, and refer to Moody Prior's critical study of blank verse in *The Language of Tragedy* (1964). For references to *blank verse* in other entries, see pages *84, 129*.

**Bloomsbury Group:** Bloomsbury Group is the name applied to an informal association of writers, artists, and intellectuals, many of whom lived in Bloomsbury, a residential district in central London. This group of friends began to meet around 1905 for conversations about the arts and issues in philosophy. Its members, who opposed the narrow post-Victorian restrictions in both the arts and morality, included the novelists Virginia Woolf and E. M. Forster, the painters Duncan Grant and Vanessa Bell (Virginia Woolf's sister), the influential art critics Clive Bell and Roger Frye, the iconoclastic biographer of Victorian personages Lytton Strachey, and the famed economist John Maynard Keynes. Some members were linked not only by common interests and viewpoints but also by complicated erotic liaisons, both heterosexual and homosexual. The Bloomsbury Group had an important influence on innovative literary, artistic, and intellectual developments in the two decades after the First World War, which ended in 1918. See Leon Edel, *Bloomsbury: A House of Lions* (1979); S. P. Rosenbaum, ed., *The Bloomsbury Group: A Collection of Memoirs and Commentary* (1995).

**Bombast:** Bombast denotes a wordy and inflated diction that is patently disproportionate to the matter that it signifies. The magniloquence of even so fine a poet as Christopher Marlowe is at times inappropriate to its sense, as when Faustus declares (*Dr. Faustus*, 1604; III. i. 47ff.):

> Now by the kingdoms of infernal rule,
> Of Styx, Acheron, and the fiery lake
> Of ever-burning Phlegethon I swear
> That I do long to see the monuments
> And situation of bright-splendent Rome;

which is to say: "By Hades, I'd like to see Rome!" Bombast is a frequent component in the *heroic drama* of the late seventeenth and early eighteenth centuries. The pompous language of that drama is parodied in Henry Fielding's *Tom Thumb the Great* (1731), as in the noted opening of Act II. v., in which the diminutive male lover cries:

> Oh! Huncamunca, Huncamunca, oh!
> Thy pouting breasts, like kettle-drums of brass,
> Beat everlasting loud alarms of joy;
> As bright as brass they are, and oh! as hard;
> Oh! Huncamunca, Huncamunca, oh!

Fielding points out in a note that this passage was specifically a *parody* of James Thomson's bombastic lines in *The Tragedy of Sophonisba* (1730):

> Oh! Sophonisba, Sophonisba, oh!
> Oh! Narva, Narva, oh!

"Bombast" originally meant "cotton stuffing," and in Elizabethan times came to be used as a metaphor for an over-elaborate style.

**bomolochos** (bōmŏl′ ŏkŏs): **343**.

**book:** In its inclusive sense, the term designates any written or printed document which is of considerable length, yet is light and durable enough to be easily portable. Studies devoted to the identification of the authorship, dates of issue, *editions*, and physical properties of books are called **bibliography**.

In ancient Greece and Rome the standard form of the book was the double papyrus roll. **Papyrus**, which had been developed in Egypt, was made from the papyrus reed, which grows profusely in the Nile delta; the stems of the reed were cut into strips, soaked, and impregnated with paste. The texts were **manuscripts** (that is, written by hand), and were inscribed in columns; as the reader went along, he unwound the papyrus from the right-hand roll and wound it on the left-hand roll.

In a very important change in the form of the book during the fifth century of the Middle Ages, papyrus rolls were superseded by the parchment or vellum codex. **Parchment** was made from the skins of sheep, goats, or calves which were stretched and scraped clean to serve as a material for writing. **Vellum** is sometimes used interchangeably with "parchment," but is more useful as a term for an especially fine type of parchment that was prepared from the delicate skin of a calf or a kid. To make a **codex** (the plural is "codices"), the parchment was cut into leaves; as in the modern printed book, the leaves were stitched together on one side and then bound. The great advantages of the codex over the roll were that the codex could be opened at any point; the text could be inscribed on both sides of a leaf; and the resulting book was able to contain a much longer text than a manuscript roll. In its early era, the codex was used primarily for biblical texts—a single volume could contain all four Gospels, where a roll had been able to encompass only a single Gospel.

In the course of the Middle Ages, many monasteries had **scriptoria**—rooms in which scribes copied out texts; often, a number of scribes copied texts that were dictated by a reader, in an early form of the mass production of books. To make especially fine codices—at first for religious, and later for secular texts, including works of literature—the manuscripts were **illuminated**; that is, they were adorned by artists with bright-colored miniature paintings and ornamental scrolls. Since all kinds of parchment were expensive, written surfaces were sometimes scraped off, then used for a new text. Such parchments are called **palimpsests** (Greek for "scraped clean"); often, the original text, or in some cases multiple layers of texts, remain visible under an ultraviolet light.

Paper, invented by the Chinese as early as the first century AD, was introduced to Europe by the Arabs in the eighth century, after which it increasingly replaced parchment. Early paper was made from linen and cotton rags; later, technology was invented for making paper from the pulp of wood and other vegetable fibers. The use of paper was essential for the invention of printing. The Chinese had been printing from carved wood blocks since the sixth century; but in 1440–50, Johannes Gutenberg introduced in Germany a new craft of printing from movable metal type, with ink, on paper, by means of a press that was tightened by turning a levered screw. Within the next half-century this cheap method of making many uniform copies of a book had spread throughout Europe, with enormous consequences for the growth of literacy and learning, and for the widespread development of the experimental sciences. (See Elizabeth Eisenstein, *The Printing Press as an Agent of Change: Communications and Cultural Transformations in Early Modern Europe*, 2 vols., 1979.)

The term **incunabula** (the singular is incunabulum) designates books that were produced in the infancy of printing, during the half-century before 1500. "Incumabula" is Latin for "swaddling clothes" or "cradle."

From the mid-seventeenth century on, there was a great increase in literacy and in the demand by the general public for literary and all other types of books. The accessibility and affordability of books was greatly expedited, beginning in the nineteenth century, by the invention of machines—powered first by steam, then by electricity—for producing paper and type, printing and binding books, and reproducing illustrations. In the twentieth century, and even more in the present era, the primacy of the printed book for recording and disseminating all forms of information has been challenged by the invention and rapid proliferation of electronic media for processing texts and images.

Refer to the entries on *book editions, book format, book history studies,* and *textual studies*. For the history of the book trade from classical Greece through the twentieth century, see F. A. Mumby, *Publishing and Bookselling: From the Earliest Times to 1870* (5th ed., 1974), and Ian Norrie, *Mumby's Publishing and Bookselling in the Twentieth Century* (1982). On the making, format, and history of printed books, see Ronald B. McKerrow, *An Introduction to Bibliography for Literary Students* (rev. 1994).

**book editions:** In present usage, **edition** designates the total copies of a book that are printed from a single setting of type or other mode of reproduction. The various "printings" or "reprints" of an edition—sometimes with some minor changes in the text—may be spaced over a period of years. We now identify as a "new edition" a printing in which substantial changes have been made in the text. A text may be revised and reprinted in this way many times, hence the terms "second edition," "third edition," etc.

A **variorum edition** designates either (1) an edition of a work that lists the textual variants in an author's manuscripts and in revisions of the printed text; an example is *The Variorum Edition of the Poems of W. B. Yeats*, ed. Peter Allt and Russell K. Alspach (1957); or else (2) an edition of a text that includes a selection of annotations and commentaries on the text by previous editors and critics. (The term "variorum" is a short form of the Latin *cum notis variorum*: "with the annotations of various persons.") *The New Variorum Edition of Shakespeare* is a variorum edition in both senses of the word.

See *book*, and refer to Ronald B. McKerrow, *An Introduction to Bibliography* (rev. 1965); Fredson Bowers, *Principles of Bibliographical Description* (1949); Philip Gaskell, *A New Introduction to Bibliography* (1972).

**book format: Format** signifies the page size, shape, and other physical features of a book. The printer begins with a large "sheet"; if the sheet is folded once so as to form two "leaves" of four pages, the book is a **folio** (the Latin word for "leaf"). When we refer to "the first Shakespeare folio," for example, we mean a volume published in 1623, the first *edition* of Shakespeare's collected plays, the leaves of which were made by a single folding of the printer's sheets. A sheet folded twice into four leaves makes a **quarto**; a sheet folded a third time into eight leaves makes an **octavo**. In a **duodecimo** volume, a sheet is folded so as to make twelve leaves. The more leaves into which a single sheet is divided, the smaller the leaf, so that these terms indicate the dimensions of a book, but only approximately, because the size of the full sheet varies, especially in modern printing. It can be said, however, that a folio is a very large book; a quarto is the next in size, with a leaf that is nearly square. The third in size, the octavo, is the most frequently used in modern printing.

As this book is open in front of you, the page on the right is called a **recto** (Latin for "on the right"), and the page on the left is called a **verso** (Latin for "turned").

The **colophon** in older books was a note at the end stating such facts as the title, author, printer, and date of issue. In modern books the colophon is ordinarily in the front, on the title page. With reference to modern books, "colophon" has come to mean, usually, the publisher's emblem, such as a torch (Harper), an owl (Holt), or a ship (Viking).

**book history studies:** Investigations of all the factors involved in the production, distribution, and reception of recorded texts. Separate stages in this process—especially with reference to literary texts—had for many centuries been subjects of inquiry; but as a defined, systematic, and widely recognized study of the overall process, book history did not emerge until the 1980s. Within a few decades, this area became the subject of special journals, books, and learned conferences, and is increasingly being taught in university courses.

Traditionally, the production and dissemination of recorded texts had been conceived mainly as a self-contained and one-way process, in which the author conceives and inscribes a text, the publisher and printer reproduce the text in multiple copies, and the competent reader interprets the text in order to reconstitute the author's originating conception. From this age-old view, the current discipline of book history differs in three principal ways:

1. Traditional dealings with each stage in the production and dissemination of literary texts had been normative and evaluative. That is, literary authors were judged to be good or bad, major or minor; bibliographers set out to establish a single valid text, free from what were called "corruptions" by agents other than the originating author (see *textual criticism*); and interpretations of the text by readers were judged to be right or wrong, good or bad, sensitive or insensitive. In contrast, current exponents of book history tend to be objective and nonjudgmental. All contributions to a recorded text, whether by the author or other agents, and whether intentional or accidental, are taken into account; literary books, together with all other texts, are regarded as "commodities" that are marketed to readers, their "consumers," in order to make a profit; and the diverse responses to the text by different classes and groups, whether elite readers or mass audiences, are paid equal and neutral attention.

2. The book historian does not view the making and distribution of a book as a one-way process from author through publisher and printer to reader. Instead, Robert Darnton—an important early formulator of the point of view and procedures of book history—proposed in 1982 that historians view the "life cycle" of a book as a "communications circuit" that runs from the author through the publisher, printer, and distributors to the reader, and back to the author, in a process within which the reader "influences the author both before and after the act of composition." ("What Is the History of Books?," in *The Kiss of Lamourette: Reflections on Cultural History*, 1990.) In accordance with this perspective, book historians conceive all stages of the life cycle of a book to be interactive. The author, for example, is subject to the demands of the publisher, who estimates the market demands of readers; while the readers also directly influence the author who, in composing a work, anticipates the preferences of a potential audience.

3. In defining the overall "communications circuit," Robert Darnton emphasized also that book history deals with "each phase of this process . . . in all its relations with other systems, economic, social, political, and cultural, in the surrounding environment." D. F. McKenzie who, like Darnton, was influential in describing and exemplifying the emerging practice of book history, described the new development in *bibliography* as "a sociology of texts" that considers "the human motives and interactions" at each point in "the production, transmission, and consumption of texts." ("The Book as an Expressive Form," in *Bibliography and the Sociology of Texts*, 1986; rev. 1999.) Book history, that is, deals with the formation and dissemination of a text, not as a self-contained process, but as one that at every stage is affected by, and in turn may influence, the economic, social, and cultural circumstances of its time and place.

Applied to the long-term development of ways of recording and communicating information, book history deals with the sequence of revolutionary changes that occurred when an oral culture was succeeded by a *manuscript* culture; when the era of written texts in turn gave way, in the mid-fifteenth century, to a primarily print culture; and when, as the result of new technologies that began in the twentieth century, printed books and materials were increasingly supplemented— and to some extent displaced—by film, television, the computer, and the World Wide Web. (See *oral poetry* and *book.*) An influential work that deals with the impact on western civilization, science, and the arts by the change from script to print is Elizabeth Eisenstein, *The Printing Press as an Agent of Change* (2 vols., 1979).

The major focus by book historians has been on the era of print, and especially on the diverse circumstances that affect each stage of the production, distribution, and reception of the printed book. To cite a few prominent examples:

D. F. McKenzie has emphasized the contributions to the book, not only by the author, the author's literary advisers, and copyeditors but also by the book designer and the printer who—often with little or no consultation with an author— determine the typography, spatial layout, illustrations, paper, and binding of a book. All such nonverbal, material features of a book, McKenzie insists, are not neutral vehicles for the printed word, but have an "expressive function" and contribute to the meaning of the verbal text. (See D. F. McKenzie, *Bibliography and the Sociology of Texts*, 1986; also, for similar views about the signifying function of the material features of a book, Jerome McGann, *The Textual Condition*, 1991.)

A prolific and influential contributor to book history is the French scholar Roger Chartier, especially in his emphasis on recorded facts about the differing ways in which diverse readers have received and responded to printed texts. He has, for example, studied the literacy rates of various classes and groups of people at different times and places. He has chronicled the shift from the public to the private reading of texts, and in private reading, the change from reading to oneself aloud to reading in silence; this last practice, according to Chartier, "fostered a solitary and private relation between the reader and his book," "radically transformed intellectual work," and greatly expanded the reader's "inner life." Chartier also analyzed the degree to which people in particular localities, employing diverse "social and cultural practices" in their reading, created a diversity of interpretations of a single text. (Roger Chartier, *The Culture of Print: Power and the Uses of Print in Early Modern Europe*, 1989; and *Forms and Meanings: Texts, Performances, and Audiences from Codex to Computer*, 1995.) Other scholars have chronicled the emergence of mass audiences for printed books and journals, and have compared the literary preferences and responses of a mass audience with those of elite readers and critics. (Richard Altick, *The English Common Reader: A Social History of the Mass Reading Public, 1800—1900*, 1957, rev. 1998; Jonathan Rose, "Rereading the English Common Reader," *Journal of the History of Ideas*, Vol. 53, 1992.) There are also numerous studies of the variety of factors that affect the reception, interpretation, and evaluation of literary books. Jane Tompkins, for example, investigated the importance of an influential coterie of friends, reviewers, and magazine editors in establishing and sustaining the reputation of a novelist. (*Sensational Designs: The Cultural Work of American Fiction, 1790—1860*, 1985.) And in *A Feeling for Books*, 1997, Janice Radway shows that the panelists in the

Book-of-the-Month Club—founded in the 1920s, and still flourishing—have made their selections not in accordance with a general criterion of literary excellence, but by matching books to the tastes and preferences of specific groups of readers in the literary marketplace.

For studies of individual stages in the production and reception of literary books that have contributed to book history, see the latter-day developments described in the entries on *author and authorship, reader-response criticism, reception-theory, sociology of literature,* and *textual criticism.* All the researchers mentioned in this entry on book history studies are represented in the anthology, *The Book History Reader,* edited by David Finkelstein and Alistair McCleery, 2002. Influential works, in addition to those already referred to, are: Marshall McLuhan, *The Gutenberg Galaxy: The Making of Typographic Man* (1962); Robert Darnton, *The Business of Enlightenment: A Publishing History of the Encyclopédie, 1775–1800* (1979); Walter J. Ong, *Orality and Literacy: The Technologizing of the Word* (1982); D. F. McKenzie, "The Sociology of a Text: Orality, Literacy and Print in Early New Zealand," *The Library,* 1984, pp. 333–65; John Sutherland, *Victorian Fiction: Writers, Publishers, Readers* (1995); Geoffrey Nunberg, ed., *The Future of the Book* (1996); Adrian Johns, *The Nature of the Book: Print and Knowledge in the Making* (1998).

**bourgeois epic** (boor′ zwä): **99**.

**bourgeois tragedy: 373**.

**bowdlerize:** To delete from an edition of a literary work passages considered by the editor to be indecent or indelicate. The word derives from the Reverend Thomas Bowdler, who tidied up his *Family Shakespeare* in 1818 by omitting, as he put it, "whatever is unfit to be read by a gentleman in a company of ladies." Jonathan Swift's *Gulliver's Travels* (1726) and *The Arabian Nights,* as well as Shakespeare's plays, are often bowdlerized in editions intended for the young; and until the 1920s, at which time the standards of literary propriety were drastically liberalized, some compilers of anthologies for college students availed themselves of Bowdler's prerogative in editing Chaucer.

**Breton lay: 170**.

**broadside ballad: 22**.

**bucolic poetry** (byookŏl′ ik): **240**.

**burlesque:** Burlesque has been succinctly defined as "an incongruous imitation"; that is, it imitates the manner (the form and style) or else the subject matter of a serious literary work or a literary *genre,* in verse or in prose, but makes the imitation amusing by a ridiculous disparity between the manner and the matter. The burlesque may be written for the sheer fun of it; usually, however, it is a form of *satire.* The butt of the satiric ridicule may be the particular work or the genre that is being imitated, or else the subject matter to which the imitation is incongruously applied, or (often) both of these together.

"Burlesque," "parody," and "travesty" are sometimes applied interchangeably; simply to equate these terms, however, is to surrender useful critical distinctions. It is better to follow the critics who use "burlesque" as the generic name and use the other terms to discriminate species of burlesque; we must keep in mind, however, that a single instance of burlesque may exploit a variety of techniques. The application of these terms will be clearer if we make two preliminary distinctions: (1) In a burlesque imitation, the form and style may be either lower or higher in level and dignity than the subject to which it is incongruously applied. (See the discussion of levels under *style*.) If the form and style are high and dignified but the subject is low or trivial, we have "high burlesque"; if the subject is high in status and dignity but the style and manner of treatment are low and undignified, we have "low burlesque." (2) A burlesque may also be distinguished according to whether it imitates a general literary type or genre, or else a particular work or author. Applying these two distinctions, we get the following species of burlesque.

I. **Varieties of high burlesque:**
  A.  A **parody** imitates the serious manner and characteristic features of a particular literary work, or the distinctive style of a particular author, or the typical stylistic and other features of a serious literary genre, and deflates the original by applying the imitation to a lowly or comically inappropriate subject. John Phillips' "The Splendid Shilling" (1705) parodied the epic style of John Milton's *Paradise Lost* (1667) by exaggerating its high formality and applying it to the description of a tattered poet composing in a drafty attic. Henry Fielding in *Joseph Andrews* (1742) parodied Samuel Richardson's novel *Pamela* (1740–41) by putting a hearty male hero in place of Richardson's sexually beleaguered heroine, and later on Jane Austen poked good-natured fun at the genre of the *gothic novel* in *Northanger Abbey* (1818). Here is Hartley Coleridge's parody of the first stanza of William Wordsworth's "She Dwelt among the Untrodden Ways," which he applies to Wordsworth himself:

> He lived amidst th' untrodden ways
> To Rydal Lake that lead,
> A bard whom there were none to praise,
> And very few to read.

From the early nineteenth century to the present, parody has been the favorite form of burlesque. Among the gifted parodists of the past century in England were Max Beerbohm (see *A Christmas Garland*, 1912) and Stella Gibbons (*Cold Comfort Farm*, 1936), and in America, James Thurber, Phyllis McGinley, and E. B. White. The novel *Possession* (1990), by the English writer A. S. Byatt, exemplifies a serious literary form which includes straight-faced parodies of Victorian poetry and prose, as well as of academic scholarly writings.

  B.  A **mock epic** or **mock-heroic** poem is that type of parody which imitates, in a sustained way, both the elaborate form and the ceremonious style of the *epic* genre, but applies it to narrate a commonplace or trivial subject matter. In a masterpiece of this type, *The Rape of the Lock* (1714), Alexander Pope views through the grandiose epic perspective a quarrel between the belles and elegants of his day over the theft of a lady's curl. The story includes such elements of traditional epic protocol as supernatural *machinery*, a voyage on board ship, a visit to the underworld, and a heroically scaled battle between the sexes—although with metaphors, hatpins, and snuff for weapons. The term *mock-heroic* is often applied to other dignified poetic forms which are purposely mismatched to a lowly subject; for example, to Thomas Gray's comic "Ode on the Death of a Favorite Cat" (1748); see under *bathos and anticlimax*.

II. **Varieties of low burlesque:**

A. The **Hudibrastic poem** takes its name from Samuel Butler's *Hudibras* (1663), which satirized rigid Puritanism by describing the adventures of a Puritan knight, Sir Hudibras. Instead of the doughty deeds and dignified style of the traditional genre of the *chivalric romance*, however, we find the knightly hero experiencing mundane and humiliating misadventures which are described in *doggerel* verses and a ludicrously colloquial idiom.

B. The **travesty** mocks a particular work by treating its lofty subject in a grotesquely undignified manner and style. As Boileau put it, describing a travesty of Virgil's Aeneid, "Dido and Aeneas are made to speak like fishwives and ruffians." The New Yorker once published a travesty of Ernest Hemingway's novel Across the River and Into the Trees (1950) with the title Across the Street and Into the Bar, and the film Young Frankenstein is a travesty of Mary Shelley's novel Frankenstein.

Another form of burlesque is the **lampoon**: a short satirical work, or a passage in a longer work, which describes the appearance and character of a particular person in a way that makes that person ridiculous. It typically employs **caricature**, which in a verbal description (as in graphic art) exaggerates or distorts, for comic effect, a person's distinctive physical features or personality traits. John Dryden's *Absalom and Achitophel* (1681) includes a famed twenty-five-line lampoon of Zimri (Dryden's contemporary, the Duke of Buckingham), which begins:

> In the first rank of these did Zimri stand;
> A man so various, that he seemed to be
> Not one, but all mankind's epitome:
> Stiff in opinions, always in the wrong;
> Was everything by starts, and nothing long. . . .

The modern sense of "burlesque" as a theater form derives, historically, from plays which mocked serious types of drama by an incongruous imitation. John Gay's *Beggar's Opera* (1728)—which in turn became the model for the German *Threepenny Opera* by Bertolt Brecht and Kurt Weill (1928)—was a high burlesque of Italian opera, applying its dignified formulas to a company of beggars and thieves. A number of the comic musical plays by Gilbert and Sullivan in the Victorian era also include elements of high burlesque of grand opera.

See George Kitchin, *A Survey of Burlesque and Parody in English* (1931); Richmond P. Bond, *English Burlesque Poetry, 1700–1750* (1932); Margaret A.

Rose, *Parody: Ancient, Modern, and Post-Modern* (1993). Anthologies: Walter Jerrold and R. M. Leonard, eds., *A Century of Parody and Imitation* (1913); Robert P. Falk, ed., *The Antic Muse: American Writers in Parody* (1955); Dwight MacDonald, ed., *Parodies: An Anthology* (1960).

**cacophony** (kăkŏf′ ŏnē): **105**.

**caesura** (sĕzyoor′ ă): **197**.

**canon of literature:** The Greek word "kanon," signifying a measuring rod or a rule, was extended to denote a list or catalogue, then came to be applied to the list of books in the Hebrew Bible and the New Testament which were designated by church authorities to be the genuine Holy Scriptures. A number of writings related to those in the Scriptures, but not admitted into the authoritative canon, are called **apocrypha**; eleven books which have been included in the Roman Catholic biblical canon are considered apocryphal by Protestants.

The term "canon" was later used to signify the list of secular works accepted by experts as genuinely written by a particular author. We speak thus of "the Chaucer canon" and "the Shakespeare canon," and refer to other works that have sometimes been attributed to an author, but on evidence that many editors judge to be inadequate or invalid, as "apocryphal." In recent decades the phrase **literary canon** has come to designate—in world literature, or in European literature, but most frequently in a national literature—those authors who, by a cumulative consensus of critics, scholars, and teachers, have come to be widely recognized as "major," and to have written works often hailed as literary *classics*. The literary works by canonical authors are the ones which, at a given time, are most kept in print, most frequently and fully discussed by literary critics and historians, and—in the present era—most likely to be included in anthologies and in the syllabi of college courses with titles such as "World Masterpieces," "Major English Authors," or "Great American Writers."

The use of the term "canon" with reference both to the books of the Bible and to secular literature obscures important differences in the two applications. The biblical canon has been established by church authorities vested with the power to make such a decision; is enforced by authorities with the power to impose religious sanctions; is explicit in the books that it lists; and is closed, permitting neither deletions nor additions. (See the entry "Canon" in *The Oxford Companion to the Bible*, 1993.) The canon of literature, on the other hand, is the product of a wavering and unofficial consensus; it is tacit rather than explicit, loose in its boundaries, and always subject to changes in the works that it includes.

The social process by which an author or a literary work comes to be widely although tacitly recognized as canonical has come to be called "canon formation." The factors in this formative process are complex and disputed. It seems clear, however, that the process involves, among other conditions, a broad concurrence of critics, scholars, and authors with diverse viewpoints and sensibilities; the persistent influence of, and reference to, an author in the work of other authors; the frequent reference to an author or work within the discourse of a cultural community; and the widespread assignment of an author or text in school and college curricula. Such factors are of course mutually interactive, and they need to be sustained over a period of time. In his "Preface to Shakespeare" (1765) Samuel Johnson said that a century is "the term commonly fixed as a test of literary merit." Some authors of the past century such as Marcel Proust, Franz Kafka, Thomas Mann, and James Joyce—probably even more recent writers such as Vladimir Nabokov and Milan Kundera—have achieved the prestige, influence, assignment in college courses, and persistence of reference in literary discourse to establish them in the European canon; others, including Yeats, T. S. Eliot, Virginia Woolf, and Robert Frost, are already secure in their national canons, at least.

At any time, the boundaries of a literary canon remain indefinite and disputable, while inside those boundaries some authors are central and others more marginal. Occasionally an earlier author who was for long on the fringe of the canon, or even outside it, gets transferred to a position of eminence. A conspicuous example was John Donne, who from the eighteenth century on was regarded mainly as an interestingly eccentric poet. T. S. Eliot, followed by Cleanth Brooks and other *New Critics* in the 1930s and later, made Donne's writings the very paradigm of the self-ironic and paradoxical poetry they most admired, and so helped elevate him to a high place within the English canon. (See *metaphysical poets.*) Since then, Donne's reputation has somewhat diminished, but he remains prominent in the canon. Once firmly established, an author shows considerable resistance to being disestablished by adverse criticism and changing literary preferences. For example, many New Critics, together with the influential F. R. Leavis in England, while lauding Donne, vigorously attacked the Romantic poet Shelley as embodying poetic qualities they strongly condemned; but although a considerable number of critics joined in this derogation of Shelley, the long-term effect was to aggrandize the critical attention and discussion that helps sustain an author's place in the canon.

Since the 1970s, the nature of canon formation, and opposition to established literary canons, has become a leading concern among critics of diverse theoretical viewpoints, whether deconstructive, feminist, Marxist, postcolonial, or new historicist (see *poststructuralism*). The debate often focuses on the practical issue of what books to assign in college curricula, especially in required "core courses" in the humanities and in Western civilization. A widespread charge is that the standard canon of great books, not only in literature but in all areas of *humanistic* study, has been determined less by artistic excellence than by the politics of power; that is, that the canon has been formed in accordance with the *ideology*, political interests, and values of a dominant class that was white, male, and European. As a result, it is frequently claimed that the canon consists mainly of works that convey and sustain racism, *patriarchy*, and imperialism, and understate or exclude interests and accomplishments of blacks, Hispanics, and other ethnic minorities, and also the achievements of women, the working class, popular culture, homosexuals, and non-European civilizations. The demand is "to open the canon" so as to make it **multicultural** instead of "Eurocentric." (As applied to literary scholarship, "multicultural" designates the movement to redress what are asserted to be the errors and injustices of a history dominated by Europe-centered historians, so as to make it represent adequately the cultural contributions of races and groups that have been hitherto marginalized or ignored. See *Multiculturalism: Roots and Realities,* ed. James Trotman, 2002.) Another demand that is frequently voiced is that the standard canon be stripped of its elitism and its "hierarchism"— that is, its built-in discriminations between high art and lower art—in order to include such cultural products as Hollywood films, television serials, popular songs, and fiction written for a mass audience. There is also a radical wing of revisionist theorists who, to further their political aim to transform the existing power structures, demand not merely the opening, but the abolition of the standard canon and its replacement by currently marginal and excluded groups and texts.

The views of defenders of the standard canon, like those of its opponents, range from moderate to extreme. The position of many moderate defenders might be summarized as follows: Whatever has been the influence of class, gender, race, and other special interests and prejudices in forming the existing canon, this is far from the whole story. The canon is the result of the concurrence of a great many (often unexpressed) norms and standards, and among these, one crucial factor has been the high intellectual and artistic quality of the canonical works themselves, and their attested power to enlighten and give delight, and to appeal to widely shared human concerns and values. (See *humanism.*) Moderate defenders agree to the desirability of enlarging the canon of texts that are assigned frequently in academic courses, in order to make the canon more broadly representative of diverse cultures, ethnic groups, classes, and interests; they point out, however, that such changes would not be a drastic innovation, since the educational canon has always been subject to deletions and additions. They emphasize also that the existing Western, English, and American canons include notable exemplars of skepticism about established ways of thinking, of political radicalism, and of the toleration of dissent—features of the accepted canon of which the present proponents of radical change are, clearly, the inheritors and beneficiaries. And however a canon is enlarged to represent other cultures and classes, moderate defenders insist on the need to maintain a continuing study of and dialogue with the diverse and long-lasting works of intellect and imagination that have shaped Western civilization and constitute much of Western culture. They point to the enduring primacy, over many centuries, of such Western authors as Homer, Plato, Dante, and Shakespeare. They also remark that many theorists who challenge the traditional English canon, when they turn from theory to applied criticism, attend preponderantly to established authors—not only Shakespeare, but also Spenser, Milton, Jane Austen, Wordsworth, George Eliot, Whitman, Henry James, and many others—and so recognize and confirm in practice the literary canon that they in theory oppose.

For discussions of the nature and formation of the literary canon, see the collection of essays edited by Robert von Hallberg, *Canons* (1984); John Guillory, *Cultural Capital: The Problem of Literary Canon Formation* (1993); and Wendell V. Harris, "Canonicity," *PMLA,* Vol. 106 (1991), pp. 110–21. Questioners or opponents of the traditional canon: Leslie A. Fiedler and Houston A. Baker, Jr., eds., *English Literature: Opening Up the Canon* (1981); Jane Tompkins, *Sensational*

*Designs: The Cultural Work of American Fiction, 1790–1860* (1985); Barbara Herrnstein Smith, *Contingencies of Value: Alternative Perspectives for Critical Theory* (1988); Jonathan Culler, *Framing the Sign: Criticism and Its Institutions* (1988), chapter 2, "The Humanities Tomorrow"; and Darryl L. Gless and Barbara H. Smith, eds., *The Politics of Liberal Education* (1990). Defenses of the traditional canon: Frank Kermode, "Prologue" to *An Appetite for Poetry* (1989); the essays in *The Changing Culture of the University*, a special issue of *Partisan Review* (Spring 1991); Harold Bloom, *The Western Canon* (1994).

For references to *canon of literature* in other entries, see pages *89, 113*.

**cardinal sins: 330**.

**caricature: 37**.

**carnivalesque: 77**.

**Caroline Age: 253**.

**carpe diem:** Carpe Diem, meaning "seize the day," is a Latin phrase from one of Horace's *Odes* (I. xi.) which has become the name for a very common literary *motif*, especially in lyric poetry. The speaker in a carpe diem poem emphasizes that life is short and time is fleeting in order to urge his auditor—who is often represented as a virgin reluctant to change her condition—to make the most of present pleasures. A frequent emblem of the brevity of physical beauty and the finality of death is the rose, as in Edmund Spenser's *The Faerie Queene*, 1590–96 (II. xii. 74–75; "Gather therefore the Rose, whilst yet is prime"), and, in the seventeenth century, Robert Herrick's "To the Virgins, to Make Much of Time" ("Gather ye rosebuds, while ye may"), and Edmund Waller's "Go, Lovely Rose." The more complex poems of this type communicate the poignant sadness—or else desperation—of the pursuit of pleasures under the sentence of inevitable death; for example, Andrew Marvell's "To His Coy Mistress" (1681) and the set of variations on the carpe diem motif in *The Rubáiyát of Omar Khayyám*, translated by the Victorian poet Edward FitzGerald. In 1747 Lady Mary Wortley Montagu wrote "The Lover: A Ballad," a brilliant counter to the carpe diem poems written by male poets; in it, the woman explains to her importunate suitor why she finds him utterly resistible.

**catalectic** (kătălek′ tĭk): **195**.

**catastrophe** (in a plot) (kătăs′ trŏf̄e): **267**; *372, 375*.

**catharsis** (kăthär′ sĭs): **371**.

**Cavalier poets: 253**; *179*.

**Celtic Revival:** The Celtic Revival, also known as the **Irish Literary Renaissance**, identifies the remarkably creative period in Irish literature from about 1880 to the death of William Butler Yeats in 1939. The aim of Yeats and other early leaders of the movement was to create a distinctive national literature by going back to Irish history, legend, and folklore, as well as to native literary models. The major writers, however, wrote not in the native Irish (one of the Celtic languages) but in English, and under the influence of various non-Irish literary forms. A number of them also turned increasingly for their subject matter to modern Irish life rather than to the ancient past.

Notable poets in addition to Yeats were AE (George Russell) and Oliver St. John Gogarty. The dramatists included Yeats himself, as well as Lady Gregory (who was also an important patron and publicist for the movement), John Millington Synge, and later Sean O'Casey. Among the novelists were George Moore and James Stephens, as well as James Joyce, who, although he abandoned Ireland for Europe and ridiculed the excesses of the nationalist writers, adverted to Irish subject matter and characters in all his writings. As these names indicate, the Celtic Revival produced some of the greatest poetry, drama, and prose fiction written in English during the first four decades of the twentieth century.

See Herbert Howarth, *The Irish Writers* (1958); Phillip L. Marcus, *Yeats and the Beginning of the Irish Renaissance* (1970), and "The Celtic Revival: Literature and the Theater," in *The Irish World: The History and Cultural Achievements of the Irish People* (1977). Declan Kiberd, *Inventing Ireland* (1996), deals with the Irish writers as exemplary modernists. For the influence of anthropology on Irish revivalists, see Gregory Castle, *Modernism and the Celtic Revival* (2001).

**character and characterization:**

1. **The character** is the name of a literary *genre*; it is a short, and usually witty, sketch in prose of a distinctive type of person. The genre was inaugurated by Theophrastus, a Greek author of the second century BC, who wrote a lively book entitled *Characters*. The form had a great vogue in the early seventeenth century; the books of characters then written by Joseph Hall, Sir Thomas Overbury, and John Earle influenced later writers of essays, history, and fiction. The titles of some of Overbury's sketches will indicate the nature of the form: "A Courtier," "A Wise Man," "A Fair and Happy Milkmaid." See Richard Aldington's anthology *A Book of "Characters"* (1924).

2. **Characters** are the persons represented in a dramatic or narrative work, who are interpreted by the reader as possessing particular moral, intellectual, and emotional qualities by inferences from what the persons say and their distinctive ways of saying it—the **dialogue**—and from what they do—the **action**. The grounds in the characters' temperament, desires, and moral nature for their speech and actions are called their **motivation**. A character may remain essentially "stable," or unchanged in outlook and disposition, from beginning to end of a work (Prospero in Shakespeare's *The Tempest*, Micawber in Charles Dickens' *David Copperfield*, 1849–50), or may undergo a radical change, either through a gradual process of development (the title character in Jane Austen's *Emma*, 1816) or as the result of a crisis (Shakespeare's *King Lear*, Pip in Dickens' *Great Expectations*). Whether a character remains stable or changes, the reader of a traditional and realistic work expects "consistency"—the character should not

suddenly break off and act in a way not plausibly grounded in his or her temperament as we have already come to know it.

E. M. Forster, in *Aspects of the Novel* (1927), introduced new terms for an old distinction by discriminating between flat and round characters. A **flat character** (also called a **type**, or "two-dimensional"), Forster says, is built around "a single idea or quality" and is presented without much individualizing detail, and therefore can be described adequately in a single phrase or sentence. A **round character** is complex in temperament and motivation and is represented with subtle particularity; such a character therefore is as difficult to describe with any adequacy as a person in real life, and like real persons, is capable of surprising us. A *humours character*, such as Ben Jonson's "Sir Epicure Mammon," has a name which says it all, in contrast to the roundness of character in Shakespeare's multifaceted Falstaff. Almost all dramas and narratives, properly enough, have some characters who serve merely as functionaries and are not characterized at all, as well as other characters who are left relatively flat: there is no need, in Shakespeare's *Henry IV, Part I*, for Mistress Quickly to be as globular as Falstaff. The degree to which, to be regarded as artistically successful, characters need to be three-dimensional depends on their function in the plot; in many types of narrative, such as in the detective story or adventure novel or farce comedy, even the protagonist is usually two-dimensional. Sherlock Holmes and Long John Silver do not require, for their excellent literary roles, the roundness of a Hamlet, a Becky Sharp, or a Jay Gatsby. In his *Anatomy of Criticism* (1957), Northrop Frye has proposed that even lifelike characters are identifiable variants, more or less individualized, of stock two-dimensional types in old literary genres, such as the self-deprecating "eiron," the boastful "alazon," and the "senex iratus," or choleric old father in classical comedy. (See *stock characters*.)

A broad distinction is frequently made between alternative methods for **characterizing** (that is, establishing the distinctive characters of) the persons in a narrative: showing and telling. In **showing** (also called "the dramatic method"), the author simply presents the characters talking and acting, and leaves it entirely up to the reader to infer the motives and dispositions that lie behind what they say and do. The author may show not only external speech and actions, but also a character's inner thoughts, feelings, and responsiveness to events; for a highly developed mode of such inner showing, see *stream of consciousness*. In **telling**, the author intervenes authoritatively in order to describe, and often to evaluate, the motives and dispositional qualities of the characters. For example, in the terse opening chapter of *Pride and Prejudice* (1813), Jane Austen first shows us Mr. and Mrs. Bennet as they talk to one another about the young man who has just rented Netherfield Park, then (in the quotation below) tells us about them, and so confirms and expands the inferences that we have begun to make from what has been shown.

> Mr. Bennet was so odd a mixture of quick parts, sarcastic humour,
> reserve, and caprice, that the experience of three-and-twenty years had
> been insufficient to make his wife understand his character. *Her* mind
> was less difficult to develop. She was a woman of mean understanding,
> little information, and uncertain temper.

Especially since the novelistic theory and practice of Flaubert and Henry James, a critical tendency has been to consider "telling" a violation of artistry and to recommend only the technique of "showing" characters; authors, it is said, should totally efface themselves in order to write "objectively," "impersonally," or "dramatically." Such judgments, however, privilege a modern artistic limitation suited to particular novelistic effects, and decry an alternative method of characterization which a number of novelists have employed to produce masterpieces. (See *point of view.*)

Innovative writers in the twentieth century—including novelists from James Joyce to French writers of the *new novel*, and authors of the dramas and novels of the *absurd* and various experimental forms—often presented the persons in their works in ways which ran counter to the earlier mode of representing lifelike characters who manifest a consistent substructure of individuality. Structuralist critics undertook to dissolve even the lifelike characters of traditional novels into a system of literary conventions and codes which are *naturalized* by the readers; that is, readers are said to project lifelikeness upon codified literary representations by assimilating them into their own prior stereotypes of individuals in real life. See *structuralist criticism* and *text and writing (écriture)*, and refer to Jonathan Culler, *Structuralist Poetics* (1975), chapter 9, "Poetics of the Novel."

See *plot* and *narrative and narratology*. For the traditional problems and methods of characterization, including discussions of showing and telling, see in addition to E. M. Forster (above), Percy Lubbock, *The Craft of Fiction* (1926); Wayne C. Booth, *The Rhetoric of Fiction* (1961), especially chapters 1–4: and W. J. Harvey, *Character and the Novel* (1965). On problems in determining dramatic character, see Bert O. States, *The Pleasure of the Play* (1994); and on the disappearance of traditional characterization in postmodern drama, Elinor Fuchs, *The Death of Character* (1996). On the formal distinction between primary characters (*protagonists*) and minor characters, see Alex Woloch, *The One vs. the Many: Minor Characters and the Space of the Protagonist in the Novel* (2003).

**character, the** (a literary form): **42**; *287*.

**characterizing: 43**. See also *distance and involvement; empathy and sympathy*.

**chiasmus** (kīăz′ mŭs): **314**.

**Chicago School** (of criticism): **126**; *135*.

**chivalric romance:** Chivalric romance (or **medieval romance**) is a type of narrative that developed in twelfth-century France, spread to the literatures of other countries, and displaced the earlier *epic* and heroic forms. ("Romance" originally signified a work written in the French language, which evolved from a dialect of the Roman language, Latin.) Romances were at first written in verse, but later in prose as well. The **romance** is distinguished from the epic in that it does not represent a heroic age of tribal wars, but a courtly and chivalric age, often one of highly developed manners and civility. Its standard plot is that of a quest undertaken by a single knight in order to gain a lady's favor; frequently its central interest is *courtly love*, together with tournaments fought and dragons and monsters slain for the damsel's sake; it stresses the chivalric ideals of courage, loyalty, honor, mercifulness to an opponent, and elaborate manners; and it delights in wonders and marvels. Supernatural events in the epic usually were attributed to the will and actions of the gods; romance shifts the supernatural to this world, and makes much of the mysterious effect of magic, spells, and enchantments.

The recurrent materials of medieval chivalric romances have been divided by scholars into four classes of subjects: (1) "The Matter of Britain" (Celtic subject matter, especially stories centering on the court of King Arthur). (2) "The Matter of Rome" (the history and legends of classical antiquity, including the exploits of Alexander the Great and of the heroes of the Trojan War); Geoffrey Chaucer's *Troilus and Criseyde* belongs to this class. (3) "The Matter of France" (Charlemagne and his knights). (4) "The Matter of England" (heroes such as King Horn and Guy of Warwick). The cycle of tales which developed around the pseudohistorical British King Arthur produced many of the finest romances, some of them (stories of Sir Perceval and the quest for the Holy Grail) with a religious instead of a purely secular content. Chrétien de Troyes, the great twelfth-century French poet, wrote Arthurian romances; German examples are Wolfram von Eschenbach's *Parzival* and Gottfried von Strassburg's *Tristan und Isolde*, both written early in the thirteenth century. *Sir Gawain and the Green Knight*, composed in fourteenth-century England, is a **metrical romance** (that is, a romance written in verse) about an Arthurian knight; and Thomas Malory's *Morte d'Arthur* (fifteenth century) is an English version in prose of the cycle of earlier metrical romances about Arthur and various of his Knights of the Round Table.

See *prose romance, Gothic romance*, and *romantic comedy*. Refer to L. A. Hibbard, *Medieval Romance in England* (rev. 1961); R. S. Loomis, *The Development of Arthurian Romance* (1963) and *The Grail* (1963); the anthology *Medieval Romances*, ed. R. S. and L. H. Loomis (1957); and *The Cambridge Companion to Medieval Romance*, ed. Roberta L. Krueger (2000). For the history of the term "romance" and modern extensions of the genre of romance, see Gillian Beer, *The Romance* (1970); and for Northrop Frye's theory of the mythical basis of the romance genre, see the entry in this *Glossary* on *myth*. For references to *chivalric romance* in other entries, see pages *15, 37, 59, 228, 252*.

**choral character: 46**.

**chorus:** Among the ancient Greeks the chorus was a group of people, wearing masks, who sang or chanted verses while performing dancelike movements at religious festivals. A similar chorus played a part in Greek tragedies, where (in the plays of Aeschylus and Sophocles) they served mainly as commentators on the dramatic actions and events who expressed traditional moral, religious, and social attitudes; beginning with Euripides, however, the chorus assumed primarily a lyrical function. The Greek ode, as developed by Pindar, was also chanted by a chorus; see *ode*. In *The Birth of Tragedy* (1872) the German classicist and philosopher Friedrich Nietzsche speculated that, at the origin of Greek tragedy, the chorus—

consisting of goat-like satyrs—were the only figures on the stage. They were presented as attendants and witnesses of the suffering, death, and self-transformation of their master, the god Dionysus. Later, in Nietzsche's view, actors were introduced to enact the event that had originally been represented only symbolically, and the chorus was reduced to the role of commentator.

Roman playwrights such as Seneca took over the chorus from the Greeks, and in the mid-sixteenth century some English dramatists (for example, Norton and Sackville in *Gorboduc*) imitated the Senecan chorus. The classical type of chorus was never widely adopted by English dramatic writers. John Milton, however, included a chorus in *Samson Agonistes* (1671), as did Shelley in *Prometheus Unbound* (1820) and Thomas Hardy in *The Dynasts* (1904–08); more recently, T. S. Eliot made effective use of the classical chorus in his religious tragedy *Murder in the Cathedral* (1935). The use in drama of a chorus of singers and dancers survives also in operas and in musical comedies.

During the Elizabethan Age the term "chorus" was applied also to a single person who, in some plays, spoke the prologue and epilogue, and sometimes introduced each act as well. This character served as the author's vehicle for commentary on the play, as well as for exposition of its subject, time, and setting, and the description of events happening offstage; examples are Christopher Marlowe's *Dr. Faustus* and Shakespeare's *Henry V*. In Shakespeare's *Winter's Tale*, the fifth act begins with "Time, the Chorus," who requests the audience that they "impute it not a crime / To me or my swift passage that I slide / O'er sixteen years" since the preceding events, then summarizes what has happened during those years and announces that the setting for this present act is Bohemia. A modern and extended use of a single character with a choral function is the Stage Manager in Thornton Wilder's *Our Town* (1938).

Modern scholars use the term **choral character** to refer to a person within the play itself who stands apart from the action and by his or her comments provides the audience with a special perspective (often an *ironic* perspective) through which to view the other characters and events. Examples in Shakespeare are the Fool in *King Lear*, Enobarbus in *Antony and Cleopatra*, and Thersites in *Troilus and Cressida*; a modern instance is Seth Beckwith in O'Neill's *Mourning Becomes Electra* (1931). "Choral character" is sometimes applied also to one or more persons in a novel who represent the point of view of a community or of a cultural group, and so provide norms by which to judge the other characters and what they do; instances are Thomas Hardy's peasants and the old black women in some of William Faulkner's novels.

For the alternative use of the term "chorus" to signify a recurrent stanza in a song, see *refrain*. Refer to A. W. Pickard-Cambridge, *Dithyramb, Tragedy and Comedy* (1927) and *The Dramatic Festivals of Athens* (1953); T. B. L. Webster, *Greek Theater Production* (1956).

**chorus** (in a song): **306.**

**Christian humanism: 145.**

**chronicle plays:** Chronicle plays were dramatic works based on the historical materials in the English *Chronicles* by Raphael Holinshed and others; see *Chronicles*. They achieved high popularity late in the sixteenth century, when the patriotic fervor following the defeat of the Spanish Armada in 1588 fostered a demand for plays dealing with English history. The early chronicle plays presented a loosely knit series of events during the reign of an English king and depended for effect mainly on a bustle of stage battles, pageantry, and spectacle. Christopher Marlowe, however, in his *Edward II* (1592) selected and rearranged materials from Holinshed's *Chronicles* to compose a unified drama of character, and Shakespeare's series of chronicle plays, encompassing the succession of English kings from Richard II to Henry VIII, includes such major artistic achievements as *Richard II, 1 Henry IV, 2 Henry IV*, and *Henry V*.

The Elizabethan chronicle plays are sometimes called **history plays**. This latter term, however, is often applied more broadly to any drama based mainly on historical materials, such as Shakespeare's Roman plays *Julius Caesar* and *Antony and Cleopatra*, and including such recent examples as Arthur Miller's *The Crucible* (1953), which treats the Salem witch trials of 1692, and Robert Bolt's *A Man for All Seasons* (1962), about the sixteenth-century judge, author, and martyr Sir Thomas More. G. B. Shaw titled one of his plays, which dealt with historical matters, *St. Joan: A Chronicle Play in Six Scenes* (1923).

E. M. W. Tillyard, *Shakespeare's History Plays* (1946); Lily B. Campbell, *Shakespeare's "Histories"* (1947); Irving Ribner, *The English History Play in the Age of Shakespeare* (rev. 1965); Max M. Reese, *The Cease of Majesty: A Study of Shakespeare's History Plays* (1962). For a *new-historicist* treatment of Shakespeare's history plays *Henry IV, 1 and 2*, and *Henry V*, see Stephen Greenblatt, "Invisible Bullets," in *Political Shakespeare: New Essays in Cultural Materialism*, ed. Jonathan Dollimore and Alan Sinfield (1985).

**chronicles:** Chronicles the predecessors of modern histories, were written accounts, in prose or verse, of national or worldwide events over a considerable period of time. If the chronicles deal with events year by year, they are often called **annals**. Unlike the modern historian, most chroniclers tended to take their information as they found it, making little attempt to separate fact from legend. The most important English examples are the *Anglo-Saxon Chronicle*, started by King Alfred in the ninth century and continued until the twelfth century, and the *Chronicles of England, Scotland, and Ireland* (1577–87) by Raphael Holinshed and other writers. The latter documents were important sources of materials for the *chronicle plays* of Shakespeare and other Elizabethan dramatists.

**chronological primitivism: 286**; *137*.

**classic, a: 211**; *38*.

**classical: 211**.

**Cliché:** Cliché is French for "stereotype"—that is, a metal plate with a raised surface of type, used for printing. In its literary application, "cliché" signifies an expression that deviates enough from ordinary usage to call attention to itself and has been used so often that it is felt to be hackneyed or cloying. "I beg your pardon" or "sincerely yours" are standard usages that do not call attention to themselves; but "point with pride," "the eternal verities," "a whole new ballgame," and "lock, stock, and barrel" are accounted as clichés; so are indiscriminate uses in ordinary talk of terms taken from specialized vocabularies such as "alienation," "identity crisis," and "interface." Some clichés are foreign phrases that are used as an arch or elegant equivalent for a common English term ("aqua pura," "terra firma"); others are over-used literary echoes. "The cup that cheers" is an inaccurate quotation from William Cowper's *The Task* (1785), referring to tea—"the cups / That cheer but not inebriate." In his *Essay on Criticism* (II. 11. 350ff.) Alexander Pope comments satirically on some clichés that early-eighteenth-century **poetasters** (untalented pretenders to the poetic art) used in order to eke out their rhymes:

> Where'er you find "the cooling western breeze,"
> In the next line, it "whispers through the trees";
> If crystal streams "with pleasing murmurs creep,"
> The reader's threatened (not in vain) with "sleep."

See Eric Partridge, *A Dictionary of Clichés* (4th ed., 1950), and Christine Ammer, *Have a Nice Day—No Problem! A Dictionary of Clichés* (1992).

**climax** (in a plot): **267**.

**climax** (rhetorical): **24**.

**close reading: 217**; *73*.

**closed couplet: 141**; *213*.

**closet drama: 84**.

**codex: 30**.

**cognitive rhetoric: 312**.

**Colonial Period: 245**; *169*.

**colophon** (kŏl′ ŏfŏn): **32**.

**comedy:** In the most common literary application, a comedy is a fictional work in which the materials are selected and managed primarily in order to interest and amuse us: the characters and their discomfitures engage our pleasurable attention rather than our profound concern, we are made to feel confident that no great disaster will occur, and usually the action turns out happily for the chief characters. The term "comedy" is customarily applied only to plays for the stage or to motion pictures; it should be noted, however, that the comic form, as just defined, also occurs in prose fiction and narrative poetry.

Within the very broad spectrum of dramatic comedy, the following types are frequently distinguished:

1. **Romantic comedy** was developed by Elizabethan dramatists on the model of contemporary *prose romances* such as Thomas Lodge's *Rosalynde* (1590), the source of Shakespeare's *As You Like It* (1599). Such comedy represents a love affair that involves a beautiful and engaging heroine (sometimes disguised as a man); the course of this love does not run smooth, yet overcomes all difficulties to end in a happy union. Many of the boy-meets-girl plots of later writers are instances of romantic comedy, as are many motion pictures, from *The Philadelphia Story* to *Sleepless in Seattle*. In *Anatomy of Criticism* (1957), Northrop Frye points out that some of Shakespeare's romantic comedies manifest a movement from the normal world of conflict and trouble into "the green world"—the Forest of Arden in *As You Like It*, or the fairy-haunted wood of *A Midsummer Night's Dream*—in which the problems and injustices of the ordinary world are dissolved, enemies reconciled, and true lovers united. Frye regards that phenomenon (together with other aspects of these comedies, such as their conclusion in the social ritual of a wedding, a feast, or a dance) as evidence that comic plots derive from primitive myths and rituals that celebrated the victory of spring over winter. (See *archetypal criticism*.) Linda Bamber's *Comic Women, Tragic Men: A Study of Gender and Genre in Shakespeare* (1982) undertakes to account for the fact that in Shakespeare's romantic comedies, the women are often superior to the men, while in his tragedies he "creates such nightmare female figures as Goneril, Regan, Lady Macbeth, and Volumnia." (See *gender criticism*.)

2. **Satiric comedy** ridicules political policies or philosophical doctrines, or else attacks deviations from the accepted social order by making ridiculous the violators of its standards of morals or manners. (See *satire*.) The early master of satiric comedy was the Greek Aristophanes, c. 450–c. 385 BC, whose plays mocked political, philosophical, and literary matters of his age. Shakespeare's contemporary, Ben Jonson, wrote satiric or (as it is sometimes called) "corrective comedy." In his *Volpone* and *The Alchemist*, for example, the greed and ingenuity of one or more intelligent but rascally swindlers, and the equal greed but stupid gullibility of their victims, are made grotesquely or repulsively ludicrous rather than lightly amusing.

3. The **comedy of manners** originated in the **New Comedy** of the Greek Menander, c. 342–292 BC (as distinguished from the **Old Comedy** represented by Aristophanes, c. 450–c. 385 BC) and was developed by the Roman dramatists Plautus and Terence in the third and second centuries BC. Their plays dealt with the vicissitudes of young lovers and included what became the *stock characters* of much later comedy, such as the clever servant, old and stodgy parents, and the wealthy rival. The English comedy of manners was early exemplified by Shakespeare's *Love's Labour's Lost* and *Much Ado about Nothing*, and was given a high polish in **Restoration comedy** (1660–1700). The Restoration form owes much to the brilliant dramas of the French writer Molière, 1622–73. It deals with the relations and intrigues of men and women living in a sophisticated upper-class society, and relies for comic effect in large part on the wit and sparkle of the dialogue—often in the form of *repartee*, a witty conversational give-and-take which constitutes a kind of verbal fencing

match—as well as on the violations of social standards and decorum by would-be wits, jealous husbands, conniving rivals, and foppish dandies. Excellent examples are William Congreve's *The Way of the World* and William Wycherley's *The Country Wife*. (See *The Cambridge Companion to English Restoration Theatre*, ed. Deborah Payne Fisk, 2000.) A middle-class reaction against what had come to be considered the immorality of situation and indecency of dialogue in the courtly Restoration comedy resulted in the *sentimental comedy* of the eighteenth century. In the latter part of the century, however, Oliver Goldsmith (*She Stoops to Conquer*) and his contemporary Richard Brinsley Sheridan (*The Rivals* and *A School for Scandal*) revived the wit and gaiety, while deleting the indecency, of Restoration comedy. The comedy of manners lapsed in the early nineteenth century, but was revived by many skillful dramatists, from A. W. Pinero and Oscar Wilde (*The Importance of Being Earnest*, 1895), through George Bernard Shaw and Noel Coward, to Neil Simon, Alan Ayckbourn, Wendy Wasserstein, and other recent and contemporary writers. Many of these comedies have also been adapted for the cinema. See David L. Hirst, *Comedy of Manners* (1979).

4. **Farce** is a type of comedy designed to provoke the audience to simple, hearty laughter—"belly laughs," in the parlance of the theater. To do so it commonly employs highly exaggerated or caricatured types of characters, puts them into improbable and ludicrous situations, and often makes free use of sexual mix-ups, broad verbal humor, and physical bustle and horseplay. Farce was a component in the comic episodes in medieval *miracle plays*, such as the Wakefield plays *Noah* and the *Second Shepherd's Play*, and constituted the matter of the Italian *commedia dell'arte* in the Renaissance. In the English drama that has best stood the test of time, farce is usually an episode in a more complex form of comedy—examples are the knockabout scenes in Shakespeare's *The Taming of the Shrew* and *The Merry Wives of Windsor*. The plays of the French playwright Georges Feydeau (1862–1921), relying in great part on sexual humor and innuendo, are true farce throughout, as is Brandon Thomas' *Charley's Aunt*, an American play of 1892 which has often been revived, and also some of the current plays of Tom Stoppard. Many of the movies by such comedians as Charlie Chaplin, Buster Keaton, W. C. Fields, the Marx brothers, and Woody Allen are excellent farce, as are the Monty Python films and television episodes. Farce is often employed in single scenes of musical revues, and is the standard fare of television "situation comedies." It should be noted that the term "farce," or sometimes "farce comedy," is applied also to plays—a supreme example is Oscar Wilde's *The Importance of Being Earnest* (1895)—in which exaggerated character-types find themselves in ludicrous situations in the course of an improbable plot, but which achieve their comic effects not by broad humor and bustling action, but by the sustained brilliance and wit of the dialogue. Farce is also a frequent comic tactic in the theater of the *absurd*. Refer to Robert Metcalf Smith and H. G. Rhoads, eds., *Types of Farce Comedy* (1928); Leo Hughes, *A Century of English Farce* (1956); and for the history of farce and low comedy from the Greeks to the present, Anthony Caputi, *Buffo: The*

*Genius of Vulgar Comedy* (1978), and Albert Bermel, *Farce: A History from Aristophanes to Woody Allen* (1990).

A distinction is often made between high and low comedy. **High comedy**, as described by George Meredith in the classic essay *The Idea of Comedy* (1877), evokes "intellectual laughter"—thoughtful laughter from spectators who remain emotionally detached from the action—at the spectacle of folly, pretentiousness, and incongruity in human behavior. Meredith finds its highest form within the comedy of manners, in the combats of wit (sometimes identified now as the "love duels") between such intelligent, highly verbal, and well-matched lovers as Benedick and Beatrice in Shakespeare's *Much Ado about Nothing* (1598–99) and Mirabell and Millamant in Congreve's *The Way of the World* (1700). **Low comedy**, at the other extreme, has little or no intellectual appeal, but undertakes to arouse laughter by jokes, or "gags," and by slapstick humor and boisterous or clownish physical activity; it is, therefore, one of the common components of farce.

See also *comedy of humours, tragicomedy*, and *wit, humor, and the comic*. On comedy and its varieties: G. E. Duckworth, *The Nature of Roman Comedy* (1952); Elder Olson, *The Theory of Comedy* (1968); Allan Rodway, *English Comedy* (1975). On the relation of comedy to myth and ritual: Northrop Frye, *Anatomy of Criticism* (1957), pp. 163–86; C. L. Barber, *Shakespeare's Festive Comedy* (1959). On comedy in cinema and television: Horace Newcomb, *Television: The Most Popular Art* (1974), chapter 2; Steve Neale and Frank Krutnik, *Popular Film and Television Comedy* (1990). There is a large collection of resources on the web: "Introduction to Greek and Roman Comedy," at http://depthome.brooklyn.cuny.edu/classics/dunkle/comedy/index.htm.

**comedy of humours:**   A type of comedy developed by Ben Jonson, the *Elizabethan* playwright, based on the ancient physiological theory of the "four humours" that was still current in Jonson's time. The **humours** were held to be the four primary fluids—blood, phlegm, choler (or yellow bile), and melancholy (or black bile)—whose "temperament" (mixture) was held to determine both a person's physical condition and type of character. An imbalance of one or another humour in a temperament was said to produce four kinds of disposition, whose names have survived the underlying theory: sanguine (from the Latin "sanguis," blood), phlegmatic, choleric, and melancholic. In Jonson's comedy of humours each of the major characters has a preponderant humour that gives him a characteristic distortion or eccentricity of disposition. Jonson expounds his theory in the "Induction" to his play *Every Man in His Humour* (1598) and exemplifies the mode in his later comedies; often he identifies the ruling disposition of a **humours character** by his or her name: "Zeal-of-the-land Busy," "Dame Purecraft," "Wellbred." The Jonsonian type of humours character appears in plays by other Elizabethans, and remained influential in the *comedies of manners* by William Wycherley, Sir George Etheredge, William Congreve, and other dramatists of the English Restoration, 1660–1700.

**comedy of manners: 49**; *51*.

**comedy, sentimental: 327**.

**comic, the: 380**; *320*.

**comic relief:** Comic relief is the introduction of comic characters, speeches, or scenes in a serious or tragic work, especially a drama. Such elements were almost universal in *Elizabethan tragedy*. Sometimes they occur merely as episodes of dialogue or horseplay for purposes of alleviating tension and adding variety. In more carefully wrought plays, however, they are integrated with the plot, in a way that counterpoints and enhances the serious or tragic significance. Examples of such complex uses of comic elements are the gravediggers in *Hamlet* (V. i.), the scene of the drunken porter after the murder of the king in *Macbeth* (II. iii.), the Falstaff scenes in *1 Henry IV*, and the roles of Mercutio and the old nurse in *Romeo and Juliet*.

See Thomas De Quincey's famed essay "On the Knocking at the Gate in *Macbeth*" (1823).

**commedia dell'arte:** Commedia dell'arte was a form of comic drama developed about the mid-sixteenth century by guilds of professional Italian actors. Playing *stock characters*, the actors largely improvised the dialogue around a given **scenario**—a term that still denotes a brief outline of a drama, indicating merely the entrances of the main characters and the general course of the action. In a typical play, a pair of young lovers outwit a rich old father ("Pantaloon"), aided by a clever and intriguing servant ("Harlequin"), in a plot enlivened by the buffoonery of "Punch" and other clowns. Wandering Italian troupes played in all the large cities of Renaissance Europe and influenced writers of comedies in Elizabethan England and later in France. Shakespeare's *The Taming of the Shrew*, Rostand's *Cyrano de Bergerac*, and Molière's *The Misanthrope* drew on conventions of the commedia. The modern puppet shows of Punch and Judy are descendants of this old Italian comedy, emphasizing its components of *farce* and buffoonery.

See Kathleen M. Lea, *Italian Popular Comedy, 1560–1620* (2 vols., 1934); Martin Green and John Swan, *The Triumph of Pierrot* (rev. 1993), traces the influence of Pierrot from 1860 to 1930 and beyond; Domenico Pietropaolo, ed., *The Science of Buffoonery: Theory and History of the Commedia dell'Arte* (1989). See also two books by Robert F. Storey: *Pierrot: A Critical History of a Mask* (1978) and *Pierrots on the Stage of Desire* (1985), which tracks the persistence of Pierrot in nineteenth-century French literature and pantomime.

**common measure** (in meter): **341**.

**Commonwealth Period: 253**.

**competence** (linguistic): **173**.

**complication** (in a plot): **267**.

**conceit:** Originally meaning a concept or image, "conceit" came to be the term for figures of speech which establish a striking parallel, usually ingeniously elaborate, between two very dissimilar things or situations. (See *figurative language*.) English poets of the sixteenth and seventeenth centuries adapted the term from the Italian "concetto." Two types of conceit are often distinguished by specific names:

1. The **Petrarchan conceit** is a type of figure used in love poems that had been novel and effective in the Italian poetry of Petrarch, but became hackneyed in some of his imitators among the Elizabethan sonneteers. (See the entry *sonnet*.) The figure consists of detailed, ingenious, and often exaggerated comparisons applied to the disdainful mistress, as cold and cruel as she is beautiful, and to the distresses and despair of her worshipful lover. (See *courtly love*.) Sir Thomas Wyatt (1503–42), for example, in the sonnet "My Galley Chargèd with Forgetfulness" that he translated from Petrarch, compares the lover's state in detail to a ship laboring in a storm. Another sonnet of Petrarch's translated by Wyatt begins with an *oxymoron* describing the opposing passions experienced by a courtly sufferer from the disease of love:

> I find no peace; and all my war is done;
> I fear and hope; I burn and freeze in ice.

Shakespeare (who at times employed this type of conceit himself) *parodied* some standard comparisons by Petrarchan sonneteers in his Sonnet 130, beginning

> My mistress' eyes are nothing like the sun;
> Coral is far more red than her lips' red:
> If snow be white, why then her breasts are dun;
> If hairs be wires, black wires grow on her head.

2. The **metaphysical conceit** is a characteristic figure in the work of John Donne (1572–1631) and other *metaphysical poets* of the seventeenth century. It was described by Samuel Johnson, in a famed passage in his "Life of Cowley," (1779–81), as "wit" which is

a kind of *discordia concors*; a combination of dissimilar images, or discovery of occult resemblances in things apparently unlike. . . . The most heterogeneous ideas are yoked by violence together.

The metaphysical poets exploited all knowledge—commonplace or esoteric, practical, theological, or philosophical, true or fabulous—for the vehicles of these figures; and their comparisons, whether succinct or expanded, were often novel and witty, and at their best startlingly effective. In sharp contrast to both the concepts and figures of conventional Petrarchism is John Donne's "The Flea," a poem that uses a flea who has bitten both lovers as the basic reference for the lyric speaker's argument against a lady's resistance to his advances. In Donne's "The Canonization," as the poetic argument develops, the comparisons for the relationship between lovers move from the area of commerce and business, through actual and mythical birds and diverse forms of historical memorials, to a climax which equates the sexual acts and the moral status of worldly lovers with the ascetic life and heavenly destination of unworldly saints. The best known sustained conceit is Donne's parallel (in "A Valediction: Forbidding Mourning") between the continuing relationship of his and his lady's soul during their physical parting, and the coordinated movements of the two feet of a draftsman's compass. An oft-cited instance of the chilly ingenuity of the metaphysical conceit when it is overdriven is Richard Crashaw's description, in his mid-seventeenth-century poem "Saint Mary Magdalene," of the tearful eyes of the repentant Magdalene as

> two faithful fountains
> Two walking baths, two weeping motions,
> Portable and compendious oceans.

The metaphysical conceit fell out of favor in the eighteenth century, when it came to be regarded as strained and unnatural. But with the strong revival of interest in the metaphysical poets during the early decades of the twentieth century, a number of modern poets exploited this type of figure. Examples are T. S. Eliot's comparison of the evening to "a patient etherized upon a table" at the beginning of "The Love Song of J. Alfred Prufrock," and the series of startling figurative vehicles in Dylan Thomas' "In Memory of Ann Jones." The vogue for such conceits extended even to popular love songs, in the 1920s and later, by well-educated composers such as Cole Porter: "You're the Cream in My Coffee" and "You're the Top."

Refer to Rosemond Tuve, *Elizabethan and Metaphysical Imagery* (1947), and K. K. Ruthven, *The Conceit* (1969).

**concrete and abstract:** In standard philosophical usage a "concrete term" is a word that denotes a particular person or physical object, and an "abstract term" denotes either a class of things or else (as in "brightness," "beauty," "evil," "despair") qualities that exist only as attributes of particular persons or things. A sentence, accordingly, is said to be concrete if it makes an assertion about a particular subject (T. S. Eliot's "Grishkin is nice . . ."), and abstract if it makes an assertion about an abstract subject (Alexander Pope's "Hope springs eternal in the human breast"). Critics of literature, however, often use these terms in an extended way: a passage is called abstract if it represents its subject matter in general or nonsensuous words or with only a thin realization of its experienced qualities; it is called concrete if it represents its subject matter with striking particularity and sensuous detail. In his "Ode to Psyche" (1820) John Keats'

> 'Mid hush'd, cool-rooted flowers, fragrant-eyed,
> Blue, silver-white, and budded Tyrian

is a concrete description of a locale which interinvolves qualities that are perceived by four different senses: hearing, touch, sight, and smell. And in the opening of his "Ode to a Nightingale," Keats communicates concretely, by a combination of literal and figurative language, how it feels, physically, to experience the full-throated song of the nightingale:

> My heart aches, and a drowsy numbness pains
> My sense, as though of hemlock I had drunk,
> Or emptied some dull opiate to the drains. . . .

It is frequently asserted that "poetry is concrete," or, as John Crowe Ransom put it in *The World's Body* (1938), that its proper subject is "the rich, contingent materiality of things." Most poetry is certainly more concrete than other modes of language, especially in its use of *imagery*. It should be kept in mind, however, that poets do not hesitate to use abstract language when the area of reference or artistic purpose calls for it. Keats, though he was one of the most concrete of poets, began *Endymion* with a sentence composed of abstract terms:

> A thing of beauty is a joy forever:
> Its loveliness increases; it will never
> Pass into nothingness; . . .

And some of the most moving and memorable passages in poetry are not concrete; for example, the statement about God in Dante's *Paradiso*, "In His will is our peace," or the bleak comment by Edgar in the last act of *King Lear*,

> Men must endure
> Their going hence, even as their coming hither;
> Ripeness is all.

See John Crowe Ransom, *The World's Body* (1938); Richard H. Fogle, *Imagery of Keats and Shelley* (1949), chapter 5.

**concrete poetry:** Concrete poetry is a recent term for an ancient poetic type, called **pattern poems**, that experiment with the visual shape in which a text is presented on the page. Some Greek poets, beginning in the third century BC, shaped a text in the form of the object that the poem describes or suggests. In the Renaissance and seventeenth century, a number of poets composed such patterned forms, in which the lines vary in length in such a way that their printed shape outlines the subject of the poem; familiar examples in English are George Herbert's "Easter Wings" and "The Altar." Prominent later experiments with pictorial or suggestive typography include Stéphane Mallarmé's *Un Coup de dés* ("A Throw of Dice," 1897) and Guillaume Apollinaire's *Calligrammes* (1918); in the latter publication, for example, Apollinaire printed the poem "Il pleut" ("It rains") so that the component letters trickle down the page.

The vogue of **concrete poetry** is a worldwide movement that was largely inaugurated in 1953 by the Swiss poet Eugen Gomringer. The practice of such poetry varies widely, but the common feature is the use of a radically reduced language, typed or printed in such a way as to force the visible text on the reader's attention as a physical object and not simply as a transparent carrier of its meanings. Many concrete poems, in fact, cannot be read at all in the conventional way, since they consist of a single word or phrase which is subjected to systematic alterations in the order and position of the component letters, or else are composed of fragments of words, or of nonsense syllables, or even of single letters, numbers, and marks of punctuation. In their shaped patterns, concrete poets often use a variety of type fonts and sizes and different colors of type, and sometimes supplement the text with drawings or photographs, while some of their shapes, called "kinetic," evolve as we turn the pages.

America had its own tradition of pattern poetry in the typographical experiments of Ezra Pound, and especially e. e. cummings; see, for example, cummings' "r-p-o-p-h-e-s-s-a-g-r" in which, to represent the way we at first perceive vaguely, then identify, the leaping insect, scrambled sequences of letters gradually order themselves into the word "grasshopper." Prominent recent practitioners of pattern poems in the shape of the things that they describe or meditate upon are May Swenson (*Iconographs*, 1970) and John Hollander (*Types of Shape*, 1991). Other Americans who have been influenced by the international vogue for concrete poetry include Emmett Williams, Jonathan Williams, and Mary Ellen Solt.

Collections of concrete poems in a variety of languages are Emmett Williams, ed., *An Anthology of Concrete Poetry* (1967); Mary Ellen Solt, ed. (with a useful historical introduction), *Concrete Poetry: A World View* (1968). For a noted early-eighteenth-century attack on pattern poems, see Addison's comments on "false wit" in the *Spectator*, Nos. 58 and 63.

**concretize** (in reading): **261**.

**confessional poetry:** Confessional poetry designates a type of narrative and lyric verse, given impetus by the American Robert Lowell's *Life Studies* (1959), which deals with the facts and intimate mental and physical experiences of the poet's own life. Confessional poetry was written in rebellion against the demand for impersonality by T. S. Eliot and the *New Critics*. By its secular subject matter, it differs from religious *spiritual autobiography* in the lineage of Augustine's *Confessions* (c. AD 400). It differs also from poems of the *Romantic Period* representing the poet's own circumstances, experiences, and feelings, such as William Wordsworth's "Tintern Abbey" and Samuel Taylor Coleridge's "Dejection: An Ode," in the candor and sometimes startling detail with which the confessional poet reveals private or clinical matters about himself or herself, including sexual experiences, mental anguish and illness, experiments with drugs, and suicidal impulses. Confessional poems were written by Allen Ginsberg, Sylvia Plath, Anne Sexton, John Berryman, and other American poets. See Diane Middlebrook, *Anne Sexton: A Biography* (1991), and "What Was Confessional Poetry?" in *The Columbia History of American Poetry*, ed. Jay Parini (1993).

**confidant:** A confidant (the feminine form is "confidante") is a character in a drama or novel who plays only a minor role in the action, but serves the protagonist as a trusted friend to whom he or she confesses intimate thoughts, problems, and feelings. In drama the confidant provides the playwright with a plausible device for communicating to the audience the knowledge, state of mind, and intentions of a principal character without the use of stage devices such as the *soliloquy* or the *aside*; examples are Hamlet's friend Horatio in Shakespeare's *Hamlet*, and Cleopatra's maid Charmian in his *Antony and Cleopatra*.

In prose fiction a famed confidant is Dr. Watson in Arthur Conan Doyle's stories about Sherlock Holmes (1887 and following). The device is particularly useful to those modern writers who, like Henry James, have largely renounced the novelist's earlier privileges of having access to a character's state of mind and of intruding into the narrative in order to communicate such information to the reader. (See *point of view*.) James applied to the confidant the term **ficelle**, French for the string by which the puppeteer manages his puppets. Discussing Maria Gostrey, Strether's confidante in *The Ambassadors*, James remarks that she is a "fi-celle" who is not, "in essence, Strether's friend. She is the reader's friend much rather" (James, *The Art of the Novel*, ed. R. P. Blackmur, 1934, pp. 321–22).

See W. J. Harvey, *Character and the Novel* (1965).

**conflict** (in a plot): **265**.

**connotation and denotation:** In a widespread literary usage, the **denotation** of a word is its primary signification or reference; its **connotation** is the range of secondary or associated significations and feelings which it commonly suggests or implies. Thus "home" denotes the house where one lives, but connotes privacy, intimacy, and coziness; that is the reason real estate agents like to use "home" instead of "house" in their advertisements. "Horse" and "steed" denote the same quadruped, but "steed" has a different connotation that derives from the chivalric or romantic narratives in which this word was often used.

The connotation of a word is only a potential range of secondary significations; which part of these connotations are evoked depends on the way the word is used in a particular context. Poems typically establish contexts that bring into play some part of the connotative as well as the denotative meaning of words. In his poem "Virtue" George Herbert wrote,

> Sweet day, so cool, so calm, so bright,
> The bridal of the earth and sky. . . .

The denotation of "bridal"—a union between human beings—serves as part of the *ground* for applying the word as a *metaphor* to the union of earth and sky; but the specific context in which the word occurs also evokes such connotations of "bridal" as sacred, joyous, and ceremonial. (Note that "marriage" although metrically and denotatively equivalent to "bridal," would have been less richly significant in this context, because more commonplace in its connotation.) Even the way a word is spelled may alter its connotation. John Keats, in a passage of his "Ode to a Nightingale" (1819),

> Charmed magic casements, opening on the foam
> Of perilous seas, in *faery* lands forlorn,

altered his original spelling of "fairy" to the old form "faery" in order to evoke the connotations of antiquity, as well as of the magic world of Spenser's *The Faerie Queene*.

**consonance: 10**.

**constative: 338**.

**constructs** (social and discursive): See *social constructs*.

**Contemporary Period: 248**. See also *Modern Period*.

**contextual criticism: 217**.

**conventions:**

1. In one sense of the term, conventions (derived from the Latin term for "coming together") are necessary, or at least convenient, devices, accepted by tacit agreement between author and audience, for solving the problems in representing reality that are posed by a particular artistic medium. In watching a modern production of a Shakespearean play, for example, the audience accepts without question the convention by which a *proscenium* stage with three walls (or if it is a **theater in the round**, with no walls) represents a room with four walls. It also accepts the convention of characters speaking in *blank verse* instead of prose, and uttering their private thoughts in *soliloquies* and *asides*, as well as the convention by which actions presented on a single stage in less than three hours may represent events which take place in a great variety of places, and over a span of many years.

2. In a second sense of the term, conventions are conspicuous features of subject matter, form, or technique that occur repeatedly in works of literature. Conventions in this sense may be recurrent types of character, turns of plot, forms of versification, or kinds of diction and style. *Stock characters* such as the Elizabethan braggart soldier, or the languishing and fainting heroine of Victorian fiction, or the sad young men of the lost-generation novels of the 1920s, were among the conventions of their literary eras. The abrupt reform of the villain at the end of the last act was a common convention of *melodrama*. *Euphuism* in prose, and the *Petrarchan* and *metaphysical conceits* in verse, were conventional devices of style. It is now just as much a literary convention to be outspoken on sexual matters as it was to be reticent in the age of Charles Dickens and George Eliot.

3. In the most inclusive sense, common in structuralist criticism, all literary works, no matter how seemingly realistic, are held to be entirely constituted by literary conventions, or "codes"—of genre, plot, character, language, and so on—which a reader *naturalizes*, by assimilating these conventions into the world of discourse and experience that, in the reader's time and place, are regarded as real, or "natural." (See *structuralist criticism* and *character and characterization*.)

**Invention** was originally a term used in theories of *rhetoric*, and later in literary criticism, to signify the "finding" of the subject matter by an orator or a poet; it then came to signify innovative elements in a work, in contrast to the deliberate "imitation" of the forms and subjects of prior literary models. (See *imitation*.) At the present time, "invention" is often opposed to "convention" (in sense 2, above) to signify the inauguration by a writer of an unprecedented subject or theme or form or style, and the resulting work is said to possess **originality**. Repeatedly in the history of literature, innovative writers such as John Donne, Walt Whitman, James Joyce, or Virginia Woolf rebel against reigning conventions of their time to produce highly original works, only to have their inventions imitated by other writers, who thereby convert literary innovations into an additional set of literary conventions. (For a discussion of the history and uses of the concept of originality, see Thomas McFarland, *Originality and Imagination*, 1985.)

There is nothing either good or bad in the extent or obviousness of conformity to pre-existing conventions; all depends on the effectiveness of the use an individual writer makes of them. The *pastoral elegy*, for example, is one of the most conspicuously convention-bound of literary forms, yet in "Lycidas" (1638) John Milton achieved what, by wide critical agreement, ranks as one of the greatest lyrics in the language. He did this by employing the ancient pastoral rituals with freshness and power, so as to absorb an individual's death into the universal human experience of mortality, and to add to his voice the resonance of earlier pastoral laments for a poet who died young.

See M. C. Bradbrook, *Themes and Conventions of Elizabethan Tragedy* (1935); Harry Levin, "Notes on Convention," in *Perspectives of Criticism* (1950); Graham Hough, *Reflections on a Literary Revolution* (1960); and the issues *On Convention* in *New Literary History*, Vols. 13–14 (1981 and 1983). For references to *conventions* in other entries, see pages *240, 271, 343*.

**conversion:** 26.

**Copernican theory** (kō̆pŭr′ nĭkan): **309**.

**copy-text:** 365.

**correspondences:** 361; *376*.

**cosmic irony:** 167.

**counterculture:** 249; *25, 69, 377*.

**country house poem:** 370.

**couplet:** 341.

**courtesy books:** 308.

**courtly love:** A doctrine of love, together with an elaborate code governing the relations between aristocratic lovers, which was widely represented in the lyric poems and *chivalric romances* of western Europe during the Middle Ages. The

development of the *conventions* of courtly love is usually attributed to the
**troubadours** (poets of Provence, in southern France) in the period from the
late eleventh century through the twelfth century. In the conventional doctrine,
love between the sexes, with its erotic and physical aspects spiritualized, is regarded as the noblest passion this side of heaven. The courtly lover idealizes and
idolizes his beloved, and subjects himself to her every whim. (This love is often
that of a bachelor knight for another man's wife, as in the stories of Tristan and
Isolde or of Lancelot and Guinevere; it must be remembered that marriage among
the upper classes in medieval Europe was usually not a relationship of love, but a
kind of business contract, for economic and political purposes.) The lover suffers
agonies of body and spirit as he is put to the test by his imperious sweetheart, but
remains devoted to her, manifesting his honor by his fidelity and his adherence to
a rigorous code of behavior, both in knightly battles and in the complex ceremonies of courtly speech and conduct.

The origins of courtly love have been traced to a number of sources: a serious
reading of the Roman poet Ovid's mock-serious book *The Remedies of Love*; an
imitation in lovers' relations of the politics of feudalism (the lover is a vassal, and
both his lady and the god of love are his lords); and especially an importation into
amatory situations of Christian concepts and ritual and the veneration of the
Virgin Mary. Thus, the lady is exalted and worshiped; the lover sins and repents;
and if his faith stays steadfast, he may be admitted at last into the lover's heaven
through his lady's "gift of grace."

From southern France the doctrines of courtly love spread to Chrétien de
Troyes (who flourished 1170–90) and other poets and romance writers in northern France; to Dante (*La Vita Nuova*, 1290–94), Petrarch, and other writers in
fourteenth-century Italy; and to the love poets of Germany and northern
Europe. For a reader of English literature the conventions of courtly love are
best known by their occurrence in the medieval romance *Sir Gawain and the
Green Knight*, in Chaucer's *Troilus and Criseyde*, and later in the Petrarchan subject
matter and the *Petrarchan conceits* of the Elizabethan sonneteers.

There has long been a debate whether medieval courtly love was limited to
literature and to elegant conversation at courts, or whether to some degree it reflected the actual sentiments and conduct in aristocratic life of the time. What is
clear is that its views about the intensity and the ennobling power of love as "the
grand passion," of the special sensibility and high spiritual status of women, and of
the complex decorum governing relations between the sexes have profoundly affected not only the literature of love but also the actual experience of "being in
love" in the Western world, through the nineteenth century and (to a diminished
extent) even into our own day of sexual candor, freedom, and the feminist movement for equivalence in the relations between the sexes. Some feminists attack the
medieval doctrine of courtly love, as well as later tendencies to spiritualize and
idealize women, as in fact demeaning to them, and a covert device to ensure their
social, political, and economic subordination to men. See *feminist criticism*.

The issue of courtly love was revisited by Jacques Lacan, and, more recently,
by Slavoj Žižek; both note that the woman in all fictions of courtly love seems to
be the same person, or rather the same nonperson, since she is no more than an

abstract ideal. What this suggests, Žižek argues, is that there is "no sexual relation" with the lady, who serves as a representation of the fact that human desire can never be fully gratified. See Lacan, *The Ethics of Psychoanalysis* (1992), 149–51; and Žižek, "Courtly Love, or Woman as Thing," in *Metastases of Enjoyment* (1994).

See also C. S. Lewis, *The Allegory of Love* (1936); A. J. Denomy, *The Heresy of Courtly Love* (1947); M. J. Valency, *In Praise of Love* (1958); F. X. Newman, ed., *The Meaning of Courtly Love* (1968); Denis de Rougemont, *Love in the Western World* (rev. 1974); Roger Boase, *The Origin and Meaning of Courtly Love: A Critical Study of European Scholarship* (1977). For skeptical views of some commonly held opinions, see D. W. Robertson, "Some Medieval Doctrines of Love," in *A Preface to Chaucer: Studies in Medieval Perspectives* (1962); Peter Dronke, *Medieval Latin and the Rise of European Love-Lyric* (1965–66); E. Talbot Donaldson, "The Myth of Courtly Love," in *Speaking of Chaucer* (1970). For reappraisals of the role of women in the tradition, see Andrée Kahn Blumstein, *Misogyny and Idealization in the Courtly Romance* (1977), and R. Howard Bloch, *Medieval Misogyny and the Invention of Western Romantic Love* (1991).

For references to *courtly love* in other entries, see pages *45, 53, 238*.

**crisis** (in a plot): **267**.

**criteria** (in criticism): **61**.

**criticism:** Criticism, or more specifically **literary criticism**, is the overall term for studies concerned with defining, classifying, analyzing, interpreting, and evaluating works of literature. **Theoretical criticism** proposes an explicit **theory** of literature, in the sense of general principles, together with a set of terms, distinctions, and categories, to be applied to identifying and analyzing works of literature, as well as the **criteria** (the standards, or norms) by which these works and their writers are to be evaluated. The earliest, and enduringly important, treatise of theoretical criticism was Aristotle's *Poetics* (fourth century BC). Among the most influential theoretical critics in the following centuries were Longinus in Greece; Horace in Rome; Boileau and Sainte-Beuve in France; Baumgarten and Goethe in Germany; Samuel Johnson, Coleridge, and Matthew Arnold in England; and Poe and Emerson in America. Landmarks of theoretical criticism in the first half of the twentieth century are I. A. Richards, *Principles of Literary Criticism* (1924); Kenneth Burke, *The Philosophy of Literary Form* (1941, rev. 1957); R. S. Crane, ed., *Critics and Criticism* (1952); Erich Auerbach, *Mimesis: The Representation of Reality in Western Literature* (trans. 1953, reissued 2003); and Northrop Frye, *Anatomy of Criticism* (1957).

Since the 1970s there have been a large number of publications— Continental, American, and English—proposing diverse radical forms of critical theory. These are listed and dated in the entry *theories and movements in criticism, recent*; each theory in that list is also given a separate entry in this *Glossary*. For a discussion of the special uses of the term "theory" in these critical movements, see *poststructuralism*.

**Practical criticism**, or **applied criticism**, concerns itself with particular works and writers; in an applied critique, the theoretical principles controlling the analysis, interpretation, and evaluation are often left implicit, or brought in only as the occasion demands. Among the more influential works of applied criticism in England and America are the literary essays of Dryden in the *Restoration*; Dr. Johnson's *Lives of the English Poets* (1779–81); Coleridge's chapters on the poetry of Wordsworth in *Biographia Literaria* (1817) and his lectures on Shakespeare; William Hazlitt's lectures on Shakespeare and the English poets, in the second and third decades of the nineteenth century; Matthew Arnold's *Essays in Criticism* (1865 and following); I. A. Richards' *Practical Criticism* (1930); T. S. Eliot's *Selected Essays* (1932); and the many critical essays by Virginia Woolf, F. R. Leavis, and Lionel Trilling. Cleanth Brooks' *The Well Wrought Urn* (1947) exemplifies the "close reading" of single texts which was the typical mode of practical criticism in the American *New Criticism*. For a more recent example of practical criticism applied to a single poetic text, see Stanley Fish, *Surprised by Sin: The Reader in Paradise Lost* (2d ed., 1998).

In practical criticism, a frequent distinction is made between impressionistic and judicial criticism:

**Impressionistic criticism** attempts to represent in words the felt qualities of a particular passage or work, and to express the responses (the "impression") that the work directly evokes from the critic. As William Hazlitt put it in his essay "On Genius and Common Sense" (1824): "You decide from feeling, and not from reason; that is, from the impression of a number of things on the mind . . . though you may not be able to analyze or account for it in the several particulars." And Walter Pater later said that in criticism "the first step toward seeing one's object as it really is, is to know one's own impression as it really is, to discriminate it, to realise it distinctly," and posed as the basic question, "What is this song or picture . . . to *me*?" (preface to *Studies in the History of the Renaissance*, 1873). At its extreme this mode of criticism becomes, in Anatole France's phrase, "the adventures of a sensitive soul among masterpieces."

**Judicial criticism**, on the other hand, attempts not merely to communicate, but to analyze and explain the effects of a work by reference to its subject, organization, techniques, and style, and to base the critic's individual judgments on specified criteria of literary excellence.

Rarely are these two modes of criticism sharply distinct in practice, but good examples of primarily impressionistic commentary can be found in the Greek Longinus (see the characterization of the *Odyssey* in his treatise *On the Sublime*), Hazlitt, Walter Pater (the locus classicus of impressionism is his description of Leonardo's *Mona Lisa* in *The Renaissance*, 1873), and some of the twentieth-century critical essays of E. M. Forster and Virginia Woolf.

Types of traditional critical theories and of applied criticism can be usefully distinguished according to whether, in defining, explaining, and judging a work of literature, they refer the work primarily to the outer world, or to the reader, or to the author, or else treat the work as an independent entity:

1. **Mimetic criticism** views the literary work as an imitation, or reflection, or representation of the world and human life, and the primary criterion applied

to a work is the "truth" and "adequacy" of its representation to the matter that it represents, or should represent. This mode of criticism, which first appeared in Plato and (in a qualified way) in Aristotle, remains characteristic of modern theories of literary realism. (See *imitation*.)

2. **Pragmatic criticism** views the work as something which is constructed in order to achieve certain effects on the audience (effects such as aesthetic pleasure, instruction, or kinds of emotion), and it tends to judge the value of the work according to its success in achieving that aim. This approach, which largely dominated literary discussion from the versified *Art of Poetry* by the Roman Horace (first century BC) through the eighteenth century, has been revived in recent *rhetorical criticism*, which emphasizes the artistic strategies by which an author engages and influences the responses of readers to the matters represented in a literary work. The pragmatic approach has also been adopted by some *structuralists* who analyze a literary text as a systematic play of codes that produce the interpretative responses of a reader.

3. **Expressive criticism** treats a literary work primarily in relation to its author. It defines poetry as an expression, or overflow, or utterance of feelings, or as the product of the poet's imagination operating on his or her perceptions, thoughts, and feelings; it tends to judge the work by its sincerity, or its adequacy to the poet's individual vision or state of mind; and it often seeks in the work evidences of the particular temperament and experiences of the author who, deliberately or unconsciously, has revealed himself or herself in it. Such views were developed mainly by romantic critics in the early nineteenth century and remain current in our own time, especially in the writings of *psychological* and *psychoanalytic critics* and in *critics of consciousness* such as Georges Poulet and the Geneva School. (For a reading of literary criticism itself as involving self-expression, see Geoffrey Galt Harpham, *The Character of Criticism*, 2006.)

4. **Objective criticism** deals with a work of literature as something which stands free from what is often called an "extrinsic" relationship to the poet, or to the audience, or to the environing world. Instead it describes the literary product as a self-sufficient and autonomous object, or else as a world-in-itself, which is to be contemplated as its own end, and to be analyzed and judged solely by "intrinsic" criteria such as its complexity, coherence, equilibrium, integrity, and the interrelations of its component elements. The conception of the self-sufficiency of an aesthetic object was proposed in Kant's *Critique of Aesthetic Judgment* (1790)—see *distance and involvement*—was taken up by proponents of *art for art's sake* in the latter part of the nineteenth century, and has been elaborated in detailed modes of applied criticism by a number of important critics since the 1920s, including the *New Critics*, the *Chicago School*, and proponents of European *formalism*.

An essential critical enterprise that the ordinary reader takes for granted is to establish a valid text for a literary work; see the entry *textual criticism*. Also, criticism is often classified into types which bring to bear upon literature various areas of knowledge, in an attempt to identify the conditions and influences that determine the particular characteristics and values of a literary work. Accordingly, we have "historical criticism," "biographical criticism," "sociological criticism" (see *sociology of literature* and *Marxist criticism*), *psychological criticism* (a subspecies is *psychoanalytic criticism*), and *archetypal* or *myth criticism* (which undertakes to explain the formation of types of literature by reference to the views about myth and ritual in modern cultural anthropology).

For a detailed discussion of the classification of traditional theories that is represented in this essay, see M. H. Abrams, *The Mirror and the Lamp* (1953), chapter 1, and "Types and Orientations of Critical Theories" in *Doing Things with Texts: Essays in Criticism and Critical Theory* (1989). On types of critical approaches, refer also to René Wellek and Austin Warren, *Theory of Literature* (rev. 1970). Histories of criticism: *Classical Criticism*, ed. George A. Kennedy (1989); Bernard Weinberg, *A History of Literary Criticism in the Italian Renaissance* (2 vols., 1963); René Wellek, *A History of Modern Criticism, 1750–1950* (7 vols., 1955ff.); *The Cambridge History of Literary Criticism* (multiple vols., 1989–). On criticism in the earlier nineteenth century see Abrams, *The Mirror and the Lamp*, and on twentieth-century criticism, S. E. Hyman, *The Armed Vision* (1948); Murray Krieger, *The New Apologists for Poetry* (1956); Jonathan Culler, *Structuralist Poetics* (1975) and *Literary Theory: A Very Short Introduction* (1997); Grant Webster, *The Republic of Letters: A History of Postwar American Literary Opinion* (1979); Frank Lentricchia, *After the New Criticism* (1980); Chris Baldick, *Criticism and Literary Theory, 1890 to the Present* (1996).

Convenient anthologies of literary criticism are A. H. Gilbert, ed., *Literary Criticism, Plato to Croce* (1962); Lionel Trilling, ed., *Literary Criticism: An Introductory Reader* (1970); Hazard Adams, ed., *Critical Theory since Plato* (2d ed., 1993).

Anthologies that focus on recent and current criticism include: Hazard Adams and Leroy Searle, eds., *Critical Theory since 1965* (1986); Vassilis Lambropoulos and David Neal Miller, eds., *Twentieth-Century Literary Theory: An Introductory Anthology* (1987); David Lodge, ed., *Modern Criticism and Theory* (1988); Robert Con Davis and Ronald Schleifer, *Contemporary Literary Criticism* (rev. 1989); and the most inclusive, Vincent Leitch and others, eds., *The Norton Anthology of Theory and Criticism* (2001). Suggested readings in current types of critical theory are included in the entry of this *Glossary* for each type.

For collections of essays on topics in recent theory and criticism, see Michael Groden and Martin Kreiswirth, eds., *The Johns Hopkins Guide to Literary Theory and Criticism* (1994); Frank Lentricchia and Thomas McLaughlin, eds., *Critical Terms for Literary Study* (2d ed., 1995).

For types of criticism, see *anxiety of influence; archetypal criticism; art for art's sake; Chicago School; contextual criticism; theories and movements in recent criticism; critics of consciousness; Darwinian literary studies; deconstruction; dialogic criticism; ecocriticism; feminist criticism; gender criticism; linguistics in modern criticism; Marxist criticism; New Criticism; new historicism; phenomenology and criticism; postcolonial studies; psychological and psychoanalytic criticism; queer theory; reader-response criticism; reception theory; rhetorical criticism; Russian formalism; semiotics; sociological criticism; speech-act theory; structuralist criticism; stylistics.*

**criticism, theories and movements in recent: 368**.

**critics of consciousness: 262**; *63, 259*.

**critique:** Critique is often used to designate an especially robust and searching kind of criticism; it suggests a rational analysis of an intellectual position, or of a work incorporating that position, with a sharp eye for errors, confusions, or harmful implications. The term glances back to the German philosopher Immanuel Kant, who wrote three *Critiques* (of Pure Reason, Practical Reason, and Judgment), published 1781–90. The fact that Kant's use of "critique" suggests a rigorous reliance on reason, implies confidence in human autonomy, and is associated with Kant's looking forward to human emancipation (see *Enlightenment*) has made the term especially congenial to Marxist thinkers. The use of "critique" is associated particularly with the writings on "critical social theory" of the Frankfurt School, a group of neo-Marxists that included Walter Benjamin, Herbert Marcuse, Theodor Adorno, Max Horkheimer, and Jürgen Habermas (see under *Marxist criticism*). For brief and influential position statements, see Horkheimer, "Traditional and Critical Theory," in *Critical Theory* (1992); and Adorno, "Resignation," in *The Culture Industry* (2001).

**cultural constructs: 219**; *132, 277, 297*. See also *social constructs*.

**cultural materialism: 224**; *185*.

**cultural poetics: 223**.

**cultural primitivism: 285**; *254*.

**cultural studies:** Cultural studies designates a recent and rapidly growing cross-disciplinary enterprise for analyzing the conditions that affect the production, reception, and cultural significance of all types of institutions, practices, and products; among these, literature is accounted as merely one of many forms of cultural "signifying practices." A chief concern is to specify the functioning of the social, economic, and political forces and power structures that are said to produce the diverse forms of cultural phenomena and to endow them with their social "meanings," their "truth," the modes of discourse in which they are discussed, and their relative value and status.

One precursor of modern cultural studies was Roland Barthes, who in *Mythologies* (1957, trans. 1972) analyzed the social conventions and "codes" that confer meanings in such social practices as women's fashions and professional wrestling. (See Barthes under *semiotics* and *structuralism*.) Another was the British school of neo-Marxist studies of literature and art—especially in their popular and working-class modes—as an integral part of the general culture. This movement was inaugurated by Raymond Williams' *Culture and Society* (1958) and by Richard Hoggart's *The Uses of Literacy* (1958, reprinted 1992), and it became institutionalized in the influential Birmingham Centre for Contemporary Cultural Studies, founded by Hoggart in 1964. In the United States, the vogue for cultural studies had its roots mainly in the mode of literary and cultural criticism known as "the new historicism," with its antecedents both in poststructural theorists such as Louis Althusser and Michel Foucault and in the treatment of culture as a set of signifying systems by Clifford Geertz and other cultural anthropologists. (See under *new historicism*.)

A prominent endeavor in cultural studies is to subvert the distinctions in traditional criticism between "high literature" and "high art" and what were considered the lower forms that appeal to a much larger body of consumers. Typically, cultural studies pay less attention to works in the established literary *canon* than to popular fiction, best-selling romances (that is, love stories), journalism, and advertising, together with other arts that have mass appeal such as cartoon comics, film, television "soap operas," and rock and *rap* music. And within the areas of literature and the more traditional arts, a frequent undertaking is to move to the center of cultural study those works that, it is claimed, have been marginalized or excluded by the *aesthetic ideology* of white European and American males, particularly the products of women, minority ethnic groups, and colonial and *postcolonial* writers. Politically radical exponents of cultural studies orient their writings and teaching toward the explicit end of reforming existing power structures and relations, which they consider to be dominated by a privileged gender, race, or class. For the contributions of Stuart Hall—a leader in British cultural studies—to discussions of culture, race, and ethnicity, see David Morley and Kuan-Hsing Chen, eds., *Stuart Hall: Critical Dialogues in Cultural Studies* (1996).

Many cultural studies are devoted to the analysis and interpretation of objects and social practices outside the realm of literature and the other arts; these phenomena are viewed as endowed with meanings that are the product of social forces and conventions, and that may either express or oppose the dominant structures of power in a culture. In theory, there is no limit to the kinds of things and patterns of behavior to which such an analysis of cultural "texts" may be applied; current studies deal with a spectrum ranging from the vogue of bodybuilding through urban street fashions, and from cross-dressing to the social gesture of smoking a cigarette.

See the journal *Cultural Studies*, 1987–; also Catherine Belsey, *Critical Practice* (1980); Andrew Ross, *No Respect: Intellectual and Popular Culture* (1989); Lawrence Grossberg, Cary Nelson, and Paula Treichler, eds., *Cultural Studies* (1992); Anthony Easthope, *Literary into Cultural Studies* (1991); Richard Klein, *Cigarettes are Sublime* (1993); Valda Blundell, John Shepherd, and Ian Taylor, eds., *Relocating Cultural Studies: Developments in Theory and Research* (1993); Terry Lovell, ed., *Feminist Cultural Studies* (2 vols., 1995); Houston A. Baker, Jr., Manthia Diawara, and Ruth H. Lindeborg, eds., *Black British Cultural Studies: A Reader* (1996); Mark Seltzer, *Serial Killers I, II, III* (1997); Mieke Bal, *The Practice of Cultural Analysis* (1997); Simon During, ed., *The Cultural Studies Reader* (2d ed., 1999); Simon During, *Cultural Studies: A Critical Introduction* (2005); Andrew Edgar and Peter Sedgwick, eds., *Cultural Theory: The Key Thinkers* (2d ed., 2007). M. Jessica Munns and Gita Rajan, eds., *A Cultural Studies Reader: History, Theory, Practice* (1995) traces cultural studies as far back as Matthew Arnold in the Victorian era, then through the structural anthropology of Claude Lévi-Strauss to many current practitioners. For references to *cultural studies* in other entries, see pages *326, 348*.

**cyberpunk: 323**.

**dactylic** (dăktĭl′ ĭk): **195**.

**Dadaism: 357**.

**Darwinian literary studies:** The application to literature of Charles Darwin's theory of evolution, especially such evolutionary concepts as the struggle for existence, and the survival of those individuals and groups best adapted to their environment. The movement was begun in the mid-1990s by scholars, dissatisfied with the prevailing literary paradigms, who argued for a wholesale refashioning of literary studies to bring them into conformity with the findings of biological science, especially the theory of evolution. Darwinian literary studies were one of several new areas of investigation that were developed simultaneously with, or soon after, Edward O. Wilson's *Sociobiology: The New Synthesis* (1975), which argued that evolutionary pressures and results play a significant role not only in animal societies, but also in human culture. These investigations applied evolutionary principles to the fields of psychology, anthropology, and epistemology (the study of how human beings acquire knowledge).

The first major publication in Darwinian literary studies was Joseph Carroll's *Evolution and Literary Theory* (1995), written in express opposition to the various modes of *poststructuralist* criticism, with their exclusive focus on textual or linguistic features and their treatment of culture in total independence from biology. Carroll proposed, instead, that literary works should be studied as articulations of the vital needs and interests of human beings, viewed as adaptively evolved organisms. This approach, he claimed, would enable critics to discover in works of literature, beneath their myriad details of character and plot, an innate structure of motives, cognitive predispositions, and behavior that, as the result of an age-old process of evolution, is specific to the human species.

Many Darwinian studies focus on the analysis of themes in literature, especially those that deal with human reproductive behavior in sexual competition and the selection of mates, and with the formation of social alliances and of family relationships. When applied even to such unlikely seeming works as those of Jane Austen, for example, such an approach stresses the fact that they typically involve men who compete for women in their socioeconomic attributes of money and rank, and women who compete for men in their attributes of youth and beauty. When applied to the Homeric epics, the Darwinian approach views these works as a series of stories in which men—Paris, for example, who abducted Helen of Troy from Agamemnon—compete with one another, fundamentally, not for power, status, or wealth, but for the most desirable sexual mates.

Such thematic analyses have been criticized as drastically reductive, even vulgar. Another, more theoretical approach has emerged in the Darwinian movement that is concerned less with the analysis of particular works than in the ways that literature in general represents the elemental features of human life. A key work of this type was Robert F. Storey's *Mimesis and the Human Animal* (1996), which proposed a "biogrammar" of the human species that stressed such aspects of literature as its representation of human sociality and of elemental human motives and mental functions. Storey then applied his biogrammar to an analysis of the major *genres* of narrative, tragedy, and comedy, which he treated as highly developed forms of evolved and adaptive—or, in tragedy, of maladaptive—responses to evolutionary pressures; each genre, he claimed, had its distinctive kind of "phylogenetic" history of adaptive evolution.

Another type of Darwinian approach to literature is the study of how the basic activities of writing and reading literary works contribute to the adaptive fitness for survival of the human organism, by developing useful patterns of response, mapping out social relations, depicting intimate kin relationships, clarifying our understanding of our fundamental nature, and in general, helping us to make sense of the environing world. Some studies in this area of literary investigation use methods, such as statistical analyses, which ally them with the social sciences rather than the *humanities*.

For an overview of Darwinian literary studies, and of their relation to other fields such as evolutionary philosophy and *ecocriticism*, see Joseph Carroll, *Literary Darwinism: Evolution, Human Nature, and Literature* (2004). The initial anthology of Darwinian approaches to literature was Jonathan Gottschall and David Sloan Wilson, eds., *The Literary Animal: Evolution and the Nature of Narrative* (2005). For a wide-ranging, undogmatic application of the Darwinian perspective to a diversity of literary texts, see David P. Barash and Nanelle R. Barash, *Madame Bovary's Ovaries: A Darwinian Look at Literature* (2005). Among other relevant studies are Marcus Nordlund, *Shakespeare and the Nature of Love: Literature, Culture, Evolution* (2007), and Jonathan Gottschall, *The Rape of Troy: Evolution, Violence, and the World of Homer* (2008).

**dead metaphor: 120**.

**death of the author: 281**.

**Decadence, the:** In the latter part of the nineteenth century, some French proponents of the doctrines of *Aestheticism*, especially Charles Baudelaire, also espoused views and values that developed into a movement called "the Decadence." The term (not regarded by its exponents as derogatory) was based on qualities attributed to the literature of Hellenistic Greece in the last three centuries BC, and to Roman literature after the death of the Emperor Augustus in AD 14. These literatures were said to possess the high refinement and subtle beauties of a culture and art that had passed their vigorous prime, but manifested a special savor of incipient decay. Such was also held to be the state of European civilization, especially in France, as it approached the end of the nineteenth century.

Many of the precepts of the Decadence were voiced by Théophile Gautier in the "Notice," describing Baudelaire's poetry, that he prefixed to an edition of Baudelaire's *Les Fleurs du mal* ("Flowers of Evil") in 1868. Central to the

Decadent movement was the view that art is totally opposed to "nature," in the sense both of biological nature and of the standard, or "natural," norms of morality and sexual behavior. The thoroughgoing Decadent writer cultivates high artifice in style and, often, the bizarre in subject matter, recoils from the fecundity and exuberance of the organic and instinctual life of nature, prefers elaborate dress over the living human form and cosmetics over the natural hue, and sometimes sets out to violate what is commonly held to be "natural" in human experience by resorting to drugs, deviancy from standard norms of behavior, and sexual experimentation, in the attempt to achieve (in a phrase echoed from the French poet Arthur Rimbaud) "the systematic derangement of all the senses." The movement reached its height in the last two decades of the nineteenth century; extreme products were the novel *À rebours* ("Against the Grain"), written by J. K. Huysmans in 1884, and some of the paintings of Gustave Moreau. This period is also known as the **fin de siècle** (end of the century); the phrase connotes the lassitude, satiety, and ennui expressed by many writers of the Decadence.

In England the ideas, moods, and behavior of the Decadence were manifested, beginning in the 1860s, in the poems of Algernon Charles Swinburne, and in the 1890s by writers such as Oscar Wilde, Arthur Symons, Ernest Dowson, and Lionel Johnson; the notable artist of the English Decadence was Aubrey Beardsley. In the search for strange sensations, a number of English Decadents of the 1890s experimented with drugs and espoused what were conventionally held to be extranatural modes of sexual experience; several of them died young. Representative literary productions are Wilde's novel *The Picture of Dorian Gray* (1891), his play *Salomé* (1893), and many of the poems of Ernest Dowson.

The emphases of the Decadence on drugged perception, sexual experimentation, and the deliberate inversion of conventional moral, social, and artistic norms reappeared, with modern variations, in the *Beat* poets and novelists of the 1950s and in the *counterculture* of the decades that followed.

See Mario Praz, *The Romantic Agony* (1933); A. E. Carter, *The Idea of Decadence in French Literature, 1830–1900* (1958); Karl Beckson, ed., *Aesthetes and Decadents of the 1890s* (1966); Richard Gilman, *Decadence: The Strange Life of an Epithet* (1979); Ian Fletcher, ed., *Decadence and the 1890s* (1979); and G. H. Pittock Murray, *Spectrum of Decadence: The Literature of the 1890s* (1993). A useful descriptive guide to books on the subject is Linda C. Dowling, *Aestheticism and Decadence: A Selective Annotated Bibliography* (1977). For references to *decadence* in other entries, see page *25*.

**decasyllabic couplet** (dĕk′ asĭlă″ bĭk): **341**.

**deconstruction:** Deconstruction, as applied in the criticism of literature, designates a theory and practice of reading that questions and claims to "subvert" or "undermine" the assumption that the system of language provides grounds that are adequate to establish the boundaries, the coherence or unity, and the determinate meanings of a literary text. Typically, a deconstructive reading sets out to show that conflicting forces within the text itself serve to dissipate the seeming definiteness of its structure and meanings into an indefinite array of incompatible and undecidable possibilities.

The originator and namer of deconstruction is the French thinker Jacques Derrida, among whose precursors were Friedrich Nietzsche (1844–1900) and Martin Heidegger (1889–1976)—German philosophers who put to radical question fundamental philosophical concepts such as "knowledge," "truth," and "identity"—as well as Sigmund Freud (1856–1939), whose *psychoanalysis* violated traditional concepts of a coherent individual consciousness and a unitary self. Derrida presented his basic views in three books, all published in 1967, entitled *Of Grammatology, Writing and Difference,* and *Speech and Phenomena*; after that date he reiterated, expanded, and applied those views in a rapid sequence of publications.

Derrida's writings are complex and elusive, and the summary here can only indicate some of their main tendencies. His vantage point is what he calls, in *Of Grammatology,* "the axial proposition that there is no outside-the-text" ("il n'y a rien hors du texte," or alternatively "il n'y a pas de hors-texte"). Like all Derrida's key terms and statements, this has multiple significations, but a primary one is that a reader cannot get beyond verbal signs to any things-in-themselves which, because they are independent of the system of language, might serve to anchor a determinable meaning.

Derrida's reiterated claim is that not only all Western philosophies and theories of language, but all Western uses of language, hence all Western culture, are **logocentric**; that is, they are centered or grounded on a "logos" (which in Greek signified both "word" and "rationality") or, in a phrase he adopts from Heidegger, they rely on "the metaphysics of presence." They are logocentric, according to Derrida, in part because they are **phonocentric**; that is, they grant, implicitly or explicitly, logical "priority," or "privilege," to speech over writing as the model for analyzing all discourse. By logos, or **presence**, Derrida signifies what he also calls an "ultimate referent"—a self-certifying and self-sufficient ground, or foundation, available to us totally outside the play of language itself, that is directly present to our awareness and serves to "center" (that is, to anchor, organize, and guarantee) the structure of the linguistic system, and as a result suffices to fix the bounds, coherence, and determinate meanings of any spoken or written utterance within that system. (On Derrida's "decentering" of structuralism, see *poststructuralism*.) Historical instances of claimed foundations for language are God as the guarantor of its validity, or a Platonic form of the true reference of a general term, or a Hegelian "telos" or goal toward which all process strives, or an intention to signify something determinate that is directly present to the awareness of the person who initiates an utterance. Derrida undertakes to show that these and all other attempts by Western philosophy to establish an absolute ground in presence, and all implicit reliance on such a ground in using language, are bound to fail. Especially, he directs his skeptical exposition against the phonocentric assumption—which he regards as central in Western theories of language—that at the instant of speaking, the "intention" of a speaker to mean something determinate by an utterance is immediately and fully present in the speaker's consciousness, and is also communicable to an auditor. (See *intention,* under *interpretation and hermeneutics*.) In Derrida's view, we must always say more, and other, than we intend to say.

Derrida expresses his alternative conception, that the play of linguistic meanings is "undecidable," in terms derived from Saussure's view that in a sign system, both the *signifiers* (the material elements of a language, whether spoken or written) and the *signifieds* (their conceptual meanings) owe their seeming identities, not to their own "positive" or inherent features, but to their "differences" from other speech sounds, written marks, or conceptual significations. (See Saussure, in *linguistics in modern criticism* and in *semiotics*.) From this view Derrida evolves his radical claim that the features that, in any particular utterance, would serve to establish the signified meaning of a word, are never "present" to us in their own positive identity, since both these features and their significations are nothing other than a network of differences. On the other hand, neither can these identifying features be said to be strictly "absent"; instead, in any spoken or written utterance, the apparent meaning is the result only of a "self-effacing" **trace**—self-effacing in that one is not aware of it—which consists of all the nonpresent differences from other elements in the language system that invest the utterance with its "effect" of having a meaning in its own right. The consequence, in Derrida's view, is that we can never, in any instance of speech or writing, have a demonstrably fixed and decidable present meaning. He concedes that the differential play (*jeu*) of language may produce the "effects" of decidable meanings in an utterance or text, but asserts that these are merely effects, and lack a ground that would justify certainty in interpretation.

In a characteristic move, Derrida coins the *portmanteau* term **différance**, in which, he says, he uses the spelling "-ance" instead of "-ence" to indicate a fusion of two senses of the French verb "différer": to be different, and to defer. This double sense points to the phenomenon that, on the one hand, a text proffers the "effect" of having a significance that is the product of its difference, but that on the other hand, since this proffered significance can never come to rest in an actual "presence"—or in a language-independent reality Derrida calls a **transcendental signified**—its determinate specification is deferred from one linguistic interpretation to another in a movement or "play," as Derrida puts it, *en abîme*—that is, in an endless regress. To Derrida's view, then, it is difference that makes possible the meaning whose possibility (as a decidable meaning) it necessarily baffles. As Derrida says in another of his coinages, the meaning of any spoken or written utterance, by the action of opposing internal linguistic forces, is ineluctably **disseminated**—a term which includes, among its deliberately contradictory significations, that of having an effect of meaning (a "semantic" effect), of dispersing meanings among innumerable alternatives, and of negating any specific meaning. There is thus no ground, in the incessant play of difference that constitutes any language, for attributing a decidable meaning, or even a finite set of determinately multiple meanings (which he calls "polysemism"), to any utterance that we speak or write. (What Derrida calls "polysemism" is what William Empson called "ambiguity"; see *ambiguity*.) As Derrida puts it in *Writing and Difference:* "The absence of a transcendental signified extends the domain and the play of signification infinitely" (p. 280).

Several of Derrida's skeptical procedures have been especially influential in deconstructive literary criticism. A cardinal procedure is to subvert the innumerable **binary oppositions**—such as speech/writing, nature/culture, truth/error, male/female—which are essential structural elements in logocentric language.

Derrida shows that such oppositions constitute a tacit hierarchy, in which the first term functions as privileged and superior and the second term as derivative and inferior. Derrida's procedure is to invert the hierarchy, by showing that the primary term can be made out to be derivative from, or a special case of, the secondary term; but instead of stopping at this reversal, he goes on to destabilize both hierarchies, leaving them in a condition of undecidability. (Among deconstructive literary critics, one such demonstration is to take the standard hierarchical opposition of literature/criticism, to invert it so as to make criticism primary and literature secondary, and then to represent, as an undecidable set of oppositions, the assertions that criticism is a species of literature and that literature is a species of criticism.) A second operation influential in literary criticism is Derrida's deconstruction of any attempt to establish a securely determinate bound, or limit, or margin, to a textual work so as to differentiate what is "inside" from what is "outside" the work. A third operation is his analysis of the inherent nonlogicality, or "rhetoricity"—that is, the inescapable reliance on *rhetorical figures* and *figurative language*—in all uses of language, including in what philosophers have traditionally claimed to be the strictly literal and logical arguments of philosophy. Derrida, for example, emphasizes the indispensable reliance in all modes of discourse on metaphors that are assumed to be merely convenient substitutes for *literal*, or "proper" meanings; then he undertakes to show, on the one hand, that metaphors cannot be reduced to literal meanings but, on the other hand, that supposedly literal terms are themselves metaphors whose metaphoric nature has been forgotten.

Derrida's characteristic way of proceeding is not to lay out his deconstructive concepts and operations in a systematic exposition, but to allow them to emerge in a sequence of exemplary close readings of passages from writings that range from Plato through Jean-Jacques Rousseau to the present era—writings that, by standard classification, are mainly philosophical, although occasionally literary. He describes his procedure as a "double reading." Initially, that is, he interprets a text as, in the standard fashion, "lisible" (readable or intelligible), since it engenders "effects" of having determinate meanings. But this reading, Derrida says, is only "provisional," as a stage toward a second, or deconstructive "critical reading," which disseminates the provisional meaning into an indefinite range of significations that, he claims, always involve (in a term taken from logic) an **aporia**—an insuperable deadlock, or "double bind," of incompatible or contradictory meanings which are "undecidable," in that we lack any sufficient ground for choosing among them. The result, in Derrida's rendering, is that each text deconstructs itself, by undermining its own supposed grounds and dispersing itself into incoherent meanings in a way, he claims, that the deconstructive reader neither initiates nor produces; deconstruction is something that simply "happens" in a critical reading. Derrida asserts, furthermore, that he has no option except to attempt to communicate his deconstructive readings in the prevailing logocentric language, hence that his own interpretive texts deconstruct themselves in the very act of deconstructing the texts to which they are applied. He insists, however, that "deconstruction has nothing to do with destruction," and that all the standard uses of language will inevitably go on; what he undertakes, he says, is merely to "situate" or "reinscribe" any text in a system of difference which shows the instability of the effects to which the text owes its seeming intelligibility.

Derrida did not propose deconstruction as a mode of literary criticism, but as a way of reading all kinds of texts so as to reveal and subvert the tacit metaphysical presuppositions of Western thought. His views and procedures, however, have been taken up by literary critics, especially in America, who have adapted Derrida's "critical reading" to the kind of *close reading* of particular literary texts which had earlier been the familiar procedure of the *New Criticism*; they do so, however, Paul de Man has said, in a way which reveals that new-critical close readings "were not nearly close enough." The end results of the two kinds of close reading are utterly diverse. New-critical explications of texts had undertaken to show that a great literary work, in the tight internal relations of its figurative and paradoxical meanings, constitutes a freestanding, bounded, and organic entity of multiplex yet determinate meanings. On the contrary, a radically deconstructive close reading undertakes to show that a literary text lacks a "totalized" boundary that makes it an entity, much less an organic unity; also that the text, by a play of internal counterforces, disseminates into an indefinite range of self-conflicting significations. Some deconstructive critics claim that a literary text is superior to non-literary texts, but only because, by its self-reference, it shows itself to be more aware of features that all texts inescapably share: its fictionality, its lack of a genuine ground, and especially its patent "rhetoricity," or use of figurative procedures —features that make any "right reading" or "correct reading" of a text impossible.

Paul de Man was the most innovative and influential of the critics who applied deconstruction to the reading of literary texts. In de Man's later writings, he represented the basic conflicting forces within a text under the headings of "grammar" (the code or rules of language) as opposed to "rhetoric" (the unruly play of figures and tropes), and aligned these with other opposed forces, such as the "constative" and "performative" linguistic functions that had been distinguished by John Austin (see *speech-act theory*). In its grammatical aspect, language persistently aspires to determinate, referential, and logically ordered assertions, which are persistently dispersed by its rhetorical aspect into an open set of nonreferential and illogical possibilities. A literary text, then, of inner necessity says one thing and performs another, or as de Man alternatively puts the matter, a text "simultaneously asserts and denies the authority of its own rhetorical mode" (*Allegories of Reading*, 1979, p. 17). The inevitable result, for a critical reading, is an aporia of "vertiginous possibilities."

Barbara Johnson, once a student of de Man's, has applied deconstructive readings not only to literary texts, but to the writings of other critics, including Derrida himself. Her succinct statement of the aim and methods of a deconstructive reading is often cited:

> *Deconstruction* is not synonymous with *destruction*. . . . The deconstruction of a text does not proceed by random doubt or arbitrary subversion, but by the careful teasing out of warring forces of signification within the text itself. If anything is destroyed in a

deconstructive reading, it is not the text, but the claim to unequivocal
domination of one mode of signifying over another.
(*The Critical Difference*, 1980, p. 5)

J. Hillis Miller, formerly the leading American representative of the *Geneva
School* of consciousness-criticism, later became one of the most prominent of de-
constructors, known especially for his application of this type of critical reading to
prose fiction. Miller's statement of his critical practice indicates how drastic the
result may be of applying to works of literature the concepts and procedures that
Derrida had developed for deconstructing the foundations of Western
metaphysics:

> Deconstruction as a mode of interpretation works by a careful and
> circumspect entering of each textual labyrinth. . . . The deconstructive
> critic seeks to find, by this process of retracing, the element in the
> system studied which is alogical, the thread in the text in question
> which will unravel it all, or the loose stone which will pull down the
> whole building. The deconstruction, rather, annihilates the ground on
> which the building stands by showing that the text has already anni-
> hilated the ground, knowingly or unknowingly. Deconstruction is not
> a dismantling of the structure of a text but a demonstration that it has
> already dismantled itself.

Miller's conclusion is that any literary text, as a ceaseless play of "irreconcilable"
and "contradictory" meanings, is "indeterminable" and "undecidable"; hence, that
"all reading is necessarily misreading." ("Stevens' Rock and Criticism as Cure, II,"
in Miller's *Theory Then and Now*, 1991, p. 126, and "Walter Pater: A Partial
Portrait," *Daedalus*, Vol. 105, 1976.)

For other aspects of Derrida's views see *poststructuralism* and refer to Geoffrey
Bennington, *Jacques Derrida* (1993). Some of the central books by Jacques Derrida
available in English, with the dates of translation into English, are *Of
Grammatology*, translated and introduced by Gayatri C. Spivak (1976); *Writing and
Difference* (1978); and *Dissemination* (1981). A useful anthology of selections from
Derrida is *A Derrida Reader: Between the Blinds*, ed. Peggy Kamuf (1991). *Acts of
Literature*, ed. Derek Attridge (1992), is a selection of Derrida's discussions of liter-
ary texts. An accessible introduction to Derrida's views is the edition by Gerald
Graff of Derrida's noted dispute with John R. Searle about the speech-act theory
of John Austin, entitled *Limited Inc.* (1988); on this dispute see also Jonathan
Culler, "Meaning and Iterability," in *On Deconstruction* (1982), and Geoffrey Galt
Harpham, "Derrida and the Ethics of Criticism," in *Shadows of Ethics: Criticism and
the Just Society* (1999). Books exemplifying types of deconstructive literary criti-
cism: Paul de Man, *Blindness and Insight* (1971), and *Allegories of Reading* (1979);
Barbara Johnson, *The Critical Difference: Essays in the Contemporary Rhetoric of
Reading* (1980), and *A World of Difference* (1987); J. Hillis Miller, *Fiction and
Repetition: Seven English Novels* (1982), *The Linguistic Moment: From Wordsworth to
Stevens* (1985), and *Theory Then and Now* (1991); Cynthia Chase, *Decomposing
Figures: Rhetorical Readings in the Romantic Tradition* (1986). Expositions of

Derrida's deconstruction and of its applications to literary criticism: Geoffrey Hartman, *Saving the Text* (1981); Jonathan Culler, *On Deconstruction* (1982); Richard Rorty, "Philosophy as a Kind of Writing," in *Consequences of Pragmatism* (1982); Michael Ryan, *Marxism and Deconstruction* (1982); Mark C. Taylor, ed., *Deconstruction in Context* (1986); Christopher Norris, *Paul de Man* (1988). For the range of deconstructive literary criticism, refer to Martin McQuillan, ed., *Deconstruction: A Reader* (2001); for a positive assessment of this criticism, see Christopher Norris, *Deconstruction: Theory and Practice* (3d ed., 2002).

Among the many critiques of Derrida and of various practitioners of deconstructive literary criticism are Terry Eagleton, *The Function of Criticism* (1984); M. H. Abrams, "The Deconstructive Angel," "How to Do Things with Texts," and "Construing and Deconstructing," in *Doing Things with Texts* (1989); John M. Ellis, *Against Deconstruction* (1989); Wendell V. Harris, ed., *Beyond Poststructuralism* (1996). Essays that oppose the theory and practice of deconstruction are collected in *The Emperor Redressed: Critiquing Critical Theory*, ed. Dwight Eddins, 1995, and *Theory's Empire: An Anthology of Dissent*, ed. Daphne Patai and Will H. Corral, 2005.

For references to *deconstruction* in other entries, see pages *8, 13, 118, 121, 146, 147, 161, 175, 218, 219, 262, 279, 312, 315, 339.*

**décor** (dā′ kōr): **330**.

**Decorum:** Decorum, as a term in literary criticism, designates the view that there should be propriety, or fitness, in the way that a literary *genre*, its subject matter, its characters and actions, and the style of its narration and dialogue are matched to one another. The doctrine has its roots in classical theory, especially in the versified essay *Art of Poetry* by the Roman Horace in the first century BC. It achieved an elaborate form in the criticism and composition of literature in the Renaissance and the *Neoclassic* age, when (as John Milton put it in his essay *Of Education*, 1644) decorum became "the grand masterpiece to observe." In its most rigid application, literary forms, characters, and style were ordered in hierarchies, or "levels," from high through middle to low, and all these elements had to be matched to one another. Thus comedy must not be mixed with tragedy, and the highest and most serious genres (epic and tragedy) must represent characters of the highest social classes (kings and nobility) acting in a way appropriate to their status and speaking in the *high style*. A number of critics in this period, however, especially in England, maintained the theory of decorum only in limited ways. Thomas Rymer (1641–1713) was an English proponent, and Samuel Johnson (1709–84) was a notable opponent of the strict form of literary decorum.

See *neoclassic and romantic, poetic diction*, and *style*, and refer to Vernon Hall, *Renaissance Literary Criticism: A Study of Its Social Content* (1945). Erich Auerbach's *Mimesis* (trans. 1953, reprinted 2003) describes the sustained conflict in postclassical Europe between the reigning doctrines of literary decorum and the example of the Bible, in which the highest matters, including the sublime tragedy of the life and passion of Christ, are intermingled with base characters and humble narrative detail, and are treated with what seemed to a classical taste a blatant indecorum of style. For Wordsworth's deliberate inversion of traditional decorum at the beginning of the nineteenth century, by investing the common, the lowly, and the trivial with high dignity and sublimity, see M. H. Abrams, *Natural Supernaturalism* (1971), pp. 390–408. For references to *decorum* in other entries, see pages *134, 213, 269, 374.*

**deep structure** (linguistic): **176**.

**defamiliarize: 127**.

**deictic** (dīk′ tĭk): **208**.

**deism:** A widespread mode of religious thought that manifested faith in human reason during the European *Enlightenment* in the latter part of the seventeenth and the eighteenth centuries. Deism has been succinctly described as "religion without revelation." The thoroughgoing deist renounced, as violating reason, all "revealed religion"—that is, all religions, including Christianity, which are based on faith in the truths revealed in special scriptures at a certain time and place, and therefore available only to particular individuals or groups. The deist instead relied on those truths which, it was claimed, prove their accord with universal human reason by the fact that they are to be found in all religions, everywhere, at all times. Accordingly the basic tenets of deism—for example, that there is a deity, discoverable by reasoning from the creation to the creator, who deserves our worship and sanctions all moral values—were, in theory, the elements shared by all particular, or "positive," religions. Many thinkers assimilated aspects of deism while remaining professing Christians. Alexander Pope, without renouncing his Catholicism, expressed succinctly the basic tenets of deism in his poem "The Universal Prayer" (1738), which begins

> Father of all! in every age,
> In every clime adored,
> By saint, by savage, and by sage,
> Jehovah, Jove, or Lord!

**deliberative oratory: 311**.

**demotic style** (dĕmŏt′ ik): **350**.

**denotation: 57**.

**denouement** (dānoomän′): **268**.

**descriptive–meditative lyric: 269**.

**deus ex machina:** Deus ex machina is Latin for "a god from a machine." It designates the practice of some Greek playwrights (especially Euripides) to end a drama with a god, lowered to the stage by a mechanical apparatus, who by his judgment and commands resolved the dilemmas of the human characters. The phrase is now used for any forced and improbable device—a telltale birthmark, an unexpected inheritance, the discovery of a lost will or letter—by which a hard-pressed author resolves a plot. Conspicuous examples occur even in major novels like Charles Dickens' *Oliver Twist* (1837–38) and Thomas Hardy's *Tess of the D'Urbervilles* (1891). The German playwright Bertolt Brecht *parodied* such devices in the mad-cap conclusion of his *Threepenny Opera* (1928). See *plot*.

**diachronic** (dīakrŏn′ ik): **172**.

**dialects: 174**.

**dialogic criticism:** Dialogic criticism is modeled on the theory and critical proce-dures of the Soviet critic Mikhail Bakhtin who, although he published his major works in the 1920s and 1930s, remained virtually unknown to the West until the 1980s, when translations of his writings gave him a wide and rapidly increasing influence. To Bakhtin a literary work is not (as in various *poststructural* theories) a text whose meanings are produced by the play of impersonal linguistic or eco-nomic or cultural forces, but a site for the dialogic interaction of multiple voices, or modes of discourse, each of which is not merely a verbal but a social phenom-enon, and as such is the product of manifold determinants that are specific to a class, social group, and speech community. A person's speech does not express a pre-existent and autonomous individuality; instead, his or her character emerges in the course of the dialogue and is composed of languages from diverse social con-texts. Each utterance, furthermore, whether in actual life or as represented in lit-erature, owes its precise inflection and meaning to a number of attendant factors—the specific social situation in which it is spoken, the relation of its speaker to an actual or anticipated listener, and the relation of the utterance to the prior utter-ances to which it is (explicitly or implicitly) a response.

Bakhtin's prime interest was in the novel, and especially in the ways that the multiple voices that constitute the text of any novel disrupt the authority of the author's single voice. In *Problems of Dostoevsky's Poetics* (1929, trans. by Caryl Emerson, 1984), he contrasts the **monologic** novels of writers such as Leo Tolstoy —which undertake to subordinate the voices of all the characters to the authoritative discourse and controlling purposes of the author—to the **dialogic form** (or "poly-phonic form") of Fyodor Dostoevsky's novels, in which the characters are liberated to speak "a plurality of independent and unmerged voices and consciousnesses, a genuine polyphony of fully valid voices." In Bakhtin's view, however, a novel can never be totally monologic, since the narrator's reports of the utterances of another character are inescapably "double-voiced" (in that we can distinguish therein the author's own accent and inflection), and also dialogic (in that the author's discourse continually reinforces, alters, or contests with the types of speech that it reports).

In *Rabelais and His World* (trans. 1984), Bakhtin proposed his widely cited concept of the **carnivalesque** in certain works of literature. This literary mode parallels the flouting of authority and temporary inversion of social hierarchies that, in many cultures, are permitted during a season of carnival. The literary work does so by introducing a mingling of voices from diverse social levels that are free to mock and subvert authority, to flout social norms by ribaldry, and to exhibit various ways of profaning what is ordinarily regarded as sacrosanct. Bakhtin traces the occurrence of the carnivalesque in ancient, medieval, and Renaissance writers (especially in Rabelais); he also asserts that the mode recurs later, especially in the play of irreverent, parodic, and subversive voices in the novels of Dostoevsky—novels that are both dialogic and carnivalesque.

In an essay on "Discourse in the Novel" (1934–35), Bakhtin develops his view that the novel is constituted by a multiplicity of divergent and contending social voices that achieve their full significance only in the process of their dialogic interaction both with each other and with the voice of the narrator. Bakhtin explicitly sets his theory against Aristotle's *Poetics*, which proposed that the primary component in narrative forms is a plot that evolves coherently from its beginning to an end in which all complications are resolved (see *plot*). Instead, Bakhtin elevates *discourse* (equivalent to Aristotle's subordinate element of *diction*) into the primary component of a narrative work; and he describes discourse as a medley of voices, social attitudes, and values that are not only opposed, but irreconcilable, with the result that the work remains unresolved and open-ended. Although he wrote during the Stalinist regime in Russia, Bakhtin's libertarian and open concept of the literary narrative is obviously, although tacitly, opposed to the Soviet version of Marxist criticism, which stresses the way a novel either reflects or distorts the true social reality, or expresses only a single dominant ideology, or should exemplify a "social realism" that accords with an authoritarian party line. See *Marxist criticism* and, for a discussion of the complex issue of Bakhtin's relation to Marxism and Soviet literary criticism, see Simon Dentith, *Bakhtinian Thought: An Introductory Reader* (1995), pp. 8–21.

Bakhtin's views have been, in some part and in diverse ways, incorporated by representatives of various types of critical theory and practice, whether traditional or *poststructural*. Among current students of literature, those who are identified specifically as "dialogic critics" follow Bakhtin's example by proposing that the primary component in the constitution of narrative works, or of literature generally —and of general culture as well—is a plurality of contending and mutually qualifying social voices, with no possibility of a decisive resolution into a monologic truth. Self-reflexively, a thoroughgoing dialogic critic, in accordance with Bakhtin's views, considers his own critical writings to be simply one voice among many in the contention of critical theories and practices, which coexist in a sustained tension of opposition and mutual definition. As Don Bialostosky, a chief spokesman for dialogic criticism, voiced its rationale and ideal:

> As a self-conscious practice, dialogic criticism turns its inescapable involvement with some other voices into a program of articulating itself with all the other voices of the discipline, the culture, or the world of cultures to which it makes itself responsible. . . . Neither a live-and-let-live relativism nor a settle-it-once-and-for-all authoritarianism but a strenuous and open-ended dialogism would keep them talking to themselves and to one another, discovering their affinities without resting in them and clarifying their differences without resolving them.
>
> ("Dialogic Criticism," in G. Douglas Atkins and Laura Morrow, eds., *Contemporary Literary Theory*, 1989, pp. 223–24)

See the related critical enterprise called *discourse analysis*; and in addition to the writings mentioned above, refer to Mikhail Bakhtin's *The Dialogic Imagination*, ed. Michael Holquist (1981), and *Speech Genres and Other Late Essays*, ed. Caryl Emerson and Michael Holquist (1986). For Bakhtin's life and intellectual views, with attention to the problem of identifying writings that Bakhtin published under the names of various of his colleagues, see Katerina Clark and Michael Holquist, *Mikhail Bakhtin* (1984), and Gary Saul Morson and Caryl Emerson, *Mikhail Bakhtin: Creation of a Poetics* (1990). An influential early exposition that publicized Bakhtin's ideas in the West was Tzvetan Todorov, *Mikhail Bakhtin: The Dialogical Principle* (1984). A later book describing the wide dissemination of these ideas is David Lodge's *After Bakhtin* (1990). For an application of dialogic criticism, see Don H. Bialostosky, *Wordsworth, Dialogics, and the Practice of Criticism* (1992). For a critical view of Bakhtin's claims, see René Wellek, *A History of Modern Criticism, 1750–1950*, Vol. 7 (1991), pp. 354–71.

For references to *dialogic criticism* in other entries, see pages *82, 282*.

**dialogic form:** 77.

**dialogue:** 42.

**diary:** 26.

**diction:** 269.

**didactic literature:** The adjective "didactic," which means "intended to give instruction," is applied to works of literature that are designed to expound a branch of knowledge, or else to embody, in imaginative or fictional form, a moral, religious, or philosophical doctrine or *theme*. (See the entry *literature*.) Such works are commonly distinguished from essentially imaginative works (sometimes called "mimetic" or "representational") in which the materials are organized and rendered, not in order to expound and enhance the appeal of the doctrine they embody, but in order to enhance the intrinsic interest of the materials themselves and their capacity to move and give artistic pleasure to an audience. In the first century BC the Roman Lucretius wrote his didactic poem *De Rerum Natura* ("On the Nature of Things") to expound and make persuasive and appealing his naturalistic philosophy and ethics, and in the same era Virgil wrote his *Georgics*, in which the poetic elements add *aesthetic* appeal to a laudation of rural life and information about the practical management of a farm. Most medieval and much Renaissance literature was didactic in intention. In the eighteenth century, a number of poets wrote **georgics** (on the model of Virgil), describing in verse such utilitarian arts as sheepherding, running a sugar plantation, and making cider. Alexander Pope's *Essay on Criticism* and his *Essay on Man* are eighteenth-century didactic poems on the subjects of literary criticism and of moral philosophy.

Such works for the most part directly describe the principles and procedures of a branch of knowledge or a craft, or else argue an explicit doctrine by proofs and examples. Didactic literature, however, may also take on the attributes of imaginative works, by embodying the doctrine in a fictional narrative or dramatic form that is intended to enhance the doctrine's human interest and persuasive force, as well as to add a dimension of pleasure in the artistry of the representation. In the various forms of *allegory*, for example, including Edmund Spenser's *The Faerie Queene* and John Bunyan's *The Pilgrim's Progress*, the purpose of enhancing and adding force to the incorporated doctrines is a primary determinant of the choice and presentation of the allegoric characters, the evolution of the plot, and the invention of fictional details. The diverse types of *satire* are didactic in that they are designed, by various devices of ridicule, to alter the reader's attitudes toward certain types of people, institutions, products, and modes of conduct. Dante's *Letter to Can Grande* tells us that he planned his fourteenth-century *Divine Comedy* to represent, in the mode of a visionary narrative, the major Christian truths and the way to avoid damnation and achieve salvation. And John Milton's *Paradise Lost* (1667) can also be called didactic to the extent that the narrative is in fact organized, as Milton claimed in his opening invocation, around his "great argument" to "assert Eternal Providence, / And justify the ways of God to men."

It will be seen from these examples that "didactic literature," as here defined, is an analytical distinction and not a derogatory term; also that the distinction is not absolute but a matter of relative emphasis on instructing and persuading an audience, as against rendering a subject in such a way as to maximize its power to move and give artistic delight in its own right. The plays of Bernard Shaw and Bertolt Brecht manifest a fine balance of didactic intention, imaginative invention, and artistic enhancement. And some literary masterpieces are primarily didactic, while others (Shakespeare's *King Lear*, Jane Austen's *Emma*, James Joyce's *Ulysses*)—even though their plots involve moral concerns and imply criteria for moral judgments—are primarily, to adopt a phrase by Samuel Taylor Coleridge, works "of pure imagination."

The term **propagandist literature** is sometimes used as the equivalent of didactic literature, but it is more useful to reserve the term for that type of didactic work which is obviously organized and rendered to induce the reader to assume a specific attitude toward, or to take direct action on, a pressing social, political, or religious issue of the time at which the work is written. Prominent and effective examples of such works are Harriet Beecher Stowe's *Uncle Tom's Cabin* (1852, attacking slavery in the South), Upton Sinclair's *The Jungle* (1906, on the horrors of the unregulated slaughtering and meat-packing industry in Chicago), and Clifford Odets' *Waiting for Lefty* (1935, a play directed against the strong-arm tactics used to suppress a taxicab drivers' union). The *socialist realism* that was the official critical doctrine of the former Soviet Union espoused what was essentially a propagandist mode of literature.

See *fiction*, and refer to John Chalker, *The English Georgic: A Study in the Development of a Form* (1969). On a useful way to distinguish between primarily didactic and primarily imaginative, or "mimetic," literature, see R. S. Crane, ed., *Critics and Criticism* (1952), especially pp. 63–68 and 589–94.

**différance** (dĭf′ ārăns″): **71**.

**difference** (in linguistics): **174**; *325*.

**dimeter** (dĭm′ ĕter): **196**.

**dirge: 92**.

**discourse: 282**; *78, 219, 257, 277*.

**discourse analysis:** Traditional linguists and philosophers of language, as well as literary students of *style* and *stylistics*, have typically focused their analyses on isolated units of language—the sentence, or even single words, phrases, and figures—in abstraction from the specific circumstances of an utterance. Discourse analysis, on the other hand, as developed in the 1970s, concerns itself with the use of language in a running discourse, continued over a number of sentences, and involving the interaction of speaker (or writer) and auditor (or reader) in a specific situational context, and within a particular framework of social and cultural conventions.

Emphasis on the meaning of a discourse as dependent on specific cultural conditions and particular circumstances derives from a number of investigators and areas of research, including the work of Hans-Georg Gadamer in *hermeneutics*, the concern of Michel Foucault with the institutional conditions and power structures that serve to make given statements accepted as authoritative or true, and the work of Clifford Geertz and other cultural anthropologists on the rootedness of linguistic and other meanings in the social forms and practices specific to a cultural community. (See the above writers, under *interpretation and hermeneutics* and *new historicism*.) The current use of discourse analysis in literary studies was given special impetus by the speech-act philosopher H. P. Grice, who in 1975 coined the term **implicature** to account for indirection in discourse; for example, to explain how we are able to identify the illocutionary force of an utterance that lacks an explicit indicator of its illocutionary intention. (See *speech-act theory*.) Thus, how can we explain the fact that the utterance, "Can you pass the salt?" although it is in the syntactical form of a question of possibility, can be used by the speaker, and correctly understood by the hearer, as a polite form of request? (H. P. Grice, "Logic and Conversation," 1975, reprinted in his *Studies in the Way of Words*, 1989.) Grice proposed that users of a language share a set of implicit expectations which he calls the "communicative presumption"—for example, that an utterance is intended by a speaker to be true, clear, and above all relevant. If an utterance seems purposely to violate these expectations, we seek to make sense of it by transferring it to a context in which it is clearly appropriate. Other language theorists have continued Grice's analysis of the underlying collective assumptions that help to make utterances meaningful and intelligible, and serve also to make a sustained discourse a coherent development of signification instead of a mere collocation of independent sentences. One such assumption is that the hearer shares with the speaker (or the reader shares with the writer) a large body of nonlinguistic knowledge and experience; another is that the speaker is using language in a way that is intentional, purposive, and in accordance with the accepted linguistic and cultural conventions; a third is that there is a shared knowledge of the complex ways in which the meaning of a locution varies with the particular situation, as well as with the type of discourse, in which it is uttered.

Some proponents of stylistics include discourse analysis within their area of investigation. (See *stylistics*.) And since the late 1970s, a number of critics have adapted discourse analysis to the examination of the *dialogue* in novels and dramas. A chief aim is to explain how the characters represented in a literary work, and also the readers of that work, are constantly able to infer correctly meanings that are not asserted or specified in a conversational interchange. The claim is that such inferences are "rule-governed," in that they depend on tacit sets of assumptions, shared by users and interpreters of discourse, that come into play to establish meanings and, furthermore, that these meanings vary systematically, in accordance with whether the rule-guided expectations are fulfilled or intentionally violated. Such explorations of conversational discourse in literature often extend to the re-analysis of *point of view* and other traditional topics in the criticism of literary narratives. (Compare the entry on *dialogic criticism*.)

See Malcolm Coulthard, *An Introduction to Discourse Analysis* (1977); Gillian Brown and George Yule, *Discourse Analysis* (1983); Teun A. van Dijk and Walter Kintsch, *Strategies of Discourse Comprehension* (1983); Dan Sperber and Deirdre Wilson, *Relevance: Communication and Cognition* (1986); Wendell V. Harris, *Interpretive Acts* (1988), chapter 2. A relevant collection of writings is Adam Jaworski and Nicholas Coupland, eds., *The Discourse Reader* (1999). For references to *discourse analysis* in other entries, see pages *79, 161, 339, 351*.

**discovery** (in a plot): **268**.

**discursive formations: 281**.

**discussion play: 287**.

**disposition** (in rhetoric): **311**.

**disseminate** (in deconstruction): **71**.

**dissociation of sensibility:** "Dissociation of sensibility" was a phrase introduced by T. S. Eliot in his essay "The Metaphysical Poets" (1921). Eliot's claim was that John Donne and the other *metaphysical poets* of the earlier seventeenth century, like the Elizabethan and Jacobean dramatists, "possessed a mechanism of sensibility which could devour any kind of experience." They manifested "a direct sensuous apprehension of thought," and felt "their thought as immediately as the odour of a rose." But "in the seventeenth century a dissociation of sensibility set in, from which we have never recovered." This dissociation of intellection from emotion and sensuous perception, according to Eliot, was greatly aggravated by the influence of John Milton and John Dryden; and most of the later poets writing in English either thought or felt, but did not think and feel, as an act of unified sensibility.

Eliot's vaguely defined distinction had a great vogue, especially among American *New Critics*. The dissociation of sensibility was said to be the feature that weakened most poetry between Milton and the later writings of W. B. Yeats, and was attributed particularly to the development, in the seventeenth century, of the scientific conception of reality as a material universe stripped of human values and feeling. (See, for example, Basil Willey, *The Seventeenth*

*Century Background*, 1934.) Especially after 1950, however, Eliot's conception of a sudden but persisting dissociation of sensibility came in for strong criticism, on the ground that it is an invalid historical claim that was contrived to support Eliot's disapproval (as a political and social conservative) of the course of English intellectual, political, and religious history after the Civil War of 1642, as well as to rationalize Eliot's particular poetic preferences.

See T. S. Eliot, "The Metaphysical Poets," in *Selected Essays* (2d ed., 1960), and "Milton II," in *On Poetry and Poets* (1957). Attacks on the validity of the doctrine are Leonard Unger, *Donne's Poetry and Modern Criticism* (1950), and Frank Kermode, *Romantic Image* (1957), chapter 8.

**dissonance** (dĭs' ŏnans): **105**.

**distance and involvement:** In his *Critique of Judgment* (1790), Immanuel Kant analyzed the experience of an aesthetic object as an act of "contemplation" which is "disinterested" (that is, independent of one's personal interests and desires) and free from reference to the object's reality, moral effect, or utility. (See *aesthetics* and *aestheticism*.) Various philosophers of art developed this concept into attempts to distinguish "aesthetic experience" from all other kinds of experience, on the basis of the impersonality and disinterestedness with which we contemplate an aesthetic object or work of art. Writing in 1912, Edward Bullough introduced the term "distance" into this type of theory. He points, for example, to the difference between our ordinary experience of a dense fog at sea—with its strains, anxiety, and fear of invisible dangers—and an aesthetic experience, in which we attend with delight to the "objective" features and sensuous qualities of the fog itself. This aesthetic mode of experiencing the fog is, Bullough affirms, the effect of "psychical distance," which "is obtained by separating the object and its appeal from one's own self, by putting it out of gear with practical needs and ends." The degree of this psychical distance varies according to the nature of the artistic object that we contemplate, and also in accordance with an "individual's capacity for maintaining a greater or lesser degree" of such distance.

In recent literary criticism the term **aesthetic distance**, or simply **distance**, is often used not only to define the nature of literary and aesthetic experience in general, but also to analyze the many devices by which authors control the degree of a reader's distance, or "detachment"—which is in inverse relationship to the degree of a reader's **involvement**, or "concern"—with the actions and fortunes of one or another character represented within a work of literature. See, for example, Wayne C. Booth's detailed analysis of the control of distance in Jane Austen's *Emma*, in *The Rhetoric of Fiction* (rev. 1983), chapter 9.

Edward Bullough's innovative essay on "Psychical Distance as a Factor in Art and an Aesthetic Principle," *British Journal of Psychology* 5 (1912), is reprinted in Melvin Rader, ed., *A Modern Book of Aesthetics* (rev. 1952). A useful review of theories of the aesthetic attitude and of aesthetic distance is Jerome Stolnitz, *Aesthetics and Philosophy of Art Criticism* (1960), chapter 2. For the view that such theories are mistaken, see George Dickie, *Art and the Aesthetic* (1974), chapters 4 and 5.

For references to *distance, aesthetic* in other entries, see pages *63, 95, 183, 355*. See also *empathy and sympathy*.

**distancing effect:** 6.

**documentary drama:** 231.

**documentary fiction:** 230.

**doggerel:** A term applied to rough, heavy-footed, and jerky *versification*, and also to verses that are monotonously regular in meter and tritely conventional in sentiment. Doggerel is usually the product of ineptitude on the part of the versifier, but is sometimes deliberately employed by poets for satiric, comic, or rollicking effect. John Skelton (1460?–1529) wrote short lines of two or three stresses, intentionally rough and variable in meter, which have come to be called **Skeltonics**; as he both described and exemplified his versification in *Colin Clout:*

> For though my rhyme be ragged,
> Tattered and jagged,
> Rudely rain-beaten,
> Rusty and moth-eaten,
> If ye take well therewith,
> It hath in it some pith.

The tumbling, broken, and comically grotesque *octosyllabic couplet*—often using double, triple, and imperfect rhymes—developed by Samuel Butler for his satiric poem *Hudibras* (1663–78) is a form of deliberate doggerel that has come to be called **Hudibrastic verse**:

> Besides, he was a shrewd philosopher,
> And had read every text and gloss over;
> Whate'er the crabbed'st author hath,
> He understood b'implicit faith.

See *meter*.

**domestic tragedy:** 373.

**double plot:** 266; *375*.

**double rhyme:** 317.

**drama:** The form of composition designed for performance in the theater, in which actors take the roles of the characters, perform the indicated actions, and utter the written dialogue. (The common alternative name for a dramatic composition is a **play**.) In **poetic drama** the dialogue is written in verse, which in English is usually *blank verse* and in French is the twelve-syllable line called an *alexandrine*. Almost all the *heroic dramas* of the English Restoration Period, however, were written in *heroic couplets* (iambic pentameter lines rhyming in pairs). A **closet drama** is written in dramatic form, with dialogue, indicated settings, and stage directions, but is intended by the author to be read rather than to be performed; examples are Milton's *Samson Agonistes* (1671), Byron's *Manfred* (1817), Shelley's *Prometheus Unbound* (1820), and Hardy's *The Dynasts* (1904–08).

For types of drama, see *absurd, literature of the; chronicle plays; comedy; comedy of humours; commedia dell'arte; drama of sensibility; epic theater; expressionism; folk drama; heroic drama; masque; melodrama; miracle plays, morality plays, and interludes; mummer's play; pantomime and dumb show; pastoral; problem play; satire; sentimental comedy; tragedy; tragicomedy*. For features of drama, see *act; atmosphere; character and characterization; deus ex machina; plot; proscenium arch; setting; theater in the round; three unities*.

**drama of sensibility: 327**; *329.*

**dramatic irony: 167**; *266.*

**dramatic lyric: 85**; *179.*

**dramatic monologue:** A **monologue** is a lengthy speech by a single person. In a play, when a character utters a monologue that expresses his or her private thoughts, it is called a *soliloquy*. **Dramatic monologue**, however, does not designate a component in a play, but a type of *lyric poem* that was perfected by Robert Browning. In its fullest form, as represented in Browning's "My Last Duchess," "The Bishop Orders His Tomb," "Andrea del Sarto," and many other poems, the dramatic monologue has the following features: (1) A single person, who is patently *not* the poet, utters the speech that makes up the whole of the poem, in a specific situation at a critical moment: the Duke is negotiating with an emissary for a second wife; the Bishop lies dying; Andrea once more attempts wistfully to believe his wife's lies. (2) This person addresses and interacts with one or more other people; but we know of the auditors' presence, and what they say and do, only from clues in the discourse of the single speaker. (3) The main principle controlling the poet's choice and formulation of what the lyric speaker says is to reveal to the reader, in a way that enhances its interest, the speaker's temperament and character.

In monologues such as "Soliloquy of the Spanish Cloister" and "Caliban upon Setebos," Browning omits the second feature, the presence of a silent auditor; but features 1 and 3 are the necessary conditions of a dramatic monologue. The third feature—the focus on self-revelation—serves to distinguish a dramatic monologue from its near relation, the **dramatic lyric**, which is also a monologue uttered in an identifiable situation at a dramatic moment. John Donne's "The Canonization" and "The Flea" (1613), for example, are dramatic lyrics that lack only one feature of the dramatic monologue: the focus of interest is primarily on the speaker's elaborately ingenious argument, rather than on the character he inadvertently reveals in the course of arguing. And although Wordsworth's "Tintern Abbey" (1798) is spoken by one person to a silent auditor (his sister) in a specific situation at a significant moment in his life, it is not a dramatic monologue proper, both because we are invited to identify the speaker with the poet himself, and because the organizing principle and focus of interest is not the revelation of the speaker's distinctive temperament, but the evolution of his observations, memories, and thoughts toward the resolution of an emotional problem.

Tennyson wrote "Ulysses" (1842) and other dramatic monologues, and the form has been used by H. D. (Hilda Doolittle), Amy Lowell, Robert Frost, E. A. Robinson, Ezra Pound, Robert Lowell, and other poets of the twentieth century. The best-known modern instance is T. S. Eliot's "The Love Song of J. Alfred Prufrock" (1915).

See Robert Langbaum, *The Poetry of Experience: The Dramatic Monologue in Modern Literary Tradition* (1957); Ralph W. Rader, "The Dramatic Monologue and Related Lyric Forms," *Critical Inquiry* 3 (1976); and Adena Rosmarin, *The Power of Genre* (1985), chapter 2, "The Dramatic Monologue."

**dramatis personae** (dräm′ ătĭs pĕrsō′ nē): **258**.

**dream allegory: 86**.

**dream vision:** Dream vision (also called **dream allegory**) is a mode of narrative widely employed by medieval poets: the narrator falls asleep, usually in a spring landscape, and dreams the events he goes on to relate; often he is led by a guide, human or animal, and the events which he dreams are at least in part an *allegory*. A very influential example is the thirteenth-century French poem *Roman de la Rose*; the greatest of medieval poems, Dante's *Divine Comedy*, is also a dream vision. In fourteenth-century England, it is the narrative mode of the fine elegy *Pearl*, of Langland's *Piers Plowman*, and of Chaucer's *The Book of the Duchess* and *The House of Fame*. After the Middle Ages the vogue of the dream allegory diminished, but it never died out, as Bunyan's prose narrative *The Pilgrim's Progress* (1678) and Keats' verse narrative *The Fall of Hyperion: A Dream* (1819) bear witness. Lewis Carroll's *Alice's Adventures in Wonderland* (1865) is in the form of a dream vision, and James Joyce's *Finnegans Wake* (1939) consists of an immense cosmic dream on the part of an archetypal dreamer.

See C. S. Lewis, *The Allegory of Love* (1938); and Howard Rollin Patch, *The Other World according to Descriptions in Medieval Literature* (1950, reprinted 1970).

**dumb show: 239**.

**duodecimo** (doo′ ŏdĕs″ ĭmō): **32**.

**dystopia** (dĭstō′ pēă): **378**.

**Early Modern** (period): **307**.

**Early National Period** (in American literature): **246**.

**echoism: 236**.

**eclectic text: 366**.

**eclogue** (ĕk′ lŏg): **240**.

**ecocentrism: 88**.

**ecocriticism:** Ecocriticism was a term coined in the late 1970s by combining "crit-icism" with a shortened form of "ecology"—the science that investigates the in-terrelations of all forms of plant and animal life with each other and with their physical habitats. "Ecocriticism" (or by alternative names, **environmental criti-cism** and **green studies**) designates the critical writings which explore the rela-tions between literature and the biological and physical environment, conducted with an acute awareness of the devastation being wrought on that environment by human activities.

Representations of the natural environment are as old as recorded literature, and were prominent in the account of the Garden of Eden in the Hebrew Bible, as well as in the *pastoral* form inaugurated by the Greek Theocritus in the third century BC and later imitated by the Roman poet Virgil—an idealized depiction of rural life, viewed as survival of the simplicity, peace, and harmony that had been lost by a complex and urban society. The nostalgic view of a return to un-spoiled nature in order to restore a lost simplicity and concord remained evident in James Thomson's long poem in blank verse *The Seasons* (1726–30), and in the widely practiced *genre* called **nature writing**: the intimate, realistic, and detailed description in prose of the natural environment, rendered as it appears to the dis-tinctive sensibility of the author. This literary form was largely initiated in England by Gilbert White's enormously popular *Natural History and Antiquities of Selborne* (1789)—his close and affectionate observations of wildlife and the natural setting in a particular area of rural England. In America, an early instance of nature writ-ing was William Bertram's *Travels* through the Carolinas, Georgia, and Florida (1791); among its successors was a classic of this genre, Henry David Thoreau's *Walden* (1854). By the mid-nineteenth century Thoreau and other writers in America and England were already drawing attention to the threats to the envi-ronment by urbanization and industrialization. Later in the century, increasing alarm at the rapidity and extent of the human despoilation of nature led to what came to be called "the environmental movement" to preserve what remained of the American wilderness; the most noted advocates were the American writers John Burroughs (1837–1921) and John Muir (1838–1914).

In the twentieth century the warnings by scientists and conservationists in-creased; two especially influential books were Aldo Leopold's *A Sand County Almanac* (1949), drawing attention to the ominous degradation of the environ-ment, and Rachel Carson's *Silent Spring* (1962), concerning the devastation in-flicted by newly developed chemical pesticides on wildlife, both on land and in water. By the latter part of the century there was a widespread realization that the earth was in an environmental crisis, brought on by the industrial and chemi-cal pollution of the "biosphere" (the thin layer of earth, water, and air essential to life), the depletion of forests and of natural resources, the relentless extinction of plant and animal species, and the explosion of the human population beyond the capacity of the earth to sustain it.

It was in this climate of crisis, or even imminent catastrophe, that ecocriticism was inaugurated. By the 1990s it had become a recognized and rapidly growing field of literary study, with its own organization (ASLE: Association for the Study of Literature and Environment), its own journal (*ISLE: Interdisciplinary Studies in*

*Literature and Environment*), numerous articles in literary and critical periodicals, a proliferation of college courses, and a series of conferences whose concern with the literature of the environment encompassed all continents. As in earlier insurgent modes such as *feminist criticism* and *queer theory*, many ecocritical writings continue to be oriented toward heightening their readers' awareness, and even toward inciting them to social and political action; but while the other movements in criticism are directed toward achieving social and political justice, a number of ecocritics are impelled by the conviction that what is at stake in their enterprise is not only the well-being but, ultimately, the survival of the human race.

Ecocritics do not share a single theoretical perspective or procedure; instead, their engagements with environmental literature manifest a wide range of traditional, *poststructural*, and *postcolonial* points of view and modes of analysis. Within this diversity, however, certain issues and concerns are recurrent:

1. It is claimed that the reigning religions and philosophies of Western civilization are deeply **anthropocentric**; that is, they are oriented to the interests of human beings, who are viewed as opposed to and superior to nature, and free to exploit natural resources and animal species for their own purposes. This viewpoint is grounded in the biblical account of the creation, in which God gave man "dominion over the fish of the sea, and over the birds of the air, and over the cattle, and over all the earth" (*Genesis* 1.26). A similar conception is manifested elsewhere in the Bible, dominated Greek and Roman philosophy, was the prevailing view in Christianity, and underlay the emergence of modern science in the Renaissance, the *humanism* of the eighteenth-century *Enlightenment*, and the triumphs of what has been called "the scientific-technological-industrial complex" in the nineteenth and twentieth centuries. A present-day countermovement, sometimes named "deep ecology," maintains that all attempts to reform particular instances of the spoliation of the natural world deal with symptoms rather than the root cause, and that the only real hope is to replace anthropocentrism by **ecocentrism**: the view that all living things and their earthly environment, no less than the human species, possess importance, value, and even moral and political rights.

2. Prominent in ecocriticism is a critique of *binaries* such as man/nature or culture/nature, viewed as mutually exclusive oppositions. It is pointed out, instead, that these entities are interconnected, and also mutually constitutive. As Wendell Berry wrote in *The Unsettling of America* (1977), "we and our country create one another, depend upon one another, are literally part of one another.... Our culture and our place are images of each other, and inseparable from each other." Our identities, or sense of self, for example, are informed by the particular place in which we live and in which we feel that we belong and are at home. On the other side, human experience of the natural environment is never a replication of the thing itself, but always mediated by the culture of a particular time and place; and its representation in a work of literature is inescapably shaped by human feelings and the human imagination. A striking example is the radical shift in the conception of the wilderness in America, from the Puritan view of it as a dark and ominous thing, possibly the abode of

demons, which needs to be overcome, appropriated, and cultivated by human beings, to the view expressed by Thoreau two centuries later that "In wildness is the preservation of the world" ("Walking," in *Excursions*, 1863). Or as the poet Gerard Manley Hopkins wrote in England some twenty years later, in "Inversnaid":

> What would the world be, once bereft
> Of wet and of wildness? Let them be left,
> O let them be left, wildness and wet;
> Long live the weeds and the wilderness yet.

3. Many ecocritics recommend, and themselves exemplify, the extension of "green reading" (that is, the analysis of the implications of a text for environmental concerns) to all literary *genres*, including prose fiction and poetry, and also to writings in the natural and social sciences. Within the literary domain, the endeavor is to elevate the status, or to include within the major *canon of literature* the hitherto undervalued forms of nature writing and of *local color* or regional fiction by authors such as Thomas Hardy, Mark Twain, and Sarah Orne Jewett.

4. A conspicuous feature in ecocriticism is the analysis of the differences in attitudes toward the environment that are attributable to a writer's race, ethnicity, social class, and gender. The writings of Annette Kolodny gave impetus to what has come to be called **ecofeminism**—the analysis of the role attributed to women in fantasies of the natural environment by male authors, as well as the study of specifically feminine conceptions of the environment in the neglected nature writings by female authors. In *The Lay of the Land: Metaphor as Experience and History in American Life and Letters* (1975), Kolodny stresses, in male-authored literature, the predominant gendering of the land as female, and the accordant tendency to resort to nature for pastoral repose, recuperation, and gratification. She also proposes a parallel between the domination and subjugation of women and the exploitation and spoliation of the land. (For an instance in which the devastation of a natural scene is figured in detail as the rape of a virgin, refer to Wordsworth's autobiographical poem "Nutting," 1800.) In a later book, *The Land before Her: Fantasy and Experiences of the American Frontiers, 1680–1860* (1984), Kolodny details the difference between the traditional representations of the frontier by male authors, and the counterview—domestic, and oriented to gardening and family concerns—in neglected narratives about the frontier by women. Other critics have pointed out that the prominent American form called the **wilderness romance**—represented by such major works as James Fenimore Cooper's Leatherstocking novels, Herman Melville's *Moby Dick*, and Mark Twain's *Huckleberry Finn*—project distinctively male imaginings of escape to an unspoiled natural environment, free of women and of an effete, woman-dominated civilization, in which the protagonist undergoes a test of his character and virility. See for example Nina Baym, "Melodramas of Beset Manhood: How Theories of American Fiction Exclude Women Writers" (1981), in *Feminism and American*

Literary History (1992); also Vera Norwood, Made from This Earth: American Women and Nature (1993).

5. There is a growing interest in the animistic religions of so-called "primitive" cultures, as well as in Hindu, Buddhist, and other religions and civilizations that lack the Western opposition between humanity and nature, and do not assign to human beings dominion over the nonhuman world. Ecocritics in the United States concern themselves especially with the oral traditions of Native Americans and with the exposition of these cultures by contemporary Native American writers such as N. Scott Momaday and Leslie Marmon Silko. The common view, it is pointed out, envisions the natural world as a living, sacred thing, in which each individual feels intimately bonded to a particular physical "place," and where human beings live in interdependence and reciprocity with other living things. See Joni Adamson, American Indian Literature, Environmental Justice, and Ecocriticism: The Middle Place (2001), and Donelle N. Dreese, Ecocriticism: Creating Self and Place in Environmental and American Indian Literatures (2002). Refer to primitivism.

Some environmental critics maintain that the ecological crisis can only be resolved by the rejection, in the West, of the Judeo-Christian religion and culture, with its anthropocentric view that human beings, because they possess souls, transcend nature and are inherently masters of the nonhuman world, and by adopting instead an ecocentric religion which promulgates the sacredness of nature and a reverence for all forms of life as intrinsically equivalent. (See for example the influential essay by the intellectual historian Lynn White, Jr., "The Historical Roots of Our Ecologic Crisis," in The Ecocentric Reader, listed below.) Other environmentalists insist, on the contrary, that the hope for radical reform lies, not in trying to assimilate an outmoded or alien religion, but in identifying and developing those strands in the human-centered religion, philosophy, and ethics of the West which maintain that the human relationship to the nonhuman world is not one of mastery, but of stewardship, and which recognize the deep human need for the natural world as something to be enjoyed for its own sake, as well as the moral responsibility of human beings to maintain and transmit a liveable, diverse, and enjoyable world to their posterity. (See the book by the Australian philosopher John Passmore, Man's Responsibility for Nature: Ecological Problems and Western Traditions, 1974. This work includes a useful survey not only of the predominantly anti-environmental religion and metaphysics of the West, but also of the recurrent counterviews that emphasize human responsibility for the natural environment and nonhuman forms of life.) Despite such disagreements, all ecocritics concur that science-based knowledge of looming ecological disaster is not enough, because knowledge can lead to effective political and social action only when informed and impelled, as it is in literature, by imagination and feeling. As P. B. Shelley wrote in his "Defense of Poetry" almost two centuries ago: "There is no want of knowledge," scientific and other, "respecting what is wisest and best in morals, government, and political economy"; what we lack is "the creative faculty to imagine that which we know" and "the generous impulse to act that which we imagine."

There are numerous anthologies of nature writing; representative recent ones are *The Norton Book of Nature Writing*, ed. Robert Finch and John Elder (1990); *American Nature Writers*, ed. John Elder (2 vols., 1996); *Literature of Nature: An International Sourcebook* (1998). The *Romantic Period* of the early nineteenth century was the turning point in the long Western tradition of human transcendence and domination over nature. The central view in innovative Romantic literature and philosophy, in England and Germany, was that the root of the modern human malaise is its separation, or "alienation," from its original unity with nature, and that the cure for this disease of civilization lies in a reunion between humanity and nature that will restore concreteness and values to a natural world in which we can once more feel thoroughly at home, in a joyous consonance and reciprocity with all living things. (See M. H. Abrams, *Natural Supernaturalism: Tradition and Revolution in Romantic Literature*, 1971, chapters 3–5, 8; also his essay "Coleridge and the Romantic Vision of the World," 1974, included in *The Correspondent Breeze: Essays on English Romanticism*, 1984.) Jonathan Bate, in *Romantic Ecology: Wordsworth and the Environmental Tradition* (1991), details the emergence, in Wordsworth and his English contemporaries and successors, of an environmental and ecological consciousness, the result of noting the destruction of forest and farm lands by urban sprawl, as well as recognizing what Wordsworth, in the eighth book of *The Excursion* (1814), called "the outrage done to nature" by newly established factories that foul the air and pollute the waterways.

Books that were important in the founding and development of ecocriticism, in addition to those already mentioned, include Leo Marx, *The Machine in the Garden: Technology and the Pastoral Ideal in America* (1964); Roderick Frazier Nash, *Wilderness and the American Mind* (1967; 3d ed., 1982); Donald Worster, *Nature's Economy: A History of Ecological Ideas* (1977); John Elder, *Imagining the Earth: Poetry and the Vision of Nature* (1985); Robert Pogue Harrison, *Forests: The Shadow of Civilization* (1992); Lawrence Buell, *The Environmental Imagination: Thoreau, Nature Writing, and the Formation of American Culture* (1995); Simon Schama, *Landscape and Memory* (1995).

The anthology *The Ecocriticism Reader: Landmarks in Literary Ecology*, ed. Cheryll Glotfelty and Harold Fromm (1996), did much, by its Introduction and selections, to give definition and impetus to the ecocritical movement. The following collections of essays indicate the scope and diversity of ecocritical writings: *Sisters of the Earth: Women's Prose and Poetry about Nature*, ed. Lorraine Anderson (1991); *Being in the World: An Environmental Reader for Writers*, ed. Scott H. Slovic and Terrell F. Dixon (1993); *The Greening of Literary Scholarship: Literature, Theory, and the Environment*, ed. Steven Rosendale (2002). Greg Garrard outlines the theory and practice of the movement in *Ecocriticism* (2004).

**ego: 291**.

**eiron** (ī′ rŏn): **343**; *165*.

**elegiac meter** (ĕlĕjī′ ăk): **92**.

**elegy:** In Greek and Roman times, "elegy" denoted any poem written in **elegiac meter** (alternating *hexameter* and *pentameter* lines). The term was also used, however, to refer to the subject matter of change and loss frequently expressed in the elegiac verse form, especially in complaints about love. In accordance with this latter usage, "The Wanderer," "The Seafarer," and other poems in Old English on the transience of all worldly things are even now called elegies. In Europe and England the word continued to have a variable application through the Renaissance. John Donne's elegies, written in the late sixteenth and early seventeenth centuries, are love poems, although they relate to the sense of elegy as lament, in that many of them emphasize mutability and loss. In the seventeenth century the term **elegy** began to be limited to its most common present usage: a formal and sustained lament in verse for the death of a particular person, usually ending in a consolation. Examples are the medieval poem *Pearl* and Chaucer's *Book of the Duchess* (elegies in the mode of *dream allegory*); Alfred, Lord Tennyson's *In Memoriam* (1850), on the death of Arthur Hallam; and W. H. Auden's "In Memory of W. B. Yeats" (1940). Occasionally the term is used in its older and broader sense, for somber meditations on mortality such as Thomas Gray's "Elegy Written in a Country Churchyard" (1757), and the *Duino Elegies* (1912–22) of the German poet Rainer Maria Rilke on the transience both of poets and of the earthly objects they write poems about.

    The **dirge** is also a versified expression of grief on the occasion of a particular person's death, but differs from the elegy in that it is short, is less formal, and is usually represented as a text to be sung; examples are Shakespeare's "Full Fathom Five Thy Father Lies" and William Collins' "A Song from Shakespeare's *Cymbeline*" (1749). **Threnody** is now used mainly as an equivalent for "dirge," and **monody** for an elegy or dirge which is presented as the utterance of a single person. John Milton describes his "Lycidas" (1638) in the subtitle as a "monody" in which "the Author bewails a learned Friend," and Matthew Arnold called his elegy on A. H. Clough "Thyrsis: A Monody" (1866).

    An important subtype of the elegy is the **pastoral elegy**, which represents both the poet and the one he mourns—who is usually also a poet—as shepherds (the Latin word for shepherd is "pastor"). This poetic form was originated by the Sicilian Greek poet Theocritus, was continued by the Roman Virgil, was developed in various European countries during the Renaissance, and remained current in English poetry through the nineteenth century. Notable English pastoral elegies are Spenser's "Astrophel," on the death of Sir Philip Sidney (1595); Milton's "Lycidas" (1638); Shelley's "Adonais" (1821); and in the Victorian age, Arnold's "Thyrsis." The pastoral elegists, from the Greeks through the Renaissance, developed a set of elaborate *conventions*, which are illustrated here by reference to "Lycidas." In addition to the fictional representation of both mourner and subject as shepherds tending their flocks (lines 23–36 and elsewhere), we often find the following conventional features:

1. The lyric speaker begins by invoking the muses, and goes on to make frequent reference to other figures from classical mythology (lines 15–22, and later).
2. All nature joins in mourning the shepherd's death (lines 37–49). (Recent critics who stress the mythic and ritual origins of poetic genres claim that this feature is a survival from primitive laments for the death of Thammuz, Adonis, or other vegetational deities who died in the autumn to be reborn in the spring. See *myth critics*.)
3. The mourner charges with negligence the nymphs or other guardians of the dead shepherd (lines 50–63).
4. There is a procession of appropriate mourners (lines 88–111).
5. The poet raises questions about the justice of fate, or else of Providence, and adverts to the corrupt conditions of his own times (lines 64–84, 113–31). Such passages, though sometimes called "digressions," are integral to the evolution of the mourner's thought in "Lycidas."
6. Post-Renaissance elegies often include an elaborate passage in which appropriate flowers are brought to deck the hearse (lines 133–51).
7. There is a closing consolation. In Christian elegies, the lyric reversal from grief and despair to joy and assurance typically occurs when the elegist comes to realize that death in this world is the entry to a higher life (lines 165–85).

In his *Life of Milton* (1779) Samuel Johnson, who disapproved both of pastoralism and mythology in modern poetry, decried "Lycidas" for "its inherent improbability," but in the elegies by Milton and other major poets the ancient rituals provide a structural frame on which they play variations with originality and power. Some of the pastoral conventions, although adapted to an industrial age and a non-Christian worldview, survive still in Walt Whitman's elegy on Lincoln, "When Lilacs Last in the Dooryard Bloom'd" (1866).

In the last two decades of the twentieth century there was a strong revival of the elegy, especially in America, to mourn the devastation and death wrought by AIDS among talented young intellectuals, poets, and artists; see Michael Klein, ed., *Poets for Life: Seventy-six Poets Respond to AIDS* (1989).

See *conventions* and *pastoral*. On the elegy, refer to T. P. Harrison, Jr., and H. J. Leon, eds., *The Pastoral Elegy: An Anthology* (1939); Peter Sacks, *The English Elegy: Studies in the Genre from Spenser to Yeats* (1985). On "Lycidas": C. A. Patrides, ed., *Milton's "Lycidas": The Tradition and the Poem* (rev. 1983), which includes a number of recent critical essays; and Scott Elledge, ed., *Milton's "Lycidas"* (1966), which reprints classical and Renaissance pastoral elegies and other texts as background to Milton's poem. For both traditional and modern forms of elegy, see the introductory materials and the poems reprinted in Sandra M. Gilbert, ed., *Inventions of Farewell: A Book of Elegies* (2001).

**Elizabethan Age: 252.**

**emblem: 359.**

**emotive language: 117**.

**empathy and sympathy:** German theorists in the nineteenth century developed
the concept of "Einfühlung" ("feeling into"), which has been translated as **empathy**. It signifies an identification of oneself with an observed person or object which
is so close that one seems to participate in the posture, motion, and sensations that
one observes. Empathy is often described as "an involuntary projection of ourselves
into an object," and is commonly explained as the result of an "inner mimicry";
that is, the observation of an object evokes incipient muscular movements which
are not experienced as one's own sensations, but as though they were attributes of
the outer object. The object may be human, or nonhuman, or even inanimate. In
thoroughly absorbed contemplation we seem empathically to pirouette with a bal-
let dancer, soar with a hawk, bend with the movements of a tree in the wind, and
even to participate in the strength, ease, and grace with which a well-proportioned
arch appears to support a bridge. When John Keats wrote in a letter that he becomes "a part of all I see," and that "if a sparrow comes before my window I take
part in its existence and pick about the gravel," he was describing an habitual experience of his intensely empathic temperament, long before the word was coined.

In literature we call "empathic" a passage which conspicuously evokes from
the reader this sense of participation with the pose, movements, and physical sensations of the object that the passage describes. An example is Shakespeare's description, in his narrative poem *Venus and Adonis* (1593), of

> the snail, whose tender horns being hit,
> Shrinks backward in his shelly cave with pain.

Another is the description of the motion of a wave in Keats' *Endymion* (1818),

> when heav'd anew
> Old ocean rolls a lengthen'd wave to the shore,
> Down whose green back the short-liv'd foam, all hoar,
> Bursts gradual, with a wayward indolence.

Also empathic is the description of a wave—experienced from the point of view
of Penelope awaiting the long-delayed return of her husband Odysseus—by
H. D. (Hilda Doolittle), in her poem, "At Ithaca":

> Over and back,
> the long waves crawl
> and track the sand with foam;
> night darkens and the sea
> takes on that desperate tone
> of dark that wives put on
> when all their love is done.

**Sympathy**, as distinguished from empathy, denotes fellow-feeling; that is,
not feeling-into the physical state and sensations, but feeling-along-with the mental state and emotions, of another human being, or of nonhuman beings to whom

we attribute human emotions. (See *personification*.) We "sympathize," for example, with the emotional experience of a child in his first attempt to recite a piece in public; we may also "empathize" as he falters in his speaking or makes an awkward gesture. Robert Burns' "To a Mouse" (1786) is an engaging expression of his quick sympathy with the terror of the "wee, sleekit, cow'rin, tim'rous beastie" whose nest he has turned up with his plow.

The engagement and control of a reader's sympathy with certain characters, and the establishment of **antipathy** toward others, is essential to the traditional literary artist. In *King Lear*, Shakespeare undertakes to make us sympathize with Cordelia, for example, and progressively with King Lear, but to make us feel horror and antipathy toward his "pelican daughters," Goneril and Regan. Our attitude in the same play toward the villainous Edmund, the bastard son of Gloucester, as managed by Shakespeare, is complex—antipathetic, yet with some element of sympathetic understanding of his distorted personality. (See *distance and involvement*.) Bertolt Brecht's *alienation effect* was designed to inhibit the sympathy of an audience with the protagonists of his plays, in order to encourage a critical attitude to the actions and social and economic realities that the plays represent.

A number of recent critical theorists stress the need to read against one's acquiescence to the sympathetic identification intended by an author. Such feminist critics as Judith Fetterley, for example, in *The Resisting Reader* (1978), propose that women should learn to read in opposition to the sympathy with male protagonists, and the derogation of women characters, that is written into the work of many male authors. (See under *feminist criticism*.) And a tendency in the *new historicism*, as well as in *postcolonial* criticism, is to recommend that the reader, even if against an author's intention, shift his or her sympathy from the dominant to the subversive characters in a literary work—from the magus Prospero, for example, in Shakespeare's *The Tempest*, to his brutish and rebellious slave Caliban, who is taken to represent the natives of the New World who were oppressed and enslaved by English and European invaders. (Some current critics claim that, whatever Shakespeare's intentions, Caliban, as he is represented, is sympathetic, and that Prospero, as he is represented, is not; also that the sympathetic admiration for Prospero in the nineteenth century depended on a willful evasion of certain aspects of the play.)

Refer to H. S. Langfeld, *The Aesthetic Attitude* (1920)—the section on empathy is reprinted in *Problems of Aesthetics* (1963), ed. Eliseo Vivas and Murray Krieger. For detailed analyses of empathic passages in literature, see Richard H. Fogle, *The Imagery of Keats and Shelley* (1949), chapter 4. See also the entry *sensibility, literature of*.

**English sonnet:** 336.

**enjambment** (ĕnjămb′ mĕnt): **197**.

**Enlightenment:** The name applied to an intellectual movement and cultural ambiance which developed in western Europe during the seventeenth century and reached its height in the eighteenth. The common element was a trust in universal and uniform human reason as adequate to solve the crucial problems and to establish the essential norms in life, together with the belief that the application of such reason was rapidly dissipating the darkness of superstition, prejudice, and barbarity, was freeing humanity from its earlier reliance on mere authority and unexamined tradition, and had opened the prospect of progress toward a life in this world of universal peace and happiness. (See the idea of *progress*.) For some thinkers the model for "reason" was the inductive procedure of science, which proceeds by reasoning from the particular facts of experience to universal laws; for others (especially Descartes and his followers), the model for "reason" was primarily geometrical—the deduction of particular truths from clear and distinct ideas which are universal, and known intuitively by "the light of reason." Many thinkers relied on reason in both these senses.

   In England the thought and the world outlook of the Enlightenment are usually traced from Francis Bacon (1561–1626) through John Locke (1632–1704) to late-eighteenth-century thinkers such as William Godwin (1756–1836); in France, from Descartes (1596–1650) through Voltaire (1694–1778) to Diderot and other editors of the great twenty-volume *Encyclopédie* (1751–72); in Germany, from Leibniz (1646–1716) to what is often said to be the highest product of the Enlightenment, the "critical philosophy" of Immanuel Kant (1724–1804). Kant's famous essay "What Is Enlightenment?" written in 1784, defines it as "the liberation of mankind from his self-caused state of minority" and the achievement of a state of maturity which is exemplified in his "determination and courage to use [his understanding] without the assistance of another." In America, Benjamin Franklin and Thomas Jefferson represented the principles of the French and English Enlightenment, which also helped shape the founding documents of the United States: the Declaration of Independence and the Constitution.

   In recent years, the Enlightenment has been the subject of vigorous reassessment and debate. See Emmanuel Chukwudi Eze, ed., *Race and the Enlightenment: A Reader* (1997), for an anthology of Enlightenment texts, many of them, from the point of view of the present, strikingly unenlightened about race. For a positive assessment of the Enlightenment's contribution to modern political and scientific attitudes, see Jonathan I. Israel, *Radical Enlightenment: Philosophy and the Making of Modernity 1650–1750* (2001).

   The Enlightenment category of the universal, which was central to eighteenth-century thinkers who sought to transcend national, linguistic, or other divisions, has been both praised as an indispensable tool of a radical social *critique* and derogated as the conceptual means by which local differences such as race, sex, ethnicity, and class are elided in the name of a dubious universality. A crucial text in the latter reassessment was Michel Foucault, "What is Enlightenment?" in

Paul Rabinow, ed., *The Foucault Reader* (1984), pp. 32–50. See also James Schmidt, ed., *What is Enlightenment?* (1996); Geoffrey Galt Harpham, "So . . . What *Is* Enlightenment?" in *Shadows of Ethics* (1999), pp. 67–98. For an anthology of Enlightenment writings, see Peter Gay, ed., *The Enlightenment: A Comprehensive Anthology* (1973). Gay has also written *The Enlightenment: An Interpretation* (2 vols., 1995, 1996); see also Ernst Cassirer, *The Philosophy of the Enlightenment* (1968). Refer to the entry *neoclassic and romantic.* For references to *Enlightenment* in other entries, see pages *65, 76, 254, 310.*

**environmental criticism: 87**.

**envoy** (in a poem): **343**.

**epic:** In its strict sense the term **epic** or **heroic poem** is applied to a work that meets at least the following criteria: it is a long verse narrative on a serious subject, told in a formal and elevated style, and centered on a heroic or quasi-divine figure on whose actions depends the fate of a tribe, a nation, or (in the instance of John Milton's *Paradise Lost*) the human race.

There is a standard distinction between traditional and literary epics. "Traditional epics" (also called "folk epics" or "primary epics") were written versions of what had originally been oral poems about a tribal or national hero during a warlike age. (See *oral poetry*.) Among these are the *Iliad* and *Odyssey* that the Greeks ascribed to Homer; the Anglo-Saxon *Beowulf*; the French *Chanson de Roland* and the Spanish *Poema del Cid* in the twelfth century; and the thirteenth-century German epic *Nibelungenlied*. "Literary epics" were composed by individual poetic craftsmen in deliberate imitation of the traditional form. Of this kind is Virgil's Latin poem the *Aeneid*, which later served as the chief model for Milton's literary epic *Paradise Lost* (1667). *Paradise Lost* in turn became, in the *Romantic Period*, a model for John Keats' fragmentary epic *Hyperion*, as well as for William Blake's several epics, or "prophetic books" (*The Four Zoas, Milton, Jerusalem*), which translated into Blake's own mythic terms the biblical narrative that had been Milton's subject.

In his *Anatomy of Criticism* (1957) Northrop Frye asserts that Homer established for his successors the "demonstration that the fall of an enemy, no less than of a friend or leader, is tragic and not comic," and that with this "objective and disinterested element," the epic acquired an authority based "on the vision of nature as an impersonal order." The epic was ranked by Aristotle as second only to tragedy, and by many Renaissance critics as the highest of all *genres*. The literary epic is certainly the most ambitious of poetic enterprises, making immense demands on a poet's knowledge, invention, and skill to sustain the scope, grandeur, and authority of a poem that tends to encompass the world of its day and a large portion of its learning. Despite numerous attempts in many languages over nearly three thousand years, we possess no more than a half-dozen such poems of indubitable greatness. Literary epics are highly conventional compositions which usually share the following features, derived by way of the *Aeneid* from the traditional epics of Homer:

1. The hero is a figure of great national or even cosmic importance. In the *Iliad* he is the Greek warrior Achilles, who is the son of the sea nymph Thetis; and Virgil's Aeneas is the son of the goddess Aphrodite. In *Paradise Lost*, Adam and Eve are the progenitors of the entire human race, or if we regard Christ as the protagonist, He is both God and man. Blake's primal figure is "the Universal Man" Albion, who incorporates, before his fall, humanity and God and the cosmos as well.

2. The setting of the poem is ample in scale, and may be worldwide, or even larger. Odysseus wanders over the Mediterranean basin (the whole of the world known at the time), and in Book XI he descends into the underworld (as does Virgil's Aeneas). The scope of *Paradise Lost* is the entire universe, for it takes place in heaven, on earth, in hell, and in the cosmic space between. (See *Ptolemaic universe*.)

3. The action involves extraordinary deeds in battle, such as Achilles' feats in the Trojan War, or a long, arduous, and dangerous journey intrepidly accomplished, such as the wanderings of Odysseus on his way back to his homeland, in the face of opposition by some of the gods. *Paradise Lost* includes the revolt in heaven by the rebel angels against God, the journey of Satan through chaos to discover the newly created world, and his desperately audacious attempt to outwit God by corrupting mankind, in which his success is ultimately frustrated by the sacrificial action of Christ.

4. In these great actions the gods and other supernatural beings take an interest or an active part—the Olympian gods in Homer, and Jehovah, Christ, and the angels in *Paradise Lost*. These supernatural agents were in the *Neoclassic Age* called the **machinery**, in the sense that they were part of the literary contrivances of the epic.

5. An epic poem is a ceremonial performance, and is narrated in a ceremonial style which is deliberately distanced from ordinary speech and proportioned to the grandeur and formality of the heroic subject and architecture. Hence Milton's **grand style**—his formal diction and elaborate and stylized syntax, which are in large part modeled on Latin poetry, his sonorous lists of names and wide-ranging *allusions*, and his imitation of Homer's *epic similes* and *epithets*.

There are also widely used epic *conventions*, or formulas, in the choice and ordering of episodes; prominent among them are these features, as exemplified in *Paradise Lost*:

1. The narrator begins by stating his **argument**, or epic theme, invokes a muse or guiding spirit to inspire him in his great undertaking, then addresses to the muse the **epic question**, the answer to which inaugurates the narrative proper (*Paradise Lost*, I. 1–49).

2. The narrative starts **in medias res** ("in the middle of things"), at a critical point in the action. *Paradise Lost* opens with the fallen angels in hell, gathering their scattered forces and determining on revenge. Not until Books V–VII does the angel Raphael narrate to Adam the events in heaven which led to this situation; while in Books XI–XII, after the fall, Michael foretells to Adam future

events up to Christ's second coming. Thus Milton's epic, although its action focuses on the temptation and fall of man, encompasses all time from the creation to the end of the world.

3. There are catalogues of some of the principal characters, introduced in formal detail, as in Milton's description of the procession of fallen angels in Book I of *Paradise Lost*. These characters are often given set speeches that reveal their diverse temperaments and moral attitudes; an example is the debate in Pandemonium, Book II.

The term "epic" is often applied, by extension, to narratives which differ in many respects from this model but manifest the epic spirit and grandeur in the scale, the scope, and the profound human importance of their subjects. In this broad sense Dante's fourteenth-century *Divine Comedy* and Edmund Spenser's late-sixteenth-century *The Faerie Queene* (1590–96) are often called epics, as are conspicuously large-scale and wide-ranging works of prose fiction such as Herman Melville's *Moby-Dick* (1851), Leo Tolstoy's *War and Peace* (1869), and James Joyce's *Ulysses* (1922); this last work achieves epic scope in representing the events of an ordinary day in Dublin (16 June 1904) by modeling them on the episodes of Homer's *Odyssey*. In a still more extended application, the Marxist critic Georg Lukács used the term **bourgeois epic** for all novels which, in his view, reflect the social reality of their capitalist age on a broad scale. In a famed sentence, Lukács said that "the novel is the epic of a world that has been abandoned by God" (*Theory of the Novel*, trans. Anna Bostock, 1971). See Lukács under *Marxist criticism*.

See *mock epic* and refer to W. W. Lawrence, *Beowulf and Epic Tradition* (1928); C. M. Bowra, *From Vergil to Milton* (1945), and *Heroic Poetry* (1952); C. S. Lewis, *A Preface to "Paradise Lost"* (1942); Brian Wilkie, *Romantic Poets and Epic Tradition* (1965); Michael Murren, *The Allegorical Epic* (1980); Andrew Ford, *Homer: The Poetry of the Past* (1992); David Quint, *Epic and Empire* (1993). For an *archetypal* conception of the epic, see Northrop Frye, *Anatomy of Criticism* (1957), pp. 315–26. For references to *epic* in other entries, see pages *36, 100, 134, 141, 143, 237*. See also *heroic drama*.

**epic question: 98**.

**epic similes:** Epic similes are formal, sustained similes in which the secondary subject, or *vehicle*, is elaborated far beyond its points of close parallel to the primary subject, or *tenor* (see under *figurative language*). This figure was imitated from Homer by Virgil, Milton, and other writers of literary *epics*, who employed it to enhance the ceremonial quality and wide-ranging reference of the narrative style. In the epic simile in *Paradise Lost* (I. 768ff.), Milton describes his primary subject, the fallen angels thronging toward their new-built palace of Pandemonium, by an elaborate comparison to the swarming of bees:

> As Bees
> In spring time, when the Sun with Taurus rides,
> Pour forth their populous youth about the Hive

> In clusters; they among fresh dews and flowers
> Fly to and fro, or on the smoothèd Plank,
> The suburb of their Straw-built Citadel,
> New rubb'd with Balm, expatiate and confer
> Their State affairs. So thick the aery crowd
> Swarm'd and were strait'n'd; . . .

**epic theater:** Epic theater is a term that the German playwright Bertolt Brecht, in the 1920s, applied to his plays. By the word "epic," Brecht signified primarily his attempt to emulate on the stage the objectivity of the narration in Homeric *epic*. By employing a detached narrator and other devices to achieve *alienation effects*, Brecht aimed to subvert the sympathy of the audience with the actors, and the identification of the actor with his role, that were features of the theater of bourgeois realism. His hope was to encourage his audience to criticize and oppose, rather than passively to accept, the social conditions and modes of behavior that the plays represent. Brecht's dramatic works continue to be produced frequently, and his epic theater has had an important influence on such playwrights as Edward Bond and Caryl Churchill in England and Tony Kushner in America.

   See Bertolt Brecht under *Marxist criticism*, and refer to John Willett, ed., *Brecht on Theatre: The Development of an Aesthetic* (1964); and Janelle Reinelt, *After Brecht: British Epic Theater* (1994).

**epideictic oratory:** (ĕpĭdīk′ tĭk): *311*; *235*.

**epigram:** The term is now used for a statement, whether in verse or prose, which is terse, pointed, and witty. The epigram may be on any subject and in any mode: amatory, elegiac, meditative, complimentary, anecdotal, or (most often) satiric. Martial, the Roman epigrammatist, established the enduring model for the caustically satiric epigram in verse.

   The verse epigram was much cultivated in England in the late sixteenth and seventeenth centuries by such poets as John Donne, Ben Jonson, and Robert Herrick. The form flourished especially in the eighteenth century, the time that Austin Dobson described as the age "of wit, of polish, and of Pope." Matthew Prior is a highly accomplished writer of epigrams, and many closed couplets by Alexander Pope and Lady Mary Wortley Montagu are detachable epigrams. In the same century, when the exiled Stuarts were still pretenders to the English throne, John Byrom proposed this epigrammatic toast:

> God bless the King—I mean the Faith's defender!
> God bless (no harm in blessing) the Pretender!
> But who pretender is or who is king—
> God bless us all! that's quite another thing.

   And here is one of Samuel Taylor Coleridge's epigrams, to show that Romanticism did not preclude wit:

*On a Volunteer Singer*

Swans sing before they die—'twere no bad thing
Should certain people die before they sing!

Many of the short poems of Walter Savage Landor (1775–1864) were fine examples of the nonsatirical epigram. Boileau and Voltaire excelled in the epigram in France, as did Lessing, Goethe, and Schiller in Germany; and in America, a number of the short poems by Ralph Waldo Emerson and Emily Dickinson may be accounted epigrams. The form continued to be cultivated by Robert Frost, Ezra Pound, Ogden Nash, Phyllis McGinley, Dorothy Parker, A. R. Ammons, Richard Wilbur, Anthony Hecht, and other poets in the twentieth century.

"Epigram" came to be applied, after the eighteenth century, to neat and witty statements in prose as well as verse; an alternative name for the prose epigram is the **apothegm**. (For the analysis of examples, see *wit, humor, and the comic.*) Such terse and witty prose statements are to be distinguished from the **aphorism**: a pithy and pointed statement of a serious maxim, opinion, or general truth. One of the best known aphorisms is also one of the shortest: *ars longa, vita brevis est* —"art is long, life is short." It occurs first in a work attributed to the Greek physician Hippocrates entitled *Aphorisms,* which consisted of tersely worded precepts on the practice of medicine. (See John Gross, ed., *The Oxford Book of Aphorisms,* 1983.)

Refer to E. B. Osborn, ed., *The Hundred Best Epigrams* (1928); Kingsley Amis, ed., *The New Oxford Book of Light Verse* (1978); Russell Baker, ed., *The Norton Book of Light Verse* (1986). For references to *epigram* in other entries, see page *381.*

**epiphany:** Epiphany means "a manifestation," or "showing forth," and by Christian thinkers was used to signify a manifestation of God's presence within the created world. In the early draft of *A Portrait of the Artist as a Young Man* entitled *Stephen Hero* (published posthumously in 1944), James Joyce adapted the term to secular experience, to signify the experience of a sudden radiance and revelation that occurs in the act of perceiving a commonplace object. "By an epiphany [Stephen] meant a sudden spiritual manifestation." "Its soul, its whatness, leaps to us from the vestment of its appearance. The soul of the commonest object . . . seems to us radiant. The object achieves its epiphany." Joyce's short stories and novels include a number of epiphanies; a climactic one is the revelation that Stephen experiences at the sight of the young girl wading on the shore of the sea in *A Portrait of the Artist,* chapter 4.

"Epiphany" has become the standard term for the description, recurrent in modern poetry and prose fiction, of the sudden flare into revelation of an ordinary object or scene. Joyce, however, had merely substituted this word for what earlier authors had called the **moment**. Thus Shelley, in his *Defense of Poetry* (1821), described the "best and happiest moments . . . arising unforeseen and departing unbidden," "visitations of the divinity," which poetry "redeems from decay." William Wordsworth was a pre-eminent poet of what he called "moments," or in more elaborate cases, "spots of time." For examples of short poems which represent a moment of revelation, see Wordsworth's "The Two April Mornings" and "The Solitary Reaper." Wordsworth's *Prelude*, like some of Joyce's narratives, is constructed as a sequence of such visionary encounters. Thus in Book VIII, lines 543–54 (1850 ed.), Wordsworth describes the "moment" when he for the first time passed in a stagecoach over the "threshold" of London and the "trivial forms / Of houses, pavement, streets" suddenly assumed a profound power and significance:

> 'twas a moment's pause,—
> All that took place within me came and went
> As in a moment; yet with Time it dwells,
> And grateful memory, as a thing divine.

See Irene H. Chayes, "Joyce's Epiphanies," reprinted in *Joyce's "Portrait": Criticisms and Critiques*, ed. T. E. Connolly (1962); Morris Beja, *Epiphany in the Modern Novel* (1971); Ashton Nichols, *The Poetics of Epiphany: Nineteenth-Century Origins of the Modern Literary Moment* (1987). On the history of the traditional "moment" in sacred writings, beginning with St. Augustine, and its conversion into the modern literary epiphany, see M. H. Abrams, *Natural Supernaturalism: Tradition and Revolution in Romantic Literature* (1971), chapters 7–8.

**episodic** (plot): **227**; *266*.

**epistolary novel** (ĕpĭs″ tōlĕr′ ē): **228**; *274*.

**Epithalamion:** Epithalamion, or in the Latin form "epithalamium," is a poem written to celebrate a marriage. Among its classical practitioners were the Greeks Sappho and Theocritus and the Romans Ovid and Catullus. The term in Greek means "at the bridal chamber," since the verses were originally written to be sung outside the bedroom of a newly married couple. The form flourished among the Neo-Latin poets of the Renaissance, who established the model that was followed by writers in the European vernacular languages. Sir Philip Sidney wrote the first English instance in about 1580, and fifteen years later Edmund Spenser wrote his great lyric "Epithalamion," a celebration of his own marriage that he composed as a wedding gift to his bride. Spenser's poem follows, in elaborately contrived numbers of stanzas and lines, the sequence of the hours during his wedding day and night and combines, with unfailing ease and dignity, Christian ritual and beliefs, pagan topics and mythology, and the local Irish setting. John Donne, Ben Jonson, Robert Herrick, and many other Renaissance poets composed wedding poems that were solemn or ribald, according to the intended audience and the poet's own temperament.

Sir John Suckling's "A Ballad upon a Wedding" is a good-humored *parody* of this upper-class poetic form, which he applies to a lower-class wedding. The tradition persists. Shelley composed an "Epithalamium"; Tennyson's *In Memoriam*, although it opens with a funeral, closes with an epithalamion; A. E. Housman spoke in the antique idiom of the bridal song in "He Is Here, Urania's Son"; and W. H. Auden wrote an "Epithalamion" in 1939.

See Robert H. Case, *English Epithalamies* (1896); Virginia J. Tufte, *The Poetry of Marriage* (1970); and (on the elaborate construction of the stanzas and lines in Spenser's "Epithalamion" to correspond with the passage of time on his wedding day) A. Kent Hieatt, *Short Time's Endless Monument* (1960).

**epithet:** Epithet: As a term in criticism, **epithet** denotes an adjective or adjectival phrase used to describe a distinctive quality of a person or thing; an example is *"silver snarling* trumpets" in John Keats's *The Eve of St. Agnes*. The term is also applied to an identifying phrase that stands in place of a noun; thus Alexander Pope's "the *glittering forfex*" is an ironically inflated epithet for the scissors with which the Baron performs his heinous act in *The Rape of the Lock* (1714). The frequent use of derogatory adjectives and phrases in *invective* has led to the mistaken notion that an "epithet" is always uncomplimentary.

**Homeric epithets** are adjectival terms—usually a compound of two words —like those which Homer in his *epic* poems used as recurrent formulas in referring to a distinctive feature of someone or something: *"fleet-footed* Achilles," *"bolt-hurling* Zeus," "the *wine-dark* sea." Buck Mulligan in James Joyce's *Ulysses* parodied the formula in his reference to "the snot-green sea." We often use "conventional epithets" in identifying historical or legendary figures, as in Charles *the Great*, Lorenzo *the Magnificent, Patient* Griselda.

**epode** (ĕ′ pōd): **235**.

**equivoque** (ĕk′ wĭvōk): **295**.

**Erziehungsroman** (ĕrtsē″ ungsrōmän″): **229**.

**eschatology** (ĕs′ kătol″ ōjē): **163**.

**essay:** Essay Any short composition in prose that undertakes to discuss a matter, express a point of view, persuade us to accept a thesis on any subject, or simply entertain. The essay differs from a "treatise" or "dissertation" in its lack of pretension to be a systematic and complete exposition, and in being addressed to a general rather than a specialized audience; as a consequence, the essay discusses its subject in nontechnical fashion, and often with a liberal use of such devices as anecdote, striking illustration, and humor to augment its appeal.

A useful distinction is that between the formal and informal essay. The **formal essay**, or **article**, is relatively impersonal: the author writes as an authority, or at least as highly knowledgeable, and expounds the subject in an orderly way. Examples will be found in various scholarly journals, as well as among the serious articles on current topics and issues in any of the magazines addressed to a thoughtful audience—*Harper's, Commentary, Scientific American*, and so on. In the **informal essay** (or "familiar" or "personal essay"), the author assumes a tone of intimacy with his audience, tends to deal with everyday things rather than with public affairs or specialized topics, and writes in a relaxed, self-revelatory, and sometimes whimsical fashion. Modern examples are to be found in any issue of *The New Yorker.*

The Greeks Theophrastus and Plutarch and the Romans Cicero and Seneca wrote essays long before the genre was given what became its standard name by Montaigne's French *Essais* in 1580. The title signifies "attempts" and was meant to indicate the tentative and unsystematic nature of Montaigne's commentary on topics such as "Of Illness" and "Of Sleeping," in contrast to formal and technical treatises on the same subjects. Francis Bacon, late in the sixteenth century, inaugurated the English use of the term in his own *Essays*; most of them are short discussions such as "Of Truth," "Of Adversity," "Of Marriage and the Single Life." Alexander Pope adopted the term for his expository compositions in verse, the *Essay on Criticism* (1711) and the *Essay on Man* (1733), but the verse essay has had few important exponents after the eighteenth century. In the early eighteenth century Joseph Addison and Sir Richard Steele's *Tatler* and *Spectator*, with their many successors, gave to the essay written in prose its standard modern vehicle, the literary periodical (earlier essays had been published in books).

In the early nineteenth century the founding of new types of magazines, and their steady proliferation, gave great impetus to the writing of essays and made them a major department of literature. This was the age when William Hazlitt, Thomas De Quincey, Charles Lamb, and, later in the century, Robert Louis Stevenson brought the English essay—and especially the personal essay—to a level that has not been surpassed. Major American essayists in the nineteenth century include Washington Irving, Emerson, Thoreau, James Russell Lowell, and Mark Twain. In our own era the many periodicals pour out scores of essays every week. Most of them are formal in type; Virginia Woolf, George Orwell, E. M. Forster, James Thurber, E. B. White, James Baldwin, Susan Sontag, and Toni Morrison, however, are notable recent practitioners of the informal essay.

See Robert Scholes and Carl H. Klaus, *Elements of the Essay* (1969); John Gross, ed., *The Oxford Book of Essays* (1991); Wendy Martin, ed., *Essays by Contemporary American Women* (1996). For a suggestive view of the tacit philosophical assumptions underlying the essay form, see Georg Lukács, "On the Nature and Form of the Essay," in *Soul and Form* (1980).

**essentialism: 146**; *221.*

**estrange: 127**.

**estrangement effect: 6**.

**ethnic writers: 250**; *28, 223.*

**ethos** (ē′ thōs): **242**.

**euphemism:** An inoffensive expression used in place of a blunt one that is felt to be disagreeable or embarrassing. Euphemisms occur frequently with reference to such subjects as religion ("Gosh darn!" for "God damn!"), death ("pass away" instead of "die"), bodily functions ("comfort station" instead of "toilet"), and sex ("to sleep with" instead of "to have sexual intercourse with").

On the extraordinary number and variety of sexual euphemisms in Shakespeare's plays, see Eric Partridge, *Shakespeare's Bawdy* (1960).

**euphony and cacophony: Euphony** is a term applied to language which strikes the ear as smooth, pleasant, and musical, as in these lines from John Keats, *The Eve of St. Agnes* (1820),

> And lucent syrops, tinct with cinnamon;
> Manna and dates, in argosy transferred
> From Fez; and spicèd dainties, every one,
> From silken Samarcand to cedar'd Lebanon.

Analysis of the passage, however, will show that what seems to be a purely auditory agreeableness is due more to the significance of the words, conjoined with the ease and pleasure of the physical act of enunciating the sequence of the speech sounds, than to the inherent melodiousness of the speech sounds themselves. The American critic John Crowe Ransom illustrated the importance of significance to euphony by altering Tennyson's "The murmur of innumerable bees" to "The murder of innumerable beeves"; the euphony is destroyed, not by changing one speech sound and inserting others, but by the change in reference.

Similarly, in **cacophony**, or **dissonance**—language which is perceived as harsh, rough, and unmusical—the discordancy is the effect not only of the sound of the words, but also of their significance, conjoined with the difficulty of enunciating the sequence of the speech sounds. Cacophony may be inadvertent, through a lapse in the writer's attention or skill, as in the unfortunate line of Matthew Arnold's fine poem "Dover Beach" (1867), "Lay like the folds of a bright girdle furled." But cacophony may also be deliberate and functional: for humor, as in Robert Browning's "Pied Piper" (1842),

> Rats!
> They fought the dogs and killed the cats . . .
> Split open the kegs of salted sprats,
> Made nests inside men's Sunday hats;

or else for other purposes, as in Thomas Hardy's attempt, in his poem "In Tenebris I," to mimic, as well as describe, dogged endurance by the difficulty of negotiating the transition in speech sounds from each stressed monosyllable to the next:

> I shall not lose old strength
> In the lone frost's black length.
> Strength long since fled!

For other sound effects see *alliteration* and *onomatopoeia*. Refer to G. R. Stewart, *The Technique of English Verse* (1930), and Northrop Frye, ed., *Sound and Poetry* (1957).

**euphuism:** A conspicuously formal and elaborate prose style which had a vogue in the 1580s in drama, prose fiction, and probably also in the conversation of English court circles. It takes its name from the moralistic prose romance *Euphues: The Anatomy of Wit*, which John Lyly wrote in 1578. In the dialogues

of this work and of *Euphues and His England* (1580), as well as in his stage comedies, Lyly exaggerated and used persistently a stylized prose which other writers
had developed earlier. The style is sententious (that is, full of moral maxims), relies
on syntactical balance and *antithesis*, reinforces the structural parallels by heavy and
elaborate patterns of *alliteration* and *assonance*, exploits the *rhetorical question*, and is
addicted to long similes and learned allusions which are often drawn from mythology and the supposed characteristics and habits of legendary animals. Here is a
brief example from *Euphues*; the character Philautus is speaking:

> I see now that as the fish *Scholopidus* in the flood Araris at the waxing
> of the Moon is as white as the driven snow, and at the waning as
> black as the burnt coal, so Euphues, which at the first encreasing of
> our familiarity, was very zealous, is now at the last cast become most
> faithless.

Shakespeare good-humoredly *parodied* this self-consciously elegant style in *Love's
Labour's Lost* and other plays; nonetheless he, like other authors of the time, profited from Lyly's explorations of the formal and rhetorical possibilities of English
prose.

See *style*; also Jonas A. Barish, "The Prose Style of John Lyly," *English Literary
History* 23 (1956), and G. K. Hunter, *John Lyly* (1962).

**exegesis** (ĕxējē′ sis): **158**.

**exemplum** (ĕxĕm′ plŭm): **9**.

**existential philosophy: 160**.

**explication: 217**; *13*.

**exposition** (in a plot): **267**.

**expressionism:** A German movement in literature and the other arts (especially the
   visual arts) which was at its height between 1910 and 1925—that is, in the period
   just before, during, and after World War I. Its chief precursors were artists and
   writers who had in various ways departed from realistic depictions of life and the
   world, by incorporating in their art visionary or powerfully emotional states of
   mind that are expressed and transmitted by means of distorted representations of
   the outer world. Among these precursors in painting were Vincent Van Gogh,
   Paul Gauguin, and the Norwegian Edvard Munch—Munch's lithograph *The Cry*
   (1894) depicting, against a bleak and stylized background, a tense figure with a
   contorted face uttering a scream of pure horror, is often taken to epitomize what
   became the expressionist mode. Prominent among the literary precursors of the
   movement in the nineteenth century were the French poets Charles Baudelaire
   and Arthur Rimbaud, the Russian novelist Fyodor Dostoevsky, the German
   philosopher Friedrich Nietzsche, and above all the Swedish dramatist August
   Strindberg.

Expressionism itself was not a concerted or well-defined movement. It can be said, however, that its central feature is a revolt against the artistic and literary tradition of *realism*, both in subject matter and in style. The expressionist artist or writer undertakes to express a personal vision—usually a troubled or tensely emotional vision—of human life and human society. This is done by exaggerating and distorting what, according to the norms of artistic realism, are objective features of the world, and by embodying violent extremes of mood and feeling. Often the work implies that what is depicted or described represents the experience of an individual standing alone and afraid in an industrial, technological, and urban society which is disintegrating into chaos. Those expressionists who were radical in their politics also projected utopian views of a future community in a regenerate world.

Expressionist painters tended to use jagged lines to depict contorted objects and forms, as well as to substitute arbitrary, often lurid colors, for natural hues; among these painters were Emil Nolde, Franz Marc, Oskar Kokoschka, and, for a time, Wassily Kandinsky. Expressionist poets (including the Germans Gottfried Benn and Georg Trakl) departed from standard meter, syntax, and poetic structure to organize their works around symbolic images. Expressionist writers of prose narratives (most eminently Franz Kafka) abandoned standard modes of characterization and plot for symbolic figures involved in an obsessive world of nightmarish events.

Drama was a prominent and widely influential form of expressionist writing. Among the better-known German playwrights were Georg Kaiser (*Gas, From Morn to Midnight*), Ernst Toller (*Mass Man*), and, in his earlier productions, Bertolt Brecht. Expressionist dramatists often represented anonymous human types instead of individualized characters, replaced plot with episodic renderings of intense and rapidly oscillating emotional states, fragmented the dialogue into exclamatory and seemingly incoherent sentences or phrases, and employed masks and abstract or lopsided and sprawling stage sets. The producer Max Reinhardt, although not himself in the movement, directed a number of plays by Strindberg and by German expressionists; in them he inaugurated such modern devices as the revolving stage and special effects in lighting and sound. This mode of German drama had an important influence on the American theater. Eugene O'Neill's *The Emperor Jones* (1920) projected, in a sequence of symbolic episodes, the individual and racial memories of a terrified African-American protagonist, and Elmer Rice's *The Adding Machine* (1923) used nonrealistic means to represent a mechanical, sterile, and frightening world as experienced by Mr. Zero, a tiny and helpless cog in the impersonal system of big business. The flexible possibilities of the medium made the motion picture an important vehicle of German expressionism. Robert Wiene's early expressionist film *The Cabinet of Dr. Caligari* (1920)—representing, in ominously distorted settings, the machinations of the satanic head of an insane asylum—as well as Friedrich Murnau's *Nosferatu* (1922) and Fritz Lang's *Metropolis* (1926) are often shown in current revivals of films.

Expressionism had begun to flag by 1925 and was finally suppressed in Germany by the Nazis in the early 1930s, but it has continued to exert influence on English and American, as well as European, art and literature. We recognize its effects, direct or indirect, on the writing and staging of such plays as Thornton Wilder's *The Skin of Our Teeth* and Arthur Miller's *Death of a Salesman*, as well as on the *theater of the absurd*; on the poetry of Allen Ginsberg and other *Beat* writers; on the prose fiction of Samuel Beckett, Kurt Vonnegut, Jr., Joseph Heller, and Thomas Pynchon; and on a number of films that exhibit the distorted perceptions and fantasies of disturbed characters, by such directors as Ingmar Bergman, Federico Fellini, and Michelangelo Antonioni.

See Richard Samuel and R. H. Thomas, *Expressionism in German Life, Literature and the Theater, 1910–1924* (1939); Walter H. Sokel, *The Writer in Extremis: Expressionism in Twentieth-Century German Literature* (1959); John Willett, *Expressionism* (1970); Donald E. Gordon, *Expressionism: Art and Idea* (1987). On the expressionist cinema: Siegfried Kracauer, *From Caligari to Hitler: A Psychological History of the German Film* (1947); Lotte Eisner, *The Haunted Screen: Expressionism in the German Cinema and the Influence of Max Reinhardt* (1969). For references to *expressionism* in other entries, see pages *203, 231*.

**expressive criticism: 63**; *135, 153, 213, 261, 289, 312, 348*.

**eye rhymes: 317**; *271*.

**fable: 8**.

**fabliau:** The medieval fabliau was a short comic or satiric tale in verse dealing realistically with middle-class or lower-class characters and delighting in the ribald; one of its favorite themes was the cuckolding of a stupid husband. (Professor Douglas Bush neatly characterized the type as "a short story broader than it is long.") The fabliau flourished in France in the twelfth and thirteenth centuries and became popular in England during the fourteenth century. Chaucer, who wrote one of the greatest serious short stories in verse, the account of Death and the rioters in "The Pardoner's Tale," also wrote one of the best fabliaux, the hilarious "Miller's Tale."

See Joseph Bédier, *Les Fabliaux* (5th ed., 1928); *Fabliaux: Ribald Tales from the Old French*, trans. Robert Hellman and Richard O'Gorman (1976); and Howard Bloch, *The Scandal of the Fabliaux* (1986).

**fabula: 209**.

**fabulation: 232**.

**fallible narrator: 276**; *166*.

**falling action: 267**.

**false wit: 380**; *193*.

**family resemblances: 136**.

**fancy and imagination:** The distinction between fancy and imagination was a key element in Samuel Taylor Coleridge's theory of poetry, as well as in his general theory of the mental processes. In earlier discussions, "fancy" and "imagination" had for the most part been used synonymously to denote a faculty of the mind which is distinguished from "reason," "judgment," and "memory," in that it receives "images" from the senses and reorders them into new combinations. In the thirteenth chapter of *Biographia Literaria* (1817), Coleridge attributes this reordering function of the sensory images to the lower faculty he calls **fancy**: "Fancy . . . has no other counters to play with, but fixities and definites. The Fancy is indeed no other than a mode of Memory emancipated from the order of time and space." To Coleridge, that is, the fancy is a mechanical process which receives the elementary images—the "fixities and definites" which come to it ready-made from the senses—and, without altering the parts, reassembles them into a different spatial and temporal order from that in which they were originally perceived. The imagination, however, which produces a much higher kind of poetry,

> dissolves, diffuses, dissipates, in order to re-create; or where this process
> is rendered impossible, yet still at all events it struggles to idealize and
> unify. It is essentially *vital*, even as all objects (*as* objects) are essentially
> fixed and dead.

Coleridge's **imagination**, that is, is able to "create" rather than merely reassemble, by dissolving the fixities and definites—the mental pictures, or images, received from the senses—and unifying them into a new whole. And while the fancy is merely mechanical, the imagination is "vital"; that is, it is an organic faculty which operates not like a sorting machine, but like a living and growing plant. As Coleridge says elsewhere, the imagination "generates and produces a form of its own," while its rules are "the very powers of growth and production." And in the fourteenth chapter of the *Biographia*, Coleridge adds his famous statement that the "synthetic" power which is the "imagination . . . reveals itself in the balance or reconciliation of opposite or discordant qualities: of sameness, with difference; of the general, with the concrete; the idea, with the image. . . ." The faculty of imagination, in other words, assimilates and synthesizes the most disparate elements into an organic whole—that is, a newly generated unity, constituted by an interdependence of parts whose identity cannot survive their removal from the whole. (See *organic form*.)

Most critics after Coleridge who distinguished fancy from imagination tended to make fancy simply the faculty that produces a lesser, lighter, or humorous kind of poetry, and to make imagination the faculty that produces a higher, more serious, and more passionate poetry. And the concept of "imagination" itself is as various as the modes of psychology that critics have adopted (associationist, Gestalt, *Freudian, Jungian*), while its processes vary according to the way in which a critic conceives of the nature of a poem (as essentially realistic or essentially visionary, as a verbal construction or as "myth," as "pure poetry" or as a work designed to produce effects on an audience).

See I. A. Richards, *Coleridge on Imagination* (1934); M. H. Abrams, *The Mirror and the Lamp* (1953), chapter 7; Richard H. Fogle, *The Idea of Coleridge's Criticism* (1962).

**fantastic literature: 276**.

**fantasy: 323**.

**farce: 50**; *52*.

**feminine ending: 197**.

**feminine rhyme: 317**.

**feminist criticism:** As a distinctive and concerted approach to literature, feminist criticism was not inaugurated until late in the 1960s. Behind it, however, lie two centuries of struggle for the recognition of women's cultural roles and achievements, and for women's social and political rights, marked by such books as Mary Wollstonecraft's A *Vindication of the Rights of Woman* (1792), John Stuart Mill's *The Subjection of Women* (1869), and the American Margaret Fuller's *Woman in the Nineteenth Century* (1845). Much of feminist literary criticism continues in our time to be interrelated with the movement by political **feminists** for social, legal, and cultural freedom and equality.

An important precursor in feminist criticism was Virginia Woolf, who, in addition to her fiction, wrote *A Room of One's Own* (1929) and numerous other essays on women authors and on the cultural, economic, and educational disabilities within what she called a "patriarchal" society, dominated by men, that have hindered or prevented women from realizing their productive and creative possibilities. (See the collection of her essays, *Women and Writing*, ed. M. Barrett, 1979.) A much more radical critical mode, sometimes called "second-wave feminism," was launched in France by Simone de Beauvoir's *The Second Sex* (1949), a wide-ranging critique of the cultural identification of women as merely the negative object, or "Other," to man as the dominating "Subject" who is assumed to represent humanity in general; the book dealt also with "the great collective myths" of women in the works of many male writers.

In America, modern feminist criticism was inaugurated by Mary Ellmann's deft and witty discussion, in *Thinking about Women* (1968), about the derogatory stereotypes of women in literature written by men, and also about alternative and subversive representations that occur in some writings by women. Even more influential was Kate Millett's hard-hitting *Sexual Politics*, published the following year. By "politics" Millett signifies the mechanisms that express and enforce the relationships of power in society; she analyzes many Western social arrangements and institutions as covert ways of manipulating power so as to establish and perpetuate the dominance of men and the subordination of women. In her book she attacks the male bias in Freud's *psychoanalytic* theory and also analyzes selected passages by D. H. Lawrence, Henry Miller, Norman Mailer, and Jean Genet as revealing the ways in which the authors, in their fictional fantasies, aggrandize their aggressive phallic selves and degrade women as submissive sexual objects.

Since 1969 there has been an explosion of feminist writings without parallel in previous critical innovations, in a movement that in its earlier stages, as Elaine Showalter remarked, displayed the urgency and excitement of a religious awakening. Current feminist criticism in America, England, France, and other countries is not a unitary theory or procedure. It manifests, among those who practice it, a great variety of critical vantage points and procedures, including adaptations of *psychoanalytic, Marxist,* and diverse *poststructuralist* theories, and its vitality is signalized by the vigor (sometimes even rancor) of the debates within the ranks of professed feminists themselves. The various feminisms, however, share certain assumptions and concepts that underlie the diverse ways that individual critics explore the factor of sexual difference and privilege in the production, the form and content, the reception, and the critical analysis and evaluation of works of literature:

1. The basic view is that Western civilization is pervasively **patriarchal** (ruled by the father)—that is, it is male-centered and controlled, and is organized and conducted in such a way as to subordinate women to men in all cultural domains: familial, religious, political, economic, social, legal, and artistic. From the Hebrew Bible and Greek philosophic writings to the present, the female tends to be defined by negative reference to the male as the human norm, hence as an Other, or kind of non-man, by her lack of the identifying male organ, of male capabilities, and of the male character traits that are presumed, in the patriarchal view, to have achieved the most important scientific and technical inventions and the major works of civilization and culture. Women themselves are taught, in the process of being socialized, to internalize the reigning patriarchal *ideology* (that is, the conscious and unconscious presuppositions about male superiority), and so are conditioned to derogate their own sex and to cooperate in their own subordination.

2. It is widely held that while one's sex as a man or woman is determined by anatomy, the prevailing concepts of **gender**—of the traits that are conceived to constitute what is masculine and what is feminine in temperament and behavior—are largely, if not entirely, *social constructs* that were generated by the pervasive patriarchal biases of our civilization. As Simone de Beauvoir put it, "One is not born, but rather becomes, a woman. . . . It is civilization as a whole that produces this creature . . . which is described as feminine." By this cultural process, the masculine in our culture has come to be widely identified as active, dominating, adventurous, rational, creative; the feminine, by systematic opposition to such traits, has come to be identified as passive, acquiescent, timid, emotional, and conventional. (See *gender criticism.*)

3. The further claim is that this patriarchal (or "masculinist," or "androcentric") ideology pervades those writings which have been traditionally considered great literature, and which until recently have been written mainly by men for men. Typically, the most highly regarded literary works focus on male protagonists—Oedipus, Ulysses, Hamlet, Tom Jones, Faust, the Three Musketeers, Captain Ahab, Huck Finn, Leopold Bloom—who embody masculine traits and ways of feeling and pursue masculine interests in masculine fields of action. To these males, the female characters, when they play a role, are marginal and subordinate, and are represented either as complementary and subservient to, or in opposition to, masculine desires and enterprises. Such works, lacking autonomous female role models, and implicitly addressed to male readers, either leave

the woman reader an alien outsider or else solicit her to "identify against herself" by taking up the position of the male subject and so assuming male values and ways of perceiving, feeling, and acting. It is often held, in addition, that the traditional categories and criteria for analyzing and appraising literary works, although represented in standard critical theory as objective, disinterested, and universal, are in fact infused with masculine assumptions, interests, and ways of reasoning, so that the standard selection and rankings, the prevailing *canon*, and the critical treatments of literary works have in fact been tacitly but thoroughly gender-biased.

A major interest of feminist critics in English-speaking countries has been to reconstitute the ways we deal with literature in order to do justice to female points of view, concerns, and values. One emphasis has been to alter the way a woman reads the literature of the past so as to make her not an acquiescent, but (in the title of Judith Fetterley's book published in 1978) *The Resisting Reader*; that is, one who resists the author's intentions and design in order, by a "revisionary rereading," to bring to light and to counter the covert sexual biases written into a literary work. Another prominent procedure has been to identify recurrent and distorting "images of women," especially in novels and poems written by men. These images are often represented as tending to fall into two antithetic patterns. On the one side we find idealized projections of men's desires (the Madonna, the Muses of the arts, Dante's Beatrice, the pure and innocent virgin, the "Angel in the House" that was represented in the writings of the Victorian poet Coventry Patmore). On the other side are demonic projections of men's sexual resentments and terrors (Eve and Pandora as the sources of all evil, destructive sensual temptresses such as Delilah and Circe, the malign witch, the castrating mother). While many feminist critics have decried the literature written by men for its depiction of women as marginal, docile, and subservient to men's interests and emotional needs and fears, some of them have also identified male writers who, in their view, have managed to rise above the sexual prejudices of their time sufficiently to understand and represent the cultural pressures that have shaped the characters of women and forced upon them their negative or subsidiary social roles. The latter class is said to include, in selected works, such authors as Chaucer, Shakespeare, Samuel Richardson, Henrik Ibsen, and George Bernard Shaw.

A number of feminists have concentrated, not on the woman as reader, but on what Elaine Showalter named **gynocriticism**—that is, a criticism which concerns itself with developing a specifically female framework for dealing with works written by women, in all aspects of their production, motivation, analysis, and interpretation, and in all literary forms, including journals and letters. Notable books in this mode include Patricia Meyer Spacks' *The Female Imagination* (1975), on English and American novels of the past three hundred years; Ellen Moers' *Literary Women* (1976), on major women novelists and poets in England, America, and France; Elaine Showalter's *A Literature of Their Own: British Women Novelists from Brontë to Lessing* (1977); and Sandra Gilbert and Susan Gubar's *The Madwoman in the Attic* (1979; rev. 2000). This last book stresses especially the psychodynamics of women writers in the nineteenth century. Its authors propose that the "anxiety of authorship," resulting from the stereotype that literary creativity is an exclusively male prerogative, effected in women writers a psychological duplicity that projected a monstrous counterfigure to the idealized heroine, typified by Bertha Rochester, the madwoman in Charlotte Brontë's *Jane Eyre*; such a figure is "usually in some sense the *author's* double, an image of her own anxiety and rage." (Refer to *influence and the anxiety of influence*.)

One concern of gynocritics is to identify distinctively feminine subject matters in literature written by women—the world of domesticity, for example, or the special experiences of gestation, giving birth, and nurturing, or mother-daughter and woman-woman relations—in which personal and affectional issues, and not external activism, are the primary interest. Another concern is to uncover in literary history a female tradition, incorporated in subcommunities of women writers who were aware of, emulated, and found support in earlier women writers, and who in turn provide models and emotional support to their own readers and successors. A third undertaking is to show that there is a distinctive feminine mode of experience, or "subjectivity," in thinking, feeling, valuing, and perceiving oneself and the outer world. Related to this is the attempt (thus far, without much agreement about details) to specify the traits of a "woman's language," or distinctively feminine *style* of speech and writing, in sentence structure, types of relations between the elements of a discourse, and characteristic figures of speech and imagery. Some feminists have turned their critical attention to the great number of women's domestic and "sentimental" novels, which are noted perfunctorily and in derogatory fashion in standard literary histories, yet which dominated the market for fiction in the nineteenth century and produced most of the best sellers of the time; instances of this last critical enterprise are Elaine Showalter's *A Literature of Their Own* (1977) on British writers, and Nina Baym's *Woman's Fiction: A Guide to Novels by and about Women in America, 1820–1870* (1978). Sandra Gilbert and Susan Gubar have described the later history of women's writings in *No Man's Land: The Place of the Woman Writer in the Twentieth Century* (2 vols., 1988–89).

The often-asserted goal of feminist critics has been to enlarge and reorder, or in radical instances entirely to displace, the literary canon—that is, the set of works which, by a cumulative consensus, have come to be considered "major" and to serve as the chief subjects of literary history, criticism, scholarship, and teaching (see *canon of literature*). Feminist studies have succeeded in raising the status of many female authors hitherto more or less scanted by scholars and critics (including Anne Finch, George Sand, Elizabeth Barrett Browning, Elizabeth Gaskell, Christina Rossetti, Harriet Beecher Stowe, and Sidonie-Gabrielle Colette) and to bring into purview other authors who have been largely or entirely overlooked as subjects for serious consideration (among them Margaret Cavendish, Aphra Behn, Lady Mary Wortley Montagu, Joanna Baillie, Kate Chopin, Charlotte Perkins Gilman, and a number of African-American writers such as Zora Neale Hurston). Some feminists have devoted their critical attention especially to the literature written by lesbian writers, or that deals with lesbian relationships in a heterosexual culture. (See *queer theory*.)

American and English critics have for the most part engaged in empirical and thematic studies of writings by and about women. The most prominent feminist critics in France, however, have occupied themselves with the "theory" of the role of gender in writing, conceptualized within various *poststructural* frames of reference, and above all Jacques Lacan's reworkings of Freudian *psychoanalysis* in terms of Saussure's linguistic theory. English-speaking feminists, for example, have drawn attention to demonstrable evidences that a male bias is encoded in our linguistic conventions; instances include the use of "man" or "mankind" for human beings in general, of "chairman" and "spokesman" for people of either sex, and of the pronouns "he" and "his" to refer back to ostensibly gender-neutral nouns such as "God," "human being," "child," "inventor," "author," and "poet." (See Sally McConnell-Ginet, Ruth Borker, and Nelly Furman, eds., *Women and Language in Literature and Society*, 1980; Deborah Cameron, *Feminism and Linguistic Theory* (2d ed., 1992); and Robin Tolmach Lakoff et al., *Language and Woman's Place: Text and Commentaries*, 2004; see also the entry *linguistics in literary criticism*.) The radical claim of some French theorists, on the other hand, is that all Western languages, in all their features, are utterly and irredeemably male-engendered, male-constituted, and male-dominated. Discourse, it is asserted, in a term proposed by Lacan, is **phallogocentric**; that is, it is centered and organized throughout by implicit recourse to the phallus (used in a symbolic sense) both as its supposed "logos," or ground, and as its prime signifier and power source. Phallogocentrism, it is claimed, manifests itself in Western discourse not only in its vocabulary and syntax, but also in its rigorous rules of logic, its proclivity for fixed classifications and oppositions, and its criteria for what is traditionally considered to be valid evidence and objective knowledge. A basic problem for such theorists is to establish the very possibility of a woman's language that will not, when a woman writes, automatically be appropriated into this phallogocentric language, since such appropriation is said to force her into complicity with linguistic features that impose on females a condition of marginality and subservience, or even of linguistic nonentity.

To evade this dilemma, Hélène Cixous posits the existence of an incipient "feminine writing" (écriture féminine) which has its source in the mother, in the stage of the mother-child relation before the child acquires the male-centered verbal language. Thereafter, in her view, this prelinguistic and unconscious potentiality manifests itself in those written texts which, abolishing all repressions, undermine and subvert the fixed signification, the logic, and the "closure" of our phallocentric language, and open out into a joyous freeplay of meanings. Alternatively, Luce Irigaray posits a "woman's writing" which evades the male monopoly and the risk of appropriation into the existing system by establishing as its generative principle, in place of the monolithic phallus, the diversity, fluidity, and multiple possibilities inherent in the structure and erotic functioning of the female sexual organs and erogenous zones, and in the distinctive nature of female sexual experiences. Julia Kristeva posits a "chora," or prelinguistic, pre-Oedipal, and unsystematized signifying process, centered on the mother, that she labels "semiotic." This process is repressed as we acquire the father-controlled, syntactically ordered, and logical language that she calls "symbolic." The semiotic process, however, can break out in a revolutionary way—her prime example is avant-garde poetry, whether written by women or by men—as a "heterogeneous destructive causality" that disrupts and disperses the authoritarian "subject" and strikes free of the oppressive order and rationality of our standard discourse which, as the product of the "law of the Father," consigns women to a negative and marginal status.

Since the 1980s a number of feminist critics have used *poststructuralist* positions and techniques to challenge the category of "woman" and other founding concepts of feminism itself. They point out the existence of differences and adversarial strands within the supposedly monolithic history of patriarchal discourse, and emphasize the inherent linguistic instability in the basic conceptions of "woman" or "the feminine," as well as the diversities within these supposedly universal and uniform female identities that result from differences in race, class, nationality, and historical situation. See Barbara Johnson, *A World of Difference* (1987); Rita Felski, *Beyond Feminist Aesthetics: Feminist Literature and Social Change* (1989); and the essays in *Feminism/ Postmodernism*, ed. Linda J. Nicholson (1990). Judith Butler, in two influential books, has opposed the notion that the feminist movement requires the concept of a feminine identity; that is, that there exist essential factors that define a woman as a woman. Instead, she elaborates the view that the fundamental features which define gender are social and cultural productions that produce the illusory effect of being natural. Butler proposes also that we consider gender as a "performative"—that to be masculine or feminine or homosexual is not something that one is, but a socially pre-established pattern of behavior that one repeatedly enacts. (For the concept of "the performative," refer to *speech-act theory*.) See Judith Butler, *Gender Trouble: Feminism and the Subversion of Identity* (1990) and *Bodies that Matter* (1993).

Feminist theoretical and critical writings, although recent in origin, expand yearly in volume and range. There exist a number of specialized feminist journals and publishing houses; almost all colleges and universities now have programs in **women's studies**—the investigation of the status and roles of women in history and in diverse institutions and activities—and courses in women's literature and feminist criticism; and ever-increasing place is given to writings by and about women in anthologies, periodicals, and conferences. Of the many critical and theoretical innovations of the past several decades, the concern with the effects of sexual differences in the writing, interpretation, analysis, and assessment of literature seems destined to have the most prominent and enduring effects on literary history, criticism, and academic instruction, when conducted by men as well as by women. (See *ecofeminism* and *gender studies*.)

In addition to the books mentioned above, the following works are especially useful. Sandra Gilbert and Susan Gubar, eds., *The Norton Anthology of Literature by Women* (2d ed., 1996)—the editorial materials provide a concise history, as well as biographies and bibliographies, of female authors since the Middle Ages. See also Jane Gallop, *The Daughter's Seduction: Feminism and Psychoanalysis* (1982), and Gayatri Chakravorty Spivak, *In Other Worlds: Essays in Cultural Politics* (1987). Histories and critiques of feminist criticism: K. K. Ruthven, *Feminist Literary Studies: An Introduction* (1984); Toril Moi, *Sexual/Textual Politics: Feminist Literary Theory* (1985)—much of this book is devoted to feminist theorists in France; Mary Evans, *Introducing Contemporary Feminist Thought* (1997); Shari Benstock, Suzanne

Ferriss, Susanne Woods., eds., *A Handbook of Literary Feminisms* (2002); Margaret Walters, *Feminism: A Very Short Introduction* (2005). Collections of essays in feminist criticism: Elaine Showalter, ed., *The New Feminist Criticism* (1985); Patrocinio P. Schweickart and Elizabeth A. Flynn, eds., *Gender and Reading: Essays on Readers, Texts, and Contexts* (1986); Robyn R. Warhol and Diane Price Herndl, eds., *Feminisms: An Anthology of Literary Theory and Criticism* (2d ed., 1997); Margo Hendricks and Patricia Parker, eds., *Women, "Race," and Writing in the Early Modern Period* (1994). For critiques of some feminist positions and views by pro-feminists, see Nina Baym, "The Madwoman and Her Languages: Why I Don't Do Feminist Literary Theory," in *Feminist Issues in Literary Scholarship*, ed. Shari Benstock (1987); Elizabeth Fox-Genovese, *Feminism without Illusions: A Critique of Individualism* (1991); Susan Gubar, *Critical Condition: Feminism at the Turn of the Century* (2000). Among the books by French feminist theorists available in English are Hélène Cixous and Catherine Clement, *The Newly Born Woman* (1986); Luce Irigaray, *Speculum of the Other Woman* (1985) and *This Sex Which Is Not One* (1985); Julia Kristeva, *Desire in Language: A Semiotic Approach to Literature and Art* (1980); *The Kristeva Reader*, ed. Toril Moi (1986). On feminist treatments of African-American women: Barbara Christian, *Black Feminist Criticism* (1985); Hazel V. Carby, *Reconstructing Womanhood: The Emergence of the Afro-American Woman Novelist* (1987); Henry L. Gates, Jr., *Reading Black, Reading Feminist: A Critical Anthology* (1990); Joy James and T. Denean Sharpley-Whiting, eds., *The Black Feminist Reader* (2000). Feminist treatments of lesbian and gay literature: Eve Kosofsky Sedgwick, *Between Men: English Literature and Male Homosocial Desire* (1985) and *Epistemology of the Closet* (1990). Feminist theater and film studies: Teresa de Lauretis, *Alice Doesn't: Feminism, Semiotics, Cinema* (1984); Sue-Ellen Case, *Feminism and Theatre* (1987); Constance Penley, *The Future of an Illusion: Film, Feminism, and Psychoanalysis* (1989); and Peggy Phenan and Lynda Hart, eds., *Acting Out: Feminist Performances* (1993).

For references to *feminist criticism* in other entries, see pages *17, 60, 95, 132, 138, 223, 259, 293, 294, 295, 302, 310, 334, 379.*

**ficelle** (fĭsĕl'): **57**.

**fiction and truth:** In an inclusive sense, **fiction** is any literary *narrative*, whether in prose or verse, which is invented instead of being an account of events that actually happened. In a narrower sense, however, fiction denotes only narratives that are written in prose (the *novel* and *short story*), and sometimes is used simply as a synonym for the novel. Literary prose narratives in which the fiction is to a prominent degree based on biographical, historical, or contemporary facts are often referred to by compound names such as "fictional biography," the *historical novel*, and the *nonfiction novel*.

Both philosophers and literary critics have concerned themselves with the logical analysis of the types of sentences that constitute a fictional text, and especially with the question of their **truth**, or what is sometimes called their "truth-value"—that is, whether, or in just what way, they are subject to the criterion of truth or falsity. Some thinkers have asserted that "fictional sentences" should be regarded as referring to a special world, "created" by the author, which is analogous to the real world, but possesses its own setting, beings, and mode of coherence. (See M. H. Abrams, *The Mirror and the Lamp*, 1953, pp. 272–85, "The Poem as Heterocosm"; James Phelan, *Worlds from Words: A Theory of Language in Fiction*, 1981.) Others, most notably I. A. Richards, have held that fiction is a form of **emotive language** composed of **pseudostatements**; and that whereas a statement in "referential language" is "justified by its truth, that is, its correspondence . . . with the fact to which it points," a pseudostatement "is justified entirely by its effect in releasing or organizing our attitudes" (I. A. Richards, *Science and Poetry*, 1926). Most current theorists, however, present an elaborated logical version of what Sir Philip Sidney long ago proposed in his *Apology for Poetry* (published 1595), that a poet "nothing affirmes, therefore never lyeth. For, as I take it, to lye is to affirm that to be true which is false." Current versions of this view hold that fictive sentences are meaningful according to the rules of ordinary, nonfictional discourse, but that, in accordance with conventions implicitly shared by the author and reader of a work of fiction, they are not put forward as assertions of fact, and therefore are not subject to the criterion of truth or falsity that applies to sentences in nonfictional discourse. See Margaret MacDonald, "The Language of Fiction" (1954), reprinted in W. E. Kennick, ed., *Art and Philosophy* (rev. 1979).

In *speech-act theory*, a related view takes the form that a writer of fiction only "pretends" to make assertions, or "imitates" the making of assertions, and so suspends the "normal illocutionary commitment" of the writer of such utterances to the claim that what he asserts is true. See John R. Searle, "The Logical Status of Fictional Discourse," in *Expression and Meaning: Studies in the Theory of Speech Acts* (1979, reprinted 1986). We find in a number of other theorists the attempt to extend the concept of "fictive utterances" to include all the genres of literature —poems, narratives, and dramas, as well as novels; all these forms, it is proposed, are imitations, or fictive representations, of some type of "natural" discourse. A novel, for example, not only is made up of fictional utterances, but is itself a fictive utterance, in that it *"represents* the verbal action of a man [that is, the narrator] reporting, describing, and referring." See Barbara Herrnstein Smith, "Poetry as Fiction," in *Margins of Discourse* (1978), and Richard Ohmann, "Speech Acts and the Definition of Literature," *Philosophy and Rhetoric* 4 (1971).

Most modern critics of prose fiction, whatever their persuasion, make an important distinction between the fictional scenes, persons, events, and dialogue that a narrator reports or describes and the narrator's own assertions about the world, about human life, or about the human situation; the central, or controlling, generalizations of the latter sort are said to be the *theme* or **thesis** of a work. These assertions by the narrator may be explicit (for example, Thomas Hardy's statement at the end of *Tess of the D'Urbervilles*, "The President of the immortals had had his sport with Tess"; or Tolstoy's philosophy of history at the end of *War and Peace*). Many such claims, however, are said to be merely "implied," "suggested," or "inferrable" from the narrator's choice and control of the fictional characters and plot of the narrative itself. It is often claimed that such generalizations by the narrator within a fictional work, whether expressed or implied, function as assertions that claim to be true about the world, and that they thereby relate the fictional narrative to the factual and moral world of actual experience. See John Hospers, "Implied Truths in Literature" (1960), reprinted in W. E. Kennick, ed., *Art and Philosophy* (rev. 1979).

A much-discussed topic, related to the question of an author's assertions and truth-claims in narrative fiction, concerns the part played by the **beliefs** of the reader. The problem raised is the extent to which a reader's own moral, religious, and social convictions, as they coincide with or diverge from those asserted or implied in a work, determine the interpretation, acceptability, and evaluation of that work by the reader. For the history and discussions of this problem in literary criticism, see William Joseph Rooney, *The Problem of "Poetry and Belief" in Contemporary Criticism* (1949); M. H. Abrams, editor and contributor, *Literature and Belief* (1957); Walter Benn Michaels, "Saving the Text: Reference and Belief," *Modern Language Notes* 93 (1978). Many discussions of the role of belief in fiction cite S. T. Coleridge's description of the reader's attitude as a "willing suspension of disbelief."

A review of theories concerning the relevance of the criterion of truth to fiction is Monroe C. Beardsley's *Aesthetics: Problems in the Philosophy of Criticism* (1958), pp. 409–19. For an analysis and critique of theories of emotive language see Max Black, "Questions about Emotive Meaning," in *Language and Philosophy* (1949), chapter 9. Gerald Graff defends the claim for propositional truth in poetry in *Poetic Statement and Critical Dogma* (1970), chapter 6. In the writings of Jacques Derrida and his followers in literary criticism, the *binary* opposition truth/falsity is one of the metaphysical presuppositions of Western thought that they put to question; see *deconstruction*. For a detailed treatment of the relationships of fictions to the real world, including a survey of the diverse views about this problem, see Peter Lamarque and Stein Haugom Olsen, *Truth, Fiction and Literature: A Philosophical Perspective* (1994).

**figural interpretation: 162**.

**figurative language:** Figurative language is a conspicuous departure from what competent users of a language apprehend as the standard meaning of words, or else the standard order of words, in order to achieve some special meaning or effect. Figures are sometimes described as primarily poetic, but they are integral to the functioning of language and indispensable to all modes of discourse.

Most modern classifications and analyses are based on the treatment of figurative language by Aristotle and later classical rhetoricians; the fullest and most influential treatment is in the Roman Quintilian's *Institutes of Oratory* (first century AD), Books VIII and IX. Since that time, figurative language has often been divided into two classes: (1) **Figures of thought**, or **tropes** (meaning "turns," "conversions"), in which words or phrases are used in a way that effects a conspicuous change in what we take to be their standard meaning. The standard meaning, as opposed to its meaning in the figurative use, is called the **literal meaning**.

(2) **Figures of speech**, or "rhetorical figures," or **schemes** (from the Greek word for "form"), in which the departure from standard usage is not primarily in the meaning of the words, but in the order or syntactical pattern of the words. This distinction is not a sharp one, nor do all critics agree on its application. For convenience of exposition, however, the most commonly identified tropes are treated here, and the most commonly identified figures of speech are collected in the article *rhetorical figures*. For recent opposition to the basic distinction between the literal and the figurative, see *metaphor, theories of*.

In a **simile**, a comparison between two distinctly different things is explicitly indicated by the word "like" or "as." A simple example is Robert Burns, "O my love's like a red, red rose." The following simile from Samuel Taylor Coleridge's "The Rime of the Ancient Mariner" also specifies the feature ("green") in which icebergs are similar to emerald:

> And ice, mast-high, came floating by,
> As green as emerald.

For highly elaborated types of simile, see *conceit* and *epic simile*.

In a **metaphor**, a word or expression that in literal usage denotes one kind of thing is applied to a distinctly different kind of thing, without asserting a comparison. For example, if Burns had said "O my love is a red, red rose" he would have uttered, technically speaking, a metaphor instead of a simile. Here is a more complex instance from the poet Stephen Spender, in which he applies several metaphoric terms to the eye as it scans a landscape:

> Eye, gazelle, delicate wanderer,
> Drinker of horizon's fluid line.[3]

For the distinction between metaphor and symbol, see *symbol*.

It should be noted that in these examples we can distinguish two elements, the metaphorical term and the subject to which it is applied. In a widely adopted usage, I. A. Richards introduced the name **tenor** for the subject ("my love" in the altered line from Burns, and "eye" in Spender's lines), and the name **vehicle** for the metaphorical term itself ("rose" in Burns, and the three words "gazelle," "wanderer," and "drinker" in Spender). In an **implicit metaphor**, the tenor is not itself specified, but only implied. If one were to say, while discussing someone's death, "That reed was too frail to survive the storm of its sorrows," the situational and verbal context of the term "reed" indicates that it is the vehicle for an implicit tenor, a human being, while "storm" is the vehicle for an aspect of a specified tenor, "sorrows." Those aspects, properties, or common associations of a vehicle which, in a given context, apply to a tenor are called by Richards the **grounds** of a metaphor. (See I. A. Richards, *Philosophy of Rhetoric*, 1936, chapters 5–6.)

All the metaphoric terms, or vehicles, cited so far have been nouns, but other parts of speech may also be used metaphorically. The metaphoric use of a verb occurs in Shakespeare's *Merchant of Venice*, V. i. 54, "How sweet the moonlight

---

[3]Lines from "Not palaces, an era's crown," from *Collected Poems, 1928–1953*, by Stephen Spender. Copyright © 1934 and renewed 1962 by Stephen Spender. Reprinted by permission.

*sleeps* upon this bank"; and the metaphoric use of an adjective occurs in Andrew Marvell's "The Garden" (1681):

> Annihilating all that's made
> To a *green* thought in a green shade.

A **mixed metaphor** conjoins two or more obviously diverse metaphoric vehicles. When used inadvertently, without sensitivity to the possible incongruity of the vehicles, the effect can be ludicrous: "Girding up his loins, the chairman plowed through the mountainous agenda." Densely figurative poets such as Shakespeare, however, often mix metaphors in a functional way. One example is Hamlet's expression of his troubled state of mind in his *soliloquy* (III. i. 59–60), "to take arms against a sea of troubles, / And by opposing end them"; another is the complex involvement of vehicle within vehicle, applied to the process of aging, in Shakespeare's Sonnet 65:

> O, how shall summer's honey breath hold out
> Against the wrackful siege of battering days?

A **dead metaphor** is one which, like "the leg of a table" or "the heart of the matter," has been used so long and become so common that we have ceased to be aware of the discrepancy between vehicle and tenor. Many dead metaphors, however, are only moribund and can be brought back to life. Someone asked Groucho Marx, "Are you a man or a mouse?" He answered, "Throw me a piece of cheese and you'll find out." The recorded history of language indicates that a great many words that we now take to be literal were, in the distant past, metaphors.

Metaphors are essential to the functioning of language and have been the subject of copious analyses, and sharp disagreements, by rhetoricians, linguists, literary critics, and philosophers of language. For a discussion of diverse views, see the entry *metaphor, theories of.*

Some tropes, sometimes classified as species of metaphor, are more frequently and usefully given names of their own:

In **metonymy** (Greek for "a change of name") the literal term for one thing is applied to another with which it has become closely associated because of a recurrent relation in common experience. Thus "the crown" or "the scepter" can be used to stand for a king and "Hollywood" for the film industry; "Milton" can signify the writings of Milton ("I have read all of Milton"); and typical attire can signify the male and female sexes: "doublet and hose ought to show itself courageous to petticoat" (Shakespeare, *As You Like It*, II. iv. 6). (For the influential distinction by the linguist Roman Jakobson between the metaphoric, or "vertical," and the metonymic, or "horizontal," dimension, in application to many aspects of the functioning of language, see under *linguistics in literary criticism*.)

In **synecdoche** (Greek for "taking together"), a part of something is used to signify the whole, or (more rarely) the whole is used to signify a part. We use the term "ten *hands*" for ten workers, or "a hundred *sails*" for ships and, in current slang, "wheels" to stand for an automobile. By a bold use of the figure, Milton describes the corrupt and greedy clergy in "Lycidas" as "blind *mouths*."

Another figure related to metaphor is **personification**, or in the Greek term, **prosopopeia**, in which either an inanimate object or an abstract concept is spoken of as though it were endowed with life or with human attributes or feelings (compare *pathetic fallacy*). Milton wrote in *Paradise Lost* (IX. 1002–3), as Adam bit into the fatal apple,

> Sky lowered, and muttering thunder, some sad drops
> Wept at completing of the mortal sin.

The second stanza of Keats' "To Autumn" finely personifies the season, autumn, as a woman carrying on the rural chores of that time of year; and in *Aurora Leigh*, I. 251–2, Elizabeth Barrett Browning wrote:

> Then, land!—then, England! oh, the frosty cliffs
> Looked cold upon me.

The personification of abstract terms was standard in eighteenth-century *poetic diction*, where it sometimes became a thoughtless formula. Coleridge cited an eighteenth-century ode celebrating the invention of inoculation against smallpox that began with this *apostrophe* to the personified subject of the poem:

> Inoculation! heavenly Maid, descend!

See Steven Knapp, *Personification and the Sublime* (1985).

The term **kenning** denotes the recurrent use, in the Anglo-Saxon *Beowulf* and poems written in other Old Germanic languages, of a descriptive phrase in place of the ordinary name for something. This type of *periphrasis*, which at times becomes a stereotyped expression, is an indication of the origin of these poems in oral tradition (see *oral poetry*). Some kennings are instances of *metonymy* ("the whale road" for the sea, and "the ring-giver" for a king); others of *synecdoche* ("the ringed prow" for a ship); still others describe salient or picturesque features of the object referred to ("foamy-necked floater" for a ship under sail, "storm of swords" for a battle).

Other departures from the standard use of words, often classified as tropes, are treated elsewhere in this *Glossary*: *aporia, conceit, epic simile, hyperbole, irony, litotes, paradox, periphrasis, pun, understatement*. Since the mid-twentieth century, especially in the *New Criticism, Russian formalism*, and Harold Bloom's theory of the *anxiety of influence*, there has been a great interest in the analysis and functioning of figurative language, which was once thought to be largely the province of pedantic rhetoricians. In deconstructive criticism, especially in the writings by Jacques Derrida and Paul de Man, the analysis of figurative language is one of the primary ways of establishing what they assert to be the uncertainty and undecidability of meaning; see *deconstruction*.

A clear summary of the classification of figures that was inherited from the classical past is Edward P. J. Corbett, *Classical Rhetoric for the Modern Student* (3d ed., 1990). Arthur Quinn's lucid and amusing booklet, *Figures of Speech: 60 Ways to Turn a Phrase* (1993), treats mainly what this *Glossary* classifies as *rhetorical figures*. René Wellek and Austin Warren, in *Theory of Literature* (rev. 1970), summarize, with bibliography, diverse treatments of figurative language; and Jonathan Culler, in *The Pursuit of Signs* (1981), discusses the concern with this topic in deconstructive theory.

For references to *figurative language* in other entries, see pages *72, 151, 176, 311*. See also *rhetorical figures; style*. Refer also to the following figures: *allusion; ambiguity; anaphora; antithesis; aporia; conceit; epic simile; epithet; hyperbole and understatement; irony; kenning; litotes; paradox; pathetic fallacy; periphrasis; pun; symbol; synesthesia*. For figures of sound, see *alliteration; onomatopoeia; rhyme*.

**figures of speech: 119**.

**figures of thought: 118**.

**fin de siècle** (făn′ dĕ syĕk′ l): **69**.

**fine arts:** Fine arts in modern usage designates primarily the five arts of *literature*, painting, sculpture, music, and architecture. Individual works of art in all these modes are held to share a defining feature: they are objects that are to be regarded with a close, exclusive, and pleasurable attention.

This grouping of the arts did not appear, in the writings of philosophers and critics, until the latter part of the eighteenth century. During some two thousand years before that time, each of these arts had been treated separately, or else classified with such practical pursuits as agriculture and carpentry. When one of the arts was compared to another, it was only in a limited way; poetry, for example, was sometimes compared to painting, but only to make the point that both represented features of the outer world, in different media. The classification of the five arts as "the fine arts" was the result, in the course of the eighteenth century, of a drastic shift in the understructure of art theory. From the ancient Greeks until the eighteenth century, theorists and critics had assumed a maker's perspective toward the product of an art, and had analyzed its attributes in terms of a construction model. That is, they regarded a work of art, such as a poem, as something that an artisan makes according (in the Latin term) to an *ars*—that is, a craft. Each of the five arts, accordingly, was held to require a special kind of skill for manipulating its specific medium—words, or paint, or marble, or musical sounds, or building materials— into a product that its maker designed to have its own kind of use, and to fulfil a particular social function. In discussions of the art of literature—the most highly developed area of art criticism—this assumption of the maker's perspective toward a literary work united such theorists, in other respects very diverse, as Aristotle, Longinus, Horace, and the rhetoricians; all their writings were oriented toward instructing a poet in how to make a good poem, as well as toward helping a reader decide whether, and in what respects, the finished poem is a good poem.

In the course of the eighteenth century, there occurred a radical shift in the treatment of the arts—a shift from a maker's perspective and a construction model to a perceiver's perspective and a contemplation model. Underlying this change was a conspicuous social phenomenon in various major cities of Europe: the establishment and rapid proliferation of institutional arrangements for making each of the five diverse arts available—usually for pay—to a large and rapidly expanding public. In literature, the change from private patronage to the commercial manufacture and public sale of literary books made poems and novels available to a large audience, who bought them to read in isolation, for no purpose other than the interest and pleasure of doing so. That period also saw the founding, for the first time, of great public museums; in each museum, paintings and sculptures from various countries and eras, and of all types, religious and secular, were extracted from their original contexts and put together in one place and for a single purpose: as objects to be contemplated and enjoyed. In that same period, public concerts were inaugurated, where large audiences gathered in order to listen to and enjoy all sorts of musical compositions, vocal and instrumental, sacred and secular. The eighteenth century was also the era in which the phenomenon of tourism developed; in England, for example, many thousands of middle–class tourists visited cathedrals and great country estates, for no other purpose than to inspect and admire their architectural achievements.

Within a single century, then, the standard way of experiencing the hitherto diverse arts had become that of confronting their already-made products as objects of pleasurable attention. In consonance with this large-scale change in the mode of experiencing the arts, theorists shifted from the maker's perspective and a construction model of art to an observer's perspective and a contemplation model. Immanuel Kant, for example, in his immensely influential *Critique of Aesthetic Judgment* (1790), defined the normative judgment of all works of art as "purely contemplative," and as "a pure disinterested delight" in an object that "pleases for its own sake." The result of this paradigm shift was to group together all five arts—so patently different in their materials, their required skills, and their social functions—into the single class of "the fine arts," consisting of objects whose reason for being was simply to be read, or looked at, or listened to, for their own sake, simply for the pleasure of doing so.

Refer to the entry *aestheticism*. For the gradual emergence during the eighteenth century of the conception of "the fine arts" as a single class, see Paul Oskar Kristeller, "The Modern System of the Arts: A Study in the History of Aesthetics," *Journal of the History of Ideas*, Vol. 12 (1951), pp. 496-527, and Vol. 13 (1952), pp. 17-46. On the social and institutional developments, and the correlative conceptual changes, that led to this classification, see M. H. Abrams, "Art-as–Such: The Sociology of Modern Aesthetics," in *Doing Things with Texts: Essays in Criticism and Critical Theory* (1989).

**folklore:** Folklore, since the mid–nineteenth century, has been the collective name applied to sayings, verbal compositions, and social rituals that have been handed down solely, or at least primarily, by word of mouth and example rather than in written form. Folklore developed, and continues even now, in communities where few if any people can read or write. It also continues to flourish among literate populations, in the form of oral jokes, stories, and varieties of wordplay; see, for example, the collection of "urban folklore" by Alan Dundes and Carl R. Pagter, *When You're up to Your Ass in Alligators: More Urban Folklore from the Paperwork Empire* (1987). Folklore includes legends, superstitions, songs, tales, proverbs, riddles, spells, and nursery rhymes; pseudoscientific lore about the weather, plants, and animals; customary activities at births, marriages, and deaths; and traditional dances and forms of drama performed on holidays or at communal gatherings. Materials from folklore have at all times been employed in sophisticated written literature. For example, the choice among the three caskets in Shakespeare's *Merchant of Venice* (II. ix.) and the superstition about a maiden's dream which is central to Keats' *Eve of St. Agnes* (1820) are both derived from folklore. Refer to A. H. Krappe, *Science of Folklore* (1930, reprinted 1974); Richard M. Dorson, ed. *Folklore and Folklife: An Introduction* (1972).

The following forms of folklore have been of special importance for later written literature:

**Folk drama** originated in primitive rites of song and dance, especially in connection with agricultural activities, which centered on vegetational deities and goddesses of fertility. Some scholars maintain that Greek *tragedy* developed from such rites, which celebrated the life, death, and rebirth of the vegetational god Dionysus. Folk dramas survive in England in the forms of the St. George play and the **mummers' play** (a mummer is a masked actor). Thomas Hardy's *The Return of the Native* (Book II, chapter 5) describes the performance of a mummers' play, and a form of this drama is still performed in America in the Kentucky mountains. See Edmund K. Chambers, *The English Folk-Play* (1933).

**Folk songs** include love songs, Christmas carols, work songs, sea chanties, religious songs, drinking songs, children's game songs, and many other types of lyric, as well as the narrative song, or traditional *ballad*. (See *oral poetry*.) All forms of folk song have been assiduously collected since the late eighteenth century, and have inspired many imitations by writers of lyric poetry, as well as by composers of popular songs in the twentieth century. Robert Burns collected and edited Scottish folk songs, restored or rewrote them, and imitated them in his own lyrics. His "A Red, Red Rose" and "Auld Lang Syne," for example, both derive from one or more folk songs, and his "Green Grow the Rashes, O" is a tidied-up version of a bawdy folk song. See J. C. Dick, *The Songs of Robert Burns* (1903); Cecil J. Sharp, *Folk Songs of England* (5 vols., 1908–12); and Alan Lomax, *The Folk Songs of North America* (1960).

The **folktale**, strictly defined, is a short narrative in prose of unknown authorship which has been transmitted orally; many of these tales eventually achieve written form. The term, however, is often extended to include stories invented by a known author—such as "The Three Bears" by Robert Southey (1774–1843) and Parson Mason L. Weems' story of George Washington and the cherry tree —which have been picked up and repeatedly narrated by word of mouth as well as in written form. Folktales are found among peoples everywhere in the world.

They include *myths, fables,* tales of heroes (whether historical like Johnny Appleseed or legendary like Paul Bunyan), and fairy tales. Many so-called "fairy tales" (the German word **Märchen** is frequently used for this type of folktale) are not stories of fairies but of various kinds of marvels; examples are "Snow White" and "Jack and the Beanstalk." Another type of folk tale, the set "joke"—that is, the comic (often bawdy) *anecdote*—is the most abundant and persistent of all; new jokes, or new versions of old jokes, continue to be a staple of social exchange, wherever people congregate in a relaxed mood.

The same, or closely similar, oral stories have turned up in Europe, Asia, and Africa, and have been embodied in the narratives of many writers. Chaucer's *Canterbury Tales* includes a number of folktales; "The Pardoner's Tale" of Death and the three rioters, for example, was of Eastern origin. See Benjamin A. Botkin, *A Treasury of American Folklore* (1944); Stith Thompson, *The Folktale* (1974); and Vladimir Propp, *Morphology of the Folktale* (1970). The standard catalogue of recurrent *motifs* in folktales throughout the world is Stith Thompson's *Motif-Index of Folk-Literature* (1932–37).

**folktale: 124**; *9.*

**foot** (in meter): **195**.

**forced rhyme: 317**; *342.*

**foregrounding: 127**.

**forensic oratory** (fōrĕn′ sĭc): **311**.

**form and structure:** "Form" is one of the most frequent terms in literary criticism, but also one of the most diverse in its meanings. It is often used merely to designate a *genre* or literary type ("the lyric form," "the short story form"), or for patterns of meter, lines, and rhymes ("the verse form," "the stanza form"). It is also, however—in a sense descended from the Latin "forma," which was equivalent to the Greek "idea"—the term for a central critical concept. In this application, the **form** of a work is the principle that determines how a work is ordered and organized; critics, however, differ greatly in their analyses of this principle. All agree that "form" is not simply a fixed container, like a bottle, into which the "content" or "subject matter" of a work is poured; but beyond this, the concept of form varies according to a critic's particular assumptions and theoretical orientation (see *criticism*).

Many *neoclassic* critics, for example, thought of the form of a work as a combination of parts, matched to each other according to the principle of *decorum*, or mutual fittingness. In the early nineteenth century Samuel Taylor Coleridge, following the lead of the German critic A. W. Schlegel, distinguished between **mechanic form**, which is a fixed, pre-existent shape such as we impose on wet clay by a mold, and **organic form**, which, Coleridge says, "is innate; it shapes as it develops itself from within, and the fullness of its development is one and the same with the perfection of its outward form." To Coleridge, in other words, as to other **organicists** in literary criticism, a good poem is like a growing plant which evolves, by an internal energy, into the organic unity that constitutes its achieved form, in which the parts are integral to and interdependent with the whole. (On organic criticism and the concept of organic form, see M. H. Abrams, *The Mirror and the Lamp,* 1953, chapters 7–8; and George Rousseau, *Organic Form,* 1972.) Many *New Critics* use the word **structure** interchangeably with "form," and regard it as primarily an equilibrium, or interaction, or ironic and paradoxical tension, of diverse words and images in an organized totality of "meanings." Various exponents of *archetypal* theory regard the form of a literary work as one of a limited number of plot shapes which it shares with myths, rituals, dreams, and other elemental and recurrent patterns of human experience. And structuralist critics conceive a literary structure on the model of the systematic way that a language is structured; see *structuralist criticism.*

In an influential critical enterprise, R. S. Crane, a leader of the **Chicago School** of criticism, revived and developed the concept of form in Aristotle's *Poetics,* and made a distinction between "form" and "structure." The form of a literary work is (in the Greek term) the "dynamis," the particular "working" or "emotional power'" that the composition is designed to effect, which functions as its "shaping principle." This formal principle controls and synthesizes the "structure" of a work—that is, the order, emphasis, and rendering of all its component subject matter and parts—into "a beautiful and effective whole of a determinate kind." See R. S. Crane, *The Languages of Criticism and the Structure of Poetry* (1953), chapters 1 and 4; also Wayne C. Booth, "Between Two Generations: The Heritage of the Chicago School," in *Profession,* Vol. 82 (Modern Language Association, 1982).

See *formalism* and refer to René Wellek, "Concepts of Form and Structure in Twentieth-Century Criticism," in *Concepts of Criticism* (1963); Kenneth Burke, *The Philosophy of Literary Form* (3d ed., 1973); and Eugène Vinaver, *Form and Meaning in Medieval Romance* (1966). See also *plot.*

**formal essay: 103**.

**formal satire: 320**.

**formalism:** A type of literary theory and analysis which originated in Moscow and St. Petersburg in the second decade of the twentieth century. At first, opponents of the movement of **Russian Formalism** applied the term "formalism" derogatorily, because of its focus on the patterns and technical devices of literature to the exclusion of its subject matter and social values; later, however, it became a neutral designation. Among the leading representatives of the movement were Boris Eichenbaum, Victor Shklovsky, and Roman Jakobson. When this critical mode was suppressed by the Soviets in the early 1930s, the center of the formalist study of literature moved to Czechoslovakia, where it was continued especially by members of the **Prague Linguistic Circle**, which included Roman Jakobson (who had emigrated from Russia), Jan Mukarovsky, and René Wellek. Beginning in the 1940s both Jakobson and Wellek continued their influential work as professors at American universities.

Formalism views *literature* primarily as a specialized use of language, and proposes a fundamental opposition between the literary (or poetical) use of language and the ordinary, "practical" use of language. It proposes that the central function of ordinary language is to communicate to auditors a message, or information, by references to the world existing outside of language. In contrast, it conceives literary language to be self-focused, in that its function is not to convey information by making extrinsic references, but to offer the reader a special mode of experience by drawing attention to its own "formal" features—that is, to the qualities and internal relations of the linguistic signs themselves. The linguistics of literature differs from the linguistics of practical discourse, because its laws are oriented toward producing the distinctive features that formalists call **literariness**. As Roman Jakobson wrote in 1921: "The object of study in literary science is not literature but literariness,' that is, what makes a given work a literary work." (See *linguistics in modern criticism*.)

The literariness of a work, as Jan Mukarovsky, a member of the Prague Circle, described it in the 1920s, consists "in the maximum of **foregrounding** of the utterance," that is, the foregrounding of "the act of expression, the act of speech itself." (To "foreground" is to bring something into prominence, to make it dominant in perception.) By "backgrounding" the referential aspect and the logical connections in language, poetry makes the words themselves "palpable" as phonic signs. The primary aim of literature in thus foregrounding its linguistic medium, as Victor Shklovsky put it in an influential formulation, is to **estrange** or **defamiliarize**; that is, by disrupting the modes of ordinary linguistic discourse, literature "makes strange" the world of everyday perception and renews the reader's lost capacity for fresh sensation. (In the *Biographia Literaria*, 1817, Samuel Taylor Coleridge had long before described the "prime merit" of a literary genius to be the representation of "familiar objects" so as to evoke "freshness of sensation"; but whereas the Romantic critic had stressed the author's ability to express a fresh mode of experiencing the world, the formalist stresses the function of purely literary devices to produce the effect of freshness in the reader's experience of a literary work.) The foregrounded properties, or "artistic devices," which estrange poetic language are often described as "deviations" from ordinary language. Such deviations, which are analyzed most fully in the writings of Roman Jakobson, consist primarily in setting up, and afterward violating, patterns in the sound and syntax of poetic language—including patterns in speech sounds, grammatical constructions, rhythm, rhyme, and stanza forms—and also in setting up prominent recurrences of key words or images.

Some of the most fruitful work of Jakobson and others, valid outside the formalist perspective, has been in the analysis of *meter* and of the repetitions of sounds in *alliteration* and *rhyme*. These features of poetry they regard not as supplementary adornments of the meaning, but as effecting a reorganization of language on the semantic as well as the phonic and syntactic levels. Formalists have also made influential contributions to the theory of prose fiction. With respect to this genre, the central formalist distinction is that between the "story" (the simple enumeration of a chronological sequence of events) and a plot. An author is said to transform the raw material of a story into a literary *plot* by the use of a variety of devices that violate sequence and that deform and defamiliarize the story elements; the effect is to foreground the narrative medium and devices themselves, and in this way to disrupt and refresh what had been our standard responses to the subject matter. (See *narrative and narratology*.)

The standard treatment of the Russian movement is by Victor Erlich, *Russian Formalism: History, Doctrine* (rev. 1981). See also R. L. Jackson and S. Rudy, eds., *Russian Formalism: A Retrospective Glance* (1985). René Wellek has described *The*

*Literary Theory and Aesthetics of the Prague School* (1969). Representative formalist writings are collected in Lee T. Lemon and Marion I. Reese, eds., *Russian Formalist Criticism: Four Essays* (1965); Ladislav Matejka and Krystyna Pomorska, eds., *Readings in Russian Poetics: Formalist and Structuralist Views* (1971); P. L. Garvin, ed., *A Prague School Reader on Esthetics, Literary Structure and Style* (1964); and Peter Steiner, ed., *The Prague School: Selected Writings, 1929–1946* (1982). A comprehensive and influential formalist essay by Roman Jakobson, "Linguistics and Poetics," is included in his *Language in Literature* (1987). Samuel Levin's *Linguistic Structures in Poetry* (1962) represents an American application of formalist principles, and E. M. Thompson has written *Russian Formalism and Anglo-American New Criticism: A Comparative Study* (1971).

American *New Criticism*, although it developed independently, is sometimes called "formalist" because, like European formalism, it stresses the analysis of the literary work as a self-sufficient verbal entity, constituted by internal relations and independent of reference either to the state of mind of the author or to the actualities of the "external" world. It also, like European formalism, conceives poetry as a special mode of language whose distinctive features are defined in terms of their systematic opposition to practical or scientific language. Unlike the European formalists, however, the New Critics did not apply the science of linguistics to poetry, and their emphasis was not on a work as constituted by linguistic devices for achieving specifically literary effects, but on the complex interplay within a work of ironic, paradoxical, and metaphoric meanings around a humanly important "theme." The main influence of Russian and Czech formalism on American criticism has been on the development of *stylistics* and of *narratology*. Roman Jakobson and Tzvetan Todorov have also been influential in introducing formalist concepts and methods into French *structuralism*.

Strong opposition to formalism, in both its European and American varieties, has been voiced by some *Marxist critics* (who view it as the product of a reactionary ideology), and more recently by proponents of *reader-response criticism, speech-act theory*, and *new historicism*; these last three types of criticism all reject the view that there is a sharp and definable division between ordinary language and literary language. In the 1990s a number of critics called for a return to a formalist mode of treating a work of literature primarily as literature, instead of with persistent reference to its stand, whether explicit or covert, on political, racial, or sexual issues. A notable instance is Frank Lentricchia's "Last Will and Testament of an Ex-literary Critic" (*Lingua Franca*, Sept./Oct. 1996), renouncing his earlier writings and teachings "about literature as a political instrument," in favor of the view "that literature is pleasurable and important, as literature, and not as an illustration of something else." (Refer to *objective criticism*, under the entry in this *Glossary* on *criticism*.) See also Harold Bloom's advocacy of reading literature not to apply or confirm a political or social theory but for the love of literature, in *The Western Canon* (1994); and the essays in *Aesthetics and Ideology*, ed. George Levine (1994).

Toward the end of the last century, the formalist approach found a number of theoretical advocates. This return to formalism, building on a renewed interest in metrics (see *meter*) and in *aesthetics*, at first was proposed primarily as a reaction against the *new historicism*; but within a few years, what became known as the **new formalism** proposed a positive program, undertaking to connect the formal aspects of literature to the historical, political, and worldly concerns, in opposition to which the formalist movement had earlier defined itself. A number of new formalists argue that the formal integrity of a work of art is what protects it against *ideology*, idealization, and the routinizing effects of everyday experience; others emphasize that the perception of aesthetic or literary form is a necessary condition of critical thought.

The first major advocate of new formalism was Susan J. Wolfson in *Formal Charges: The Shaping of Poetry in British Romanticism* (1997). Wolfson and Marshall Brown edited a collection of new-formalist essays, *Reading for Form* (2006). See also W. J. T. Mitchell, "The Commitment to Form," *PMLA*, Vol. 118 (March 2003); and for an appreciative overview of the new-formalist movement, Marjorie Levenson, "What Is New Formalism?" *PMLA*, Vol. 122 (March 2007). For references to formalism (in literary criticism) in other entries, see pages *218, 261*.

**free verse:** Free verse is sometimes referred to as "open form" verse, or by the French term **vers libre**. Like traditional verse, it is printed in short lines instead of in continuous lines of prose, but it differs from such verse by the fact that its rhythmic pattern is not organized into a regular metrical form—that is, into feet, or recurrent units of weak- and strong-stressed syllables. (See *meter*.) Most free verse also has irregular line lengths, and either lacks rhyme or else uses it only sporadically. (*Blank verse* differs from unrhymed free verse in that it is metrically regular.)

Within these broad boundaries, there is a great diversity in the measures that are labeled free verse. An approximation to one modern form occurs in the King James translation of the biblical Psalms and Song of Solomon, which imitates in English prose the parallelism and cadences of Hebrew poetry. In the nineteenth century William Blake, Matthew Arnold, and other poets in England and America experimented with departures from regular meters; and in 1855 Walt Whitman startled the literary world with his *Leaves of Grass* by using verse lines of varying length which depended for rhythmic effects not on recurrent metric feet, but on cadenced units and on the repetition, balance, and variation of words, phrases, clauses, and lines. French *Symbolist* poets in the latter part of the nineteenth century, and American and English poets of the twentieth century, especially after World War I, began the present era of the intensive use of free verse. It has been employed by Rainer Maria Rilke, Jules Laforgue, T. S. Eliot, Ezra Pound, William Carlos Williams, and numberless contemporary poets in all the Western languages. Most of the verse in English that is published today is nonmetrical.

Among the many modes of open versification in English, we can make a broad distinction between the long-lined and often orotund verses of poets like Whitman and Allen Ginsberg, of which a principal origin is the translated poetry of the Hebrew Bible, and the shorter-lined, conversational, often ironic forms employed by the majority of writers in free verse. In the latter type, poets yield up the drive, beat, and song achievable by traditional meters in order to exploit other rhythmic possibilities. A poem by e. e. cummings will illustrate the effects that become available when the verse is released from a regular line and reiterative beat. Instead, cummings uses conspicuous visual cues—the variable positioning, spacing, and length of words, phrases, and lines—to control pace, pause, and emphasis in the reading, and also to achieve an alternation of suspension and relief, in accordance as the line endings work against or coincide with the pull toward closure of the units of syntax.

*Chanson Innocente*[4]

in Just-
spring        when the world is mud-
luscious the little
lame balloonman

whistles      far      and wee

and eddieandbill come
running from marbles and
piracies and it's
spring

when the world is puddle-wonderful

the queer
old balloonman whistles
far      and      wee
and bettyandisbel come dancing
from hop-scotch and jump-rope and

it's
spring
and
     the
          goat-footed
balloonMan        whistles
far
and
wee

In the following passage from Langston Hughes' free-verse poem "Mother to Son," the second and sixth lines are metrically parallel (in that both fall into fairly regular *iambic pentameter*) in order to enhance their opposition in reference; while the single word "bare," constituting a total verse line, is rhymed with "stair" in the long line to which "bare" contrasts starkly, in meaning as in length:

> *Mother to Son*[5]
>
> Well, son, I'll tell you:
> Life for me ain't been no crystal stair.
> It's had tacks in it,
> And splinters,
> And boards torn up,
> And places with no carpet on the floor—
> Bare.

A very short poem by A. R. Ammons exemplifies the unobtrusive way in which, even as he departs from them, a free-verse poet can recall and exploit traditional stanza forms and meters:

> *Small Song*[6]
>
> The reeds give
> way to the
>
> wind and give
> the wind away

The visual pattern of the printed poem signals that we are to read it as consisting of four equal lines of three words each, and as divided into two stanzaic *couplets*. The first line of each stanza ends with the same word, "give," not only to achieve tension and release in the suspended syntax of each of the verb phrases, but also, by means of the parallelism, to enhance our surprise at the shift of meaning from "give way" (surrender) to "give . . . away" (reveal, with a suggestion also of yield up). The poet also adapts standard metric feet to his special purposes: the poem is framed by opening and closing with a regular *iambic* foot, yet is free to mimic internally the resistance to the wind in the recurrent strong stresses in the first stanza (The réeds gíve / wáy) and the graceful yielding to the wind in the succession of light iambs in the second stanza (And gíve / theˇ wínd aˇwáy).

A number of contemporary poets and critics have called—in a movement sometimes labeled as "the new formalism"—for a return from free verse to the meters, rhyme, and stanza forms of traditional English versification. For discussions see Alan Shapiro, "The New Formalism," *Critical Inquiry*, Vol. 14 (1987); and Dana Gioia, "Notes on the New Formalism," in *Conversant Essays*, ed. James McCorkle (1990).

See Percy Mansell Jones, *The Background of Modern French Poetry* (1951); Donald Wesling, "The Prosodies of Free Verse," in *Twentieth-Century Literature in Retrospect*, ed. Reuben A. Brower (1971); Walter Sutton, *American Free Verse*

---

[5]"Mother to Son" by Langston Hughes from Collected Poems. Reprinted by permission of Harold Ober Associates, Inc.

[6]"Small Song" is reprinted from The Really Short Poems of A. R. Ammons, by permission of W. W. Norton & Company, Inc. Copyright © 1990 by A. R. Ammons.

(1973); Paul Fussell, *Poetic Meter and Poetic Form* (rev. 1979); Charles O. Hartman, *Free Verse: An Essay on Prosody* (1980). Timothy Steele's *Missing Measures: Modern Poetry and the Revolt against Meter* (1990) is a history of free verse by a writer who argues for a return to metrical versification. For references to *free verse* in other entries, see pages *199, 288*.

**Freudian criticism:** See *psychological and psychoanalytic criticism*.

**Freytag's Pyramid: 267**.

**gangsta rap: 244**.

**gay studies: 296**; *132*.

**gender: 111**; *293*.

**gender criticism:** Gender criticism, like the **gender studies** of which it is a part, is based on the premise that, while sex (a person's identification as male or female) is determined by anatomy, gender (masculinity or femininity in personality traits and behavior) can be largely independent of anatomy, and is a *social construction* that is diverse, variable, and dependent on historical circumstances. Gender criticism analyzes differing conceptions of gender and their role in the writing, reception, subject matter, and evaluation of literary works.

　　Gender studies have an obvious (and sometimes contentious) overlap with *feminist criticism, gay studies*, and *lesbian studies*; the distinguishing attribute of gender studies has come to be their special attention to the roles of males, and of varying conceptions of masculinity, in the course of social, political, and artistic history. A field of scholarship known as **men's studies** was established early in the 1980s on the model of the pre-existing field of *women's studies*. Proponents of men's studies did not contest the overall fact of *patriarchy*—male privilege and domination over women throughout the social history of the West—but undertook to complicate and subtilize the opposition of oppressors and victims by stressing the variety of male roles, or "masculinities," the internal stresses within each concept of masculinity, and the degree to which patriarchal dominance tended to distort the characters of men as well as women. Early on, a number of feminist scholars decried men's studies as in fact complicit with the patriarchy they ostensibly opposed, and as reinforcing the predominant place of the male in scholarship and the college curriculum. In the course of time, however, tensions have lessened, while a number of courses in women's studies have broadened their scope so as to become, in effect, gender studies. (See Harry Brod, ed., *The Making of Masculinities: The New Men's Studies*, 1987; Alice Jardine and Paul Smith, eds., *Men in Feminism*, 1987; Judith Kegan Gardiner, ed., *Masculinity Studies and Feminist Theory: New Directions*, 2002.)

　　Gender studies are indebted to the social historian Michel Foucault, who analyzed all sexual identities, whether perceived to be normal or transgressive, as constructed and reconstructed in various eras of social discourses under the impulse of the power-drive. In addition, two feminist scholars wrote books that were not only important for gay/lesbian as well as feminist studies, but also helped to give impetus and shape to men's studies and to the analysis of the nature and plurality of masculinities. In 1985 Eve Kosofsky Sedgwick published *Between Men: English Literature and Male Homosocial Desire*, which proposed that there is a large "homosocial spectrum" of male-to-male bondings, ranging from fierce rivalry through a variety of relationships within families, friendships, and all-male societies and organizations, to patently erotic desires and intimacies; she also held that these relationships were crossed, concealed, or distorted by a pervasive homophobia— the fear that one's bondings to other men, whatever its type, should appear to be homosexual, to oneself as well as to other people. In 1990 Judith Butler published *Gender Trouble: Feminism and the Subversion of Identity*. In it she argued that gender is not an innate or essential identity, but a contingent and variable construct that mandates a "performance"—that is, a particular set of practices which an individual acquires from the discourse of his or her social era and strives to enact. (Refer to the comments on Foucault, Sedgwick, and Butler in the entries *feminist criticism* and *queer theory*.)

The predominant emphasis on same-sex desires and on intersexual rivalries in forming masculine and other gender categories has been countered by a number of scholars who insist on the importance of such nonsexual factors as race, ethnicity, economic arrangements, and social class in establishing different types and ideals of manhood. David Leverenz, for example, in *Manhood and the American Renaissance* (1989), attributes the chief influence in fashioning American "ideologies of manhood" to altering economic conditions and class structures. Leverenz stresses the primacy, from the mid-nineteenth century into the present, of the economic era of competitive individualism in establishing middle-class norms of manhood that are based on male rivalry in the working arena, and points out the pervasive effect of the struggle for dominance and status, not of men against women, but of men against other men. James Eli Adams' *Dandies and Desert Saints: Styles of Victorian Masculinity* (1995) analyzes the multiplicity, the multiple determinants, the surprising interrelationships, and the internal strains and instabilities of diverse Victorian masculinities and ideals of "manliness." He identifies shared interests that were dependent on social class, occupation, political allegiance, and religious beliefs, as well as same-sex desires and object-choices, which bonded Victorian men into a diversity of tight-knit groups and sometimes secret communities, and describes the mixed feelings of suspicion, fear, and allure exerted on outsiders by such closed male fellowships, including those that did not have a homosexual component.

Scholars of gender, and particularly of masculinities, focus on eras when rapid changes in social conditions have produced conspicuous strains and alterations in gender-norms. The Victorian period has been a favorite one for these investigations. Another is the present era, in which the vogue of gender studies has itself served to make even more uncertain, precarious, and mutable the gender roles that such studies subject to analytic scrutiny.

Gender studies are interdisciplinary, and are conducted by sociologists, cultural anthropologists, and social historians, as well as by scholars of literature and cinema. The following books indicate the range of these studies: Joseph H. Pleck, *The Myth of Masculinity* (1981); Carroll Smith-Rosenberg, *Disorderly Conduct:*

*Visions of Gender in Victorian America* (1985); Peter G. Filene, *Him/Her/Self: Sex Roles in Modern America* (rev. 1986); Teresa de Lauretis, *Technologies of Gender: Essays on Theory, Film, and Fiction* (1987); Mary Poovey, *Uneven Developments: The Ideological Work of Gender in Mid-Victorian England* (1988); Rita Felski, *The Gender of Modernity* (1995). Consult also the essays collected in Joseph A. Boone and Michael Cadden, eds., *Engendering Men: The Question of Male Feminist Criticism* (1990); Michael Roper and James Tosh, eds., *Manful Assertions: Masculinities in Britain since 1800* (1991); David Glover and Cora Kaplan, eds., *Genders* (2000); Rachel Adams and David Savran, eds., *The Masculinity Studies Reader* (2002). See also Eve Kosofsky Sedgwick, "Gender Criticism: What Isn't Gender," in Stephen Greenblatt and Giles Gunn, eds., *Redrawing the Boundaries: The Transformation of English and American Literary Studies* (1992).

**gender studies: 132**.

**generative linguistics: 176**.

**Geneva School** (of criticism): **261**.

**genres:** A term, French in origin, that denotes types or classes of *literature*. The genres into which literary works have been grouped at different times are very numerous, and the criteria on which the classifications have been based are highly variable. Since the writings of Plato and Aristotle, however, there has been an enduring division of the overall literary domain into three large classes, in accordance with who speaks in the work: *lyric* (uttered throughout in the first person), *epic* or *narrative* (in which the narrator speaks in the first person, then lets the characters speak for themselves); and *drama* (in which the characters do all the talking). A similar tripartite scheme, elaborated by German critics in the late eighteenth and early nineteenth centuries, was echoed by James Joyce in his *Portrait of the Artist as a Young Man* (1916), chapter 5, and functions still in critical discourse and in the general distinction, in college catalogues, between courses in poetry, prose fiction, and drama.

Within this overarching division, Aristotle and other classical critics identified a number of more specific genres. Many of the ancient names, including *epic, tragedy, comedy*, and *satire*, have remained current to the present day; to them have been added, over the last three centuries, such relative newcomers as *biography, essay*, and *novel*. A glance at the genres in prose and verse listed at the end of this entry will indicate the crisscrossing diversity of the classes and subclasses to which individual works of literature have been assigned.

Through the Renaissance and much of the eighteenth century, the recognized genres—or poetic **kinds** as they were then called—were widely thought to be fixed literary types, somewhat like species in the biological order of nature. Many *neoclassic* critics insisted that each kind must remain "pure" (there must, for example, be no "mixing" of tragedy and comedy), and also proposed *rules* which specified the subject matter, structure, style, and emotional effect proper to each kind. At that time the genres were also commonly ranked in a hierarchy (related to the ranking of social classes, from royalty and the nobility down to peasants—see *deco-*

*rum)*, ranging from epic and tragedy at the top to the pastoral, short lyric, epigram, and other types—then considered to be minor genres—at the bottom. Shakespeare satirized the pedantic classifiers of his era in Polonius' catalogue (*Hamlet*, II. ii.) of types of drama: "tragedy, comedy, history, pastoral, pastoral-comical, historical-pastoral, tragical-historical, tragical-comical-historical-pastoral. . . ."

In the course of the eighteenth century the emergence of new types of literary productions—such as the novel, and the poem combining description, philosophy, and narrative (James Thomson's *Seasons*, 1726–30)—helped weaken confidence in the fixity and stability of literary genres. And in the late eighteenth and early nineteenth century, the extraordinary rise in the prominence and prestige of the short lyric poem, and the concurrent shift in the basis of critical theory to an *expressive* orientation (see the entry *criticism*), effected a drastic alteration both in the conception and ranking of literary genres, with the lyric displacing epic and tragedy as the quintessentially poetic type. From the *Romantic Period* on, a decreasing emphasis on the generic conception of literature was indicated by the widespread use of criteria for evaluating literature which—unlike the criteria in *neoclassic* criticism, which tended to be specific to a particular genre—were broadly applicable to all literary works: criteria such as "sincerity," "intensity," "organic unity," and "high seriousness." In the *New Criticism* of the mid-twentieth century, with its ruling concept of the uniqueness of each literary work, genre ceased to play more than a subordinate role in critical analysis and evaluation. For the changes in the nineteenth century in the classification and ranking of the genres, see M. H. Abrams, *The Mirror and the Lamp* (1953), especially chapters 1, 4, and 6; on the continuance, as well as changes, of writings in the traditional genres during the Romantic Period, see Stuart Curran, *Poetic Form and British Romanticism* (1986).

After 1950 or so, an emphasis on generic types was revived by some critical theorists, although on varied principles of classification. R. S. Crane and other Chicago critics have defended the utility for practical criticism of a redefined distinction among genres, based on Aristotle's *Poetics*, in which works are classified in accordance with the similarity in the principles by which they are organized in order to achieve a particular kind of emotional effect; see R.S. Crane, ed., *Critics and Criticism* (1952), pp. 12–24, 546–63, and refer to the *Chicago school* in this *Glossary*. Northrop Frye has proposed an *archetypal* theory in which the four major genres (comedy, romance, tragedy, and satire) are held to manifest the enduring forms bodied forth by the human imagination, as represented in the archetypal myths correlated with the four seasons (*Anatomy of Criticism*, 1957, pp. 158–239). Other current theorists conceive genres as social formations on the model of social institutions, such as the state or church, rather than on the model of biological species. By *structuralist critics* a genre is conceived as a set of constitutive conventions and codes, altering from age to age, but shared by a kind of implicit contract between writer and reader. These codes make possible the writing of a particular literary text, although the writer may play against, as well as with, the prevailing generic conventions. In the reader, these conventions generate a set of expectations, which may be controverted rather than satisfied, but enable the reader to make the work intelligible—that is, to *naturalize* it, by relating it to the world as defined and ordered by codes in the prevailing culture.

Many current critics regard genres as more or less arbitrary modes of classification, whose justification is their convenience in discussing literature. Some critics have applied to generic classes the philosopher Ludwig Wittgenstein's concept of **family resemblances**. That is, they propose that, in the loosely grouped family of works that make up a genre, there are no essential defining features, but only a set of family resemblances; each member shares some of these resemblances with some, but not all, of the other members of the genre. (For a description and discussion of Wittgenstein's view, see Maurice Mandelbaum, "Family Resemblances and Generalization Concerning the Arts," *American Philosophical Quarterly*, Vol. 2 (1965), pp. 219–28, and Carlo Ginzburg, "Family Resemblances and Family Trees: Two Cognitive Metaphors," *Critical Inquiry*, Vol. 30 (2004), pp. 537–56.) There has also been interest in the role that generic assumptions have played in shaping the work that an author composes, as well as in establishing expectations that alter the way that a reader will interpret and respond to a particular work. Whatever the present skepticism, however, about the old belief that genres constitute inherent species in the realm of literature, the fact that generic distinctions remain indispensable in literary discourse is attested by the unceasing publication of books whose titles announce that they deal with tragedy, the lyric, pastoral, the novel, or another of the many types and subtypes into which literature has over the centuries been classified.

Reviews of traditional theories of genre are René Wellek and Austin Warren, *Theory of Literature* (3d ed., 1973), chapter 17, and the readable short survey by Heather Dubrow, *Genre* (1982). For more recent developments see Paul Hernadi, *Beyond Genre: New Directions in Literary Classification* (1972); Alastair Fowler, *Kinds of Literature: An Introduction to the Theory of Genres and Modes* (1982); Adena Rosmarin, *The Power of Genre* (1985); and David Duff, ed., *Modern Genre Theory* (2000). For a Marxist approach, see Fredric Jameson, "Magical Narratives: On the Dialectical Use of Genre Criticism," chapter two of *The Political Unconscious: Narrative as a Socially Symbolic Act* (1981); for a deconstructive approach, see Jacques Derrida, "The Law of Genre," *Critical Inquiry* (Autumn 1980; reprinted in W. J. T. Mitchell, ed., *On Narrative*, 1981); and for an approach indebted to discourse analysis, see John Frow, *Genre* (2006). See the special issue of *PMLA*, Vol.122:5 (October 2007) on "Remapping Genre."

For references to *genre* in other entries, see pages *16, 42, 207, 217.* For prose genres, see *autobiography; biography; the character; drama; essay; exemplum; fable; fantastic literature; nature writing; novel; parable; satire; short story.* For verse genres, see *ballad; chivalric romance; drama; emblem poem; epic; epigram; fable; fabliau; georgic; lai; light verse; lyric; occasional poem; pastoral; rap; satire.*

**Georgian period:** 256.

**Georgian poets:** 256.

**georgic** (jôr′ jik): **79**.

**golden age:** The term derives from the *chronological primitivism* that was propounded in the Greek poet Hesiod's *Works and Days* (eighth century BC), as well as by many later Greek and Roman writers. The earliest period of human history, regarded as a state of perfect felicity, was called "the golden age," and the continuous decline of human well-being through time was expressed by the sequence "the silver age" and "the bronze age," ending with the present sad condition of humanity, "the iron age." See *primitivism and progress* and, for renderings of the golden age in the guise of a carefree rural existence, *pastoral*. Refer to Harry Levin, *The Myth of the Golden Age in the Renaissance* (1969).

**Gothic novel:** The word **Gothic** originally referred to the Goths, an early Germanic tribe, then came to signify "germanic," then "medieval." "Gothic architecture" now denotes the medieval form of architecture, characterized by the use of the high pointed arch and vault, flying buttresses, and intricate recesses, which spread through western Europe between the twelfth and sixteenth centuries.

    The **Gothic novel**, or in an alternative term, **Gothic romance**, is a type of prose fiction which was inaugurated by Horace Walpole's *The Castle of Otranto: A Gothic Story* (1764)—the subtitle denotes its setting in the Middle Ages—and flourished through the early nineteenth century. Some writers followed Walpole's example by setting their stories in the medieval period; others set them in a Catholic country, especially Italy or Spain. The locale was often a gloomy castle furnished with dungeons, subterranean passages, and sliding panels; the typical story focused on the sufferings imposed on an innocent heroine by a cruel and lustful villain, and made bountiful use of ghosts, mysterious disappearances, and other sensational and supernatural occurrences (which in a number of novels turned out to have natural explanations). The principal aim of such novels was to evoke chilling terror by exploiting mystery and a variety of horrors. Many of them are now read mainly as period pieces, but the best opened up to fiction the realm of the irrational and of the perverse impulses and nightmarish terrors that lie beneath the orderly surface of the civilized mind. Examples of Gothic novels are William Beckford's *Vathek* (1786)—the setting of which is both medieval and Oriental and the subject both erotic and sadistic—Ann Radcliffe's *The Mysteries of Udolpho* (1794) and other highly successful romances, and Matthew Gregory Lewis' *The Monk* (1796), which exploited, with considerable literary skill, the shock effects of a narrative involving rape, incest, murder, and diabolism. Jane Austen made good-humored fun of the more decorous instances of the Gothic vogue in *Northanger Abbey* (written 1798, published 1818).

    The term "Gothic" has also been extended to a type of fiction which lacks the exotic setting of the earlier romances, but develops a brooding *atmosphere* of gloom and terror, represents events that are uncanny or macabre or melodramatically violent, and often deals with aberrant psychological states. In this extended sense the term "Gothic" has been applied to William Godwin's *Caleb Williams* (1794), Mary Shelley's remarkable and influential *Frankenstein* (1818), and the novels and tales of terror by the German E. T. A. Hoffmann. Still more loosely, "Gothic" has been used to describe elements of the macabre and terrifying that are included in such later works as Emily Brontë's *Wuthering Heights*, Charlotte Brontë's *Jane Eyre*, Charles Dickens' *Bleak House* (for example, chapters 11, 16, and 47) and *Great Expectations* (the Miss Havisham episodes). Critics have recently drawn attention to the many women writers of Gothic fiction, and have explained features of the mode as the result of the suppression of female sexuality, or else as a challenge to the gender hierarchy and values of a male-dominated culture. See *feminist criticism* and refer to Sandra Gilbert and Susan Gubar, *The Madwoman in the Attic* (1979), and Juliann E. Fleenor, ed., *The Female Gothic* (1983).

America, especially the American South, has been fertile in Gothic fiction in the extended sense, from the novels of Charles Brockden Brown (1771–1810) and the terror tales of Edgar Allan Poe to William Faulkner's *Sanctuary* and *Absalom, Absalom!* and some of the fiction of Truman Capote. The nightmarish realm of uncanny terror, violence, and cruelty opened by the Gothic novel continued to be explored in novels such as Daphne du Maurier's popular *Rebecca* (1938) and Iris Murdoch's *The Unicorn*; it is also exploited by authors of horror fiction such as H. P. Lovecraft and Stephen King, and by the writers and directors of innumerable horror movies.

See G. R. Thompson, ed., *The Gothic Imagination: Essays in Dark Romanticism* (1974); William Patrick Day, *In the Circles of Fear and Desire* (1985); David Punter, *The Literature of Terror: A History of Gothic Fiction from 1765 to the Present* (1979; 2d ed., 1996); Eugenia DeLamotte, *Perils of the Night* (1990); Anne Williams, *Art of Darkness* (1995); Victor Sage and Allan Lloyd Smith, eds., *Modern Gothic: A Reader* (1996); Fred Botting, *Gothic* (1996); E. J. Clery and Robert Miles, eds., *Gothic Documents: A Sourcebook, 1700-1820* (2000). On "American Gothic"—and especially the "southern Gothic"—see Chester E. Eisinger, "The Gothic Spirit in the Forties," *Fiction in the Forties* (1963). For references to *Gothic novel* in other entries, see pages *228, 255, 355*.

**grammar: 173**; *347*.

**grammar of narration: 208**.

**grand style: 98**.

**Graveyard Poets:** A term applied to eighteenth-century poets who wrote meditative poems, usually set in a graveyard, on the theme of human mortality, in moods which range from elegiac pensiveness to profound gloom. Examples are Thomas Parnell's "Night-Piece on Death" (1721), Edward Young's long *Night Thoughts* (1742), and Robert Blair's "The Grave" (1743). The vogue resulted in one of the best-known English poems, Thomas Gray's "Elegy Written in a Country Churchyard" (1751). The writing of graveyard poems spread from England to Continental literature in the second part of the century and is represented in America by William Cullen Bryant's "Thanatopsis" (1817).

See Amy Louise Reed, *The Background of Gray's Elegy* (1924). Edith M. Sickels, in *The Gloomy Egoist* (1932), follows the evolution of graveyard and other melancholy verse through the Romantic Period. For the vogue in Europe, refer to Paul Von Tieghem, *Le Pré-romantisme* (3 vols., 1924–47).

**Great Chain of Being:** The conception of the Great Chain of Being is grounded in ideas about the nature of God, or (in metaphysical terms) the First Cause, in the Greek philosophers Plato, Aristotle, and Plotinus, and was developed by later thinkers into a comprehensive philosophy to account for the origin, types, and relationships of all living things in the universe. This worldview was already prevalent in the Renaissance, but was refined and greatly developed by the German philosopher Gottfried Leibniz early in the eighteenth century, and then adopted by a number of thinkers of the *Enlightenment*. In its comprehensive eighteenth-century form, the Great Chain of Being was based on the concept that the essential "excellence" of God consists in His limitless creativity—that is, in an unstinting, unjealous overflow of His own being into the fullest possible variety of other beings. From this premise were deduced three consequences:

1. Plenitude. The universe is absolutely full of every possible kind and variety of life; no conceivable species of being remains unrealized.
2. Continuity. Each species differs from the next by the least possible degree, and so merges all but imperceptibly into the species most nearly related to it.
3. Gradation. The existing species exhibit a hierarchy of status, and so compose a great chain, or ladder, of being, extending from the lowliest condition of the merest existence up to God Himself. In this chain human beings occupy the middle position between the animal kinds and the angels, who are purely spiritual beings.

On these concepts Leibniz and other thinkers also grounded what is called **philosophical optimism**—the view that this is "the best of all possible worlds," but only in the special sense that this is the best world whose existence is logically possible. The reasoning underlying this claim is that, since God's bountifulness consists in His creation of the greatest possible variety of graded beings, aspects of created life that to our limited human point of view seem to be deficient or evil can be recognized, from an overall cosmic viewpoint, to follow necessarily from the very excellence of the divine nature. This excellence logically entails that there must be a progressive set of limitations, hence increasing "evils," as we move downward along the chain of being. As Voltaire ironically summarized this mode of optimism in his era, "This is the best of all possible worlds, and everything in it is a necessary evil."

With remarkable precision and economy, Alexander Pope compressed the basic concepts that make up the Great Chain of Being into a half-dozen or so *heroic couplets*, in Epistle I of his *Essay on Man* (1732–34):

> Of systems possible, if 'tis confessed
> That Wisdom Infinite must form the best,
> Where all must full or not coherent be,
> And all that rises rise in due degree;
> Then in the scale of reasoning life, 'tis plain,
> There must be, somewhere, such a rank as man. . . .
> See, through this air, this ocean, and this earth,
> All matter quick, and bursting into birth. . . .

> Vast Chain of Being! which from God began,
> Natures ethereal, human, angel, man,
> Beast, bird, fish, insect, what no eye can see,
> No glass can reach! from Infinite to thee,
> From thee to nothing. . . .

Philosophical optimism is one type of what is known as a **theodicy**. This term, compounded of the Greek words for "God" and "right," designates any system of thought which sets out to reconcile the assumption that God is perfectly good with the fact that evil exists. Milton's "great argument" in *Paradise Lost*, by which he undertakes to "assert Eternal Providence / And justify the ways of God to men" (I. 24–26) is an example of a traditional Christian theodicy, explaining evil as the result of "man's first disobedience" in Eden to a perfectly just God, which "Brought death into the world, and all our woe."

See A. O. Lovejoy's classic work in the history of ideas, *The Great Chain of Being* (1936); also E. M. W. Tillyard, *The Elizabethan World Picture* (1943), chapters 4–5, which deals with the prevalence of the conception in Shakespeare's lifetime.

**green studies: 87.**

**grounds** (of a metaphor): **119**.

**gull** (in drama): **344**.

**gynocriticism: 112**.

**hagiography** (hăg′ ē̄ŏg″ răfē): **25**.

**haiku** (sometimes spelled **hokku**): Haiku is a Japanese poetic form that represents—in seventeen syllables that are ordered into three lines of five, seven, and five syllables—the poet's emotional or spiritual response to a natural object, scene, or season of the year. The strict form, which relies on the short, uniform, and unstressed syllabic structure of the Japanese language, is extremely difficult in English; most poets who attempt the haiku loosen the rule for the number and pattern of the syllables. The haiku greatly influenced Ezra Pound and other Imagists, who set out to reproduce both the brevity and the precision of the image in the Japanese original. Ezra Pound's "In a Station of the Metro" is a well-known instance of the haiku in the loosened English form; see this poem under *imagism*.

Earl R. Miner, *The Japanese Tradition in British and American Literature* (1958); R. H. Blyth, *A History of Haiku* (2 vols., 1963–64); Bruce Ross, ed., *Haiku Moment: An Anthology of Contemporary North American Haiku* (1993).

**hamartia** (hämärtē′ a): **371**.

**Harlem Renaissance:** A period of remarkable creativity in literature, music, dance, painting, and sculpture by African-Americans, from the end of the First World War in 1917 through the 1920s. In the course of the mass migrations to the urban

North in order to escape the legal segregation of the American South—and also in order to take advantage of the jobs opened to African-Americans at the beginning of the War—the population of the region of Manhattan known as Harlem became almost exclusively black, and developed into the vital center of African-American culture in America. Distinguished writers who were part of the movement included the poets Countee Cullen, Langston Hughes (who also wrote novels and plays), Claude McKay, and Sterling Brown; the novelists Jean Toomer (whose inventive *Cane*, 1923, included verse and drama as well as prose fiction), Jessie Fauset, and Wallace Thurman; and many essayists, memoirists, and writers in diverse modes such as James Weldon Johnson, Marcus Garvey, and Arna Bontemps.

The Great Depression of 1929 and the early 1930s brought the period of buoyant Harlem culture—which had been fostered by prosperity in the publishing industry and the art world—effectively to an end. Zora Neale Hurston's novel *Their Eyes Were Watching God* (1937), and her other works, however, are widely accounted as late products of the Harlem Renaissance.

See *The New Negro: An Interpretation* (1925), an anthology edited by Alain Locke that did much to define the spirit of the Harlem Renaissance; Arna Bontemps, ed., *The Harlem Renaissance Remembered* (1972); David Levering Lewis, ed., *The Portable Harlem Renaissance Reader* (1994); David Levering Lewis, *When Harlem Was in Vogue* (1997); Steven Watson, *The Harlem Renaissance: Hub of African-American Culture, 1920-1930* (1995); Cheryl Wall, *Women of the Harlem Renaissance* (1995); George Hutchinson, *The Harlem Renaissance in Black and White* (1995); William L. Andrews, Frances Smith Foster, Trudier Harris, eds., *The Concise Oxford Companion to African American Literature* (2001).

**hegemony** (hĕ jĕm′ ŏnē): **185**.

**heptameter** (hĕptăm′ ĕter): **196**.

**hermeneutic circle** (hĕr′ mĕnoo″ tĭk): **158**.

**hermeneutics: 158**; *81*.

**hermeneutics of suspicion: 283**; *161, 184*.

**hero** (in a narrative): **265**; *14*.

**heroic couplet:** Lines of iambic pentameter (see *meter*) which rhyme in pairs: *aa, bb, cc*, and so on. The adjective "heroic" was applied in the later seventeenth century because of the frequent use of such couplets in heroic (that is, *epic*) poems and in *heroic dramas*. This verse form was introduced into English poetry by Geoffrey Chaucer (in *The Legend of Good Women* and most of *The Canterbury Tales*), and has been in constant use ever since. From the age of John Dryden through that of Samuel Johnson, the heroic couplet was the predominant English measure for all the poetic kinds; some poets, including Alexander Pope, used it almost to the exclusion of other meters.

In that era, usually called the *Neoclassic Period*, the poets wrote **closed couplets**, in which the end of each pair of lines tends to coincide with the end either of a sentence or of a self-sufficient unit of syntax. The sustained employment of the closed heroic couplet meant that two lines had to serve something of the function of a stanza. In order to maximize the interrelationships of the component parts of the couplet, neoclassic poets often used an end-stopped first line (that is, made the end of the line coincide with a pause in the syntax), and also broke many single lines into subunits by balancing the line around a strong *caesura*, or medial pause in the syntax.

The following passage from John Denham's *Cooper's Hill* (which he added in the version of 1655) is an early instance of the artful management of the closed couplet that fascinated later neoclassic poets; they quoted it and commented upon it again and again, and used it as a model for exploiting the potentialities of this verse form. (See the comment on *Cooper's Hill* under *topographical poetry*.) Note how Denham achieves diversity within the straitness of his couplets by shifts in the position of the caesuras, by the use of rhetorical balance and *antithesis* between the single lines and between the two halves within a single line, and by the variable positioning of the adjectives in the second couplet. Note also the framing and the emphasis gained by inverting the iambic foot that begins the first line and the last line, and by manipulating similar and contrasting vowels and consonants. The poet is addressing the River Thames:

> O could I flow like thee, and make thy stream
> My great example, as it is my theme!
> Though deep, yet clear; though gentle, yet not dull;
> Strong without rage, without o'erflowing full.

And here is a passage from Alexander Pope, the greatest master of the metrical, syntactical, and rhetorical possibilities of the closed heroic couplet ("Of the Characters of Women," 1735, lines 243–48):

> See how the world its veterans rewards!
> A youth of frolics, an old age of cards;
> Fair to no purpose, artful to no end,
> Young without lovers, old without a friend;
> A fop their passion, but their prize a sot;
> Alive, ridiculous, and dead, forgot!

These closed neoclassic couplets contrast with the "open" pentameter couplets quoted from Keats' *Endymion* (1818) in the entry on *meter*. In the latter, the pattern of stresses varies often from the iambic norm, the syntax is unsymmetrical, and the couplets run on freely, with the rhyme serving to color rather than to stop the verse.

See George Williamson, "The Rhetorical Pattern of Neoclassical Wit," *Modern Philology*, Vol. 33 (1935); W. K. Wimsatt, "One Relation of Rhyme to Reason (Alexander Pope)," in *The Verbal Icon* (1954); William Bowman Piper, *The Heroic Couplet* (1969). For references to *heroic couplet* in other entries, see pages *139, 369.*

**heroic drama:** Heroic drama was a form mainly specific to the *Restoration Period*, though instances continued to be written in the early eighteenth century. As

John Dryden defined it: "An heroic play ought to be an imitation, in little, of an heroic poem; and consequently . . . love and valour ought to be the subject of it" (Preface to *The Conquest of Granada*, 1672). By "heroic poem" he meant *epic*, and the plays attempted to emulate the epic by employing as protagonist a large-scale warrior whose actions involve the fate of an empire, and by having all the characters speak in an elevated style, usually cast in the epigrammatic form of the closed *heroic couplet*. A noble hero and heroine are typically represented in a situation in which their passionate love conflicts with the demands of honor and with the hero's patriotic duty to his country; if the conflict ends in disaster, the play is called an **heroic tragedy**. Often the central dilemma is patently contrived and the characters seem to modern readers to be statuesque and unconvincing, while the attempt to sustain a high epic style swells sometimes into *bombast*, as in this utterance from Dryden's *Love Triumphant* (1693): "What woods are these? I feel my vital heat / Forsake my limbs, my curdled blood retreat."

Dryden is the major writer of this dramatic form; *The Conquest of Granada* is one of the better heroic tragedies, but Dryden's most successful achievement is *All for Love* (1678), which is an adaptation to the heroic formula of Shakespeare's *Antony and Cleopatra*. Other heroic dramatists were Nathaniel Lee (*The Rival Queens*) and Thomas Otway, whose *Venice Preserved* is a fine tragedy that transcends the limitations of the form. We also owe indirectly to heroic tragedy two very amusing *parodies* of the type: the Duke of Buckingham's *The Rehearsal* (1672) and Henry Fielding's *The Tragedy of Tragedies, or the Life and Death of Tom Thumb the Great* (1731).

See Bonamy Dobrée, *Restoration Tragedy* (1929); Allardyce Nicoll, *Restoration Drama* (1955); Arthur C. Kirsch, *Dryden's Heroic Drama* (1965). For references to *heroic drama* in other entries, see pages *22, 84, 141, 254.*

**hokku:** 140.

**Homeric epithet:** 103.

**homonyms:** 295.

**homostrophic** (hǒ′ mō strō″ fĭk): **236**.

**Horatian ode:** 236.

**Horatian satire:** 321.

**hubris** (hyoo′ brĭs): **371**.

**Hudibrastic poem** (hyoo′ dĭbrăs″ tik): **37**.

**Hudibrastic verse:** 84.

**humanism:** In the sixteenth century the word **humanist** was coined to signify one who taught or wrote in the "studia humanitatis," or "humanities"—that is, grammar, rhetoric, history, poetry, and moral philosophy, as distinguished from fields less concerned with the moral and imaginative aspects and activities of man, such as mathematics, natural philosophy, and theology. At that time, these studies focused on classical, especially Roman, culture; and they put great emphasis on learning to speak and write good Latin. Scholarly humanists recovered, edited, and expounded many ancient texts in Greek and Latin, and so contributed greatly to the store of materials and ideas in the European *Renaissance*. These humanists also wrote many works concerned with educational, moral, and political themes, based largely on classical writers such as Aristotle, Plato, and above all, Cicero. In the nineteenth century a new word, **humanism**, came to be applied to the view of human nature, the general values, and the educational ideas common to many Renaissance humanists, as well as to a number of later writers in the same tradition.

Typically, Renaissance humanism assumed the dignity and central position of human beings in the universe; emphasized the importance in education of studying classical imaginative and philosophical literature, although with emphasis on its moral and practical rather than its aesthetic values; and insisted on the primacy, in ordering human life, of reason (considered the universal and defining human faculty) as opposed to the instinctual appetites and the "animal" passions. Many humanists also stressed the need, in education, for a rounded development of an individual's diverse powers—physical, mental, artistic, and moral—as opposed to a merely technical or specialized kind of training.

In our time the term "humanist" often connotes those thinkers who base truth on human experience and reason and who base values on human nature and culture, as distinguished from those who regard religious revelation as the warrant for basic truth and values. With few exceptions, however, Renaissance humanists were pious Christians who incorporated the concepts and ideals inherited from pagan antiquity into the frame of the Christian creed. The result was that they tended to emphasize the values achievable by human beings in this world rather than in an afterlife, and to minimize the earlier Christian emphasis on the innate corruption of human beings and on the ideals of asceticism and of withdrawal from this world in a preoccupation with the world hereafter. It has become common to refer to this synthesis of classical and Christian views, typical of writers such as Sir Philip Sidney, Edmund Spenser, and John Milton, as **Christian humanism**.

The rapid advance in the achievements and prestige of the natural sciences and technology after the Renaissance sharpened, in later heirs of the humanistic tradition, the need to defend the role of the humanities in a liberal education against the encroachments of the sciences and the practical arts. As Samuel Johnson, the eighteenth-century humanist who had once been a schoolmaster, wrote in his *Life of Milton* (1779):

> The truth is, that the knowledge of external nature, and the sciences
> which that knowledge requires or includes, are not the great or the
> frequent business of the human mind. . . . We are perpetually moralists,
> but we are geometricians only by chance. . . . Socrates was rather of
> opinion that what we had to learn was, how to do good, and avoid evil.

Matthew Arnold, a notable proponent of humanism in the *Victorian Period*, strongly defended the central role of humane studies in general education. Many of Arnold's leading ideas are adaptations of the tenets of the older humanism—his view, for example, that culture is a perfection "of our humanity proper, as distinguished from our animality," and consists of "a harmonious expansion of *all* the powers which make the beauty and worth of human nature"; his emphasis on knowing "the best that is known and thought in the world," with the assumption that much of what is best is in the writings of classical antiquity; and his conception of poetry as essentially "a criticism of life."

In the 1890s the German philosopher Wilhelm Dilthey developed a highly influential distinction between the natural sciences, which aim at an abstract and reductive "explanation" of the world, and the "human sciences" (the humanities), which aim to achieve an "understanding" of the full, concrete world of actual experience—the lived human world, for example, that is represented in works of literature. (See in the entry *interpretation and hermeneutics*.)

In the last century the American movement of 1910–33 known as the **New Humanism**, under the leadership of Irving Babbitt and Paul Elmer More, argued for a return to a primarily humanistic education, and for a very conservative view of moral, political, and literary values that is grounded mainly on classical literature. (See Irving Babbitt, *Literature and the American College*, 1908; and Norman Foerster, ed., *Humanism and America*, 1930.) But in the present age of proliferating demands for specialists in the sciences, technology, and the practical arts, the broad humanistic base for a general education has been greatly eroded. In most colleges the earlier humanistic view of the aims of a liberal education survives mainly in the requirement that all students in the liberal arts must take at least one course in the group called **the humanities**, which comprises literature, philosophy, music, languages, and sometimes history.

It is notable that a number of structuralist and poststructuralist philosophical and critical theories were expressly antihumanistic, not only in the sense that they undertook to subvert many of the values proposed by traditional humanism, but in the more radical sense that they undertook to "decenter," or to eliminate entirely, the focus on the human being, or *subject*, as the major object of study and the major agency in effecting scientific, cultural, and literary achievements. "Man," as Michel Foucault put it in a widely quoted affirmation, "is a simple fold in our language" who is destined to "disappear as soon as that knowledge has found a new form." In the realm of literary and critical theory, some *structuralists* conceived of a human author as simply a "space" in which linguistic and cultural codes come together to effect a text; *deconstructionists* tended to reduce the human subject to one of the "effects" engendered by the differential play of language; and a number of *Marxist* and *new-historicist* critics analyzed the subject as a construction that is produced by the ideological "discursive formations," particular to a time and culture, which the author-as-subject acquires and transmits in his or her literary productions. (See *subject*, under *poststructuralism*.)

Diverse poststructural and other opponents of humanism assert that human-centered systems of norms and values are based on the fallacy of **essentialism**—that is, the view (which antihumanists assume to be mistaken) that there is an essential human nature, or set of defining human features, which is innate, universal, and independent of historical and cultural differences. In response, the philosopher Martha Nussbaum has mounted a defense of essentialism, insisting that we are able to formulate, from within our own historical and cultural situation, a set of basic features, functions, and needs that constitute the specifically human form of life and are shared by human beings across all divisions of time, place, and culture. These common features include the knowledge that we are mortal, and have an instinctual aversion to death; the fact that we live an embodied life, hence have nutritional, sexual, and other needs and desires and a sensibility to pleasure and pain; the cognitive ability to perceive, think, and imagine, together with the practical ability to plan the means to achieve our aims; the capacity to experience emotions such as grief, anger, fear, and love; and a sense of relatedness and affiliation to other human beings. Possessing such capacities, we are able to recognize ourselves in others and to acknowledge our common humanity, whatever our individual and cultural differences. Conversely, if an individual does not have one or more of these features, we consider him to be, to that extent, lacking in humanity. Nussbaum holds that such essentialism provides adequate grounds for establishing basic human norms and values, and also that it is in fact indispensable to justify claims for social and political justice on behalf of any oppressed, excluded, or marginalized minority. (See Martha Nussbaum, "Social Justice and Universalism: In Defense of an Aristotelian Account of Human Functioning," *Modern Philology*, Vol. 90, supplement, May 1993. In *Women and Human Development: The Capabilities Approach*, 2000, Nussbaum proposes a somewhat revised list of human capabilities, in a book oriented toward establishing the ground for freedom and justice for women, across all national and cultural differences; see chapter 1, "In Defense of Universal Values.")

The linguist and social philosopher Noam Chomsky also supports human essentialism; not, like Nussbaum, on the basis of shared human capabilities, but on the basis of a biologically determined "universal grammar," fixed in the human brain, which enables the "rule-bound creativity" of the production and under-standing of language. (See Chomsky under *linguistics in literary criticism.*) This uni-versal genetic inheritance, in Chomsky's view, constitutes the very core of human nature. He maintains that the anti-essentialist view of poststructural theorists—that all human attitudes, beliefs, and norms are social constructions within particular cultures—abets efforts by dominant social and political groups to shape such atti-tudes and norms to their own purposes. Only the conviction that human beings have an innate and determinate human nature can provide the grounds on which to resist such impositions on human liberty. (See Chomsky, *Reflections on Language,* 1975, and for evidence drawn from diverse fields to support Chomsky's genetic view of an essential human nature, Steven Pinker, *The Blank Slate: The Modern Denial of Human Nature,* 2002.)

A number of feminists, gay and lesbian critics, and proponents of ethnic *mul-ticulturalism* are adherents of "identity politics," and stake out a position which dif-fers from both the humanistic and poststructural views of the nature and valid role of the human *subject.* Like traditional humanists, **identity theorists** reject the ex-treme poststructural claims that the human subject is no more than a social con-struction or textual effect, and reposition the subject—as a particular sexual, gender-specific, or ethnic identity—at the center of the scene of writing, interpre-tation, and political action. In opposition to traditional humanists, on the other hand, identity theorists emphasize the identity of the subject as a representative of one or another group, rather than as a representative of universal humanity. (On current conflicts about "identity" among advocates of political activism see Jonathan Culler, *Literary Theory: A Very Short Introduction,* 1997, chapter 8; also refer to the entries in this *Glossary* on *feminist criticism, postcolonial studies,* and *queer theory.*)

On the concept and history of humanism: Douglas Bush, *The Renaissance and English Humanism* (1939); P. O. Kristeller, *The Classics and Renaissance Thought* (1955); H. I. Marrou, *A History of Education in Antiquity* (1956); R. S. Crane, *The Idea of the Humanities* (2 vols., 1967); Tony Davies, *Humanism* (2d ed., 2008); Tzvetan Todorov, *Imperfect Garden: The Legacy of Humanism* (2002). On the New Humanism in the early twentieth century: Claes G. Ryn, *Will, Imagination and Reason: Irving Babbitt and the Problem of Reality* (1986). For antihumanist critiques or deconstruction of the human subject, see the references under *poststructuralism, deconstruction,* and *new historicism.* For opposition to such views and defenses of the humanist position in authorship, interpretation, and criticism, see Commission on the Humanities, *The Humanities in American Life: Report of the Commission on the Humanities* (1980); Richard Levin, "Bashing the Bourgeois Subject," in *Textual Practice,* Vol. 3 (1989); Clara Claiborne Park, *Rejoining the Common Reader* (1991); M. H. Abrams, "What Is a Humanistic Criticism?" in *The Emperor Redressed: Critiquing Critical Theory,* ed. Dwight Eddins (1995); Richard A. Etlin, *In Defense of Humanism: Value in Arts and Letters* (1996); Alvin Kernan, ed., *What's Happened to the Humanities?* (1997); David A. Hollinger, ed., *The Humanities and the Dynamics of Inclusion Since World War II* (2006). On the recur-rent claim of a "crisis in the humanities," see Geoffrey Galt Harpham, "Beyond and Beneath the 'Crisis in the Humanities,'" *New Literary History,* Vol. 36

(2005); Kwame Anthony Appiah, *Cosmopolitanism: Ethics in a World of Strangers* (2006).

For references to *humanism* in other entries, see pages *39, 40, 88, 158, 212, 280, 348.*

**humanist: 144**; *307.*

**humanities, the: 145**; *158.*

**humor: 381.**

**humours character: 51**; *43.*

**humours, four: 51.**

**hybridization** (in literary cultures): **277.**

**hymn:** Hymn in current usage denotes a song that celebrates God or expresses religious feelings and is intended primarily to be sung as part of a religious service. (See *lyric.*) The term derives from the Greek *hymnos*, which originally signified songs of praise that were for the most part addressed to the gods, but in some instances to human heroes or to abstract concepts. The early Christian Churches, following classical examples, introduced the singing of hymns as part of the liturgy; some of these consisted of the texts or paraphrases of Old Testament psalms, but others were composed as songs of worship by churchly authors of the time. The writing of religious lyric poems set to music continued through the Middle Ages and into the Protestant Reformation; Martin Luther himself (1483–1546) composed both the German words and the music of hymns, including "A Mighty Fortress Is Our God," which is now sung by most Christian denominations.

The writing of religious hymns, some of them metrical versions of the psalms and others original, continued through the Renaissance and was supplemented by a revival of "literary hymns" on secular or even pagan subjects—a classical type which had been kept alive through the Middle Ages by a number of neo-Latin poets, and was now composed to be read rather than sung. Edmund Spenser's *Fowre Hymns* (1596) are distinguished examples of such literary hymns; the first two celebrate earthly love and beauty, and the second two celebrate heavenly (that is, Christian) love and beauty. The tradition of writing hymns on secular subjects continued into the nineteenth century, and produced such examples as James Thomson's "A Hymn on the Seasons" (1730), Keats' "Hymn to Apollo," and Shelley's "Hymn of Apollo" and "Hymn of Pan"; the last three of these hymns, it should be noted, like many of the original Greek hymns, are addressed to pagan gods.

The secular hymns were often long and elaborate compositions that verged closely upon another form of versified praise, the *ode*. These hymns, as well as many religious instances such as the great "Hymn" that constitutes all but the brief introduction of Milton's "On the Morning of Christ's Nativity" (1629), were formal compositions that were intended only to be read. The other type of hymn—the short religious lyric written for public singing—was revived, and developed into its modern form, by the notable eighteenth-century hymnists of personal religious emotions, including Isaac Watts, Charles and John Wesley, and William Cowper; a successor in the next century was John Henry Newman, author of "Lead, Kindly Light." In America the poets John Greenleaf Whittier, Oliver Wendell Holmes, and Henry Wadsworth Longfellow wrote hymns, but the greatest and best-known American devotional songs are the anonymous *African-American* type that we call **spirituals**, such as "Swing Low, Sweet Chariot" and "Go Down, Moses." (James Weldon Johnson and J. Rosamond Johnson, *Book of American Negro Spirituals*, 1925–26.)

See the anthology, *New Oxford Book of Christian Verse*, ed. Donald Davie (1982); and refer to C. S. Phillipe, *Hymnody Past and Present* (1937); Louis F. Benson, *The English Hymn* (1962); P. S. Diehl, *The Medieval European Religious Lyric* (1985); and the article "Hymn" in *The New Princeton Encyclopedia of Poetry and Poetics* (1993).

**hyperbole and understatement:** The figure of speech, or *trope*, called **hyperbole** (Greek for "overshooting") is bold overstatement, or the extravagant exaggeration of fact or of possibility. It may be used either for serious or ironic or comic effect. Iago says gloatingly of Othello (III. iii. 330ff.):

> Not poppy nor mandragora,
> Nor all the drowsy syrups of the world,
> Shall ever medicine thee to that sweet sleep
> Which thou ow'dst yesterday.

Famed examples in the seventeenth century are Ben Jonson's gallantly hyperbolic compliments to his lady in "Drink to me only with thine eyes," and the ironic hyperboles in "To His Coy Mistress," by which Andrew Marvell attests how infinitely slowly his "vegetable love should grow"—if he had "but world enough and time." The "tall talk" or **tall tale** of the American West is a form of mainly comic hyperbole. There is the story of a cowboy in an eastern restaurant who ordered a steak well done. "Do you call this well done?" he roared at the server. "I've seen critters hurt worse than that get well!"

The contrary figure is **understatement** (the Greek term is **meiosis**, "lessening"), which deliberately represents something as very much less in magnitude or importance than it really is, or is ordinarily considered to be. The effect is usually ironic. It is savagely (and complexly) ironic in Jonathan Swift's *A Tale of a Tub* (1704), in which the narrator asserts the "superiority" of "that Wisdom, which converses about the surface" to "that pretended Philosophy which enters into the Depth of Things," giving as example that "last week I saw a Woman *flay'd*, and you will hardly believe how much it altered her Person for the worse." The understatement is comically ironic in Mark Twain's comment, "The reports of my death are greatly exaggerated." Some critics extend "meiosis" to the use in literature of a simple, unemphatic statement to enhance the effect of a deeply pathetic or tragic event; an example is the line at the close of the narrative in William Wordsworth's "Michael" (1800): "And never lifted up a single stone."

A special form of understatement is **litotes** (Greek for "plain" or "simple"), the assertion of an affirmative by negating its contrary: "He's not the brightest man in the world" meaning "He is stupid." The figure is frequent in Anglo-Saxon poetry, where the effect is usually one of grim irony. In *Beowulf*, after Hrothgar has described the ghastly mere where the monster Grendel dwells, he comments, "That is not a pleasant place."

**hypermedia: 150**.

**hypertext:** Hypertext designates a nonsequential kind of text, achieved by embedding within it a number of links and references to other texts; the result is to make the experience of reading the hypertext nonlinear, open, and variable. That is, the reader of the hypertext, instead of reading along a single verbal line, is free to branch off into other texts at will. (This *Glossary* can be accounted a form of hypertext, in that the italicized terms invite readers to suspend forward progress while they look ahead or back in order to consult other relevant entries.) The term was coined in the 1960s, but later was applied specifically to texts on a computer, in which browsers and hyperlinks enable the reader to move instantly from one document to another. The use of the nonsequential mode in other media, such as sound, graphics, and video, is referred to as **hypermedia**.

   See George P. Landow, ed., *Hyper/Text/Theory* (1994).

**hypotactic style** (hī′ pōtăk″ tik): **351**.

**iambic** (īăm′ bik): **195**; *28, 131*.

**icon** (in semiotics) (ī kŏn): **324**.

**iconography** (īkŏnŏ′ grăf ē): **163**.

**id: 291**.

**identity theorists: 147**.

**ideology** (īdēŏl′ ŏjē): **181**; *4, 19, 39, 219, 277, 302, 364*.

**idyll: 240**.

**illocutionary act** (īl′ ōkyoo″ shŭnāry): **338**.

**illuminated** (books): **31**.

**Imagery:** This term is one of the most common in criticism, and one of the most variable in meaning. Its applications range all the way from the "mental pictures" which, it is sometimes claimed, are experienced by the reader of a poem, to the totality of the components which make up a poem. Examples of this range of usage are the statements by the poet C. Day Lewis, in his *Poetic Image* (1948, pp. 17–18), that an image "is a picture made out of words," and that "a poem may itself be an image composed from a multiplicity of images." Three discriminable uses of the word, however, are especially frequent; in all these senses imagery is said to make poetry *concrete*, as opposed to *abstract*:

1. "Imagery" (that is, "images" taken collectively) is used to signify all the objects and qualities of sense perception referred to in a poem or other work of literature, whether by literal description, by *allusion*, or in the *vehicles* (the secondary references) of its similes and metaphors. In William Wordsworth's "She Dwelt among the Untrodden Ways" (1800), the imagery in this broad sense includes the literal objects the poem refers to (for example, "untrodden ways," "springs," "grave"), as well as the "violet" of the metaphor and the "star" of the simile in the second stanza. The term "image" should not be taken to imply a visual reproduction of the object denoted; some readers of the passage experience visual images and some do not; and among those who do, the explicitness and details of the pictures vary greatly. Also, "imagery" in this usage includes not only visual sense qualities, but also qualities that are auditory, tactile (touch), thermal (heat and cold), olfactory (smell), gustatory (taste), and kinesthetic (sensations of movement). In his *In Memoriam* (1850), No. 101, for example, Tennyson's imagery encompasses not only things that are visible, but also qualities that are smelled, tasted, or heard, together with a suggestion, in the adjective "summer," of warmth:

> Unloved, that beech will gather brown, . . .
> And many a rose-carnation feed
> With summer spice the humming air. . . .

2. Imagery is used, more narrowly, to signify only specific descriptions of visible objects and scenes, especially if the description is vivid and particularized, as in this passage from Marianne Moore's "The Steeple-Jack":

> a sea the purple of the peacock's neck is
> paled to greenish azure as Dürer changed
> the pine tree of the Tyrol to peacock blue and guinea
>    grey.[7]

3. Commonly in recent usage, imagery signifies *figurative language*, especially the *vehicles* of metaphors and similes. Critics after the 1930s, and notably the *New Critics*, went far beyond earlier commentators in stressing imagery, in this sense, as the essential component in poetry, and as a major factor in poetic meaning, structure, and effect.

Using the term in this third sense, Caroline Spurgeon, in *Shakespeare's Imagery and What It Tells Us* (1935), made statistical counts of the referents of the figurative vehicles in Shakespeare, and used the results as clues to Shakespeare's personal experiences, interests, and temperament. Following the lead of several earlier critics,

---

[7]Lines from "The Steeplejack" by Marianne Moore, from *The Complete Poems of Marianne Moore*. Copyright © 1951. Reprinted with permission from Faber & Faber Ltd.

she also pointed out the frequent occurrence in Shakespeare's plays of image clusters (recurrent groupings of seemingly unrelated metaphors and similes). She also presented evidence that a number of the individual plays have characteristic image *motifs* (for example, animal imagery in *King Lear*, and the figures of disease, corruption, and death in *Hamlet*); her view was that these elements established the overall tonality or *atmosphere* of a play. Many critics in the next few decades joined Spurgeon in the search for images, image clusters, and "thematic imagery" in works of literature. Some *New Critics* held that the implicit interactions of the imagery—in distinction from explicit statements by the author or the overt speeches and actions of the characters—were the way that the controlling literary subject, or *theme*, worked itself out in many plays, poems, and novels. See, for example, the critical writings of G. Wilson Knight; Cleanth Brooks on *Macbeth* in *The Well Wrought Urn* (1947), chapter 2; and Robert B. Heilman, *This Great Stage: Image and Structure in "King Lear"* (1948).

See also H. W. Wells, *Poetic Imagery* (1924); Richard H. Fogle, *The Imagery of Keats and Shelley* (1949); Norman Friedman, "Imagery: From Sensation to Symbol," *Journal of Aesthetics and Art Criticism* 12 (1953); Frank Kermode, *Romantic Image* (1957). For references to *imagery* in other entries, see pages 55, 152.

**imaginary** (in Lacanian criticism): **294**.

**imagination: 109**.

**Imagism:** Imagism was a poetic vogue that flourished in England, and even more vigorously in America, approximately between the years 1912 and 1917. It was planned and exemplified by a group of English and American writers in London, partly under the influence of the poetic theory of T. E. Hulme, as a revolt against what Ezra Pound called the "rather blurry, messy . . . sentimentalistic mannerish" poetry at the turn of the century. Pound, the first leader of the movement, was soon succeeded by Amy Lowell; after that Pound sometimes referred to the movement, slightingly, as "Amygism." Other leading participants, for a time, were H. D. (Hilda Doolittle), D. H. Lawrence, William Carlos Williams, John Gould Fletcher, and Richard Aldington. The Imagist proposals, as voiced by Amy Lowell in her preface to the first of three anthologies called *Some Imagist Poets* (1915–17), were for a poetry which, abandoning conventional limits on poetic materials and versification, is free to choose any subject and to create its own rhythms, uses common speech, and presents an "image" (vivid sensory description) that is hard, clear, and concentrated. (See *imagery*.)

The typical Imagist poem is written in *free verse* and undertakes to render as precisely, vividly, and tersely as possible, and without comment or generalization, the writer's impression of a visual object or scene; often the impression is rendered by means of metaphor, or by juxtaposing, without indicating a relationship, the description of one object with that of a second and diverse object. This famed example by Ezra Pound exceeds other Imagist poems in the degree of its concentration:

*In a Station of the Metro*

The apparition of these faces in the crowd,
Petals on a wet, black bough.[8]

In this poem Pound, like a number of other Imagists, was influenced by the Japanese *haiku*.

Imagism was too restrictive to endure long as a concerted movement, but it served to inaugurate a distinctive feature of *modernist* poetry. Almost every major poet from the 1920s through the middle of the twentieth century, including W. B. Yeats, T. S. Eliot, and Wallace Stevens, manifests some influence by the Imagist experiments with the presentation of precise, clear images that are juxtaposed without specifying their interrelationships.

See T. E. Hulme, *Speculations*, ed. Herbert Read (1924); *The Imagist Poem*, ed. William Pratt (1963); Hugh Kenner, *The Pound Era* (1971); Glenn Hughes, *Imagism and the Imagists: A Study in Modern Poetry* (1973); J. B. Harmer, *Victory in Limbo: Imagism, 1908–1917* (1975). For references to *imagism* in other entries, see page *248*.

**imitation:** In literary criticism the word **imitation** has two frequent but diverse applications: (1) to define the nature of literature and the other arts, and (2) to indicate the relationship of one literary work to another literary work which served as its model.

1. In his *Poetics*, Aristotle defines poetry as an imitation (in Greek, **mimesis**) of human actions. (See *criticism*.) By "imitation" he means something like "representation," in its root sense: the poem imitates by taking an instance of human action and re-presenting it in a new "medium"—that of words. By distinguishing differences in the artistic media, in the kind of actions imitated, and in the manner of imitation (for example, dramatic or narrative), Aristotle first distinguishes poetry from other arts, and then makes distinctions between the various poetic kinds, such as drama and epic, tragedy and comedy. From the sixteenth through the eighteenth century the term "imitation" was a central term in discussing the nature of poetry. Critics differed radically, however, in their concept of the nature of the mimetic relationship, and of the kinds of things in the external world that works of literature imitate, or ought to imitate, so that theories of imitation varied in the kind of art they recommended, from a strict realism to a remote idealism. With the emergence in the early nineteenth century of an *expressive criticism* (the view that poetry is essentially an expression of the poet's feelings or imaginative process), imitation tended to be displaced from its central position in literary theory (see *criticism*). In the last half-century, however, the use of the term has been revived, especially by R. S. Crane and other *Chicago critics*, who ground their theory on the analytic method and basic distinctions of Aristotle's *Poetics*. Many *Marxist critics* also propose a view

---

[8]Lines from "In a Station of the Metro" from *Personae* by Ezra Pound. Copyright 1926 by Ezra Pound. Reprinted by permission of New Directions Publishing Corporation and Faber & Faber Ltd.

of literature as an imitation, or, in their preferred term, "reflection," of social reality.

2. Greek and Roman rhetoricians and critics often recommended that a poet should "imitate" the established models in a particular literary *genre*. The notion that the proper procedure for poets, with the rare exception of an "original genius," was to imitate the normative forms and styles of the Greek and Roman masters continued to be influential through the eighteenth century. All the major critics, however, also insisted that mere copying was not enough—that a good literary work must imitate the form and spirit rather than the detail of the classic models, and that success can be achieved only by a poet who possesses an innate poetic talent. (See *neoclassic*.)

In a specialized use of the term in this second sense, "imitation" was also used to describe a literary work which deliberately echoed an older work but adapted it to subject matter in the writer's own age, usually in a satirical fashion. In the poems that Alexander Pope called *Imitations of Horace* (1733 and following), for example, an important part of the intended effects depend on the reader's recognition of the resourcefulness and wit with which Pope accommodated to contemporary circumstances the structure, details, and even the wording of one or another of Horace's Roman satires.

On "imitation" as a term used to define literature see R. S. Crane, ed., *Critics and Criticism* (1952); M. H. Abrams, *The Mirror and the Lamp* (1953), chapters 1–2; and Erich Auerbach, *Mimesis* (trans. 1953, reprinted 2003). On Pope's "imitations" of Horace and other ancient masters see R. A. Brower, *Alexander Pope: The Poetry of Allusion* (1959). For denials, on various grounds, that literature can be claimed to be an imitation of reality, see *Russian formalism, structuralist criticism, deconstruction, new historicism*, and *text and writing (écriture)*. Among modern defenses of the view that literature is mimetic, in the broad sense that it has reference beyond the text to the world of human experience, see Gerald Graff, *Literature against Itself* (1979); A. D. Nuttall, *A New Mimesis: Shakespeare and the Representation of Reality* (1983); and Robert Alter, "Mimesis and the Motives for Fiction," in his *Motives for Fiction* (1984).

For references to *imitation* in other entries, see pages *59, 63, 212, 311, 339*.

**imperfect rhyme: 317**.

**impersonal** (narrator): **273**.

**implicature: 81**.

**implicit metaphor: 119**.

**implied auditor: 258**.

**implied author: 259**.

**implied reader: 299**.

**impressionistic criticism: 62**; *355*.

**in medias res** (in mā′ dēäs rās′): **98**.

**incidents** (in a plot): **266**.

**incremental repetition: 22**.

**incunabula** (ĭn′ kyoonăb″ yoolă): **31**.

**index** (in semiotics): **324**.

**indexicals: 208**.

**indirect satire: 321**.

**influence and the anxiety of influence:** Critics and historians of literature have for many centuries discussed what was called the **influence** of an author, or of a literary tradition, upon a later author, who was said to adopt, and at the same time to alter, aspects of the subject matter, form, or style of the earlier writer or writers. Among traditional topics for discussion, for example, have been the influence of Homer on Virgil, of Virgil on Milton, of Milton on Wordsworth, or of Wordsworth on Wallace Stevens. The **anxiety of influence** is a phrase used by the influential contemporary critic Harold Bloom to identify his radical revision of this standard theory that influence consists in a direct "borrowing," or assimilation, of the materials and features found in earlier writers. Bloom's own view is that in the composition of any poem, influence is inescapable, but that it evokes in the author an anxiety that compels a drastic distortion of the work of a predecessor. He applies this concept of anxiety to the reading as well as the writing of poetry.

In Bloom's theory a poet (especially since the time of Milton) is motivated to compose when his imagination is seized upon by a poem or poems of a "precursor." The "belated" poet's attitudes to his precursor, like those in Freud's analysis of the Oedipal relationship of son to father, are ambivalent; that is, they are compounded not only of admiration but also (since any strong poet feels a compelling need to be autonomous and original) of hate, envy, and fear of the precursor's preemption of the descendant's imaginative space. The belated poet safeguards his sense of his own freedom and priority by reading a parent poem "defensively," in such a way as to distort it beyond his own conscious recognition. Nonetheless, he cannot avoid embodying the distorted parent poem into his own hopeless attempt to write an unprecedentedly original poem; the most that even the best belated poet can achieve is to write a poem so "strong" that it effects an illusion of "priority"—that is, a double illusion that it has escaped the precursor poem's precedence in time, and that it exceeds it in greatness.

Bloom identifies six distortive processes which operate in the self-defensive reading of a precursor; he calls these processes "revisionary ratios" and defines them mainly on the model of Freud's defense mechanisms (see *psychoanalytic criticism*). He also equates these distortive mechanisms with the devices by which the medieval Kabbalists reinterpreted the Hebrew Bible, as well as with various types of literary *tropes* (see *figurative language*). Since in Bloom's view the revisionary ratios are the categories through which all of us, whether or not we are ourselves poets, inescapably read our precursors, his conclusion is that we can never know "the poem-in-itself"; all interpretation is "a necessary misprision," and all "reading is therefore misprision—or misreading." A "weak misreading" is an attempt (doomed to fail) to get at what a text really means, while a "strong misreading" is one in which an individual reader's defenses are unconsciously licensed to recast, innovatively, the text that the reader undertakes to interpret.

Since Bloom conceives that "every poem is a misinterpretation of a parent poem," he recommends that literary critics boldly practice what he calls **antithetical criticism**—that is, that they learn "to read any poem as its poet's deliberate misinterpretation, *as a poet*, of a precursor poem or of poetry in general." The results of such "strong readings" will be antithetical both to what the poet himself thought he meant and to what standard weak misreadings have made out the poem to mean. In his own powerfully individualistic writings, Bloom applies such antithetical criticism to poets ranging from the eighteenth century through the major Romantics, and Yeats and Stevens, to contemporary poets such as A. R. Ammons and John Ashbery. He is aware that, by the terms of his theory, his own interpretations both of poets and critics are necessarily misreadings. His claim is that his antithetical interpretations are strong, and therefore "interesting," misreadings, and so will take their place in the accumulation of misreadings which constitutes the history both of poetry and of criticism, at least since the seventeenth century—although this history is bound to be tragic, since as time goes on there will be a constant decrease in the area of imaginative possibilities that are left open to poets.

As Bloom points out, a precursor of his views was Walter Jackson Bate's *The Burden of the Past and the English Poet* (1970), which described the struggles by poets, since 1660, to overcome the inhibitive effect of fear that their predecessors might have exhausted all the possibilities of writing great and original poems. Bloom presented his own theory of reading and writing poetry in *The Anxiety of Influence* (1973), then elaborated the theory, and demonstrated its application to diverse poetic texts, in three rapidly successive books, *A Map of Misreading* (1975), *Kabbalah and Criticism* (1975), and *Poetry and Repression* (1976), as well as in a number of writings concerned with individual poets. See also the collection of Bloom's writings, *Poetics of Influence*, ed. John Hollander (1988). For analyses and critiques of this theory of literature see Frank Lentricchia, *After the New Criticism* (1980), chapter 9; David Fite, *Harold Bloom: The Rhetoric of Romantic Vision* (1985); M. H. Abrams, "How to Do Things with Texts," in *Doing Things with Texts* (1989). Bloom proposed his theory, it will have been noted, with respect to male poets; for an application of the concept of anxiety of influence to women writers, see Sandra Gilbert and Susan Gubar, *The Madwoman in the Attic* (rev. 2000), discussed in the entry *feminist criticism*.

**intentional fallacy:** Intentional fallacy signifies what is claimed to be the error of interpreting and evaluating a literary work by reference to evidence, outside the text itself, for the intention—the design and purposes—of its author. The term was proposed by W. K. Wimsatt and Monroe C. Beardsley in "The Intentional Fallacy" (1946), reprinted in Wimsatt's *The Verbal Icon* (1954). They asserted that an author's intended aims and meanings in writing a literary work—whether these are asserted by the author or merely inferred from our knowledge of the author's life and opinions—are irrelevant to the literary critic, because the meaning, structure, and value of a text are inherent within the finished, freestanding, and public work of literature itself. Reference to the author's supposed purposes, or else to the author's personal situation and state of mind in writing a text, is held to be a harmful mistake, because it diverts our attention to such "external" matters as the author's biography, or psychological condition, or creative process, which we substitute for the proper critical concern with the "internal" constitution and inherent value of the literary product. (See *objective criticism*, under *criticism*.)

   This claim, which was central in the *New Criticism*, has been strenuously debated, and was reformulated by both of its original proponents. (See Wimsatt, "Genesis: An Argument Resumed," in *Day of the Leopards*, 1976; and Beardsley, *Aesthetics*, 1958, pp. 457–61, and *The Possibility of Criticism*, 1970, pp. 16–37.) A view acceptable to many traditional critics (but not to *structuralist* and *poststructuralist* theorists) is that in the exceptional instances—for example, in Henry James' prefaces to his novels—where we possess an author's express statement about his artistic intentions in a literary work, that statement should constitute evidence for an interpretive hypothesis, but should not in itself be determinative. If the author's stated intentions do not accord with the text, they should be qualified or rejected in favor of an alternative interpretation that conforms more closely to the shared, or "public," linguistic and literary conventions that the text itself incorporates.

   Compare *affective fallacy*. For diverse views of the role of authorial intentions in establishing a text and in interpreting the meanings of a text, see *interpretation and hermeneutics* and *textual criticism*. A detailed objection to Wimsatt and Beardsley's original essay is E. D. Hirsch's "Objective Interpretation" (1960), reprinted as an appendix to his *Validity in Interpretation* (1967). An anthology of discussions of this topic in literary criticism is David Newton–de Molina, *On Literary Intention* (1976). Ronald Dworkin discusses parallels between the role of intention in legal interpretation and literary interpretation, in "Law as Interpretation," *The Politics of Interpretation*, ed. W. J. T. Mitchell (1983). For references to *intentional fallacy* in other entries, see pages *161, 217*.

**interior monologue: 345.**

**interlude** (in drama): **201.**

**internal rhyme: 316.**

**interpellation: 184.**

**interpretation and hermeneutics:** In the narrow sense, to interpret a work of literature is to specify the meanings of its language by analysis, paraphrase, and commentary; usually such **interpretation** focuses on especially obscure, ambiguous, or figurative passages. In a broader sense, to interpret a work of literature is to make clear the artistic features and purport in the overall work of which language serves as the medium. Interpretation in this sense includes the analysis of such matters as the work's *genre*, component elements, form and structure, theme, and effects (see *criticism*).

The term **hermeneutics** originally designated the formulation of principles of interpretation that apply specifically to the Bible; the principles incorporated both the rules governing a valid reading of the biblical text, and **exegesis**, or commentary on the application of the meanings expressed in the text. Since the nineteenth century, however, "hermeneutics" has come to designate the theory of interpretation in general—that is, a formulation of the principles and methods involved in getting at the meaning of all written texts, including legal, historical, and literary, as well as biblical texts.

The German theologian Friedrich Schleiermacher, in a series of lectures in 1819, was the first to frame a theory of "general hermeneutics" as "the art of understanding" texts of every kind. Schleiermacher's views were developed in the 1890s by the influential philosopher Wilhelm Dilthey (1833–1911), who proposed a science of hermeneutics designed to serve as the basis for interpreting all forms of writing in the "human sciences": that is, in the *humanities* and the social sciences, as distinguished from the natural sciences. Dilthey regarded the human sciences as ways of dealing with the temporal, concrete, "lived experience" of human beings. He proposed that whereas the aim of the natural sciences is to achieve "explanation" by means of static, reductive categories, the aim of hermeneutics is to establish a general theory of "understanding." The understanding of a verbal text consists in "the interpretation of *works*, works in which the texture of inner life comes fully to expression." And in literature above all, "the inner life of man finds its complex, exhaustive, and objectively intelligible expression." (See *humanism*.)

In formulating the way in which we come to understand the meaning of a text, Dilthey gave the name the **hermeneutic circle** to a procedure Schleiermacher had earlier described. That is, in order to understand the determinate meanings of the verbal parts of any linguistic whole, we must approach the parts with a prior sense of the meaning of the whole; yet we can know the meaning of the whole only by knowing the meanings of its constituent parts. This circularity of the interpretive process applies to the interrelations between the single words within any sentence and the sentence as a whole, as well as to interrelations between all the sentences and the work as a whole. Dilthey maintained that the hermeneutic circle is not a vicious circle, in that we can achieve a valid interpretation by a mutually qualifying interplay between our evolving sense of the whole and our retrospective understanding of its component parts.

Interest in the theory of interpretation revived strongly in the 1950s and 1960s, concurrently with the turn of Western philosophy to focus on the uses and meanings of language, and the turn of literary criticism—exemplified by the

*New Criticism* in America—to the conception of a literary work as a linguistic object and to the view that the primary task of criticism is to interpret its verbal meanings and their interrelations. There have been two main lines of development in recent hermeneutics:

1. One development, represented notably by the Italian theorist Emilio Betti and the American E. D. Hirsch, takes off from Dilthey's claim that a reader is able to achieve an objective interpretation of an author's expressed meaning. In his *Validity in Interpretation* (1967), followed by *The Aims of Interpretation* (1976), Hirsch asserts that "a text means what its author meant," specifies that this meaning is "the verbal meaning which an author intends," and undertakes to show that such verbal meaning is in principle determinate (even if in some instances determinately ambiguous, or multiply significant), that it remains stable through the passage of time, and that it is in principle reproducible by each competent reader. The author's verbal **intention** is not the author's overall state of consciousness at the time of writing, but only the intention-to-mean something which, by recourse to preexisting linguistic conventions and norms, gets actualized in words, and so may be shared by readers who are competent in the same conventions and norms and know how to apply them in their interpretive practice. If a text is read independently of reference to the author's intentions, Hirsch asserts, it remains indeterminate—that is, capable of an indefinite diversity of meanings. A reader arrives at a determinate interpretation by using an implicit logic of validation (capable of being made explicit by the hermeneutic theorist), which serves to specify the author's intention, by reference not only to the general conventions and norms of a language, but also to all evidence, whether internal or external to the text, concerning "relevant aspects in the author's outlook" or "horizon." Relevant external references include the author's cultural milieu and personal prepossessions, as well as the literary and generic conventions that were available to the author at the time when the work was composed.

   Hirsch reformulates Dilthey's concept of the hermeneutic circle as follows: a competent reader forms an "hypothesis" as to the meaning of a part or whole of a text which is "corrigible"—that is, the hypothesis can be either confirmed or disconfirmed by continuing reference to the text; if disconfirmed, it is replaced by an alternative hypothesis which conforms more closely to all the components of the text. Since the interpreted meanings of the components of a text are to some degree constituted by the hypotheses one brings to their interpretation, such a procedure can never achieve absolute certainty as to a text's correct meaning. The most a reader can do is to arrive at the most probable meaning of a text; but this logic of highest probability, Hirsch insists, is adequate to yield objective knowledge, confirmable by other competent readers, concerning the determinate and stable meanings both of the component passages and of the artistic whole in a work of literature.

   Hirsch follows traditional hermeneutics in making an essential distinction between verbal meaning and significance. The **significance** of a text to a reader is the relation of its verbal meaning to other matters, such as the personal situation, beliefs, and responses of the individual reader, or the prevailing cultural milieu of the reader's own era, or a particular set of concepts or values, and so on. The **verbal meaning** of a text, Hirsch asserts—the meaning intended by the writer—is determinate and stable; its significance, however—what makes the text alive and resonant for diverse readers in diverse times—is indeterminate and ever-changing. Verbal meaning is the particular concern of hermeneutics; textual significance, in its many aspects, is one of the concerns of literary criticism.

2. The second line of development in recent hermeneutics takes off from Dilthey's view that the genuine understanding of literary and other humanistic texts consists in the reader's re-experience of the "inner life" that the texts express. A primary thinker in this development is Martin Heidegger, whose *Being and Time* (1927, trans. 1962) incorporated the act of interpretation into an **existential philosophy**—that is, a philosophy centered on "Dasein," or what it is to-be-in-the-world. Heidegger's student Hans Georg Gadamer adapted Heidegger's philosophy into an influential theory of textual interpretation, *Truth and Method* (1960, trans. 1975). The philosophical premise is that temporality and historicality—a situation in one's present that looks back to the past and anticipates the future—is inseparably a part of each individual's being; that the process of understanding something, involving an act of interpretation, goes on not only in reading verbal texts but in all aspects of human experience; and that language, like temporality, pervades all aspects of that experience. In applying these philosophical assumptions to the understanding of a literary text, Gadamer translates the traditional hermeneutic circle into the metaphors of dialogue and fusion. Readers bring to a text a "pre-understanding," which is constituted by their own temporal and personal "horizons." They should not, as "subjects," attempt to analyze and dissect the text as an autonomous "object." Instead the reader, as an "I," situated in his or her present time, addresses questions to the text as a "Thou," but with a receptive openness that simply allows the matter of the text—by means of their shared heritage of language—to speak in responsive dialogue, and to readdress its own questions to the reader. The understood meaning of the text is an event which is always the product of a "fusion of the horizons" that a reader brings to the text and that the text brings to the reader.

Gadamer insists that (unlike most theories of interpretation) this hermeneutics is not an attempt to establish norms or rules for a correct interpretation, but an attempt simply to describe how we in fact succeed in understanding texts. Nonetheless his theory has the consequence that the search for a determinate meaning of a text which remains stable through the passage of time becomes a will-o'-the-wisp. Since the meaning of a text "is always codetermined" by the particular temporal and personal horizon of the individual reader, there cannot be one stable "right interpretation"; the meaning of a text is always to an important extent its meaning that it has here, now, for me. To Gadamer's view that the historical and personal relativity of meaning is inescapable, Hirsch replies that a reader in the present, by reconstructing the linguistic, literary, and cultural conditions of its author, is often able adequately to determine the original and unchanging verbal meaning intended by the writer of a text in the past; and that insofar as Gadamer is right about the unbridgeable gap between the meaning of a text then and its meaning now, he is referring to the ever-alterable "significance" contributed by each reader, in his or her time and personal and social circumstances, to the text's stable verbal meaning.

Traditional literary critics had tacitly assumed that to interpret a text correctly is to approximate the meaning intended by its author, long before theorists such as Hirsch undertook to define and justify this view. Even the *New Critics* took for granted that the meaning of a text is the meaning that the author intended; what some of these critics called the *intentional fallacy* merely designates the supposed error, in interpreting a text, of employing clues concerning an author's intention which are "external" to the "internal" actualization of that intention in the language of the text itself. Most traditional philosophers, including recent "ordinary language philosophers," have also held that to understand an utterance involves reference to the writer's intention, which we infer from our awareness of the writer's linguistic assumptions. H. P. Grice, for example, proposed in the 1950s an influential account of verbal meaning as a speaker's intention in an utterance to produce a specific effect in a hearer, by means of the hearer's recognition of the speaker's intention in making that utterance. (See under *discourse analysis.*) In *Speech Acts* (1970), John Searle accepted this description, with the qualification that the speaker can express, and so enable the hearer to recognize, his or her intention only insofar as the expression conforms to the conventions or rules of their common language. In a later refinement of this view, Searle makes a distinction between the speaker's intention which determines the kind and meaning of a *speech act*, and the speaker's intention to communicate that meaning to a hearer; see his *Intentionality* (1983), chapter 6. On this issue in ordinary-language philosophy, see also P. F. Strawson, "Intention and Convention in Speech Acts," in Jay F. Rosenberg and Charles Travis, eds., *Readings in the Philosophy of Language* (1971).

A radical departure from the traditional author-oriented views of a determinate intended meaning occurs in a number of *structural* and *poststructural* theories. (See *author and authorship.*) Some theorists, rejecting any control of interpretation by reference to an author, or *subject*, and his or her intention, insist that the meanings of a text are rendered "undecidable" by the self-conflicting workings of language itself, or alternatively that meanings are entirely relative to the particular interpretive strategy that is brought into play by the reader. (See *deconstruction* and *reader-response criticism.*) Other current theorists, although they may admit that the manifest meanings of a text are specified by the intentions of the author, regard such meanings merely as disguises, or displacements, of the real meanings, which are the unconscious motives and needs of the author, or else the suppressed political realities and power-relationships of the social structure of an historical era. (See *psychoanalytic criticism, Marxist criticism, new historicism.*) Paul Ricoeur has labeled such modes of reading, exemplified by Marx, Nietzsche, and Freud, the *hermeneutics of suspicion*, in that they approach a text as a veiled or mystified set of representations, whose real meaning, or *subtext*, needs to be deciphered by the knowing reader.

In addition to the titles listed above, refer to Richard E. Palmer, *Hermeneutics: Interpretation Theory in Schleiermacher, Dilthey, Heidegger, and Gadamer* (1969), an informative review of the history and conflicting theories of interpretation from the standpoint of an adherent to Gadamer's theory. See also *Literary Criticism and Historical Understanding*, ed. Phillip Damon (1967); *The Conflict of Interpretations: Essays in Hermeneutics* (1974) by the French philosopher Paul Ricoeur; the anthology of essays *Hermeneutics: Questions and Prospects*, ed. Gary Shapiro and Alan Sica (1984); Wendell V. Harris, *Interpretive Acts: In Search of Meaning* (1988); Francis-Noël Thomas, *The Writer Writing* (1992), chapter 2, "'Intentions' and 'Purposes'." In *Multiple Authorship and the Myth of Solitary Genius* (1991), Jack Stillinger points out that reference to authorial intention in order to determine meaning is complicated by the fact that often a number of persons collaborate in producing a literary or other published text; see under *textual criticism*. John R. Searle distinguishes three different meanings of "intention" in diverse discussions of the interpretation of literary texts, in "Literary Theory and Its Discontents," *The Emperor Redressed*, ed. Dwight Eddins (1995).

For references to *interpretation* in other entries, see pages *260, 305*.

**interpretation, typological and allegorical:** The **typological** (or **figural**) mode of interpreting the Bible was inaugurated by St. Paul and developed by the early Church Fathers as a way of reconciling the history, prophecy, and laws of the Hebrew Scriptures with the narratives and teachings of the Christian Scriptures. As St. Augustine expressed its principle: "In the Old Testament the New Testament is concealed; in the New Testament the Old Testament is revealed." In typological theory, that is, the key persons, actions, and events in the Old Testament are viewed as "figurae" (Latin for "figures") which were historical realities, but also "prefigure" those persons, actions, and events in the New Testament that are similar to them in some aspect, function, or relationship. Often the Old Testament figures are called **types** and their later correlatives in the New Testament are called **antitypes**. The Old Testament figure or type is held to be a prophecy or promise of the higher truth that is "fulfilled" in the New Testament, according to a plan which is eternally present in the mind of God but manifests itself to human beings only in the two scriptural revelations separated by a span of time.

To cite a few of the very many instances of typological interpretation: Adam was said to be a figure (or in alternative terms, a "type," "image," or "shadow") of Christ. One of the analogies cited between prefiguration and fulfillment was that between the creation of Eve from Adam's rib and the flow of blood from the side of the crucified Christ; another was the analogy between the tree that bore the fruit occasioning Adam's original sin and the cross which bore as its fruit Christ, the Redeemer of that sin. In a similar fashion the manna provided the children of Israel in the wilderness (Exodus 16) was held to prefigure the Eucharist, and the relationship between the Egyptian servant girl Hagar and Sarah (Genesis 16) was held to prefigure the relationship between the earthly Jerusalem of the Old Testament and the heavenly Jerusalem of the New Testament. By some interpreters, elements of New Testament history were represented as in their turn prefiguring the events that will come to be fulfilled in "the last days" of Christ's Second Coming and Last Judgment.

The **allegorical interpretation** of the Bible had its roots in Greek and Roman thinkers who treated classical myths as allegorical representations of abstract cosmological, philosophical, or moral truths. The method was applied to narratives in the Hebrew Scriptures by the Jewish philosopher Philo (died AD 50) and was adapted to Christian interpretation by Origen in the third century. The fundamental distinction in the allegorical interpretation of the Bible is between the "literal" (or "historical," or "carnal") meaning of the text—the historical truth that it specifically signifies—and the additional "spiritual" or "mystical" or "allegoric" meaning that it signifies by analogy. (Refer to the entry *allegory*.)

The spiritual aspect of a text's literal meaning was often in turn subdivided into two or more levels; some interpreters specified as many as seven, or even twelve levels. By the twelfth century, however, biblical interpreters widely agreed in finding a **fourfold meaning** in many biblical passages. A typical set of distinctions, as proposed by St. Thomas Aquinas and others, specifies (1) the literal or historical meaning, which is a narrative of what in fact happened; (2) the allegorical meaning proper, which is the New Testament truth, or else the prophetic reference to the Christian Church, that is signified by a passage in the Old Testament; (3) the tropological meaning, which is the moral truth or doctrine signified by the same passage; and (4) the anagogical meaning, or reference of the passage to Christian **eschatology**, that is, the events that are to come in "the last days" of Christ's judgment and the life after death of individual souls.

We can distinguish between the typological and allegorical mode of interpretation by saying that typology is horizontal, in that it relates items in two texts (the Old and New Testaments) that are separated in time, while allegorical interpretation is vertical, in that it uncovers multiple layers of significance in a single textual item. The two interpretive methods, however, were often applied simultaneously, and in many instances fused, by biblical exegetes. Both methods flourished into the eighteenth century and recur recognizably in later periods. They were employed in sermons and in a great variety of writings on religious matters, and were adapted to **iconography**—that is, representations of biblical and nonbiblical persons and events intended to have allegoric or symbolic significance—in painting and sculpture. Medieval and later poets sometimes adopted the typological and allegorical principles— originally developed for interpreting the Bible—in composing their own writings on religious subjects. Dante, for example, in a letter written in 1319 to his friend and patron Can Grande della Scala, announced that he composed his *Divine Comedy* to signify a double subject, literal and allegorical, and that the allegorical subject can in turn be subdivided into allegorical, moral, and anagogical meanings. Scholars have analyzed the adaptation of typological and allegorical procedures by many later poets who wrote on religious themes, including Edmund Spenser, George Herbert, John Milton, and (in a late and highly individual revival of the mode) William Blake.

The American scholar D. W. Robertson and others have proposed that not only writings on religious subjects but also many seemingly secular poems of the Middle Ages—including the *Roman de la Rose*, the works of Chaucer and

Chrétien de Troyes, and medieval love lyrics—were expressly written to incorporate typological and allegorical modes of theological and moral references. The
validity, however, of extending these interpretive modes to secular literature is
strongly disputed; see the suggested readings below. In *The Genesis of Secrecy: On
the Interpretation of Narrative* (1979), the British critic Frank Kermode adapted the
ancient interpretive distinction between carnal and spiritual meanings to his analysis of levels of meaning in recent works of prose fiction.

   On the various modes of biblical interpretation, see F. W. Farrar, *History of
Interpretation* (1886), Beryl Smalley, *The Study of the Bible in the Middle Ages* (rev.
1952), and the notable study by Henri de Lubac, *Exégèse Médiévale: les quatre sens
de l'écriture* (4 vols., 1959–74; rev. 1993). A classic discussion of typological, or figural, interpretation is Erich Auerbach's "Figura" in his *Scenes from the Drama of
European Literature* (1959). Philip Rollinson, in *Classical Theories of Allegory and
Christian Culture* (1981), relates early medieval interpretation of the Bible to modes
of literary interpretation in classical times. An American application in the eighteenth century of the old interpretive modes is Jonathan Edwards' *Images or
Shadows of Divine Things*, ed. Perry Miller (1948). For uses of typological and alle-
goric materials by various literary authors, see Rosemund Tuve, *A Reading of
George Herbert* (1952) and *Allegorical Imagery* (1966); J. H. Hagstrum, *William
Blake: Poet and Painter* (1964); P. J. Alpers, *The Poetry of "The Faerie Queene"*
(1967); and the essays on a number of authors in Paul Miner, ed., *Literary Uses of
Typology* (1977). For the extension of typological and allegoric methods to the
analysis of secular medieval poems, see D. W. Robertson, Jr., "Historical
Criticism," in *English Institute Essays, 1950*, ed. A. S. Downer (1951), and *A
Preface to Chaucer: Studies in Medieval Perspectives* (1962). The validity of such an
extension is attacked by several scholars in *Critical Approaches to Medieval
Literature*, ed. Dorothy Bethurum (1960), and by R. S. Crane, "On Hypotheses
in 'Historical Criticism,'" in *The Idea of the Humanities* (1967, Vol. 2, pp. 236–
60). On the application of biblical allegorization to later literary forms see, in ad-
dition to Kermode (above), Northrop Frye, *The Great Code: The Bible and
Literature* (1982); and Stephen Prickett, ed., *Reading the Text: Biblical Criticism and
Literary Theory* (1991).

**interpretive communities: 301**.

**intertextuality: 364**; *12*.

**intonation: 175**.

**intrigue: 266**.

**introspection: 345**.

**intrusive** (narrator): **272**.

**invective:** Invective is the denunciation of a person by the use of derogatory *epithets*.
   Thus Prince Hal, in Shakespeare's *1 Henry IV*, calls the corpulent Falstaff "this
   sanguine coward, this bedpresser, this horseback-breaker, this huge hill of flesh."
   (In the context of the play, there is in this instance of invective an undertone of

affection, as often when friends, secure in an intimacy that ensures they will not be taken literally, resort to derogatory name-calling in the exuberance of their affection.)

In his *Discourse Concerning Satire* (1693), John Dryden described the difference in efficacy, as a put-down, between the directness of invective and the indirectness of *irony*, in which a speaker maintains the advantage of cool detachment by leaving it to the circumstances to convert bland compliments into insults:

> How easy is it to call rogue and villain, and that wittily! But how hard
> to make a man appear a fool, a blockhead, or a knave, without using
> any of those opprobrious terms. . . . There is . . . a vast difference
> between the slovenly butchering of a man, and the fineness of a stroke
> that separates the head from the body, and leaves it standing in its place.

**irony:** In Greek comedy the character called the *eiron* was a dissembler, who characteristically spoke in understatement and deliberately pretended to be less intelligent than he was, yet triumphed over the *alazon*—the self-deceiving and stupid braggart. (See in Northrop Frye, *Anatomy of Criticism*, 1957.) In most of the modern critical uses of the term "irony," there remains the root sense of dissembling, or of hiding what is actually the case; not, however, in order to deceive, but to achieve special rhetorical or artistic effects.

**Verbal irony** (which was traditionally classified as one of the *tropes*) is a statement in which the meaning that a speaker implies differs sharply from the meaning that is ostensibly expressed. The ironic statement usually involves the explicit expression of one attitude or evaluation, but with indications in the overall speech-situation that the speaker intends a very different, and often opposite, attitude or evaluation. Thus in Canto IV of Alexander Pope's *The Rape of the Lock* (1714), after Sir Plume, egged on by the ladies, has stammered out his incoherent request for the return of the stolen lock of hair, the Baron answers:

> "It grieves me much," replied the Peer again,
> "Who speaks so well should ever speak in vain."

This is a straightforward case of an ironic reversal of the surface statement (of which one effect is to give pleasure to the reader) because there are patent clues, established by the preceding narrative, that the Peer is not in the least aggrieved and does not think that poor Sir Plume has spoken at all well. A more complex instance of irony is the famed sentence with which Jane Austen opens *Pride and Prejudice* (1813): "It is a truth universally acknowledged that a single man in

possession of a good fortune must be in want of a wife"; part of the ironic implication (based on assumptions that Austen assumes the audience shares with her) is
that a single woman is in want of a rich husband. Sometimes the use of irony by
Pope and other masters is very complicated: the meaning and evaluations may be
subtly qualified rather than simply reversed, and the clues to the ironic counter-
meanings under the literal statement—or even to the fact that the author intends
the statement to be understood ironically—may be oblique and unobtrusive. That
is why recourse to irony by an author tends to convey an implicit compliment to
the intelligence of readers, who are invited to associate themselves with the author
and the knowing minority who are not taken in by the ostensible meaning. That
is also why many literary ironists are misinterpreted and sometimes (like Daniel
Defoe and Jonathan Swift in the eighteenth century) get into serious trouble
with the obtuse authorities. Following the intricate and shifting maneuvers of
great ironists like Plato, Swift, Austen, or Henry James is a test of skill in reading
between the lines.

Some literary works exhibit **structural irony**; that is, the author, instead of
using an occasional verbal irony, introduces a structural feature that serves to sustain a duplex meaning and evaluation throughout the work. One common literary device of this sort is the invention of a **naive hero**, or else a naive narrator or
spokesman, whose invincible simplicity or obtuseness leads him to persist in putting an interpretation on affairs which the knowing reader—who penetrates to,
and shares, the implied point of view of the authorial presence behind the naive
*persona*—just as persistently is called on to alter and correct. (Note that verbal
irony depends on knowledge of the fictional speaker's ironic *intention*, which is
shared both by the speaker and the reader; structural irony depends on a knowledge of the author's ironic intention, which is shared by the reader but is not intended by the fictional speaker.) One example of the naive spokesman is Swift's
well-meaning but insanely rational and morally obtuse economist who writes the
"Modest Proposal" (1729) to convert the excess children of the oppressed and
poverty-stricken Irish into a financial and gastronomical asset. Other examples
are Swift's stubbornly credulous Gulliver, the self-deceiving and paranoid mono-
loguist in Browning's "Soliloquy of the Spanish Cloister" (1842), and the insane
editor, Kinbote, in Vladimir Nabokov's *Pale Fire* (1962). A related structural device for sustaining ironic qualification is the use of the *fallible narrator*, in which the
teller of the story is a participant in it. Although such a narrator may be neither
stupid, credulous, nor demented, he nevertheless manifests a failure of insight, by
viewing and appraising his own motives, and the motives and actions of other
characters, through what the reader is intended to recognize as the distorting perspective of the narrator's prejudices and private interests. (See *point of view*.)

In *A Rhetoric of Irony* (1974) Wayne Booth identifies as **stable irony** that in
which the speaker or author makes available to the reader an assertion or position
which, whether explicit or implied, serves as a firm ground for ironically qualifying or subverting the surface meaning. **Unstable irony**, on the other hand, offers
no fixed standpoint which is not itself undercut by further ironies. The literature
of the *absurd* typically presents such a regression of ironies. At an extreme, as in
Samuel Beckett's drama *Waiting for Godot* (1955) or his novel *The Unnamable*

(1960), there is an endless regress of ironic undercuttings. Such works suggest a denial that there is any secure evaluative standpoint, or even any determinable rationale, in the human situation.

**Sarcasm** in common parlance is sometimes used as an equivalent for all forms of irony, but it is far more useful to restrict it only to the crude and taunting use of apparent praise for dispraise: "Oh, you're God's great gift to women, you are!" The difference in application of the two terms is indicated by the difference in their etymologies; whereas "irony" derives from "eiron," a "dissembler," "sarcasm" derives from the Greek verb "sarkazein," "to tear flesh." An added clue to sarcasm is the exaggerated inflection of the speaker's voice.

The term "irony," qualified by an adjective, is used to identify various literary devices and modes of organization:

**Socratic irony** takes its name from the fact that, as he is represented in Plato's dialogues (fourth century BC), the philosopher Socrates usually dissembles by assuming a pose of ignorance, an eagerness to be instructed, and a modest readiness to entertain opinions proposed by others; although these, upon his continued questioning, turn out to be ill-grounded or to lead to absurd consequences.

**Dramatic irony** involves a situation in a play or a narrative in which the audience or reader shares with the author knowledge of present or future circumstances of which a character is ignorant; in that situation, the literary character unknowingly acts in a way we recognize to be grossly inappropriate to the actual circumstances, or expects the opposite of what we know that fate holds in store, or says something that anticipates the actual outcome, but not at all in the way that the character intends. Writers of Greek tragedy, who based their plots on legends whose outcome was already known to their audience, made frequent use of this device. Sophocles' *Oedipus the King*, for example, is a very complex instance of **tragic irony**, for the king ("I, Oedipus, whom all men call great") engages in a hunt for the incestuous father-murderer who has brought a plague upon Thebes; the object of the hunt turns out (as the audience, but not Oedipus, has known right along) to be the hunter himself; and the king, having achieved a vision of the terrible truth, blinds himself. Dramatic irony occurs also in comedy. A comic example of dramatic irony is the scene in Shakespeare's *Twelfth Night* (II. v.) in which Malvolio struts and preens in anticipation of a good fortune that the audience knows is based on a fake letter; the dramatic irony is heightened for the audience by Malvolio's ignorance of the presence of the hidden hoaxers, who gleefully comment on his incongruously complacent speech and actions.

**Cosmic irony** (or "the irony of fate") is attributed to literary works in which a deity, or else fate, is represented as though deliberately manipulating events so as to lead the protagonist to false hopes, only to frustrate and mock them. This is a favorite structural device of Thomas Hardy. In his *Tess of the D'Urbervilles* (1891) the heroine, having lost her virtue because of her innocence, then loses her happiness because of her honesty, finds it again only by murder, and having been briefly happy, is hanged. Hardy concludes: "The President of the Immortals, in Aeschylean phrase, had ended his sport with Tess."

**Romantic irony** is a term introduced by Friedrich Schlegel and other German writers of the late eighteenth and early nineteenth centuries to designate a mode of dramatic or narrative writing in which the author builds up the illusion of representing reality, only to shatter the illusion by revealing that the author, as artist, is the creator and arbitrary manipulator of the characters and their actions. The concept owes much to Laurence Sterne's presentation of a self-conscious and willful narrator in his *Tristram Shandy* (1759–67). Byron's great narrative poem *Don Juan* (1819–24) persistently uses this device for ironic and comic effect, letting the reader into the narrator's confidence, and so revealing the latter to be nothing more than a fabricator of fiction who is often at a loss for matter to sustain his story and undecided about how to continue it. (See Anne Mellor, *English Romantic Irony*, 1980.) This type of irony, involving a *self-conscious narrator*, has become a recurrent mode in the modern form of *involuted fiction*.

A number of writers associated with the *New Criticism* used "irony," although in a greatly extended sense, as a general criterion of literary value. This use is based largely on two literary theorists. T. S. Eliot praised a kind of "wit" (characteristic, in his view, of seventeenth-century *metaphysical poets* but absent in the Romantic poets) which is an "internal equilibrium" that implies the "recognition," in dealing with any one kind of experience, "of other kinds of experience which are possible." ("Andrew Marvell," 1921, in *Selected Essays*, 1960.) And I. A. Richards defined irony in poetry as an equilibrium of opposing attitudes and evaluations (*Principles of Literary Criticism*, 1924, chapter 32):

> Irony in this sense consists in the bringing in of the opposite, the complementary impulses; that is why poetry which is exposed to it is not of the highest order, and why irony itself is so constantly a characteristic of poetry which is.

Such observations were developed by Robert Penn Warren, Cleanth Brooks, and other New Critics into the claim that poems in which the writer commits himself or herself unreservedly to a single attitude or outlook, such as love or admiration or idealism, are of an inferior order because they are vulnerable to the reader's ironic skepticism; the greatest poems, on the other hand, are invulnerable to external irony because they already incorporate the poet's own "ironic" awareness of opposite and complementary attitudes. See Robert Penn Warren, "Pure and Impure Poetry" (1943), in *Critiques and Essays in Criticism*, ed. Robert W. Stallman (1949); Cleanth Brooks, "Irony as a Principle of Structure" (1949), in *Literary Opinion in America*, ed. M. D. Zabel (3d ed., 1962).

See D. C. Muecke, *Irony* (1970); A. E. Dyson, *The Crazy Fabric, Essays in Irony* (1965); Wayne C. Booth, *A Rhetoric of Irony* (1974). Linda Hutcheon, *Irony's Edge: The Theory and Politics of Irony* (1995). A suggestive and wide-ranging earlier exploration of the mode is Søren Kierkegaard's *The Concept of Irony* (1841; trans. Lee M. Capel, 1965). For references to *irony* in other entries, see page *217*.

**irregular ode: 235**.

**Italian sonnet: 336**.

**ivory tower:** A phrase taken from the biblical Song of Songs 7:4, in which the lover says to the beloved woman, "Thy neck is as a tower of ivory." In the 1830s the French critic Sainte-Beuve applied the phrase "tour d'ivoire" to the stance of the poet Alfred de Vigny, to signify his isolation from everyday life and his exaltation of art above all practical concerns. Since then "ivory tower" is often used (usually in a derogatory way) to signify an attitude or a way of life which is isolated from the everyday world and indifferent or hostile to practical affairs; more specifically, it is used to signify a theory and practice of art which insulates it from moral, political, and social concerns or effects. (See *aestheticism.*)

**Jacobean Age: 252.**

**jeremiad:** A term derived from the Old Testament prophet Jeremiah, who in the seventh century BC attributed the calamities of Israel to its violation of the covenant with Jehovah and return to pagan idolatry, denounced with gloomy eloquence its religious and moral iniquities, and called on the people to repent and reform in order that Jehovah might restore them to His favor and renew the ancient covenant. As a literary term, **jeremiad** is applied to any work which, with a magniloquence like that of the Old Testament prophet (although it may be in secular rather than religious terms), accounts for the misfortunes of an era as a just penalty for its social and moral wrongdoings, but usually holds open the possibility for reforms that will bring a happier future.

In the *Romantic Period*, powerful passages in William Blake's "prophetic poems" constitute short jeremiads, and the term is often applied to those of Thomas Carlyle's writings in which he uses a resonant biblical idiom to denounce the social and economic misdeeds of the *Victorian Period* and to call for drastic reforms. The jeremiad, in its original religious mode, was a familiar genre in the sermons and writings of the *Colonial Period* in America, at a time when it was a commonplace that the colonies in New England were the "New Israel" with which God had covenanted a glorious future. The misfortunes of the colonists, accordingly, were attributed to deviations from the divine commands and described as punishments inflicted by God on His chosen people for their own ultimate benefit. In the words of Increase Mather, "God does not punish . . . other Nations until they have filled up the Measure of their sins, and then he utterly destroyeth them; but if our Nation forsake the God of their Fathers never so little," He punishes us in order "that so he may prevent our destruction" (*The Day of Trouble Is Near*, 1674). Since that era the prophetic stance and denunciatory rhetoric of the jeremiad has been manifested by many orators and writers, religious and secular, into the present time. See Sacvan Bercovitch, *The American Jeremiad* (1978), and George P. Landow, *Elegant Jeremiahs: The Sage from Carlyle to Mailer* (1986).

**journal: 26.**

**judicial criticism: 62.**

**juncture** (in linguistics): **175**.

**Jungian criticism: 293**; *16.*

**Juvenalian satire: 321**.

**kenning: 121**.

**kinds** (of literature): **134**.

**Künstlerroman** (kunst′ lĕrōmän″): **229**.

**Lacanian literary criticism: 293**.

**lai:** A name originally applied to a variety of poems by medieval French writers in the latter part of the twelfth and the thirteenth centuries. Some lais were lyric, but most were short narratives written in *octosyllabic couplets*. Marie de France, who wrote in the French language although probably in England at the court of King Henry II, composed a number of notable poems of this sort; they are called "Breton lais" because most of their narratives are drawn from Arthurian and other Celtic legends. ("Breton" refers to Brittany, which was a Celtic part of France; see *chivalric romance*.) The Anglicized term **Breton lay** was applied in the fourteenth century to English poems written on the model of the narratives of Marie de France; they included *Sir Orfeo*, the *Lay of Launfal*, and Chaucer's "The Franklin's Tale." Later still, **lay** was used by English poets simply as a synonym for song, or as an archaic word for a fairly short narrative poem (for example by Sir Walter Scott in his *Lay of the Last Minstrel*, 1805).

  See Roger S. Loomis, ed., *Arthurian Literature in the Middle Ages* (1959); and the Introduction by Charles W. Dunn to *Lays of Courtly Love*, trans. Patricia Terry (1963).

**lampoon: 37**.

**langue** (in linguistics) (läng): **173**; *281, 325, 347.*

**latent content: 290**.

**lay** (song): **170**.

**Lebenswelt: 260**; *261.*

**legend: 206**.

**leitmotif** (līt″ mōtēf′): **205**.

**lesbian studies: 296**; *132.*

**light verse:** Light verse is a term applied to a great variety of poems that use an ordinary speaking voice and a relaxed manner to treat their subjects gaily, or play-fully, or wittily, or with good-natured *satire*. The subject matter of light verse need not be in itself petty or inconsequential; the defining quality is the *tone* of voice used, and the attitude of the lyric or narrative speaker toward the subject. Thomas Love Peacock's "The War Song of Dinas Vawr" (1829) begins

> The mountain sheep are sweeter,
> But the valley sheep are fatter;
> We therefore deemed it meeter
> To carry off the latter.

And it ends

> We brought away from battle,
> And much their land bemoaned them,
> Two thousand head of cattle,
> And the head of him who owned them:
> Ednyfed, king of Dyfed,
> His head was borne before us;
> His wine and beasts supplied our feasts,
> And his overthrow, our chorus.

The dispassionate attitude, brisk colloquialism, and pat rhymes convert what could be a matter for epic or tragedy into a comic narrative that qualifies as light verse.

**Vers de société (society verse)** is the very large subclass of light verse that deals with the relationships, concerns, and doings of polite, upper-class society. It is often satiric, but in the mode of badinage rather than severity; and when it deals with love it does so as a sexual game, or flirtatiously, or in the mode of elegant and witty compliment, rather than with passion or high seriousness. The tone is usually urbane, the style deft, and the form polished and sometimes contrived with technical virtuosity; most poems using intricate French stanza forms, such as the *villanelle*, are society verse. (See Carolyn Wells, ed., *A Vers de Société Anthology*, reprinted 1976.)

Nursery rhymes and other children's verses are another type of light verse. Edward Lear ("The Jumblies," "The Owl and the Pussy Cat") and Lewis Carroll ("Jabberwocky," *The Hunting of the Snark*) made children's **nonsense verses** into a Victorian specialty. Lear is also notable for popularizing the **limerick**, which is a largely oral form of light verse that everyone knows and many of us have practiced. (See *oral poetry.*) The name is probably derived from a convivial song with the refrain "Will you come up to Limerick?" (Limerick is a county in Ireland.) It consists of a single five-line stanza in *anapestic* meter, rhyming *aabba*, with the third and fourth lines shortened from three feet to two feet. Some limericks are decorous but many are ribald. Here is a limerick about the limerick by the scholar and humorist Professor Morris Bishop which is itself decorous, but indicates a propensity toward the alternative mode:

> The limerick is furtive and mean;
> You must keep her in close quarantine,
> Or she sneaks to the slums

> And promptly becomes
> Disorderly, drunk and obscene.[9]

An accessible collection is *The Penguin Book of Limericks*, ed. E. O. Parrott (1983). For scholarly editions of the ribald variety of the form, largely from oral sources, refer to G. Legman's two volumes, *The Limerick: 1700 Examples, with Notes, Variants, and Index* (1969); and *The New Limerick: 2750 Unpublished Examples, American and British* (1977).

Fine artificers of light and society verse are John Skelton (c. 1460–1529), the *Cavalier poets* of the early seventeenth century, and John Dryden, Matthew Prior, Lady Mary Wortley Montagu, Alexander Pope, W. S. Gilbert, and Austin Dobson. Modern practitioners include Ezra Pound, W. H. Auden, e. e. cummings, Ogden Nash, Marianne Moore, Edna St. Vincent Millay, Dorothy Parker, Phyllis McGinley, Morris Bishop, John Betjeman, A. R. Ammons, John Updike, and Ishmael Reed.

See *epigram*. Refer to *Worldly Muse: An Anthology of Serious Light Verse*, ed. A. J. M. Smith (1951); *The Fireside Book of Humorous Poetry*, ed. W. Cole (1959); *The New Oxford Book of Light Verse*, ed. Kingsley Amis (1978); *The Norton Book of Light Verse*, ed. Russell Baker (1986).

**limerick: 171**; *238*.

**limited point of view: 273**.

**line** (of verse): **194**.

**linguistics in literary criticism: Linguistics** is the systematic study of the elements of language and the principles governing their combination and organization. An older term for the scientific study of the constitution and history of language was **philology**—a term that is still sometimes used as synonymous with linguistics. Through the nineteenth century, philology was mainly "comparative" (the analysis of similarities and differences within a family of related languages) and "historical" (the analysis of the evolution of a family of languages, or of changes within a particular language, over a long course of time). This latter study of the changes in language over a span of time has come to be called **diachronic**; the important developments in twentieth-century linguistics came with the shift to the **synchronic** study of the systematic interrelations of the components of a single language at a particular time. A major contributor to modern synchronic linguistics was Ferdinand de Saussure, a French-speaking Swiss whose lectures on language as a self-sufficient system, delivered 1907–11, were published from students' notes in 1916, three years after Saussure's death; these lectures have been translated as *Course in General Linguistics* (1916). (See Saussure under *semiotics*.) Important contributions were also made by American "descriptive" or "structural" linguists, notably Edward Sapir and Leonard Bloomfield, who set out to devise a

---

[9]From *A Bowl of Bishop* by Morris Bishop. Copyright © 1954 by Morris Bishop. Used by permission of Doubleday, a division of Random House.

linguistic theory and vocabulary adequate to analyze, as modes of verbal "behavior," various Native American languages. Both Continental and American linguistics have been applied to the analysis of the distinctive uses of language in literary texts (see *Russian formalism* and *stylistics*), and Saussure's concepts and procedures in analyzing a language have been adopted as a model for analyzing the forms and organization of large-scale literary structures (see *structuralist criticism*).

As an empirical, fact-based study of language, philology has often appealed to students of literature who seek to ground their enterprise on hard evidence, rather than what they consider to be *subjective* responses and judgments. Several influential critics, including Paul de Man, Edward Said, and the medievalist Lee Patterson, in articles called a "Return to Philology," argued that literary criticism needed to recover the discipline and rigor of traditional linguistic studies. Such calls for what is often termed a **new philology** have been especially strong in disciplines such as classics and medieval studies, where textual criticism has always been a central concern. In these latter studies, the phrase "new philology" designates a movement to reorient philological study away from its traditional focus on establishing an authoritative text, to a concern with the effect on the reader of the material and verbal particularities of each manuscript text; refer to *book history studies*.

On calls for a return to philology, see Paul de Man, "The Return to Philology," in *The Resistance to Theory* (1986); Edward Said, "The Return to Philology," in *Humanism and Democratic Criticism* (2004); Jan Ziolkowski, *On Philology* (1990); Lee Patterson, "The Return to Philology," in John van Engen, ed., *The Past and Future of Medieval Studies* (1994); and Seth Lehrer, ed., *Literary History and the Challenge of Philology: The Legacy of Erich Auerbach* (1996). On the new philological movement in medieval studies, see also Stephen Nichols, ed., "The New Philology," a special issue of the journal *Speculum*, Vol. 65 (1990).

The following linguistic terms and concepts are often employed by current critics and theorists of literature:

Saussure introduced an important distinction between langue and parole. A **parole** is any particular meaningful utterance, spoken or written. The **langue** is the implicit system of elements, of distinctions and oppositions, and of principles of combination, which make it possible, within a language community, for a speaker to produce and the auditor to understand a particular parole. The linguist's primary concern, in Saussure's view, is to establish the nature of the underlying linguistic system, the langue. The American linguist Noam Chomsky has substituted for Saussure's langue and parole the distinction between **competence** (the tacit knowledge possessed by native speakers who have mastered, or "internalized," the implicit conventions and rules of a language system that make possible the production and understanding of well-formed and meaningful sentences) and **performance** (the actual utterance of particular sentences). Competent speakers know how to produce such sentences, without being able to specify the conventions and rules that enable them to do so; the function of the linguist is to identify and make explicit the system of linguistic conventions and rules that the speaker unknowingly puts into practice.

Modern linguists commonly distinguish three aspects that together constitute the **grammar**—the components, and the principles of ordering the components

—in any "natural language" (English, French, Japanese, and so on): (1) **phonology**, the study of the elementary speech sounds; (2) **morphology**, the study of the ordering of speech sounds into the smallest meaningful groups (*morphemes* and words); and (3) **syntax**, the study of the way that sequences of words are ordered into phrases, clauses, and sentences. Structural linguists usually represent these three aspects as manifesting parallel principles of distinctions and ordering, although on successively higher and more complex levels of organization. A fourth aspect of language sometimes included within the area of linguistics is **semantics**, the study of the meaning of words and of the combination of words in phrases, sentences, and larger linguistic units. In the area of semantics, Saussure introduced the terminology of the *sign* (a single word) as constituted by an inseparable union of **signifier** (the speech sounds or written marks composing the sign) and **signified** (the conceptual meaning of the sign).

1. One branch of phonology is **phonetics**, the physical description of the elementary speech sounds in all known languages and the way they are produced by the vocal apparatus. The "phonetic alphabet" is a standardized set of symbols for representing in written form all these speech sounds. Another branch is "phonemics," which deals with **phonemes**: the smallest units of speech sound which, within any one natural language, are functional—that is, which cannot vary without changing the word of which they are a part into a different word. Thus in the English word represented by the spelling "pin," if we change only the initial speech sound, we get three different words, pin–tin–din; if we change only the medial sound, we get pin–pen–pun; if we change only the final sound, we get pin–pit–pill. From the matrix of such changes, we determine that each of the individual units represented by the spelling p, t, d; i, e, u; and n, t, l function as differentiating phonemes within the English language. Each language has its own system of phonemes which both overlaps with and diverges from the phonemic system of any other language. The imperfect success that a native speaker of one language, such as German or French, manifests in adapting his habitual pronunciations to the phonemic system of a different language, such as English, is a major feature of what we identify as a "foreign accent."

   Even within a single language, however, a native speaker will vary the pronunciation of a single phonemic unit within different combinations of speech sounds, and will also vary the pronunciation from one utterance to another. Even greater phonetic differences are apparent between two native speakers, especially if they speak the **dialects** of diverse regions, or of diverse social groups. Saussure proposed the principle that what we identify as "the same phoneme" within a language is not determined by the physical features of the speech sound itself, but by its **difference** from all other phonemes in that language—that is, by the differentiability, within a given language, between a particular speech unit and all other functional speech units. Saussure's important claim is that the principle of difference, rather than any "positive" property, functions to establish identity not only for phonemes, but for units on all levels of linguistic organization, including both signs and the concepts that the signs signify. All these types of items, then, are systemic facts that achieve an identity only within a particular language, and vary between one language and another. (This claim, that seeming identities are in fact constituted by networks of differences, has been adopted and generalized as a central feature in *structuralism, semiotics,* and *deconstruction.*)

2. The next level of analysis, after phonology, is morphology—the combination of phonemes into morphemes and into words. A **morpheme** is the smallest meaningful unit of speech sounds within any one language; that is, a morphemic unit, composed of one or more phonemes, is a unit that recurs in a language with the same, or at least similar, meaning. Some morphemes, such as "man," "open," and "run" in English, constitute complete words; others, however, occur only as parts of words. For example the noun "grace" is a word that is a single morpheme. If we prefix to the root element, "grace," the morpheme "dis-," it becomes a different word with a sharply different meaning: "disgrace"; if we add to the root the morphemic suffix "-ful," the noun functions as an adjective, "graceful"; if we add to these two morphemes the further suffix, "-ly," the resulting word functions as an adverb, "gracefully"; if we prefix to this form either the morphemic "dis-" or "un-," we get the adverbial words, each composed of four morphemes, "disgracefully" and "ungracefully."

We find also an interesting set of phoneme combinations which do not constitute specific morphemes, yet are experienced by speakers of English as having a common, though very loose-boundaried, area of meaning. Examples are the initial sounds represented by "fl-" in the set of words "flash, flare, flame, flicker, flimmer," all of which signify a kind of moving light; while in the set "fly, flip, flap, flop, flit, flutter," the same initial sounds all signify a kind of movement in air. The terminal sounds represented by "-ash," as they occur in the set "bash, crash, clash, dash, flash, gash, mash, slash," have an overlapping significance of sudden or violent movement. Such combinations of phonemes are sometimes called "phonetic intensives," or else instances of **sound-symbolism**; they are important components in the type of words, exploited especially by poets, in which the sounds of the words seem peculiarly appropriate to their significance. See *onomatopoeia,* and refer to Leonard Bloomfield, *Language* (1933), pp. 244–46; I. A. Richards, *The Philosophy of Rhetoric* (1936), pp. 57–65.

Phonemes, morphemes, and words are all said to be "segments" of the stream of speech sounds which constitute an utterance. Linguists also distinguish **suprasegmental** features of language, consisting of stress, juncture, and intonation, all of which function morphemically, in that they alter the identity and significance of the segments in an utterance. A shift in **stress**—that is, of relative forcefulness, or loudness, of a component element in an utterance— from the first to the second syllable converts the noun "ínvalid" into the adjective "inválid," and the noun "cónvict" into the verb "convíct." **Juncture** denotes the transition in an utterance between adjacent speech sounds, whether within a word, between words, or between groups of words. Linguists distinguish various functional classes of junctures in English utterances. **Intonation** is the variation of pitch, or voice melody, in the course of an utterance. We utter the assertion "He is going home" with a different intonation from that of the question "Is he going home?"; and the use of the question intonation even with the assertive sequence of words "He is going home?" will make the sentence function to an auditor not as an assertion, but as a question. Uttering the following three words so as to alter the relative stress in the ways indicated, and at the same time using a variety of intonational patterns and pauses, will reveal the extent to which suprasegmental features can affect the significance of a sentence constituted by the same words: "Í like you." "I líke you." "I like yóu."

3. The third level of analysis (after the level of phonemes and the level of the combination of phonemes into morphemes and words) is syntax: the combination of words into phrases, clauses, and sentences. Analysis of speech performances (paroles) in any language reveals regularities in such constructions, which are explained by postulating syntactic **rules** that are operative within the linguistic system, or langue, which has been mastered by competent speakers and auditors. (These purely "descriptive" rules, or general regularities of syntax in common speech, are to be distinguished from the "prescriptive" rules of grammar which are presented in school handbooks designed to teach the "correct usage" of upper-class standard English.) A widely used distinction, developed by Roman Jakobson, is that between the rules governing **paradigmatic** relations (the "vertical" relations between any single word in a sentence and other words that are phonologically, syntactically, or semantically similar, and which can be substituted for it), and **syntagmatic** relations (the "horizontal" relations which determine the possibilities of putting words in a sequence so as to make a well-formed syntactic unit). On the phonemic and morphemic levels, a similar distinction is made between paradigmatic relations among single elements and syntagmatic relations of sequences of elements. This paradigmatic-syntagmatic distinction parallels the distinction made by Jakobson between metaphoric (vertical) and metonymic (horizontal) relations in analyzing *figurative language*.

Noam Chomsky in *Syntactic Structures* (1957) initiated what is known as **transformational-generative grammar**. Chomsky's persistent emphasis is on the central feature he calls "creativity" in language—the fact that a competent native speaker can produce a meaningful sentence which has no exact precedent in the speaker's earlier linguistic experience, as well as the fact that competent auditors can understand the sentence immediately, although it is equally new to them. To explain this "rule-bound creativity" of a language, Chomsky proposed that native speakers' and listeners' competence consists in their mastery of a set of generative and transformational rules. This mode of linguistics is called **generative** in that it undertakes to establish a finite system of rules that will suffice to "generate"—in the sense that it will adequately account for—the totality of syntactically "well-formed" sentences that are possible in a given language. It is **transformational** in that it postulates, in the **deep structure** of a language system, a set of "kernel sentences" (such as "John is building a house") which, in accordance with diverse rules of transformation, serve to produce a great variety of sentences on the

**surface structure** of a language system (for example, the passive form "The house is being built by John" and the question form "Is John building a house?" as well as a large number of more complex derivatives from the simple kernel sentence). Debates concerning Chomsky's views are included in Louise M. Antony and Norbert Hornstein, eds., *Chomsky and His Critics* (2003).

For diverse applications of the concepts and methods of modern linguistics to the criticism of literature, see *deconstruction, Russian formalism, semiotics, structuralism,* and *stylistics.* For Saussure's theories refer to Ferdinand de Saussure, *Course in General Linguistics,* trans. Wade Baskin (1966), and the concise analysis by Jonathan Culler, *Ferdinand de Saussure* (rev. 1986). For American linguistics: George L. Trager and Henry Lee Smith, Jr., *An Outline of English Structure* (1957); Zellig S. Harris, *Structural Linguistics* (2d ed., 1960); Leonard Bloomfield, *Language* (1994). On transformational-generative grammar: Noam Chomsky, *Selected Readings,* ed. J. P. B. Allen and Paul Van Buren (1971); *The Structure of Language,* ed. Jerry A. Fodor and Jerrold J. Katz (1964); John Lyons, *Noam Chomsky* (1970). Useful reviews of Continental and American linguistics and of their applications in literary criticism are included in Karl D. Uitti, *Linguistics and Literary Theory* (1969); William H. Youngren, *Semantics, Linguistics, and Criticism* (1972); Jonathan Culler, *The Pursuit of Signs* (1981); Nigel Fabb and others, eds., *The Linguistics of Writing: Arguments between Language and Literature* (1987); Jan Ziolkowski, ed., *On Philology* (1990); Roger Fowler, *Linguistic Criticism* (2d ed., 1996). A comprehensive account of the role of the concept of language in literary theory is Geoffrey Galt Harpham, *Language Alone: The Critical Fetish of Modernity* (2002). See also Roman Jakobson's influential essay "Linguistics and Poetics," in his *Language in Literature* (1987), and the expansion of Jakobson's basic distinction between the horizontal and vertical dimensions of language in David Lodge, *The Modes of Modern Writing: Metaphor, Metonymy, and the Typology of Modern Literature* (1977).

Issues of gender and language are addressed in Barrie Thorne, Cheris Kramerae, Nancy Henley, eds., *Language, Gender, and Society* (1983); Dale Spender, *Man Made Language* (2d ed., 1985); Joyce Penfield, ed., *Women and Language in Transition* (1987); Deborah Cameron, *Feminism and Linguistic Theory* (2d ed., 1992); Sally Johnson and Ulrike Hanna Meinhof, eds., *Language and Masculinity* (1997). (Refer to *feminist criticism* and *gender criticism.*) For references to *linguistics* in other entries, see pages *71, 147, 324.*

**literal meaning: 118**; *72, 189.*

**literariness: 127.**

**literary ballad: 22.**

**literary canon: 38.**

**literary criticism: 61.** See *criticism, literary.*

**literature** (from the Latin *litteraturae,* "writings"): Literature has been commonly used since the eighteenth century, equivalently with the French *belles lettres* ("fine letters"), to designate fictional and imaginative writings—poetry, prose fiction, and drama. (See *genres*.) In an expanded use, it designates also any other writings (including philosophy, history, and even scientific works addressed to a general audience) that are especially distinguished in form, expression, and emotional power. It is in this larger sense of the term that we call "literary" the philosophical writings of Plato and William James, the historical writings of Edward Gibbon, the scientific essays of Thomas Henry Huxley, and the psychoanalytic lectures of Sigmund Freud, and include them in the reading lists of some courses in literature. Confusingly, however, "literature" is sometimes applied also, in a sense close to the Latin original, to all written works, whatever their kind or quality. This all-inclusive use is especially frequent with reference to the sum of works that deal with a particular subject matter. At a major American university that includes a College of Agriculture, the Chairman of the Division of Literature once received this letter: "Dear Sir, Kindly send me all your literature concerning the use of cow manure as a fertilizer."

In its application to imaginative writing, "literature" has an evaluative as well as descriptive function, so that its proper use has become a matter of contention. Modern critical movements, aiming to correct what are seen as historical injustices, stress the strong but covert role played by gender, race, and class in establishing what has, in various eras, been accounted as literature, or in forming the ostensibly timeless criteria of great and *canonical* literature, or in distinguishing between "high literature" and the literature addressed to a mass audience. See, for example, the entries on *cultural studies, feminist criticism, gender criticism, Marxist criticism*, and *new historicism*. For the historical development of the concept of a work of literature as a *fine art* that is autonomous, and to be enjoyed for its own sake, see M. H. Abrams, "Art-as-Such: The Sociology of Modern Aesthetics," in *Doing Things with Texts* (1984); and Pierre Bourdieu, *The Rules of Art: Genesis and Structure of the Literary Field* (1995). For references to *literature* in other entries, see pages *79, 126, 134, 182, 220, 347.*

**literature of fact: 230**.

**literature of sensibility: 326**.

**literature of the absurd: 1**.

**litotes** (lī′ tŏtēz): **149**.

**local color:** The detailed representation in prose fiction of the setting, dialect, customs, dress, and ways of thinking and feeling which are distinctive of a particular region, such as Thomas Hardy's "Wessex" or Rudyard Kipling's India. After the Civil War a number of American writers exploited the literary possibilities of local color in various parts of America; for example, the West (Bret Harte), the Mississippi region (Mark Twain), the South (George Washington Cable), the Midwest (E. W. Howe, Hamlin Garland), and New England (Sarah Orne Jewett and Mary Wilkins Freeman). The term "local color fiction" is often applied to works which, like O. Henry's or Damon Runyon's stories set in New York City, rely for their interest mainly on a sentimental or comic representation of the surface particularities of a region; the term "regional fiction" is then used to distinguish those works which deal with more deep-seated, complex, and general human characteristics and problems. See *regional novel*.

**local poetry: 369.**

**logocentric** (lōgō sĕn′ trik): **70.**

**loose sentence: 350.**

**Lost Generation: 248.**

**low burlesque: 37.**

**low comedy: 57.**

**low style: 350.**

**lyric:** In the most common use of the term, a **lyric** is any fairly short poem, uttered by a single speaker, who expresses a state of mind or a process of perception, thought, and feeling. Many lyric speakers are represented as musing in solitude. In *dramatic lyrics*, however, the lyric speaker is represented as addressing another person in a specific situation; instances are John Donne's "Canonization" and William Wordsworth's "Tintern Abbey."

Although the lyric is uttered in the first person, the "I" in the poem need not be the poet who wrote it. In some lyrics, such as John Milton's sonnet "When I consider how my light is spent" and Samuel Taylor Coleridge's "Frost at Midnight," the references to the known circumstances of the author's life make it clear that we are to read the poem as a personal expression. Even in such **personal lyrics**, however, both the character and utterance of the speaker may be formalized and altered by the author in a way that is conducive to the desired artistic effect. In a number of lyrics, the speaker is a conventional period-figure, such as the long-suffering suitor in the Petrarchan sonnet (see *Petrarchan conceit*), or the courtly, witty lover of the *Cavalier* poems. And in some types of lyrics, the speaker is obviously an invented figure remote from the poet in character and circumstance. (See *persona, confessional poetry*, and *dramatic monologue* for distinctions between personal and invented lyric speakers.)

The lyric genre comprehends a great variety of utterances. Some, like Ben Jonson's "To the Memory of . . . William Shakespeare" and Walt Whitman's ode on the death of Abraham Lincoln, "O Captain, My Captain," are ceremonial poems uttered in a public voice on a public occasion. Among the lyrics in a more private mode, some are simply a brief, intense expression of a mood or state of feeling; for example, Shelley's "To Night," or Emily Dickinson's "Wild Nights, Wild Nights," or this fine medieval song:

> Fowles in the frith,
> The fisshes in the flood,
> And I mon waxe wood:
> Much sorwe I walke with
> For best of bone and blood.

But the genre also includes extended expressions of a complex evolution of fee-lingful thought, as in the long elegy and the meditative ode. And within a lyric, the process of observation, thought, memory, and feeling is organized in a variety of ways. For example, in "love lyrics" the speaker may simply express an enam-ored state of mind in an ordered form, as in Robert Burns' "O my love's like a red, red rose," and Elizabeth Barrett Browning's "How do I love thee? Let me count the ways"; or may gallantly elaborate a compliment (Ben Jonson's "Drink to me only with thine eyes"); or may deploy an argument to take advantage of fleeting youth and opportunity (Andrew Marvell's "To His Coy Mistress," or Shakespeare's first seventeen sonnets addressed to a male youth); or may express a cool response to an importunate lover (Christina Rossetti's "No, thank you, John"). In other kinds of lyrics the speaker manifests and celebrates a particular disposition and set of values (John Milton's "L'Allegro" and "Il Penseroso"); or expresses a sustained process of observation and meditation in the attempt to re-solve an emotional problem (Wordsworth's "Ode: Intimations of Immortality," Arnold's "Dover Beach"); or is exhibited as making and justifying the choice of a way of life (Yeats' "Sailing to Byzantium").

In the original Greek, "lyric" signified a song rendered to the accompaniment of a lyre. In some current usages, lyric still retains the sense of a poem written to be set to music; the *hymn*, for example, is a lyric on a religious subject that is in-tended to be sung. The adjectival form "lyrical" is sometimes applied to an ex-pressive, song-like passage in a narrative poem, such as Eve's declaration of love to Adam, "With thee conversing I forget all time," in Milton's *Paradise Lost*, IV, 639–56.

See *genre* for the broad distinction between the three major poetic classes of drama, narrative (or epic), and lyric, and also for the sudden elevation of lyric, in the Romantic period, to the status of the quintessentially poetic mode. For sub-classes of the lyric, see *aubade, dramatic monologue, elegy, epithalamion, hymn, ode, sonnet*. Refer to Norman Maclean, "From Action to Image: Theories of the Lyric in the 18th Century," in *Critics and Criticism*, ed. R. S. Crane (1952); Maurice Bowra, *Mediaeval Love-Song* (1961); Chaviva Hošek and Patricia Parker, eds., *Lyric Poetry: Beyond New Criticism* (1985); David Lindley, *Lyric* (1985); Helen Vendler, *The Music of What Happens* (1988).

For references to *lyric* in other entries, see pages *134, 235, 336*. For types of lyric, see *aubade; dramatic monologue; elegy; epithalamion; folk song; haiku; ode; sonnet*.

**machinery** (in an epic): **98**; *37*.

**magazines: 333**.

**magic realism: 232**.

**malapropism:** Malapropism is that type of **solecism** (the conspicuous and unin-tended violation of standard diction or grammar) which mistakenly uses a word in place of another that it resembles; the effect is usually comic. The term derives from Mrs. Malaprop in Richard Brinsley Sheridan's comedy *The Rivals* (1775), who in the attempt to display a copious vocabulary said things such as "a progeny of learning," "as headstrong as an allegory on the banks of the Nile," and "he is the very pineapple of politeness." In an early radio comedy "The Easy Aces," Jane Ace, an inveterate malapropist, remarked: "He got so excited, he ran around like a chicken with its hat off."

**manifest content: 290.**

**manifesto: 213**.

**manuscripts: 30.**

**Märchen** (měr′ shěn): **125**.

**Marxist criticism:** Marxist criticism, in its diverse forms, grounds its theory and practice on the economic and cultural theory of Karl Marx (1818–83) and his fellow-thinker Friedrich Engels (1820–95), and especially on the following claims:

1. In the last analysis, the evolving history of humankind, of its social groupings and relations, of its institutions, and of its ways of thinking are largely determined by the changing mode of its "material production"—that is, of its overall economic organization for producing and distributing material goods.
2. Changes in the fundamental mode of material production effect changes in the class structure of a society, establishing in each era dominant and subordinate classes that engage in a struggle for economic, political, and social advantage.
3. Human consciousness is constituted by an **ideology**—that is, the beliefs, values, and ways of thinking and feeling through which human beings perceive, and by recourse to which they explain, what they take to be reality. An ideology is, in complex ways, the product of the position and interests of a particular class. In any historical era, the dominant ideology embodies, and serves to legitimize and perpetuate, the interests of the dominant economic and social class.

Ideology was not much discussed by Marx and Engels after *The German Ideology*, which they wrote jointly in 1845–46, but it has become a key concept in Marxist criticism of literature and the other arts. Marx inherited the term from French philosophers of the late eighteenth century, who used it to designate the study of the way that all general concepts develop from particular sense perceptions. In the present era, "ideology" is used in a variety of non–Marxist ways, ranging from a derogatory name for any set of political ideas that are held dogmatically and applied rigorously, to a neutral name for ways of perceiving and thinking that are specific to an individual's race, sex, nationality, education, or ethnic group. In its distinctively Marxist use, the reigning ideology in any era is conceived to be, ultimately, the product of its economic structure and the resulting class relations and class interests. In a famed architectural metaphor, Marx represented ideology as a "superstructure" of which the concurrent socioeconomic system is the "base." Friedrich Engels described ideology as "a false consciousness," and many later Marxists consider it to be constituted largely by unconscious prepossessions that are illusory, in contrast to the "scientific" (that is, Marxist) knowledge of the economic determinants, historical evolution, and present constitution of the social world. A further claim is that, in the era of capitalist economic organization that emerged in the West during the eighteenth century, the reigning ideology incorporates the interests of the dominant and exploitative class, the "bourgeoisie," who own the means of production and distribution, as opposed to the "proletariat," or wage-earning working class. This ideology, it is claimed, to those who live in and with it, seems a natural and inevitable way of seeing, explaining, and dealing with the environing world, but in fact has the hidden function of legitimizing and maintaining the position, power, and economic interests of the ruling class. Bourgeois ideology is regarded as both producing and permeating the social and cultural institutions, beliefs, and practices of the present era—including religion, morality, philosophy, politics, and the legal system, as well as (although in a less direct way) literature and the other arts.

In accordance with some version of the views just outlined, a Marxist critic typically undertakes to explain the *literature* in any historical era, not as works created in accordance with timeless artistic criteria, but as "products" of the economic and ideological determinants specific to that era. What some Marxist critics themselves decried as "vulgar Marxism" analyzed a "bourgeois" literary work as in direct correlation with the present stage of the class struggle and demanded that such works be replaced by a "social realism" that would represent the true reality and progressive forces of our time; in practice, this usually turned out to be the demand that literature conform to an official party line. More flexible Marxists, on the other hand, building upon scattered comments on literature in Marx and Engels themselves, grant that traditional literary works possess a degree of autonomy that enables some of them to transcend the prevailing bourgeois ideology sufficiently to represent (or in the frequent Marxist equivalent, to **reflect**) aspects of the "objective" reality of their time. (See *imitation*.)

The Hungarian thinker Georg Lukács, one of the most widely influential of Marxist critics, represents such a flexible view of the role of ideology. He proposed that each great work of literature creates "its own world," which is unique and seemingly distinct from "everyday reality." But masters of realism in the novel such as Balzac or Tolstoy, by "bringing to life the greatest possible richness of the objective conditions of life," and by creating "typical" characters who manifest the essential tendencies and determinants of their epoch, succeed—often "in opposition to [the author's] own conscious ideology"—in producing a fictional world which is a "reflection of life in the greatest concreteness and clarity and with all its motivating contradictions." That is, the fictional world of such great writers accords with the Marxist conception of the real world as constituted by class conflict, economic and social "contradictions," and the alienation of the individual under capitalism. (See *bourgeois epic*, under *epic*, and refer to Georg Lukács, *Writer and Critic and Other Essays*, trans. 1970; the volume also includes Lukács' useful review of the foundational tenets of Marxist criticism, in "Marx and Engels on Aesthetics.")

While lauding nineteenth-century literary realism, Lukács attacked modernist experimental writers as "decadent" instances of concern with the subjectivity of the alienated individual in the fragmented world of our late stage of capitalism. (See *modernism*.) He thereby inaugurated a vigorous debate among Marxist critics about the political standing of formal innovators in twentieth-century literature. In opposition to Lukács, the **Frankfurt School** of German Marxists, especially Theodor Adorno and Max Horkheimer, lauded modernist writers such as James Joyce, Marcel Proust, and Samuel Beckett, proposing that their formal experiments, by the very fact that they fragment and disrupt the life they "reflect," establish a distance and detachment that serve as an implicit critique—or yield a "negative knowledge"—of the dehumanizing institutions and processes of society under capitalism. Adorno and Horkheimer attempted, after World War II, to explain "why humanity, instead of entering into a truly human condition" (as Marxists had predicted) "is sinking into a new kind of barbarism." See the entry *critique*, and refer to *The Essential Frankfurt School Reader*, ed. Andrew Arato and Eike Gebhardt (1982), and for an authoritative history of the Frankfurt School, Martin Jay, *The Dialectical Imagination* (1996).

Two rather maverick German Marxists, Bertolt Brecht and Walter Benjamin, who also supported modernist and nonrealistic art, have had considerable influence on non-Marxist as well as Marxist criticism. In his critical theory, and in his own dramatic writings (see *epic theater*), Bertolt Brecht rejected what he called the "Aristotelian" concept that a tragic play is an imitation of reality, with a unified plot and a universal theme that establishes an identification of the audience with the hero and produces a catharsis of the spectator's emotions. (See Aristotle, under *tragedy* and *plot*.) Brecht proposes instead that the illusion of reality should be deliberately shattered by an episodic plot, by protagonists who do not attract the audience's sympathy, by a striking theatricality in staging and acting, and by other ways of baring the artifice of drama so as to produce an "alienation effect" (see under *distance and involvement*). The result of such alienation, Brecht asserts, will be to jar audiences out of their passive acceptance of modern capitalist society as a natural way of life, into an attitude not only (as in Adorno) of critical understanding of capitalist shortcomings, but of active cooperation with the forces of change.

Another notable critic, Walter Benjamin, was both an admirer of Brecht and briefly an associate of the Frankfurt School. Particularly influential was Benjamin's attention to the effects of changing material conditions in the production of the arts, especially the recent developments of the mass media that have promoted, he said, "a revolutionary criticism of traditional concepts of art." In his essay "The Work of Art in the Age of Mechanical Reproduction," Benjamin proposes that modern technical innovations such as photography, the phonograph, the radio, and especially the cinema, have transformed the very concept and status of a work of art. Formerly an artist or author produced a work which was a single object, regarded as the special preserve of the bourgeois elite, around which developed a quasi-religious "aura" of uniqueness, autonomy, and aesthetic value independent of any social function—an aura which invited in the spectator a passive attitude of absorbed contemplation in the object itself. (See *aestheticism*.) The new media not only make possible the infinite and precise reproducibility of the objects of art, but effect the production of works which, like the motion pictures, are specifically designed to be reproduced in multiple copies. Such modes of art, Benjamin argues, by destroying the mystique of the unique work of art as a subject for pure contemplation, make possible a radical role for works of art by opening the way to "the formulation of revolutionary demands in the politics of art." (Benjamin's writings are available in Walter Benjamin, *Selected Writings*, 4 vols., 2002–04. Useful collections of essays by the Marxist critics Lukács, Brecht, Adorno, and Horkheimer are R. Taylor, ed., *Aesthetics and Politics*, 1977; and Roger S. Gottlieb, ed., *An Anthology of Western Marxism: From Lukács and Gramsci to Socialist-Feminism*, 1989.)

The second half of the twentieth century witnessed a resurgence of Marxist criticism, marked by an openness, on some level of literary analysis, to other current critical perspectives; a flexibility which acknowledges that Marxist critical theory is itself, at least to some degree, an evolving historical process; a subtilizing of the concept of ideology as applied to literary content; and a tendency to grant an increased role to nonideological and distinctively artistic determinants of literary structures and values.

In the 1960s the influential French Marxist Louis Althusser assimilated the *structuralism* then current into his view that the structure of society is not a monolithic whole, but is constituted by a diversity of "nonsynchronous" social formations, or "ideological state apparatuses," including religious, legal, political, and literary institutions. Each of these possesses a "relative autonomy"; only "in the last instance" is the ideology of a particular institution determined by its material base in contemporary economic production. In an influential reconsideration of the general nature of ideology, Althusser opposes its definition as simply "false consciousness." He declares instead that the ideology of each mode of state apparatus is different, and operates by means of a discourse which **interpellates** (calls upon) the individual to take up a pre-established "subject position"—that is, a position as a person with certain views and values, which, however, in every instance serve the ultimate interests of the ruling class. (See *discourse* and *subject* under *poststructuralism*.) Althusser affirms, furthermore, that a great work of literature is not a mere product of ideology, because its fiction establishes for the reader a distance from which to recognize, hence expose, "the ideology from which it is born . . . from which it detaches itself as art, and to which it alludes." Pierre Macherey, in *A Theory of Literary Production* (1966, trans. 1978), stressed the supplementary claim that a literary text not only distances itself from its ideology by its fiction and form, but also exposes the "contradictions" that are inherent in that ideology by its "silences" or "gaps"—that is, by what the text fails to say because its inherent ideology makes it impossible to say it. Combining Marxism and *Freudianism*, Macherey asserts that such textual "absences" are symptoms of ideological repressions of the contents in the text's own "unconscious." The aim of Marxist criticism, Macherey asserts, is to make these silences "speak" and so to reveal, behind what an author consciously intended to say, the text's unconscious content—that is, its repressed awareness of the flaws, stresses, and incoherence in the very ideology that it incorporates. (See *hermeneutics of suspicion*.)

Between 1929 and 1935 the Italian Communist Antonio Gramsci, while imprisoned by the fascist government, wrote approximately thirty documents on political, social, and cultural subjects, known as the "prison notebooks." Gramsci maintains the original Marxist distinction between the economic base and the cultural superstructure, but replaces the claim that culture is a disguised "reflection" of the material base with the concept that the relationship between the two is one of "reciprocity," or interactive influence. Gramsci places special emphasis on the popular, as opposed to the elite elements of culture, ranging from *folklore* and popular music to the cinema. Gramsci's most widely echoed concept is that of **hegemony**: that a social class achieves a predominant influence and power, not by direct and overt means, but by succeeding in making its ideological views so pervasive that the subordinate classes unwittingly accept and participate in their own oppression. The concept of hegemony, unlike the classical Marxist conception of ideology, implies an openness to negotiation and exchange, as well as conflict, between classes, and so refashions Marxist categories to fit a modern, post-industrial society in which diverse concepts and ideas, apart from "modes of production," play a leading role. Another appealing feature of Gramsci's thought to recent theorists is his emphasis on the role of intellectuals and opinion makers in helping people understand how they can effect their own transformation. Especially since Gramsci's prison writings began to be translated into English in 1971, they have had a strong influence on literary and social critics such as Terry Eagleton in England and Fredric Jameson and Edward Said in America, who argue for the power of literary culture to intervene in and transform existing economic and political arrangements and activities. (See Gramsci, *Selections from Cultural Writings*, trans. William Boelhower, 1985; David Forgacs, ed., *The Antonio Gramsci Reader: Selected Writings 1916–1935*, 2000; Chantal Mouffe, ed., *Gramsci and Marxist Theory*, 1979.)

Gramsci's writings also inspired a number of **post-Marxist** thinkers, who sought to adapt Marxism to *poststructural* discourse. Among these was a leader of the British Cultural Studies movement, Stuart Hall. (See *cultural studies*, also *cultural materialism* under the entry *new historicism*.) Hall insisted that ideology must not be considered a "false consciousness" or kind of concealment, but rather as a multifaceted force in the struggle for cultural power, carried on in the mode of the production of meaning. All "meaning," Hall said, "is always a social production, a practice. The world has to be *made to mean*." (See Hall, "The Recovery of 'Ideology,'" in Michael Gurevitch and others, eds., *Culture, Society and the Media*, 1982.)

Also strongly influenced by Gramsci were Ernesto Laclau and Chantal Mouffe, who in *Hegemony and Socialist Strategy* (1985) argued for an understanding of society grounded, not in economic determinism, but in the nature of language. Adapting the linguistic view of Ferdinand de Saussure that the identity of a sign and of its significance was not intrinsic, but determined by its position in a differential system, they argued that such "unfixity" was "the condition of every social identity," so that the place of power in a society can be legitimately occupied by anyone or any group. With the aid of Sausserian language theory, Laclau and Mouffe propose a view of society that, instead of being strictly determined by

modes of production and the laws of economics, is open to innovation, transformation, and self-invention. (For Saussure's linguistic theory, see under *linguistics in
literary criticism* and *semiotics*. For post-Marxist theory in general, refer to Geoffrey
Galt Harpham, *Language Alone: The Critical Fetish of Modernity*, 2002, pp. 70–141.)

In England the many social and critical writings of Raymond Williams manifest an adaptation of Marxist concepts to his humanistic concern with the overall
texture of an individual's "lived experience." A leading theorist of Marxist criticism in England is Terry Eagleton, who expanded and elaborated the concepts
of Althusser and Macherey into his view that a literary text is a special kind of
production in which ideological discourse—described as any system of mental representations of lived experience—is reworked into a specifically literary discourse.
In recent years Eagleton has been increasingly hospitable to the tactical use, for
dealing with ideology in literature, of concepts derived from *deconstruction* and
from Lacan's version of Freudian *psychoanalysis*. Eagleton views such poststructuralist analyses as useful to Marxist critics of literary texts insofar as they serve to
undermine reigning beliefs and certainties, but solely as preliminary to the properly Marxist enterprise of exposing their ideological motivation and to the application of the criticism of literature toward politically desirable ends.

The most prominent American theorist, Fredric Jameson, is also the most
eclectic of Marxist critics. In *The Political Unconscious: Narrative as a Socially
Symbolic Act* (1981), Jameson expressly adapts to his critical enterprise such seemingly incompatible viewpoints as the medieval theory of fourfold levels of meaning in the *allegorical interpretation* of the Bible, the *archetypal criticism* of Northrop
Frye, *structuralist criticism*, Lacan's reinterpretations of Freud, *semiotics*, and *deconstruction*. These modes of criticism, Jameson asserts, are applicable at various stages of
the critical interpretation of a literary work; but Marxist criticism, he contends,
"subsumes" all the other "interpretive modes," by retaining their positive findings
within a "political interpretation of literary texts" which stands as the "final" or
"absolute horizon of all reading and all interpretation." This last-analysis "political
interpretation" of a literary text involves an exposure of the hidden role of the
"political unconscious"—a concept which Jameson describes as his "collective,"
or "political," adaptation of the Freudian concept that each individual's unconscious is a repository of repressed desires. (See *psychological and psychoanalytic criticism*.)
In a mode similar to Macherey, Jameson affirms that in any literary product of
our late capitalist era, the "rifts and discontinuities" in the text, and especially
those elements which, in the French phrase, are its "non-dit" (its not-said), are
symptoms of the repression by a predominant ideology of the contradictions of
"History" into the depths of the political unconscious; and the content of this repressed History, Jameson asserts, is the revolutionary process of "the collective
struggle to wrest a realm of Freedom from a realm of Necessity." In the final stage
of an interpretation, Jameson holds, the Marxist critic "rewrites," in the mode of
"allegory," the literary text "in such a way that the [text] may be seen as the . . .
reconstruction of a prior historical or ideological *subtext*"—that is, of the text's unspoken, because repressed and unconscious, awareness of the ways it is determined
not only by current ideology, but also by the long-term process of true "History."
(See *allegory*.)

Refer to *sociology of literature*, and for the Marxist wing of the new historicism, see *cultural materialism* under the entry *new historicism*. Useful introductions to Marxist criticism in general are the essays in Maynard Solomon, ed., *Marxism and Art: Essays Classic and Contemporary* (1979); Terry Eagleton and Drew Milne, eds., *Marxist Literary Theory: A Reader* (1996). In addition to the writings listed above, refer to Georg Lukács, *Studies in European Realism* (1950); Raymond Williams, *Culture and Society, 1780–1950* (1960) and *Marxism and Literature* (1977); Peter Demetz, *Marx, Engels and the Poets: Origins of Marxist Literary Criticism* (1967); Walter Benjamin, *Illuminations* (trans. 1968); Louis Althusser, *Lenin and Philosophy, and Other Essays* (1969, trans. 1971), and *For Marx* (1996); Fredric Jameson, *Marxism and Form* (1971), and *Late Marxism: Adorno, or the Persistence of the Dialectic* (1996); Lee Baxandall and Stefan Morawski, eds., *Marx and Engels on Literature and Art* (1973); Terry Eagleton, *Criticism and Ideology* (1976) and *Marxism and Literary Criticism* (1976); Chris Bullock and David Peck, eds., *Guide to Marxist Literary Criticism* (1980); Michael Ryan, *Marxism and Deconstruction* (1982); J. J. McGann, *The Romantic Ideology* (1983); J. G Merquior, *Western Marxism* (1986). Various essays by Gayatri Chakravorty Spivak assimilate Marxist concepts both to *deconstruction* and to the viewpoint of *feminist criticism*; see, for example, her "Displacement and the Discourse of Women," in *Displacement: Derrida and After*, ed. Mark Krupnick (1983). For Derrida's "reading" of Marx, see his *Specters of Marx: The State of the Debt, the Work of Mourning, and the New International* (1994). For a sharp critique of recent theorists of Marxist criticism, see Frederick Crews, "Dialectical Immaterialism," in *Skeptical Engagements* (1986); also Richard Levin, "The New Interdisciplinarity in Literary Criticism," in Nancy Easterlin and Barbara Riebling, eds., *After Poststructuralism: Interdisciplinarity and Literary Theory*, 1993. Marxist concerns also serve to form the *new formalism* in literary criticism; see Robert Kaufman, "Red Kant, or The Persistence of the Third Critique in Adorno and Jameson," *Critical Inquiry*, Vol. 26 (2000).

For references to *Marxist criticism* in other entries, see pages *8, 65, 78, 128, 146, 161, 224, 230, 281, 334.*

**masculine ending: 197**.

**masculine rhyme: 317**.

**masque:** The masque (a variant spelling of "mask") was inaugurated in Renaissance Italy and flourished in England during the reigns of Elizabeth I, James I, and Charles I. In its full development, it was an elaborate form of court entertainment that combined poetic drama, music, song, dance, splendid costuming, and stage spectacle. A plot—often slight, and mainly mythological and allegorical—served to hold together these diverse elements. The speaking characters, who wore masks (hence the title), were often played by amateurs who belonged to courtly society. The play concluded with a dance in which the players doffed their masks and were joined by the audience.

In the early seventeenth century in England the masque drew upon the finest artistic talents of the day, including Ben Jonson for the poetic script (for example, *The Masque of Blacknesse* and *The Masque of Queens*) and Inigo Jones, the architect, for the elaborate sets, costumes, and stage machinery. Each lavish production cost a fortune; it was literally the sport of kings and queens, until both court and drama were abruptly ended by the Puritan triumph of 1642. The two examples best known to modern readers are the masque-within-a-play in the fourth act of Shakespeare's *The Tempest*, and Milton's sage and serious revival of the form, *Comus*, with songs by the composer Henry Lawes, which was presented at Ludlow Castle in 1634. The jubilant fourth act which Shelley added to his poetic drama *Prometheus Unbound* (1819) was modeled on the Renaissance masque, as are two dramas by the American poet Robert Frost, *A Masque of Reason* (1945) and *A Masque of Mercy* (1947). Edgar Allen Poe's lurid tale, "The Masque of the Red Death," depicts not a dramatic masque, but a masquerade ball, conducted by a medieval prince and his courtiers in defiance of a lethal plague that was ravishing the land. At this ball, a ghastly masked intruder turns out to be the Red Death itself.

The **antimasque** was a form developed by Ben Jonson. In it the characters were grotesque and unruly, the action ludicrous, and the humor broad; it served as a foil and countertype to the elegance, order, and ceremony of the masque proper, which preceded it in a performance.

See Allardyce Nicoll, *Stuart Masques and the Renaissance Stage* (1937). Stephen Orgel and Roy Strong, in *Inigo Jones: The Theatre of the Stuart Court* (2 vols., 1973), discuss Jones' contributions to the masque, with copious illustrations.

**mechanic form: 125**.

**medieval romance: 44**.

**medieval tragedy: 372**.

**meiosis** (mīō′ sĭs): **149**.

**melodrama:** "Melos" is Greek for song, and the term "melodrama" was originally applied to all musical plays, including opera. In early-nineteenth-century London, many plays were produced with a musical accompaniment that (as in modern motion pictures) served simply to fortify the emotional tone of the various scenes; the procedure was developed in part to circumvent the Licensing Act (1737), which allowed "legitimate" plays only as a monopoly of the Drury Lane and Covent Garden theaters, but permitted musical entertainments elsewhere. The term "melodrama" is now often applied to some of the typical plays, especially during the *Victorian Period*, that were written to be produced to musical accompaniment.

The Victorian melodrama can be said to bear the relation to tragedy that *farce* does to comedy. Typically, the protagonists are *flat* types: the hero is great-hearted, the heroine pure as the driven snow, and the villain a monster of malignity. (The sharply contrasted good guys and bad guys of the movie western and some television dramas are modern derivatives from standard types in the old melodramas.) The plot revolves around malevolent intrigue and violent action, while the credibility of both character and plot is often sacrificed for violent effect and emotional opportunism. Nineteenth-century melodramas such as *Under the*

*Gaslight* (1867) and the temperance play *Ten Nights in a Barroom* (1858) are still sometimes produced—less for thrills, however, than for laughs. Recently, the composer Stephen Sondheim converted George Dibdin Pitt's Victorian thriller *Sweeney Todd, The Barber of Fleet Street* (1842) into a highly effective musical drama.

The terms "melodrama" and "melodramatic" are also, in an extended sense, applied to any literary work or episode, whether in drama or prose fiction, that relies on implausible events and sensational action. Melodrama, in this sense, was standard fare in cowboy-and-Indian and cops-and-robber types of silent films, and remains alive and flourishing in current cinematic and television productions.

See M. W. Disher, *Blood and Thunder: Mid-Victorian Melodrama and Its Origins* (1949) and *Plots That Thrilled* (1954); Frank Rahill, *The World of Melodrama* (1967); R. B. Heilman, *Tragedy and Melodrama* (1968); David Thorburn, "Television Melodrama," *Television as a Cultural Force*, ed. Douglass Cater (1976); Bruce McConachie, *Melodramatic Formations: American Theatre and Society, 1820–1870* (1992).

**memoir: 26**.

**Menippean satire** (mĕnĭp′ ēăn): **321**.

**men's studies: 132**.

**metafiction: 232**; *276*.

**metaphor: 119**; *57, 358*.

**metaphor, theories of:** When someone says, discussing John's eating habits, "John is a pig," and when Coleridge writes in "The Ancient Mariner"

> The moonlight steeped in silentness
> The steady weathercock,

we recognize that the noun "pig" and the verb "steeped" are metaphors, and have no trouble understanding them. (See *metaphor* under *figurative language*.) But after twenty-five centuries of discussions of metaphor by rhetoricians, grammarians, and literary critics—in which during the last half-century they have been joined by many philosophers—there is no general agreement about the way we identify metaphors, how we are able to understand them, and what (if anything) they serve to tell us. Following is a brief summary of the most prominent among competing theories of metaphor:

1. The similarity view. This was the traditional way of analyzing metaphors, from the time that Aristotle introduced it in the fourth century BC until the recent past. It holds that a metaphor is a departure from the *literal* (that is, what a competent speaker experiences as the standard) use of language which serves as a condensed or elliptical *simile*, in that it involves an implicit comparison between two disparate things. (The two things in the examples cited above are John's eating habits and those of a pig, and the event of something being steeped—soaked

in a liquid—and the appearance of the moonlit landscape.) This view usually assumes that the features being compared pre-existed the use of the metaphor; that the metaphor can be translated into a statement of literal similarity without loss of cognitive content (that is, of the information it conveys); and also that a metaphor serves mainly to enhance the rhetorical force and stylistic vividness and pleasantness of a discourse.

2.  The interaction view. In *The Philosophy of Rhetoric* (1936) I. A. Richards introduced the terms *vehicle* for the metaphorical word (in the two examples, "pig" and "steeped") and *tenor* for the subject to which the metaphorical word is applied (John's eating habits and the moonlit landscape). In place of the similarity view, he proposed that a metaphor works by bringing together the disparate "thoughts" of the vehicle and tenor so as to effect a meaning that "is a resultant of their interaction" and that cannot be duplicated by literal assertions of a similarity between the two elements. He also asserted that metaphor cannot be viewed simply as a rhetorical or poetic departure from ordinary usage, in that it permeates all language and affects the ways we perceive and conceive the world. Almost twenty years later, in an influential essay entitled "Metaphor" (1954–55), the philosopher Max Black refined and greatly expanded Richards' treatment. Black proposed that each of the two elements in a metaphor has a "system of associated commonplaces," consisting of the properties and relations that we commonly attach to the object, person, or event. When we understand a metaphor, the system of commonplaces associated with the "subsidiary subject" (equivalent to I. A. Richards' "vehicle") interacts with the system associated with the "principal subject" (Richards' "tenor") so as to "filter" or "screen" that system, and thus effects a new way of perceiving and conceiving the principal subject. This process, by which one complex set of associations serves to select and reorganize a second set, Black claims, is a "distinctive *intellectual* operation." He also claims that, in place of saying that metaphors simply formulate a pre-existing similarity between the two subjects, "it would be more illuminating in some of these cases to say that the metaphor *creates* the similarity."

Before Max Black's essay, philosophers had paid only passing attention to metaphor. The reigning assumption had been that the main function of language is to communicate truths, and that truths can be clearly communicated only in literal language. For the most part, accordingly, philosophers had adverted to metaphor only to warn against its intrusion into rational discourse, as opposed to poetry and oratory, on the ground that figurative language, as John Locke had said in his *Essay Concerning Human Understanding* (1690), serves only "to insinuate wrong ideas, move the passions, and thereby mislead the judgment." Black's essay, however, helped inaugurate a philosophical concern with metaphor which, since the 1960s, has resulted in a flood of publications. Many of these writings restate, with various qualifications, refinements, and expansions, either the similarity or interaction views of metaphor. Within these contributions, however, one can identify two additional views, both of which have been influential in literary theory as well as in philosophy:

3.  The pragmatic view. In an essay entitled "What Metaphors Mean" (1978), Donald Davidson mounted a challenge to the standard assumption that there

is a metaphorical meaning as distinct from a literal meaning. "Metaphors," he claims, "mean what the words, in their most literal interpretation, mean, and nothing more." The question of metaphor is pragmatic, not semantic; that is, it is the use of a literal statement in such a way as to "suggest," or "intimate," or "lead us to notice" what we might otherwise overlook. In a chapter on "Metaphor" in *Expression and Meaning* (1979), John Searle also rejected the similarity and interaction views, on the grounds that at best they serve to explain, and that only in part and in a misleading way, how some metaphors come to be used and understood. In consonance with his overall *speech-act theory*, Searle proposed that to explain metaphor we must distinguish between "word, or sentence meaning" (what the word or sentence means literally) and a particular speaker's "utterance meaning" (the metaphorical meaning that a speaker uses the literal word or sentence meaning to express). Searle goes on to propose a set of implicit principles, shared by the speaker and interpreter, to explain how a speaker can use a sentence with a literal meaning to say something with a very different metaphorical meaning, as well as to clarify how a hearer recognizes and proceeds to interpret a literal sentence that is used metaphorically.

4. The cognitive (or conceptual) view. This treatment of metaphor, prominent since about 1980, begins by rejecting the assumption in many earlier theories that the ordinary, normal use of language is literal, from which metaphor is a deviation for special rhetorical and poetic purposes. Instead it claims that the ordinary use of language is pervasively and indispensably metaphorical, and that metaphor persistently and profoundly structures the ways human beings perceive, what they know, and how they think.

George Lakoff and Mark Turner in *More than Cool Reason* (1979) provide a short and accessible introduction to this cognitive view, with special attention to its relevance for the analysis of metaphors in poetry. They conceive metaphor to be a projection and mapping across what they call "conceptual domains"; that is, its use is basically a cognitive mental process, of which the metaphorical word, phrase, or sentence is only the linguistic aspect and expression. To identify the two elements that compose a metaphor, the authors replace "vehicle" and "tenor," or "primary" and "secondary," with the terms "source domain" and "target domain." In using and understanding a metaphor, part of the conceptual structure of the source domain is "mapped" onto the conceptual structure of the target domain, in a one-way "transaction" (as distinct from an "interaction") which may alter and reorganize the way we perceive or think about the latter element.

A distinctive procedure in this view is to identify a number of "basic conceptual metaphors" that pervade discourse in our Western culture, but are so common and operate so automatically that for the most part we use them without noticing them. Some of the most common basic metaphors are Purposes Are Destinations; Time Moves; Time Is A Reaper; Life Is A Journey; Life Is A Play; People Are Plants. Such metaphors establish cross-conceptual mappings that manifest themselves in our ordinary speech as well as in the greatest poetry. People Are Plants, for example, is a type of cognitive mapping that underlies such everyday expressions as "She's in the flower of youth," "She's a late bloomer," and "He's withering fast," no less than it does King Lear's "Ripeness is all." The difference between trivially conventional and innovatively poetic uses of a basic metaphor, by this analysis, is a difference not in cognitive kind, but in the range and diversity of application, and in the skill manifested in its verbal expression. And in all uses (including in the language of the sciences) cross-domain metaphors play an ineradicable part in determining what we know, how we reason, what values we assign, and the ways we conduct our lives.

Vigorous debates about metaphor continue apace. A plausible conclusion is that the diverse accounts of metaphor need not be mutually exclusive, in that each is directed especially to a particular one of many kinds of metaphor or functions of metaphor, or focuses on a different moment in the process of recognizing and understanding a metaphor, or is adapted to the perspective of a preferred mode of philosophy.

Mark Johnson, ed., *Philosophical Perspectives on Metaphor* (1981) includes, among others, the writings on metaphor (mentioned above) by Richards, Black, Davidson, and Searle; Sheldon Sacks, ed., *On Metaphor* (1987), contains essays by both philosophers and literary critics; and Andrew Ortony, ed., *Metaphor and Thought* (2d ed., 1993) includes an essay by George Lakoff that summarizes the cognitive treatments of metaphor. On the cognitive view, see also George Lakoff and Mark Johnson, *Metaphors We Live By* (1980); and Mark Turner, *Death Is the Mother of Beauty* (1987). For earlier treatments of the pervasive cognitive function of metaphors, see Stephen C. Pepper, *World Hypotheses* (1942), on the "root metaphors" that generate the major philosophical worldviews; and M. H. Abrams, *The Mirror and the Lamp* (1953), on the diverse "constitutive metaphors" that provide the structure and categories of divergent theories of literature and the other arts. See also Paul Ricoeur, *The Rule of Metaphor* (1977), and for an influential essay on metaphor by a *deconstructive* theorist, Jacques Derrida, "White Mythology," in *Margins of Discourse* (1982). For references to *theories of metaphor* in other entries, see pages *311, 313*.

**metaphysical conceit: 53**; *23, 245*.

**metaphysical poets:** John Dryden said in his *Discourse Concerning Satire* (1693) that John Donne in his poetry "affects the metaphysics," meaning that Donne employs the terminology and abstruse arguments of the medieval Scholastic philosophers. In 1779 Samuel Johnson extended the term "metaphysical" from Donne to a school of poets, in the acute and balanced critique which he incorporated in his "Life of Cowley." The name is now applied to a group of seventeenth-century poets who, whether or not directly influenced by Donne, employ similar poetic procedures and imagery, both in secular poetry (Cleveland, Marvell, and Cowley) and in religious poetry (Herbert, Vaughan, Crashaw, and Traherne).

Attempts have been made to demonstrate that these poets had in common a philosophical worldview. The term "metaphysical," however, fits these very diverse writers only if it is used, as Johnson used it, to indicate a common poetic style, use of figurative language, and way of organizing the meditative process or the poetic argument. Donne set the metaphysical mode by writing poems which are sharply opposed to the rich mellifluousness and the idealized view of human nature and of sexual love which had constituted a central tradition in Elizabethan poetry, especially in Spenser and the writers of *Petrarchan sonnets*; Donne's poems are opposed also to the fluid, regular versification of Donne's contemporaries, the *Cavalier poets*. Instead, Donne wrote in a diction and meter modeled on the rough give-and-take of actual speech, and often organized his poems as an urgent or heated argument—with a reluctant mistress, or an intruding friend, or God, or death, or with himself. He employed a subtle and often deliberately outrageous logic; he was realistic, ironic, and sometimes cynical in his treatment of the complexity of human motives, especially in the sexual relationship; and whether playful or serious, and whether writing the poetry of love or of intense religious experience, he was above all "witty," making ingenious use of *paradox, pun,* and startling parallels in simile and metaphor (see *metaphysical conceit* and *wit*). The beginnings of four of Donne's poems will illustrate the shock tactic, the dramatic form of direct address, the rough idiom, and the rhythms of the living voice that are characteristic of his metaphysical style:

> Go and catch a falling star,
> Get with child a mandrake root . . .

> For God's sake hold your tongue, and let me love.

> Busy old fool, unruly sun . . .

> Batter my heart, three-personed God. . . .

Some, not all, of Donne's poetic procedures have parallels in each of his contemporaries and successors whom literary historians usually group as metaphysical poets.

These poets have had admirers in every age, but beginning with the *Neoclassic Period* of the later seventeenth century, they were by most critics and readers regarded as interesting but perversely ingenious and obscure exponents of *false wit*, until a drastic revaluation after World War I elevated Donne, and to a lesser extent Herbert and Marvell, high in the hierarchy of English poets (see *canon of literature*). This reversal owed much to H. J. C. Grierson's Introduction to *Metaphysical Lyrics and Poems of the Seventeenth Century* (1912), was given strong impetus by T. S. Eliot's essays "The Metaphysical Poets" and "Andrew Marvell" (1921), and was continued by a great number of commentators, including F. R. Leavis in England and especially the American *New Critics*, who tended to elevate the metaphysical style into the model of their ideal poetry of irony, paradox, and "unified sensibility." (See *dissociation of sensibility*.) More recently, Donne has lost this exemplary status, but continues to occupy a firm position as a prominent poet in the English canon.

See F. R. Leavis, *Revaluation: Tradition and Development in English Poetry* (1936); Cleanth Brooks, *Modern Poetry and the Tradition* (1939); Rosemund Tuve, *Elizabethan and Metaphysical Imagery* (1947); J. E. Duncan, *The Revival of Metaphysical Poetry* (1959); Helen Gardner, ed., *John Donne: A Collection of Critical Essays* (1962). F. J. Warnke, *European Metaphysical Poetry* (1961), treats the continental vogue of this style. For references to *metaphysical poets* in other entries, see pages *39, 53, 168, 239, 248, 380.*

**meter:** Meter is the recurrence, in regular units, of a prominent feature in the sequence of speech sounds of a language. There are four main types of meter in European languages: (1) In classical Greek and Latin, the meter was **quantitative**; that is, it was established by the relative duration of the utterance of a syllable, and consisted of recurrent patterns of long and short syllables. (2) In French and many other Romance languages, the meter is **syllabic**, depending on the number of syllables within a line of verse, without regard to the fall of the stresses. (3) In the older Germanic languages, including Old English, the meter is **accentual**, depending on the number of stressed syllables within a line, without regard to the number of intervening unstressed syllables. (4) The fourth type of meter, combining the features of the two preceding types, is **accentual-syllabic**, in which the metric units consist of a recurrent pattern of stresses on a recurrent number of syllables. The stress-and-syllable type has been the predominant meter of English poetry since the fourteenth century.

There is considerable dispute about the most valid or useful way to analyze and classify English meters. This entry will begin by presenting a traditional accentual-syllabic analysis which has the virtues of being simple, widely used, and applicable to by far the greater part of English poetry from Chaucer to the present. Major departures from this stress-and-syllable meter will be described in the latter part of the entry.

In all sustained spoken English we sense a **rhythm**; that is, a recognizable although varying pattern in the beat of the **stresses**, or **accents** (the more forcefully uttered, hence louder syllables) in the stream of speech sounds. In meter, this rhythm is structured into a recurrence of regular—that is, approximately equivalent—units of stress pattern. Compositions written in meter are also known as **verse**.

We attend, in reading verse, to the individual **line**, which is a sequence of words printed as a separate entity on the page. The meter is determined by the pattern of stronger and weaker stresses on the syllables composing the words in the verse line; the stronger is called the "stressed" syllable and all the weaker ones the "unstressed" syllables. (What the ear perceives as a strong stress is not an absolute quantity, but is relative to the degree of stress in the adjacent syllables.) Three major factors determine where the stresses (in the sense of the relatively stronger stresses or accents) will fall in a line of verse: (1) Most important is the "word accent" in words of more than one syllable; in the noun "áccent" itself, for example, the stress falls on the first syllable. (2) There are also many monosyllabic words in the language, and on which of these—in a sentence or a phrase—the stress will fall depends on the grammatical function of the word (we normally put stronger stress on nouns, verbs, and adjectives, for example, than on articles or prepositions), and depends also on the "rhetorical accent," or the emphasis we give a word because we want to enhance its importance in a particular utterance. (3) Another determinant of perceived stress is the prevailing "metrical accent," which is the beat that we have come to expect, in accordance with the stress pattern that was established earlier in the metrical composition.

If the prevailing stress pattern enforces a drastic alteration of the normal word accent, we get a **wrenched accent**. Wrenching may be the result of a lack of metrical skill; it was, however, conventional in the *folk ballad* (for example, "fair ladíe," "far countrée"), and is sometimes deliberately used for comic effects, as in Lord Byron's *Don Juan* (1819–24) and in the verses of Ogden Nash.

It is possible to distinguish a number of degrees of syllabic stress in English speech, but the most common and generally useful fashion of analyzing and classifying the standard English meters is "binary." That is, we distinguish only two categories—strong stress and weak stress—and group the syllables into metric feet according to the patterning of these two degrees. A **foot** is the combination of a strong stress and the associated weak stress or stresses which make up the recurrent metric unit of a line. The relatively stronger-stressed syllable is called, for short, "stressed"; the relatively weaker-stressed syllables are called "light," or most commonly, "unstressed."

The four standard feet distinguished in English are:

1. **Iambic** (the noun is "iamb"): an unstressed syllable followed by a stressed syllable.

    Thĕ cúr | fĕw tólls | thĕ knéll | ŏf pár | tĭng dáy. |

    (Thomas Gray, "Elegy Written in a Country Churchyard")

2. **Anapestic** (the noun is "anapest"): two unstressed syllables followed by a stressed syllable.

    Thĕ Ăs sýr | iăn căme dówn | lĭke ă wólf | ŏn thĕ fóld. |

    (Lord Byron, "The Destruction of Sennacherib")

3. **Trochaic** (the noun is "trochee"): a stressed followed by an unstressed syllable.

    Thére thĕy | áre, mў | fíf tў | mén ănd | wó mĕn. |

    (Robert Browning, "One Word More")

    Most trochaic lines lack the final unstressed syllable—in the technical term, such lines are **catalectic**. So in Blake's "The Tiger":

    Tí gĕr! | tí gĕr! | búrn ĭng | bríght |
    Ín thĕ | fó rĕst | óf thĕ | níght. |

4. **Dactylic** (the noun is "dactyl"): a stressed syllable followed by two unstressed syllables.

    Éve, wĭth hĕr | bás kĕt, wăs |
    Déep ĭn thĕ | bélls ănd grăss. |

    (Ralph Hodgson, "Eve")

    Iambs and anapests, since the strong stress is at the end, are called "rising meter"; trochees and dactyls, with the strong stress at the beginning, are called "falling meter." Iambs and trochees, having two syllables, are called "duple meter"; anapests and dactyls, having three syllables, are called "triple meter." It should be noted that the iamb is by far the commonest English foot; some metric theorists treat other types of stress patterns as variants of the iamb. (For the development of the iambic line in English, see John Thompson, *The Founding of English Metre*, 1961.)

Two other feet are often distinguished by special titles, although they occur in English meter only as occasional variants from standard feet:

**Spondaic** (the noun is "spondee"): two successive syllables with approximately equal strong stresses, as in each of the first two feet of this line:

Góod stróng| thíck stú|pĕ fý| ĭng ín|cĕnse smóke.|

(Browning, "The Bishop Orders His Tomb")

**Pyrrhic** (the noun is also "pyrrhic"): a foot composed of two successive syllables with approximately equal light stresses, as in the second and fourth feet in this line:

Mý wăy | ĭs tŏ | bĕ gín | wĭth thĕ | bĕ gín nĭng|

(Byron, *Don Juan*)

This latter term is used only infrequently. Some traditional metrists deny the existence of a true pyrrhic, on the grounds that the prevailing metrical accent—in the above instance, iambic—always imposes a slightly stronger stress on one of the two syllables.

A metric line is named according to the number of feet composing it:

| | |
|---|---|
| **monometer:** | one foot |
| **dimeter:** | two feet |
| **trimeter:** | three feet |
| **tetrameter:** | four feet |
| **pentameter:** | five feet |
| **hexameter:** | six feet (an **Alexandrine** is a line of six iambic feet) |
| **heptameter:** | seven feet (a **fourteener** is another term for a line of seven iambic feet—hence, of fourteen syllables; it tends to break into a unit of four feet followed by a unit of three feet) |
| **octameter:** | eight feet |

To describe the meter of a line we name (1) the predominant foot and (2) the number of feet it contains. In the illustrations above, for example, the line from Gray's "Elegy" is "iambic pentameter," and the line from Byron's "The Destruction of Sennacherib" is "anapestic tetrameter."

To **scan** a passage of verse is to go through it line by line, analyzing the component feet, and also indicating where any major pauses in the phrasing fall within a line. Here is a **scansion**, signified by conventional symbols, of the first five lines from John Keats' *Endymion* (1818). The passage was chosen because it exemplifies a flexible and variable rather than a highly regular metrical pattern.

1. Ă thíng | ŏf béau | tў ís | ă jóy | fŏr é vĕr: |
2. Ĭts lóve | lĭ nĕss | ĭn créas | ĕs; // ít | wĭll név ĕr |
3. Páss ĭn | tŏ nóth | ĭng nĕss, | // bŭt stíll | wĭll kéep |

4. Ă bów | ĕr quí | ĕt fŏr | ŭs, // ánd | ă sléep |
5. Fúll ŏf | swĕet dréams, | ănd héalth, | ănd quí | ĕt bréath ĭng. |

The prevailing meter is iambic pentameter. As in all fluent verse, however, there are many variations upon the basic iambic foot; these are sometimes called "substitutions." Thus:

1. The closing feet of lines 1, 2, and 5 end with an extra unstressed syllable, and are said to have a **feminine ending**. In lines 3 and 4, the closing feet, because they are standard iambs, end with a stressed syllable and are said to have **masculine endings**.
2. In lines 3 and 5, the opening iambic feet have been "inverted" to form trochees. (This initial position is the most common place for inversions in iambic verse.)
3. I have marked the second foot in line 2, and the third foot of line 3 and line 4, as pyrrhics (two unstressed syllables); these help to give Keats' verses their rapid movement. This is a procedure in scansion about which metric analysts disagree: some will feel enough of a metric beat to mark all these feet as iambs; others will mark still other feet (for example, the third foot of line 1) as pyrrhics also. And some metrists prefer to use symbols measuring two degrees of strong stress, and will indicate a difference in the feet, as follows:

Ĭts ló've | lĭ néss | ĭn cŕeas | ĕs.

Notice, however, that these are differences only in nuance; analysts agree that the prevailing pulse of Keats' versification is iambic throughout, and that despite many variations, the felt norm is of five stresses in the verse line.

Two other elements are important in the metric movement of Keats' passage: (1) In lines 1 and 5, the pause in the reading—which occurs naturally at the end of a sentence, clause, or other syntactic unit—coincides with the end of the line; such lines are called **end-stopped**. Lines 2 through 4, on the other hand, are called **run-on lines** (or in a term derived from the French, they exhibit **enjambment**—"a striding-over"), because the pressure of the incompleted syntactic unit toward closure carries on over the end of the verse line. (2) When a strong phrasal pause falls within a line, as in lines 2, 3, and 4, it is called a **caesura**—indicated in the quoted passage by the conventional symbol //. The management of these internal pauses is important for giving variety and for providing expressive emphases in the long pentameter line.

To understand the use and limitations of an analysis such as this, we must realize that a prevailing metric pattern (iambic pentameter, in the passage from Keats) establishes itself as a perceived norm which controls the reader's expectations, even though the number of lines that deviate from the norm may exceed the number that fit the norm exactly. In addition, scansion is an abstract scheme which deliberately omits notation of many aspects of the actual reading of a poem that contribute importantly to its pace, rhythm, and total impression. It does not specify, for example, whether the component words in a metric line are short words or long words, or whether the strong stresses fall on short vowels or long vowels; it does not give any indication of the *intonation*—the overall rise and fall in the pitch and loudness of the voice—which we use to bring out the meaning and rhetorical effect of these poetic lines; nor does it indicate the interplay of the metric stresses with the rhythms and lengths of the varied phrasal and clausal structures within a sustained poetic passage. Such details are omitted in order to lay bare the essential metric skeleton; that is, the pattern of the stronger and weaker stresses in the syllabic sequence of a verse line. Moreover, an actual reading of a poem, if it is a skillful reading, will not accord mechanically with the scansion. There is a marked difference between the scansion, as an abstract metrical norm, and a skilled and expressive oral reading, or **performance**, of a poem; and no two competent readers will perform the same lines in precisely the same way. But in a performance, the metric norm indicated by the scansion is sensed as an implicit understructure of pulses; in fact, the interplay of an expressive performance, sometimes with and sometimes against this underlying structural pattern, gives tension and vitality to our experience of verse.

We need to note, finally, that some kinds of versification which occur in English poetry differ from the syllable-and-stress type already described:

1. **Strong-stress meters** or **accentual verse**. In this meter, native to English and other Germanic languages, only the beat of the strong stresses counts in the scanning, while the number of intervening light syllables is highly variable. Usually there are four strong-stressed syllables in a line, whose beat is emphasized by *alliteration*. This was the meter of Old English poetry and continued to be the meter of many Middle English poems, until Chaucer and others popularized the syllable-and-stress meter. In the opening passage, for example, of *Piers Plowman* (later fourteenth century) the four strong stresses (always divided by a medial caesura) are for the most part reinforced by alliteration (see *alliterative meter*); the light syllables, which vary in number, are recessive and do not assert their individual presence:

> In a sómer séson, // whan sóft was the sónne,
> I shópe me in shróudes, // as Í a shépe were,
> In hábits like an héremite, // unhóly of wórkes,
> Went wýde in this wórld, // wónders to hére.

Strong-stress meter survives in some *folk* poetry and in traditional children's rhymes such as "Hickory, dickory, dock" and was revived as an artful literary meter by Samuel Taylor Coleridge in *Christabel* (1816), in which each line has four strong stresses but the number of syllables within a line varies from four to twelve.

What G. M. Hopkins in the later nineteenth century called his **sprung rhythm** is a variant of strong-stress meter: each foot, as he describes it, begins with a stressed syllable, which may either stand alone or be associated with from one to three (occasionally even more) light syllables. Two six-stress lines from Hopkins' "The Wreck of the *Deutschland*" indicate the variety of the rhythms in this meter, and also exemplify its most striking feature: the great weight of the strong stresses, and the frequent juxtaposition of strong stresses (*spondees*) at any point in the line. The stresses in the second line were marked in a manuscript by Hopkins himself; they indicate that in complex instances, his metric decisions may seem arbitrary:

> The | sóur | scythe | crínge, and the | bléar | sháre | cóme. |
> Our | héarts' chárity's | héarth's | fíre, our | thóughts' chivalry's |
> thróng's | Lórd. |

(See Marcella M. Holloway, *The Prosodic Theory of Gerard Manley Hopkins*, 1947.) A number of modern metrists, including T. S. Eliot and Ezra Pound, skillfully interweave both strong-stress and syllable-and-stress meters in some of their versification.

2. *Quantitative meters* in English are written in imitation of classical Greek and Latin versification, in which the metrical pattern is not determined by the stress but by the "quantity" (duration of pronunciation) of a syllable, and the foot consists of a combination of "long" and "short" syllables. Sir Philip Sidney, Edmund Spenser, Thomas Campion, and other Elizabethan poets experimented with this meter in English, as did Coleridge, Tennyson, Henry Wadsworth Longfellow, and Robert Bridges later on. The strong accentual character of English, however, as well as the indeterminateness of the duration of a syllable in the English language, makes it impossible to sustain a quantitative meter for any length. See Derek Attridge, *Well-Weighted Syllables: Elizabethan Verse in Classical Meters* (1974).

3. In *free verse* (discussed in a separate entry), the component lines have no (or only occasional) metric feet, or uniform stress patterns.

George Saintsbury, *Historical Manual of English Prosody* (1910), is a well-illustrated treatment of traditional syllable-and-stress metrics. For later discussions of this and alternative metric theories see Seymour Chatman, *A Theory of Meter* (1965); and W. K. Wimsatt and Monroe C. Beardsley, "The Concept of Meter" (1959). This last essay is reprinted in W. K. Wimsatt, *Hateful Contraries* (1965), and in Harvey Gross, ed., *The Structure of Verse* (1966)—an anthology that reprints other useful essays, including Northrop Frye, "The Rhythm of Recurrence," and Yvor Winters, "The Audible Reading of Poetry." See also W. K. Wimsatt, ed., *Versification: Major Language Types* (1972); Paul Fussell, *Poetic Meter and Poetic Form* (rev. 1979); John Hollander, *Rhyme's Reason: A Guide to English Verse* (1981); T. V. F. Brogan, *English Versification, 1570–1980* (1981); Robert Pinsky, *The Sounds of Poetry: A Brief Guide* (1998); Amittai Aviram, *Telling Rhythm: Body and Meaning in Poetry* (1994); Philip Hobsbaum, *Metre, Rhythm, and Verse Form* (1996); Thomas Carper and Derek Attridge, *Meter and Meaning: An Introduction to Rhythm in Poetry* (2003). For responses by contemporary poets to David Baker's contention that there are only iambic feet in English, see David Baker, ed., *Meter in English: A Critical Engagement* (1996). For references to *meter* in other entries, see pages *129, 288*. See also *alliterative meter; blank verse; doggerel; free verse.*

**miracle plays, morality plays, and interludes:** Miracle plays, morality plays, and interludes are types of late-medieval drama, written in a variety of verse forms.

The **miracle play** had as its subject either a story from the Bible, or else the life and martyrdom of a saint. In the usage of some historians, however, "miracle play" denotes only dramas based on saints' lives, and the term **mystery play** is applied only to dramas based on the Bible. "Mystery" is used in the archaic sense (probably derived from the Latin *ministerium*, "work," "occupation") of the "trade" conducted by each of the medieval guilds which sponsored these plays.

The plays representing biblical narratives originated within the church in about the tenth century, in dramatizations of brief parts of the Latin liturgical service, called **tropes**, especially the "Quem quaeritis" ("Whom are you seeking") trope portraying the visit of the three Marys to the tomb of Christ. Gradually these evolved into complete plays which were written in English instead of in Latin, produced under the auspices of the various trade guilds, and acted on stages set outside the church. The miracle plays written in England are of unknown authorship. In the fourteenth century there developed in cities such as York and Chester the practice, on the feast of Corpus Christi (sixty days after Easter), of putting on great "cycles" of such plays, representing crucial events in the biblical history of mankind from the Creation and Fall of man, through the Nativity, Crucifixion, and Resurrection of Christ, to the Last Judgment. The precise way that the plays were staged is a matter of scholarly debate, but it is widely agreed that each scene was played on a separate "pageant wagon" which was drawn, in sequence, to one after another fixed station in a city, at each of which some parts of the cycle were enacted. The biblical texts were greatly expanded in these plays, and the unknown authors added scenes, comic as well as serious, of their own invention. For examples of the variety, vitality, and power of these dramas, see the Wakefield "Noah" and "Second Shepherd's Play," and the Brome "Abraham and Isaac."

**Morality plays** were dramatized *allegories* of a representative Christian life in the plot form of a quest for salvation, in which the crucial events are temptations, sinning, and the climactic confrontation with death. The usual protagonist represents Mankind, or Everyman; among the other characters are personifications of virtues, vices, and Death, as well as angels and demons who contest for the prize of the soul of Mankind. A character known as the **Vice** often played the role of the tempter in a fashion both sinister and comic; he is regarded by some literary historians as a precursor both of the cynical, ironic villain and of some of the comic figures in Elizabethan drama, including Shakespeare's Falstaff. The best-known morality play is the fifteenth-century *Everyman*, which is still given an occasional performance; other notable examples, written in the same century, are *The Castle of Perseverance* and *Mankind*.

**Interlude** (Latin, "between the play") is a term applied to a variety of short stage entertainments, such as secular *farces* and witty dialogues with a religious or political point. In the late fifteenth and early sixteenth centuries, these little dramas were performed by bands of professional actors; it is believed that they were often put on between the courses of a feast or between the acts of a longer play. Among the better-known interludes are John Heywood's farces of the first half of the sixteenth century, especially *The Four PP* (that is, the Palmer, the Pardoner, the 'Pothecary, and the Peddler, who engage in a lying contest), and *Johan Johan the Husband, Tyb His Wife, and Sir John the Priest*.

Until the middle of the twentieth century, concern with medieval drama was scholarly rather than critical. Since that time a number of studies have dealt with the relationships of the texts to the religious and secular culture of medieval Europe, and have stressed the artistic excellence and power of the plays themselves. See Karl Young, *The Drama of the Medieval Church* (2 vols., 1933); Arnold Williams, *The Drama of Medieval England* (1961); T. W. Craik, *The Tudor Interlude* (1962); David M. Bevington, *From Mankind to Marlowe* (1962); V. A. Kolve, *The Play Called Corpus Christi* (1966); Rosemary Woolf, *The English Mystery Plays* (1972); Jerome Taylor and Alar Nelson, eds., *Medieval English Drama: Essays Critical and Contextual* (1972); Robert Potter, *The English Morality Play* (1975). For references to *miracle play* in other entries, see pages *252, 372, 374*.

**mirror stage: 294**.

**mise en scene** (mē′ zän sĕn′): **330**.

**mixed metaphor: 120**.

**mock epic: 36**.

**mock heroic: 36**; *24*.

**Modern Period: 256**; *362*.

**modernism and postmodernism:** The term **modernism** is widely used to identify new and distinctive features in the subjects, forms, concepts, and styles of literature and the other arts in the early decades of the twentieth century, but especially after World War I (1914–18). The specific features signified by "modernism" (or by the adjective **modernist**) vary with the user, but many critics agree that it involves a deliberate and radical break with some of the traditional bases not only of Western art, but of Western culture in general. Important intellectual precursors of modernism, in this sense, are thinkers who had questioned the certainties that had supported traditional modes of social organization, religion, and morality, and also traditional ways of conceiving the human self—thinkers such as Friedrich Nietzsche (1844–1900), Karl Marx, Sigmund Freud, and James G. Frazer, whose 12-volume *The Golden Bough* (1890–1915) stressed the correspondence between central Christian tenets and pagan, often barbaric, myths and rituals.

Literary historians locate the beginning of the modernist revolt as far back as the 1890s, but most agree that what is called **high modernism**, marked by an unexampled scope and rapidity of change, came after the First World War. The year 1922 alone was signalized by the appearance of such monuments of modernist innovation as James Joyce's *Ulysses*, T. S. Eliot's *The Waste Land*, and Virginia Woolf's *Jacob's Room*, as well as many other experimental works of literature. The catastrophe of the war had shaken faith in the moral basis, coherence, and durability of Western civilization and raised doubts about the adequacy of traditional literary modes to represent the harsh and dissonant realities of the postwar world. T. S. Eliot wrote in a review of Joyce's *Ulysses* in 1923 that the inherited mode of ordering a literary work, which assumed a relatively coherent and stable social order, could not accord with "the immense panorama of futility and anarchy which is contemporary history." Like Joyce and like Ezra Pound in his *Cantos*, Eliot experimented with new forms and a new style that would render contemporary disorder, often contrasting it to a lost order and integration that, he claimed, had been based on the religion and myths of the cultural past. In *The Waste Land* (1922), for example, Eliot replaced the standard syntactic flow of poetic language by fragmented utterances, and substituted for the traditional type of coherent poetic structure a deliberate dislocation of parts, in which very diverse components are related by connections that are left to the reader to discover, or invent. Major works of modernist fiction, following Joyce's *Ulysses* and his even more radical *Finnegans Wake* (1939), subvert the basic conventions of earlier prose fiction by breaking up the narrative continuity, departing from the standard ways of representing characters, and violating the traditional syntax and coherence of narrative language by the use of *stream of consciousness* and other innovative modes of narration. Gertrude Stein—often linked with Joyce, Pound, Eliot, and Woolf as a trail-blazing modernist—experimented with **automatic writing** (writing that has been freed from control by the conscious, purposive mind) and other modes of language that achieved their effects by violating the norms of standard English syntax and sentence structure. Among other European and American writers who are central representatives of modernism are the novelists Marcel Proust, Thomas Mann, André Gide, Franz Kafka, Dorothy Richardson, and William Faulkner; the poets Stéphane Mallarmé, William Butler Yeats, Rainer Maria Rilke, Marianne Moore, William Carlos Williams, and Wallace Stevens; and the dramatists August Strindberg, Luigi Pirandello, Eugene O'Neill, and Bertolt Brecht. Their new forms of literary construction and rendering had obvious parallels in the break away from representational conventions in the artistic movements of *expressionism* and *surrealism*, in the modernist paintings and sculpture of Cubism, Futurism, and Abstract Expressionism, and in the violations of standard conventions of melody, harmony, and rhythm by the modernist musical composers Stravinsky, Schoenberg, and their radical followers.

A prominent feature of modernism is the phenomenon called the **avant-garde** (a French military metaphor: "advance-guard"); that is, a small, self-conscious group of artists and authors who deliberately undertake, in Ezra Pound's phrase, to "make it new." By violating the accepted conventions and proprieties, not only of art but of social discourse, they set out to create ever-new artistic forms and styles and to introduce hitherto neglected, and sometimes forbidden, subject matter. Frequently, avant-garde artists represent themselves as "alienated" from the established order, against which they assert their own autonomy; a prominent aim is to shock the sensibilities of the conventional reader and to challenge the norms and pieties of the dominant bourgeois culture. See Renato Poggioli, *The Theory of the Avant-Garde* (1968). Peter Bürger's *Theory of the Avant-Garde* (1984) is a neo-Marxist analysis both of modernism and of its distinctive cultural formation, the avant-garde.

The term **postmodernism** is often applied to the literature and art after World War II (1939–45), when the effects on Western morale of the First World War were greatly exacerbated by the experience of Nazi totalitarianism and mass extermination, the threat of total destruction by the atomic bomb, the progressive devastation of the natural environment, and the ominous fact of over-population. Postmodernism involves not only a continuation, sometimes carried to an extreme, of the countertraditional experiments of modernism, but also diverse attempts to break away from modernist forms which had, inevitably, become in their turn conventional, as well as to overthrow the elitism of modernist "high art" by recourse for models to the "mass culture" in film, television, newspaper cartoons, and popular music. Many of the works of postmodern literature—by Jorge Luis Borges, Samuel Beckett, Vladimir Nabokov, Thomas Pynchon, Roland Barthes, and many others—so blend literary genres, cultural and stylistic levels, the serious and the playful, that they resist classification according to traditional literary rubrics. And these literary anomalies are paralleled in other arts by phenomena like pop art, op art, the musical compositions of John Cage, and the films of Jean-Luc Godard and other directors.

An undertaking in some postmodernist writings—prominently in Samuel Beckett and other authors of the literature of the *absurd*—is to subvert the foundations of our accepted modes of thought and experience so as to reveal the meaninglessness of existence and the underlying "abyss," or "void," or "nothingness" on which any supposed security is conceived to be precariously suspended. Postmodernism in literature and the arts has parallels with the movement known as poststructuralism in linguistic and literary theory; poststructuralists undertake to subvert the foundations of language in order to demonstrate that its seeming meaningfulness dissipates, for a rigorous inquirer, into a play of conflicting indeterminacies, or else undertake to show that all forms of cultural discourse are manifestations of the reigning ideology, or of the relations and constructions of power, in contemporary society. (See *poststructuralism*.)

For some postmodernist developments in literature, see literature of the *absurd, antihero, antinovel, Beat writers, concrete poetry, metafiction, new novel*. On modernism, refer to Richard Ellmann and Charles Feidelson, eds., *The Modern Tradition: Backgrounds of Modern Literature* (1965); Irving Howe, ed., *The Idea of the Modern in Literature and the Arts* (1967); Lionel Trilling, *Beyond Culture* (1968); Paul de Man, "Literary History and Literary Modernity," in *Blindness and Insight* (1971); Hugh Kenner, *The Pound Era* (1971); David Perkins, *A History of Modern Poetry: From the 1890s to the High Modernist Mode* (1976); Peter Nicholls, *Modernisms: A Literary Guide* (1995); Christopher Butler, *Early Modernism: Literature, Music, and Painting in Europe, 1900–1916* (1994); Malcolm Bradbury and James McFarlane, eds., *Modernism: 1890–1930/A Guide to European Literature* (1991); Michael North, *The Dialect of Modernism: Race, Language, and Twentieth-Century Literature* (1998); Michael Levenson, ed., *The Cambridge Companion to Modernism* (1999). See also the journal *Modernism/Modernity*.

On postmodernism, see Clement Greenberg, *The Notion of Post-Modern* (1980); J. F. Lyotard, *The Postmodern Condition* (trans. 1984); Andreas Huyssen, *After the Great Divide: Modernism, Mass Culture, Postmodernism* (1986); David Harvey, *The Condition of Postmodernity: An Enquiry into the Origins of Cultural Change* (1989); John McGowan, *Postmodernism and Its Critics* (1991); Fredric Jameson, *Postmodernism* (1991); Ingeborg Hoesterey, ed., *Zeitgeist in Babel: The Postmodernist Controversy* (1991); Stuart Sim, ed., *The Routledge Companion to Postmodernism* (2001); Victor E. Taylor and Charles E. Winquist, eds., *Encyclopedia of Postmodernism* (2003).

On the massive impact on culture and literature of the two World Wars, see Paul Fussell, *Wartime: Understanding and Behavior in the Second World War* (1989), and *The Great War and Modern Memory* (2000).

On modern and postmodern drama: Austin Quigley, *The Modern Stage and Other Worlds* (1985); William B. Worthen, *Modern Drama and the Rhetoric of Theater* (1992); Debora Geis, *Postmodern Theatric(k)s* (1993). For references to *modernism* in other entries, see pages *183, 248, 256, 280*.

**modernist: 202**; *153*.

**moment, the: 101**.

**monody: 92**.

**monologic: 77**.

**monologue: 85**.

**monometer** (mŏnŏm′ ĕter): **196**.

**mood: 18**.

**morality play: 201**; *8, 252, 344, 372, 374*.

**morpheme: 175**.

**morphology:** 174.

**motif and theme:** A **motif** is a conspicuous element, such as a type of event, device, reference, or formula, which occurs frequently in works of literature. The "loathly lady" who turns out to be a beautiful princess is a common motif in *folklore*, and the man fatally bewitched by a fairy lady is a motif adopted from folklore in Keats' "La Belle Dame sans Merci" (1820). Common in lyric poems is the **ubi sunt motif**, the "where-are" formula for lamenting the vanished past ("Where are the snows of yesteryear?"), and also the *carpe diem* motif, whose nature is sufficiently indicated by Robert Herrick's title "To the Virgins, to Make Much of Time." An **aubade**—from the Old French "alba," meaning dawn—is an early-morning song whose usual motif is an urgent request to a beloved to wake up. A familiar example is Shakespeare's "Hark, hark, the lark at heaven's gate sings."

An older term for recurrent poetic concepts or formulas is the **topos** (Greek for "a commonplace"); Ernst R. Curtius, *European Literature and the Latin Middle Ages* (trans. 1953), treats many of the ancient literary topoi. The term "motif," or else the German **leitmotif** (a guiding motif), is also applied to the frequent repetition, within a single work, of a significant verbal or musical phrase, or set description, or complex of images, as in the operas of Richard Wagner or in novels by Thomas Mann, James Joyce, Virginia Woolf, and William Faulkner. See *imagery*; and for a *deconstructive* treatment of recurrent elements or motifs in prose fiction, see J. Hillis Miller, *Fiction and Repetition* (1982).

**Theme** is sometimes used interchangeably with "motif," but the term is more usefully applied to a general concept or doctrine, whether implicit or asserted, which an imaginative work is designed to involve and make persuasive to the reader. John Milton states as the explicit theme of *Paradise Lost* to "assert Eternal Providence, / And justify the ways of God to men"; see *didactic literature* and *fiction and truth*. Some critics have claimed that all nontrivial works of literature, including lyric poems, involve an implicit theme which is embodied and dramatized in the evolving meanings and imagery; see, for example, Cleanth Brooks, *The Well Wrought Urn* (1947). And *archetypal critics* trace such recurrent themes as that of the scapegoat, or the journey underground, through myths and social rituals, as well as literature. For a discussion of the overlapping applications of the critical terms "subject," "theme," and "thesis" see Monroe C. Beardsley, *Aesthetics* (1958, pp. 401–11).

**motivation:** 42.

**movements in recent criticism:** 368.

**multiculturalism:** 39.

**multiple authorship:** 367; *19*.

**multiple meaning:** 12.

**mummers' play:** 124.

**mystery play: 200**.

**myth:** In classical Greek, "mythos" signified any story or plot, whether true or invented. In its central modern significance, however, a myth is one story in a **mythology**—a system of hereditary stories of ancient origin which were once believed to be true by a particular cultural group, and which served to explain (in terms of the intentions and actions of deities and other supernatural beings) why the world is as it is and things happen as they do, to provide a rationale for social customs and observances, and to establish the sanctions for the rules by which people conduct their lives. Most myths are related to social **rituals**—set forms and procedures in sacred ceremonies—but anthropologists disagree as to whether rituals generated myths or myths generated rituals. If the protagonist is a human being rather than a supernatural being, the traditional story is usually called not a myth but a **legend**. If the hereditary story concerns supernatural beings who are not gods, and the story is not part of a systematic mythology, it is usually classified as a *folktale*.

The French structuralist Claude Lévi-Strauss departed from the traditional views just described, to treat the myths within each culture as signifying systems whose true meanings are unknown to their proponents. He analyzes the myths of a particular culture as composed of signs which are to be identified and interpreted by the cultural anthropologist on the model of the linguistic theory of Ferdinand de Saussure. See Lévi-Strauss, "The Structural Study of Myth," in *Structural Anthropology* (1968), and refer to *structuralist criticism* and *semiotics*. Another influential contribution to the theory of myths is the German intellectual historian Hans Blumenberg's *Work on Myth* (1979, trans. 1985). Among other things, Blumenberg proposes that the function of myth is to help human beings cope with the inexorability of reality and the course of events—a need that is not outmoded by scientific advances and rationality; that myths evolve according to a "Darwinism of words," in which those forms and variations survive that cope most effectively with the changing social environment; and that myth is best conceived not as a collection of fixed and final stories, but as "a work"—an ongoing and ever-changing process that is expressed in oral and written narratives and involves the diverse ways in which these narratives are received and appropriated.

It can be said that a mythology is a religion which we do not believe. Poets, however, after having ceased to believe them, have persisted in using the myths of Jupiter, Venus, Prometheus, Wotan, Adam and Eve, and Jonah for their plots, episodes, or allusions; as Coleridge said, "still doth the old instinct bring back the old names." The term "myth" has also been extended to denote supernatural tales that are deliberately invented by their authors. Plato in the fourth century BC used such invented myths in order to project philosophical speculation beyond the point at which certain knowledge is possible; see, for example, his "Myth of Er" in Book X of *The Republic*. The German *Romantic* authors F. W. J. Schelling and Friedrich Schlegel proposed that to write great literature, modern poets must develop a new unifying mythology which will synthesize the insights of the myths of the Western past with the new discoveries of philosophy and the physical sciences. In the same period in England William Blake, who felt "I must create a system or be enslaved by another man's," incorporated in his poems a system of mythology he had himself created by fusing hereditary myths, biblical history and prophecy, and his own intuitions, visions, and intellection. A number of modern writers have also asserted that an integrative mythology, whether inherited or invented, is essential to literature. James Joyce in *Ulysses* and *Finnegans Wake*, T. S. Eliot in *The Waste Land*, Eugene O'Neill in *Mourning Becomes Electra*, and many other writers have deliberately woven their modern materials on the pattern of ancient myths, while W. B. Yeats, like his admired predecessor Blake, undertook to construct his own systematic mythology, which he expounded in *A Vision* (1926) and embodied in a number of remarkable lyric poems such as "The Second Coming" and "Byzantium."

Around the middle of the twentieth century, "myth" became a prominent term in literary analysis. A large group of writers, the **myth critics**—including Robert Graves, Francis Fergusson, Maud Bodkin, Richard Chase, and (the most influential) Northrop Frye—viewed the genres and individual plot patterns of many works of literature, including what on the surface are highly sophisticated and realistic works, as recurrences of basic mythic formulas. As Northrop Frye put it, "the typical forms of myth become the conventions and genres of literature." According to Frye's theory, there are four main narrative genres—comedy, romance, tragedy, and irony (satire)—and these are "displaced" modes of the four elemental forms of myth that are associated with the seasonal cycle of spring, summer, autumn, and winter. (See *archetypal criticism* and *genre*.)

A reader needs to be alert to the bewildering variety of applications of the term "myth" in contemporary criticism. In addition to those already described, its uses range all the way from signifying any widely held fallacy ("the myth of progress," "the American success myth") to denoting the solidly and detailedly imagined realm within which a fictional narrative is enacted ("Faulkner's myth of Yoknapatawpha County," "the mythical world of *Moby-Dick*").

For classical mythology see H. J. Rose, *A Handbook of Greek Mythology* (1939), and on the use of classical myths in English literature, Douglas Bush, *Mythology and the Renaissance Tradition in English Poetry* (rev. 1963) and *Mythology and the Romantic Tradition in English Poetry* (rev. 1969). Among studies of myths especially influential for modern literature and criticism are James G. Frazer, *The Golden Bough* (rev., 1911); Jessie L. Weston, *From Ritual to Romance* (1920); Jane E. Harrison, *Themis* (2d ed., 1927); F. R. R. S. Raglan, *The Hero* (1936). On "myth critics" see William Righter, *Myth and Literature* (1975); and for instances of the theory and practice of myth criticism, Francis Fergusson, *The Idea of a Theater* (1949); Richard Chase, *Quest for Myth* (1949); Philip Wheelwright, *The Burning Fountain* (1954); Leslie Fiedler, *Love and Death in the American Novel* (1960); John B. Vickery, ed., *Myth and Literature* (1966); Northrop Frye, *Anatomy of Criticism* (1957) and "Literature and Myth" in *Relations of Literary Study*, ed. James Thorpe (1967). This last essay has a useful bibliography of the theory and history of myths, as well as of major exponents of myth criticism. See *archetypal criticism; folklore*.

**myth critics: 207**; *16, 93, 293.*

**mythoi** (mĭth′ oy): **16**.

**mythology: 206**.

**mythos: 265**.

**naive hero: 166**.

**narratee: 209**; *258*.

**narration, grammar of:** The **grammar of narration** is the analysis of special and distinctive grammatical usages that occur in fictional *narratives*. Its systematic study was begun by Käte Hamburger in *The Logic of Literature* (1957, trans. 1973). One focus of such analysis is the special play of **deictics**, also known as **indexicals** or **shifters**—that is, words and phrases such as "now," "then," "here," "there," "today," "last week," as well as personal pronouns ("I," "you") and some tenses of verbs—whose reference depends on the particular speaker and his or her position in place and time. In many narratives, usually in a way not explicitly noticed by the reader, the references of such terms constantly shift or merge, as the narration moves from the narrator, by whom the events are told in the past tense (for example, then and there), to a character in the narration, for whom the action is present (for example, here and now). Another notable grammatical usage in narration has been called **free indirect discourse** (equivalent to the French "style indirect libre"), or "represented speech and thought." These terms refer to the way, in many narratives, that the reports of what a character says and thinks shift in pronouns, adverbs, tense, and grammatical mode, as we move—or sometimes hover—between the direct narrated representation of these events as they occur to the character and the indirect representation of such events by the narrator of the story. Thus, a direct representation, "He thought, 'I will see her home now, and may then stop at my mother's'," might shift, in an "indirect representation," to "He thought that he would see her home and then maybe stop at his mother's." In a further shift to "free indirect representation" the sentence might change to "He would see her home then, and might afterward stop at his mother's." Refer to *narrative and narratology*, and see Roy Pascal, *The Dual Voice: Free Indirect Speech and Its Functioning in the Nineteenth-Century European Novel* (1977); Dorrit Cohn, *Transparent Minds: Narrative Modes for Presenting Consciousness in Fiction* (1978); Ann Banfield, *Unspeakable Sentences: Narration and Representation in the Language of Fiction* (1982).

**narrative and narratology:** A **narrative** is a story, whether told in prose or verse, involving events, characters, and what the characters say and do. Some literary forms such as the novel and short story in prose, and the epic and romance in verse, are explicit narratives that are told by a *narrator*. In drama, the narrative is not told, but evolves by means of the direct presentation on stage of the actions and speeches of the characters. (Refer to *genres*.) It should be noted that there is an implicit narrative element even in many *lyric* poems. In William Wordsworth's "The Solitary Reaper," for example, we infer from what the lyric speaker says that, coming unexpectedly in the Scottish Highlands upon a girl reaping and singing, he stops, attends, meditates, and then resumes his climb up the hill.

**Narratology** denotes a concern, which became prominent in the mid-twentieth century, with the general theory and practice of narrative in all literary forms. It deals especially with types of narrators, the identification of structural elements and their diverse modes of combination, recurrent narrative devices, and the analysis of the kinds of *discourse* by which a narrative gets told, as well as with the **narratee**—that is, the explicit or implied person or audience to whom the narrator addresses the narrative. Recent narratological theory picks up and elaborates upon many topics in traditional treatments of fictional narratives, from Aristotle's *Poetics* in the fourth century BC to Wayne Booth's *The Rhetoric of Fiction* (rev. 1983); this theory, however, deals with such topics in terms of concepts and analytic procedures that derive from developments in *Russian formalism* and especially in French *structuralism*. Narratologists, accordingly, do not treat a narrative in the traditional way, as a fictional representation of life and the world, but as a systematic and purely formal construction. A primary interest of structural narratologists is in the way that narrative discourse fashions a **story**—a mere sequence of events in time—into the organized and meaningful structure of a literary *plot*. (The Russian formalists had made a parallel distinction between the **fabula**—the elemental materials of a story—and the **syuzhet**, the concrete representation used to convey the story.) The general undertaking is to determine the rules, or codes of composition, that are manifested by the diverse forms of plot, and also to formulate the "grammar" of narrative in terms of structures and narrative formulas that recur in many stories, whatever the differences in the narrated subject matters. In *Narrative Discourse* (1980), followed by *Figures of Literary Discourse* (1982), the French structuralist critic Gérard Genette presented influential analyses of the complex interrelationships between a story and the types of discourse in which the story is narrated, and greatly subtilized the treatment of *point of view* in narrative fiction.

In the 1970s the historian Hayden White set out to demonstrate that the narratives written by historians are not simple representations of a sequence of facts, nor the revelation of a design inherent in events themselves. Instead, White analyzes historical narratives as shaped by the imposition on events of cultural patterns similar to the narratological, *archetypal*, and other structural concepts that had been applied in the criticism of literature; see his *Metahistory* (1973) and *The Content of the Form: Narrative Discourse and Historical Representation* (1987). The philosopher W. B. Gallie has written an influential book on the kind of explanation and understanding that, in the writing of history, is achieved by narration instead of propositional statements and logical arguments; see W. B. Gallie, *Philosophy and the Historical Understanding* (1964); also Arthur C. Danto, *Narration and Knowledge* (1985).

A book which did much to inaugurate modern narratology was *The Morphology of the Folktale* by the Russian formalist Vladimir Propp (trans. 1970). For later developments in narrative theory see, in addition to Genette (above), Tzvetan Todorov, *The Poetics of Prose* (trans. 1977); Seymour Chatman, *Story and Discourse: Narrative Structure in Fiction and Film* (1978); Robert Alter, *The Art of Biblical Narrative* (1981); Wallace Martin, *Recent Theories of Narrative* (1986); Gerald Prince, *A Dictionary of Narratology* (1987); Paul Ricoeur, *Time and*

*Narrative* (3 vols., 1984–88); Peter Brooks, *Reading for the Plot: Design and Intention in Narrative* (1992); Mieke Bal, *Narratology: Introduction to the Theory of Narrative* (rev. 1997); Seymour Chatman, *Coming to Terms: The Rhetoric of Narration in Fiction and Film* (1990); David Herman, ed., *Narratologies: New Perspectives on Narrative Analysis* (1999). Some cognitive psychologists and literary theorists have proposed that narrative, or the telling of diverse "stories" about how one thing leads to another, is the basic means by which we make sense of the world, provide meaning to our experiences, and organize our lives. See Jerome Bruner, *Acts of Meaning* (1990), and *Actual Worlds, Possible Minds* (1986); and Mark Turner, *The Literary Mind* (1996). For some narratological contributions to older analyses of how a story gets told, see *point of view*. For references to *narrative* in other entries, see pages *134, 265.*

**narratology: 209**; *127, 128, 268.*

**narrator: 272**; *208.*

**natural geniuses: 211**.

**naturalism: 303**; *216.*

**Naturalistic Period: 247**.

**naturalize** (in reading): **364**; *44, 58, 136, 267.*

**nature writing: 87**; *214.*

**negative capability:** The poet John Keats introduced this term in a letter written in December 1817 to define a literary quality "which Shakespeare possessed so enormously—I mean *Negative Capability*, that is, when man is capable of being in uncertainties, mysteries, doubts, without any irritable reaching after fact and reason." Keats contrasted to this quality the writing of Coleridge, who "would let go by a fine isolated verisimilitude . . . from being incapable of remaining content with half knowledge," and went on to express the general principle "that with a great poet the sense of beauty overcomes every other consideration, or rather obliterates all consideration."

The elusive term has entered critical circulation and has accumulated a large body of commentary. When conjoined with observations in other letters by Keats, "negative capability" can be taken (1) to characterize an impersonal, or objective, author who maintains *aesthetic distance*, as opposed to a subjective author who is personally involved with the characters and actions represented in a work of literature, and as opposed also to an author who uses a literary work to present and to make persuasive his or her personal beliefs; and (2) to suggest that, when embodied in a beautiful artistic form, the literary subject matter, concepts, and characters are not subject to the ordinary standards of evidence, truth, and morality, as we apply these standards in the course of our everyday experience.

Refer to *distance and involvement* and *objective and subjective*. On the diverse interpretations of Keats' "negative capability," see W. J. Bate, *John Keats* (1963).

**neoclassic and romantic:** The simplest use of these extremely variable terms is as noncommittal names for periods of literature. In this application, the "Neoclassic Period" in England spans the 140 years or so after the Restoration (1660), and the "Romantic Period" is usually taken to extend approximately from the outbreak of the French Revolution in 1789—or alternatively, from the publication of *Lyrical Ballads* in 1798—through the first three decades of the nineteenth century. With reference to American literature, the term "neoclassic" is rarely applied to eighteenth-century writers; on the other hand, 1830–65, the era of Emerson, Thoreau, Poe, Melville, and Hawthorne, is sometimes called "the American Romantic Period." (See *periods of English literature* and *periods of American literature*.) "Neoclassic" and "romantic" are frequently applied also to periods of German, French, and other Continental literatures, but with differences in the historical spans they identify.

Historians have often tried to "define" neoclassicism or romanticism, as though each term denoted an essential feature which was shared, to varying degrees, by all the major writings of an age. But the multiplex course of literary events has not formed itself around such simple entities, and the numerous and conflicting single definitions of neoclassicism and romanticism are either so vague as to be next to meaningless or so specific as to fall far short of equating with the great range and variety of the literary phenomena. A more useful undertaking is simply to specify some salient attributes of literary theory and practice that were shared by a number of prominent writers in the Neoclassic Period in England, and that serve to distinguish them from many outstanding writers of the Romantic Period. The following list of ideas and characteristics that were shared, between 1660 and the late 1700s, by authors such as John Dryden, Alexander Pope, Joseph Addison, Jonathan Swift, Samuel Johnson, Oliver Goldsmith, and Edmund Burke, may serve as an introductory sketch of some prominent features of **neoclassic** literature:

1. These authors exhibited a strong traditionalism, which was often joined to a distrust of radical innovation and was evidenced above all in their great respect for **classical** writers—that is, the writers of ancient Greece and Rome—who were thought to have achieved excellence, and established the enduring models, in all the major literary *genres*. Hence the term "neoclassic." (It is from this high estimate of the literary achievements of classical antiquity that the term "**a classic**" has come to be applied to any later literary work that is widely agreed to have achieved excellence and to have set a standard in its kind. See the entry *canon of literature* and T. S. Eliot's *What Is a Classic?* 1945.)

2. Literature was conceived to be primarily an "art"; that is, a set of skills which, although it requires innate talents, must be perfected by long study and practice and consists mainly in the deliberate adaptation of known and tested means to the achievement of foreseen ends upon the audience of readers. (See *pragmatic criticism*, under *criticism*.) The neoclassic ideal, founded especially on Horace's Roman *Ars Poetica* (first century BC), is the craftsman's ideal, demanding finish, correction, and attention to detail. Special allowances were often made for the unerring and innovative freedom of what were called **natural geniuses**, and

also for felicitous strokes, available even to some less gifted poets, which occur without premeditation and achieve, as Alexander Pope said (in his deft and comprehensive summary of neoclassic principles *An Essay on Criticism*, 1711), "a grace beyond the reach of art." But the prevailing view was that a natural genius such as Homer or Shakespeare is extremely rare, and probably a thing of the past, and that to even the best of artful poets, literary "graces" come only occasionally. The representative neoclassic writer commonly strove, therefore, for "correctness," was careful to observe the complex demands of stylistic *decorum*, and for the most part respected the established "rules" of his art. The neoclassic **rules of poetry** were, in theory, the essential properties of the various *genres* (such as epic, tragedy, comedy, pastoral) that have been abstracted from classical works whose long survival has proved their excellence. Such properties, many critics believed, must be embodied in modern works if these too are to be excellent and to survive through the ages. In England, however, many critics were dubious about some of the rules accepted by Italian and French critics, and opposed the strict application of rules such as the *three unities* in drama.

3. Human beings, and especially human beings as an integral part of a social organization, were regarded as the primary subject matter of the major forms of *literature*. Poetry was held to be an *imitation* of human life—in a common phrase, "a mirror held up to nature." And by the human actions it imitates, and the artistic form it gives to the imitation, poetry is designed to yield both instruction and pleasure to the people who read it. Not art for art's sake, but art for humanity's sake, was a central ideal of neoclassic *humanism*.

4. Both in the subject matter and the appeal of art, emphasis was placed on what human beings possess in common—representative characteristics and widely shared experiences, thoughts, feelings, and tastes. "True wit," Pope said in a much-quoted passage of his *Essay on Criticism*, is "what oft was thought but ne'er so well expressed." That is, a primary aim of poetry is to give new and consummate expression to the great commonplaces of human wisdom, whose universal acceptance and durability are the best warrant of their importance and truth. Some critics also insisted, it should be noted, on the need to balance or enhance the general, typical, and familiar with the opposing qualities of novelty, particularity, and invention. Samuel Johnson substituted for Pope's definition of true wit the statement that wit "is at once natural and new" and praised Shakespeare because, while his characters are species, they are all "discriminated" and "distinct." But there was wide agreement that the general nature and the shared values of humanity are the basic source and test of art, and also that the fact of universal human agreement, everywhere and always, is the best test of moral and religious truths, as well as of artistic values. (Compare *deism*.)

5. Neoclassic writers, like the major philosophers of the time, viewed human beings as limited agents who ought to set themselves only accessible goals. Many of the great works of the period, satiric and didactic, attack human "pride"—interpreted as presumption beyond the natural limits of the species— and enforce the lesson of the golden mean (the avoidance of extremes) and of

humanity's need to submit to its restricted position in the cosmic order—an order sometimes envisioned as a natural hierarchy, or *Great Chain of Being*. In art, as in life, what was for the most part praised was the law of measure and the acceptance of limits upon one's freedom. The poets admired extremely the great genres of epic and tragedy, but wrote their own masterpieces in admittedly lesser and less demanding forms such as the essay in verse and prose, the comedy of manners, and especially satire, in which they felt they had more chance to equal or surpass their classical and English predecessors. They submitted to at least some "rules" and other limiting conventions in literary subjects, structure, and diction. Typical was their choice, in many poems, to write within the extremely tight limits of the *closed couplet*. But a distinctive quality of the urbane poetry of the Neoclassic Period was, in the phrase often quoted from Horace, "the art that hides art"; that is, the seeming freedom and ease with which, at its best, it meets the challenge set by traditional and highly restrictive patterns.

Here are some aspects in which **romantic** aims and achievements, as manifested by many prominent and innovative writers during the late eighteenth and early nineteenth centuries, differ most conspicuously from their neoclassic precursors:

1. The prevailing attitude favored innovation over traditionalism in the materials, forms, and style of literature. Wordsworth's preface to the second edition of *Lyrical Ballads* in 1800 was written as a poetic **manifesto**, or statement of revolutionary aims, in which he denounced the upper-class subjects and the *poetic diction* of the preceding century and proposed to deal with materials from "common life" in "a selection of language really used by men." Wordsworth's serious or tragic treatment of lowly subjects in common language violated the neoclassic rule of *decorum*, which asserted that the serious genres should deal only with the momentous actions of royal or aristocratic characters in an appropriately elevated style. Other innovations in the period were the exploitation by Samuel Taylor Coleridge, John Keats, and others of the realm of the supernatural and of "the far away and the long ago"; the assumption by William Blake, William Wordsworth, and Percy Bysshe Shelley of the persona of a poet-prophet who writes a visionary mode of poetry; and the use of poetic *symbolism* (especially by Blake and Shelley) deriving from a worldview in which objects are charged with a significance beyond their physical qualities. "I always seek in what I see," as Shelley said, "the likeness of something beyond the present and tangible object."

2. In his preface to *Lyrical Ballads*, Wordsworth repeatedly declared that good poetry is "the spontaneous overflow of powerful feelings." According to this view, poetry is not primarily a mirror of men in action; on the contrary, its essential component is the poet's own feelings, while the process of composition, since it is "spontaneous," is the opposite of the artful manipulation of means to foreseen ends stressed by the neoclassic critics. (See *expressive criticism*.) Wordsworth carefully qualified this radical doctrine by describing his poetry as "emotion recollected in tranquility," by specifying that a poet's spontaneity is the result of a prior process of deep reflection, and by granting that it

may be followed by second thoughts and revisions. But the immediate act of composition, if a poem is to be genuine, must be spontaneous—that is, unforced, and free of what Wordsworth decried as the "artificial" rules and conventions of his neoclassic predecessors. "If poetry comes not as naturally as the leaves to a tree," Keats wrote, "it had better not come at all." The philosophical-minded Coleridge substituted for neoclassic "rules," which he describes as imposed on the poem from without, the concept of inherent organic "laws"; that is, he conceives that each poetic work, like a growing plant, evolves according to its own internal principles into its final *organic form*.

3. To a remarkable degree external nature—the landscape, together with its flora and fauna—became a persistent subject of poetry, and was described with an accuracy and sensuous nuance unprecedented in earlier writers. It is a mistake, however, to describe the romantic poets as simply "nature poets." (See *nature writing*, under *ecocriticism*.) While many major poems by Wordsworth and Coleridge—and to a great extent by Shelley and Keats—set out from and return to an aspect or change of aspect in the landscape, the outer scene is not presented for its own sake but as a stimulus for the poet to engage in the most characteristic human activity, that of thinking. Representative Romantic works are in fact poems of feelingful meditation which, although often stimulated by a natural phenomenon, are concerned with central human experiences and problems. Wordsworth asserted, in what he called a "Prospectus" to his major poems, that it is "the Mind of Man" which is "My haunt, and the main region of my song."

4. Neoclassic poetry was about other people, but many Romantic poems, long and short, invited the reader to identify the protagonists with the poets themselves, either directly, as in Wordsworth's *Prelude* (1805, rev. 1850) and a number of lyric poems (see *lyric*), or in altered but recognizable form, as in Lord Byron's *Childe Harold* (1812–18). In prose we find a parallel vogue in the revealingly personal essays of Charles Lamb and William Hazlitt and in a number of spiritual and intellectual autobiographies: Thomas De Quincey's *Confessions of an English Opium Eater* (1822), Coleridge's *Biographia Literaria* (1817), and Thomas Carlyle's fictionalized self-representation in *Sartor Resartus* (1833–34). And whether romantic subjects were the poets themselves or other people, they were no longer represented as part of an organized society but, typically, as solitary figures engaged in a long, and sometimes infinitely elusive, quest; often they were also social nonconformists or outcasts. Many important romantic works had as protagonist the isolated rebel, whether for good or ill: Prometheus, Cain, the Wandering Jew, the Satanic hero-villain, or the great outlaw.

5. What seemed to a number of political liberals the infinite social promise of the French Revolution in the early 1790s fostered the sense in Romantic writers that theirs was a great age of new beginnings and high possibilities. Many writers viewed a human being as endowed with limitless aspiration toward an infinite good envisioned by the faculty of imagination. "Our destiny," Wordsworth says in a visionary moment in *The Prelude*, "our being's heart

and home, / Is with infinitude, and only there," and our desire is for "something evermore about to be." "Less than everything," Blake announced, "cannot satisfy man." Humanity's undaunted aspirations beyond its assigned limits, which to the neoclassic moralist had been its tragic error of generic "pride," now became humanity's glory and a mode of triumph, even in failure, over the pettiness of circumstance. In a parallel way, the typical neoclassic judgment that the highest art is the perfect achievement of limited aims gave way to dissatisfaction with rules and inherited restrictions. According to a number of Romantic writers, the highest art consists in an endeavor beyond finite human possibility; as a result, neoclassical satisfaction in the perfectly accomplished, because limited, enterprise was replaced in writers such as Blake, Wordsworth, Coleridge, and Shelley, by a preference for the glory of the imperfect, in which the artist's very failure attests the grandeur of his aim. Also, Romantic writers once more entered into competition with their greatest predecessors in audacious long poems in the most exacting genres: Wordsworth's *Prelude* (a rerendering, at epic length and in the form of a spiritual autobiography, of central themes of John Milton's *Paradise Lost*); Blake's visionary and prophetic epics; Shelley's *Prometheus Unbound* (emulating Greek drama); Keats' Miltonic epic *Hyperion*; and Byron's ironic conspectus of contemporary European civilization, *Don Juan*.

See *Enlightenment*, and refer to R. S. Crane, "Neoclassical Criticism," in *Dictionary of World Literature*, ed. Joseph T. Shipley (rev. 1970); A. O. Lovejoy, *Essays in the History of Ideas* (1948); James Sutherland, *A Preface to Eighteenth Century Poetry* (1948); W. J. Bate, *From Classic to Romantic* (1948); Harold Bloom, *The Visionary Company: A Reading of English Romantic Poetry* (1961); René Wellek, "The Concept of Romanticism in Literary History" and "Romanticism Re-examined," in *Concepts of Criticism* (1963); Northrop Frye, ed., *Romanticism Reconsidered* (1963), and *A Study of English Romanticism* (1968); M. H. Abrams, *The Mirror and the Lamp: Romantic Theory and the Critical Tradition* (1953), and *Natural Supernaturalism: Tradition and Revolution in Romantic Literature* (1971); Thomas McFarland, *Romanticism and the Forms of Ruin* (1981); Marilyn Butler, *Romantics, Rebels and Reactionaries: English Literature and Its Background 1760–1830* (1982); Jerome McGann, *The Romantic Ideology* (1983); Marilyn Gaull, *English Romanticism: The Human Context* (1988); Philippe Lacoue-Labarthe and Jean-Luc Nancy, *The Literary Absolute: The Theory of Literature in German Romanticism* (trans. 1988); Isaiah Berlin, *The Crooked Timber of Humanity: Chapters in the History of Ideas* (1990); Stuart Curran, ed., *The Cambridge Companion to British Romanticism* (1993). Hugh Honour, in his books on *Neo-classicism* (1969) and on *Romanticism* (1979), stresses the visual arts. A collection of essays that define or discuss Romanticism is Robert F. Gleckner and Gerald E. Enscoe, eds., *Romanticism: Points of View* (rev. 1975); see also *An Oxford Companion to the Romantic Age: British Culture 1776–1832* (2001). In *Poetic Form and British Romanticism* (1986), Stuart Curran stresses the relationship of innovative Romantic forms to the traditional poetic genres.

For references to *neoclassic* in other entries, see pages *125, 135, 154, 254, 381.* See also *closed couplet; decorum; deism; Enlightenment; Great Chain of Being; humanism; primitivism; satire.*

**Neoclassic Period: 253**; *141, 193.*

**neoclassic poetic diction: 269**.

**Neoplatonism** (nēōplāt′ ŏnism): **263**.

**New Comedy: 49**.

**New Criticism:** This term, made current by the publication of John Crowe Ransom's *The New Criticism* in 1941, came to be applied to a theory and practice that remained prominent in American literary criticism until late in the 1960s. The movement derived in considerable part from elements in I. A. Richards' *Principles of Literary Criticism* (1924) and *Practical Criticism* (1929) and from the critical essays of T. S. Eliot. It opposed a prevailing interest of scholars, critics, and teachers of that era in the biographies of authors, in the social context of literature, and in literary history by insisting that the proper concern of literary criticism is not with the external circumstances or effects or historical position of a work, but with a detailed consideration of the work itself as an independent entity. Notable critics in this mode were the southerners Cleanth Brooks and Robert Penn Warren, whose textbooks *Understanding Poetry* (1938) and *Understanding Fiction* (1943) did much to make the New Criticism the predominant method of teaching literature in American colleges, and even in high schools, for the next two or three decades. Other prominent writers of that time—in addition to Ransom, Brooks, and Warren—who are often identified as New Critics are Allen Tate, R. P. Blackmur, and William K. Wimsatt.

A very influential English critic, F. R. Leavis, in turning his attention from background, sources, and biography to the detailed analysis of "literary texts themselves," shared some of the concepts of the New Critics and their analytic focus on what he called "the words on the page." He differed from his American counterparts, however, in his insistence that great literary works are a concrete and life-affirming enactment of moral and cultural values; he stressed also the essential role in education of what he called "the Great Tradition" of English literature in advancing the values of culture and "civilization" against the antagonistic forces in modern life. See F. R. Leavis, *Revaluation: Tradition and Development in English Poetry* (1936); *Education and the University* (1943, 2d ed. 1948); *The Great Tradition: George Eliot, Henry James, Joseph Conrad* (1948); also Anne Sampson, *F. R. Leavis* (1992).

The New Critics differed from one another in many ways, but the following points of view and procedures were shared by many of them:

1. A poem, it is held, should be treated as such—in Eliot's words, "primarily as poetry and not another thing"—and should therefore be regarded as an independent and self-sufficient verbal object. The first law of criticism, John Crowe Ransom said, "is that it shall be objective, shall cite the nature of the object"

and shall recognize "the autonomy of the work itself as existing for its own sake." (See *objective criticism*.) New Critics warn the reader against critical practices which divert attention from the poem itself (see *intentional fallacy* and *affective fallacy*). In analyzing and evaluating a particular work, they eschew reference to the biography and temperament and personal experiences of the author, to the social conditions at the time of its production, or to its psychological and moral effects on the reader; they also tend to minimize recourse to the place of the work in the history of literary forms and subject matter. Because of its focus on the literary work in isolation from its attendant circumstances and effects, the New Criticism is often classified as a type of critical *formalism*.

2. The principles of the New Criticism are basically verbal. That is, literature is conceived to be a special kind of language whose attributes are defined by systematic opposition to the language of science and of practical and logical discourse, and the explicative procedure is to analyze the meanings and interactions of words, *figures of speech*, and *symbols*. The emphasis is on the "organic unity," in a successful literary work, of its overall structure with its verbal meanings, and we are warned against separating the two by what Cleanth Brooks called "the heresy of paraphrase."

3. The distinctive procedure for a New Critic is **explication**, or **close reading**: the detailed analysis of the complex interrelationships and *ambiguities* (multiple meanings) of the verbal and figurative components within a work. "Explication de texte" (stressing all kinds of information, whether internal or external, relevant to the full understanding of a word or passage) had long been a formal procedure for teaching literature in French schools, but the explicative analyses of internal verbal interactions characteristic of the New Criticism derives from such books as I. A. Richards' *Practical Criticism* (1929) and William Empson's *Seven Types of Ambiguity* (1930).

4. The distinction between literary *genres*, although acknowledged, does not play an essential role in the New Criticism. The essential components of any work of literature, whether lyric, narrative, or dramatic, are conceived to be words, images, and symbols rather than character, thought, and plot. These linguistic elements, whatever the genre, are often said to be organized around a central and humanly significant *theme*, and to manifest high literary value to the degree that they manifest *"tension," "irony,"* and *"paradox"* in achieving a "reconciliation of diverse impulses" or an "equilibrium of opposed forces." The form of a work, whether or not it has characters and plot, is said to be primarily a "structure of meanings," which evolve into an integral and freestanding unity mainly through a play and counterplay of "thematic imagery" and "symbolic action."

The basic orientation and modes of analysis in the New Criticism were adapted to the **contextual criticism** of Eliseo Vivas and Murray Krieger. Krieger defined contextualism as "the claim that the poem is a tight, compelling, finally closed context," which prevents "our escape to the world of reference and action beyond," and requires that we "judge the work's efficacy as an aesthetic object." (See Murray Krieger, *The New Apologists for Poetry*, 1956, and *Theory of Criticism*, 1976.) The revolutionary thrust of the mode had lost much of its force by the 1960s, when it gave way to various newer theories of criticism, but it has left a deep and enduring mark on the criticism and teaching of literature, in its primary emphasis on the individual work and in the variety and subtlety of the devices that it made available for analyzing its internal relations. *Lyric Poetry: Beyond New Criticism*, eds. Chaviva Hošek and Patricia Parker (1985), is a collection of *structuralist, poststructuralist*, and other essays which—often in express opposition to the New Criticism—exemplify the diverse newer modes of "close reading"; some of these essays claim that competing forces within the language of a lyric poem preclude the possibility of the unified meaning that was a central tenet of the New Critics.

Central instances of the theory and practice of New Criticism are Cleanth Brooks, *The Well Wrought Urn* (1947), and W. K. Wimsatt, *The Verbal Icon* (1954). The enterprises of New Criticism are privileged over alternative approaches to literature in René Wellek and Austin Warren, *Theory of Literature* (3d ed., 1964), which became a standard reference book in the graduate study of literature. Robert W. Stallman's *Critiques and Essays in Criticism, 1920–1948* (1949) is a convenient collection of essays in this critical mode; the literary journal *The Explicator* (1942ff.), devoted to the close reading of single poems, was a characteristic product of its approach to literary texts, as are the items listed in *Poetry Explication: A Checklist of Interpretation Since 1924 of British and American Poems Past and Present*, ed. Joseph M. Kuntz (3d ed., 1980). See also W. K. Wimsatt, ed., *Explication as Criticism* (1963); the review of the movement by René Wellek, *A History of Modern Criticism*, Vol. 6 (1986); and the spirited retrospective defense of New Criticism by its chief exponent, Cleanth Brooks, "In Search of the New Criticism" (1983), reprinted in Brooks, *Community, Religion, and Literature* (1995). For critiques of the theory and methods of the New Criticism, see R. S. Crane, ed., *Critics and Criticism, Ancient and Modern* (1952), and *The Languages of Criticism and the Structure of Poetry* (1953); Gerald Graff, *Poetic Statement and Critical Dogma* (1970); Terry Eagleton, *Literary Theory: An Introduction* (1993); Susan Wolfson, *Formal Charges* (1997). For references to *New Criticism* in other entries, see pages *62, 73, 82, 128, 135, 152, 157, 159, 161, 168, 218, 220, 234, 239, 249, 256, 300, 363.* See also *affective fallacy; ambiguity; form and structure; intentional fallacy; tension.*

**new formalism** (in literary criticism): **128**.

**new formalism** (in writing poetry): **131**.

**new historicism:** New historicism, since the early 1980s, has been the accepted name for a mode of literary study that its proponents oppose to the *formalism* they attribute both to the *New Criticism* and to the critical *deconstruction* that followed it. In place of dealing with a text in isolation from its historical context, new historicists attend primarily to the historical and cultural conditions of its production, its meanings, its effects, and also of its later critical interpretations and evaluations. This is not simply a return to an earlier kind of literary scholarship, for the views and practices of the new historicists differ markedly from those of earlier scholars who had adverted to social and intellectual history as a "background" against which to set a work of literature as an independent entity, or had viewed literature as a "reflection" of the worldview characteristic of a period. Instead, new historicists conceive of a literary text as "situated" within the totality of the institutions, social practices, and discourses that constitute the culture of a particular time and place, and with which the literary text interacts as both a product and a producer of cultural energies and codes.

What is most distinctive in this mode of historical study is mainly the result of concepts and practices of literary analysis and interpretation that have been assimilated from various recent poststructural theorists (see *poststructuralism*). Especially prominent are (1) The views of the revisionist Marxist thinker Louis Althusser that ideology manifests itself in different ways in the discourse of each of the semi-autonomous institutions of an era, including literature, and also that ideology operates covertly to form and position the users of language as the "subjects" in a discourse, in a way that in fact "subjects" them—that is, subordinates them—to the interests of the ruling classes; see *ideology* under *Marxist criticism*, and *subject* under *poststructuralism*. (2) Michel Foucault's view that the *discourse* of an era, instead of reflecting pre-existing entities and orders, brings into being the concepts, oppositions, and hierarchies of which it speaks; that these elements are both products and propagators of "power," or social forces; and that as a result, the particular discursive formations of an era determine what is at the time accounted to be "knowledge" and "truth," as well as what is considered to be humanly normal as against what is considered to be criminal, or insane, or sexually deviant; see Foucault under *poststructuralism*. (3) The central concept in *deconstructive* criticism that all texts involve modes of signification that war against each other, merged with Mikhail Bakhtin's concept of the dialogic nature of many literary texts, in the sense that they incorporate a number of conflicting voices that represent diverse social classes and interests; see *dialogic criticism*. (4) Developments in cultural anthropology, especially Clifford Geertz' view that a culture is constituted by distinctive sets of signifying systems, and his use of what he calls **thick descriptions** —the close analysis, or "reading," of a particular social production or event so as to recover the meanings it has for the people involved in it, as well as to discover, within the overall cultural system, the network of conventions, codes, and modes of thinking with which the particular item is implicated, and which invest the item with those meanings.

In an oft-quoted phrase, Louis Montrose described the new historicism as "a reciprocal concern with the historicity of texts and the textuality of history." That is, history is conceived to be not a set of fixed, objective facts but, like the literature with which it interacts, a text that itself needs to be interpreted. Any text, on the other hand, is conceived as a discourse which, although it may seem to present, or reflect, an external reality, in fact consists of what are called **representations**—that is, verbal formations which are the "ideological products" or **cultural constructs** of the historical conditions specific to an era. Many historicists claim also that these cultural and ideological representations in texts serve mainly to reproduce, confirm, and propagate the complex power structures of domination and subordination which characterize a given society.

Despite their common perspective on literary writings as mutually implicative with all other components of a culture, we find considerable diversity and disagreements among individual exponents of the new historicism. The following proposals, however, occur frequently in their writings, sometimes in an extreme and sometimes in a qualified form. All of them are formulated in opposition to views that, according to new historicists, were central ideological constructs in traditional literary criticism. A number of historicists assign the formative period of most such constructs to the early era of capitalism in the seventeenth and eighteenth centuries.

1.  Literature does not occupy a "trans-historical" *aesthetic* realm which is independent of the economic, social, and political conditions specific to an era, nor is literature subject to timeless criteria of artistic value. Instead, a literary text is simply one of many kinds of texts—religious, philosophical, legal, scientific, and so on—all of which are formed and structured by the particular conditions of a time and place, and among which the literary text has neither unique status nor special privilege. A related fallacy of mainstream criticism, according to new historicists, was to view a literary text as an autonomous body of fixed meanings that cohere to form an organic whole in which all conflicts are artistically resolved. (See, for example, *New Criticism.*) On the contrary, it is claimed, many literary texts consist of a diversity of dissonant voices, and these voices express not only the orthodox, but also the subordinated and subversive forces of the era in which the text was produced. Furthermore, what may seem to be the artistic resolution of a literary plot, yielding pleasure to the reader, is in fact deceptive, for it is an effect that serves to cover over the unresolved conflicts of power, class, gender, and diverse social groups that make up the tensions that underlie the surface meanings of a literary text.

    Some new historicists nonetheless maintain the distinction between literary and nonliterary works, as well as between major and lesser works of literary artistry. As Stephen Greenblatt has said, "Major works of art remain centrally important, but they are jostled now by an array of other texts and images." The confrontation of such works with minor or nonliterary works, he claims, in fact serves to explain what it means to be major, and indicate why it is that works that are major have outlasted the others.

2.  History is not a homogeneous and stable pattern of facts and events which serve as the "background" to the literature of an era, or which literature can be said simply to reflect, or which can be adverted to (as in early *Marxist criticism*) as the "material" conditions that, in a unilateral way, determine the particularities of a literary text. In contrast to such views, a literary text is said by new historicists to be thoroughly "embedded" in its context, and in a constant interaction and interchange with other components inside the network of institutions, beliefs, and cultural power relationships, practices, and products that, in their ensemble, constitute what we call history. New historicists commonly regard even the conceptual "boundaries" by which we currently discriminate between *literature* and nonliterary texts to be a construct of post-Renaissance ideological formations. They continue to make use of such discriminations,

but only for tactical convenience in conducting critical discussion, and stress that one must view all boundaries between types of discourse as entirely permeable to interchanges of diverse elements and forces. Favored terms for such interchanges—whether among the modes of discourse within a single literary text, or among diverse kinds of texts, or between a text and its institutional and cultural context—are "negotiation," "commerce," "exchange," "transaction," and "circulation." Such metaphors are intended not only to denote the two-way, oscillatory relationships among literary and other components of a culture, but also to indicate, by their obvious origin in the monetary discourse of the marketplace, the degree to which the operations and values of modern consumer capitalism saturate the literary and aesthetic, as well as all other institutions and relations. As Stephen Greenblatt has expressed such a view, the "negotiation" that results in the production and circulation of a work of art involves a "mutually profitable exchange"—including "a return normally measured in pleasure and interest"—in which "the society's dominant currencies, money and prestige, are invariably involved." ("Toward a Poetics of Culture," in *The New Historicism*, ed. H. Aram Veeser, 1989.)

3. The humanistic concept of an essential human nature that is shared by the author of a literary work, the characters within the work, and the audience the author writes for, is another of the widely held ideological illusions that, according to many new historicists, were generated primarily by a capitalist culture. They also attribute to this "bourgeois" and "essentialist humanism" the view that a literary work is the imaginative creation of a free, or "autonomous," author who possesses a unified, unique, and enduring personal identity. (See *essentialism* in the entry *humanism*, also *author and authorship*.) In the epilogue to *Renaissance Self-Fashioning* (1980) Stephen Greenblatt says that, in the course of writing the book, he lost his initial confidence in "the role of human autonomy," for "the human subject itself began to seem remarkably unfree, the ideological product of the relations of power in a particular society." An area of contest among new historicists is the extent to which an author, despite being a *subject* who is constructed and positioned by the play of power and ideology within the discourse of a particular era, may retain some scope for individual initiative and "agency." A number of historicists who ascribe a degree of freedom and initiative to an individual author do so, however, not as in traditional criticism, in order to account for an author's literary invention and distinctive artistry, but in order to keep open the theoretical possibility that an individual author can intervene so as to inaugurate radical changes in the social power structure of which that individual's own "subjectivity" and function are themselves a product.

4. Like the authors who produce literary texts, their readers are *subjects* who are constructed and positioned by the conditions and ideological formations of their own era. All claims, therefore, for the possibility of a disinterested and objective interpretation and evaluation of a literary text—such as Matthew Arnold's behest that we see a work "as in itself it really is"—are among the illusions of a humanistic idealism. Insofar as the ideology of readers conforms to the ideology of the writer of a literary text, the readers will tend to *naturalize*

the text—that is, interpret its culture-specific and time-bound representations as though they were the features of universal and permanent human nature and experience. On the other hand, insofar as the readers' ideology differs from that of the writer, they will tend to **appropriate** the text—that is, interpret it so as to make it conform to their own cultural prepossessions.

New historicists acknowledge that they themselves, like all authors, are "subjectivities" that have been shaped and informed by the circumstances and discourses specific to their era, hence that their own critical writings in great part construct, rather than discover ready-made, the textual meanings they describe and the literary and cultural histories they narrate. To mitigate the risk that they will unquestioningly appropriate texts that were written in the past, they stress that the course of history between the past and present is not coherent, but exhibits discontinuities, breaks, and ruptures; by doing so, they hope to "distance" and "estrange" an earlier text and so sharpen their ability to detect its differences from their present ideological assumptions. Some historicists present their readings of texts written in the past as (in their favored metaphor) "negotiations" between past and present. In this two-way relationship, the features of a cultural product, which are identifiable only relative to their differences from the historicist's subject-position, in return make possible some degree of insight into the forces and configurations of power—especially with respect to class, gender, race, and ethnicity—that prevail in the historicist's present culture and serve to shape the historicist's own ideology and interpretations.

The concepts, themes, and procedures of new historicist criticism took shape in the late 1970s and early 1980s, most prominently in writings by scholars of the English Renaissance. They directed their attention especially to literary forms such as the pastoral and masque, and above all drama; emphasized the role in shaping a text of social and economic conditions such as literary patronage, censorship, and the control of access to printing; analyzed texts as discursive "sites" which enacted and reproduced the interests and power of the Tudor monarchy; but were alert to detect within such texts the voices of the oppressed, the marginalized, and the dispossessed. At almost the same time, students of the English Romantic period developed parallel conceptions of the intertextuality of literature and history, and similar views that the "representations" in literary texts are not reflectors of reality but "concretized" forms of ideology. Historicists of Romantic literature, however, in distinction from most Renaissance historicists, often name their critical procedures **political readings** of a literary text—readings in which they stress quasi-Freudian mechanisms such as "suppression," "displacement," and "substitution" by which, they assert, a writer's political ideology (in a process of which the writer remains largely or entirely unaware) inevitably disguises, or entirely elides into silence and "absence," the circumstances and contradictions of contemporary history. The primary aim of a political reader of a literary text is to undo these ideological disguises and suppressions in order to uncover its *subtext* of historical and political conflicts and oppressions which are the text's true, although covert or unmentioned, subject matter. (On such textual "silences," see Pierre Macherey and Fredric Jameson, under *Marxist criticism*.)

In the course of the 1980s, the characteristic viewpoints and practices of new historicism spread rapidly to all periods of literary study, and were increasingly represented, described, and debated in conferences, books, and periodical essays. The interpretive procedures of this critical mode have interacted with the earlier concern of *feminist* critics, who stressed the role of male power structures in forming dominant ideological and cultural constructs. New historicist procedures also have parallels in the critics of *African-American* and other *ethnic* literatures, who stress the role of culture formations dominated by white Europeans in suppressing, marginalizing, or distorting the achievements of nonwhite and non-European peoples. In the 1990s, various forms of new historicism, and related types of criticism that stress the embeddedness of literature in historical circumstances, replaced deconstruction as the reigning mode of *avant-garde* critical theory and practice.

Stephen Greenblatt inaugurated the currency of the label "new historicism" in his Introduction to a special issue of *Genre*, Vol. 15 (1982). He prefers, however, to call his own critical enterprise **cultural poetics**, in order to highlight his concern with literature and the arts as integral with other social practices that, in their complex interactions, make up the general culture of an era. Greenblatt's essay entitled "Invisible Bullets" in *Shakespearean Negotiations* (1988) serves to exemplify the interpretive procedures of the leading exponent of this mode of criticism, who often inaugurates a commentary on a work of literature with an unexpected historical anecdote, or with a "luminous" interpretive detail in a marginal literary text, or in a nonliterary text. In this essay, Greenblatt begins by reading a selection from Thomas Harriot's *A Brief and True Report of the New Found Land of Virginia*, written in 1588, as a representative discourse of the English colonizers of America which, without its author's awareness, serves to confirm "the Machiavellian hypothesis of the origin of princely power in force and fraud," but nonetheless draws its "audience irresistibly toward the celebration of that power." Greenblatt also asserts that Harriot tests the English power structure that he attests by recording in his *Report* the countervoices of the Native Americans who are being appropriated and oppressed by that power. Greenblatt then identifies parallel modes of power discourse and counterdiscourse in the dialogues in Shakespeare's *Tempest* between Prospero the imperialist appropriator and Caliban the expropriated native of his island, and goes on to find similar discursive configurations in the texts of Shakespeare's *Henry IV, 1 and 2*, and *Henry V*. In Greenblatt's reading, the dialogue and events of the Henry plays reveal the degree to which princely power is based on predation, calculation, deceit, and hypocrisy; at the same time, the plays do not scruple to record the dissonant and subversive voices of Falstaff and various other representatives of Elizabethan subcultures. These counterestablishment discourses in Shakespeare's plays, however, in fact are so managed as to maneuver their audience to accept and even glorify the power structure to which that audience is itself subordinated. Greenblatt applies to these plays a conceptual pattern, the **subversion-containment dialectic**, which has been a central concern of new historicist critics of Renaissance literature. The thesis is that, in order to sustain its power, any durable political and cultural order not only to some degree allows, but actively fosters "subversive" elements and forces, yet in such a way as more effectively to "contain" such challenges to the existing order. (Foucault had established such a conception by his claim that, under a dominating "regimen of truth," all attempts at opposition to power cannot help but be "complicitous" with it.) This view of the general triumph of containment over the forces of subversion has been criticized as "pessimistic" and "quietist" by the group of new historicists known as "cultural materialists," who insist on the capacity of subversive ideas and practices—including those manifested in their own critical writings—to effect drastic social changes.

**Cultural materialism** is a term, employed by the British neo-Marxist critic Raymond Williams, which has been adopted by a number of other British scholars, especially those concerned with the literature of the Renaissance, to indicate the Marxist orientation of their mode of new historicism—Marxist in that they retain a version of Marx's view of cultural phenomena as a "superstructure" which, in the last analysis, is determined by the "material" (that is, economic) "base." (See *Marxist criticism.*) They insist that, whatever the "textuality" of history, a culture and its literary products are always to an important degree conditioned by the material forces and relations of production in their historical era. They are particularly interested in the political significance, and especially the subversive aspects and effects, of a literary text, not only in its own time, but also in later versions that have been revised for the theater and the cinema. Cultural materialists stress that their criticism is itself oriented toward political "intervention" in their own era, in an express "commitment," as Jonathan Dollimore and Alan Sinfield have put it, "to the transformation of a social order which exploits people on grounds of race, gender, and class." (Foreword to *Political Shakespeare: New Essays in Cultural Materialism*, 1985. See also the comment on Stuart Hall, in the entry *Marxist criticism.*) Similar views are expressed by those American exponents of the new literary history who are political activists; indeed, some of them claim that if new historicists limit themselves to analyzing examples of class dominance and exploitation in literary texts, but stop short of a commitment to remake the present social order, they have been co-opted into "complicity" with the *formalist* literary criticism that they set out to displace. For the connections between North American forms of historicism and British cultural materialism, see Kiernan Ryan, ed., *New Historicism and Cultural Materialism: A Reader* (1996), and John Brannigan, *New Historicism and Cultural Materialism* (1998).

See *cultural studies*, which are closely related to the new historicism. For writers especially influential in forming the concepts and practices of the new historicism, see Louis Althusser, *Lenin and Philosophy, and Other Essays* (1969, trans. 1971); Louis McKay, *Foucault: A Critical Introduction* (1994); and Clifford Geertz, "Thick Description: Toward an Interpretive Theory of Culture," in *The Interpretation of Cultures* (1973). *The New Historicism*, ed. H. Aram Veeser (1989), is a useful collection of essays by Louis Montrose, Stephen Greenblatt, and other prominent historicists who focus on the Renaissance; see also Veeser's *The New Historicism Reader* (1994); the essays in Jeffrey N. Cox and Larry J. Reynolds, eds., *New Historical Literary Study* (1993); Stephen Greenblatt, ed., *Representing the English Renaissance* (1988), and his *Learning to Curse: Essays in Early Modern Culture* (1990); the survey in Paul Hamilton, *Historicism: The New Critical Idiom* (1996). See also Catherine Gallagher and Stephen Greenblatt, *Practicing New*

*Historicism* (2000). For a *feminist* application of new historicism, refer to Margaret W. Ferguson, Maureen Quilligan, and Nancy J. Vickers, eds., *Rewriting the Renaissance: The Discourses of Sexual Difference in Early Modern Europe* (1986). Treatments of Romantic literature that exemplify a new historicist orientation include Jerome J. McGann, *The Romantic Ideology: A Critical Investigation* (1983); Marjorie Levinson, *Wordsworth's Great Period Poems* (1986); Clifford Siskin, *The Historicity of Romantic Discourse* (1988); Alan Liu, *Wordsworth: The Sense of History* (1989); and Marjorie Levinson and others, *Rethinking Historicism: Critical Readings in Romantic History* (1989). For new historicist criticism focused on literature after the Romantic period, see Catherine Gallagher, *The Industrial Reformation of English Fiction: Social Discourse and Narrative Form, 1832–1867* (1985), and Walter Benn Michaels, *The Gold Standard and the Logic of Naturalism: American Literature at the Turn of the Century* (1987). Refer also to the journal *Representations*. In "What Is New Formalism?" (*PMLA*, Vol. 122, 2007), Marjorie Levinson stresses the connection between new historicism and the revival of critical interest in questions of literary form; see *new formalism*.

Jonathan Dollimore and Alan Sinfield present writings by British cultural materialists in *Political Shakespeare: New Essays in Cultural Materialism* (1985), as does John Drakakis in *Alternative Shakespeares* (1985); see also Raymond Williams, *Marxism and Literature* (1977), and Terry Eagleton, *Marxism and Literary Criticism* (1976). Walter Cohen, "Political Criticism of Shakespeare," in Jean E. Howard and Marion F. O'Connor, eds., *Shakespeare Reproduced: The Text in History and Ideology* (1987), interrogates new historicism from a Marxist point of view; while J. Hillis Miller, in his presidential address to the Modern Language Association on "The Triumph of Theory" (*PMLA*, Vol. 102, 1987, pp. 281–91), does so from the point of view of deconstructive criticism. Feminist critiques of new historicism are Lynda Boose, "The Family in Shakespeare Studies," *Renaissance Quarterly*, Vol. 40 (1987); and Carol Thomas Neely, "Constructing the Subject: Feminist Practice and the New Renaissance Discourse" (*English Literary Renaissance*, Vol. 18, 1988). Critiques of some forms of new historicism from more traditional critical positions are Edward Pechter, "The New Historicism and Its Discontents," *PMLA*, Vol. 102 (1987); M. H. Abrams, "On Political Readings of *Lyrical Ballads*," in *Doing Things with Texts: Essays in Criticism and Critical Theory* (1989); Richard Levin, "Unthinkable Thoughts in the New Historicizing of English Renaissance Drama," *New Literary History*, Vol. 21 (1989–90), pp. 433–47; and Brook Thomas, *The New Historicism and Other Old-Fashioned Topics* (1991). For tendencies in the writing of general history closely parallel to the new historicism in literary studies, see Dominick La Capra, *History and Criticism* (1985); and Lynn Hunt, ed., *The New Cultural History* (1989). For references to *new historicism* in other entries, see pages *18, 47, 95, 128, 147, 161, 281, 283, 335, 374.*

**New Humanism: 145.**

**new novel: 231**; *44, 268*

**new philology: 173.**

**novel:** The term "novel" is now applied to a great variety of writings that have in common only the attribute of being extended works of *fiction* written in prose. As an extended narrative, the novel is distinguished from the *short story* and from the work of middle length called the *novelette*; its magnitude permits a greater variety of characters, greater complication of plot (or plots), ampler development of milieu, and more sustained exploration of character and motives than do the shorter, more concentrated modes. As a narrative written in prose, the novel is distinguished from the long narratives in verse of Geoffrey Chaucer, Edmund Spenser, and John Milton which, beginning with the eighteenth century, the novel has increasingly supplanted. Within these limits the novel includes such diverse works as Samuel Richardson's *Pamela* and Laurence Sterne's *Tristram Shandy*; Jane Austen's *Emma* and Virginia Woolf's *Orlando*; Charles Dickens' *Pickwick Papers* and Henry James' *The Wings of the Dove*; Leo Tolstoy's *War and Peace* and Franz Kafka's *The Trial*; Ernest Hemingway's *The Sun Also Rises* and James Joyce's *Finnegans Wake*; Doris Lessing's *The Golden Notebook* and Vladimir Nabokov's *Lolita*.

The term for the novel in most European languages is **roman**, which is derived from the medieval term, the *romance*. The English name for the form, on the other hand, is derived from the Italian **novella** (literally, "a little new thing"), which was a short tale in prose. In fourteenth-century Italy there was a vogue for collections of such tales, some serious and some scandalous; the best known of these collections is Boccaccio's *Decameron*, which is still available in English translation at any well-stocked bookstore. Currently the term "novella" (or in the German form, *Novelle*) is often used as an equivalent for *novelette:* a prose fiction of middle length, such as Joseph Conrad's *Heart of Darkness* or Thomas Mann's *Death in Venice*. (See under *short story*.)

Long narrative romances in prose were written by Greek writers as early as the second and third centuries AD. Typically they dealt with separated lovers who, after perilous adventures and hairbreadth escapes, are happily reunited at the end. The best known of these Greek romances, influential in later European literature, were the *Aethiopica* by Heliodorus and the charming pastoral narrative

*Daphnis and Chloe* by Longus. Thomas Lodge's *Rosalynde* (the model for Shakespeare's *As You Like It*) and Sir Philip Sidney's *Arcadia* were Elizabethan continuations of the pastoral romance of the ancient Greeks. (See *romance* and *pastoral*.)

Another important predecessor of the later novel was the **picaresque narrative**, which emerged in sixteenth-century Spain; see Michael Alpert, trans., *Lazarillo de Tormes and The Swindler* (2003), and Giancarlo Maiorino, *At the Margins of the Renaissance: Lazarillo de Tormes and the Picaresque Art of Survival* (2003). The most popular instance, however, *Gil Blas* (1715), was written by the Frenchman Le Sage. "Picaro" is Spanish for "rogue," and a typical story concerns the escapades of an insouciant rascal who lives by his wits and shows little if any alteration of character through a long succession of adventures. Picaresque fiction is realistic in manner, **episodic** in structure (that is, composed of a sequence of events held together largely because they happened to one person), and often satiric in aim. The first, and very lively, English example was Thomas Nashe's *The Unfortunate Traveller* (1594). We recognize the survival of the picaresque type in many later novels such as Mark Twain's *The Adventures of Tom Sawyer* (1876), Thomas Mann's *The Confessions of Felix Krull* (1954), and Saul Bellow's *The Adventures of Augie March* (1953). The development of the novel owes much to prose works which, like the picaresque story, were written to deflate romantic or idealized fictional forms. Cervantes' great quasi-picaresque narrative *Don Quixote* (1605) was the single most important progenitor of the modern novel; in it, an engaging madman who tries to live by the ideals of chivalric romance in the everyday world is used to explore the relationships of illusion and reality in human life.

After these precedents and many others—including the seventeenth-century *character* (a brief sketch of a typical personality or way of life) and Madame de La Fayette's psychologically complex study of character, *La Princesse de Clèves* (1678) —what is recognizably the novel as we now think of it appeared in England in the early eighteenth century. In 1719 Daniel Defoe wrote *Robinson Crusoe* and in 1722, *Moll Flanders*. Both of these are still picaresque in type, in the sense that their structure is episodic rather than in the organized form of a *plot*; while Moll is herself a colorful female version of the old picaro—"twelve Year a Whore, five times a Wife (whereof once to her own Brother), Twelve Year a Thief, Eight Year a Transported Felon in Virginia," as the title page resoundingly informs us. But *Robinson Crusoe* is given an enforced unity of action by its focus on the problem of surviving on an uninhabited island, and both stories present so convincing a central character, set in so solid and detailedly realized a world, that Defoe is often credited with writing the first **novel of incident**.

The credit for having written the first English **novel of character**, or "psychological novel," is almost unanimously given to Samuel Richardson for his *Pamela; or, Virtue Rewarded* (1740). Pamela is the story of a sentimental but shrewd young woman who, by prudently safeguarding her beleaguered chastity, succeeds in becoming the wife of a wild young gentleman instead of his debauched servant girl. The distinction between the novel of incident and the novel of character cannot be drawn sharply; but in the novel of incident the greater interest is in what the *protagonist* will do next and on how the story will turn out; in the novel of character, it is on the protagonist's motives for what he or she does, and on how the protagonist as a person will turn out. On twentieth-century developments in the novel of character see Leon Edel, *The Modern Psychological Novel* (rev. 1965). For an account, in the mode of *cultural studies*, of the genesis of the conception of character in the novel, see Deidre S. Lynch, *The Economy of Character: Novels, Market Culture, and the Business of Inner Meaning* (1998).

*Pamela*, like its greater and tragic successor, Richardson's *Clarissa* (1747–48), is an **epistolary novel**; that is, the narrative is conveyed entirely by an exchange of letters. Later novelists have preferred alternative devices for limiting the narrative *point of view* to one or another single character, but the epistolary technique is still occasionally revived—for example, in Mark Harris' hilarious novel *Wake Up, Stupid* (1959) and Alice Walker's *The Color Purple* (1982). See Linda Kauffman, *Special Delivery: Epistolary Modes in Modern Fiction* (1992).

Novels may have any kind of plot form—tragic, comic, satiric, or romantic. A common distinction—which was described by Hawthorne, in his preface to *The House of the Seven Gables* (1851) and elsewhere, and has been adopted and expanded by a number of recent critics—is that between two basic types of prose fiction: the realistic novel (which is the novel proper) and the romance. The **realistic novel** can be described as the fictional attempt to give the effect of *realism*, by representing complex characters with mixed motives who are rooted in a social class, operate in a developed social structure, interact with many other characters, and undergo plausible, everyday modes of experience. This novelistic mode, rooted in such eighteenth-century writers as Defoe and Fielding, achieved a high development in the master novelists of the nineteenth century, including Jane Austen, George Eliot, Anthony Trollope, William Dean Howells, and Henry James in England and America; Stendhal, George Sand, Balzac, and Flaubert in France; and Turgenev and Tolstoy in Russia. If, as in the writings of Jane Austen, Edith Wharton, and John P. Marquand, a realistic novel focuses on the customs, conversation, and ways of thinking and valuing of the upper social class, it is often called a **novel of manners**. The **prose romance**, on the other hand, has as its precursors the *chivalric romance* of the Middle Ages and the *Gothic novel* of the later eighteenth century. It usually deploys characters who are sharply discriminated as heroes or villains, masters or victims; its protagonist is often solitary, and relatively isolated from a social context; it tends to be set in the historical past, and the *atmosphere* is such as to suspend the reader's expectations that are based on everyday experience. The plot of the prose romance emphasizes adventure, and is frequently cast in the form of the quest for an ideal, or the pursuit of an enemy; and the nonrealistic and occasionally melodramatic events are claimed by some critics to project in symbolic form the primal desires, hopes, and terrors in the depths of the human mind, and to be therefore analogous to the materials of dream, myth, ritual, and folklore. Examples of romance novels are Walter Scott's *Rob Roy* (1817), Alexandre Dumas' *The Three Musketeers* (1844–45), Emily Brontë's *Wuthering Heights* (1847), and an important line of American narratives which extends from Edgar Allan Poe, James Fenimore Cooper, Nathaniel Hawthorne, and Herman Melville to recent writings of William Faulkner and Saul Bellow. Martin Green, in *Dreams of Adventure, Deeds of Empire* (1979), distinguishes a special type of romance, "the adventure novel," which deals with masculine adventures in the newly colonized non-European world. Defoe's *Robinson Crusoe* (1719) is an early prototype; some later instances are H. Rider Haggard's *King Solomon's Mines* (1886), Robert Louis Stevenson's *Treasure Island* (1883), and Rudyard Kipling's *Kim* (1901).

Refer to Laurie Langbauer, *Women and Romance: The Consolations of Gender in the English Novel* (1990); Deborah Ross, *The Excellence of Falsehood: Romance, Realism, and Women's Contribution to the Novel* (1991). On the realistic novel in the nineteenth century see Harry Levin, *The Gates of Horn: A Study of Five French Realists* (1963); Ioan Williams, *The Realist Novel in England* (1975); G. J. Becker, *Master European Realists* (1982). On the prose romance in America, see Richard Chase, *The American Novel and Its Tradition* (1957); Northrop Frye, "The Mythos of Summer: Romance," in *Anatomy of Criticism* (1957); Joel Porte, *The Romance in America* (1969); Michael D. Bell, *The Development of American Romance* (1980); and for a skeptical view of the usual division between novel and romance, Nina Baym, *Novels, Readers, and Reviewers: Responses to Fiction in Antebellum America* (1984).

Other often identified subclasses of the novel are based on differences in subject matter, emphasis, and artistic purpose:

**Bildungsroman** and **Erziehungsroman** are German terms signifying "novel of formation" or "novel of education." The subject of these novels is the development of the protagonist's mind and character, in the passage from childhood through varied experiences—and often through a spiritual crisis—into maturity, which usually involves recognition of one's identity and role in the world. The mode began in Germany with K. P. Moritz's *Anton Reiser* (1785–90) and Goethe's *Wilhelm Meister's Apprenticeship* (1795–96); it includes Charlotte Brontë's *Jane Eyre* (1847), George Eliot's *The Mill on the Floss* (1860), Charles Dickens' *Great Expectations* (1861), Somerset Maugham's *Of Human Bondage* (1915), and Thomas Mann's *The Magic Mountain* (1924). An important subtype of the Bildungsroman is the **Künstlerroman** ("artist-novel"), which represents the growth of a novelist or other artist from childhood into the stage of maturity that signalizes the recognition of the protagonist's artistic destiny and mastery of an artistic craft. Dickens' *David Copperfield* (1849–50) can be considered an early instance of this type; later and more developed examples include some major novels of the twentieth century: Marcel Proust's *Remembrance of Things Past* (1913–27), James Joyce's *A Portrait of the Artist as a Young Man* (1914–15), Thomas Mann's *Tonio Kröger* (1903) and *Dr. Faustus* (1947), and André Gide's *The Counterfeiters* (1926). See Lionel Trilling, "The Princess Casamassima," in *The Liberal Imagination* (1950); Maurice Beebe, *Ivory Towers and Sacred Founts: The Artist as Hero in Fiction* (1964); Jerome H. Buckley, *Season of Youth: The Bildungsroman from Dickens to Golding* (1974); Martin Swales, *The German Bildungsroman from Wieland to Hesse* (1978); Thomas L. Jeffers, *Apprenticeships: The Bildungsroman from Goethe to Santayana* (2005). In *Unbecoming Women: British Women Writers and the Novel of Development* (1993), Susan Fraiman analyzes novels about "growing up female"; she proposes that they put to question the "enabling fiction" that the *Bildungsroman* is a "progressive development" toward "masterful selfhood."

The **social novel** emphasizes the influence of the social and economic conditions of an era on shaping characters and determining events; often it also embodies an implicit or explicit thesis recommending political and social reform. Examples of social novels are Harriet Beecher Stowe's *Uncle Tom's Cabin* (1852), Upton Sinclair's *The Jungle* (1906), John Steinbeck's *The Grapes of Wrath* (1939), Nadine Gordimer's *Burger's Daughter* (1979). A Marxist version of the social novel, representing the hardships suffered by the oppressed working class, and usually written to incite the reader to radical political action, is called the **proletarian novel** (see *Marxist criticism*). Proletarian fiction flourished especially during the great economic depression of the 1930s. An English example is Walter Greenwood's *Love on the Dole* (1933); American examples are Grace Lumpkin's *To Make My Bread* (1932), about a mill strike in North Carolina, and Robert Cantwell's *Laugh and Lie Down* (1931), about the harshness of life in a lumber mill city in the Northwest.

Some realistic novels make use of events and personages from the historical past to add interest and picturesqueness to the narrative. What we usually specify as the **historical novel**, however, began in the nineteenth century with Sir Walter Scott. The historical novel not only takes its setting and some characters and events from history, but makes the historical events and issues crucial for the central characters and the course of the narrative. Some of the greatest historical novels also use the protagonists and actions to reveal what the author regards as the deep forces that impel the historical process. Examples of historical novels are Scott's *Ivanhoe* (1819), set in the period of Norman domination of the Saxons at the time of Richard I; Dickens' *A Tale of Two Cities* (1859), set in Paris and London during the French Revolution; George Eliot's *Romola* (1863), in Florence during the Renaissance; Tolstoy's *War and Peace* (1869), in Russia during the invasion by Napoleon; and Margaret Mitchell's *Gone with the Wind* (1936), in Georgia during the Civil War and Reconstruction. An influential treatment of the form was by the Marxist scholar and critic Georg Lukács, *The Historical Novel* (1937, trans. 1962); a comprehensive later commentary is by Harry E. Shaw, *The Forms of Historical Fiction: Sir Walter Scott and His Successors* (1983).

One twentieth-century variant of the historical novel is known as **documentary fiction**, which incorporates not only historical characters and events, but also reports of everyday events in contemporary newspapers: John Dos Passos, *USA* (1938); E. L. Doctorow, *Ragtime* (1975) and *Billy Bathgate* (1989). Another recent offshoot is the form that one of its innovators, Truman Capote, named the **non-fiction novel**. This uses a variety of novelistic techniques, such as deviations from the temporal sequence of events and descriptions of a participant's state of mind, to give a graphic rendering of recent people and happenings, and is based not only on historical records but often on personal interviews with the chief agents. Truman Capote's *In Cold Blood* (1965) and Norman Mailer's *The Executioner's Song* (1979) are instances of this mode; both offer a detailed rendering of the life, personality, and actions of murderers, based on a sustained series of prison interviews with the protagonists themselves. Other examples of this form are the writings of John McPhee, which the author calls **literature of fact**; see his *Levels of the Game* (1969) and *The Deltoid Pumpkin Seed* (1973). A third variant is the *fabulative* historical novel that interweaves history with fantasized, even fantastic events: John Barth, *The Sot-Weed Factor* (1960, rev. 1967); Thomas Pynchon, *Gravity's Rainbow* (1973). See John Hollowell, *Fact and Fiction: The New Journalism and the Nonfiction Novel* (1977); Barbara Foley, *Telling the Truth: The Theory and Practice of Documentary Fiction* (1986); and Barbara Lounsberry, *The Art of Fact: Contemporary Artistic Nonfiction* (1990). Cushing Strout, in *The Veracious Imagination* (1981), studies such developments in recent novels, as well as the related form called **documentary drama** in theater, film, and television, which combines fiction with history, journalistic reports, and biography.

The **regional novel** emphasizes the setting, speech, and social structure and customs of a particular locality, not merely as *local color*, but as important conditions affecting the temperament of the characters and their ways of thinking, feeling, and interacting. Instances of such localities are "Wessex" in Thomas Hardy's novels, and "Yoknapatawpha County," Mississippi, in Faulkner's. Stella Gibbons wrote a witty *parody* of the regional novel in *Cold Comfort Farm* (1936). For a discussion of regionalism centered on the Maine author Sarah Orne Jewett, see chapter 4 in Bill Brown, *A Sense of Things* (2003).

Beginning with the second half of the nineteenth century, the novel displaced all other literary forms in popularity. The theory as well as the practice of the novelistic art has received the devoted attention of some of the greatest masters of modern literature—Flaubert, Henry James, Proust, Mann, Joyce, and Virginia Woolf. (Henry James' prefaces, gathered into one volume as *The Art of the Novel*, ed. R. P. Blackmur, 1934, exemplify the care and subtlety that have been lavished on this craft.) There has been constant experimentation with new fictional methods, such as management of the *point of view* to minimize or eliminate the apparent role of the author-narrator or, at the opposite extreme, to foreground the role of the author as the inventor and controller of the fiction; the use of *symbolist* and *expressionist* techniques and of devices adopted from the art of the cinema; the dislocation of time sequence; the adaptation of forms and motifs from myths and dreams; and the exploitation of *stream of consciousness* narration in a way that converts the story of outer action and events into a drama of the life of the mind.

Such experimentation reached a radical extreme in the second half of the twentieth century (see *postmodernism*). Vladimir Nabokov was a supreme technician who wrote **involuted novels** (a work whose subject incorporates an account of its own genesis and development—for example, his *Pale Fire*); employed multilingual puns and jokes; incorporated esoteric data about butterflies (a subject in which he was an accomplished scientist); adopted strategies from chess, crossword puzzles, and other games; parodied other novels (and his own as well); and set elaborate traps for the unwary reader. This was also the era of what is sometimes called the **antinovel**—that is, a work which is deliberately constructed in a negative fashion, relying for its effects on the deletion of standard elements, on violating traditional norms, and on playing against the expectations established in the reader by the novelistic methods and conventions of the past. Thus Alain Robbe-Grillet, a leader among the exponents of the **nouveau roman** (the **new novel**) in France, wrote *Jealousy* (1957), in which he left out such standard elements as plot, characterization, descriptions of states of mind, locations in time and space, and frame of reference to the world in which the work is set. We are simply presented in this novel with a sequence of perceptions, mainly visual, which we may *naturalize* (that is, make intelligible in the mode of standard narrative procedures) by postulating that we are occupying the physical space and sharing the hyperacute observations of a jealous husband, from which we may infer also the tortured state of his disintegrating mind. Other new novelists are Nathalie Sarraute and Philippe Sollers. See Roland Barthes, *Writing Degree Zero* (trans. 1967), and Stephen Heath, *The Nouveau Roman: A Study in the Practice of Writing* (1972).

The term **magic realism**, originally applied in the 1920s to a school of surrealist German painters, was later used to describe the prose fiction of Jorge Luis Borges in Argentina, as well as the work of writers such as Gabriel García Márquez in Colombia, Isabel Allende in Chile, Günter Grass in Germany, Italo Calvino in Italy, and John Fowles and Salman Rushdie in England. These writers weave, in an ever-shifting pattern, a sharply etched *realism* in representing ordinary events and details together with fantastic and dreamlike elements, as well as with materials derived from myth and fairy tales. See, for example, Gabriel García Márquez's *One Hundred Years of Solitude* (1967). Robert Scholes has popularized **metafiction** (an alternative is **surfiction**) as an overall term for the growing class of novels which depart from realism and foreground the roles of the author in inventing the fiction and of the reader in receiving the fiction. Scholes has also popularized the term **fabulation** for a current mode of freewheeling narrative invention. Fabulative novels violate, in various ways, standard novelistic expectations by drastic—and sometimes highly effective—experiments with subject matter, form, style, temporal sequence, and fusions of the everyday, the fantastic, the mythical, and the nightmarish, in renderings that blur traditional distinctions between what is serious or trivial, horrible or ludicrous, tragic or comic. Recent fabulators include Thomas Pynchon, John Barth, Donald Barthelme, William Gass, Robert Coover, and Ishmael Reed. See Raymond Federman, *Surfiction* (1975); Robert Scholes, *Fabulation and Metafiction* (1979)—an expansion of his *The Fabulators* (1967); James M. Mellard, *The Exploded Form: The Modernist Novel in America* (1980); and Patricia Waugh, *Metafiction* (1984). For an account of metafiction from a *feminist* viewpoint, see Joan Douglas Peters, *Feminist Metafiction and the Evolution of the British Novel* (2002). Refer also to the entries in this *Glossary* on the literature of the *absurd* and *black humor*.

See *fiction* and *narrative and narratology*. Histories of the novel: E. A. Baker, *History of the English Novel* (12 vols., 1924ff.); Arnold Kettle's Marxist survey, *An Introduction to the English Novel* (2 vols., 1951); Dorothy Van Ghent, *The English Novel: Form and Function* (1953); Ian Watt, *The Rise of the Novel* (1957); Michael McKeon, *The Origins of the English Novel 1600–1740* (1987; 2d ed., 2002); J. Paul Hunter, *Before Novels: The Cultural Contexts of Eighteenth-Century English Fiction* (1990); Nancy Armstrong, *Desire and Domestic Fiction: A Political History of the Novel* (1990); *The Columbia History of the British Novel*, ed. John Richetti (1994); and *The Columbia History of the American Novel*, ed. Emory Elliott (1991). *The Novel*, ed. Franco Moretti (2 vols., 2006), consists of essays by many critics on the history, forms, and themes of the novel as an international literary type.

Michael McKeon, ed., *Theory of the Novel: A Historical Approach* (2000), gathers essays in literary criticism of the novel, from its beginnings to the present. On the art of the novel: Percy Lubbock, *The Craft of Fiction* (1921); E. M. Forster, *Aspects of the Novel* (1927); and three later influential books—Wayne C. Booth, *The Rhetoric of Fiction* (rev. 1983); Frank Kermode, *The Sense of an Ending* (1968); and David Lodge, *The Art of Fiction* (1992). Philip Stevick, ed., *The Theory of the Novel* (1967) is a collection of influential essays by various critics; J. Hillis Miller applies a deconstructive mode of criticism in *Fiction and Repetition* (1982); and Daniel Schwarz, *The Humanistic Heritage* (1986), reviews theories of prose fiction from 1900 to the present. The Czech émigré writer Milan Kundera has written three notable meditations on the novel in Europe: *The Art of the Novel* (2003), *Testaments Betrayed: An Essay in Nine Parts* (1995), and *The Curtain: An Essay in Seven Parts* (2006).

For additional types of the novel, see *absurd, literature of the; fantastic literature; Gothic novel; magic realism; novel of sensibility; novelette; realism and naturalism; science fiction; utopias and dystopias.* For features of the novel, see *atmosphere; character and characterization; confidant; distance and involvement; frame story; local color; narration, grammar of; persona, tone, and voice; plot; point of view; realism and naturalism; setting; stock character; stock situations; stream of consciousness.*

**novel of character: 227.**

**novel of incident: 227.**

**novel of manners: 228.**

**novel of sensibility: 328**; *329.*

**novelette: 332**; *226.*

**novella** (nōvĕl′ ă): **226.**

**Novelle** (nōvĕl′ ĕ): **332.**

**objective and subjective:** The social critic John Ruskin complained in 1856 that "German dullness and English affectation have of late much multiplied among us the use of two of the most objectionable words that were ever coined by the troublesomeness of metaphysicians—namely, 'objective' and 'subjective'." Ruskin was at least in part right. The words were imported into English criticism from the post-Kantian German critics of the late eighteenth and early nineteenth centuries, and they have certainly been troublesome. Amid the great variety of sometimes conflicting ways in which the opposition has been applied to literature, one is sufficiently widespread to be worth specifying. A **subjective** work is one in which the author incorporates personal experiences, or projects into the narrative his or her personal disposition, judgments, values, and feelings. An **objective** work is one in which the author presents the invented situation or the fictional characters and their thoughts, feelings, and actions and undertakes to remain detached and noncommittal. Thus a subjective *lyric* is one in which we are invited to associate the "I," or lyric speaker, with the poet (Coleridge's "Frost at Midnight," Wordsworth's "Tintern Abbey," Shelley's "Ode to the West Wind," Sylvia Plath's "Daddy"); in an objective lyric the speaker is obviously an invented character, or else is simply a lyric voice without specific characteristics (Robert Browning's "My Last Duchess," T. S. Eliot's "The Love Song of J. Alfred Prufrock," Wallace Stevens' "Sunday Morning"). A subjective novel is one in which the author (or at any rate the narrator) intervenes to comment and deliver judgments about the characters and actions represented; an objective novel is one in which the author is self-effacing and tries to create the effect that the story tells itself. Critics agree, however, that the difference between a subjective and objective literary work is not absolute, but a matter of degree. See *confessional poetry, distance and involvement, negative capability, persona*, and *point of view*.

On the introduction of the terms "objective" and "subjective" into English criticism and the variousness of their application, see M. H. Abrams, *The Mirror and the Lamp* (1953), pp. 235–44. For their uses in modern criticism of the novel, see Wayne C. Booth, *The Rhetoric of Fiction* (rev. 1983), chapter 3.

**objective correlative:** This term, which had been coined by the American painter and poet Washington Allston (1779–1843), was introduced by T. S. Eliot, rather casually, into his essay "Hamlet and His Problems" (1919); its subsequent vogue in literary criticism, Eliot said, astonished him. "The only way of expressing emotion," Eliot wrote, "is by finding an 'objective correlative'; in other words, a set of objects, a situation, a chain of events which shall be the formula of that *particular* emotion," and which will evoke the same emotion from the reader. Eliot's formulation has been often criticized for falsifying the way a poet actually composes, on the ground that no object or situation is in itself a "formula" for an emotion, but depends for its emotional significance and effect on the way it is rendered and used by a particular poet. The vogue of Eliot's concept of an outer correlative for inner feelings was due in part to its accord with the campaign of the *New Criticism* against vagueness of description and the direct statement of feelings in poetry—an oft-cited example was Shelley's "Indian Serenade": "I die, I faint, I fail"—and in favor of definiteness, impersonality, and descriptive concreteness.

See Eliseo Vivas, "The Objective Correlative of T. S. Eliot," reprinted in *Critiques and Essays in Criticism*, ed. Robert W. Stallman (1949).

**objective criticism: 63**; *157, 217*.

**objective** (narrator): **273**.

**occasional poems:** Occasional poems are written to celebrate or memorialize a particular occasion, such as a birthday, a marriage, a death, a military engagement or victory, the dedication of a public building, or the opening performance of a play. Edmund Spenser's "Epithalamion," on the occasion of his own marriage; John Milton's "Lycidas," on the death of the young poet Edward King; Andrew Marvell's "An Horatian Ode upon Cromwell's Return from Ireland"; and Alfred, Lord Tennyson's "The Charge of the Light Brigade" are all poems that have long survived their original occasions, and W. B. Yeats' "Easter, 1916" and W. H.

Auden's "September 1, 1939" are notable later examples. England's poet laureate is often called on to meet the emergency of royal anniversaries and important public events with an appropriate occasional poem.

**octameter** (ŏktăm′ ĕtcr): **196**.

**octave** (ŏk′ tāv): **336**.

**octavo** (ŏktāv′ ō): **32**.

**octosyllabic couplet** (ŏk′ tō sĭlăb″ ik): **341**; *84, 170*.

**ode:** In its traditional application, "ode" denotes a long lyric poem that is serious in subject and treatment, elevated in style, and elaborate in its stanzaic structure. Norman Maclean said that the term now calls to mind a *lyric* which is "massive, public in its proclamations, and Pindaric in its classical prototype" ("From Action to Image," in *Critics and Criticism*, ed. R. S. Crane, 1952). The prototype was established by the Greek poet Pindar, whose odes were modeled on the songs by the *chorus* in Greek drama. His complex stanzas were patterned in sets of three: moving in a dance rhythm to the left, the chorus chanted the **strophe**; moving to the right, the **antistrophe**; then, standing still, the **epode**.

The **regular** or **Pindaric ode** in English is a close imitation of Pindar's form, with all the strophes and antistrophes written in one *stanza* pattern, and all the epodes in another. This form was introduced into England by Ben Jonson's ode "To the Immortal Memory and Friendship of That Noble Pair, Sir Lucius Cary and Sir H. Morison" (1629); the typical construction can be conveniently studied in this poem or in Thomas Gray's "The Progress of Poesy" (1757). The **irregular ode** was introduced in 1656 by Abraham Cowley, who imitated the Pindaric style and matter but disregarded the recurrent stanzaic pattern in each strophic triad; instead, he allowed each stanza to establish its own pattern of varying line lengths, number of lines, and rhyme scheme. This type of irregular stanzaic structure, which is free to alter in accordance with shifts in subject and mood, has been the most common for the English ode ever since; Wordsworth's "Ode: Intimations of Immortality" (1807) is representative.

Pindar's odes were **encomiastic**; that is, they were written to praise and glorify someone—in the instance of Pindar, the ode celebrated a victorious athlete in the Olympic games. (See *epideictic*, under *rhetoric*.) The earlier English odes, and many later ones, were also written to eulogize something, such as a person (John Dryden's "Anne Killigrew"), or the arts of music or poetry (Dryden's "Alexander's Feast"), or a time of day (Collins' "Ode to Evening"), or abstract concepts (Gray's "Hymn to Adversity" and Wordsworth's "Ode to Duty"). Romantic poets perfected the personal ode of description and passionate meditation, which is stimulated by (and sometimes at its close reverts to) an aspect of the outer scene and turns on the attempt to solve either a personal emotional problem or a generally human one (Wordsworth's "Intimations" ode, Coleridge's "Dejection: An Ode," Shelley's "Ode to the West Wind"). Recent examples of this latter type are Allen Tate's "Ode to the Confederate Dead" and Wallace Stevens' "The Idea of Order at Key West." (See *descriptive-meditative lyric*, in the entry *topographical poetry*.)

The **Horatian ode** was originally modeled on the matter, tone, and form of the odes of the Roman Horace. In contrast to the passion, visionary boldness, and formal language of Pindar's odes, many Horatian odes are calm, meditative, and colloquial; they are also usually **homostrophic** (that is, written in a single repeated stanza form), and shorter than the Pindaric ode. Examples are Marvell's "An Horatian Ode upon Cromwell's Return from Ireland" (1650) and Keats' ode "To Autumn" (1820).

See Robert Shafer, *The English Ode to 1660* (1918); G. N. Shuster, *The English Ode from Milton to Keats* (1940, reprinted 1964); Carol Maddison, *Apollo and the Nine: A History of the Ode* (1960)—this book includes a discussion of the odes of Pindar and Horace (chapter 2); John Heath-Stubbs, *The Ode* (1969); Paul H. Fry, *The Poet's Calling in the English Ode* (1980). For references to the *ode* in other entries, see pages *45, 148, 313, 355.*

**Oedipus complex: 292**.

**Old Comedy: 49**.

**Old English Period: 251**.

**omniscient point of view: 272**.

**onomatopoeia:** Onomatopoeia, sometimes called **echoism**, is used both in a narrow and in a broad sense.

1. In the narrow and most common use, onomatopoeia designates a word, or a combination of words, whose sound seems to resemble closely the sound it denotes: "hiss," "buzz," "rattle," "bang." There is no exact duplication, however, of nonverbal by verbal sounds; the perceived similarity is due as much to the meaning, and to the sensation of articulating the words, as to their sounds. Two lines of Alfred, Lord Tennyson's "Come Down, O Maid" (1847) are often cited as a skillful instance of onomatopoeia:

> The moan of doves in immemorial elms,
> And murmuring of innumerable bees.

The American critic John Crowe Ransom remarked that by making only two changes in the speech sounds of the last line, we lose the echoic effect because we change the meaning drastically: "And murdering of innumerable beeves."

The sounds seemingly mimicked by onomatopoeic words need not be pleasant ones. Robert Browning liked to represent squishy and scratchy sounds, as in "Meeting at Night" (1845):

> As I gain the cove with pushing prow,
> And quench its speed i' the slushy sand.
> A tap at the pane, the quick sharp scratch
> And blue spurt of a lighted match. . . .

Compare *euphony* and *cacophony*.

2. In the broad sense, "onomatopoeia" is applied to words or passages which seem to correspond to, or to strongly suggest, what they denote in any way whatever—in size, movement, tactile feel, duration, or force, as well as sound (see *sound symbolism*). Alexander Pope recommends such extended verbal mimicry in his *Essay on Criticism* (1711) when he says that "the sound should seem an echo of the sense," and goes on to illustrate his maxim by mimicking two different kinds of action or motion by the metrical movement and by the difficulty or ease of utterance, in conjunction with the signification, of the poetic lines that describe them:

> When Ajax strives some rock's vast weight to throw,
> The line too labors, and the words move slow;
> Not so when swift Camilla scours the plain,
> Flies o'er th' unbending corn, and skims along the main.

**opsis** (ŏp′ sĭs): **330**.

**oral poetry:** Oral poetry, or "oral formulaic poetry," is composed and transmitted by singers or reciters; in its older instances, the recitations were sometimes accompanied by a harp or a drum, or by other musical instruments. Its origins are prehistoric, yet it continues to flourish even now among populations which for the most part cannot read or write. Oral poetry includes both narrative forms (see *epic* and *ballad*) and lyric forms (see *folk songs*). There is no fixed version of an oral composition, since each performer tends to render it differently, and sometimes introduces differences between one performance and the next. Such poems, however, typically incorporate verbal formulas—set words, word patterns, refrains, and set-pieces of description—which help a performer to improvise a narrative or song on a given theme, and also to recall and repeat, although often with variations, a poem that has been learned from someone else. (For examples of such formulas, see *ballad, epic,* and *refrain*.)

Oral ballads and songs have been collected and published ever since the eighteenth century. The systematic analysis of oral formulaic poetry in its origins and early renderings, however, was begun in the 1930s by the American scholar Milman Parry on field trips to Yugoslavia, the last place in Europe where the custom of composing and transmitting oral poetry, especially heroic narratives of warfare, still survived. Albert B. Lord and other successors continued Parry's work, and also applied the principles of this contemporary oral poetry retrospectively to an analysis of the constitution of the Homeric epics, the Anglo-Saxon *Beowulf*, the Old French *Chanson de Roland*, and other epic poems which, although they survive only in a written form, had originated and evolved as oral formulaic poetry. Research into oral literary performances is also being carried on in Africa, Asia, and other parts of the world where the ancient tradition maintains its vitality. Walter J. Ong, *Orality and Literacy: The Technologizing of the Word* (1982) analyzes the effects on literary compositions of the shift from an oral to a print culture. For current modes of primarily oral poetry within a print culture, see *limerick* (under *light verse*) and *rap poetry* (under *performance poetry*).

A description of Milman Parry's work is in *Serbocroatian Heroic Songs*, ed. Albert B. Lord, Vol. 1; see also Albert B. Lord, *The Singer of Tales* (1960, reprinted 1968); Adam Parry, ed., *The Making of Homeric Verse: The Collected Papers of Milman Parry* (1971); Ruth Finnegan, *Oral Poetry: Its Nature, Significance and Social Context* (1977); and J. M. Foley, *Oral Traditional Literature* (1980, reprinted 1983). For references to *oral poetry* in other entries, see pages *19, 22, 97, 121, 243.*

**organic form: 125**; *109.*

**organicist: 125**; *3.*

**orientalism: 277.**

**originality: 59.**

**ottava rima** (ŏtäv′ ă rē′ mă): **342.**

**over-reading: 13.**

**oxymoron** (ŏxĭmō′ rŏn): **239.**

**palimpsest: 31.**

**palinode:** Palinode from the Greek for "song again," is a poem or poetic passage in which the poet renounces or retracts an earlier poem, or an earlier type of subject matter. An elaborate and charming example is the Prologue to *The Legend of Good Women* in which Geoffrey Chaucer, contrite after being charged by the God of Love with having slandered women lovers in *Troilus and Criseyde* and in his translation of the *Romance of the Rose*, does penance by writing this poem on women who were saints in their fidelity to the creed of love. (Refer to *courtly love.*) Palinodes are especially common in love poetry. The Elizabethan sonnet by Sir Philip Sidney, "Leave me, O love which reachest but to dust," is a palinode renouncing the poetry of sexual love for that of heavenly love.

**pantomime and dumb show: Pantomime** is acting on the stage without speech, using only posture, gesture, bodily movement, and exaggerated facial expression to **mime** ("mimic") a character's actions and to express a character's feelings. Elaborate pantomimes, halfway between drama and dance, were put on in ancient Greece and Rome, and the form was revived, often for comic effect, in Renaissance Europe. Mimed dramas enjoyed a vogue in eighteenth-century England, and in the twentieth century the silent movies encouraged a brief revival of the art and produced a superlative pantomimist in Charlie Chaplin. Miming survived into the recent past with French masters such as Marcel Marceau in the theater and Jacques Tati in the cinema. England still retains the institution of the Christmas pantomime, which enacts children's nursery rhymes, or familiar children's stories such as "Puss in Boots," in a blend of miming, music, and dialogue. In America and many other countries, circus clowns are expert pantomimists, and miming has recently been revived in the theater for the deaf.

A **dumb show** is an episode of pantomime introduced into a spoken play. It was a common device in Elizabethan drama, in imitation of its use by Seneca, the Roman writer of tragedies. Two well-known dumb shows are the preliminary episode, summarizing the action to come, of the play-within-a-play in *Hamlet* (III. ii.), and the miming of the banishment of the Duchess and her family in John Webster's *The Duchess of Malfi* (III. iv.).

See R. J. Broadbent, *A History of Pantomime* (1901).

**papyrus: 30**.

**parable: 9**.

**paradigmatic** (in linguistics): **176**.

**paradox:** Paradox A paradox is a statement which seems on its face to be logically contradictory or absurd, yet turns out to be interpretable in a way that makes sense. An instance is the conclusion to John Donne's sonnet "Death, Be Not Proud":

> One short sleep past, we wake eternally
> And death shall be no more; *Death, thou shalt die.*

The paradox is used occasionally by almost all poets, but was a persistent and central device in seventeenth-century *metaphysical poetry*, both in its religious and secular forms. Donne, who wrote a prose collection titled *Problems and Paradoxes*, exploited the figure constantly in his poetry. "The Canonization," for example, is organized as an extended proof, full of local paradoxes, of the paradoxical thesis that sexual lovers are saints. Paradox is also a frequent component in verbal *wit*.

If the paradoxical utterance conjoins two terms that in ordinary usage are contraries, it is called an **oxymoron**; an example is Alfred, Lord Tennyson's "O *Death in life*, the days that are no more." The oxymoron was a familiar type of *Petrarchan conceit* in Elizabethan love poetry, in phrases like "pleasing pains," "I burn and freeze," "loving hate." It is also a frequent figure in devotional prose and religious poetry as a way of expressing the Christian mysteries, which transcend human sense and logic. So John Milton describes the appearance of God, in *Paradise Lost* (III, 380):

> Dark with excessive bright thy skirts appear.

Paradox was a prominent concern of many *New Critics*, who extended the term from its limited application to a type of *figurative language* so as to encompass all surprising deviations from, or qualifications of, common perceptions or commonplace opinions. It is in this expanded sense that Cleanth Brooks is able to claim, with some plausibility, that "the language of poetry is the language of paradox," in *The Well Wrought Urn* (1947). See also *deconstruction* for the claim that all uses of language disseminate themselves into the unresolvable paradox called an *aporia*. For references to *paradox* in other entries, see pages *193, 217*.

**paralipsis** (părălĭp´ sĭs): **315**.

**parallelism: 14**.

**paranomasia** (părănōmā´ zya): **295**.

**pararhyme: 317**.

**paratactic style: 350**.

**parchment: 30**.

**parody: 36**; *30, 77, 102, 106, 231, 241*.

**parole** (in linguistics): **173**; *281, 325*.

**partial rhyme: 317**.

**pastoral:** The originator of the pastoral was the Greek poet Theocritus, who in the third century BC wrote poems representing the life of Sicilian shepherds. ("Pastor" is Latin for "shepherd.") Virgil later imitated Theocritus in his Latin *Eclogues,* and in doing so established the enduring model for the traditional **pastoral**: a deliberately conventional poem expressing an urban poet's nostalgic image of the supposed peace and simplicity of the life of shepherds and other rural folk in an idealized natural setting. The *conventions* that hundreds of later poets imitated from Virgil's imitations of Theocritus include a shepherd reclining under a spreading beech tree and meditating on the rural muse, or piping as though he would ne'er grow old, or engaging in a friendly singing contest, or expressing his good or bad fortune in a love affair, or grieving over the death of a fellow shepherd. From this last type developed the *pastoral elegy,* which persisted long after the other traditional types had lost their popularity. Other terms often used synonymously with pastoral are **idyll**, from the title of Theocritus' pastorals; **eclogue** (literally, "a selection"), from the title of Virgil's pastorals; and **bucolic poetry**, from the Greek word for "herdsman."

Classical poets often described the pastoral life as possessing features of the mythical *golden age.* Christian pastoralists conjoined the golden age of pagan fable with the Garden of Eden in the Bible, and also exploited the religious symbolism of "shepherd" (applied to the ecclesiastical or parish "pastor," and to the figure of Christ as the Good Shepherd) to give many pastoral poems a Christian range of reference. In the Renaissance the traditional pastoral was also adapted to diverse satirical and allegorical uses. Edmund Spenser's *Shepherd's Calendar* (1579), which popularized the mode in English poetry, included most of the varieties of pastoral poems current in that period.

Such was the attraction of the pastoral dream that Renaissance writers incorporated it into various other literary forms. Sir Philip Sidney's *Arcadia* (1581–84) was a long pastoral *romance* written in an elaborately artful prose. (**Arcadia** was a mountainous region of Greece which Virgil substituted for Theocritus' Sicily as his idealized pastoral milieu.) There was also the pastoral lyric (Christopher Marlowe's "The Passionate Shepherd to His Love"), and the pastoral drama. John Fletcher's *The Faithful Shepherdess* is an example of this last type, and Shakespeare's *As You Like It*, based on the contemporary pastoral romance *Rosalynde* by Thomas Lodge, is set in the forest of Arden, a green refuge from the troubles and complications of ordinary life where enmities are reconciled, problems resolved, and the course of true love made to run smooth.

The last important series of traditional pastorals, and an extreme instance of their calculated and graceful display of high artifice, was Alexander Pope's *Pastorals* (1709). Five years later John Gay, in his *Shepherd's Week*, wrote a *parody* of the type by applying its elegant formulas to the crudity of actual rustic manners and language; by doing so, he inadvertently showed later poets the way to the seriously realistic treatment of rural life. In 1783 George Crabbe published *The Village* specifically in order to

> paint the cot
> As Truth will paint it and as bards will not.

How far the term then lost its traditional application to a poetry of aristocratic artifice is indicated by Wordsworth's title for his realistic rendering of a rural tragedy in 1800: "Michael, A Pastoral Poem."

In recent decades the term "pastoral" has been expanded in various ways. William Empson, in *Some Versions of Pastoral* (1935), identified as pastoral any work which opposes simple to complicated life, to the advantage of the former: the simple life may be that of the shepherd, the child, or the working man. In Empson's view this literary mode serves as an oblique way to criticize the values and hierarchical class structure of the society of its time. Empson accordingly applies the term to works ranging from Andrew Marvell's seventeenth-century poem "The Garden" to Lewis Carroll's *Alice in Wonderland* and the modern *proletarian novel*. Other critics apply the term "pastoral" to any work which represents a withdrawal to a place apart that is close to the elemental rhythms of nature, where the protagonist gains a new perspective on the complexities, frustrations, and conflicts of the social world. On the continuation of the pastoral strain in "nature writers," see *ecocriticism*.

W. W. Greg, *Pastoral Poetry and Pastoral Drama: A Literary Inquiry, with Special Reference to the Pre-Restoration Stage in England* (1906); the Introduction to *English Pastoral Poetry from the Beginnings to Marvell*, ed. Frank Kermode (1952); Thomas G. Rosenmeyer, *The Green Cabinet: Theocritus and the European Pastoral Lyric* (1969); Andrew V. Ettin, *Literature and the Pastoral* (1985); Paul Alpers, *What Is Pastoral?* (1996); Annabel Patterson, *Pastoral and Ideology, Virgil to Valéry* (1987). For references to *pastoral* in other entries, see page 87.

**pastoral elegy:** 92; *59, 240.*

**pathetic fallacy:** A phrase invented by John Ruskin in 1856 to signify any representation of inanimate natural objects that ascribes to them human capabilities, sensations, and emotions (*Modern Painters*, Vol. 3, chapter 12). As used by Ruskin—for whom "truth" was a primary criterion of art—the term was derogatory; for, he claimed, such descriptions do not represent the "true appearances of things to us" but "the extraordinary, or false appearances, when we are under the influence of emotion, or contemplative fancy." Two of Ruskin's examples are the lines

> The spendthrift crocus, bursting through the mould
> Naked and shivering, with his cup of gold,

and Coleridge's description in "Christabel" of

> The one red leaf, the last of its clan,
> That dances as often as dance it can.

These passages, Ruskin says, however beautiful, are false and "morbid." Only in the greatest poets is the use of the pathetic fallacy valid, and then only at those rare times when it would be inhuman to resist the pressure of powerful feelings to humanize the perceived fact. Ruskin's contention would make just about all poets, including Shakespeare, "morbid." "Pathetic fallacy" is now used mainly as a neutral name for a procedure in which human traits are ascribed to natural objects in a way that is less formal and more indirect than in the figure called *personification*.

See Josephine Miles, *Pathetic Fallacy in the Nineteenth Century* (1942); Harold Bloom, ed., *The Literary Criticism of John Ruskin* (1965), Introduction and pp. 62–78.

**pathos:** Pathos in Greek meant the passions, or suffering, or deep feeling generally, as distinguished from **ethos**, a person's overall disposition or character. In modern criticism, however, pathos is applied in a much more limited way to a scene or passage that is designed to evoke the feelings of tenderness, pity, or sympathetic sorrow from the audience. In the *Victorian* era some prominent writers exploited pathos beyond the endurance of many readers today—examples are the rendering of the death of Little Nell in Charles Dickens' *The Old Curiosity Shop* and of the death of Little Eva in Harriet Beecher Stowe's *Uncle Tom's Cabin*. (See *sentimentalism*.) To many modern readers, the greatest passages of pathos do not dwell on the details of suffering but achieve their effect by understatement and suggestion. Examples are the speech of King Lear when he is briefly reunited with Cordelia (IV. vii. 59ff.), beginning

> Pray, do not mock me.
> I am a very foolish fond old man,

and William Wordsworth's terse and indirect revelation of the grief of the old father for the loss of his son in *Michael* (1800), ll. 465–66:

> Many and many a day he thither went,
> And never lifted up a single stone.

**patriarchal:** 111; *39, 132.*

**pattern poem: 55**.

**pentameter** (pĕntăm′ ĕter): **196**.

**perfect rhyme: 317**.

**performance** (in linguistics): **173**.

**performance** (of a poem): **198**.

**performance poetry:** Since the seventeenth century, poetry—like other forms of literature—has been composed primarily for printing. In recent years, however, the ancient tradition of composing poetry specifically for oral performance before an audience has been revived in a number of modes, some of which involve extemporizing the poem during the performance itself. Taken together, these compositions can be accounted the first widespread and sustained revival of oral poetry since the beginning of the print culture in the fifteenth century. (See *oral poetry*; also *printing*, under *Renaissance*.) During the rebellious 1960s, for example, **poetry happenings** (public recitations, often to musical accompaniment) were an integral part of the countercultural scene. Later, other marginalized groups produced similar performances, usually in urban settings and before audiences who regarded poetry in print as academic and elitist. The **poetry slam** emerged in the 1980s as competitions in which rival poets were set a time limit, then scored for their oral productions by members of the audience; the poetry at such events was marked by emphatic rhythms, succinctness, clarity, and hipness. For essays by various inquirers about the public performance of printed poems, as well as about contemporary poems composed for public performance, see Charles Bernstein, ed., *Close Listening: Poetry and the Performed Word* (1998). The anthology *Poetry Nation*, ed. Regie Cabico, Todd Swift, and Bob Holman (1998), traces the genealogy of various modes of "alternative" poetry that fuse oral and printed traditions to the performances of the Beat Generation, especially Allen Ginsberg. (See under *Beat Writers*.)

The most widely known and practiced performance poetry is **rap**, an element in **hip-hop**; the latter term since the 1980s has come to designate a cultural movement among urban African-American youths that originated in New York and was marked by distinctive clothing, graffiti, break dancing, and music, especially rap. Both the music and verse form of rap had complex origins in African, *African-American*, and West Indian musical traditions. The verbal component, technically speaking, consists of an irregular meter, in verse lines of variable length and a varying number of mainly sequential rhymes, in which there is a frequent use of *partial* and *forced rhymes* (see *meter* and *rhyme*). "To rap" is slang for "to talk," and rap verse is spoken, in a heavily stressed beat, over an accompaniment of bass, percussion, and sometimes other musical instruments. Often the accompaniment is punctuated by "scratching" (the sounds made by rotating a phonograph record to and fro on a turntable so that the needle moves back and forth in the groove) and by "sampling" (the insertion of fragments of recorded music). In the mode known as **freestyling**, or **battle-rapping**, rap verses are improvised during performance, often in competitions between rival rappers. A rapper's distinctive style, in versification, pace, and voice quality, is called his or her "flow."

In its early years rap usually conveyed a contentious and anti–establishment message, and in the 1980s the genre came to be dominated by the highly aggressive form, originating on the West Coast, called **gangsta rap** ("gangster rap"), which flaunted (sometimes in a self-mocking way) its transgressive stance against propriety, law, and conventional morality by celebrating violence, misogyny, homophobia, and a candid desire for material goods and sex. Soon, however, rap became less iconoclastic, although much of it continued to express defiance and challenge, as in this passage from "Poetry," by the rapper KRS-One, recorded in 1987.

> Difficult, isn't it
> My point? You're missing it
> Your head is in front of my hand
> So I'm dissing it![10]

Increasingly, women rappers and white rappers entered the field that was originally the preserve of urban African-American males, and it became common for rap to voice moderate and even mainstream values. In 1989, for example, Queen Latifah recorded a moral warning, "The Evil That Men Do"; this is an excerpt:

> Tell me, don't you think it's a shame
> When someone can put a quarter in a video game
> But when a homeless person approaches you on the street
> You can't treat him the same
> It's time to teach the deaf, the dumb, the blind
> That black on black crime only shackles and binds
> You to a doom, a fate worse than death
> But there's still time left
> To stop puttin' your conscience on cease,
> And bring about some type of peace. . . . [11]

In recent years rap has achieved a remarkable and wide-ranging popularity. The lyrics are composed in many languages, and the form attracts enthusiastic audiences—in personal, recorded, and televised performances—in most countries of the world.

See Nelson George, *Hip Hop America* (1999); and Michael Eric Dyson, *Know What I Mean?: Reflections on Hip Hop* (2007). For a discussion of rap in relation to other African-American modes of expression, refer to Tricia Rose, *Black Noise:*

---

[10]Lines from "Poetry" as performed by KRS-One. Lyrics written by Lawrence Parker/Scott Sterling. Copyright © 1986 Zomba Enterprises Inc. (ASCAP)/BDP Music. All rights for the US administered by Zomba Enterprises Inc. (ASCAP). Used by permission of BMG Music Publishing, Inc.

[11]Lines from "Evil That Men Do" by Dana Owens, as performed by Queen Latifah. Copyright © 1987 WB Music Corp. (ASCAP) and Queen Latifah Music Inc. (ASCAP). All rights administered by WB Music Corp. All rights reserved. Used by permission of Warner Bros. Publications U.S., Miami, FL, 33014.

*Rap Music and Black Culture in Contemporary America* (1994). The online encyclopedia Wikipedia has informative articles on performance poetry, hip-hop, rap, and related topics: refer to *http://en.wikipedia.org/wiki/MainPage*. For references to *performance poetry* in other entries, see page *25*.

**performative** (in speech–act theory): **338**.

**performative** (in poststructural theory): **339**; *298*.

**periodic sentence: 350**.

**periods of American literature:** The division of American literature into convenient historical segments, or "periods," lacks the degree of consensus among literary scholars that we find with reference to English literature; see *Periods of English Literature*. The many syllabi of college surveys reprinted in *Reconstructing American Literature* (ed. Paul Lauter, 1983), and the essays in *Redefining American Literary History*, ed. A. LaVonne Brown Ruoff and Jerry W. Ward (1990), demonstrate how variable are the temporal divisions and their names, especially since the efforts to do justice to literature written by women and by ethnic minorities. Some recent historians, anthologists, and teachers of American literature simply divide their survey into dated sections, without affixing period names. A prominent tendency, however, is to recognize the importance of major wars in marking significant changes in literature. This tendency, as the scholar Cushing Strout has remarked, "suggests that there is an order in American political history more visible and compelling than that indicated by specifically literary or intellectual categories."

The following divisions of American literary history recognize the importance assigned by many literary historians to the Revolutionary War (1775–81), the Civil War (1861–65), World War I (1914–18), and World War II (1939–45). Under these broad divisions are listed some of the more widely used terms to distinguish periods and subperiods of American literature. These terms, it will be noted, are diverse in kind; they may signify a span of time, or a type of political organization, or a prominent intellectual or imaginative mode, or a predominant literary form.

**1607–1775**. This overall era, from the founding of the first settlement at Jamestown to the outbreak of the American Revolution, is often called the **Colonial Period**. Writings were for the most part religious, practical, or historical. Notable among the seventeenth-century writers of journals and narratives about the founding and early history of some of the colonies were William Bradford, John Winthrop, and the theologian Cotton Mather. In the following century Jonathan Edwards was a major philosopher as well as theologian, and Benjamin Franklin an early American master of lucid and cogent prose. Not until 1937, when Edward Taylor's writings were first published from manuscript, was Taylor discovered to have been an able religious poet in the *metaphysical* style of the English devotional poets Herbert and Crashaw. Anne Bradstreet was the chief Colonial poet of secular and domestic as well as religious subjects.

The publication in 1773 of *Poems on Various Subjects* by Phillis Wheatley, then a nineteen-year-old slave who had been born in Africa, inaugurated the long and distinguished, but until recently neglected, line of **black writers** (or by what has come to be the preferred name, **African–American writers**) in America. The complexity and diversity of the African-American cultural heritage—both Western and African, oral and written, slave and free, Judeo-Christian and pagan, plantation and urban, integrationist and black nationalist—have effected tensions and fusions that, over the course of time, have produced a highly innovative and distinctive literature, as well as musical forms that have come to be considered America's most important contribution to the Western musical tradition. See J. Saunders Redding, *To Make a Poet Black* (1939; reissued 1986); Houston A. Baker, Jr., *Black Literature in America* (1971); Bernard W. Bell, *The Afro-American Novel and Its Tradition* (1987); Henry L. Gates, Jr., *Figures in Black* (1987) and ed. *Black Literature and Literary Theory* (1984); also Henry L. Gates, Jr., Nellie Y. McKay, and others, eds., *The Norton Anthology of African-American Literature* (1997).

The period between the Stamp Act of 1765 and 1790 is sometimes distinguished as the **Revolutionary Age**. It was the time of Thomas Paine's influential revolutionary tracts; of Thomas Jefferson's "Statute of Virginia for Religious Freedom," "Declaration of Independence," and many other writings; of *The Federalist Papers* in support of the Constitution, most notably those by Alexander Hamilton and James Madison; and of the patriotic and satiric poems by Philip Freneau and Joel Barlow.

**1775–1865**. The years 1775–1828, the **Early National Period** ending with the triumph of Jacksonian democracy in 1828, signalized the emergence of a national imaginative literature, including the first American stage comedy (Royall Tyler's *The Contrast*, 1787), the earliest American novel (William Hill Brown's *The Power of Sympathy*, 1789), and the establishment in 1815 of the first enduring American magazine, *The North American Review*. Washington Irving achieved international fame with his essays and stories; Charles Brockden Brown wrote distinctively American versions of the *Gothic novel* of mystery and terror; the career of James Fenimore Cooper, the first major American novelist, was well launched; and William Cullen Bryant and Edgar Allan Poe wrote poetry that was relatively independent of English precursors. In the year 1760 was published the first of a long series of **slave narratives** and autobiographies written by *African-American* slaves who had escaped or been freed. Most of these were published between 1830 and 1865, including Frederick Douglass' *Narrative of the Life of Frederick Douglass* (1845) and Harriet Jacobs' *Incidents in the Life of a Slave Girl* (1861).

The span 1828–65 from the Jacksonian era to the Civil War, often identified as the **Romantic Period in America** (see *Neoclassic and Romantic*), marks the full coming of age of a distinctively American literature. This period is sometimes known as the **American Renaissance**, the title of F. O. Matthiessen's influential book (1941) about its outstanding writers, Ralph Waldo Emerson, Henry David Thoreau, Edgar Allan Poe, Herman Melville, and Nathaniel Hawthorne (see also *symbolism*); it is also sometimes called the **Age of Transcendentalism**, after the philosophical and literary movement, centered on Emerson, that was dominant in New England (see *Transcendentalism*). In all the major genres except drama, writers produced works of an originality and excellence not exceeded in later American literature. Emerson, Thoreau, and the early feminist Margaret Fuller shaped the ideas, ideals, and literary aims of many contemporary and later American writers. It was the age not only of continuing writings by William Cullen Bryant, Washington Irving, and James Fenimore Cooper, but also of the novels and short stories of Poe, Hawthorne, Melville, Harriet Beecher Stowe, and the southern novelist William Gilmore Simms; of the poetry of Poe, John Greenleaf Whittier, Emerson, Henry Wadsworth Longfellow, and the most innovative and influential of all American poets, Walt Whitman; and of the beginning of distinguished American criticism in the essays of Poe, Simms, and James Russell Lowell. The tradition of *African-American* poetry by women was continued by Francis Ellen Watkins Harper, and the African-American novel was inaugurated by William Wells Brown's *Clotel* (1853) and by Harriet E. Wilson's *Our Nig* (1859).

**1865–1914**. The cataclysm of the bloody Civil War and Reconstruction, followed by a burgeoning industrialism and urbanization in the North, profoundly altered American self-awareness, and also American literary modes. 1865–1900 is often known as the **Realistic Period**, by reference to the novels by Mark Twain, William Dean Howells, and Henry James, as well as by John W. DeForest, Harold Frederic, and the *African-American* novelist Charles W. Chesnutt. These works, though diverse, are often labeled "realistic" in contrast to the "romances" of their predecessors in prose fiction: Poe, Hawthorne, and Melville (see *prose romance* and *realism*). Some realistic authors grounded their fiction in a regional milieu; these include (in addition to Mark Twain's novels on the Mississippi River region) Bret Harte in California, Sarah Orne Jewett in Maine, Mary Wilkins Freeman in Massachusetts, and George W. Cable and Kate Chopin in Louisiana. (See *regional novel.*) Chopin has become prominent as an early and major *feminist* novelist. Whitman continued writing poetry up to the last decade of the century, and (unknown to him and almost everyone else) was joined by Emily Dickinson; although only seven of Dickinson's more than a thousand short poems were published in her lifetime, she is now recognized as one of the most distinctive and eminent of American poets. Sidney Lanier published his experiments in versification based on the meters of music; the *African-American* author Paul Laurence Dunbar wrote both poems and novels between 1893 and 1905; and in the 1890s Stephen Crane, although he was only twenty nine when he died, published short poems in free verse that anticipate the experiments of Ezra Pound and the *Imagists*, and wrote also the brilliantly innovative short stories and short novels that look forward to two later narrative modes: naturalism and impressionism. The years 1900–14—although James, Howells, and Mark Twain were still writing, and Edith Wharton was publishing her earlier novels—are sometimes discriminated as the **Naturalistic Period**, in recognition of the powerful although sometimes crudely wrought novels by Frank Norris, Jack London, and Theodore Dreiser, which typically represent characters who are joint victims of their instinctual drives and of external sociological forces; see *naturalism*, under *realism and naturalism*.

**1914–1939**. The era between the two world wars, marked by the trauma of the great economic depression beginning in 1929, was that of the emergence of what is still known as "modern literature," which in America reached an eminence rivaling that of the American Renaissance of the mid-nineteenth century; unlike most of the authors of that earlier period, however, the American modernists also achieved widespread international recognition and influence. (See *modernism.*) *Poetry* magazine, founded in Chicago by Harriet Monroe in 1912, published many innovative authors. Among the notable poets were Edgar Lee Masters, Edwin Arlington Robinson, Robert Frost, Carl Sandburg, Wallace Stevens, William Carlos Williams, Ezra Pound, Robinson Jeffers, Marianne Moore, T. S. Eliot, Edna St. Vincent Millay, and e. e. cummings—authors who wrote in an unexampled variety of poetic modes. These included the *Imagism* of Amy Lowell, H. D. (Hilda Doolittle), and others; the metric poems by Frost and the free-verse poems by Williams in the American vernacular; the formal and ty-pographic experiments of cummings; the poetic naturalism of Jeffers; and the as-similation to their own distinctive uses by Pound and Eliot of the forms and pro-cedures of French *symbolism*, merged with the intellectual and figurative methods of the English *metaphysical poets*. Among the major writers of prose fiction were Edith Wharton, Sinclair Lewis, Ellen Glasgow, Willa Cather, Gertrude Stein, Sherwood Anderson, John Dos Passos, F. Scott Fitzgerald, William Faulkner, Ernest Hemingway, Thomas Wolfe, and John Steinbeck. America produced in this period its first great dramatist in Eugene O'Neill, as well as a group of distin-guished literary critics that included Van Wyck Brooks, Malcolm Cowley, T. S. Eliot, Edmund Wilson, and the irreverent and caustic H. L. Mencken.

The literary productions of this era are often subclassified in a variety of ways. The flamboyant and pleasure-seeking 1920s are sometimes referred to as "the Jazz Age," a title popularized by F. Scott Fitzgerald's *Tales of the Jazz Age* (1922). The same decade was also the period of the Harlem Renaissance, which produced ma-jor writings in all the literary forms by Countee Cullen, Langston Hughes, Claude McKay, Jean Toomer, Zora Neale Hurston, and many other *African-American* wri-ters. (See *Harlem Renaissance.*)

Many prominent American writers of the decade following the end of World War I, disillusioned by their war experiences and alienated by what they perceived as the crassness of American culture and its "puritanical" repressions, are often tagged (in a term first applied by Gertrude Stein to young Frenchmen of the time) as the **Lost Generation**. A number of these writers became expatriates, moving either to London or to Paris in their quest for a richer literary and artistic milieu and a freer way of life. Ezra Pound, Gertrude Stein, and T. S. Eliot lived out their lives abroad, but most of the younger "exiles," as Malcolm Cowley called them (*Exile's Return*, 1934), came back to America in the 1930s. Hemingway's *The Sun Also Rises* and Fitzgerald's *Tender Is the Night* are novels that represent the mood and way of life of two groups of American expatriates. In "the radical '30s," the period of the Great Depression and of the economic and social reforms in the New Deal inaugurated by President Franklin Delano Roosevelt, some authors joined radical political movements, and many others dealt in their literary works with pressing social issues of the time—including, in the novel, William Faulkner, John Dos Passos, James T. Farrell, Thomas Wolfe, and John Steinbeck, and in the drama, Eugene O'Neill, Clifford Odets, and Maxwell Anderson.

**1939 to the Present**, the **contemporary period**. World War II, and espe-cially the disillusionment with Soviet Communism consequent upon the Moscow trials for alleged treason and Stalin's signing of the Russo-German pact with Hitler in 1939, largely ended the literary radicalism of the 1930s. A final blow to the very few writers who had maintained intellectual allegiance to Soviet Russia came in 1991 with the collapse of Russian Communism and the dissolution of the Soviet Union. For several decades the *New Criticism*—dominated by conservative southern writers, the **Agrarians**, who in the 1930s had championed a return from an industrial to an agricultural economy—typified the prevailing critical tendency to isolate literature from the life of the author and from society and to conceive a work of literature, in formal terms, as an organic and autonomous entity. (See John L. Stewart, *The Burden of Time: The Fugitives and Agrarians*, 1965.) The eminent and influential critics Edmund Wilson and Lionel Trilling, however—as well as other critics grouped with them as the **New York Intellectuals**, including Philip Rahv, Alfred Kazin, and Irving Howe—continued through the 1960s to deal with a work of literature humanistically and historically, in the context of its author's life, temperament, and social milieu, and in terms of the work's moral and imaginative qualities and its consequences for society. See V. B. Leitch, *American Literary Criticism from the Thirties to the Eighties*, 1988, chapter 4. (For a discussion of radically new developments in American literary theory and criticism in the 1970s and later, see *poststructuralism*.)

The 1950s, while often regarded in retrospect as a period of cultural conformity and complacency, was marked by the emergence of vigorous anti-establishment and anti-traditional literary movements: the *Beat writers* such as Allen Ginsberg and Jack Kerouac; the American exemplars of the literature of the *absurd*; the **Black Mountain Poets**, Charles Olson, Robert Creeley, and Robert Duncan; and the **New York Poets**, Frank O'Hara, Kenneth Koch, and John Ashbery. It was also a time of *confessional poetry* and the literature of extreme sexual candor, marked by the emergence of Henry Miller as a notable author (his autobiographical and fictional works, begun in the 1930s, had earlier been available only under the counter) and the writings of Norman Mailer, William Burroughs, and Vladimir Nabokov (*Lolita* was published in 1955). The **counterculture** of the 1960s and early 1970s continued some of these modes, but in a fashion made extreme and fevered by the rebellious youth movement and the vehement and sometimes violent opposition to the war in Vietnam; for an approving treatment of this movement, see Theodore Roszak, *The Making of a Counter Culture* (1969), and for a later retrospective, Morris Dickstein, *Gates of Eden: American Culture in the Sixties* (1978). See *modernism and postmodernism*, and for radical developments of this era in African-American literature, see *Black Arts Movement*.

Important American writers after World War II include, in prose fiction, Vladimir Nabokov (who emigrated to America in 1940), Eudora Welty, Robert Penn Warren, Bernard Malamud, James Gould Cozzens, Saul Bellow, Mary McCarthy, Norman Mailer, John Updike, Kurt Vonnegut, Jr., Thomas Pynchon, John Barth, Donald Barthelme, E. L. Doctorow, and Cynthia Ozick; in poetry, Marianne Moore, Robert Penn Warren, Theodore Roethke, Elizabeth Bishop, Richard Wilbur, Robert Lowell, Allen Ginsberg, Adrienne Rich, Sylvia Plath, A. R. Ammons, and John Ashbery; and in drama, Thornton

Wilder, Lillian Hellman, Arthur Miller, Tennessee Williams, Edward Albee, and a number of more recent playwrights, including Sam Shepard, David Mamet, Tony Kushner, and Wendy Wasserstein. Many of the most innovative and distinguished literary works of the later decades of the twentieth century have been written by writers who are often identified as belonging to one or another "minority," or **ethnic** literary group. (An "ethnic group" consists of individuals who are distinguishable, within a majority cultural and social system, by shared characteristics such as race, religion, language, cultural modes, and national origin.) There is, however, much contention, both within and outside these groups, whether it is more just and enlightening to consider such writers simply as part of the American mainstream or to stress what is called "the identity" of each writer as a participant in an ethnic culture with its distinctive subject matter, themes, and formal features. This is the era of the notable *African-American* novelists and essayists Ralph Ellison, James Baldwin, Richard Wright, Albert Murray, Gloria Naylor, Alice Walker, and Toni Morrison; the poets Amiri Baraka (LeRoi Jones), Gwendolyn Brooks, Maya Angelou, and Rita Dove; and the dramatists Lorraine Hansberry and August Wilson. (For some developments in popular modes of versification, see *performance poetry*.) It is also the era of the emergence of such prominent minority novelists as Leslie Marmon Silko (Native American); Oscar Hijuelos and Sandra Cisneros (Hispanic); and Maxine Hong Kingston and Amy Tan (Chinese-American). See Houston A. Baker, ed., *Three American Literatures: Essays in Chicano, Native American, and Asian-American Literature for Teachers of American Literature* (1982).

The contemporary literary scene in America is crowded and varied, and these lists could readily be expanded. We must await the passage of time to determine which writers now active will emerge as enduringly major figures in the *canon* of American literature.

**periods of english literature:** For convenience of discussion, historians divide the continuity of English literature into segments of time that are called "periods." The exact number, dates, and names of these periods vary, but the list below conforms to widespread practice. The list is followed by a brief comment on each period, in chronological order.

| | |
|---|---|
| 450–1066 | Old English (or Anglo-Saxon) Period |
| 1066–1500 | Middle English Period |
| 1500–1660 | The Renaissance (or Early Modern) |
| 1558–1603 | Elizabethan Age |
| 1603–1625 | Jacobean Age |
| 1625–1649 | Caroline Age |
| 1649–1660 | Commonwealth Period (or Puritan Interregnum) |
| 1660–1785 | The Neoclassical Period |
| 1660–1700 | The Restoration |
| 1700–1745 | The Augustan Age |

1745–1785    The Age of Sensibility (or Age of Johnson)

1785–1832    The Romantic Period

1832–1901    The Victorian Period

   1848–1860    The Pre-Raphaelites

   1880–1901    Aestheticism and Decadence

1901–1914    The Edwardian Period

1910–1936    The Georgian Period

1914–          The Modern Period

   1945–          Postmodernism

The **Old English Period**, or the **Anglo-Saxon Period**, extended from the invasion of Celtic England by Germanic tribes (the Angles, Saxons, and Jutes) in the first half of the fifth century to the conquest of England in 1066 by the Norman French under the leadership of William the Conqueror. Only after they had been converted to Christianity in the seventh century did the Anglo-Saxons, whose earlier literature had been oral, begin to develop a written literature. (See *oral poetry*.) A high level of culture and learning was soon achieved in various monasteries; the eighth-century churchmen Bede and Alcuin were major scholars who wrote in Latin, the standard language of international scholarship. The poetry written in the vernacular Anglo-Saxon, known also as Old English, included *Beowulf* (eighth century), the greatest of Germanic epic poems, and such lyric laments as "The Wanderer," "The Seafarer," and "Deor," all of which, although composed by Christian writers, reflect the conditions of life in the pagan past. Caedmon and Cynewulf were poets who wrote on biblical and religious themes, and there survive a number of Old English lives of saints, sermons, and paraphrases of books of the Bible. Alfred the Great, a West Saxon king (871–99) who for a time united all the kingdoms of southern England against a new wave of Germanic invaders, the Vikings, was no less important as a patron of literature than as a warrior. He himself translated into Old English various books of Latin prose, supervised translations by other hands, and instituted the Anglo-Saxon Chronicle, a continuous record, year by year, of important events in England.

See S. B. Greenfield, *A Critical History of Old English Literature* (1965); C. L. Wrenn, *A Study of Old English Literature* (1966).

**Middle English Period**. The four and a half centuries between the Norman Conquest in 1066, which effected radical changes in the language, life, and culture of England, and about 1500, when the standard literary language (deriving from the dialect of the London area) had become recognizably "modern English"—that is, close enough to the language we speak and write to be intelligible to a present-day reader.

The span from 1100 to 1350 is sometimes discriminated as the **Anglo-Norman Period**, because the non-Latin literature of that time was written mainly in Anglo-Norman, the French dialect spoken by the invaders, who had established themselves as the ruling class of England, and who shared a literary culture with French-speaking areas of mainland Europe. Among the important and influential works from this period are Marie de France's *Lais* (c.1180—which may have been written while Marie was at the royal court in England), Guillaume de Lorris' and Jean de Meun's *Roman de la Rose* (1225?– 75?), and Chrétien de Troyes' *Erec et Enide* (the first Arthurian romance, c.1165) and *Yvain* (c.1177–81). When the native vernacular—descended from Anglo-Saxon, but with extensive lexical and syntactic elements assimilated from Anglo-Norman, and known as **Middle English**—came into general literary use, it was at first mainly the vehicle for religious and homiletic writings. The first great age of primarily secular literature—rooted in the Anglo-Norman, French, Irish, and Welsh, as well as the native English literature—was the second half of the four-teenth century. This was the age of Chaucer and John Gower, of William Langland's great religious and satirical poem *Piers Plowman*, and of the anonymous master who wrote four major poems in complex *alliterative meter*, including *Pearl* (an elegy) and *Sir Gawain and the Green Knight*. This last work is the most accom-plished of the English *chivalric romances* in verse; the most notable prose romance was Thomas Malory's *Morte d'Arthur*, written a century later. The outstanding poets of the fifteenth century were the "Scottish Chaucerians," who included King James I of Scotland and Robert Henryson. The fifteenth century was more important for popular literature than for the artful literature addressed to the upper classes: it was the age of many excellent songs, secular and religious, and of diverse *folk ballads*, as well as the flowering time of the *miracle* and *morality plays*, which were written and produced for the general public.

See W. L. Renwick and H. Orton, *The Beginnings of English Literature to Skelton* (rev. 1952); H. S. Bennett, *Chaucer and the Fifteenth Century* (1947); Edward Vasta, ed., *Middle English Survey: Critical Essays* (1965).

The **Renaissance**, 1500–1660. There is an increasing use by historians of the term *early modern* to denote this era: see the entry *Renaissance*.

**Elizabethan Age**. Strictly speaking, the period of the reign of Elizabeth I (1558–1603); the term "Elizabethan," however, is often used loosely to refer to the late sixteenth and early seventeenth centuries, even after the death of Elizabeth. This was a time of rapid development in English commerce, maritime power, and nationalist feeling—the defeat of the Spanish Armada occurred in 1588. It was a great (in drama the greatest) age of English literature—the age of Sir Philip Sidney, Christopher Marlowe, Edmund Spenser, William Shakespeare, Sir Walter Raleigh, Francis Bacon, Ben Jonson, and many other extraordinary writers of prose and of dramatic, lyric, and narrative poetry. A number of scholars have looked back on this era as one of intellectual coherence and social order; an influential example was E. M. W. Tillyard's *The Elizabethan World Picture* (1943). Recent historical critics, however, have emphasized its intellectual uncertainties and political and social conflicts; see *new historicism*.

**Jacobean Age**. The reign of James I (in Latin, "Jacobus"), 1603–25, which followed that of Queen Elizabeth. This was the period in prose writings of Bacon, John Donne's sermons, Robert Burton's *Anatomy of Melancholy*, and the King James translation of the Bible. It was also the time of Shakespeare's greatest trage-dies and tragicomedies, and of major writings by other notable poets and playwrights including Donne, Ben Jonson, Michael Drayton, Lady Mary Wroth, Sir Francis Beaumont and John Fletcher, John Webster, George Chapman, Thomas Middleton, Philip Massinger, and Elizabeth Cary, whose notable biblical drama *The Tragedy of Mariam, the Faire Queene of Jewry* was the first long play by an Englishwoman to be published.

See Basil Willey, *The Seventeenth Century Background* (1934); Douglas Bush, *English Literature in the Earlier Seventeenth Century* (1945); C. V. Wedgwood, *Seventeenth Century English Literature* (1950).

**Caroline Age**. The reign of Charles I, 1625–49; the name is derived from "Carolus," the Latin version of "Charles." This was the time of the English Civil War fought between the supporters of the king (known as "Cavaliers") and the supporters of Parliament (known as "Roundheads," from their custom of wearing their hair cut short). John Milton began his writing during this period; it was the time also of the religious poet George Herbert and of the prose writers Robert Burton and Sir Thomas Browne.

Associated with the court were the **Cavalier poets**, writers of witty and polished lyrics of courtship and gallantry. The group included Richard Lovelace, Sir John Suckling, and Thomas Carew. Robert Herrick, although a country parson, is often classified with the Cavalier poets because, like them, he was a **Son of Ben** —that is, an admirer and follower of Ben Jonson—in many of his lyrics of love and gallant compliment.

See Robin Skelton, *Cavalier Poets* (1960).

The **Commonwealth Period**, also known as the **Puritan Interregnum**, extends from the end of the Civil War and the execution of Charles I in 1649 to the restoration of the Stuart monarchy under Charles II in 1660. In this period England was ruled by Parliament under the Puritan leader Oliver Cromwell; his death in 1658 marked the dissolution of the Commonwealth. Drama almost disappeared for eighteen years after the Puritans closed the public theaters in September 1642, not only on moral and religious grounds, but also to prevent public assemblies that might foment civil disorder. It was the age of Milton's political pamphlets, of Hobbes' political treatise *Leviathan* (1651), of the prose writers Sir Thomas Browne, Thomas Fuller, Jeremy Taylor, and Izaak Walton, and of the poets Henry Vaughan, Edmund Waller, Abraham Cowley, Sir William Davenant, and Andrew Marvell.

The **Neoclassical Period**, 1660–1785; see the entry *neoclassic and romantic.*

**Restoration**. This period takes its name from the restoration of the Stuart line (Charles II) to the English throne in 1660, at the end of the *Commonwealth*; it is specified as lasting until 1700. The urbanity, wit, and licentiousness of the life centering on the court, in sharp contrast to the seriousness and sobriety of the earlier Puritan regime, is reflected in much of the literature of this age. The theaters came back to vigorous life after the revocation of the ban placed on them by the Puritans in 1642, although they became more exclusively oriented toward the aristocratic classes than they had been earlier. Sir George Etherege, William Wycherley, William Congreve, and John Dryden developed the distinctive comedy of manners called *Restoration comedy*, and Dryden, Thomas Otway, and other playwrights developed the even more distinctive form of tragedy called *heroic drama.* Dryden was the major poet and critic, as well as one of the major dramatists. Other poets were the satirists Samuel Butler and the Earl of Rochester; notable writers in prose, in addition to the masterly Dryden, were Samuel Pepys, Sir William Temple, the religious writer in vernacular English John Bunyan, and the philosopher John Locke. Aphra Behn, the first Englishwoman to earn her living by her pen and one of the most inventive and versatile authors of the age, wrote poems, highly successful plays, and *Oroonoko,* the tragic story of a noble African slave, an important precursor of the *novel.*

See Basil Willey, *The Seventeenth Century Background* (1934); L. I. Bredvold, *The Intellectual Milieu of John Dryden* (1932).

**Augustan Age**. The original Augustan Age was the brilliant literary period of Virgil, Horace, and Ovid under the Roman emperor Augustus (27 BC–AD 14). In the eighteenth century and later, however, the term was frequently applied also to the literary period in England from approximately 1700 to 1745. The leading writers of the time (such as Alexander Pope, Jonathan Swift, and Joseph Addison) themselves drew the parallel to the Roman Augustans, and deliberately imitated their literary forms and subjects, their emphasis on social concerns, and their ideals of moderation, decorum, and urbanity. (See *neoclassicism.*) A major representative of popular, rather than classical, writing in this period was the novelist, journalist, and pamphleteer Daniel Defoe. Lady Mary Wortley Montagu was a brilliant letter writer in a great era of letter writing; she also wrote poems of wit and candor that violated the conventional moral and intellectual roles assigned to women in the Augustan era.

**Age of Sensibility**. The period between the death of Alexander Pope in 1744, and 1785, which was one year after the death of Samuel Johnson and one year before Robert Burns' *Poems, Chiefly in Scottish Dialect.* (Alternative dates frequently proposed for the end of this period are 1789 and 1798; see *Romantic Period.*) An older name for this half-century, the **Age of Johnson**, stresses the dominant position of Samuel Johnson (1709–84) and his literary and intellectual circle, which included Oliver Goldsmith, Edmund Burke, James Boswell, Edward Gibbon, and Hester Lynch Thrale. These authors on the whole represented a culmination of the literary and critical modes of *neoclassicism* and the worldview of the *Enlightenment.* The more recent name, "Age of Sensibility," puts its stress on the emergence, in other writers of the 1740s and later, of new cultural attitudes, theories of literature, and types of poetry; we find in this period, for example, a growing sympathy for the Middle Ages, a vogue of *cultural primitivism*, an awakening interest in ballads and other folk literature, a turn from neoclassic "correctness" and its emphasis on judgment and restraint to an emphasis on instinct and feeling, the development of a *literature of sensibility*, and above all the exaltation by some critics of "original genius" and a "bardic" poetry of the sublime and visionary imagination. Thomas Gray expressed this anti-neoclassic sensibility and set of values in his "Stanzas to Mr. Bentley" (1752):

> But not to one in this benighted age
> Is that diviner inspiration given,
> That burns in Shakespeare's or in Milton's page,
> The pomp and prodigality of Heaven.

Other poets who showed similar shifts in thought and taste were William Collins and Joseph and Thomas Warton (poets who, together with Gray, began in the 1740s the vogue for what Samuel Johnson slightingly referred to as "ode, and elegy, and sonnet"), Christopher Smart, and William Cowper. Thomas Percy published his influential *Reliques of Ancient English Poetry* (1765), which included many *folk ballads* and a few medieval metrical romances, and James Macpherson in the same decade published his greatly altered (and in considerable part fabricated) versions of the poems of the Gaelic bard Ossian (Oisin) which were enormously popular throughout Europe. This was also the period of the great novelists, some realistic and satiric and some "sentimental": Samuel Richardson, Henry Fielding, Tobias Smollett, and Laurence Sterne.

See Northrop Frye, "Toward Defining an Age of Sensibility," in *Fables of Identity* (1963), and ed. *Romanticism Reconsidered* (1965); F. W. Hilles and Harold Bloom, eds., *From Sensibility to Romanticism* (1965).

**Romantic Period**. The Romantic Period in English literature is dated as beginning in 1785 (see *Age of Sensibility*)—or alternatively in 1789 (the outbreak of the French Revolution), or in 1798 (the publication of William Wordsworth's and Samuel Taylor Coleridge's *Lyrical Ballads*)—and as ending either in 1830 or else in 1832, the year in which Sir Walter Scott died and the passage of the Reform Bill signaled the political preoccupations of the Victorian era. For some prominent characteristics of the thought and writings of this remarkable and diverse literary period, as well as for a list of suggested readings, see *neoclassic and romantic*. The term is often applied also to literary movements in European countries and America; see *periods of American literature*. Romantic characteristics are usually said to have been manifested first in Germany and England in the 1790s, and not to have become prominent in France and America until two or three decades after that time. Major English writers of the period, in addition to Wordsworth and Coleridge, were the poets Robert Burns, William Blake, Lord Byron, Percy Bysshe Shelley, John Keats, and Walter Savage Landor; the prose writers Charles Lamb, William Hazlitt, Thomas De Quincey, Mary Wollstonecraft, and Leigh Hunt; and the novelists Jane Austen, Sir Walter Scott, and Mary Shelley. The span between 1786 and the close of the eighteenth century was that of the *Gothic romances* by William Beckford, Matthew Gregory Lewis, William Godwin, and, above all, Ann Radcliffe.

**Victorian Period**. The beginning of the Victorian Period is frequently dated 1830, or alternatively 1832 (the passage of the first Reform Bill), and sometimes 1837 (the accession of Queen Victoria); it extends to the death of Victoria in 1901. Historians often subdivide the long period into three phases: Early Victorian (to 1848), Mid-Victorian (1848–70), and Late Victorian (1870–1901). Much writing of the period, whether imaginative or didactic, in verse or in prose, dealt with or reflected the pressing social, economic, religious, and intellectual issues and problems of that era. (For a summary of these issues, and also for the derogatory use of the term "Victorian," see *Victorian* and *Victorianism*.) Among the notable poets were Alfred, Lord Tennyson, Robert Browning, Elizabeth Barrett Browning, Christina Rossetti, Matthew Arnold, and Gerard Manley Hopkins (whose remarkably innovative poems, however, did not become known until they were published, long after his death, in 1918). The most prominent essayists were Thomas Carlyle, John Ruskin, Arnold, and Walter Pater; the most distinguished of many excellent novelists (this was a great age of English prose fiction) were Charlotte and Emily Brontë, Charles Dickens, William Makepeace Thackeray, Elizabeth Gaskell, George Eliot, George Meredith, Anthony Trollope, Thomas Hardy, and Samuel Butler.

For prominent literary movements during the Victorian era, see the entries on *Pre-Raphaelites, Aestheticism*, and *Decadence*.

**Edwardian Period**. The span between the death of Victoria (1901) and the beginning of World War I (1914) is named for King Edward VII, who reigned from 1901 to 1910. Poets writing at the time included Thomas Hardy (who gave up novels for poetry at the beginning of the century), Alfred Noyes, William Butler Yeats, and Rudyard Kipling; dramatists included Henry Arthur Jones, Arthur Wing Pinero, James Barrie, John Galsworthy, George Bernard Shaw, and the playwrights of the *Celtic Revival* such as Lady Gregory, Yeats, and John M. Synge. Many of the major achievements were in prose fiction—works by Thomas Hardy, Joseph Conrad, Ford Madox Ford, John Galsworthy, H. G. Wells, Rudyard Kipling, and Henry James, who published his major final novels, *The Wings of the Dove, The Ambassadors*, and *The Golden Bowl*, between 1902 and 1904.

**Georgian Period** is a term applied both to the reigns in England of the four successive Georges (1714–1830) and (more frequently) to the reign of George V (1910–36). The term **Georgian poets** usually designates a group of writers in the latter era who loomed large in four anthologies entitled *Georgian Poetry*, which were published by Edward Marsh between 1912 and 1922. Marsh favored writers we now tend to regard as relatively minor poets such as Rupert Brooke, Walter de la Mare, Ralph Hodgson, W. H. Davies, and John Masefield. "Georgian poetry" has come to connote verse which is mainly rural in subject matter, deft and delicate rather than bold and passionate in manner, and traditional rather than experimental in technique and form.

**Modern Period**. The application of the term "modern," of course, varies with the passage of time, but it is frequently applied specifically to the literature written since the beginning of World War I in 1914; see *modernism and postmodernism*. This period has been marked by persistent and multidimensioned experiments in subject matter, form, and style, and has produced major achievements in all the literary genres. Among the notable writers are the poets W. B. Yeats, Wilfred Owen, T. S. Eliot, W. H. Auden, Robert Graves, Dylan Thomas, and Seamus Heaney; the novelists Joseph Conrad, James Joyce, D. H. Lawrence, Dorothy Richardson, Virginia Woolf, E. M. Forster, Aldous Huxley, Graham Greene, Doris Lessing, and Nadine Gordimer; the dramatists G. B. Shaw, Sean O'Casey, Noel Coward, Samuel Beckett, Harold Pinter, Caryl Churchill, Brendan Behan, Frank McGuinness, and Tom Stoppard. The modern age was also an important era for literary criticism; among the innovative and influential English critics were T. S. Eliot, I. A. Richards, Virginia Woolf, F. R. Leavis, and William Empson. (See *New Criticism*.)

This entry has followed what has been the widespread practice of including under "English literature" the works of **anglophone authors**—that is, authors who speak and write in the English language—in all the British Isles. A number of the writers listed above were in fact natives of Ireland, Scotland, and Wales. Of the Modern Period especially it can be said that much of the greatest "English" literature was written by the Irish writers Yeats, Shaw, Joyce, O'Casey, Beckett, Iris Murdoch, and Seamus Heaney. And in recent decades, some of the most notable achievements in the English language have been written by authors who are natives of recently liberated English colonies (often referred to as **postcolonial authors**), including the Rhodesian Doris Lessing; The South Africans Nadine Gordimer, Athol Fugard, and J. M. Coetzee; the West Indians V. S. Naipaul and Derek Walcott; the Nigerians Chinua Achebe and Wole Soyinka; and the Indian novelists R. K. Narayan, Anita Desai, and Salman Rushdie. See Terry Eagleton, *Exiles and Emigrés* (1975), and refer to *postcolonial studies*.

The **Postmodern Period** is applied to the era after World War II (1939–45). See *modernism and postmodernism* and, for innovations during the postmodern period in critical theory and practice, *poststructuralism*. Refer also to *Periods of American Literature*.

**peripety** (pĕrĭp' ĕtē): **268**; *372*.

**periphrasis** (pĕrĭf' răsĭs): **269**; *121*.

**perlocutionary act: 338**.

**persona, tone, and voice:** These terms reflect the tendency in recent criticism to think of narrative and lyric works of literature as a mode of speech, or in what is now a favored term, as *discourse*. To conceive a work as an utterance suggests that there is a speaker who has determinate personal qualities, and who expresses attitudes both toward the characters and materials within the work and toward the audience to whom the work is addressed. In his *Rhetoric* (fourth century BC), Aristotle, followed by other Greek and Roman rhetoricians, pointed out that an orator projects in the course of his oration an *ethos*, that is, a personal character, which itself functions as a means of persuasion. For example, if the impression a speaker projects is that of a person of rectitude, intelligence, and goodwill, the audience is instinctively inclined to give credence to such a speaker's arguments. The current concern with the nature and function of the author's presence in a work of imaginative literature is related to this traditional concept, and is part of the rhetorical emphasis in modern criticism. (See *rhetoric, rhetorical criticism*, and *speech-act theory*.)

Specific applications of the terms "persona," "tone," and "voice" vary greatly and involve difficult concepts in philosophy and social psychology—concepts such as "the self," "personal identity," "role-playing," and "sincerity." This essay will merely sketch some central uses of these terms that have proved helpful in analyzing the experience of diverse works of literature.

**Persona** was the Latin word for the mask worn by actors in the classical theater, from which was derived the term **dramatis personae** for the list of characters who play a role in a drama, and ultimately the English word "person," a particular individual. In recent literary discussion "persona" is often applied to the first-person speaker who tells the story in a narrative poem or novel, or whose voice we hear in a lyric poem. Examples of personae, in this broad application, are the visionary first-person narrator of John Milton's *Paradise Lost* (who in the opening passages of various books of that epic discourses at some length about himself); the Gulliver who tells us about his misadventures in *Gulliver's Travels*; the "I" who carries on most of the conversation in Alexander Pope's satiric dialogue *Epistle to Dr. Arbuthnot*; the genial narrator of Henry Fielding's *Tom Jones*, who pauses frequently for leisurely discourse with his reader; the speaker who talks first to himself, then to his sister, in William Wordsworth's "Tintern Abbey"; the Duke who tells the emissary about his former wife in Robert Browning's "My Last Duchess"; and the fantastic "biographer" who narrates Virginia Woolf's *Orlando*. Calling all such diverse speakers "personae" serves to indicate that they are all, to some degree, adapted to the generic and formal requirements and the artistic aims of a particular literary work. We need, however, to go on to make distinctions between such speakers as Jonathan Swift's Gulliver and Browning's Duke, who are entirely fictional characters very different from their authors; the narrators in Pope's *Epistle* and Fielding's *Tom Jones*, who are presented as closer to their authors, although clearly shaped to fit the roles they are designed to play in those works; and the speakers in the autobiographical passages in *Paradise Lost*, in "Tintern Abbey," and in "Ode to a Nightingale," where we are invited to attribute the voice we hear, and the sentiments it utters, to the poet in his own person.

In an influential discussion, I. A. Richards defined **tone** as the expression of a literary speaker's "attitude to his listener." "The tone of his utterance reflects . . . his sense of how he stands toward those he is addressing" (*Practical Criticism*, 1929, chapters 1 and 3). In a more complex definition, the Soviet critic Mikhail Bakhtin said that tone, or "intonation," is "oriented *in two directions:* with respect to the listener as ally or witness and with respect to the object of the utterance as the third, living participant whom the intonation scolds or caresses, denigrates or magnifies." ("Discourse in Life and Discourse in Art," in Bakhtin's *Freudianism: A Marxist Critique*, trans. 1976.) The sense in which the term is used in recent criticism is suggested by the phrase "tone of voice," as applied to nonliterary speech. The way we speak reveals, by subtle clues, our conception of, and attitude toward, the things we are talking about, our personal relationship to our auditor, and also our assumptions about the social level, intelligence, and sensitivity of that auditor. The tone of a speech can be described as critical or approving, formal or intimate, outspoken or reticent, solemn or playful, arrogant or prayerful, angry or loving, serious or ironic, condescending or obsequious, and so on through numberless possible nuances of relationship and attitude both to object and auditor. In a literary narrative, the *narratee* (the person or persons to whom the narrator addresses the story) is sometimes explicitly identified, but at other times remains an **implied auditor**, revealed only by what the narrator implicitly takes for granted as needing or not needing explanation or justification, and by the tone of the narrator's address. *Feminist critics*, for example, point out that much of the literature by male authors assumes a male readership who share the narrator's views, interests, and values. See Judith Fetterley, *The Resisting Reader* (1978).

Some current critical uses of "tone" are broader, and coincide in reference with what other critics prefer to call "voice."

**Voice**, in a recently evolved usage, signifies the equivalent in imaginative literature to Aristotle's "ethos" in a speech of persuasive rhetoric, and suggests also the traditional rhetorician's concern with the importance of the physical voice in an oration. The term in criticism points to the fact that we are aware of a voice beyond the fictitious voices that speak in a work, and a persona behind all the dramatic personae, and behind even the first-person narrator. We have the sense, that is, of a pervasive authorial presence, a determinate intelligence and moral sensibility, who has invented, ordered, and rendered all these literary characters and materials in just this way. The particular qualities of the author's ethos, or voice, in Henry Fielding's novel *Tom Jones* (1749) manifest themselves, among other things, in the fact that he has chosen to create the wise, ironic, and worldly persona who ostensibly tells the story and talks to the reader about it. The sense of a distinctive authorial presence is no less evident in the work of recent writers who, unlike Fielding, pursue a strict policy of authorial noninterference and by effacing themselves, try to give the impression that the story tells itself (see *point of view*). There is great diversity in the quality of the authorial mind, temperament, and sensibility which, by inventing, controlling, and rendering the particular fiction, pervades works—all of them "objective" or impersonal in narrative technique—such as James Joyce's *Ulysses*, Virginia Woolf's *Mrs. Dalloway*, Ernest Hemingway's "The Killers," and William Faulkner's *The Sound and the Fury*. For a particular emphasis on the importance of the author's implicit presence as this is sustained from work to work, see *critics of consciousness*. For a discussion of the relation between a poet's speaking voice in real life and the qualities of his or her poem, refer to Francis Berry, *Poetry and the Physical Voice* (1962).

Of the critics listed below who deal with this concept, Wayne C. Booth prefers the term **implied author** over "voice," in order better to indicate that the reader of a work of fiction has the sense not only of the timbre and tone of a speaking voice, but of a total human presence. Booth's view is that this implied author is "an ideal, literary, created version of the real man"—that is, the implied author, although related to the actual author, is nonetheless part of the total fiction, whom the author gradually brings into being in the course of his composition, and who plays an important role in the overall effect of a work on the reader. Critics such as Walter J. Ong, on the other hand, distinguish between the author's "false voice" and his "true voice," and regard the latter as the expression of the author's genuine self or identity; as they see it, to discover one's true "voice" is to discover oneself. All of these critics agree, however, that the sense of a convincing authorial voice and presence, whose values, beliefs, and moral vision serve implicitly as controlling forces throughout a work, helps to sway the reader to yield the imaginative consent without which a poem or novel would remain an elaborate verbal game.

Refer to Bakhtin's view of the multiplex voices in narrative fiction, in the entry *dialogic criticism*. See Richard Ellmann, *Yeats: The Man and the Masks* (1948), which discusses Yeats' theory of a poet's "masks" or "personae," both in his life and his art; Reuben Brower, "The Speaking Voice," in *Fields of Light* (1951); Wayne C. Booth, *The Rhetoric of Fiction* (rev. 1983), chapter 3; W. J. Ong, *The Barbarian Within* (1962); J. O. Perry, ed., *Approaches to the Poem* (1965)—in which section 3, "Tone, Voice, Sensibility," includes selections from I. A. Richards, Reuben Brower, and W. J. Ong; Walter J. Slatoff, *With Respect to Readers* (1970); Lionel Trilling, *Sincerity and Authenticity* (1972); and Robert C. Elliott, *The Literary Persona* (1982). For references to *persona* in other entries, see pages *312, 313*.

**personal lyrics:** 179.

**personification:** 121; *7, 95, 269, 330*. See also *invocation; pathetic fallacy*.

**Petrarchan conceit** (pĕträr′ kan): **53**; *60, 179, 239, 336*.

**Petrarchan sonnet:** 336; *193*.

**phallogocentric** (fălŏg′ ōsĕn″ trik): **114**.

**phenomenological criticism:** 261.

**phenomenology and criticism:** The philosophical perspective and method called **phenomenology** was established by the German thinker Edmund Husserl (1859–1938). Husserl set out to analyze human consciousness—that is, to describe the concrete **Lebenswelt** (lived world), as this is experienced independently of any prior suppositions, whether these suppositions come from philosophy or from common sense. He proposes that consciousness is a unified **intentional** act. By "intentional" he does not mean that it is deliberately willed, but that it is always directed to an "object"; in other words, to be conscious is always to be conscious of something. Husserl's claim is that in this unitary act of consciousness, the thinking subject and the object it "intends," or is aware of, are interinvolved and reciprocally implicative. In order to free itself of prior conceptions, the phenomenological analysis of consciousness begins with an "epoché" (suspension) of all presuppositions about the nature of experience, and this suspension involves "bracketing" (holding in abeyance) the question whether or not the object of consciousness is real—that is, whether or not the object exists outside the consciousness which "intends" it.

Phenomenology had widespread philosophical influence after it was put forward by Husserl in 1900 and later, and was diversely developed by Martin Heidegger in Germany and Maurice Merleau-Ponty in France. It greatly influenced Hans-Georg Gadamer and other theorists concerned with analyzing the conscious activity of understanding language (see *interpretation and hermeneutics*), and, directly or indirectly, affected the way in which many critics analyze the experience of literature.

In the 1930s the Polish theorist Roman Ingarden (1893–1970), who wrote his books in both Polish and German, adapted the phenomenological viewpoint and concepts to a formulation of the way we understand and respond to a work of literature. In Ingarden's analysis, a literary work originates in the intentional acts of consciousness of its author—"intentional" in the phenomenological sense that the acts are directed toward an object. These acts, as recorded in a text, make it possible for a reader to re-experience the work in his or her own consciousness. The recorded text contains many elements which are potential rather than fully realized, as well as many "places of indeterminacy" in what it sets forth. An "active reading" responds to the sequence of the printed words by a temporal process of consciousness which "fills out" these potential and indeterminate aspects of the text, and in so doing, in Ingarden's term, the reading **concretizes** the schematic literary work. Such a reading is said to be "co-creative" with the conscious processes recorded by the author, and to result in an actualized "aesthetic object" within the reader's consciousness which does not depict a reality that exists independently of the work, but instead constitutes a "quasi-reality"—that is to say, its own fictional world. See Roman Ingarden, *The Literary Work of Art* (1931, trans. 1973), and *The Cognition of the Literary Work of Art* (1937, trans. 1973); also, the exposition in Eugene Falk, *The Poetics of Roman Ingarden* (1981). For German critics strongly influenced by Ingarden, see Wolfgang Iser under *reader-response criticism*, and Hans Robert Jauss under *reception theory*.

The term **phenomenological criticism** is often applied specifically to the theory and practice of the **Geneva School** of critics, most of whose members taught at the University of Geneva, and all of whom were joined by friendship, interinfluence, and their general approach to literature. The older members of the Geneva School were Marcel Raymond and Albert Beguin; later members were Jean Rousset, Jean-Pierre Richard, and, most prominently, Georges Poulet. J. Hillis Miller, who for six years was a colleague of Poulet's at Johns Hopkins University, was in his earlier career (before turning to *deconstructive criticism*) the leading American representative of the Geneva School of criticism, and applied this critical mode to the analysis of a variety of American and English authors.

Geneva critics regard each work of literature as a fictional world that is created out of the *Lebenswelt* of its author and embodies the author's unique mode of consciousness. In its approach to literature as primarily subjective, this criticism is opposed to the objective approach of *formalism*, both in its European variety and in American *New Criticism*. Its roots instead go back through the nineteenth century to that type of romantic *expressive criticism* which regarded a literary work as the revelation of the personality of its author, and also proposed that the awareness of this personality is the chief aim and value of reading literature. (As early as 1778, for example, the German critic Johann Gottfried Herder wrote: "This *living reading*, this divination into the soul of the author, is the sole mode of reading, and the most profound means of self-development.") In the course of time, however, Geneva critics assimilated a number of the concepts and methods of Husserl, Heidegger, and other phenomenologists. In the view of the Geneva critics the "cogito," or distinctive formations of consciousness, of the individual author—related to, but not identical with, the author's "empirical," or biographical, self—pervades a work of literature, manifesting itself as the subjective correlate of the "contents" of the work; that is, of the objects, characters, imagery, and style into which the author's personal mode of awareness and feeling imaginatively projects itself. (For a related critical concept see *voice*; refer also to *objective and subjective*.) By "bracketing" their own prepossessions and particularities, the readers of a literary work make themselves purely and passively receptive, and so are capable of achieving participation, or even identity, with the immanent consciousness of its author. Their undertaking to read a work so as to experience the mode of consciousness of its author, and then to reproject this consciousness in their own critical writing about that work, underlies the frequent application to the Geneva School of the term **critics of consciousness** and the description of their aim in a critical reading of works of literature as "consciousness of the consciousness of another." As Georges Poulet put it in "Phenomenology of Reading" (1969): "When I read as I ought . . . with the total commitment required of any reader," then "I am thinking the thoughts of another. . . . But I think it as my very own. . . . My consciousness behaves as though it were the consciousness of another." (It should be noted that whereas the philosopher Husserl's aim in phenomenology was to describe the essential features of consciousness which are shared by all human beings, the Geneva critics' quite different aim is to identify—and also to identify oneself with—the unique consciousness of each individual author.)

Within this framework, critics of consciousness differ in the extent to which they attend to specific elements in the "external" contents, formal structure, and style of a text, on their way toward isolating its author's "interior" mode of consciousness. A conspicuous tendency of most of these critics is to put together widely separated passages within a single work, on the principle, as J. Hillis Miller says in his book *Charles Dickens*, that since all these passages "reveal the persistence of certain obsessions, problems, and attitudes," the critic may, by analyzing them, "glimpse the original unity of a creative mind." Furthermore the critics of consciousness often treat a single work not as an individual entity, but as part of the collective body of an author's writings, in order, as Miller said of Dickens, "to identify what persists through all the swarming multiplicity of his novels as a view of the world which is unique and the same." Georges Poulet has also undertaken, in a number of books, to tell the history of the varying imaginative treatments of the topic of time throughout the course of Western literature, regarding these treatments as correlative with diverse modes of lived experience. In these histories Poulet sets out to identify "for each epoch a consciousness common to all contemporary minds"; he claims, however, that within this shared period-consciousness, the consciousness of each author also manifests its uniqueness. The influence of the criticism of consciousness reached its height in the 1950s and 1960s, then gave way to the explicitly opposed critical modes of *structuralism* and *deconstruction*. Many of its concepts and procedures, however, survive in some forms of *reader-response criticism* and *reception aesthetic*.

Robert R. Magliola, *Phenomenology and Literature* (1977), deals with various types of phenomenological poetics and criticism in the context of an exposition of Husserl, Heidegger, and other phenomenological philosophers. Brief introductions to the Geneva School of criticism are Georges Poulet, "Phenomenology of Reading," *New Literary History* 1 (1969–70), and J. Hillis Miller, "The Geneva School . . . ," in *Modern French Criticism*, ed. J. K. Simon (1972). In "Geneva or

Paris? The Recent Work of Georges Poulet," *University of Toronto Quarterly*, Vol. 39 (1970), Miller indicates his own transition from the criticism of consciousness to the very different critical mode of *deconstruction*. A detailed study of the Geneva School is Sarah Lawall's *Critics of Consciousness: The Existential Structures of Literature* (1968); see also Michael Murray, *Modern Critical Theory: A Phenomenological Introduction* (1976). Among the writings of Geneva critics and other critics of consciousness available in English are Georges Poulet, *Studies in Human Time* (1949), *The Interior Distance* (1952), and *The Metamorphoses of the Circle* (1961); Jean Starobinski, *The Invention of Liberty, 1700–1789* (1964); Gaston Bachelard, *Subversive Humanist: Texts and Reading*, ed. Mary M. Jones (1991); J. Hillis Miller, *Charles Dickens: The World of His Novels* (1959), *The Disappearance of God* (1963), and *Poets of Reality* (1965). Other critical works influenced by phenomenology are Paul Brodtkorb, *Ishmael's White World: A Phenomenological Reading of Moby Dick* (1965); David Halliburton, *Edgar Allan Poe: A Phenomenological View* (1973); and Bruce Johnson, *True Correspondence: A Phenomenology of Thomas Hardy's Novels* (1983).

**philology: 172**.

**philosophical optimism: 139**.

**phoneme** (fō′ nēm): **174**.

**phonetics** (fōnĕt′ ĭks): **174**.

**phonocentric** (fōnōsĕn′ trĭk): **70**.

**phonology: 174**.

**picaresque narrative** (pĭk′ ărĕsk″): **227**; *266*.

**Pindaric ode: 235**.

**Platonic love:** In Plato's *Symposium* 210–212, Socrates recounts the doctrine about Eros (love) that, he modestly says, has been imparted to him by the wise woman Diotima. She bids us not to linger in the love evoked by the beauty in a single human body, but to mount up as by a stair, "from one going on to two, and from two to all fair forms," then up from the beauty of the body to the beauty of the mind, until we arrive at a final contemplation of the Idea, or Form, of "beauty absolute, separate, simple, and everlasting." From this beauty, in its own realm of Ideas, the human soul is in exile; and of this ideal beauty, the beauties of the body and of the world perceived by the senses are only distant, distorted, and impermanent reflections. Plotinus and other **Neoplatonists** (the "new Platonists," a school of Platonic philosophers of the third to the fifth century) developed the view that all beauty in the sensible world—as well as all goodness and truth—is an "emanation" (radiation) from the One or Absolute, which is the source of all being and all value. Christian thinkers of the Italian Renaissance, merging this impersonal Absolute with the personal God of the Bible, developed the theory that genuine beauty of the body is only the outer manifestation of a moral and spiritual beauty of the soul, which in turn is rayed out from the absolute beauty of the one

God Himself. The Platonic lover is irresistibly attracted to the bodily beauty of a beloved person, but reveres it as a sign of the spiritual beauty that it shares with all other beautiful bodies, and at the same time regards it as merely the lowest rung on a ladder that leads up from sensual desire to the pure contemplation of Heavenly Beauty in God.

Highly elaborated versions of this conception of Platonic love are to be found in Dante, Petrarch, and other writers of the thirteenth and fourteenth centuries, and in many Italian, French, and English authors of sonnets and other love poems during the Renaissance. See, for example, the exposition in Book IV of Castiglione's *The Courtier* (1528), and in Edmund Spenser's "An Hymn in Honor of Beauty." As Spenser wrote in one of the sonnets he called *Amoretti* (1595):

> Men call you fayre, and you doe credit it. . . .
> But only that is permanent and free
> From frayle corruption, that doth flesh ensew.
> That is true beautie: that doth argue you
> To be divine and borne of heavenly seed:
> Derived from that fayre spirit, from whom al true
> And perfect beauty did at first proceed.

From this complex religious and philosophical doctrine, the modern notion that Platonic love is simply love that stops short of sexual gratification is a drastic reduction.

The concept of Platonic love fascinated many later poets, especially Shelley; an example is his poem "Epipsychidion" (1821). But his friend Byron took a skeptical view of such lofty claims for the human Eros-impulse. "Oh Plato! Plato!" Byron sighed,

> you have paved the way,
> With your confounded fantasies, to more
> Immoral conduct by the fancied sway
> Your system feigns o'er the controlless core
> Of human hearts, than all the long array
> Of poets and romancers. . . .

(*Don Juan*, I. cxvi.)

See Plato's *Symposium* and *Phaedrus*, and the exposition of Plato's doctrine of Eros (which Plato applied to male/male relationships) in G. M. A. Grube, *Plato's Thought* (1935), chapter 3. For a cognitive and moral assessment of Plato's doctrines of love and desire, see Martha Craven Nussbaum, *Love's Knowledge: Essays on Philosophy and Literature* (1990), especially chapter 3. Refer to Paul Shorey, *Platonism Ancient and Modern* (1938); George Santayana, "Platonic Love in Some Italian Poets," in *Selected Critical Writings*, ed. Norman Henfrey (2 vols., 1968), I, pp. 41–59. See *courtly love*.

**play** (drama): **84**.

**plot:** The plot (which Aristotle termed the **mythos**) in a dramatic or narrative work is constituted by its events and actions, as these are rendered and ordered toward achieving particular artistic and emotional effects. This description is deceptively simple, because the actions (including verbal discourse as well as physical actions) are performed by particular characters in a work, and are the means by which they exhibit their moral and dispositional qualities. Plot and character are therefore interdependent critical concepts—as Henry James has said, "What is character but the determination of incident? What is incident but the illustration of character?" (See *character and characterization*.) Notice also that a plot is distinguishable from the *story*—that is, a bare synopsis of the temporal order of what happens. When we summarize the story in a literary work, we say that first this happens, then that, then that. . . . It is only when we specify how this is related to that, by causes and motivations, and in what ways all these matters are rendered, ordered, and organized so as to achieve their particular effects, that a synopsis begins to be adequate to the plot. (On the distinction between story and plot see *narrative and narratology*.)

There are a great variety of plot forms. For example, some plots are designed to achieve tragic effects, and others to achieve the effects of comedy, romance, satire, or of some other *genre*. Each of these types in turn exhibits diverse plot patterns, and may be represented in the mode either of drama or of narrative, and either in verse or in prose. The following terms, widely current in traditional criticism, are useful in distinguishing the component elements of plots and in helping to discriminate types of plots, and of the characters appropriate to them, in both narrative and dramatic literature.

The chief character in a plot, on whom our interest centers, is called the **protagonist** (or alternatively, the **hero** or **heroine**), and if the plot is such that he or she is pitted against an important opponent, that character is called the **antagonist**. Elizabeth Bennet is the protagonist, or heroine, of Jane Austen's *Pride and Prejudice* (1813); Hamlet is the protagonist and King Claudius the antagonist in Shakespeare's play, and the relation between them is one of **conflict**. If the antagonist is evil, or capable of cruel and criminal actions, he or she is called the **villain**. Many, but far from all, plots deal with a conflict; Thornton Wilder's play *Our Town* (1938), for example, does not. In addition to the conflict between individuals, there may be the conflict of a protagonist against fate, or against the circumstances that stand between him and a goal he has set himself; and in some works (as in Henry James' *Portrait of a Lady*) the chief conflict is between opposing desires or values in the protagonist's own temperament. For the recent employment of an anti-traditional protagonist, see *antihero*.

A character in a work who, by sharp contrast, serves to stress and highlight the distinctive temperament of the protagonist is termed a **foil**. Thus Laertes the man of action is a foil to the dilatory Hamlet; the firebrand Hotspur is a foil to the cool and calculating Prince Hal in Shakespeare's *1 Henry IV*; and in *Pride and Prejudice*, the gentle and compliant Jane Bennet serves as a foil to her strong-willed sister Elizabeth. ("Foil" originally signified "leaf," and came to be applied to the thin sheet of bright metal placed under a jewel to enhance its brilliance.)

If a character initiates a scheme which depends for its success on the ignorance or gullibility of the person or persons against whom it is directed, it is called an **intrigue**. Iago is a villain who intrigues against Othello and Cassio in Shakespeare's tragedy *Othello*. A number of comedies, including Ben Jonson's *Volpone* (1607) and many *Restoration* plays (for example, William Congreve's *The Way of the World* and William Wycherley's *The Country Wife*), have plots which turn largely on the success or failure of an intrigue.

As a plot evolves it arouses expectations in the audience or reader about the future course of events and actions and how characters will respond to them. A lack of certainty on the part of a concerned reader about what is going to happen, especially to characters with whom the reader has established a bond of sympathy, is known as **suspense**. If what in fact happens violates the expectations we have formed, it is known as **surprise**. The interplay of suspense and surprise is a prime source of vitality in a traditional plot. The most effective surprise, especially in realistic narratives, is one which turns out, in retrospect, to have been grounded in what has gone before, even though we have hitherto made the wrong inference from the given facts of circumstance and character. As E. M. Forster put it, the shock of the unexpected, "followed by the feeling, 'oh, that's all right' is a sign that all is well with the plot." A "surprise ending," in the pejorative sense, is one in which the author resolves the plot without adequate earlier grounds in characterization or events, often by the use of highly unlikely coincidence; there are numerous examples in the short stories of O. Henry. (For one type of manipulated ending, see *deus ex machina*.) *Dramatic irony* is a special kind of suspenseful expectation, when the audience or readers foresee the oncoming disaster or triumph but the character does not.

A plot is commonly said to have **unity of action** (or to be "an artistic whole") if it is apprehended by the reader or auditor as a complete and ordered structure of actions, directed toward the intended effect, in which none of the prominent component parts, or **incidents**, is nonfunctional; as Aristotle put this concept (*Poetics*, section 8), all the parts are "so closely connected that the transposal or withdrawal of any one of them will disjoint and dislocate the whole." Aristotle claimed that it does not constitute a unified plot to present a series of episodes which are strung together simply because they happen to a single character. Many *picaresque narratives*, nevertheless, such as Daniel Defoe's *Moll Flanders* (1722), have held the interest of readers for centuries with such an *episodic* plot structure; while even so tightly integrated a plot as that of Henry Fielding's *Tom Jones* (1749) introduces, for variety's sake, a long story by the Man of the Hill, which is related to the main plot only by parallels and contrasts.

A successful later development which Aristotle did not foresee is the type of structural unity that can be achieved with **double plots**, familiar in *Elizabethan* drama. In this form, a **subplot**—a second story that is complete and interesting in its own right—is introduced into the play; when skillfully invented and managed, the subplot serves to broaden our perspective on the main plot and to enhance rather than diffuse the overall effect. The integral subplot may have the relation of analogy to the main plot (the Gloucester story in *King Lear*), or else of counterpoint against it (the comic subplot involving Falstaff in *1 Henry IV*).

Edmund Spenser's *The Faerie Queene* (1590–96) is an instance of a narrative romance which interweaves main plot and a multiplicity of subplots into an intricately interrelated structure, in a way that the critic C. S. Lewis compares to the **polyphonic** art of contemporary Elizabethan music, in which two or more diverse melodies are carried on simultaneously.

The order of a unified plot, Aristotle pointed out, is a continuous sequence of beginning, middle, and end. The **beginning** initiates the main action in a way which makes us look forward to something more; the **middle** presumes what has gone before and requires something to follow; and the **end** follows from what has gone before but requires nothing more; we feel satisfied that the plot is complete. The structural beginning (sometimes also called the "initiating action," or "point of attack") need not be the initial stage of the action that is brought to a climax in the narrative or play. The epic, for example, plunges *in medias res*, "in the middle of things" (see *epic*), many short stories begin at the point of the climax itself, and the writer of a drama often captures our attention in the opening scene with a representative incident, related to and closely preceding the event which precipitates the central situation or conflict. Thus Shakespeare's *Romeo and Juliet* opens with a street fight between the servants of two great houses, and his *Hamlet* with the apparition of a ghost; the **exposition** of essential prior matters —the feud between the Capulets and Montagues, or the posture of affairs in the Royal House of Denmark—Shakespeare weaves rapidly and skillfully into the dialogue of these startling initial scenes. In the novel, the modern drama, and especially the motion picture, such exposition is sometimes managed by **flashbacks**: interpolated narratives or scenes (often justified, or *naturalized*, as a memory, a reverie, or a confession by one of the characters) which represent events that happened before the time at which the work opened. Arthur Miller's play *Death of a Salesman* (1949) and Ingmar Bergman's film *Wild Strawberries* (1957) make persistent and skillful use of this device.

The German critic Gustav Freytag, in *Technique of the Drama* (1863), introduced an analysis of plot that is known as **Freytag's Pyramid**. He described the typical plot of a five-act play as a pyramidal shape, consisting of a rising action, climax, and falling action. Although the total pattern that Freytag described applies only to a limited number of plays, various of his terms are frequently echoed by critics of prose fiction as well as drama. As applied to *Hamlet*, for example, the **rising action** (a section that Aristotle had called the **complication**) begins, after the opening scene and exposition, with the ghost's telling Hamlet that he has been murdered by his brother Claudius; it continues with the developing conflict between Hamlet and Claudius, in which Hamlet, despite setbacks, succeeds in controlling the course of events. The rising action reaches the **climax** of the hero's fortunes with his proof of the King's guilt by the device of the play within a play (III. ii.). Then comes the **crisis**, the reversal or "turning point" of the fortunes of the protagonist, in his failure to kill the King while he is at prayer. This inaugurates the **falling action**; from now on the antagonist, Claudius, largely controls the course of events, until the **catastrophe**, or outcome, which is decided by the death of the hero, as well as of Claudius, the Queen, and Laertes. "Catastrophe" is usually applied to tragedy only; a more general term for this precipitating final scene, which is applied to both comedy and tragedy, is the **de-nouement** (French for "unknotting"): the action or intrigue ends in success or failure for the protagonist, the conflicts are settled, the mystery is solved, or the misunderstanding cleared away. A frequently used alternative term for the outcome of a plot is the **resolution**.

In many plots the denouement involves a **reversal**, or in Aristotle's Greek term, **peripety**, in the protagonist's fortunes, whether to the protagonist's failure or destruction, as in tragedy, or success, as in comic plots. The reversal frequently depends on a **discovery** (in Aristotle's term, **anagnorisis**). This is the recognition by the protagonist of something of great importance hitherto unknown to him or to her: Cesario reveals to the Duke at the end of Shakespeare's *Twelfth Night* that he is really Viola; the fact of Iago's lying treachery dawns upon Othello; Fielding's Joseph Andrews, in his comic novel by that name (1742), discovers on the evidence of a birthmark—"as fine a strawberry as ever grew in a garden"—that he is in reality the son of Mr. and Mrs. Wilson.

Since the 1920s, a number of writers of prose fiction and drama—building on the example of Laurence Sterne's *Tristram Shandy*, as early as 1759–67—have deliberately designed their works to frustrate the expectations of chronological order, coherence, reliable narration, and resolution that the reader or auditor has formed by habituation to traditional plots; some writers have even attempted to dispense altogether with a recognizable plot. (See, for example, literature of the *absurd, modernism and postmodernism, antinovel,* the *new novel.*) Also, various recent types of critical theory have altered or supplemented many traditional concepts in the classification and analysis of plots. The *archetypal critic* Northrop Frye reduced all plots to four types that, he claims, reflect the myths corresponding to the four seasons of the year. Structuralist critics, who conceive diverse plots as sets of alternative conventions and codes for constructing a fictional narrative, analyze and classify these conventional plot forms on the model of linguistic theory. (See *structuralist criticism* and *narratology,* and the discussion of plots in Jonathan Culler, *Structuralist Poetics,* 1975, pp. 205–24.) And some recent critical theorists have undertaken to explode entirely the traditional treatments of plots, on the ground that any notion of the "unity" of a plot and of its "teleological" progress toward a resolution are illusory, or else that the resolution itself is only a facade to mask the irreconcilable conflicts and contradictions (whether psychological or social) that are the basic components of any literary text. See under *poststructuralism.*

For recent developments in the concept of plot, see *narrative and narratology.* Refer to Aristotle, *Poetics*; E. M. Forster, *Aspects of the Novel* (1927); R. S. Crane, "The Concept of Plot and the Plot of *Tom Jones,*" in Crane, ed., *Critics and Criticism* (1952); Wayne C. Booth, *The Rhetoric of Fiction* (rev. 1983); Elder Olson, *Tragedy and the Theory of Drama* (1966); Robert Scholes and Robert Kellogg, *The Nature of Narrative* (1966); Frank Kermode, *The Sense of an Ending: Studies in the Theory of Fiction* (1967); Eric S. Rabkin, *Narrative Suspense* (1974); Tzvetan Todorov, *The Poetics of Prose* (trans. 1977); Seymour Chatman, *Story and Discourse: Narrative Structure in Fiction and Film* (1980); Peter Brooks, *Reading for the Plot: Design and Invention in Narrative* (1984). For references to *plot* in other entries, see pages *127, 332.*

**plurisignation: 12**.

**poetaster** (pō″ ĕtăs′ tĕr): **48**.

**poetic diction:** The term **diction** signifies the kinds of words, phrases, and sentence structures, and sometimes also of figurative language, that constitute any work of literature. A writer's diction can be analyzed under a great variety of categories, such as the degree to which the vocabulary and phrasing is abstract or concrete, Latin or Anglo-Saxon in origin, colloquial or formal, technical or common. See *style* and *poetic license.*

Many poets in all ages have used a distinctive language, a "poetic diction," which includes words, phrasing, and figures not current in the ordinary discourse of the time. (See *poetic license.*) In modern discussion, however, the term **poetic diction** is applied especially to poets who, like Edmund Spenser in the Elizabethan age or G. M. Hopkins in the Victorian age, deliberately employed a diction that deviated markedly not only from common speech, but even from the writings of other poets of their era. And in a frequent use, "poetic diction" is narrowed to specify the special style developed by *neoclassic* writers of the eighteenth century who, like Thomas Gray, believed that "the language of the age is never the language of poetry" (letter to Richard West, 1742). This **neoclassic poetic diction** was in large part derived from the characteristic usage of admired earlier poets such as the Roman Virgil, Edmund Spenser, and John Milton, and was based primarily on the reigning principle of *decorum,* according to which a poet must adapt the "level" and type of his diction to the mode and status of a particular genre (see *style*). Formal satire, such as Alexander Pope's "Epistle to Dr. Arbuthnot" (1735), because it represented a poet's direct commentary on everyday matters, permitted—indeed required—the use of language really spoken by urbane and cultivated people of the time. But what were ranked as the higher genres, such as epic, tragedy, and ode, required a refined and elevated poetic diction to raise the style to the level of the form. On the other hand, pastoral and descriptive poems, which involved references to lowly materials, used a special diction to invest such materials with the dignity and elegance that were considered appropriate to poetry.

Prominent characteristics of this eighteenth-century poetic diction were its *archaism* and its use of recurrent *epithets*; its preference for resounding words derived from Latin ("refulgent," "irriguous," "umbrageous"); the frequent *invocations* to, and *personifications* of, abstractions and inanimate objects; and above all, the persistent use of **periphrasis** (a roundabout, elaborate way of saying something) to avoid what were regarded as low, technical, or commonplace terms by means of a substitute phrase that was thought to be of higher dignity and decorum. Among the many periphrases in James Thomson's *The Seasons* (1726–30) are "the finny tribe" for "fish," "the bleating kind" for "sheep," and "from the snowy leg . . . the inverted silk she drew" instead of "she took off her silk stocking." The following stanza from Thomas Gray's excellent period piece, "Ode on a Distant Prospect of Eton College" (1747), manifests all these devices of neoclassic poetic diction. Contemporary readers took special pleasure in the ingenuity of the periphrases by which Gray, to achieve the stylistic elevation appropriate to an ode, managed to describe schoolboys at play while evading the use of common—hence what were considered to be unpoetic—words such as "swim," "cage," "boys," "hoop," and "bat":

> Say, Father Thames, for thou hast seen
> Full many a sprightly race
> Disporting on thy margent green
> The paths of pleasure trace;
> Who foremost now delight to cleave
> With pliant arm thy glassy wave?
> The captive linnet which enthrall?
> What idle progeny succeed
> To chase the rolling circle's speed,
> Or urge the flying ball?

In William Wordsworth's famed attack on the neoclassic doctrine of a special language for poetry, in his preface of 1800 to *Lyrical Ballads*, he claimed that there is no "*essential* difference between the language of prose and metrical composition"; decried the poetic diction of eighteenth-century writers as "artificial," "vicious," and "unnatural"; set up as the criterion for a valid poetic language that it be, not a matter of artful contrivance, but the "spontaneous overflow of powerful feelings"; and, by a drastic reversal of the class hierarchy of linguistic decorum, claimed that the best model for the natural expression of feeling is not an idealized version of upper-class speech, but the actual speech of "humble and rustic life."

See Thomas Quayle, *Poetic Diction: A Study of Eighteenth-Century Verse* (1924); Geoffrey Tillotson, "Eighteenth-Century Poetic Diction" (1942), reprinted in *Eighteenth-Century English Literature*, ed. James L. Clifford (1959); J. Arthos, *The Language of Natural Description in Eighteenth-Century Poetry* (1949); M. H. Abrams, "Wordsworth and Coleridge on Diction and Figures," in *The Correspondent Breeze* (1984). For general treatments of the diverse vocabularies of poets, refer to Owen Barfield, *Poetic Diction* (rev. 1973), and Winifred Novotny, *The Language Poets Use* (1962). For references to *poetic diction* in other entries, see pages *15, 75, 350.*

**poetic drama: 84.**

**poetic justice:** Poetic justice was a term coined by Thomas Rymer, an English critic of the later seventeenth century, to signify the distribution, at the end of a literary work, of earthly rewards and punishments in proportion to the virtue or vice of the various characters. Rymer's view was that a poem (in a sense that includes dramatic tragedy) is an ideal realm of its own, and should be governed by ideal principles of *decorum* and morality and not by the random way things often work out in the actual world. No important critics or literary writers since Rymer's day have acceded, in any but a highly qualified way, to his rigid recommendation of poetic justice; it would, for example, destroy the possibility of tragic suffering, which exceeds what the protagonist has deserved because of his or her *tragic flaw*, or error of judgment.

See Introduction to *The Critical Works of Thomas Rymer*, ed. Curt A. Zimansky (1956); M. A. Quinlan, *Poetic Justice in the Drama* (1912); Martha C. Nussbaum, *Poetic Justice: The Literary Imagination and Public Life* (1995).

**poetic license:** John Dryden in the late seventeenth century defined poetic license as "the liberty which poets have assumed to themselves, in all ages, of speaking things in verse which are beyond the severity of prose." In its most common use the term is confined to *poetic diction* alone, to justify the poet's departure from the rules and conventions of standard spoken and written prose in matters such as syntax, word order, the use of archaic or newly coined words, and the conventional use of *eye-rhymes* (wind-bind, daughter-laughter). The degree and kinds of linguistic freedom assumed by poets have varied according to the conventions of each age, but in every case the justification of the freedom lies in the success of the effect. The sustained opening sentence of Milton's *Paradise Lost* (1667), for example, departs radically, but with eminent success, from the colloquial language of his time in the choice and order of words, in idiom and figurative construction, and in syntax, to achieve a distinction of language and grandeur of announcement commensurate with Milton's high subject and the tradition of the epic form.

In a broader sense "poetic license" is applied not only to diction, but to all the ways in which poets and other literary authors are held to be free to violate, for special effects, the ordinary norms not only of common discourse but also of literal and historical truth, including the devices of meter and rhyme, the recourse to literary *conventions*, and the representation of fictional characters and events. In *1 Henry IV*, for example, Shakespeare follows Samuel Daniel's history in verse of the Wars of the Roses by making the valiant Hotspur much younger than he was in fact, in order to serve as a more effective *foil* to the apparently dissolute Prince Hal. A special case is **anachronism**—the placing of an event or person or thing outside of its historical era. Shakespeare described his Cleopatra as wearing Elizabethan corsets; and in *Julius Caesar*, which is set in ancient Rome, he introduced a clock that strikes the hour. The term "poetic license" is sometimes extended to a poet's violation of fact from ignorance, as well as by design. It need not diminish our enjoyment of the work that Shakespeare attributed a seacoast to landlocked Bohemia in *The Winter's Tale*, or that Keats, in writing "On First Looking into Chapman's Homer" (1816), mistakenly made Cortez instead of Balboa the discoverer of the Pacific Ocean.

See Geoffrey N. Leech, A *Linguistic Guide to English Poetry* (1969), chapter 3, "Varieties of Poetic License." For the view by *Russian Formalists* that varieties of poetic license are used to freshen our perceptions both of literary language and of the world it represents, see Victor Erlich, *Russian Formalism* (1965).

**poetry happenings: 243**.

**poetry slam: 243**.

**point of view:** Point of view signifies the way a story gets told—the mode (or modes) established by an author by means of which the reader is presented with the characters, dialogue, actions, setting, and events which constitute the *narrative* in a work of fiction. The question of point of view has always been a practical concern of the novelist, and there have been scattered observations on the matter in critical writings since the emergence of the modern *novel* in the eighteenth century. Henry James' prefaces to his various novels, however—collected as *The Art of the Novel* in 1934—and Percy Lubbock's *The Craft of Fiction* (1926), which codified and expanded upon James' comments, made point of view one of the most prominent and persistent concerns in modern treatments of the art of prose fiction.

Authors have developed many different ways to present a story, and many single works exhibit a diversity of methods. The simplified classification below, however, is widely recognized and can serve as a preliminary frame of reference for analyzing traditional types of narration and for determining the predominant type in mixed narrative modes. It deals first with by far the most widely used modes, first-person and third-person narration. It establishes a broad distinction between these two modes, then divides third-person narratives into subclasses according to the degree and kind of freedom or limitation which the author assumes in getting the story across to the reader. It then goes on to deal briefly with the rarely used mode of second-person narration.

In a **third-person narrative**, the **narrator** is someone outside the story proper who refers to all the characters in the story by name, or as "he," "she," "they." Thus Jane Austen's *Emma* begins: "Emma Woodhouse, handsome, clever, and rich, with a comfortable home and happy disposition, seemed to unite some of the best blessings of existence; and had lived nearly twenty-one years in the world with very little to distress or vex her." In a **first-person narrative**, the narrator speaks as "I," and is to a greater or lesser degree a participant in the story, or else is the *protagonist* of the story. J. D. Salinger's *The Catcher in the Rye* (1951), an instance of the latter type, begins: "If you really want to hear about it, the first thing you'll really want to know is where I was born, and what my lousy childhood was like, and how my parents were occupied and all before they had me, and all that David Copperfield kind of crap. . . ."

I.    **Third-person points of view**

A.    **The omniscient point of view.** This is a common term for the many and varied works of fiction written in accord with the *convention* that the narrator knows everything that needs to be known about the agents, actions, and events, and has privileged access to the characters' thoughts, feelings, and motives; also that the narrator is free to move at will in time and place, to shift from character to character, and to report (or conceal) their speech, doings, and states of consciousness.

Within this mode, the **intrusive narrator** is one who not only reports, but also comments on and evaluates the actions and motives of the characters, and sometimes expresses personal views about human life. Most works are written according to the convention that the omniscient narrator's reports and judgments are to be taken as **authoritative** by the reader, and so serve to establish what counts as the true facts and values within the fictional

world. This is the fashion in which many of the greatest novelists have written, including Henry Fielding, Jane Austen, Charles Dickens, William
Makepeace Thackeray, George Eliot, Thomas Hardy, Fyodor Dostoevsky,
and Leo Tolstoy. (In Fielding's *Tom Jones* and Tolstoy's *War and Peace*,
1869, the intrusive narrator goes so far as to interpolate commentary, or
short essays suggested by the subject matter of the novels.) On the other
hand, the omniscient narrator may choose to be **unintrusive** (alternative
terms are **impersonal** or **objective**). Flaubert in *Madame Bovary* (1857),
for example, for the most part describes, reports, or "shows" the action in
dramatic scenes without introducing his own comments or judgments.
More radical instances of the unintrusive narrator, who gives up even the
privilege of access to inner feelings and motives, are to be found in a number of Ernest Hemingway's short stories; for example, "The Killers" and "A
Clean, Well-Lighted Place." (See *showing and telling*, under *character*.) For an
extreme use of impersonal representation, see the comment on Robbe-
Grillet's *Jealousy*, under *novel*.

Gérard Genette subtilized in various ways the analysis of third-person
point of view. For example, he distinguishes between **focus of narration**
(who tells the story) and **focus of character** (who perceives what is narrated
in one or another section of the story). In Henry James' *What Maisie Knew*,
for example, the focus of narration is an adult who tells the story, but his
focus is on events as they are perceived and interpreted by the character
Maisie, a child. Both the focus of narration and the focus of character (that
is, of perception) in a single story may shift rapidly from the narrator to a
character in the story, and from one character to another. In *To the
Lighthouse*, Virginia Woolf shifts the focus of character in turn to each of the
principal participants in the story; and Hemingway's *short story*, "The Short
Happy Life of Francis Macomber," is a third-person narrative in which the
focus of perception is, in various passages, the narrator, the hunter Wilson,
Mrs. Macomber, Mr. Macomber, and even, briefly, the hunted lion. See
Gérard Genette, *Narrative Discourse: An Essay in Method* (1972, trans. 1980).
For an analysis of the grammatical shift in pronouns, indicators of time and
place, and the tenses of verbs as the focus and the mode of narration shifts
within a story, see *free indirect discourse*, under *narration, grammar of*.

B. **The limited point of view.** The narrator tells the story in the third person,
but stays inside the confines of what is perceived, thought, remembered, and
felt by a single character (or at most by very few characters) within the story.
Henry James, who refined this narrative mode, described such a selected
character as his "focus," or "mirror," or "center of consciousness." In a
number of James' later works all the events and actions are represented as
they unfold before, and filter to the reader through, the particular perceptions, awareness, and responses of only one character; for example, Strether
in *The Ambassadors* (1903). A short and artfully sustained example of this limited point of view in narration is Katherine Mansfield's story "Bliss" (1920).
Later writers developed this technique into *stream-of-consciousness* narration, in
which we are presented with outer perceptions only as they impinge on the

continuous current of thought, memory, feelings, and associations which constitute a particular observer's total awareness. The limitation of point of view represented both by James' "center of consciousness" narration and by the "stream-of-consciousness" narration sometimes used by James Joyce, Virginia Woolf, William Faulkner, and others, is often said to exemplify the "self-effacing author," or "objective narration," more effectively than does the use of an unintrusive but omniscient narrator. In the latter instance, it is said, the reader remains aware that someone, or some outside voice, is telling us about what is going on; the alternative mode, in which the point of view is limited to the consciousness of a character within the story itself, gives readers the illusion of experiencing events that evolve before their own eyes. For a revealing analysis, however, of the way even an author who restricts the narrative center of consciousness to a single character nonetheless communicates authorial judgments on people and events, and also controls the judgments evoked from the reader, see Ian Watt, "The First Paragraph of *The Ambassadors:* An Explication," reprinted in David Lodge, ed., *Twentieth Century Literary Criticism: A Reader* (1972). See also *persona, tone, and voice.*

II.  **First-person points of view**

This mode, insofar as it is consistently carried out, limits the matter of the narrative to what the first-person narrator knows, experiences, infers, or finds out by talking to other characters. We distinguish between the narrative "I" who is only a fortuitous witness and auditor of the matters he relates (Marlow in *Heart of Darkness* and other works by Joseph Conrad); or who is a participant, but only a minor or peripheral one, in the story (Ishmael in Herman Melville's *Moby-Dick* , Nick in F. Scott Fitzgerald's *The Great Gatsby*); or who is himself or herself the central character in the story (Daniel Defoe's *Moll Flanders*, Charlotte Brontë's *Jane Eyre* and *Villette*, Charles Dickens' *Great Expectations*, Mark Twain's *The Adventures of Huckleberry Finn*, J. D. Salinger's *The Catcher in the Rye*). Ralph Ellison's *Invisible Man* manifests a complex narrative mode in which the protagonist is the first-person narrator, whose *focus of character* is on the perceptions of a third party—white America—to whose eyes the protagonist, because he is black, is "invisible." For a special type of first-person narrative, see *epistolary novel*, under *novel*.

III.  **Second-person points of view**

This name has been given to a mode in which the story gets told solely, or at least primarily, as an address by the narrator to someone he calls by the second-person pronoun "you," who is represented as experiencing that which is narrated. This form of narration occurred in occasional passages of traditional fiction, but has been exploited in a sustained way only since the latter part of the twentieth century and then only rarely; the effect is of a virtuoso performance. The French novelist Michel Butor in *La Modification* (1957, trans. as *Second Thoughts* in 1981), the Italian novelist Italo Calvino in *If on a Winter's Night a Traveler* (trans. 1981), and the American novelist Jay McInerney in *Bright Lights, Big City* (1984), all tell their story with "you" as the *narratee*. McInerney's *Bright Lights, Big City*, for example, begins:

You are not the kind of guy who would be at a place like this at this time of the morning. But here you are, and you cannot say that the terrain is entirely unfamiliar, though the details are fuzzy. You are at a nightclub talking to a girl with a shaved head. The club is either Heartbreak or the Lizard Lounge.

This second person may turn out to be a specific fictional character, or the reader of the story, or even the narrator himself or herself, or not clearly or consistently the one or the other; and the story may unfold by shifting between telling the narratee what he or she is now doing, has done in the past, or will or is commanded to do in the future. Italo Calvino uses the form to achieve a complex and comic form of *involuted fiction*, by involving "you," the reader, in the fabrication of the narrative itself. His novel opens:

You are about to begin reading Italo Calvino's new novel, *If on a winter's night a traveler*. Relax. Concentrate. . . . Best to close the door, the TV is always on in the next room. Tell the others right away, "No, I don't want to watch TV!" . . . Or if you prefer, don't say anything; just hope they'll leave you alone.

Refer to Bruce Morrissette, "Narrative 'You' in Contemporary Literature," *Comparative Literature Studies*, Vol. 2 (1965); Brian Richardson; "The Poetics and Politics of Second-Person Narrative," *Genre*, Vol. 24 (1991); Monika Fludernick, "Second-Person Narrative as a Test Case for Narratology," *Style*, Vol. 28 (1994); and "Second-Person Narrative: A Bibliography," *Style*, Vol. 28 (1994).

Two other frequently discussed narrative tactics are relevant to a consideration of points of view:

The **self-conscious narrator** shatters any illusion that he or she is telling something that has actually happened by revealing to the reader that the narration is a work of fictional art, or by flaunting the discrepancies between its patent fictionality and the reality it seems to represent. This can be done either seriously (Henry Fielding's narrator in *Tom Jones* and Marcel in Marcel Proust's *Remembrance of Things Past*, 1913–27) or for primarily comic purposes (Tristram in Laurence Sterne's *Tristram Shandy*, 1759–67, and the narrator of Lord Byron's versified *Don Juan*, 1819–24), or for purposes which are both serious and comic (Thomas Carlyle's *Sartor Resartus*, 1833–34). See Robert Alter, *Partial Magic: The Novel as a Self-Conscious Genre* (1975), and refer to *romantic irony*, under the entry *irony*.

One variety of self-conscious narrative exploited in recent prose fiction is called the **self-reflexive novel**, or the *involuted novel*, which incorporates into its narration reference to the process of composing the fictional story itself. An early modern version, André Gide's *The Counterfeiters* (1926), is also one of the most intricate. As the critic Harry Levin summarized its self-involution: it is "the diary of a novelist who is writing a novel [to be called *The Counterfeiters*] about a novelist who is keeping a diary about the novel he is writing"; the nest of Chinese boxes was further multiplied by Gide's publication, also in 1926, of his own *Journal of The Counterfeiters*, kept while he was composing the novel. Vladimir Nabokov is an ingenious exploiter of involuted fiction; for example, in *Pale Fire* (1962). See *metafiction* under the entry *novel*.

We ordinarily accept what a narrator tells us as authoritative. The **fallible** or **unreliable narrator**, on the other hand, is one whose perception, interpretation, and evaluation of the matters he or she narrates do not coincide with the opinions and norms implied by the author, which the author expects the alert reader to share. (See the commentary on reliable and unreliable narrators in Wayne C. Booth, *The Rhetoric of Fiction*, rev. 1983.) Henry James made repeated use of the narrator whose excessive innocence, or oversophistication, or moral obtuseness, makes him a flawed and distorting "center of consciousness" in the work; the result is an elaborate structure of ironies. (See *irony*.) Examples of James' use of a fallible narrator are his short stories "The Aspern Papers" and "The Liar." *The Sacred Fount* and *The Turn of the Screw* are works by James in which, according to some critics, the clues for correcting the views of the fallible narrator are inadequate, so that what we are meant to take as factual within the story, and the evaluations intended by the author, remain problematic. See, for example, the remarkably diverse critical interpretations collected in A *Casebook on Henry James' "The Turn of the Screw,"* ed. Gerald Willen (1960), and in *The Turn of the Screw* (2d ed.) ed. Deborah Esch and Jonathan Warren (1999). The critic Tzvetan Todorov, on the other hand, has classified *The Turn of the Screw* as an instance of **fantastic literature**, which he defines as deliberately designed by the author to leave the reader in a state of uncertainty whether the events are to be explained by reference to natural causes (as hallucinations caused by the protagonist's repressed sexuality) or to supernatural causes. See Todorov's *The Fantastic: A Structural Approach to a Literary Genre* (trans. Richard Howard, 1973); also Eric S. Rabkin, *The Fantastic in Literature* (1976).

Drastic experimentation in recent prose fiction has complicated in many ways traditional renderings of point of view, not only in second-person, but also in first- and third-person narratives; see *fiction; persona, tone, and voice*; and *postmodernism*. On point of view, in addition to the writings mentioned above, refer to Norman Friedman, "Point of View in Fiction," *PMLA*, Vol. 70 (1955); Leon Edel, *The Modern Psychological Novel* (rev. 1964), chapters 3–4; Wayne C. Booth, *The Rhetoric of Fiction* (rev. 1983); Franz Stanzel, *A Theory of Narrative* (1979, trans. 1984); Susan Lanser, *The Narrative Act: Point of View in Fiction* (1981); Wallace Martin, *Recent Theories of Narrative* (1986). For references to *point of view* in other entries, see pages *57, 82, 209, 228, 231, 259*.

**positivism: 379**.

**postcolonial studies.** The critical analysis of the history, culture, literature, and modes of discourse that are specific to the former colonies of England, Spain, France, and other European imperial powers. These studies have focused especially on the Third World countries in Africa, Asia, the Caribbean islands, and South America. Some scholars, however, extend the scope of such analyses also to the discourse and cultural productions of countries such as Australia, Canada, and New Zealand, which achieved independence much earlier than the Third World countries. Postcolonial studies sometimes also encompass aspects of British literature in the eighteenth and nineteenth centuries, viewed through a perspective that reveals the ways in which the social and economic life represented in that literature was tacitly underwritten by colonial exploitation.

An important text in establishing the theory and practice in this field of study was *Orientalism* (1978) by the Palestinian-American scholar Edward Said, which applied a revised form of Michel Foucault's historicist critique of discourse (see under *new historicism*) to analyze what he called "cultural imperialism." This mode of imperialism imposed its power not by force, but by the effective means of disseminating in subjugated colonies a Eurocentric *discourse* that assumed the normality and pre-eminence of everything "occidental," correlatively with its representations of the "oriental" as an exotic and inferior other. The term **orientalism** is now sometimes applied to cultural imperialism by means of the control of discourse, not only in the orient, but anywhere in the world.

Since the 1980s, such analysis has been supplemented by other theoretical principles and procedures, including Althusser's redefinition of the Marxist theory of *ideology* and the *deconstructive* theory of Derrida. The rapidly expanding field of postcolonial studies, as a result, is not a unified movement with a distinctive methodology. One can, however, identify several central and recurrent issues:

1. The rejection of the "master narrative" of Western imperialism—in which the colonial "other" is not only subordinated and marginalized, but in effect deleted as a cultural agency—and its replacement by a counter-narrative in which the colonial cultures fight their way back into a world history written by Europeans. In the influential book *The Empire Writes Back: Theory and Practice in Post-Colonial Literatures* (2d ed., 2002), Bill Ashcroft, Gareth Griffiths, and Helen Tiffin stress what they term the **hybridization** of colonial languages and cultures, in which imperialist importations are superimposed on indigenous traditions; they also draw attention to a number of postcolonial countertexts to the *hegemonic* texts that present a Eurocentric version of colonial history.

2. An abiding concern with the construction, within Western discursive practices, of the colonial and postcolonial "subject," as well as of the categories by means of which this subject conceives itself and perceives the world within which it lives and acts. (See *social constructs* and *subject*, under *poststructuralism*.) The **subaltern** has become a standard way to designate the colonial subject that has been constructed by European discourse and internalized by colonial peoples who employ this discourse; "subaltern" is a British word for someone of

inferior military rank, and combines the Latin terms for "under" *(sub)* and "other" *(alter)*. A recurrent topic of debate is how, and to what extent, a subaltern subject, writing in a European language, can manage to serve as an agent of resistance against, rather than of compliance with, the very discourse that has created its subordinate identity. See, for example, Gayatri Chakravorty Spivak, "Can the Subaltern Speak?" (1988), reprinted in *The Postcolonial Studies Reader*, listed below.

3. A major element in the postcolonial agenda is to disestablish Eurocentric norms of literary and artistic values, and to expand the literary *canon* to include colonial and postcolonial writers. In the United States and Britain, there is an increasingly successful movement to include, in the standard academic curricula, the brilliant and innovative novels, poems, and plays by such postcolonial writers in the English language as the Africans Chinua Achebe and Wole Soyinka, the Caribbean islanders V. S. Naipaul and Derek Walcott, and the authors from the Indian subcontinent G. V. Desani and Salman Rushdie. Compare *ethnic writers* under *periods of American literature*, and see Homi Bhabha, *The Location of Culture* (1994). For a survey of the large and growing body of *anglophone* literature by postcolonial writers throughout the world, see Martin Coyle and others, *Encyclopedia of Literature and Criticism* (1990), pp. 1113–1236; and Gaurav Desai and Supriya Nair, *Postcolonialisms: An Anthology of Cultural Theory and Criticism* (2005).

Postcolonial scholarship also studies forms of imperialism other than European, including the domination of some southern-hemisphere groups or nations by other southern-hemisphere groups or nations. This rethinking of empire has brought the United States into focus as an object of postcolonial scholarship, both as a contemporary empire and as itself a postcolonial nation. See Amy Kaplan and Donald E. Pease, eds., *Cultures of United States Imperialism* (1993). In recent years, scholars in postcolonial studies have turned their attention to identities in a globalized world where large groups of people have, for various reasons, left their homelands, producing diasporas, population flows, and émigré groups. See Rey Chow, *Writing Diaspora: Tactics of Intervention in Contemporary Cultural Studies* (1993) and *The Protestant Ethnic and the Spirit of Capitalism* (2002); and Arjun Appadurai, *Modernity at Large: Cultural Dimensions of Globalization* (1996).

Comprehensive anthologies: Henry Schwarz and Sangeeta Ray, eds., *A Companion to Postcolonial Studies* (2000); and David Theo Goldberg and Ato Quayson, eds., *Relocating Postcolonialism* (2002). In addition to titles listed above, refer also to Frantz Fanon, *The Wretched of the Earth* (trans. 1963), and *Black Skin, White Masks* (trans. 1967); Gayatri Chakravorty Spivak, *In Other Worlds* (1987), and Ranajit Guha and Gayatri Chakravorty Spivak, eds., *Selected Subaltern Studies* (1988); Christopher L. Miller, *Theories of Africans: Francophone Literature and Anthropology in Africa* (1990); Homi K. Bhabha, ed., *Nation and Narration* (1990); Aijaz Ahmad, *In Theory: Classes, Nations, Literatures* (1992); Edward W. Said, *Culture and Imperialism* (1993); Chris Weedon, *Feminist Practice and Poststructuralist Theory* (2d ed., 1997); Robert J. C. Young, *Postcolonialism: An Historical Introduction* (2001); and Neil Lazarus, ed., *The Cambridge Companion to Postcolonial Literary Studies* (2004).

Anne McClintock, Aamir Mufti, Ella Shohat, eds., *Dangerous Liaisons: Gender, Nation, and Postcolonial Perspectives* (1997), stresses the convergence of postcolonial studies and *feminism*. Much postcolonial inquiry takes its point of departure from theories of nationalism; often cited are Benedict Anderson, *Imagined Communities: Reflections on the Origin and Spread of Nationalism* (rev. 1991), and Partha Chatterjee, *Nationalist Thought and the Colonial World* (1993). See also *Interventions: International Journal of Postcolonial Studies*. For references to *postcolonial studies* in other entries, see pages *95, 257*.

**post-Marxism:** 185.

**postmodern period:** 257.

**postmodernism:** 203; *319*.

**poststructuralism:** Poststructuralism designates a broad variety of critical perspectives and procedures that in the 1970s displaced structuralism from its prominence as the radically innovative way of dealing with language and other signifying systems. A conspicuous announcement to American scholars of the poststructural point of view was Jacques Derrida's paper on "Structure, Sign and Play in the Discourse of the Human Sciences," delivered in 1966 to an International Colloquium at Johns Hopkins University. (The paper is included in Derrida's *Writing and Difference*, 1978.) Derrida attacked the systematic, quasi-scientific pretensions of the strict form of structuralism—derived from Saussure's concept of the structure of language and represented by the cultural anthropologist Claude Lévi-Strauss—by asserting that the notion of a systemic structure, whether linguistic or other, presupposes a fixed "center" that serves to organize and regulate the structure yet itself "escapes structurality." In Saussure's theory of language, for example, this center is assigned the function of controlling the endless differential play of internal relationships, while remaining itself outside of, and immune from, that play. (See *structuralism*.) As Derrida's other writings made clear, he regarded this incoherent and unrealizable notion of an ever-active yet always absent center as only one of the many ways in which all of Western thinking is "logocentric" or dependent on the notion of a self-certifying foundation, or absolute, or essence, or ground, which is ever-needed but never present. (See *deconstruction*.)

Other contemporary thinkers, including Michel Foucault, Jacques Lacan, and (in his later phase) Roland Barthes, although in diverse ways, also undertook to "decenter" or "undermine" or "subvert" traditional claims for the existence of self-evident foundations that guarantee the validity of all knowledge and truth, and establish the possibility of determinate communication. This **antifoundationalism** in philosophy, conjoined with skepticism about traditional conceptions of meaning, knowledge, truth, value, and the subject or "self," is evident in some (although not all) current exponents of diverse modes of literary studies, including *feminist, new historicist*, and *reader-response* criticism. In its extreme forms, the poststructural claim is that the workings of language inescapably undermine meanings in the very process of making such meanings possible, or else that every mode of discourse "constructs," or constitutes, the very facts or truths or knowledge that it claims to discover.

"Postmodern" is sometimes used in place of, or interchangeably with, "poststructural." It is more useful, however, to follow the example of those who apply "postmodern" to developments in literature and other arts, and reserve "poststructural" for theories of criticism and of intellectual inquiries in general. (See *modernism and postmodernism*.)

Salient features or themes that are shared by diverse types of poststructural thought and criticism include the following:

1. The primacy of theory. Since Plato and Aristotle, discourse about poetry or literature has involved a "theory," in the traditional sense of a conceptual scheme, or set of principles, distinctions, and categories—sometimes explicit, but often only implied in critical practice—for identifying, classifying, analyzing, and evaluating works of literature. (See *criticism*.) In poststructural criticism what is called "theory" came to be foregrounded, so that many critics felt it incumbent to "theorize" their individual positions and practices. The nature of theory, however, was conceived in a new and very inclusive way; for the word **theory**, standing without qualification, often designated an account of the general conditions of signification that determine meaning and interpretation in all domains of human action, production, and intellection. In most cases, this account was held to apply not only to verbal language, but also to psychosexual and sociocultural signifying systems. As a consequence, the pursuit of literary criticism was conceived to be integral with all the other pursuits traditionally classified as the "human sciences," and to be inseparable from consideration of the general nature of human "subjectivity," and also from reference to all forms of social and cultural phenomena. Often the theory of signification was granted primacy in the additional sense that, when common experience in the use or interpretation of language does not accord with what the theory entails, such experience is rejected as unjustified and illusory, or else is accounted an ideologically imposed concealment of the actual operation of the signifying system.

   A prominent aspect of poststructural theories is that they are posed in opposition to inherited ways of thinking in all provinces of knowledge. That is, they expressly "challenge" and undertake to "destabilize," and in many instances to "undermine" and "subvert," what they identify as the foundational assumptions, concepts, procedures, and findings in traditional modes of discourse in Western civilization (including literary criticism). In a number of politically oriented critics, this questioning of established ways of thinking and of formulating knowledge is joined to an adversarial stance toward the established institutions, class structures, and practices of economic and political power and social organization.

2. The decentering of the **subject**. The oppositional stance of many poststructural critics is manifested in a sharp critique of what they call "humanism"; that is, of the traditional view that the human being or human author is a coherent identity, endowed with purpose and initiative, whose design and intentions effectuate the form and meaning of a literary or other product. (See *humanism*.) For such traditional terms as "human being" or "individual" or "self" poststructuralists

tend to substitute "subject," because this word is divested of the connotation that it has originating or controlling power, and instead suggests that the human being is "subjected to" the play of external forces; and also because the word suggests the grammatical term, the "subject" of a sentence, which is an empty slot, to be filled by whoever happens to be speaking at a particular time and place. *Structuralism* had already tended to divest the subject of operative initiative and control, evacuating the purposive human agent into a mere location, or "space," wherein the differential elements and codes of a systematic *langue* precipitate into a particular *parole*, or signifying product. Derrida, however, by deleting the structural linguistic "center," had thereby also eliminated the possibility of a controlling agency in language, leaving the use of language an unregulatable and undecidable play of purely relational elements. In the view of many deconstructive critics, the subject or author or narrator of a text becomes itself a purely linguistic product—as Paul DeMan has put it in *Allegories of Reading* (1979), we "rightfully reduce" the subject "to the status of a mere grammatical pronoun." Alternatively, the subject–author is granted at most the function of trying (although always vainly) to "master" the incessant freeplay of the decentered signifiers. For a collection of essays on "the subject" in writings on politics, philosophy, psychoanalysis, and history, see Eduardo Cadava, Peter Connor, Jean-Luc Nancy, eds., *Who Comes After the Subject?* (1991).

Michel Foucault and Roland Barthes both signalized this evacuation of the traditional conception of the author by announcing the "disappearance of the author," or even more melodramatically, "the **death of the author**." (Foucault, "What Is an Author," 1969, in *Language, Counter-Memory, Practice*, 1977; Barthes, "The Death of the Author," 1968, in *Image, Music, Text*, 1977.) They did not mean to deny that a human individual is a necessary link in the chain of events that results in a parole or text. What they denied was the validity of the "function," or "role" hitherto assigned in Western discourse to a uniquely individual and purposive author, who is conceived as the "cogito," or origin of all knowledge; as the initiator, purposive planner, and (by his or her intentions) the determiner of the form and meanings of a text; and as the "center," or organizing principle, of the matters treated in traditional literary criticism and literary history. In addition, a number of current forms of *psychoanalytic, Marxist*, and *new historicist* criticism manifest a similar tendency to decenter, and in extreme cases to delete, what is often called the "agency" of the author as a self-coherent, purposive, and determinative human being. Instead, the human agent is said to be a disunified subject that is the product of diverse psychosexual conditions, and subjected to the uncontrollable workings of unconscious compulsions. Alternatively, the subject is held to be no more than a "construction" by current forms of ideology; or a "site" traversed by the *cultural constructs* and the *discursive formations* engendered by the conceptual and power configurations in a given era. (See *author and authorship*.)

3. Reading, texts, and writing. The decentering or deletion of the author leaves the reader, or interpreter, as the focal figure in poststructural accounts of signifying practices. This figure, however, like the author, is stripped of the traditional attributes of purposiveness and initiative and converted into an impersonal process

called "reading." What this reading engages is no longer called a literary "work" (since this traditional term implies a purposive human maker of the product); instead, reading engages a "text"—that is, a structure of signifiers regarded merely as a given for the reading process. Texts in their turn (especially in deconstructive criticism) lose their individuality, and are often represented as manifestations of *écriture*—that is, of an all-inclusive "textuality," or writing-in-general, in which the traditional "boundaries" between literary, philosophical, historical, legal, and other classes of texts are considered to be both artificial and superficial. See *text and writing (écriture)*.

A distinctive poststructural view is that no text can mean what it seems to say. To a deconstructive critic, for example, a text is a chain of signifiers whose seeming determinacy of meaning, and seeming reference to an extra-textual world, are no more than "effects" produced by the differential play of conflicting internal forces which, on closer analysis, turn out to deconstruct the text into an undecidable scatter of opposed significations. In the representation of Roland Barthes, the "death" of the author frees the reader to enter the literary text in whatever way he or she chooses, and the intensity of pleasure yielded by the text becomes proportionate to the reader's abandonment of limits on its signifying possibilities. In Stanley Fish's version of *reader-response criticism*, all the meanings and formal features seemingly found in a text are projected into the printed marks by each individual reader; any agreement about meaning between two individuals is contingent upon their happening to belong to a single one among many diverse "interpretive communities."

4. The concept of discourse. Literary critics had long made casual use of the term "discourse," especially in application to passages representing conversations between characters in a literary work, and in the 1970s there developed a critical practice called *discourse analysis* which focuses on such conversational exchanges. This type of criticism (as well as the *dialogic criticism* inaugurated by Mikhail Bakhtin) deals with literary discourse as conducted by human characters whose voices engage in a dynamic interchange of beliefs, attitudes, sentiments, and other expressions of states of consciousness.

In poststructural criticism, **discourse** has become a very prominent term, supplementing (and in some cases displacing) "text" as the name for the verbal material which is the primary concern of literary criticism. In poststructural usage, however, the term is not confined to conversational passages but, like "writing," designates all verbal constructions and implies the superficiality of the boundaries between literary and nonliterary modes of signification. Most conspicuously, discourse has become the focal term among critics who oppose the deconstructive concept of a "general text" that functions independently of particular historical conditions. Instead, they conceive of discourse as social parlance, or language-in-use, and consider it to be both the product and manifestation not of a timeless linguistic system, but of particular social conditions, class structures, and power relationships that alter drastically in the course of history. In Michel Foucault, discourse-as-such is the central subject of analytic concern. Foucault conceives that "discourse" is to be analyzed as totally anonymous, in that it is simply "situated at the level of the 'it is said' *(on dit).*" (*The Archaeology* *of Knowledge*, 1972, pp. 55, 122.) For example, *new historicists* (for whom, in this respect, Foucault serves as a model) may attend to all Renaissance references to usury as part of an anonymous "discourse," which circulates through legal, religious, philosophical, and economic writings of the era; it circulates also through those literary writings, such as Shakespeare's sonnets or *The Merchant of Venice*, in which usury is alluded to, whether literally or figuratively. Any allusion to usury is conceived to be better understood if it is referred to the total body of discourse on that topic, as well as to the social forces and institutions that have produced the conception of usury at that time and in that place.

5. Many socially oriented analysts of discourse share with other poststructuralists the conviction (or at any rate the strong suspicion) that no text means what it seems to say, or what its writer intended to say. But whereas deconstructive critics attribute the subversion of the apparent meaning to the unstable and self-conflicting nature of language itself, social analysts of discourse—and also *psychoanalytic critics*—view the surface, or "manifest" meanings of a text as a disguise, or substitution, for underlying meanings which cannot be overtly said, because they are suppressed by psychic, or ideological, or discursive necessities. By some critics, the covert meanings are regarded as having been suppressed by all three of these forces together. Both the social and psychoanalytic critics of discourse therefore interpret the manifest meanings of a text as a distortion, displacement, or total "occlusion" of its real meanings; and these real meanings, in accordance with the critic's theoretical orientation, turn out to be either the writer's psychic and psycholinguistic compulsions, or the material realities of history, or the social power structures of domination, subordination, and marginalization that obtained when the text was written. The widespread poststructural view that the surface or overt meanings of a literary or other text serve as a "disguise" or "mask" of its real meanings, or **subtext**, has been called, in a phrase taken from the French philosopher of language Paul Ricoeur, a **hermeneutics of suspicion**.

6. Many poststructural theorists propose or assume an extreme form of both cognitive and evaluative relativism. The claim is that, in the absence of an absolute and atemporal standard or foundation or center, all asserted truths and values are relative to the predominant culture at a given time and place; or to a particular economic, social, ethnic, or interpretive class; or to the psychic configuration of a particular individual or type of individuals. Such a general relativism is affirmed even by some theorists who are also political activists, and advocate (by explicit or implicit appeal to social justice as a fundamental value) emancipation and equality for sexual, racial, ethnic, or other oppressed, marginalized, or excluded minorities.

The primacy of "theory" in poststructural criticism has evoked countertheoretical challenges, most prominently in an essay "Against Theory" by Steven Knapp and Walter Benn Michaels (1982). Defining theory (in consonance with the widespread poststructural use of the term) as "the attempt to govern interpretations of particular texts by appealing to an account of interpretation in general," the two authors claim that this is an impossible endeavor "to stand outside practice in order to govern practice from without," assert that accounts of interpretation in general entail no consequences for the actual practice of interpretation, and conclude that all theory "should therefore come to an end." Such a conclusion is supported by a number of writers, including Stanley Fish and the influential philosophical pragmatist Richard Rorty, who (despite disagreements in their supporting arguments) agree that no general account of interpretation entails particular consequences for the actual practice of literary interpretation and criticism. (See W. J. T. Mitchell, ed., *Against Theory: Literary Studies and the New Pragmatism,* 1985, which includes the initiating essay plus a supplementary essay by Knapp and Michaels, together with essays and critiques by Fish, Rorty, E. D. Hirsch, and others.) The French philosopher Jean-François Lyotard has also mounted an influential attack against "theory," which he regards as an attempt to impose a common vocabulary and set of principles in order illegitimately to control and constrain the many independent "language-games" that constitute discourse; see his *The Postmodern Condition* (1984). One response to this skepticism about the efficacy of theory on practice (a skepticism that is often labeled the **new pragmatism**) is that, while no general theory of meaning entails consequences for the practice of interpretation (in the strict logical sense of "entails"), it is a matter of common observation that diverse current theories have in actual fact served both to foster and to corroborate diverse and novel interpretive practices by literary critics. (For a view of both the inescapability and practical functioning of literary and artistic theory in traditional criticism, see M. H. Abrams, "What's the Use of Theorizing about the Arts?" 1972, reprinted in *Doing Things with Texts,* 1989.)

Jonathan Culler's *Literary Theory: A Very Short Introduction* (1997) analyzes the issues and debates that cut across the boundaries of diverse poststructural theories. See also Richard Harland, *Superstructuralism: The Philosophy of Structuralism and Post-Structuralism* (1987); Anthony Easthope, *British Poststructuralism since 1968* (1988). Anthologies that include important poststructural essays and selections: David Lodge, ed., *Modern Criticism and Theory* (1988); K. M. Newton, ed., *20th-Century Literary Theory* (1988); Robert Con Davis and Ronald Schleifer, eds., *Contemporary Literary Criticism* (rev. 1989). The most inclusive collection, with extensive bibliographies, is Vincent Leitch, ed., *The Norton Anthology of Theory and Criticism* (2001). For discussions and critiques of poststructuralist theories and practices from diverse points of view: Fredric Jameson, *Poststructuralism; or The Cultural Logic of Late Capitalism* (1991); John McGowan, *Postmodernism and Its Critics* (1991); Jonathan Arac and Barbara Johnson, eds., *Consequences of Theory* (1991); Dwight Eddin, ed., *The Emperor Redressed: Critiquing Critical Theory* (1995); James Battersby, *Reason and the Nature of Texts* (1996); Wendell V. Harris, ed., *Beyond Structuralism* (1996); Daphne Patai and Will H. Corral, eds., *Theory's Empire: An Anthology of Dissent* (2005).

For references to *poststructuralism* in other entries, see pages *18, 39, 67, 77, 114, 147, 219, 249, 294, 348, 368.*

**practical criticism: 62**.

**pragmatic criticism: 63**; *211, 312.*

**Prague Linguistic Circle: 126**.

**Pre-Raphaelites:** In 1848 a group of English artists, including Dante Gabriel Rossetti, William Holman Hunt, and John Millais, organized the "Pre-Raphaelite Brotherhood." Their aim was to replace the reigning academic style of painting by a return to the truthfulness, simplicity, and spirit of devotion which they attributed to Italian painting before the time of Raphael (1483–1520) and the other painters of the high Italian *Renaissance*. The ideals of this group of painters were taken over by a literary movement which included Dante Gabriel Rossetti himself (who was a poet as well as a painter), his sister Christina Rossetti, William Morris, and Algernon Swinburne. Dante Gabriel Rossetti's poem "The Blessed Damozel" typifies the medievalism, the pictorial realism with symbolic overtones, and the union of flesh and spirit, sensuousness and religiousness, associated with the earlier writings of this school. See also Christina Rossetti's remarkable poem "Goblin Market" (1862) and William Morris' narrative in verse *The Earthly Paradise* (1868–70).

   Graham Hough, *The Last Romantics* (1949); T. J. Barringer, *Reading the Pre-Raphaelites* (1999); Jan Marsh and Pamela Gerrish Nun, *Pre-Raphaelite Women Artists* (1999); Christopher Wood, *The Pre-Raphaelites* (2d ed., 2001); Elizabeth Helsinger, *Poetry and the Pre-Raphaelite Arts: William Morris and Dante Gabriel Rossetti* (2007).

**presence** (in deconstruction): **70**.

**primitivism and progress:** A **primitivist** is someone who prefers what is "natural" (in the sense of that which exists prior to or independently of human culture, reasoning, and contrivance) to what is "artificial" (in the sense of what human beings achieve by thought, activities, laws and conventions, and the complex arrangements of a civilized society). A useful, although not mutually exclusive, distinction has been made between two manifestations of primitivism:

1. **Cultural primitivism** is the preference for what is conceived to be "nature" and "the natural" over "art" and "the artificial" in any area of human culture and values. As the intellectual historian A. O. Lovejoy has neatly summarized it, the "natural" is "a thing you reach by going back and leaving out." For example, in ethics a cultural primitivist lauds the natural (that is, the innate) instincts and passions over the dictates of reason and prudential forethought. In social philosophy, the ideal is the simple and natural forms of social and political order in place of the anxieties and frustrations engendered by a complex and highly developed social organization. In milieu, a primitivist prefers outdoor "nature," unmodified by human intervention, to cities or artful gardens. And in literature and the other arts, the primitivist lauds spontaneity, the free expression of emotion, and the intuitive productions of "natural genius," as against a calculated adaptation of artistic means to foreseen ends and a conformity to "artificial" forms, rules, and conventions. Typically, the cultural primitivist asserts that in the modern world, the life, activities, and products of "primitive" people—who are considered to live in a way more accordant to

"nature" because they are isolated from civilization—are at least in some ways preferable to the life, activities, and products of people living in a highly developed society, especially in cities. The eighteenth-century cult of the **Noble Savage**—who was conceived to be "naturally" intelligent, moral, and possessed of high dignity in thought and deed—and the concurrent vogue of "natural" poetry written by supposedly uneducated peasants or working folk, were both aspects of primitivism. Cultural primitivism has played an especially prominent and persistent role in American thought and literature, where the "new world" was early conceived in terms both of the classical *golden age* of the distant past and the Christian millennium of the future. The American Indian was sometimes identified with the legendary Noble Savage, and the American pioneer was often represented as a new Adam who had cut free from the artifice and corruptions of European civilization in order to reassume a "natural" life of freedom, innocence, and simplicity. See Henry Nash Smith, *Virgin Land* (1950), and R. W. B. Lewis, *The American Adam* (1955).

2. **Chronological primitivism** designates the belief that the ideal era of humanity's way of life lay in the very distant past, when men and women lived naturally, simply, and freely, and that the process of history has been a gradual "decline" from that happy stage into an increasing degree of artifice, complexity, inhibitions, prohibitions, and consequent anxieties and discontents in the psychological, social, and cultural realms. In its extreme form, the ideal era is postulated as having existed in "the state of nature," before social organization and civilization had even begun; more commonly, it is placed at some later stage of development, and sometimes as late as the era of classical Greece. Many, but not all, cultural primitivists are also chronological primitivists.

A historical concept that is antithetic to chronological primitivism emerged in the seventeenth century and reached its height in the nineteenth century. This is the idea of **progress**: the doctrine that—by virtue of the development and exploitation of art, science, and technology, and by the application of human rationality—the course of history represents an overall improvement in the life, morality, and happiness of human beings from early barbarity to the present stage of civilization. Sometimes it is also claimed that this historical progress of humanity will continue indefinitely, possibly to end in a final stage of social, rational, and moral perfection. (See *Enlightenment* and *utopia*.)

Primitivism is as old as humanity's recorded intellection and imaginings, and is reflected in myths of a vanished age of gold and a lost Garden of Eden. It achieved a special vogue, however, in the eighteenth century, by way of reaction to the prevailing stress on artfulness and the refinements of civilization during the *Neoclassic Period*, in a European movement in which Jean-Jacques Rousseau (1712–78) was a central figure. D. H. Lawrence (1885–1930) is a later example of a broadly primitivistic thinker, in his laudation of the spontaneous instinctual life, his belief in an ancient, vanished condition of humanity's personal and social wholeness, his high regard for "primitive" modes of life that still survive outside the bounds of sophisticated societies, and his attacks on the disintegrative effects of modern science and technology and on the economy and culture these developments have generated. There are also strains of cultural primitivism in, for example, James Fenimore Cooper's *Leather-Stocking Tales*, in Mark Twain's *Huckleberry Finn*, and in the outlook and lifestyle of dropouts and various kinds of subcultures in our own time, as well as in the establishment of communes whose ideal is a radically simplified individual and social life close to the soil. (Refer to *ecocriticism*.) But most men and women, and many writers of literature, are primitivists in some moods, longing to escape from the complexities, fever, anxieties, and "alienation" of modern civilization into what are taken to be the elemental simplicities of a lost natural life. That imagined life may be identified with the individual's own childhood, or with the prehistoric or classical or medieval past, or may be conceived as existing still in some primitive, carefree, faraway place on earth.

See H. N. Fairchild, *The Noble Savage* (1928); J. B. Bury, *The Idea of Progress* (1932); Lois Whitney, *Primitivism and the Idea of Progress* (1934); A. O. Lovejoy and George Boas, *Primitivism and Related Ideas in Antiquity* (1948); A. O. Lovejoy, *Essays in the History of Ideas* (1948); Clifford Geertz, *Local Knowledge* (1983). Marianna Torgovnick's *Gone Primitive: Savage Intellects, Modern Lives* (1990) argues that modern Western culture has been formed in dialectical opposition to presumably nonmodern or premodern cultures. Friedrich Nietzsche's *The Genealogy of Morals* (1887) and Sigmund Freud's *Civilization and Its Discontents* (1949; see *psychoanalysis*) involve aspects of cultural primitivism, in their stress on the compelling needs of the body and of the elemental human instincts, especially sexuality, which require a complex and perhaps impossible reconciliation with the repressions and inhibitions that are inescapable in a civilized society. A work of radical cultural primitivism that was influential on the rebellious youth movements of the 1960s and 1970s is Norman O. Brown's *Life Against Death* (1959); refer to *Beat writers*, and to the *contemporary period*, under *periods of American literature*.

**printing: 307.**

**problem play:** A type of drama that was popularized by the Norwegian playwright Henrik Ibsen. In problem plays, the situation faced by the protagonist is put forward by the author as a representative instance of a contemporary social problem; often the dramatist manages—by the use of a character who speaks for the author, or by the evolution of the plot, or both—to propose a solution to the problem which is at odds with prevailing opinion. The issue may be the inadequate autonomy, scope, and dignity allotted to women in the middle-class nineteenth-century family (Ibsen's *A Doll's House*, 1879); or the morality of prostitution, regarded as a typical product of the economic system in a capitalist society (George Bernard Shaw's *Mrs. Warren's Profession*, 1898); or the crisis in racial and ethnic relations in present-day America (in numerous current dramas and films). Compare *social novel*.

A subtype of the modern problem play is the **discussion play**, in which the social issue is not incorporated into a plot but expounded in the give and take of a sustained debate among the characters. See Shaw's *Getting Married*, and Act III of his *Man and Superman*; also his book on Ibsen's plays, *The Quintessence of Ibsenism* (1891).

   In a specialized application, the term **problem plays** is sometimes applied to
a group of Shakespeare's plays, also called "bitter comedies"—especially *Troilus
and Cressida, Measure for Measure*, and *All's Well That Ends Well*—which explore
ignoble aspects of human nature, and in which the resolution of the plot seems
to many readers to be problematic, in that it does not settle or solve, except su-
perficially, the moral problems raised in the play. By extension, the term came to
be applied also to other Shakespearean plays which explore the dark side of human nature, or which seem to leave unresolved the issues that arise in the course
of the action. See A. P. Rossiter, "The Problem Plays," in *Shakespeare: Modern
Essays in Criticism*, ed. Leonard F. Dean (rev. 1967).

**progress, idea of: 286**; *96.*

**proletarian novel: 230**; *334.*

**propagandist literature: 80.**

**properties** (stage): **330.**

**proscenium arch** (prōsēn′ ēŭm): **3**; *58.*

**prose:** Prose is an inclusive term for all discourse, spoken or written, which is not
   patterned into the lines either of metric verse or of free verse. (See *meter.*) It is
   possible to discriminate a great variety of nonmetric types of discourse, which
   can be placed along a spectrum according to the degree to which they exploit,
   and make prominent, modes of formal organization. At one end is the irregular,
   and only occasionally formal, prose of ordinary conversation. Distinguished written discourse, in what John Dryden called "that other harmony of prose," is no
   less an art than distinguished verse; in all literatures, in fact, artfully written prose
   seems to have developed later than written verse. As written prose gets more "literary"—whether its function is descriptive, expository, narrative, or expressive—it
   exhibits more patent, though highly diverse, modes of rhythm and other formal
   features. The prose translations of the poetic books of the Old Testament in the
   King James Bible, for example, have a repetition, balance, and contrast of clauses
   which approximate the form that in the nineteenth century was named "the prose
   poem." **Prose poems** are compact, rhythmic, and usually sonorous compositions
   which exploit the poetic resources of language for poetic ends, but are written as a
   continuous sequence of sentences without line breaks. Early examples of prose
   poems are, in French, Charles Baudelaire's *Little Poems in Prose* (1869) and
   Arthur Rimbaud's *Illuminations* (1886), and in English, excerptible passages in
   Walter Pater's prose essays, such as his famous meditation on Leonardo da
   Vinci's painting the *Mona Lisa*, in *The Renaissance* (1873). John Ashbery's *Three
   Poems* (1972) are prose poems, in that they are printed continuously, without broken lines. Farther still along the formal spectrum, we leave the domain of prose,
   by the use of line breaks and the controlled rhythms, pauses, syntactical suspen-
   sions, and cadences that identify *free verse*. At the far end of the spectrum we get
   the regular, recurrent units of weaker and stronger stressed syllables that constitute
   the meters of English verse.

See *style* (including the list of readings), and for a special form of elaborately formal prose, *euphuism*. Refer to George Saintsbury, *A History of English Prose Rhythm* (1912); George L. Trager and Henry Lee Smith, Jr., *An Outline of English Structure* (1951); Robert Adolphe, *The Rise of Modern Prose Style* (1968). E. D. Hirsch discusses the development of English prose in *The Philosophy of Composition* (1977), pp. 51–72. See also Richard A. Lanham, *Analyzing Prose* (2d ed., 2003). On the prose poem, refer to Jonathan Monroe, *A Poverty of Objects: The Prose Poem and the Politics of Genre* (1987); and David Lehman, ed., *Great American Prose Poems: From Poe to the Present* (2003). For prose forms of literature, see the references under "genre."

**prose poem:** 288.

**prose romance:** 228; *49*.

**prosody:** Prosody signifies the systematic study of **versification** in poetry; that is, the principles and practice of *meter, rhyme*, and *stanza* forms. Sometimes the term "prosody" is extended to include also the study of speech-sound patterns and effects such as *alliteration, assonance, euphony*, and *onomatopoeia*.

**prosopopoeia** (prŏsō′ pŏpē″ a): **121.**

**prospect poem:** 369.

**protagonist:** 265; *272*.

**proverbs:** 10.

**pseudostatements:** 117.

**psychoanalytic criticism:** 290; *110, 155, 161, 281, 283, 300, 373, 381*.

**psychobiography:** 292.

**psychological and psychoanalytic criticism: Psychological criticism** deals with a work of literature primarily as an expression, in an indirect and fictional form, of the state of mind and the structure of personality of the individual author. This approach emerged in the early decades of the nineteenth century, as part of the romantic replacement of earlier mimetic and pragmatic views by an *expressive* view of the nature of literature; see *criticism*. By 1827 Thomas Carlyle could say that the usual question "with the best of our own critics at present" is one "mainly of a psychological sort, to be answered by discovering and delineating the peculiar nature of the poet from his poetry." During the *Romantic Period*, we find widely practiced all three types of the critical procedures (still current today) that are based on the assumption that the details and form of a work of literature are correlated with its author's distinctive mental and emotional traits: (1) reference to the author's personality in order to explain and interpret a literary work; (2) reference to literary works in order to establish, biographically, the personality of the author; and (3) the mode of reading a literary work specifically in order to experience the distinctive subjectivity, or consciousness, of its author (see *critics of consciousness*). We even find that John Keble, in a series of Latin lectures *On the Healing Power of Poetry*—published in 1844, but delivered more than ten years earlier—proposed a thoroughgoing proto-Freudian literary theory. "Poetry," Keble claimed, "is the indirect expression . . . of some overpowering emotion, or ruling taste, or feeling, the direct indulgence whereof is somehow repressed"; this repression is imposed by the author's sentiments of "reticence" and "shame"; the conflict between the need for expression and the compulsion to repress such self-revelation is resolved by the poet's ability to give "healing relief to secret mental emotion, yet without detriment to modest reserve" by a literary "art which under certain veils and disguises . . . reveals the fervent emotions of the mind"; and this disguised mode of self-expression serves as "a safety valve, preserving men from madness." (The emergence and the varieties of romantic psychological criticism are described in M. H. Abrams, *The Mirror and the Lamp*, 1953, chapters 6 and 9.) In the present era many critics make at least passing references to the psychology of an author in discussing works of literature, with the notable exception of those whose critical premises invalidate such reference; mainly proponents of *formalism, New Criticism, structuralism, deconstruction.*

Since the 1920s, a widespread form of psychological literary criticism has come to be **psychoanalytic criticism**, whose premises and procedures were established by Sigmund Freud (1856–1939). Freud had developed the dynamic form of psychology that he called "psychoanalysis" as a procedure for the analysis and therapy of neuroses, but soon expanded it to account for many developments and practices in the history of civilization, including warfare, mythology, and religion, as well as literature and the other arts. Freud's brief comment on the workings of the artist's imagination at the end of the twenty-third lecture of his *Introduction to Psychoanalysis* (1920), supplemented by relevant passages in the other lectures in that book, set forth the theoretical framework of what is sometimes called "classical" psychoanalytic criticism. Freud proposes that *literature* and the other arts, like dreams and neurotic symptoms, consist of the imagined, or fantasied, fulfillment of wishes that are either denied by reality or are prohibited by the social standards of morality and propriety. The forbidden, mainly sexual ("libidinal") wishes come into conflict with the "censor" (the internalized representative within each individual of a society's standards of morality and propriety) and are repressed by the censor into the unconscious realm of the artist's mind, but are permitted to achieve a fantasied satisfaction in distorted forms that serve to disguise their real motives and objects from the conscious mind. The chief mechanisms that effect these disguises of unconscious wishes are (1) "condensation" (the omission of parts of the unconscious material and the fusion of several unconscious elements into a single entity); (2) "displacement" (the substitution for an unconscious object of desire by one that is acceptable to the conscious mind); and (3) "symbolism" (the representation of repressed, mainly sexual, objects of desire by nonsexual objects which resemble them or are associated with them in prior experience). The disguised fantasies that are evident to consciousness are called by Freud the **manifest content** of a dream or work of literature; the unconscious wishes that find a semblance of satisfaction in this distorted form he calls the **latent content**.

Also present in the unconscious of every individual, according to Freud, are residual traces of prior stages of psychosexual development, from earliest infancy onward, which have been outgrown, but remain as "fixations" in the unconscious of the adult. When triggered by some later event in adult life, a repressed wish is revived and motivates a fantasy, in disguised form, of a satisfaction that is modeled on the way that the wish had been gratified in infancy or early childhood. The chief enterprise of the psychoanalytic critic, in a way that parallels the enterprise of the psychoanalyst as a therapist, is to decipher the true content, and thereby to explain the emotional effects on the reader, of a literary work by translating its manifest elements into the latent, unconscious determinants that constitute their real but suppressed meanings.

Freud also asserts, however, that artists possess special abilities that differentiate them radically from the patently neurotic personality. The artistic person, for example, possesses to an especially high degree the power to **sublimate** (that is, to shift the instinctual drives from their original sexual goals to nonsexual "higher" goals, including the discipline of becoming proficient as an artist); the ability to elaborate fantasied wish fulfillments into the manifest features of a work of art in a way that conceals or deletes their merely personal elements, and so makes them capable of satisfying the unconscious desires of people other than the individual artist; and the "puzzling" ability—which Freud elsewhere says is a power of "genius" that psychoanalysis cannot explain—to mold an artistic medium into "a faithful image of the creatures of his imagination," as well as into a satisfying artistic form. The result is a fantasied wish fulfillment of a complex and artfully shaped sort that not only allows the artist to overcome, at least partially and temporarily, personal conflicts and repressions, but also makes it possible for the artist's audience "to obtain solace and consolation from their own unconscious sources of gratification which had become inaccessible" to them. Literature and art, therefore, unlike dreams and neuroses, may serve the artist as a mode of fantasy that opens "the way back to reality."

This outline of Freud's theory of art in 1920 was elaborated and refined, but not radically altered, by the later developments in his theory of mental structures, dynamics, and processes. Prominent among these developments was Freud's model of the mind as having three functional aspects: the **id** (which incorporates libidinal and other desires), the **superego** (the internalization of social standards of morality and propriety), and the **ego** (which tries as best it can to negotiate the conflicts between the insatiable demands of the id, the impossibly stringent requirements of the superego, and the limited possibilities of gratification offered by reality). Freud has himself summarized for a general audience his later theoretical innovations, with his remarkable power for clear and dramatic exposition, in *New Introductory Lectures on Psychoanalysis* (1933) and *An Outline of Psychoanalysis* (1939).

Freud asserted that many of his views had been anticipated by insightful authors in Western literature, and he himself applied psychoanalysis to brief discussions of the latent content in the manifest characters or events of literary works including Shakespeare's *Hamlet, Macbeth, A Midsummer Night's Dream,* and *King Lear.* He also wrote a brilliant analysis of Fyodor Dostoevsky's *The Brothers*

*Karamazov* and a full-length study, *Delusion and Dream* (1917), of the novel *Gradiva* by the Danish writer Wilhelm Jensen. Especially after the 1930s, a number of writers produced critical analyses, modeled on classical Freudian theory, of the lives of authors and of the content of their literary works. One of the best-known books in this mode is *Hamlet and Oedipus* (1949) by the psychoanalyst Ernest Jones. Building on earlier suggestions by Freud himself, Jones explained Hamlet's inability to make up his mind to kill his uncle by reference to his **Oedipus complex**— that is, the repressed but continuing presence in the adult's unconscious of the male infant's desire to possess his mother and to have his rival, the father, out of the way. (Freud derived the term from Sophocles' Greek tragedy *Oedipus the King*, whose protagonist has unknowingly killed his father and married his mother.) Jones proposes that Hamlet's conflict is "an echo of a similar one in Shakespeare himself," and goes on to account for the audience's powerful and continued response to the play, over many centuries, as a result of the repressed Oedipal conflict that is shared by all men. In more recent decades there has been increasing emphasis by Freudian critics, in a mode suggested by Freud's later writings, on the role of "ego psychology" in elaborating the manifest content and artistic form of a work of literature; that is, on the way that the "ego," in contriving the work, consciously manages to mediate between the conflicting demands of the id, the superego, and the limits imposed by reality. On such developments see Frederick C. Crews, "Literature and Psychology," in *Relations of Literary Study*, ed. James Thorpe (1967), and the issue on "Psychology and Literature: Some Contemporary Directions," in *New Literary History*, Vol. 12 (1980). Norman Holland is a leading exponent of the application of psychoanalytic concepts not (as in most earlier criticism) to the relation of the author to the work, but to the relation of the reader to the work, explaining each reader's individual response as the product of a "transactive" engagement between his or her unconscious desires and defenses and the fantasies that the author has projected in the literary text; see under *reader-response criticism*.

The term **psychobiography** designates an account of the life of an author (see *biography*) that focuses on the subject's psychological development, relying for evidence both on external sources and on the author's own writings. It stresses the role of unconscious and disguised motives in forming the author's personality, and is usually written in accordance with a version, or a revision, of the Freudian theory of the stages of psychosexual development. A major exemplar of the mode was Erik H. Erikson's *Young Man Luther* (1958), in which Erikson stressed the importance of Luther's adolescent "identity crisis." Other notable instances of literary psychobiography are Leon Edel, *Henry James* (5 vols., 1953–72), and Justin Kaplan, *Mark Twain and His World* (1974). Prominent and diverse examples of Freudian literary criticism can be found in the collections listed below. It should be noted, in addition, that many modern literary critics, like many modern authors, owe some debt to Freud; such major critics, for example, as Kenneth Burke, Edmund Wilson, and Lionel Trilling assimilated central Freudian concepts into their overall critical views and procedures.

Carl G. Jung is sometimes called a psychoanalyst, but although he began as a disciple of Freud, his mature version of depth psychology is very different from that of his predecessor, and what we call **Jungian criticism** of literature departs radically from psychoanalytic criticism. Jung's emphasis is not on the individual unconscious, but on what he calls the "collective unconscious," shared by all individuals in all cultures, which he regards as the repository of "racial memories" and of primordial images and patterns of experience that he calls *archetypes*. He does not, like Freud, view literature as a disguised form of libidinal wish fulfillment that to a large extent parallels the fantasies of a neurotic personality. Instead, Jung regards great literature as, like the *myths* whose patterns recur in diverse cultures, an expression of the archetypes of the collective racial unconscious. A great author possesses, and provides for readers, access to the archetypal images buried in the racial memory, and so succeeds in revitalizing aspects of the psyche which are essential both to individual self-integration and to the mental and emotional well-being of the human race. Jung's theory of literature has been a cardinal formative influence on *archetypal criticism* and *myth criticism*. See Jung, *Contributions to Analytic Psychology* (1928) and *Modern Man in Search of a Soul* (1933); also Edward Glover, *Freud or Jung* (1950).

Since the development of *structural* and *poststructural* theories, there has been a strong revival of Freudian theories, although in diverse reformulations of the classical Freudian scheme. Close attention to Freud's writings, and frequently the assimilation of some version of Freud's ideas to their own views and procedures, are features of the criticism of many current writers, whether they are Marxist, Foucauldian, or Derridean in theoretical commitment or primary focus. Harold Bloom's theory of the *anxiety of influence* specifically adapts to the composition and reading of poetry Freud's concepts of the Oedipus complex and of the distorting operation of defense mechanisms in dreams. A number of *feminist critics* have attacked the male-centered nature of Freud's theory—especially evident in such crucial conceptions as the Oedipus complex and "penis envy" on the part of the female child; but many feminists have also adapted a revised version of Freudian concepts and mental mechanisms to their analyses of the writing and reading of literary texts. See Juliet Mitchell, *Psychoanalysis and Feminism* (1975); Mary Jacobus, *Reading Woman* (1986); Nancy Chodorow, *Feminism and Psychoanalytic Theory* (1990); Elisabeth Young-Bruehl, *Freud on Women: A Reader* (1992); Rosalind Minsky, ed., *Psychoanalysis and Gender: An Introductory Reader* (1996).

Jacques Lacan, "the French Freud," developed a *semiotic* version of Freud, converting the basic concepts of psychoanalysis into formulations derived from the linguistic theory of Ferdinand de Saussure, and applying these concepts not to the mental processes of human individuals, but to the operations of the process of signification. (See under *linguistics in literary criticism*.) Typical is Lacan's oft-quoted dictum, "The unconscious is structured like a language." His procedure is to recast Freud's key concepts and mechanisms into the linguistic mode, viewing the human mind not as pre-existent to, but as constituted by, the language we use. In Lacan's revision, for example, both *gender* and desire are not producers, but products of the signifying system. Especially important in **Lacanian literary criticism** is Lacan's reformulation of Freud's concepts of the early stages of psycho-sexual development and the formation of the Oedipus complex into the distinction between a prelinguistic stage of development that he calls the **imaginary** and the stage after the acquisition of language that he calls the **symbolic**. In the imaginary stage, there is no clear distinction between the subject and an object, or between the individual self and other selves. Intervening between these two stages is what Lacan calls the **mirror stage**, the moment when the infant learns to identify with his or her image in a mirror, and so begins to develop a sense of a separate self, and an (illusory) understanding of oneself as an autonomous subject, that is later enhanced by what is reflected back to it from encounters with other people. When it enters the symbolic, or linguistic, stage, the infant subject assimilates the inherited system of linguistic differences, hence is constituted by the symbolic, as it learns to accept its predetermined "position" in such linguistic oppositions as male/female, father/son, mother/daughter. This symbolic realm of language, in Lacan's theory, is the realm of the law of the father, in which the "phallus" (used in a symbolic sense to stand for male privilege and authority) is "the privileged signifier" that serves to establish the mode for all other signifiers. In a parallel fashion, Lacan translates Freud's views of the mental workings of dream formation into textual terms of the play of *signifiers*, converting Freud's distorting defense mechanisms into linguistic figures of speech. And according to Lacan, all processes of linguistic expression and interpretation, driven by "desire" for a lost and unachievable object, move incessantly (as in Derrida's theory of *deconstruction*) along a chain of unstable signifiers, without any possibility of coming to rest on a fixed signified, or presence. (See Jacques Lacan, *Ecrits: A Selection*, 1977; *The Four Fundamental Concepts of Psychoanalysis*, 1998; and *The Seminar of Jacques Lacan: The Ethics of Psychoanalysis, 1959–60*, 1997. See also Lacan's much discussed reading of Edgar Allan Poe's short story *The Purloined Letter* as an allegory of the workings of the linguistic signifier, in *Yale French Studies*, Vol. 48, 1972; and Malcolm Bowie, *Lacan*, 1991.) Lacan's notions of the inalienable split, or "difference," that inhabits the self, and of the endless chain of displacements in the quest for meaning, have made him a prominent reference in *poststructural* theorists. And his distinction between the pre-Oedipal, maternal stage of the prelinguistic imaginary and the "phallocentric" stage of symbolic language has been exploited at length by a number of French feminists; see Hélène Cixous, Luce Irigaray, and Julia Kristeva under *feminist criticism*.

See Jerome Neu, ed., *The Cambridge Companion to Freud* (1991). Many of Freud's psychoanalytic writings on literature and the arts have been collected by Benjamin Nelson, ed., *Sigmund Freud on Creativity and the Unconscious* (1958). Anthologies of psychoanalytic criticism by various authors are William Phillips, ed., *Art and Psychoanalysis* (1957), and Leonard and Eleanor Manheim, eds., *Hidden Patterns: Studies in Psychoanalytic Literary Criticism* (1966). Useful discussions and developments of Freudian literary theory are Frederick J. Hoffman, *Freudianism and the Literary Mind* (rev. 1957), which also describes Freud's wide influence on writers and critics; Norman N. Holland, *Holland's Guide to Psychoanalytic Psychology and Literature-and-Psychology* (1990); and Peter Brooks, *Psychoanalysis and Storytelling* (1994). Elizabeth Wright, *Psychoanalytic Criticism: Theory in Practice* (1984), reviews various developments in psychoanalytic theories and their applications to literary criticism. For two major traditional critics who have to an important extent adapted Freudian concepts to their general enterprise, see Edmund Wilson, *The Wound and the Bow* (1941), and Lionel Trilling, "Freud and Literature," in *The Liberal Imagination* (1950). Frederick C. Crews, who in 1966 wrote an exemplary Freudian critical study, *The Sins of the Fathers: Hawthorne's Psychological Themes*, later retracted his Freudian commitment; see his *Skeptical Engagements* (1986). For *feminist* views and adaptations of Jacques Lacan, see Jane Gallop, *Reading Lacan* (1985); Shoshana Felman, *Jacques Lacan and the Adventure of Insight* (1987); and Elizabeth Grosz, *Jacques Lacan: A Feminist Introduction* (1990). In recent years Slavoj Žižek has argued for the primacy of Lacan as an ethical and political thinker. See *The Sublime Object of Ideology* (1989) and *Looking Awry: An Introduction to Jacques Lacan through Popular Culture* (1991).

**Ptolemaic universe** (tŏl′ ĕmā″ ik): **309**.

**pun:** Pun (which traditional rhetoricians call **paranomasia**) denotes a play on words that are either identical in sound (**homonyms**) or very similar in sound, but are sharply diverse in significance; an example is the last word in the title of Oscar Wilde's comedy, *The Importance of Being Earnest* (1895). Puns have often had serious literary uses. The authority of the Pope in Roman Catholicism goes back to the Greek pun uttered by Jesus in Matthew 16:18, "Thou art Peter [Petros] and upon this rock [petra] I will build my church." Shakespeare and other writers used puns seriously as well as for comic purposes. In *Romeo and Juliet* (III. i. 101) Mercutio, bleeding to death, says grimly, "Ask for me tomorrow and you shall find me a grave man"; and John Donne's solemn "Hymn to God the Father" (1633) puns throughout on his own name and the past participle "done." Milton was an inveterate inventor of serious puns in *Paradise Lost*. In the eighteenth century and thereafter, however, the literary use of the pun has been almost exclusively comic. A major exception is James Joyce's *Finnegans Wake* (1939), which exploits puns throughout in order to help sustain its complex effect, at once serious and comic, of multiple levels of meaning; see *portmanteau word*.

A special type of pun, known as the **equivoque**, is the use of a single word or phrase which has two disparate meanings, in a context which makes both meanings equally relevant. An example is the phrase "come to dust" in a song from Shakespeare's *Cymbeline*: "Golden lads and girls all must, / As chimney sweepers, come to dust." An epitaph suggested for a bank teller contains a series of equivocal phrases:

> He checked his cash, cashed in his checks,
> And left his window. Who is next?

And an *epigram* by Hilaire Belloc (1870–1953) ends in an equivoque:

> When I am done, I hope it can be said:
> His sins were scarlet, but his books were read.

Refer to Jonathan Culler, ed., *On Puns: The Foundation of Letters* (1988).

**Puritan Interregnum: 253**.

**purple patch:** A translation of Horace's Latin phrase "purpureus . . . pannus" in his versified *Ars Poetica* (first century BC). It signifies a marked heightening of style in rhythm, diction, repetitions, and figurative language that makes a passage of verse or prose—especially a descriptive passage—stand out from its context. The term is sometimes applied without derogation to a set piece, separable and quotable, in which an author rises to an occasion. An example is the eulogy of England by the dying John of Gaunt in Shakespeare's *Richard II* (II. i. 40ff.), beginning:

> This royal throne of kings, this scept'red isle,
> This earth of majesty, this seat of Mars,
> This other Eden, demi-paradise. . . .

Other well-known examples are Lord Byron's depiction of the Duchess of Richmond's ball on the eve of Waterloo in *Childe Harold's Pilgrimage*, Canto III, xxi–xxviii (1816), and Walter Pater's prose description of the *Mona Lisa* in his essay on Leonardo da Vinci in *The Renaissance* (1873). Usually, however, "purple passage" connotes disparagement, implying that one has self-consciously girded oneself to perform a piece of fine writing. In Stella Gibbons' satiric novel, *Cold Comfort Farm*, the fictional narrator is proud of her purple descriptive passages, and follows the example of Baedeker's guidebooks by marking them with varying numbers of asterisks: "Dawn crept over the Downs like a sinister white animal, followed by the snarling cries of the wind eating its way between the black boughs of the thorns."

**pyrrhic** (pĭr' ĭk): **196**.

**quantitative meter: 194**; *199*.

**quarto: 32**.

**quatrain: 341**.

**queer reading: 297**.

**queer theory:** Queer theory is often used to designate the combined area of gay and lesbian studies, together with the theoretical and critical writings about all modes of variance—such as cross-dressing, bisexuality, and transsexuality—from society's normative model of sexual identity, orientation, and activities. The term "queer" was originally derogatory, used to stigmatize male and female same-sex love as deviant and unnatural; since the early 1990s, however, it has been increasingly adopted by gays and lesbians themselves as a noninvidious term to identify a way of life and an area for scholarly inquiry. (See Teresa de Lauretis, *Queer Theory: Lesbian and Gay Sexualities*, 1991; and Annamarie Jagose, *Queer Theory: An Introduction*, 1996.)

   Both **lesbian studies** and **gay studies** began as "liberation movements"—in parallel with the movements for *African-American* and *feminist* liberation—during the anti–Vietnam War, anti-establishment, and countercultural ferment of the late 1960s and 1970s. Since that time these studies have maintained a close relation to the activists who strive to achieve, for gays and lesbians, political, legal, and economic rights equal to those of the heterosexual majority. Through the 1970s, the two movements were primarily separatist: gays often thought of themselves as quintessentially male, while many lesbians, aligning themselves with the feminist movement, characterized the gay movement as sharing the antifemale attitudes of the reigning patriarchal culture. There has, however, been a growing recognition (signalized by the adoption of the joint term "queer") of the degree to which the two groups share a history as a despised and suppressed minority and possess common political and social aims.

In the 1970s, researchers for the most part assumed that there was a fixed, unitary identity as a gay man or as a lesbian that has remained stable through human history. A major endeavor was to identify and reclaim the works of nonheterosexual writers from Plato to Walt Whitman, Oscar Wilde, Marcel Proust, Andre Gide, W. H. Auden, and James Baldwin, and from the Greek poet Sappho of Lesbos to Virginia Woolf, Adrienne Rich, and Audre Lorde. The list included writers (William Shakespeare and Christina Rossetti are examples) who represented in their literary works homoerotic subject matter, but whose own sexuality the available biographical evidence leaves uncertain. (See Claude J. Summers, *The Gay and Lesbian Literary Heritage: A Reader's Companion to the Writers and Their Works, from Antiquity to the Present*, 1995.) In the 1980s and 1990s, however—in large part because of the assimilation of the viewpoints and analytic methods of Derrida, Foucault, and other *poststructuralists*—the earlier assumptions about a unitary and stable gay or lesbian identity were frequently put to question, and historical and critical analyses of sexual differences became increasingly subtle and complex.

A number of queer theorists, for example, adopted the deconstructive mode of dismantling the key binary oppositions of Western culture, such as male/female, heterosexual/homosexual, and natural/unnatural, by which a spectrum of diverse things is forced into only two categories, and in which the first category is assigned privilege, power, and centrality, while the second is derogated, subordinated, and marginalized. (See under *deconstruction*.) In an important essay of 1980, "Compulsive Heterosexuality and Lesbian Existence," Adrienne Rich posited what she called the "lesbian continuum" as a way of stressing how far-ranging and diverse is the spectrum of love and bonding among women, including female friendship, the family relationship between mother and daughter, and women's partnerships and social groups, as well as overtly physical same-sex relations. Later theorists such as Eve Sedgwick and Judith Butler undertook to invert the standard hierarchical opposition by which homosexuality is marginalized and made unnatural, by stressing the extent to which the ostensible normativity of heterosexuality is based on the suppression and denial of same-sex desires and relationships. **Queer reading** has become the term for interpretive activities that undertake to subvert and confound the established verbal and cultural boundaries between male/female, homosexual/heterosexual, and normal/abnormal.

Another prominent theoretical procedure has been to undo the "essentialist" assumption that heterosexual and homosexual are universal and transhistorical types of human subjects, or identities, by historicizing these categories—that is, by proposing that they are cultural and discursive *constructs* that emerged under special ideological conditions in a particular culture at a particular time. (See *essentialism*, under *humanism*.) A central text is the first volume of Michel Foucault's *History of Sexuality* (1976), which claims that, while there had long been a social category of sodomy as a transgressive human act, the "homosexual," as a special type of human *subject* or identity, was a construction of the medical and legal discourse of the latter part of the nineteenth century. In a further development of constructionist theory, Judith Butler, in *Gender Trouble: Feminism and the Subversion of Identity* (1990), described the categories of gender and of sexuality as *performative*, in the sense that the features which a cultural discourse institutes as masculine or feminine, heterosexual or homosexual, it also makes happen, by establishing an identity that the socialized individual assimilates and the patterns of behavior that he or she enacts. Homosexuality, by this view, is not a particular identity that effects a pattern of action, but a socially pre-established pattern of action that produces the effect of originating in a particular identity. A fundamental constructionist text, frequently cited in the arguments against essentialism, is "One Is Not Born a Woman" (1981) by Monique Wittig, in *The Straight Mind and Other Essays* (1992).

The constructionist view has been elaborated by considering the cross-influences of race and of economic class in producing the identities and modes of behavior of gender and sexuality. (See, for example, Barbara Smith, "Toward a Black Feminist Criticism," 1977, reprinted in *Within the Circle: An Anthology of African-American Literary Criticism from the Harlem Renaissance to the Present*, ed. Angelyn Mitchell, 1994; and Ann Allen Stickley, "The Black Lesbian in American Literature: An Overview," in *Conditions: Five Two*, 1979.) Sustained debate among queer theorists concerns the risk of a radical constructionism, which would dissolve a lesbian or gay identity into a purely discursive product specific to a particular culture, as against the need to affirm a special and enduring identity in order to signalize and celebrate it, as well as to establish a basis for concerted political action.

A number of journals are now devoted to queer theory and to lesbian, gay, and transgender studies and criticism; the field has also become the subject of regularly scheduled learned conferences, and has been established in the curriculum of the humanities and social sciences in a great many colleges and universities. Anthologies: Karla Jay and Joanne Glasgow, eds., *Lesbian Texts and Contexts: Radical Revisions* (1990); Diana Fuss, ed., *Inside/Out: Lesbian Theories, Gay Theories* (1991); and Henry Abelove, Michèle Aina Barale, and David M. Halperin, eds., *The Lesbian and Gay Studies Reader* (1993), which includes selections by almost all the theorists and critics mentioned in this entry. *Out Takes: Essays on Queer Theory and Film*, ed. Ellis Hanson (1999), is a collection of essays in queer criticism devoted to a variety of motion pictures. There is a large and rapidly growing body of books on these subjects. In addition to the texts listed above, see Eve Kosofsky Sedgwick, *Between Men: English Literature and Male Homosocial Desire* (1985) and *Epistemology of the Closet* (1990); Diana Fuss, *Essentially Speaking: Feminism, Nature, and Difference* (1989); Richard Dyer, *Now You See It: Studies on Lesbian and Gay Film* (1990); Gregory W. Bredbeck, *Sodomy and Interpretation, Marlowe to Milton* (1991); Susan J. Wolfe and Julia

Penelope, eds., *New Lesbian Criticism: Literary and Cultural Readings* (1992); Judith Butler, *Bodies that Matter* (1993); Michael Warner, ed., *Fear of a Queer Planet* (1993); Lee Edelman, *Homographesis: Essays in Gay Literary and Cultural Theory* (1994); Gregory Woods, *A History of Gay Literature: The Male Tradition* (1998). See also the readings listed under *feminist criticism* and *gender studies*. For references to *queer theory* in other entries, see pages *113, 339.*

**rap: 243**; *28, 238.*

**reader-response criticism:** Reader-response criticism does not designate any one critical *theory*, but rather a focus on the process of reading a literary text that is shared by many of the critical modes, American and European, which have come into prominence since the 1960s. Reader-response critics turn from the traditional conception that a text embodies an achieved set of meanings, and focus instead on the ongoing mental operations and responses of readers as their eyes follow a text on the page before them. In the more drastic forms of such criticism, matters that had been considered by critics to be features of the literary work itself (including narrator, plot, characters, style, and structure, as well as meanings) are dissolved into an evolving process, consisting primarily of diverse expectations, and the violations, deferments, satisfactions, and restructurings of expectations, in the flow of a reader's experience. Reader-response critics of all theoretical persuasions agree that, at least to some considerable degree, the meanings of a text are the "production" or "creation" of the individual reader, hence that there is no one "correct" meaning for all readers either of the linguistic parts or of the artistic whole of a text. Where these critics importantly differ is (1) in their view of the primary factors that shape a reader's responses; (2) in the place at which they draw the line between what is "objectively" given in a text and the "subjective" responses of an individual reader; and as a result of this difference, (3) in their conclusion about the extent, if any, to which a text controls, or at least "constrains," a reader's responses, so as to justify the rejection of at least some readings as misreadings, even if, as most reader-response critics assert, we are unable to demonstrate that any single reading is the correct reading.

The following is a brief survey of the more prominent forms of reader-response criticism:

The German critic Wolfgang Iser developed the phenomenological analysis of the reading process proposed by Roman Ingarden, but whereas Ingarden had limited himself to a description of reading in general, Iser applied his theory to the analysis of many individual works of literature, especially prose fiction. (For a discussion of Ingarden's views, see *phenomenology and criticism.*) In Iser's view the literary text, as a product of the writer's intentional acts, in part controls the reader's responses, but always contains (to a degree that has greatly increased in many modern literary texts) a number of "gaps" or "indeterminate elements." These the reader must fill in by a creative participation with what is given in the text before him. The experience of reading is an evolving process of anticipation, frustration, retrospection, reconstruction, and satisfaction. Iser distinguishes between the **implied reader**, who is established by a particular text itself as someone who is expected to respond in specific ways to the "response-inviting structures" of the text, and the "actual reader," whose responses are inevitably colored by his or her accumulated private experiences. In both cases, however, the process of the reader's consciousness serves to constitute both the partial patterns (which we ordinarily attribute to objective features of the work itself) and the coherence, or unity, of the work as a whole. As a consequence, literary texts always permit a varied range of possible meanings. The fact, however, that the author's intentional acts establish limits, as well as incentives, to the reader's creative additions to a text allows us to reject some readings as misreadings. (For an application of phenomenological analysis to the history, from era to era, of ever-altering reader responses to a given text, see *reception theory*.)

French *structuralist criticism*, as Jonathan Culler said in *Structuralist Poetics* (1975), "is essentially a theory of reading" which aims to "specify how we go about making sense of texts" (pp. viii, 128). As practiced by critics such as Culler in the course of his book, criticism stresses literary conventions, codes, and rules which, having been assimilated by competent readers, serve to structure their reading experience and so make possible, at the same time as they impose constraints on, the partially creative activity of interpretation. The structuralist Roland Barthes, however, in his later theory encouraged a mode of reading that opens the text to an endless play of alternative meanings. And the poststructuralist movement of *deconstruction* is a theory of reading that specifically subverts the structuralist view that interpretation is in some part controlled by linguistic and literary codes, and instead proposes a "creative" reading of any text as a play of "differences" that generate innumerable, mutually contradictory, and "undecidable" meanings.

American proponents of reader-response types of interpretive theory often begin by rejecting the claim of the American *New Criticism* that a literary work is a self-sufficient object invested with publicly available meanings, whose internal features and structure should be analyzed without "external" reference to the responses of its readers (see *affective fallacy*). In radical opposition to this view, these newer critics turn their attention exclusively from the verbal text to the reader's responses; they differ greatly, however, in the factors to which they attribute the formation of these responses.

David Bleich, in *Subjective Criticism* (1978), undertakes to show, on the basis of classroom experiments, that any purportedly "objective" reading of a text, if it is more than an empty derivation from theoretical formulas, turns out to be based on a response that is not determined by the text, but is instead a "subjective process" determined by the distinctive personality of the individual reader. In an alternative analysis of reading, Norman Holland accounts for the responses of a reader to a text by recourse to Freudian concepts (see *psychoanalytic criticism*). The subject matter of a work of literature is a projection of the fantasies—engendered by the interplay of unconscious needs and defenses—that constitute the particular "identity" of its author. The individual reader's "subjective" response to a text is a "transactive" encounter between the fantasies projected by its author and the particular defenses, expectations, and wish-fulfilling fantasies that make up the reader's own identity. In this transactive process the reader transforms the fantasy content, "which he has created from the materials of the story his defenses admitted,"

into a unity, or "meaningful totality," that constitutes the reader's particular interpretation of the text. There is no universally determinate meaning of a work; two
readers will agree in their interpretation only insofar as their "identity themes" are
sufficiently alike to enable each to fit the other's re-creation of a text to his or her
own distinctive pattern of responses.

In his theory of reading, Harold Bloom also employs psychoanalytic concepts;
in particular, he adapts Freud's concept of the mechanisms of defense against the
revelation to consciousness of repressed desires to his own view of the process of
reading as the application of "defense mechanisms" against the "influence," or
threat to the reader's imaginative autonomy, of the poet whose text is being
read. Bloom applies Freudian concepts in a much more complex way than
Holland; he arrives, however, at a parallel conclusion that there can be no determinate or correct meaning of a text. All "reading is . . . misreading"; the only
difference is that between a "strong" misreading and a "weak" misreading. (See
*anxiety of influence*.)

Stanley Fish is the proponent of what he calls **affective stylistics**. In his earlier writings Fish represented the activity of reading as one that converts the spatial
sequence of printed words on a page into a temporal flow of experience in a
reader who has acquired a "literary competence." In following the printed text
with his eye, the reader makes sense of what he has so far read by anticipating
what is still to come. These anticipations may be fulfilled by what follows in the
text; often, however, they will turn out to have been mistaken. But since, according to Fish, "the meaning of an utterance" is the reader's "experience—all of it,"
and the reader's mistakes are "part of the experience provided by the author's language," these mistakes are an integral part of the meaning of a text. (See
"Literature in the Reader: Affective Stylistics," published in 1970 and reprinted
with slight changes in *Self-Consuming Artifacts: The Experience of Seventeenth
Century Literature*, 1974, and in *Is There a Text in This Class?* 1980.) Fish's analyses
of large-scale literary works were designed to show a coherence in the kinds of
mistakes, constitutive of specific types of meaning-experience, which are effected
in the reader by the text of John Milton's *Paradise Lost*, and by various essayists and
poets of the seventeenth century.

Fish's early claim was that he was describing a universal process in the competent reading of literary texts. In later publications, however, he introduced the
concept of **interpretive communities**, each of which is composed of members
who share a particular reading "strategy," or "set of community assumptions."
Fish, in consequence, now presented his own affective stylistics as only one of
many alternative modes of interpretation, which his earlier writings were covertly
attempting to persuade his readers to adopt. He also proposed that each communal strategy in effect "creates" all the seemingly objective features of the text itself,
as well as the "intentions, speakers, and authors" that we may infer from the text.
The result is that there can be no universal "right reading" of any text; the validity
of any reading, however obvious it may seem to a reader, will always depend on
the assumptions and strategy of reading that he or she happens to share with other
members of a particular interpretive community. Fish's claim is that all values, as
well as meanings, of a text are relative to the concept or scheme of a particular

interpretive community; furthermore, that such conceptual schemes are "incommensurable," in that there is no available standpoint, outside of all interpretive communities, for translating the discourse of one community into that of another, or for mediating between them. (See Fish, *Is There a Text in This Class? The Authority of Interpretive Communities*, 1980; and for a concise exposition of philosophical critiques of Fish's claims for interpretive and evaluative relativism and incommensurability, see James Battersby, *Reason and the Nature of Texts*, 1996.) In a later book, *Doing What Comes Naturally: Change, Rhetoric, and the Practice of Theory in Literary and Legal Studies* (1989), Fish analyzes, and defends, the role of the professional "interpretive community" of academic critics in literary studies; he also extends his views of literary interpretation into the domain of legal interpretation.

Since the early 1980s, as part of a widespread tendency to stress cultural and political factors in the study of literature, reader-response critics have increasingly undertaken to "situate" a particular reading of a text in its historical setting, in the attempt to show the extent to which the responses that constitute both the interpretation and evaluation of literature have been determined by a reader's *ideology* and by built-in biases about race, class, or gender. See Peter J. Rabinowitz, *Before Reading: Narrative Conventions and the Politics of Interpretation*, 1987; and for *feminist* emphasis on the male biases that affect the responses of readers, Judith Fetterley, *The Resisting Reader* (1978); and Elizabeth A. Flynn and Patrocinio Schweikart, eds., *Gender and Reading: Essays on Readers, Texts, and Contexts* (1986).

A survey of a number of reader-response theories of criticism is included in Steven Mailloux's own contribution to this mode in *Interpretive Conventions* (1982); another survey from the point of view of deconstructive theory is Elizabeth Freund, *The Return of the Reader: Reader-Response Criticism* (1987). Anthologies of diverse reader-response essays: Susan Suleiman and Inge Crossman, eds., *The Reader in the Text* (1980); Jane P. Tompkins, ed., *Reader-Response Criticism* (1980). Important early instances of a criticism that is focused on the reader: Walter J. Slatoff, *With Respect to Readers* (1970); Louise Rosenblatt, *The Reader, the Text, the Poem* (1978); Umberto Eco, *The Role of the Reader* (trans. 1979).

In addition to the titles mentioned in this essay, the following are prominent exemplars of reader-response criticism: Stanley Fish, *Surprised by Sin: The Reader in "Paradise Lost"* (1967); Norman Holland, *The Dynamics of Literary Response* (1968) and *Five Readers Reading* (1975); Wolfgang Iser, *The Implied Reader* (1974) and *The Act of Reading: A Theory of Aesthetic Response* (1978). For critiques of Fish's "affective stylistics": Jonathan Culler, *The Pursuit of Signs* (1981); Eugene Goodheart, *The Skeptic Disposition in Contemporary Criticism* (1984); M. H. Abrams, "How to Do Things with Texts," in *Doing Things with Texts* (1989). For references to *reader-response criticism* in other entries, see pages *5, 161, 262, 282, 292, 305, 313.*

**realism and naturalism: Realism** is applied by literary critics in two diverse ways: (1) to identify a movement in the writing of novels during the nineteenth century that included Honoré de Balzac in France, George Eliot in England, and William

Dean Howells in America (see *realistic novel*, under *novel*), and (2) to designate a recurrent mode, in various eras and literary forms, of representing human life and experience in literature.

Realistic fiction is often opposed to romantic fiction. The *romance* is said to present life as we would have it be—more picturesque, fantastic, adventurous, or heroic than actuality; realism, on the other hand, is said to represent life as it really is. This distinction in terms solely of subject matter, while relevant, is clearly inadequate. Casanova, T. E. Lawrence, and Winston Churchill were people in real life, but their biographies demonstrate that truth can be stranger than literary realism. It is more useful to identify realism in terms of the intended effect on the reader: realistic fiction is written to give the effect that it represents life and the social world as it seems to the common reader, evoking the sense that its characters might in fact exist, and that such things might well happen. To achieve such effects, the novelists we identify as realists may or may not be selective in subject matter—although most of them prefer the commonplace and the everyday, represented in minute detail, over rarer aspects of life—but they must render their materials in ways that make them seem to their readers the very stuff of ordinary experience. For example, Daniel Defoe in the early eighteenth century dealt with the extraordinary adventures of a shipwrecked mariner named Robinson Crusoe and with the extraordinary misadventures of a woman named Moll Flanders; but he made his novels seem to readers a mirror held up to reality by his reportorial manner of rendering all the events, whether ordinary or extraordinary, in the same circumstantial, matter-of-fact, and seemingly unselective way. Both the fictions of Franz Kafka and the present-day novels of *magic realism* achieve their effects in large part by exploiting a realistic manner in rendering events that are in themselves fantastic, absurd, or flatly impossible.

*Russian formalists*, followed more systematically by *structuralist critics*, proposed that both the selection of subject matter and the techniques of rendering in a realistic novel depend on their accordance with literary *convention* and codes which the reader has learned to interpret, or *naturalize*, in a way that makes the text seem a reflection of everyday reality. (See Roland Barthes, "The Reality Effect," in *French Literary Theory Today*, ed. Tzvetan Todorov, 1982; and Jonathan Culler, *Structuralist Poetics*, 1975, chapter 7, "Convention and Naturalization.") Some theorists draw the conclusion that, since all literary representations are constituted by arbitrary conventions, there is no valid ground for holding any one kind of fiction to be more realistic than any other. It is a matter of common experience, however, that some novels in fact produce on the reader the effect of representing the ordinary course of events. Skepticism about the possibility of fictional realism is not an empirical doctrine which is based on the widespread experience of readers of literature, but a metaphysical doctrine that denies the existence of any objective reality that is independent of altering human conventions and cultural formations. (For philosophical discussions of conventionality and reality, see the essays by Hilary Putnam, Nelson Goodman, and Menachem Brinker in *New Literary History*, Vol. 13, 1981, and Vol. 14, 1983.)

**Naturalism** is sometimes claimed to give an even more accurate depiction of life than realism. But naturalism is not only, like realism, a special selection of subject matter and a special way of rendering those materials; it is a mode of fiction that was developed by a school of writers in accordance with a particular philosophical thesis. This thesis, a product of post-Darwinian biology in the nineteenth century, held that a human being exists entirely in the order of nature and does not have a soul nor any access to a religious or spiritual world beyond the natural world; and therefore, that such a being is merely a higher-order animal whose character and behavior are entirely determined by two kinds of forces: heredity and environment. Each person inherits compulsive instincts—especially hunger, the drive to accumulate possessions, and sexuality—and is then subjected to the social and economic forces in the family, the class, and the milieu into which that person is born. The French novelist Émile Zola, beginning in the 1870s, did much to develop this theory in what he called "le roman expérimental" (that is, the novel organized in the mode of a scientific experiment on the behavior, under given conditions, of the characters it depicts). Zola and later naturalistic writers, such as the Americans Frank Norris, Stephen Crane, and Theodore Dreiser, try to present their subjects with scientific objectivity and with elaborate documentation, sometimes including an almost medical frankness about activities and bodily functions usually unmentioned in earlier literature. They tend to choose characters who exhibit strong animal drives such as greed and sexual desire, and who are helpless victims both of glandular secretions within and of sociological pressures without. The end of the naturalistic novel is usually "tragic," but not, as in classical and Elizabethan *tragedy*, because of a heroic but losing struggle of the individual mind and will against gods, enemies, and circumstances. Instead the protagonist of the naturalistic plot, a pawn to multiple compulsions, usually disintegrates, or is wiped out.

Aspects of the naturalistic selection and management of subject matter and its austere or harsh manner of rendering its materials are apparent in many modern novels and dramas, such as Hardy's *Jude the Obscure*, 1895 (although Hardy largely substituted a cosmic determinism for biological and environmental determinism), various plays by Eugene O'Neill in the 1920s, and Norman Mailer's novel of World War II, *The Naked and the Dead*. An enlightening exercise is to distinguish the diverse ways in which the relationship between the sexes is represented in a romance (Richard Blackmore's *Lorna Doone*, 1869), an ironic comedy of manners (Jane Austen's *Pride and Prejudice*, 1813), a realistic novel (William Dean Howells' *A Modern Instance*, 1882), and a naturalistic novel (Émile Zola's *Nana*, 1880, or Theodore Dreiser's *An American Tragedy*, 1925). Movements originally opposed both to nineteenth-century realism and naturalism (although some modern works, such as Joyce's *Ulysses*, 1922, combine aspects of these and other novelistic modes) are *expressionism* and *symbolism* (see *Symbolist Movement*).

See *socialist realism*, and refer to Erich Auerbach, *Mimesis: The Representation of Reality in Western Literature* (reprinted 2003); Ian Watt, *The Rise of the Novel* (1957); Ernst Gombrich, *Art and Illusion* (1960); Harry Levin, *The Gates of Horn: A Study of Five French Realists* (1963); René Wellek, "The Concept of Realism in Literary Scholarship," in *Concepts of Criticism* (1963); J. P. Stern, *On Realism* (1973); Ioan Williams, *The Realist Novel in England* (1975); George Levine, *The Realistic Imagination* (1981); Donald Pizer, *Realism and Naturalism in Nineteenth-Century*

*American Literature* (rev. 1984); Walter Benn Michaels, *The Gold Standard and the Logic of Naturalism* (1987); James Nagel and Thomas Quirk, eds., *The Portable American Realism Reader* (1997); Harry E. Shaw, *Narrating Reality: Austen, Scott, Eliot* (1999).

**realistic novel: 228**.

**Realistic Period** (in American literature): **247**.

**reception aesthetic: 305**; *300*.

**reception history: 305**.

**reception theory:** Reception theory is the application to literary history of a form of *reader-response* theory that was proposed by Hans Robert Jauss in "Literary History as a Challenge to Literary Theory" (in *New Literary History*, Vol. 2, 1970–71). Like other reader-response criticism, it focuses on the reader's reception of a text; its prime interest, however, is not on the response of a single reader at a given time, but on the altering responses, interpretive and evaluative, of the general reading public over the course of time. Jauss proposes that although a text has no "objective meaning," it does contain a variety of objectively describable features. The response of a particular reader, which constitutes for that reader the meaning and aesthetic qualities of a text, is the joint product of the reader's own "horizon of expectations" and the confirmations, disappointments, refutations, and reformulations of these expectations when they are "challenged" by the features of the text itself. Since the linguistic and aesthetic expectations of the general population of readers change over the course of time, and since later readers and critics have access not only to the literary text but also to the published responses of earlier readers, there develops an evolving historical "tradition" of critical interpretations and evaluations of a given literary work. Following concepts proposed by Hans-Georg Gadamer (see under *interpretation and hermeneutics*), Jauss represents this tradition as a continuing "dialectic," or "dialogue," between a text and the ever-altering horizons of successive readers; in itself, a literary text possesses no fixed and final meanings or value.

This mode of studying literary reception as a dialogue, or "fusion" of horizons, has a double aspect. As a **reception aesthetic**, it "defines" the meaning and aesthetic qualities of any individual text as a set of implicit semantic and aesthetic "potentialities" which become manifest only as they are realized by the cumulative responses of readers over the course of time. In its other aspect as a **reception history**, this mode of study also transforms the history of literature—traditionally conceived as an account of the successive production of a variety of works with relatively fixed meanings and values—by making it a history that requires an "ever-necessary retelling," since it narrates the changing yet cumulative way that selected texts are interpreted and assessed, as the horizons of successive generations of readers alter over the passage of time.

See Hans Robert Jauss, *Towards an Aesthetic of Reception* (1982), and *The Aesthetic Experience and Literary Hermeneutics* (1982); and for a history and discussion of this viewpoint, Robert C. Holub, *Reception Theory: A Critical Introduction* (1984).

**recto: 32**.

**recuperation** (in reading): **364**.

**reflection** (in Marxist criticism): **182**.

**Reformation: 308**.

**refrain:** A line, or part of a line, or a group of lines, which is repeated in the course of a poem, sometimes with slight changes, and usually at the end of each *stanza*. The refrain occurs in many *ballads* and work poems, and is a frequent element in Elizabethan songs, where it may be merely a nonverbal carrier of the melodic line, as in Shakespeare's "It Was a Lover and His Lass": "With a hey, and a ho, and a hey nonino." A famous refrain is that which closes each stanza in Edmund Spenser's "Epithalamion" (1594)—"The woods shall to me answer, and my echo ring"—in which sequential changes indicate the altering sounds during the successive hours of the poet's wedding day. The refrain in Spenser's "Prothalamion"—"Sweet Thames, run softly, till I end my song"—is echoed ironically in Part III of T. S. Eliot's *The Waste Land* (1922), where it is applied to the Thames in the modern age of polluted rivers.

A refrain may consist only of a single word—"Nevermore," as in Poe's "The Raven" (1845)—or of an entire stanza. If the stanza refrain occurs in a song, which all the auditors join in singing, it is called the **chorus**; for, example, in "Auld Lang Syne" and many other songs by Robert Burns in the late eighteenth century.

**regional novel: 231**; *247*.

**regular ode: 235**.

**Renaissance:** Renaissance ("rebirth") is the name commonly applied to the period of European history following the Middle Ages; it is usually said to have begun in Italy in the late fourteenth century and to have continued, both in Italy and other countries of Western Europe, through the fifteenth and sixteenth centuries. In this period the European arts of painting, sculpture, architecture, and literature reached an eminence not exceeded in any age. The development came late to England in the sixteenth century, and did not have its flowering until the Elizabethan and Jacobean periods; sometimes, in fact, John Milton (1608–74) is described as the last great Renaissance poet. (See *periods of English literature*.)

Many attempts have been made to define "the Renaissance" in a brief statement, as though a single essence underlay the complex features of the intellectual and cultural life of a great variety of European countries over several hundred years. It has, for example, been described as the birth of the modern world out of the ashes of the Dark Ages; as the discovery of the world and the discovery of man; and as the era of the emergence of untrammeled individualism in life, thought, religion, and art. Recently some historians, finding that attributes similar to these were present in various people and places in the Middle Ages, and also that many elements long held to be medieval survived into the Renaissance, have denied that the Renaissance ever existed. This skeptical opinion serves as a reminder that history is a continuous process, and that "periods" are not intrinsic in history, but invented by historians. Nonetheless, the division of the temporal continuum into named segments is an all but indispensable convenience in discussing history. Furthermore, during the span of time called "the Renaissance," it is possible to identify a number of events and discoveries which, beginning approximately in the fifteenth century, clearly effected distinctive changes in the beliefs, productions, and manner of life of many people in various countries, especially those in the upper and the intellectual classes.

Beginning in the 1940s, a number of historians have replaced (or else supplemented) the term "Renaissance" with **early modern** to designate the span from the end of the Middle Ages until late in the seventeenth century. The latter term looks forward rather than back, emphasizing the degree to which the time, instead of being mainly a rebirth of the classical past, can be viewed, in its innovations and intellectual concerns, as a precursor of our present time. (See Leah S. Marcus, "Renaissance/Early Modern Studies," in *Redrawing the Boundaries*, ed. Stephen Greenblatt and Giles Gunn, 1992.)

The innovations during this period may be regarded as putting a strain on the relatively closed and stable world of the great civilization of the later Middle Ages, when most of the essential and permanent truths about God, man, and the universe were considered to be adequately known. The full impact of many developments in the Renaissance did not make itself felt until the Enlightenment in the later seventeenth and the eighteenth centuries, but the fact that they occurred in this period indicates the vitality, the restless curiosity, and the imaginative audacity of many people of the era, whether scholars, thinkers, artists, or adventurers. Prominent among these developments were:

1. The new learning. Renaissance scholars of the classics, called *humanists*, revived the knowledge of the Greek language, discovered and disseminated a great number of Greek manuscripts, and added considerably to the number of Roman authors and works which had been known during the Middle Ages. The result was to open up a sense of the vastness of the historical past, as well as to enlarge immensely the stock of ideas, materials, literary forms, and styles available to Renaissance writers. In the mid fifteenth century the invention of **printing** on paper from movable type (for which Johann Gutenberg of Mainz, Germany, is usually given credit, although the Chinese had developed a similar mode of printing several centuries earlier) made books for the first time cheap and plentiful, and floods of publications, ancient and modern, poured from the presses of Europe to satisfy the demands of the expanding population who had learned to read. The rapidity and range of the spread of ideas, discoveries, and types of literature in the Renaissance was made possible by this new technology of printing. (See *book* and *book history studies*.) The technology reached England in 1476, when William Caxton set up a press at Westminster, where

he published, among many other books, Chaucer's *Canterbury Tales* and Malory's *Le Morte D'Arthur*.

The humanistic revival sometimes resulted in pedantic scholarship, sterile imitations of ancient works and styles, and a rigidly authoritarian rhetoric and literary criticism. It also bred, however, the gracious and tolerant humanity of an Erasmus, and the high concept of a cultivated Renaissance aristocracy expressed in Baldassare Castiglione's *Il Cortegiano* ("The Courtier"), published in 1528. This was the most admired and widely translated of the many Renaissance **courtesy books**, or books on the character, obligations, and training of the man of the court. It sets up the ideal of the completely rounded or **Renaissance man**, developed in all his faculties and skills—physical, intellectual, and artistic. He is especially trained to be a warrior and statesman, but is capable also as athlete, philosopher, artist, conversationalist, and man of society. The courtier's relationships to women, and women's to men, are represented in accordance with the quasi-religious code of *Platonic love*, and his activities and productions are crowned by the grace of **sprezzatura**—the Italian term for the seeming spontaneity and casual ease with which a trained person may meet the requirements of complex and exacting rules. Leonardo da Vinci in Italy and Sir Philip Sidney in England are often represented as embodying the many aspects of the courtly ideal.

2. The new religion. The **Reformation** led by Martin Luther (1483–1546) was a successful heresy which struck at the very foundations of the institutionalism of the Roman Catholic Church. This early Protestantism was grounded on each individual's inner experience of spiritual struggle and salvation. Faith (based on the word of the Bible) alone was thought sufficient to save, and salvation itself was regarded as a direct transaction with God in the theater of the individual soul, without the need of intermediation by church, priest, or sacrament. For this reason Protestantism is sometimes said to have been an extreme manifestation of "Renaissance individualism" in northern Europe; it soon, however, developed its own type of institutionalism in the theocracy proposed by John Calvin (1509–64) and his Puritan followers. Although England officially broke with the Catholic Church during the reign of Henry VIII, the new religious establishment (the Anglican Church), headed by the monarch, retained many of the characteristics of the old church while embracing selected Protestant theological principles. The result was a political and theological compromise that remained the subject of heated debate for centuries.

3. The new world. In 1492 Christopher Columbus, acting on the persisting and widespread belief in the old Greek idea that the world is a globe, sailed west to find a new commercial route to the East, only to be frustrated by the unexpected barrier of a new continent. The succeeding explorations of this continent and its native populations, and its settlement by Europeans, gave new materials to the literary imagination. The magic world of Shakespeare's *The Tempest*, for example, as well as the treatment of its native inhabitants by Prospero and others, is based on a contemporary account of a shipwreck on Bermuda and other writings about voyages to the New World. More important for English literature, however, was the fact that economic exploitation of

the new world—often cruel, oppressive, and devastating to the native peoples —put England at the center, rather than as heretofore at the edge, of the chief trade routes, and so helped establish the commercial prosperity that in England, as in Italy earlier, was a necessary though not sufficient condition for the development of a vigorous intellectual and artistic life.

4. The new cosmos. The cosmos of medieval astronomy and of medieval Christian theology was **Ptolemaic** (that is, based on the Greek astronomer Ptolemy, second century) and pictured a stationary earth around which rotated the successive spheres of the moon, the various planets, and then the fixed stars. Heaven, or the Empyrean, was thought to be situated above the spheres, and Hell to be situated either at the center of the earth (as in Dante's *Inferno*) or else below the system of the spheres (as in John Milton's *Paradise Lost*). In 1543 Copernicus published his new hypothesis concerning the astronomic system; this gave a much simpler and more coherent explanation of accumulating observations of the actual movements of the heavenly bodies, which had led to ever greater complications within the scheme of the Ptolemaic world picture. The **Copernican theory** proposed a system in which the center is the sun, not the earth, and in which the earth is not stationary, but only one planet among many planets, all of which revolve around the sun.

5. Investigations have not borne out the earlier assumption by historians that the world picture of Copernicus and of the scientists who followed him (sometimes referred to as the **new philosophy**) delivered an immediate and profound shock to the theological and secular beliefs of thinking people. For example in 1611, when Donne wrote in "The First Anniversary" that "new Philosophy calls all in doubt," for "the Sun is lost, and th' earth," he did so only to support the ancient theme, or literary *topos*, of the world's decay, and to enforce a traditional Christian "contemptus mundi" (contempt for the worldly). Still later, Milton in *Paradise Lost* (1667) expressed a suspension of judgment between the Ptolemaic and Copernican theories; he adopted, however, the older Ptolemaic scheme as the cosmic setting for his poem, because it was more firmly traditional and better adapted to his narrative purposes.

6. Much more important, in the long run, was the effect on opinion of the general principles and methods of the **new science** developed by the great successors of Copernicus in the late sixteenth and early seventeenth centuries, such as the physicists Johannes Kepler and Galileo and the English physician and physiologist William Harvey. Even after Copernicus, the cosmos of many writers in the Elizabethan era (exemplified in a number of Shakespeare's plays) not only remained Ptolemaic, it also remained an animate cosmos that was invested with occult powers and inhabited by demons and spirits, and was widely believed to control men's lives by stellar influences and to be itself subject to control by the powers of witchcraft and of magic. The universe that emerged in the course of the seventeenth century, as a product of the scientific procedure of posing hypotheses that could be tested by precisely measured observations, was the physical one propounded by the French philosopher René Descartes (1596–1650). "Give me extension and motion," Descartes wrote, "and I will construct the

universe." The universe of Descartes and the new science consisted of extended particles of matter which moved in space according to fixed mathematical laws, free from interference by angels, demons, human prayer, or occult magical powers. This universe was, however, subject to the manipulations of experimental scientists who set out in this way to discover the laws of nature, and who, in the phrase of the English thinker Francis Bacon, had learned to obey nature in order to be her master. In Descartes and other philosophers, the working hypotheses of the scientists about the physical world were converted into a philosophical worldview, which was made current by popular expositions, and—together with the methodological principle that a controlled observation is the criterion of truth in many areas of knowledge—helped constitute the climate of eighteenth-century opinion known as the *Enlightenment*.

Joan Kelly inaugurated a spirited debate among *feminist* and other scholars with her essay, published in 1977, "Did Women Have a Renaissance?" (in *Women, History and Theory*, 1984). Her own answer to the question, based primarily on evidence from central Italy, was that women did not. For a book by a feminist scholar who counters this claim, by reference to women's changing roles in the family, in the church, and in positions of political and cultural power, see Margaret L. King, *Women of the Renaissance* (1991).

Refer to J. Burckhardt, *Civilization of the Renaissance in Italy* (first published in 1860); E. A. Burtt, *The Metaphysical Foundations of Modern Science* (rev. 1932); C. S. Lewis, *English Literature in the 16th Century* (1954); Marjorie Nicolson, *Science and Imagination* (1956); Thomas S. Kuhn, *The Copernican Revolution* (1957); Paul O. Kristeller, *Renaissance Thought: The Classic, Scholastic, and Humanistic Strains* (rev. 1961); John R. Hale, *The Civilization of Europe in the Renaissance* (1993).

**Renaissance** (historical period): **252**; *144, 285*.

**Renaissance, American: 246**.

**Renaissance, Harlem: 140**.

**Renaissance, Irish Literary: 41**.

**Renaissance man: 308**.

**repartee** (rĕp′ ärtē″): **381**; *49*.

**representation** (in new historicism): **219**.

**resolution** (of a plot): **268**.

**Restoration: 253**; *142*.

**Restoration comedy: 49**; *253, 381*.

**revenge tragedy: 372**.

**reversal** (in a plot): **268**; *331*.

**Revolutionary Age** (in American literature): **246**.

**rhetoric:** In his *Poetics* the Greek philosopher Aristotle defined poetry as a mode of *imitation*—a fictional representation in a verbal medium of human beings thinking, feeling, acting, and interacting—and focused his discussion on elements such as plot, character, thought, and diction within the work itself. In his *Rhetoric*, on the other hand, Aristotle defined rhetorical discourse as the art of "discovering all the available means of persuasion in any given case," and focused his discussion on the means and devices that an orator uses in order to achieve the intellectual and emotional effects on an audience that will persuade them to accede to the orator's point of view. Most of the later rhetoricians of the classical era concurred in the view that the concern of rhetoric is with the type of discourse whose chief aim is to persuade an audience to think and feel or act in a particular way. (A notable exception is the major Roman rhetorician Quintilian who, in the first century, gave rhetoric a moral basis by defining it as the art "of a good man skilled in speaking.") In a broad sense, then, rhetoric can be described as the study of language in its practical uses, focusing on the persuasive and other effects of language, and on the means by which one can achieve those effects on auditors or readers.

Following Aristotle's lead, classical theorists analyzed an effective rhetorical discourse as consisting of three components: *invention* (the finding of arguments or proofs), **disposition** (the arrangement of such materials), and *style* (the choice of words, verbal patterns, and rhythms that will most effectively express and convey these materials). This last topic of "style" came to include extensive classifications and analyses of figurative language. Rhetoricians also discriminated three main classes of oratory, each of which uses characteristic devices to achieve its distinctive type of persuasive effect:

1. **Deliberative**—to persuade an audience (such as a legislative assembly) to approve or disapprove of a matter of public policy, and to act accordingly.
2. **Forensic**—to achieve (for example, in a judicial trial) either the condemnation or approval of some person's actions.
3. **Epideictic**—"display rhetoric," used on appropriate, usually ceremonial, occasions to enlarge upon the praiseworthiness (or sometimes, the blameworthiness) of a person or group of persons, and in so doing, to display the orator's own talents and skill in rising to the rhetorical demands of the occasion. Abraham Lincoln's "Gettysburg Address" is a famed instance of epideictic oratory. In America, it remains traditional for a chosen speaker to meet the challenge of the Fourth of July or other dates of national significance by appropriately ceremonious oratory. The *ode* is a poetic form often used for epideictic purposes.

*Figurative language*, although dealt with at length in classical and later traditional rhetorics, had been considered as only one element of style and, often, as subordinated to the overall aim of persuasion. Within the past century, however, the analysis of the types and functions of figurative language has been increasingly excerpted from this rhetorical context and made an independent and central concern, not only by critics of literature but also by language theorists and by philosophers. (See *metaphor, theories of.*) Some recent theorists regard all modes of discourse to be constituted by "rhetorical" and figurative elements which are inherently nonreferential and counterlogical, and therefore subvert attempts to speak or write in ways that have decidable meanings, or logical coherence, or reference to a world beyond language. (See *deconstruction*.) Other theorists undertake to develop a **cognitive rhetoric**, from the viewpoint of "cognitive science"—that is, representations of the most general operations of the mind and brain (based in part on the workings of high-level computers), which cut across the standard distinctions between literary and nonliterary, and between rhetorical and nonrhetorical mental and linguistic processes. See Mark Turner, *Reading Minds: The Study of English in the Age of Cognitive Science* (1991) and *The Literary Mind* (1996).

Refer to *ethos* (the rhetorical concept of a speaker's projected character that functions as a means of persuasion) under *persona, tone, and voice*; also *rhetorical criticism*. See Aristotle's *Rhetoric*, ed. Lane Cooper (1932), and George A. Kennedy, ed., *Aristotle on Rhetoric* (1991); Quintilian, *Institutes of Oratory* (4 vols., Loeb Classical Library, 1920–22); M. L. Clarke, *Rhetoric at Rome: A Historical Survey* (1953); George Kennedy, *The Art of Persuasion in Greece* (1963); Edward P. J. Corbett, *Classical Rhetoric for the Modern Student* (4th ed., 1998); Thomas O. Sloane, ed., *Encyclopedia of Rhetoric* (2001). For a brief history of rhetoric, from the Greeks to the revived interest among contemporary theorists, see Renato Barilli, *Rhetoric* (trans. 1989). Walter J. Ong, in *Orality and Literacy: The Technologizing of the Word* (1982), discusses the central and pervasive role of rhetoric in Western education through the eighteenth century, and the attendant view that the oral rather than the written mode is the paradigmatic use of language.

For references to *rhetoric* in other entries, see page *312*.

**rhetorical criticism:** The Roman Horace in his versified *Art of Poetry* (first century BC) declared that the aim of a poet is either to instruct or delight a reader, and preferably to do both. This view, by making poetry a calculated means to achieve effects on its audience, breaks down Aristotle's distinction between imitative poetry and persuasive rhetoric (see *rhetoric*). Such *pragmatic criticism* became the dominant form of literary theory from late classical times through the eighteenth century. Discussions of poetry in that long span of time absorbed and expanded upon the analytic terms that had been developed in traditional rhetoric, and represented a poem mainly as a deployment of established artistic means for achieving foreseen effects upon its readers. The triumph in the early nineteenth century of *expressive* theories of literature (which conceive a work primarily as the expression of the feelings, temperament, and mental powers of the author), followed by the prominence, beginning in the 1920s, of *objective* theories of literature (which maintain that a work should be considered as an object in itself, independently of the attributes and intentions of the author and the responses of a reader), served to diminish, and sometimes to eliminate, rhetorical considerations in literary criticism. (See under *criticism*.)

Since the late 1950s, however, there has been a strong revival of interest in literature as a mode of communication from author to reader, and this has led to the development of a **rhetorical criticism** which, without departing from a primary focus on the literary work itself, undertakes to identify and analyze those elements within a poem or a prose narrative which are there primarily in order to effect certain responses in a reader. As Wayne Booth said in the preface to his influential book *The Rhetoric of Fiction* (rev. 1983), his subject is "the rhetorical resources available to the writer of epic, novel, or short story as he tries, consciously or unconsciously, to impose his fictional world upon the reader." A number of recent critics of prose fiction and of narrative and non-narrative poems have emphasized the author's use of a variety of means—including the authorial presence or "voice" that he or she projects—in order to engage the interest and guide the imaginative and emotional responses of the readers to whom, whether consciously or not, the literary work is addressed. (See *persona, tone, and voice.*) Since the 1960s there has also emerged a reader-response criticism which focuses upon a reader's interpretive responses to the sequence of words in a literary text; most of its representatives, however, either ignore or reject the rhetorical view that such responses are effected by devices that, for the most part, are contrived for that purpose by the author. (See *reader-response criticism.*)

For recent examples of the rhetorical criticism of poetry and fiction see (in addition to Wayne Booth) Kenneth Burke, *A Rhetoric of Motives* (1955); M. H. Nichols, *Rhetoric and Criticism* (1963); Donald C. Bryant, ed., *Papers in Rhetoric and Poetic* (1965); Edward P. J. Corbett, ed., *Rhetorical Analyses of Literary Works* (1969); Brian Vickers, *Classical Rhetoric in English Poetry* (2d ed., 1989).

**rhetorical figures:** It is convenient to list under this heading some common "figures of speech" which, according to the traditional analysis, depart from what is experienced by competent users as the standard, or "literal," use of language mainly by the arrangement of their words to achieve special effects, and not, like metaphors and other *tropes*, by a radical change in the meaning of the words themselves. (See *figurative language.*) A number of current theorists, however, reject the distinction between figures of speech and tropes; some reject even the general distinction between literal and figurative language. (See *metaphor, theories of.*)

**Anaphora** (Greek for "repetition") is the deliberate repetition of a word or phrase at the beginning of each one of a sequence of sentences, paragraphs, lines of verse, or *stanzas*. "A Song" by the seventeenth-century English poet Thomas Carew begins:

> Ask me no more where Jove bestows,
> When June is past the fading rose. . . .

Each of the remaining four stanzas also begins with the words: "Ask me no more." Anaphora is notably frequent in the Bible and in verse or prose strongly influenced by the Bible, such as Walt Whitman's poems, or sermons by eloquent black preachers. In the powerful address to Civil Rights marchers by the Reverend Martin Luther King, Jr. in front of the Lincoln Memorial in 1963, five successive sentences begin, "I have a dream," and six later sentences begin "Let freedom ring."

An **apostrophe** is a direct and explicit address either to an absent person or to an abstract or nonhuman entity. Often the effect is of high formality, or else of a sudden emotional impetus. Many *odes* are constituted throughout in the mode of such an address to a listener who is not literally able to listen. So John Keats begins his "Ode on a Grecian Urn" (1820) by apostrophizing the Urn—"Thou still unravished bride of quietness"—and directs the entirety of the poem to the Urn and to the figures represented on it. Samuel Taylor Coleridge's fine lyric "Recollections of Love" (1817) is an apostrophe addressed to an absent woman; at the end of the poem, Coleridge, while speaking still to his beloved, turns by a sudden impulse to apostrophize also the River Greta:

> But when those meek eyes first did seem
> To tell me, Love within you wrought—
> O Greta, dear domestic stream!
> Has not, since then, Love's prompture deep,
> Has not Love's whisper evermore
> Been ceaseless, as thy gentle roar?
> Sole voice, when other voices sleep,
> Dear under-song in clamor's hour.

Many apostrophes, as in these examples from Keats and Coleridge, imply a *person-ification* of the nonhuman object that is addressed. (See Jonathan Culler, "Apostrophe," in *The Pursuit of Signs*, 1981.)

If such an address is to a god or muse or other supernatural being to assist the poet in his composition, it is called an **invocation**. An invocation often serves to establish the authoritative or prophetic identity of the poetic *voice*; thus John Milton invokes divine guidance at the opening of *Paradise Lost*:

> And chiefly Thou, O Spirit, that dost prefer
> Before all temples th' upright heart and pure,
> Instruct me. . . .

**Chiasmus** (derived from the Greek term for the letter X, or for a crossover) is a sequence of two phrases or clauses which are parallel in syntax, but which reverse the order of the corresponding words. So in this line from Pope, the verb first precedes, then follows, the adverbial phrase:

> *Works* without show, and without pomp *presides*.

The crossover is sometimes reinforced by alliteration and other similarities in the length and component sounds of words, as in Pope's summary of the common fate of coquettes after marriage:

> *A fop* their *passion*, but their *prize* a *sot*.

In Yeats' "An Irish Airman Foresees His Death" (1919), the chiasmus consists in a reversal of the position of an entire phrase:

> The years to come seemed *waste of breath*,
> A *waste of breath* the years behind.[12]

---

[12]Lines from "An Irish Airman Foresees His Death" reprinted with permission of Scribner, an imprint of Simon and Schuster Adult Publishing, from *The Poems of W. B. Yeats: A New Edition*, edited by Richard J. Finneran. Copyright © 1919 by Macmillan Publishing Company, renewed 1947 by Bertha Georgie Yeats.

And as a reminder that all figures of speech are used in prose as well as in verse, here is an instance of chiasmus in the position of the two adjectives in Shelley's *Defence of Poetry* (1821): "Poetry is the record of the best and happiest moments of the happiest and best minds."

In **paralipsis** someone says that he need not, or will not, say something, then proceeds to do so. The most familiar use of the figure is on public occasions in which an introducer says that a speaker needs no introduction, then goes on to introduce him or her, often at considerable length. The classic literary example is Mark Antony's funeral oration, in the third act of Shakespeare's *Julius Caesar*, which is constructed around the repeated and devastatingly ironic use of this figure. The speech begins, for example, with the statement "I came to bury Caesar, not to praise him," then proceeds to eulogize Caesar and to incite his auditors against the "honorable men" who have assassinated him.

A **rhetorical question** is a sentence in the grammatical form of a question which is not asked in order to request information or to invite a reply, but to achieve a greater expressive force than a direct assertion. In everyday discourse, for example, if we utter the rhetorical question "Isn't it a shame?" it functions as a forceful alternative to the assertion "It's a shame." (In terms of modern *speech-act theory*, its "illocutionary force" is not to question but to assert.) The figure is often used in persuasive discourse, and tends to impart an oratorical tone to an utterance, whether in prose or verse. When "fierce Thalestris" in Alexander Pope's *The Rape of the Lock* (1714) asks Belinda,

> Gods! Shall the ravisher display your hair,
> While the fops envy, and the ladies stare?

she does not stay for an answer, which she obviously thinks should be "No!" (A common form of rhetorical question is one that won't take "Yes" for an answer.) Shelley's "Ode to the West Wind" (1820) closes with the most famous rhetorical question in English:

> O, Wind,
> If Winter comes, can Spring be far behind?

This figure was a favorite of W. B. Yeats. A well-known instance is "Among School Children," which ends with the rhetorical question, "How can we know the dancer from the dance?" In this instance the poetic context probably indicates that the question is left hanging because it is unanswerable, posing a problem for which there is no certain solution. In a *deconstructive* reading of this and other examples in his *Allegories of Reading* (1979), Paul de Man proposed that it is impossible to decide, not only what the answer is to the question, but also whether it is or is not a question.

**Zeugma** in Greek means "yoking"; in the most common present usage, it is applied to expressions in which a single word stands in the same grammatical relation to two or more other words, but with an obvious shift in its significance. Sometimes the word is literal in one relation and metaphorical in the other. Here are two examples of zeugma in Pope:

> Or *stain* her honour, or her new brocade.
>
> *Obliged* by hunger, and request of friends.

Byron uses zeugma for grimly comic effects in his description of a shipwreck in *Don Juan* (1819–24), Canto 2:

> And the waves oozing through the port-hole *made*
> His berth a little damp, and him afraid.
>
> The loud tempests *raise*
> The waters, and repentance for past sinning.

To achieve the maximum of concentrated verbal effects within the tight limits of the *closed couplet*, Pope in the early eighteenth century exploited all the language patterns described in this entry with supreme virtuosity. He is an English master of the rhetorical figures, as Shakespeare is of tropes.

Other linguistic patterns or "schemes" that are sometimes classified as rhetorical figures are treated elsewhere in this *Glossary*; see *antithesis, alliteration, assonance*, rhetorical *climax* (under *bathos*), and *parallelism*. For concise definitions and examples of additional figures of speech which are less commonly referred to in literary analyses, see Edward P. J. Corbett, *Classical Rhetoric for the Modern Student* (4th ed., 1998), and Arthur Quinn's entertaining and informative *Figures of Speech: Sixty Ways to Turn a Phrase* (1993). See references under "figurative language."

**rhetorical question: 315**.

**rhyme:** In English versification, standard rhyme consists of the repetition, in the rhyming words, of the last stressed vowel and of all the speech sounds following that vowel: láte-fáte; fóllow-hóllow.

**End rhymes**, by far the most frequent type, occur at the end of a verse line. **Internal rhymes** occur within a verse line, as in the Victorian poet Algernon Swinburne's

> Sister, my sister, O *fleet sweet* swallow.

A stanza from Coleridge's "The Rime of the Ancient Mariner" illustrates the patterned use both of internal rhymes (within lines 1 and 3) and of an end rhyme (lines 2 and 4):

> In mist or *cloud*, on mast or *shroud*,
> It perched for vespers *nine*;
> Whiles all the *night*, through fog-smoke *white*,
> Glimmered the white moon-*shine*.

The numbered lines in the following stanza of Wordsworth's "The Solitary Reaper" (1807) are followed by a column which, in the conventional way, marks the terminal rhyme elements by a corresponding sequence and repetition of the letters of the alphabet:

1. Whate'er her theme, the maiden sang    *a*

2. As if her song could have no *ending;*    *b*

3. I saw her singing at her work    *c*

4. And o'er the sickle *bending*—    *b*

5. I listened, motionless and *still;*    *d*

6. And as I mounted up the *hill,*    *d*

7. The music in my heart I *bore,*    *e*

8. Long after it was heard no *more.*    *e*

Lines 1 and 3 do not rhyme with any other line. Both in lines 5 and 6 and in lines 7 and 8 the rhyme consists of a single stressed syllable, and is called a **masculine rhyme**: stíll–híll, bóre–móre. In lines 2 and 4, the rhyme consists of a stressed syllable followed by an unstressed syllable, and is called a **feminine rhyme**: éndĭng–béndĭng.

A feminine rhyme, since it involves the repetition of two syllables, is also known as a **double rhyme**. A rhyme involving three syllables is called a **triple rhyme**; such rhymes, since they coincide with surprising patness, usually have a comic quality. In *Don Juan* (1819–24) Byron often uses triple rhymes such as comparison–garrison, and sometimes intensifies the comic effect by permitting the pressure of the rhyme to force a distortion of the pronunciation. This maltreatment of words, called **forced rhyme**, in which the poet gives the effect of seeming to surrender helplessly to the exigencies of a difficult rhyme, has been comically exploited by the poet Ogden Nash:

> Farewell, farewell, you old rhinocerous,
> I'll stare at something less prepocerous.[13]

If the correspondence of the rhymed sounds is exact, it is called **perfect rhyme**, or else "full" or "true rhyme." Until recently almost all English writers of serious poems have limited themselves to perfect rhymes, except for an occasional *poetic license* such as **eye-rhymes**: words whose endings are spelled alike, and in most instances were once pronounced alike, but have in the course of time acquired a different pronunciation: prove–love, daughter–laughter. Many modern poets, however, deliberately supplement perfect rhyme with **imperfect rhyme** (also known as **partial rhyme**, or else as "near rhyme," **slant rhyme**, or **pararhyme**). This effect is fairly common in *folk songs* such as children's verses, and it was employed occasionally by various writers of art lyrics such as Henry Vaughan in the seventeenth, William Blake in the late eighteenth, and very frequently by Emily Dickinson in the nineteenth century. More recently, Gerard Manley Hopkins, W. B. Yeats, Wilfred Owen, and other poets have systematically exploited partial rhymes, in which the vowels are only approximate or else

---

[13]Lines from "The Rhinoceros" by Ogden Nash, from *Verses from 1929 On* by Ogden Nash. Copyright © 1933 by Ogden Nash, renewed. Reprinted by permission of Curtis Brown, Ltd.

quite different, and occasionally even the rhymed consonants are similar rather than identical. Wilfred Owen, in 1917–18, wrote the following six-line stanza using only two sets of partial rhymes, established at the ends of the first two lines:

> The centuries will burn rich loads
>    With which we groaned,
> Whose warmth shall lull their dreamy lids,
>    While songs are crooned.
> But they will not dream of us poor lads,
>    Lost in the ground.[14]

In his poem "The Force That Through the Green Fuse Drives the Flower" (1933), Dylan Thomas uses, very effectively, such distantly approximate rhymes as (with masculine endings) trees–rose, rocks–wax, tomb–worm, and (with feminine endings) flower–destroyer–fever.

    **Rime riche** (French for "rich rhyme") is the repetition of the consonant that precedes, as well as the one that follows, the last stressed vowel; the resulting pair of words are pronounced alike but have different meanings: stare-stair, night-knight. The device is common in French poetry and was adopted by Geoffrey Chaucer. Early in the General Prologue to *The Canterbury Tales*, for example, he rhymes "seke," which has two diverse meanings, "seek" and "sick." The pilgrims go to Canterbury

> the holy blissful martyr for to seke
> That hem hath holpen whan they were seke.

The use of rime riche is very rare in English poetry after Chaucer.

    The passages quoted above will illustrate some of the many effects that can be achieved by the device that has been called "making ends meet in verse"—the pleasure of the expected yet varying chime; the reinforcement of syntax and rhetorical emphasis when a strong masculine rhyme concurs with the end of a clause, sentence, or stanza; the sudden grace of movement that may be lent by a feminine rhyme; the broadening of the comic by a pat coincidence of sound; the haunting effect of the limited *consonance* in partial rhymes. Cunning artificers in verse make rhyme more than an auxiliary sound effect; they use it to enhance, or contribute to, or counterpoint the significance of the words. When Pope in the early eighteenth century satirized two contemporary pedants in the lines

> Yet ne'er one sprig of laurel graced these ribalds,
> From slashing Bentley down to piddling Tibalds,

the rhyme of "Tibalds," as W. K. Wimsatt has said, demonstrates "what it means to have a name like that," with its implication that the scholar is as graceless as his appellation. And in one of its important functions, rhyme ties individual lines into the larger pattern of a *stanza*.

---

[14]Lines from "Miners" by Wilfred Owen, from *The Collected Poems of Wilfred Owen*. Copyright 1963 Chatto & Windos, Ltd. Reprinted by permission of New Directions Publishing Corporation.

See George Saintsbury, *History of English Prosody* (3 vols., 1906–10); W. K. Wimsatt, "One Relation of Rhyme to Reason," in *The Verbal Icon* (1954); Donald Wesling, *The Chances of Rhyme: Device and Modernity* (1980); John Hollander, *Rhyme's Reason: A Guide to English Verse* (1981). For an analysis of the complex interrelations between sound repetitions and meaning, see Roman Jakobson, "Linguistics and Poetics," in his *Language and Literature* (1987). For references to rhyme in other entries, see page *127*.

**rhythm: 194**.

**rime riche: 318**.

**rime royal: 342**.

**rising action: 267**.

**rituals: 206**.

**roman** (the genre) (rōmän′): **226**.

**roman à clef** (French for "novel with a key"): Roman à clef is a work of prose fiction in which the author expects the knowing reader to identify, despite their altered names, actual people of the time. The mode was begun in seventeenth-century France with novels such as Madeleine de Scudéry's *Le Grand Cyrus* (1649–53). An English example is Thomas Love Peacock's *Nightmare Abbey* (1818), whose characters are entertaining *caricatures* of such contemporary literary figures as Coleridge, Byron, and Shelley. A later instance is Aldous Huxley's *Point Counter Point* (1928), which represents, under fictional names, well-known English personages of the 1920s such as the novelist D. H. Lawrence, the critic Middleton Murry, and the right-wing political extremist Oswald Mosely.

**romance, the: 44**; *8*. See also *prose romance; chivalric romance; Gothic romance; romantic comedy; wilderness romance*.

**romantic** (ideas and aims): **213**; *206*.

**romantic comedy: 49**; *344*.

**romantic irony: 167**.

**Romantic Period: 255**; *20, 22, 56, 91, 135, 169, 289, 361, 363*.

**Romantic Period in America: 246**.

**round character: 43**.

**rules** (linguistic): **176**.

**rules** (neoclassic): **212**.

**run-on lines: 197**.

**Russian formalism: 126**; *6, 209, 303, 346, 352*. See also *formalism*.

**sarcasm: 167.**

**satire:** Satire can be described as the literary art of diminishing or derogating a subject by making it ridiculous and evoking toward it attitudes of amusement, contempt, scorn, or indignation. It differs from the *comic* in that comedy evokes laughter mainly as an end in itself, while satire derides; that is, it uses laughter as a weapon, and against a butt that exists outside the work itself. That butt may be an individual (in "personal satire"), or a type of person, a class, an institution, a nation, or even (as in the Earl of Rochester's "A Satyr against Mankind," 1675, and much of Jonathan Swift's *Gulliver's Travels*, 1726, especially Book IV) the entire human race. The distinction between the comic and the satiric, however, is sharp only at its extremes. Shakespeare's Falstaff is mainly a comic creation, presented primarily for our enjoyment; the puritanical Malvolio in Shakespeare's *Twelfth Night* is for the most part comic but has aspects of satire directed against the type of the fatuous and hypocritical Puritan; Ben Jonson's *Volpone* (1607) clearly satirizes the type of person whose cleverness—or stupidity—is put at the service of his cupidity; and John Dryden's *MacFlecknoe* (1682), while representing a permanent type of the pretentious *poetaster*, satirized specifically the living author Thomas Shadwell.

Satire has usually been justified by those who practice it as a corrective of human vice and folly; Alexander Pope, for example, remarked that "those who are ashamed of nothing else are so of being ridiculous." Its frequent claim (not always borne out in the practice) has been to ridicule the failing rather than the individual, and to limit its ridicule to corrigible faults, excluding those for which a person is not responsible. As Swift said, speaking of himself in his *ironic* "Verses on the Death of Dr. Swift" (1739):

> Yet malice never was his aim;
> He lashed the vice, but spared the name . . . .
> His satire points at no defect,
> But what all mortals may correct . . . .
> He spared a hump, or crooked nose,
> Whose owners set not up for beaux.

Satire occurs as an incidental element within many works whose overall mode is not satiric—in a certain character or situation, or in an interpolated passage of ironic commentary on some aspect of the human condition or of contemporary society. But for some literary writings, verse or prose, the attempt to diminish a subject by ridicule is the primary organizing principle, and these works constitute the formal *genre* labeled "satires." In discussing such writings the following distinctions are useful:

1. Critics make a broad division between formal (or "direct") satire and indirect satire. In **formal satire** the satiric *persona* speaks out in the first person. This "I" may address either the reader (as in Pope's *Moral Essays*, 1731–35), or else a character within the work itself, who is called the **adversarius** and whose major artistic function is to elicit and add credibility to the satiric speaker's comments. (In Pope's "Epistle to Dr. Arbuthnot," 1735, Arbuthnot serves as adversarius.) Two types of formal satire are commonly distinguished, taking their names from the great Roman satirists Horace

and Juvenal. The types are defined by the character of the persona whom the author presents as the first-person satiric speaker, and also by the attitude and *tone* that such a persona manifests toward both the subject matter and the readers of the work.

In **Horatian satire** the speaker manifests the character of an urbane, witty, and tolerant man of the world, who is moved more often to wry amusement than to indignation at the spectacle of human folly, pretentiousness, and hypocrisy, and who uses a relaxed and informal language to evoke from readers a wry smile at human failings and absurdities—sometimes including his own. Horace himself described his aim as "to laugh people out of their vices and follies." Pope's *Moral Essays* and other formal satires for the most part sustain an Horatian stance.

In **Juvenalian satire** the character of the speaker is that of a serious moralist who uses a dignified and public style of utterance to decry modes of vice and error which are no less dangerous because they are ridiculous, and who undertakes to evoke from readers contempt, moral indignation, or an unillusioned sadness at the aberrations of humanity. Samuel Johnson's "London" (1738) and "The Vanity of Human Wishes" (1749) are distinguished instances of Juvenalian satire. In its most denunciatory instances, this mode of satire resembles the *jeremiad*, whose model is not Roman but Hebraic.

2. **Indirect satire** is cast in some other literary form than that of direct address to the reader. The most common indirect form is that of a fictional narrative, in which the objects of the satire are characters who make themselves and their opinions ridiculous or obnoxious by what they think, say, and do, and are sometimes made even more ridiculous by the author's comments and narrative style.

One type of indirect satire is **Menippean satire**, modeled on a Greek form developed by the Cynic philosopher Menippus. It is sometimes called **Varronian satire**, after a Roman imitator, Varro; Northrop Frye, in *Anatomy of Criticism*, pp. 308–12, suggests an alternative name, the **anatomy**, after a major English instance of the type, Burton's *Anatomy of Melancholy* (1621). Such satires are written in prose, usually with interpolations of verse, and constitute a miscellaneous form often held together by a loosely constructed narrative. A prominent feature is a series of extended dialogues and debates (often conducted at a banquet or party) in which a group of loquacious eccentrics, pedants, literary people, and representatives of various professions or philosophical points of view serve to make ludicrous the attitudes and viewpoints they typify by the arguments they urge in their support. Examples are Rabelais' *Gargantua and Pantagruel* (1564), Voltaire's *Candide* (1759), Thomas Love Peacock's *Nightmare Abbey* (1818) and other satiric fiction, and Aldous Huxley's *Point Counter Point* (1928); in this last novel, as in those of Peacock, the central satiric scenes are discussions and disputes during a weekend at a country manor. Frye also classifies Lewis Carroll's two books about Alice in Wonderland as "perfect Menippean satires."

It should be noted that any narrative or other literary vehicle can be adapted to the purposes of indirect satire. John Dryden's *Absalom and*

*Achitophel* turns Old Testament history into a satiric allegory on *Restoration* political maneuverings. In *Gulliver's Travels* Swift converts to satiric use the early eighteenth-century accounts of voyage and discovery, and his *Modest Proposal* is written in the form of a project in political economy. Many of Joseph Addison's *Spectator* papers are satiric essays; Byron's *Don Juan* is a versified satiric form of the old episodic *picaresque* fiction; Ben Jonson's *The Alchemist*, Molière's *The Misanthrope*, Wycherley's *The Country Wife*, and Shaw's *Arms and the Man* are satiric plays; and Gilbert and Sullivan's *Patience*, and other works such as John Gay's eighteenth-century *Beggar's Opera* and its modern adaptation by Bertolt Brecht, *The Threepenny Opera* (1928), are satiric operettas. T. S. Eliot's *The Waste Land* (1922) employs motifs from myth in a work which can be considered by and large as a verse satire directed against what Eliot perceives as the spiritual dearth in twentieth-century life. The greatest number of modern satires, however, are written in prose, and especially in novelistic form; for example Evelyn Waugh's *The Loved One*, Joseph Heller's *Catch*-22, and Kurt Vonnegut, Jr.'s *Player Piano* and *Cat's Cradle*. Charlie Chaplin's *Modern Times* (1936) and *The Great Dictator* (1940) are classic instances of dramatic satire in the cinema. Much of the satiric thrust in current *black humor* is directed against what the author conceives to be the widespread contemporary condition of social cruelty, inanity, or chaos.

Effective English satire has been written in every period beginning with the Middle Ages. Pieces in the English *Punch* and the American *New Yorker* demonstrate that formal essayistic satire, like satiric novels, plays, and cinema, still commands a wide audience; and W. H. Auden is a twentieth-century author who wrote superb satiric poems. The proportioning of the examples in this article, however, indicates how large the Restoration and eighteenth century loom in satiric achievement: the century and a half that included Dryden, the Earl of Rochester, Samuel Butler, Wycherley, Aphra Behn, Addison, Pope, Lady Mary Wortley Montagu, Swift, Gay, Fielding, Johnson, Oliver Goldsmith, and late in the period (it should not be overlooked) the Robert Burns of "The Holy Fair" and "Holy Willie's Prayer" and the William Blake of *The Marriage of Heaven and Hell*. This same span of time was also in France the period of such major satirists as Boileau, La Fontaine, and Voltaire, as well as Molière, the most eminent of all satirists in drama. In the nineteenth century, American satire broke free of English domination with the light satiric touch of Washington Irving's *Sketch Book*, the deft satiric essays of Oliver Wendell Holmes (*The Autocrat of the Breakfast Table*), and above all the satiric essays and novels of Mark Twain.

See also *light verse*. The articles on *burlesque*, on *irony*, and on *wit, humor, and the comic* describe some of the derogatory modes and devices available to satirists. Consult James Sutherland, *English Satire* (1958); Gilbert Highet, *The Anatomy of Satire* (1962); Alvin B. Kernan, *The Plot of Satire* (1965); Matthew Hodgart, *Satire* (1969); Charles Sanders, *The Scope of Satire* (1971); Michael Seidel, *Satiric Inheritance, Rabelais to Sterne* (1979); Dustin Griffin, *Satire: A Critical Reintroduction* (1994); Fredric V. Bogel, *The Difference Satire Makes: Rhetoric and Reading from Jonson to Byron* (2001). Anthologies: Ronald Paulson, ed., *Satire: Modern Essays in Criticism* (1971); Ashley Brown and John L. Kimmey, eds., *Satire: An Anthology*

(1977), which includes both satiric writings and critical essays on satire. For references to *satire* in other entries, see pages *8, 35, 80, 378, 382.*

**satiric comedy: 49**.

**scan: 196**.

**scansion** (skăn′ shŭn): **196**.

**scenario: 52**.

**scene** (in drama): **3**.

**schemes** (figures of speech): **119**.

**science fiction and fantasy:** These terms encompass novels and short stories that represent an imagined reality that is radically different in its nature and functioning from the world of our ordinary experience. Often the setting is another planet, or this earth projected into the future, or an imagined parallel universe. The two terms are not sharply discriminated, but by and large the term **science fiction** is applied to those narratives in which—unlike in pure **fantasy**—an explicit attempt is made to render plausible the fictional world by reference to known or imagined scientific principles, or to a projected advance in technology, or to a drastic change in the organization of society.

Mary Shelley's remarkable *Frankenstein* (1818) is often considered a precursor of science fiction, but the basing of fictional worlds on explicit and coherently developed scientific principles did not occur until later in the nineteenth century, in such writings as Jules Verne's *Journey to the Center of the Earth* and H. G. Wells' *The War of the Worlds*. More recent important authors of science fiction include Isaac Asimov, Arthur Clarke, Ray Bradbury, J. G. Ballard, and Doris Lessing. Science fiction is also frequently represented in television and film; a notable instance is the *Star Trek* series.

Fantasy is as old as the fictional *utopias*, and its *satiric* forms have an important precursor in the extraordinary countries portrayed in Jonathan Swift's *Gulliver's Travels* (1726). Among the notable recent writers of fantasy are C. S. Lewis and J. R. R. Tolkien (*The Hobbit, The Lord of the Rings*), whose works incorporate materials from classical, biblical, and medieval sources. Ursula Le Guin is a major author of both science fiction and works of fantasy.

Some instances of science fiction and fantasy project a future utopia (Le Guin's *The Dispossessed*), or else attack an aspect of current science or society by imagining their dystopian conclusion (George Orwell's *Nineteen Eighty-Four*, 1949, and Margaret Atwood's *The Handmaid's Tale*, 1986); and many writers use their imaginary settings, as Swift had in *Gulliver's Travels*, for political and social satire (Aldous Huxley's *Brave New World* and much of Vonnegut's prose fiction). See *utopia and dystopia* and *satire*.

**Cyberpunk** emerged in the 1970s as a *postmodern* form of science fiction in which the events take place partially or entirely within the "virtual reality" formed by computers or computer networks, in which the characters may be either human or artificial intelligences. A well-known instance is William Gibson's

*Neuromancer*. See the essays in *Fiction 2000: Cyberpunk and the Future of Narrative*, eds. George Slusser and Tom Shippey (1992).

For other novelistic forms that depart radically from the world of ordinary experience, see *magic realism* and *metafiction*, under *novel*. Refer to Kingsley Amis, *New Maps of Hell: A Survey of Science Fiction* (1960); H. Bruce Franklin, *Future Perfect: American Science Fiction of the Nineteenth Century* (rev. 1978); Robert Scholes and Eric S. Rabkin, *Science Fiction: History, Science, Vision* (1977); Ursula K. Le Guin, *The Language of the Night: Essays on Fantasy and Science Fiction* (1979); Gary K. Wolfe, *Critical Terms for Science Fiction and Fantasy* (1986); Jane Donawerth, *Frankenstein's Daughters: Women Writing Science Fiction* (1997).

**scriptoria:** 30.

**second-person points of view:** 274.

**self-conscious narrator:** 275; *168*.

**self-reflexive novel:** 275.

**semantics:** 174.

**semiology:** 324.

**semiotics:** At the end of the nineteenth century Charles Sanders Peirce, the American philosopher, proposed and described a study that he called "semiotic," and in his *Course in General Linguistics* (1915) the Swiss linguist Ferdinand de Saussure independently proposed a science that he called "semiology." Since then **semiotics** and **semiology** have become alternative names for the systematic study of signs, as these function in all areas of human experience. The consideration of **signs** (conveyors of meaning) is not limited to explicit systems of communication such as language. The Morse code, traffic signs and signals, and a great diversity of other human activities and productions—our bodily postures and gestures, the social rituals we perform, the kinds of clothes we wear, the meals we serve, the buildings we inhabit, the objects we deal with—also convey common meanings to members who participate in a particular culture, and so can be analyzed as signs which function in diverse modes of signifying systems. Although the study of language (the use of specifically verbal signs) is technically regarded as only one branch of the general science of semiotics, *linguistics*, the highly developed science of language, in fact has for the most part supplied the basic concepts and methods that a semiotician applies to the study of other social sign systems.

C. S. Peirce distinguished three classes of signs, defined in terms of the kind of relation that exists between a signifying item and that which it signifies: (1) An **icon** functions as a sign by means of inherent similarities, or shared features, with what it signifies; examples are the similarity of a portrait to the person it depicts, or the similarity of a map to the geographical area it stands for. (2) An **index** is a sign which bears a natural relation of cause or of effect to what it signifies; thus, smoke is a sign indicating fire, and a pointing weathervane indicates the direction of the wind. (3) In the **symbol** (or in a less ambiguous term, the "**sign proper**"), the relation between the signifying item and what it signifies is not a natural one, but entirely a matter of social convention. The gesture of shaking hands, for example, in some cultures is a conventional sign of greeting or parting, and a red traffic light conventionally signifies "Stop!" The major and most complex examples of this third type of purely conventional sign, however, are the words that constitute a language.

Ferdinand de Saussure introduced many of the terms and concepts exploited by current semioticians; see Saussure under *linguistics in modern criticism*. Most important are the following: (1) A sign consists of two inseparable components or aspects, the *signifier* (in language, a set of speech sounds, or of marks on a page) and the *signified* (the concept, or idea, which is the meaning of the sign). (2) A verbal sign, in Saussure's term, is "arbitrary." That is, with the minor exception of *onomatopoeia* (words which we perceive as similar to the sounds they signify), there is no inherent, or natural, connection between a verbal signifier and what it signifies. (3) The identity of all elements of a language, including its words, their component speech sounds, and the concepts the words signify, are not determined by "positive qualities," or objective features in these elements themselves, but by *differences*, or a network of relationships, consisting of distinctions and oppositions from other speech sounds, other words, and other signifieds that obtain only within a particular linguistic system. (4) The aim of linguistics, or of any other semiotic enterprise, is to regard the *parole* (a single verbal utterance, or a particular use of a sign or set of signs) as only a manifestation of the *langue* (that is, the general system of implicit differentiations and rules of combination which underlie and make possible a particular use of signs). The focus of semiotic interest, accordingly, is not in interpreting a particular instance of signification but in establishing the general signifying system that each particular instance relies upon.

Modern semiotics, like structuralism, has developed in France under the aegis of Saussure, so that many semioticians are also structuralists. They deal with any set of social phenomena or social productions as "texts"; that is, as constituted by self-sufficient, self-ordering, hierarchical structures of differentially determined signs, codes, and rules of combination and transformation which make the texts "meaningful" to members of a particular society who are competent in that signifying system. (See *structuralist criticism*.) Claude Lévi-Strauss, in the 1960s and later, inaugurated the application of semiotics to cultural anthropology, and also established the foundations of French structuralism in general, by using Saussure's linguistics as a model for analyzing, in primitive societies, a great variety of phenomena and practices, which he treated as quasi-languages that manifest the structures of an underlying signifying system. These include kinship systems, totemic systems, ways of preparing food, myths, and prelogical modes of interpreting the world. Jacques Lacan has applied semiotics to Freudian psychoanalysis—interpreting the unconscious, for example, as (like language) a structure of signs (see Lacan under *psychological and psychoanalytic criticism*). Michel Foucault developed a mode of semiotic analysis to deal with the changing medical interpretations of symptoms of disease; the diverse ways of identifying, classifying, and treating insanity; and the altering conceptions of human sexuality (see under *poststructuralism*). Roland Barthes, explicitly applying Saussurean principles and methods, has written semiotic analyses of the constituents and codes of the differential sign systems in advertisements which describe and promote women's fashions, as well as analyses of many "bourgeois myths" about the world which, he claims, are exemplified in such social sign systems as professional wrestling matches, children's toys, cookery, and the striptease. (See his *Mythologies*, trans. 1972.) In his earlier writings Barthes was also a major exponent of *structuralist criticism*, which deals with a literary text as "a second-order semiotic system"; that is, it views a literary text as employing the first-order semiotic system of language to form a secondary semiotic structure, in accordance with a specifically literary system of conventions and codes.

For a related field of study, which can be characterized as the semiotics of culture, see *cultural studies*. Introductions to the elements of semiotic theory are included in Terence Hawkes, *Structuralism and Semiotics* (1977); Jonathan Culler, *The Pursuit of Signs* (1981); Robert Scholes, *Semiotics and Interpretation* (1982); also in the anthologies, Thomas A. Sebeok, ed., *The Tell-Tale Sign: A Survey of Semiotics* (1975); and Robert E. Innis, ed., *Semiotics: An Introductory Anthology* (1985). See also Umberto Eco, *A Theory of Semiotics* (1976); Roland Barthes, *Elements of Semiology* (trans. 1967); Thomas A. Sebeok, *Semiotics in the United States* (1991). Among the semiotic analyses of diverse social phenomena available in English are Claude Lévi-Strauss, *Structural Anthropology* (1968) and *The Raw and the Cooked* (1966); Roland Barthes, *Selected Writings*, ed. Susan Sontag (1983); Jacques Lacan, *The Language of the Self: The Function of Language in Psychoanalysis* (1968); and Michel Foucault, *The Archaeology of Knowledge* (1972), *Madness and Civilization* (1965), and *The Birth of the Clinic* (1973). On semiotics and literary analysis, see Maria Corti, *An Introduction to Literary Semiotics* (1978); Michael Riffaterre, *Semiotics of Poetry* (1978); and, in application to dramatic literature, Marvin Carlson, *Theatre Semiotics: Signs of Life* (1990). For a critical view of semiotics, see J. G. Merquior, *From Prague to Paris* (1986).

For references to *semiotics* in other entries, see pages *171, 175, 293*.

**sensibility, literature of:** When a contemporary critic talks of a poet's **sensibility**, the reference is to a characteristic way of responding, in perception, thought, and feeling, to experience; and when T. S. Eliot claimed that a *dissociation of sensibility* set in with the poetry of John Milton and John Dryden, he signified that there occurred at that time a division between a poet's sensuous, intellectual, and emotional modes of experience. When a literary historian, however, talks of the **literature of sensibility**, the reference is to a particular cultural phenomenon of the eighteenth century. This type of literature was fostered by the moral philosophy that had developed as a reaction against seventeenth-century Stoicism (which emphasized reason and the unemotional will as the sole motives to virtue), and even more importantly, as a reaction against Thomas Hobbes' claims, in *Leviathan*

(1651), that a human being is innately selfish and that the mainsprings of human behavior are self-interest and the drive for power and status. In opposition to such views, many sermons, philosophical writings, and popular tracts and essays proclaimed that "benevolence"—wishing other persons well—is an innate human sentiment and motive, and that the central elements in morality are the feelings of sympathy and "sensibility"—that is, a hair-trigger responsiveness to another person's distresses and joys. (See *empathy and sympathy*.) "Sensibility" also connoted an intense emotional responsiveness to beauty and *sublimity*, whether in nature or in art, and such responsiveness was often represented as an index to a person's gentility—that is, to one's upper-class status.

Emphasis on the human capability for sympathy and wishing others well—an important contribution was Adam Smith's *The Theory of Moral Sentiments* (1759)—helped to develop social consciousness and a sense of communal responsibility in an era of expanding commercialism and of an economy based on self interest. (For a recent application of Smith's *Theory of the Moral Sentiments* to literature, see Martha Craven Nussbaum, *Love's Knowledge*, 1990, chapter 14.) Highly exaggerated forms of sympathy and manifestations of benevolence, however, became prominent in eighteenth-century culture and literature. It was a commonplace in widespread views of morality that readiness to shed a sympathetic tear, quite apart from moral actions, is the sign both of polite breeding and a virtuous heart; and such a view was often accompanied by the observation that sympathy with another's grief, unlike personal grief, is a pleasurable emotion, hence to be sought as a value in itself. Common phrases in the cult of sensibility were the *oxymorons* "the luxury of grief," "pleasurable sorrows," and "the sadly pleasing tear." A late-eighteenth-century mortuary inscription in Dorchester Abbey reads:

> Reader! If thou hast a Heart fam'd for Tenderness and Pity,
> Contemplate this Spot. In which are deposited the Remains of a
> Young Lady. . . . When Nerves were too delicately spun to bear the
> rude Shakes and Jostlings which we meet with in this transitory world,
> Nature gave way; She sunk and died a Martyr to Excessive Sensibility.

It is clear that much of what in that age was called, with approval, "sensibility" we now call, with disapproval, *sentimentalism*.

In literature these ideas and tendencies were reflected in the **drama of sensibility**, or **sentimental comedy**, which were representations of middle-class life that replaced the tough amorality and the comic or satiric representation of aristocratic sexual license in *Restoration comedy*. In the contemporary plays of sensibility, Oliver Goldsmith remarked in his "Comparison between Sentimental and Laughing Comedy" (1773), "the virtues of private life are exhibited rather than the vices exposed, and the distresses rather than the faults of mankind make our interest in the piece"; the characters, "though they want humor, have abundance of sentiment and feeling"; with the result, he added, that the audience "sit at a play as gloomy as at the tabernacle." Plays such as Richard Steele's *The Conscious Lovers* (1722) and Richard Cumberland's *The West Indian* (1771) present monumentally benevolent heroes and heroines of the middle class, whose dialogue abounds with elevated moral sentiments and who, prior to the manipulated happy ending, suffer tribulations designed to evoke from the audience the maximum of pleasurable tears.

The **novel of sensibility**, or **sentimental novel**, of the latter part of the eighteenth century similarly emphasized the tearful distresses of the virtuous, either at their own sorrows or at those of their friends; some of them represented in addition a sensitivity to beauty or sublimity in natural phenomena which also expressed itself in tears. Samuel Richardson's *Pamela; or, Virtue Rewarded* (1740) exploits sensibility in some of its scenes; and Laurence Sterne, in *Tristram Shandy* and *A Sentimental Journey*, published in the 1760s, gives us his own inimitable compound of sensibility, self-irony, and innuendo. The vogue of sensibility was international. Jean-Jacques Rousseau's novel *Julie, or the New Héloise* (1761) dealt with lovers who manifest sensibility, and in his autobiography, *The Confessions* (written 1764–70), Rousseau represented himself, in some circumstances and moods, as a man of extravagant sensibility. Goethe's novel *The Sorrows of Young Werther* (1774) was an enormously popular presentation of the aesthetic sensitivities and finespun emotional tribulations of a young man who, frustrated in his love for a woman betrothed to another, and in general unable to adapt his sensibility to the demands of ordinary life, finally shoots himself.

An extreme English instance of the sentimental novel is Henry Mackenzie's *The Man of Feeling* (1771), which represents a hero of such exquisite sensibility that he goes into a decline from excess of pent-up tenderness toward a young lady, and dies in the perturbation of finally declaring to her his emotion. "If all his tears had been tears of blood," declares an editor of the novel, Hamish Miles, "the poor man could hardly have been more debile." Jane Austen's gently satiric treatment of a young woman of sensibility in *Sense and Sensibility* (begun 1797, published 1811) marks the decline of the fashion; but the exploitation of the mode of literary sensibility survives in such later novelistic episodes as the death of Little Nell in Charles Dickens' *Old Curiosity Shop* (1841) and the death of Little Eva in Harriet Beecher Stowe's *Uncle Tom's Cabin* (1852). Sentimentality is exploited also in Victorian *melodramas*, as well as in many movies that Hollywood labeled "tearjerkers."

In *The Politics of Sensibility* (1996), Markman Ellis departs from the usual derogatory treatment of the sentimental novels of the later eighteenth century, by arguing that they contributed to movements for social reform, including opposition to slavery, criticism of the questionable morality involved in some commercial and business practices, and the movement for the reformation and relief of prostitutes.

In America, sentimental novels were referred to as "woman's fiction" or "domestic novels," and often involved the story of a young girl who must make her way in the world unprotected. See Nina Baym, *Woman's Fiction: A Guide to Novels by and about Women in America, 1820-70* (2d ed., 1993). According to Jane Tompkins, many novels denigrated by sophisticated readers as overly sentimental or merely popular in fact represented attempts to reorganize culture from the women's point of view, and in some cases achieved devastating critiques of American society. See "Sentimental Power: *Uncle Tom's Cabin* and the Politics of Literary History," chapter 5 in *Sensational Designs: The Cultural Work of American Fiction, 1790-1860* (1985).

See *Age of Sensibility* under *periods of English literature*. Refer to Arthur Sherbo, *English Sentimental Drama* (1957); R. P. Utter and G. B. Needham, *Pamela's Daughters* (1963); R. S. Crane, "Suggestions toward a Genealogy of the 'Man of Feeling'," in *The Idea of the Humanities* (2 vols., 1967); Janet Todd, *Sensibility: An Introduction* (1986); John Mullan, *Sentiment and Sociability: The Language of Feeling in the Eighteenth Century* (1988); G. J. Barker-Benfield, *The Culture of Sensibility: Sex and Society in Eighteenth-Century Britain* (1992); Claude Rawson, *Satire and Sentiment 1660–1830* (1994); Jerome McGann, *The Poetics of Sensibility* (1996); Paul Goring, *Rhetoric of Sensibility in Eighteenth-Century Culture* (2005).

**sentimental comedy: 327**; *50.*

**sentimental novel: 328**.

**sentimentalism:** Sentimentalism is now a derogatory term applied to what is perceived to be an excess of emotion to an occasion, and especially to an overindulgence in the "tender" emotions of pathos and sympathy. Since what constitutes emotional excess or overindulgence is relative both to the judgment of the individual and to large-scale historical changes in culture and in literary fashion, what to the common reader of one age is a normal and laudable expression of humane feeling may seem sentimental to many later readers. The emotional responses of a lover that Shelley expresses and tries to evoke from the reader in his "Epipsychidion" (1821) seemed sentimental to the *New Critics* of the 1930s and later, who insisted on the need for an ironic counterpoise to intense feeling in poetry. Most readers now find both the *drama of sensibility* and the *novel of sensibility* of the eighteenth century ludicrously sentimental, and respond with jeers instead of tears to once celebrated episodes of pathos, such as many of the death scenes, especially those of children, in some Victorian novels and dramas. A staple in current anthologies of bad poetry are sentimental poems which were doubtless written, and by some people read, with deep and sincere feeling. A useful distinction between sentimental and nonsentimental is one which does not depend on the intensity and type of the feeling expressed or evoked, but labels as sentimental a work or passage in which the feeling is rendered in commonplaces and *clichés*, instead of being freshly verbalized and sharply realized in the details of the representation.

See *pathos*, and *sensibility, literature of*, and refer to I. A. Richards, *Practical Criticism* (1929), chapter 6; the discussion of sentimentality by Monroe C. Beardsley, "Bad Poetry," in *The Possibility of Criticism* (1970). Suzanne Clark has written a *feminist* reconsideration of sentimentalism in literature, *Sentimental Modernism and the Revolution of the Word* (1991), and Shirley Samuels has edited a collection of essays on *Culture of Sentiment: Race, Gender, and Sentimentality in Nineteenth-Century America* (1992).

**sestet: 336**.

**sestina** (sěstē′ na): **343**.

# 330 SEVEN DEADLY SINS

**setting:** The overall setting of a narrative or dramatic work is the general locale, historical time, and social circumstances in which its action occurs; the setting of a single episode or scene within the work is the particular physical location in which it takes place. The overall setting of *Macbeth*, for example, is medieval Scotland, and the setting for the particular scene in which Macbeth comes upon the witches is a blasted heath. The overall setting of James Joyce's *Ulysses* is Dublin on June 16, 1904, and its opening episode is set in the Martello Tower overlooking Dublin Bay. In works by writers such as Edgar Allan Poe, Thomas Hardy, and William Faulkner, both the overall and individual settings are important elements in generating the *atmosphere* of their works. The Greek term **opsis** ("scene," or "spectacle") is now occasionally used to denote a particular visible or picturable setting in any work of literature, including a lyric poem.

When applied to a theatrical production, "setting" is synonymous with **décor**, which is a French term denoting both the scenery and the **properties**, or movable pieces of furniture, on the stage. The French **mise en scène** ("placing on stage") is sometimes used in English as another synonym for "setting"; it is more useful, however, to apply the term more broadly, as the French do, to signify a director's overall conception, staging, and directing of a theatrical performance.

**seven cardinal virtues: 330**.

**seven deadly sins:** In medieval and later Christian theology these sins were usually identified as Pride, Covetousness, Lust, Envy, Gluttony, Anger, and Sloth. They were called "deadly" because they were considered to put the soul of anyone manifesting them in peril of eternal perdition; such sins could be expiated only by absolute penitence. Among them, Pride was often considered primary, since it was believed to have motivated the original fall of Satan in heaven. **Sloth** was accounted a deadly sin because it signified not simply laziness, but a torpid and despondent spiritual condition that threatened to make a person despair of any chance of achieving divine Grace. Alternative names for sloth were **accidie**, "dejection," and "spiritual dryness"; it was probably a condition close to that which present-day psychiatrists diagnose as acute depression.

The seven deadly sins (or in an alternative term, **cardinal sins**) were defined and discussed at length by such major theologians as Gregory the Great and Thomas Aquinas, and served as the topic of countless sermons. They also played an important role in many works of medieval and Renaissance literature—sometimes in elaborately developed *personifications*—including William Langland's *Piers Plowman* (B, Passus 5), Geoffrey Chaucer's "Parson's Tale," William Dunbar's "The Dance of the Sevin Deidly Synnis," and Edmund Spenser's *Faerie Queene* (Book I, Canto 4). See Morton W. Bloomfield, *The Seven Deadly Sins* (1952).

The seven deadly or cardinal sins were balanced by the **seven cardinal virtues**. Three of these, called the "theological virtues" because they were stressed in the New Testament, were Faith, Hope, and Charity (that is, Love)—see St. Paul's *I Corinthians* 13:13: "And now abideth faith, hope, and charity, these three." The other four, the "natural virtues," were derived from the moral philosophy of the ancient Greeks: justice, prudence, temperance, and fortitude.

Refer to Robert W. Ackerman, *Backgrounds to Medieval English Literature* (1966). For essays on the seven deadly sins written in 1962 by eminent English authors, see W. H. Auden, Cyril Connolly, Patrick Leigh-Fermor, Edith Sitwell, Christopher Sykes, Evelyn Waugh, and Angus Wilson, *Seven Deadly Sins: Common Reader Edition* (2002).

**Shakespearean sonnet: 336**.

**shifters** (in grammar): **208**.

**short short story: 332**.

**short story:** A short story is a brief work of prose fiction, and most of the terms for analyzing the component elements, the types, and the narrative techniques of the *novel* are applicable to the short story as well. The short story differs from the **anecdote**—the unelaborated narration of a single incident—in that, like the novel, it organizes the action, thought, and dialogue of its characters into the artful pattern of a plot, directed toward particular effects on an audience. (See *narrative and narratology*.) And as in the novel, the plot form may be comic, tragic, romantic, or satiric; the story is presented to us from one of many available *points of view*; and it may be written in the mode of fantasy, realism, or naturalism.

In the **tale**, or "story of incident," the focus of interest is primarily on the course and outcome of the events, as in Edgar Allan Poe's *The Gold Bug* (1843) and in other tales of detection, in many of the stories of O. Henry (1862–1910), and in the stock but sometimes well-contrived western and adventure stories in popular magazines. "Stories of character" focus instead on the state of mind and motivation, or on the psychological and moral qualities, of the protagonists. In some of the stories of character by Anton Chekhov (1860–1904), the Russian master of the form, nothing more happens than an encounter and conversation between two people. Ernest Hemingway's classic "A Clean, Well-Lighted Place" consists only of a curt conversation between two waiters about an old man who each day gets drunk and stays on in the café until it closes, followed by a brief meditation on the part of one of the waiters. In some stories there is a balance of interest between external action and character. Hemingway's "The Short Happy Life of Francis Macomber" is as violent in its packed events as any sensational adventure tale, but every particular of the action and dialogue is contrived to test and reveal, with a surprising set of *reversals*, the moral quality of all three protagonists.

The short story differs from the novel in the dimension that Aristotle called "magnitude," and this limitation of length imposes differences both in the effects that the story can achieve and in the choice and elaboration of the elements to achieve those effects. Edgar Allan Poe, who is sometimes called the originator of the short story as an established *genre*, was at any rate its first critical theorist. He defined what he called "the prose tale" as a narrative which can be read at one sitting of from half an hour to two hours, and is limited to "a certain unique or single effect" to which every detail is subordinate (review of Nathaniel Hawthorne's *Twice Told Tales*, 1842). Poe's comment applies to many short stories, and points to the economy of management which the tightness of the form always imposes in some degree. We can say that, by and large, the short story writer introduces a limited number of persons, cannot afford the space for a leisurely analysis and sustained development of character, and cannot develop as dense and detailed a social milieu as does the novelist. The author often begins the story close to, or even on the verge of, the climax, minimizes both prior exposition and the details of the *setting*, keeps the complications down, and clears up the denouement quickly—sometimes in a few sentences. (See *plot.*) The central incident is often selected to manifest as much as possible of the protagonist's life and character, and the details are devised to carry maximum import for the development of the plot. This spareness in the narrative often gives the artistry in a good short story higher visibility than the artistry in the more capacious and loosely structured novel.

Many distinguished short stories depart from this paradigm in various ways. It must be remembered that the name covers a great diversity of prose fiction, all the way from the **short short story**, which is a slightly elaborated anecdote of perhaps five hundred words, to such long and complex forms as Herman Melville's *Billy Budd* (c. 1890), Henry James' *The Turn of the Screw* (1898), Joseph Conrad's *Heart of Darkness* (1902), and Thomas Mann's *Mario and the Magician* (1930). In such works, the status of middle length between the tautness of the short story and the expansiveness of the novel is sometimes indicated by the name **novelette**, or *novella*. This form has been especially exploited in Germany (where it is called the **Novelle**) after it was introduced by Goethe in 1795 and carried on by Heinrich von Kleist and many other writers; the genre has also been the subject of special critical attention by German theorists.

The short narrative, in both verse and prose, is one of the oldest and most widespread of literary forms; the Hebrew Bible, for example, includes the stories of Jonah, Ruth, and Esther. Some of the narrative types which preceded the modern short story, treated elsewhere in this *Glossary*, are the *fable*, the *exemplum*, the *folktale*, the *fabliau*, and the *parable*. Early in its history, there developed the device of the **frame-story**: a preliminary narrative within which one or more of the characters proceeds to tell a series of short narratives. This device was widespread in the oral and written literature of the East and Middle East, as in the collection of stories called *The Arabian Nights* (see the Introduction to *The Arabian Nights*, trans. Husain Haddawy, 1990). This device was used by a number of other writers, including Boccaccio for his prose *Decameron* (1353) and by Chaucer for his versified *Canterbury Tales* (c. 1387). In the latter instance, Chaucer developed the frame-story of the journey, dialogue, and interactions of the Canterbury pilgrims to such a degree that the frame itself approximated the form of an organized plot. Within Chaucer's frame-plot, each story constitutes a complete and rounded narrative, yet functions also both as a means of characterizing the teller and as a vehicle for the quarrels and topics of argument en route. In its more recent forms, the frame-story may enclose either a single narrative (Henry James' *The Turn of the Screw*) or a sequence of narratives (Joel Chandler Harris' stories as told by Uncle Remus, 1881 and later; see under *beast fable*).

The type of prose narrative which approximates the present concept of the short story was developed, beginning in the early nineteenth century, in order to satisfy the need for short fiction by the many **magazines** (periodical collections of diverse materials, including essays, reviews, verses, and prose stories) that were inaugurated at that time. Among the early practitioners were Washington Irving, Hawthorne, and Poe in America, Sir Walter Scott and Mary Shelley in England, E. T. A. Hoffmann in Germany, Balzac in France, and Gogol, Pushkin, and Turgenev in Russia. Since then, almost all the major novelists in all the European languages have also written notable short stories. The form has flourished especially in America; Frank O'Connor has called it "the national art form," and its American masters include (in addition to the writers mentioned above) Mark Twain, William Faulkner, Katherine Anne Porter, Eudora Welty, Flannery O'Connor, John O'Hara, J. F. Powers, John Cheever, and J. D. Salinger.

See Sean O'Faolain, *The Short Story* (1948, reprinted 1964); Frank O'Connor, *The Lonely Voice: A Study of the Short Story* (1962); R. L. Pattee, *The Development of the American Short Story* (rev. 1966); Julie Brown, ed., *American Women Short Story Writers* (1995); Malcolm Bradbury, ed., *The Penguin Book of Modern British Short Stories* (1987); John Updike, ed., *The Best American Short Stories of the Century* (1999). On the novella: Ronald Paulson, *The Novelette Before 1900* (1968); Mary Doyle Springer, *Forms of the Modern Novella* (1976); Martin Swales, *The German Novelle* (1977). For references to the *short story* in other entries, see page *226*.

**showing** (in narrative): **43**; *273*.

**sign: 324**.

**sign proper** (in semiotics): **324**.

**significance** (in interpretation): **159**.

**signified** (in linguistics): **174**; *325*.

**signifier: 174**; *325*.

**simile** (sĭm′ ĭlē): **119**; *189, 358*.

**Skeltonics: 84**.

**slant rhyme: 317**.

**slave narratives: 246**.

**sloth: 330**.

**social constructs: 297**. See also *cultural constructs*.

**social novel: 230**.

**social theory of textual criticism: 366**.

**Socialist Realism:** Socialist Realism was a term used by Marxist critics for novels which, they claimed, reflected social reality—that is, novels that accorded with the Marxist view that the struggle between economic classes is the essential dynamic of society. After the 1930s "Socialist Realism" was the officially sanctioned artistic mode for communist writers until the dissolution of the Soviet Union in 1991. In its crude version, it served as a term of approval for novels that adhered to the party line by stressing the oppression of workers by bourgeois capitalists, the virtues of the proletariat, and the felicities of life under a communist regime. A flexible Marxist critic such as Georg Lukács, on the other hand, applied complex criteria of narrative realism to analyze and laud the traditional classics of European realistic fiction.

See *Marxist criticism, proletarian novel,* and *realism,* and refer to Georg Lukács, *Studies in European Realism* (trans. 1964); Mark Slonim, *Soviet Russian Literature* (1967); and George Bisztray, *Marxist Models of Literary Realism* (1978).

**society verse: 171**.

**sociology of literature:** Most literary historians and critics have taken some account of the relation of individual authors to the circumstances of the social and cultural era in which they live and write, as well as of the relation of a literary work to the segment of society that its fiction represents or to the audience toward which the work is addressed. (For major exceptions in recent types of criticism see *Russian formalism, New Criticism, structuralism, deconstruction.*) The term "sociology of literature," however, is applied only to the writings of those historians and critics whose primary, and sometimes exclusive, interest is in the ways that the subject matter and form of a literary work are affected by such circumstances as its author's class status, gender, and political and other interests; the ways of thinking and feeling characteristic of its era; the economic conditions of the writer's profession and of the publication and distribution of books; and the social class, conceptions, and values of the audience to which an author addresses the literary product, or to which it is made available. Sociological critics treat a work of literature as inescapably conditioned—in the choice and development of its subject matter, the ways of thinking it incorporates, its evaluations of the modes of life it renders, and even in its formal qualities—by the social, political, and economic organization and forces of its age. Such critics also tend to view the interpretation and assessment of a literary work by a reading public as shaped by the circumstances specific to that public's time and place. The French historian Hippolyte Taine is sometimes considered the first modern sociologist of literature in his *History of English Literature* (1863), which analyzed a work as determined by three factors: its author's "race," geographical and social "milieu," and historical "moment."

For prominent sociological emphases in recent critical writings, see *feminist criticism*—which emphasizes the role of male interests and assumptions as determinants of the content, values, and interpretations of the standard literary *canon*—and also *Marxist criticism.* (For an influential Marxist version, see Lucien Goldmann, *Essays on Method in the Sociology of Literature,* 1980. For approaches by the *Frankfurt School* of Marxist criticism, see two essays by Leo Lowenthal, both titled

"On Sociology of Literature," 1932, 1948, reprinted in *Literature and Mass Culture*, 1984.) It should be noted that Marx's view of the economic basis of social organization, class *ideologies*, and class conflict has influenced the work of many critics who, although not committed to Marxist doctrine, stress the sociological context and content of works of literature. The most thoroughgoing treatments of literary works as cultural products that are embedded in the circumstances and discourses of a time and place are by advocates of the current modes of criticism called the *new historicism*. For late developments in the sociology of literary texts, see *book history studies*.

See the readings listed under *authors and authorship, book history studies, feminist criticism, Marxist criticism,* and *new historicism*. Refer also to the pioneering study by Alexandre Beljame, *Men of Letters and the English Public*—that is, in the eighteenth century (1883, trans. 1948); Levin Schücking, *The Sociology of Literary Taste* (rev. 1941); Hugh Dalziel Duncan, *Language and Literature in Society, with a Bibliographical Guide to the Sociology of Literature* (1953); Pierre Bourdieu, *The Field of Cultural Production: Essays in Art and Literature* (1996). Bourdieu's views have been applied to the formation of the *canon of literature* by John Guillory in *Cultural Capital* (1995). See also two books on the sociology of the production of popular literature and its audience by Janice Radway, *A Feeling for Books: The Book-of-the-Month Club, Literary Taste, and Middle-Class Desire* (1997), and *Reading the Romance: Women, Patriarchy, and Popular Literature* (1991). Collections of essays in sociological criticism include Joseph P. Strelka, ed., *Literary Criticism and Sociology* (1973); Elizabeth and Tom Burns, eds., *Sociology of Literature and Drama: Selected Readings* (1973); and the issue of *Critical Inquiry* devoted to the sociology of literature, Vol. 14 (Spring 1988).

**socratic irony: 167**.

**solecism** (sŏl′ ĕsĭsm): **180**.

**soliloquy:** Soliloquy is the act of talking to oneself, whether silently or aloud. In drama it denotes the *convention* by which a character, alone on the stage, utters his or her thoughts aloud. Playwrights have used this device as a convenient way to convey information about a character's motives and state of mind, or for purposes of exposition, and sometimes in order to guide the judgments and responses of the audience. Christopher Marlowe's *Dr. Faustus* (first performed in 1594) opens with a long expository soliloquy, and concludes with another which expresses Faustus' frantic mental and emotional state during his belated attempts to escape damnation. The best-known of dramatic soliloquies is Hamlet's speech which begins "To be or not to be." (Compare *monologue*.)

A related stage device is the **aside**, in which a character expresses to the audience his or her thought or intention in a short speech which, by convention, is inaudible to the other characters on the stage. Both devices, common in Elizabethan and later drama, were largely rejected by dramatists in the later nineteenth century, when the increasing requirement that plays convey the illusion of real life impelled writers to exploit indirect means for conveying exposition and guidance to the audience. Eugene O'Neill, however, revived and extended the soliloquy and aside and made them basic devices throughout his play *Strange Interlude* (1928). For references to *soliloquy* in other entries, see page *58*.

**Son of Ben: 253**.

**sonnet:** A *lyric* poem consisting of a single *stanza* of fourteen iambic pentameter lines linked by an intricate rhyme scheme. (Refer to *meter* and *rhyme*.) There are two major patterns of rhyme in sonnets written in the English language:

1. The **Italian** or **Petrarchan sonnet** (named after the fourteenth-century Italian poet Petrarch) falls into two main parts: an **octave** (eight lines) rhyming *abbaabba* followed by a **sestet** (six lines) rhyming *cdecde* or some variant, such as *cdccdc*. Petrarch's sonnets were first imitated in England, both in their stanza form and their subject—the hopes and pains of an adoring male lover—by Sir Thomas Wyatt in the early sixteenth century. (See *Petrarchan conceit*.) The Petrarchan form was later used, and for a variety of subjects, by Milton, Wordsworth, Christina Rossetti, D. G. Rossetti, and other sonneteers, who sometimes made it technically easier in English (which does not have as many rhyming possibilities as Italian) by introducing a new pair of rhymes in the second four lines of the octave.

2. The Earl of Surrey and other English experimenters in the sixteenth century also developed a stanza form called the **English sonnet**, or else the **Shakespearean sonnet**, after its greatest practitioner. This sonnet falls into three *quatrains* and a concluding *couplet: abab cdcd efef gg*. There was a notable variant, the **Spenserian sonnet**, in which Spenser linked each quatrain to the next by a continuing rhyme: *abab bcbc cdcd ee*.

John Donne shifted from the hitherto primary subject, sexual love, to a variety of religious themes in his *Holy Sonnets*, written early in the seventeenth century; and Milton, in the latter part of that century, expanded the range of the sonnet to other matters of serious concern. Except for a lapse in the English *Neoclassic Period*, the sonnet has remained a popular form to the present day and includes among its distinguished practitioners, in the nineteenth century, Wordsworth, Keats, Elizabeth Barrett Browning, Christina Rossetti, and Dante Gabriel Rossetti, and in the twentieth century, Edwin Arlington Robinson, Edna St. Vincent Millay, W. B. Yeats, Robert Frost, W. H. Auden, and Dylan Thomas. The stanza is just long enough to permit a fairly complex lyric development, yet so short and so exigent in its rhymes as to pose a standing challenge to the ingenuity and artistry of the poet. The rhyme pattern of the Petrarchan sonnet has on the whole favored a statement of a problem, situation, or incident in the octave, with a resolution in the sestet. The English form sometimes uses a similar division of material, but often presents instead a repetition-with-variation of a statement in each of the three quatrains; in either case, the final couplet in the English sonnet usually imposes an *epigrammatic* turn at the end. In Drayton's fine Elizabethan sonnet in the English form "Since there's no help, come let us kiss and part," the lover brusquely declares in the first quatrain, then reiterates in the second, that he is glad that the affair is cleanly ended, then hesitates at the finality of the parting in the third quatrain, and in the concluding couplet suddenly drops his swagger to make one last plea. Here are the third quatrain and couplet:

> Now at the last gasp of love's latest breath,
> When, his pulse failing, passion speechless lies,
> When faith is kneeling by his bed of death,
> And innocence is closing up his eyes;
>> Now if thou wouldst, when all have given him over,
>> From death to life thou mightst him yet recover.

Following Petrarch's early example, a number of Elizabethan authors arranged their poems into **sonnet sequences**, or **sonnet cycles**, in which a series of sonnets are linked together by exploring the varied aspects of a relationship between lovers, or else by indicating a development in the relationship that constitutes a kind of implicit plot. Shakespeare ordered his sonnets in a sequence, as did Sidney in *Astrophel and Stella* (1580) and Spenser in *Amoretti* (1595). Later examples of the sonnet sequence on various subjects are Wordsworth's *The River Duddon*, D. G. Rossetti's *House of Life*, Elizabeth Barrett Browning's *Sonnets from the Portuguese*, and the American poet William Ellery Leonard's *Two Lives*. Dylan Thomas' *Altarwise by Owl-light* (1936) is a sequence of ten sonnets which are abstruse meditations on the poet's own life. George Meredith's *Modern Love* (1862), which concerns a bitterly unhappy marriage, is sometimes called a sonnet sequence, even though its component poems consist not of fourteen but of sixteen lines.

On the early history of the sonnet and its development in England through Milton, see Michael R. G. Spiller, *The Development of the Sonnet: An Introduction* (1992). See also L. G. Sterner, *The Sonnet in American Literature* (1930); J. B. Leishman, *Themes and Variations in Shakespeare's Sonnets* (1963); Michael R. G. Spiller, *The Sonnet Sequence: A Study of the Strategies* (1997); Helen Vendler, *The Art of Shakespeare's Sonnets* (1997). Arthur Marotti relates the vogue of the sonnet sequences to the politics and system of literary patronage in Elizabethan England, in "Love Is Not Love: Elizabethan Sonnet Sequences and the Social Order," *ELH*, Vol. 49 (1982).

**sonnet cycle:** 337.

**sonnet sequence:** 337; *12.*

**sound symbolism:** 175.

**speech–act theory:** Speech-act theory, developed by the philosopher John Austin, was described most fully in his posthumous book *How to Do Things with Words* (1962), and was explored and expanded by other "ordinary-language philosophers," including John Searle and H. P. Grice. Austin's theory is directed against traditional tendencies of philosophers (1) to analyze the meaning of isolated sentences, abstracted from the context of a discourse and from the attendant circumstances in which a sentence is uttered; and (2) to assume, in what Austin calls a logical obsession, that the standard sentence—of which other types are merely variants—is a statement that describes a situation or asserts a fact and can be judged to be either true or false. John Searle's adoption and elaboration of Austin's speech-act theory opposes to these views the claim that when we attend to the overall linguistic and situational context—including the institutional conditions that govern many uses of language—we find that in speaking or writing we perform simultaneously three, and sometimes four, distinguishable kinds of **speech acts**: (1) We utter a sentence; Austin called this act a "locution." (2) We refer to an object, and predicate something about that object. (3) We perform an illocutionary act. (4) Often, we also perform a perlocutionary act.

The **illocutionary act** performed by a locution may indeed be the one stressed by traditional philosophy and logic, to assert that something is true, but it may instead be one of very many other possible speech acts, such as questioning, commanding, promising, warning, praising, thanking, and so on. A sentence consisting of the same words in the same grammatical form, such as "I will leave you tomorrow," may in a particular verbal and situational context turn out to have the "illocutionary force" either of an assertion, a promise, or a threat. In an illocutionary act that is not an assertion, the prime criterion (although the utterance may make reference to some state of affairs) is not its truth or falsity, but whether or not the act has been performed successfully, or in Austin's term, "felicitously." A felicitous performance of a particular illocutionary act depends on its meeting "appropriateness conditions" which obtain for that type of act; these conditions are tacit linguistic and social (or institutional) conventions, or rules, that are shared by competent speakers and interpreters of a language. For example, the successful performance of an illocutionary act of promising, such as "I will come to see you tomorrow," depends on its meeting its special set of appropriateness conditions: the speaker must be capable of fulfilling his promise, must intend to do so, and must believe that the listener wants him to do so. Failing the last condition, for example, the same verbal utterance might have the illocutionary force of a threat.

In *How to Do Things with Words*, John Austin established an initial distinction between two broad types of locutions: **constatives** (sentences that assert something about a fact or state of affairs and are adjudged to be true or false) and **performatives** (sentences that are actions which accomplish something, such as questioning, promising, praising, and so on). As he continued his subtle analysis, however, Austin showed that this initial division of utterances into two sharply exclusive classes does not hold, in that many performatives also involve reference to a state of affairs, while constatives also perform an illocutionary action. Austin, however, drew special attention to the "explicit performative," which is a sentence whose utterance itself, when executed under appropriate institutional and other conditions, brings about the state of affairs that it signifies. Examples are "I name this ship the Queen Elizabeth"; "I apologize"; "I call this meeting to order"; "Let spades be trumps."

If an illocutionary act has an effect on the actions or state of mind of the hearer which goes beyond merely understanding what has been said, it is also a **perlocutionary** act. Thus, the utterance "I am going to leave you," with the illocutionary force of a warning, may not only be understood as such, but may have (or fail to have) the additional perlocutionary effect of frightening the hearer. Similarly, by the illocutionary act of promising to do something, one may please (or else anger) the hearer; and by asserting something, one may have the effect either of enlightening, or of inspiring, or of intimidating the hearer. Some perlocutionary effects are intended by the speaker; others occur without the speaker's intention, and even against that intention. For a useful exploration of the relations, in diverse cases, of illocutionary and perlocutionary speech acts, see Ted Cohen, "Illocutions and Perlocutions," in *Foundations of Language*, Vol. 9 (1973).

A number of deconstructive theorists have proposed that the use of language in fictional literature (which Austin had excluded from his consideration of what he called "seriously" intended speech acts) is in fact a prime instance of the *performative*, in that it does not refer to a pre-existing state of affairs, but brings about, or brings into being, the characters, action, and world that it describes. On the other hand, since performative linguistic acts can't avoid recourse to statement and assertion, some deconstructive theorists convert Austin's constative/performative distinction into an undecidable deadlock, or oscillation, of irreconcilable oppositions. See *deconstruction* and refer to Barbara Johnson, "Poetry and Performative Language: Mallarmé and Austin," in *The Critical Difference* (1980); Sandra Petrey, *Speech Acts and Literary Theory* (1990); Jonathan Culler, *Literary Theory: A Very Short Introduction* (1997), chapter 7, "Performative Language." Judith Butler has proposed that the terms we use to identify a person's gender and sexuality are modes of performative language, in that the reiterated application of such terms to persons, in accordance with the linguistic conventions that govern their use, in fact bring about (or cause persons to "perform") the identities and the modes of behavior that they purport to describe. See Judith Butler, *Gender Trouble: Feminism and the Subversion of Identity* (1990) and *Excitable Speech* (1997); also refer to *queer theory*.

Since 1970 speech-act theory has influenced in conspicuous and varied ways the practice of literary criticism. When applied to the analysis of direct discourse by a character within a literary work, it provides a systematic but sometimes cumbersome framework for identifying the unspoken presuppositions, implications, and effects of speech acts which competent readers and critics have always taken into account, subtly though unsystematically. (See *discourse analysis*.) Speech-act theory has also been used in a more radical way, however, as a model on which to recast the theory of literature in general, and especially the theory of prose narratives (see *fiction and truth*). What the author of a fictional work—or else what the author's invented narrator—narrates is held to constitute a "pretended" set of assertions, which are intended by the author, and understood by the competent reader, to be free from a speaker's ordinary commitment to the truth of what he or she asserts. Within the frame of the fictional world that the narrative thus sets up, however, the utterances of the fictional characters—whether these are assertions or promises or marital vows—are held to be responsible to ordinary illocutionary commitments. Alternatively, some speech-act theorists propose a new version of mimetic theory (see *imitation*). Traditional mimetic critics had claimed that *literature* imitates reality by representing in a verbal medium the setting, actions, utterances, and interactions of human beings. Some speech–act theorists, on the other hand, propose that all literature is simply "mimetic discourse." A lyric, for example, is said to be an imitation of that form of ordinary discourse in which we express our feelings about something, and a novel is an imitation of a particular form of written discourse, such as biography (Henry Fielding's *The History of Tom Jones*, 1749), or autobiography (Charles Dickens' *David Copperfield*, 1849–50), or even a scholar's annotated edition of a poetic text (Nabokov's *Pale Fire*, 1962). See Barbara Herrnstein Smith, *On the Margins of Discourse: The Relation of Literature to Language* (1978).

For basic philosophical treatments of speech acts see John Austin, *How to Do Things with Words* (1962); John R. Searle, *Speech Acts: An Essay in the Philosophy of Language* (1970); and H. P. Grice, "Logic and Conversation," in *Syntax and Semantics*, Vol. 3 (1975). On the application of speech-act theory to metaphor and to literary dialogue, see *metaphor, theories of*, and *discourse analysis*. Among the attempts to model the general theory of literature, or at least of prose fiction, on the theory of speech acts are Richard Ohmann, "Speech Acts and the Definition of Literature," *Philosophy and Rhetoric*, Vol. 4 (1971); John R. Searle, "The Logical Status of Fictional Discourse," in his *Expression and Meaning* (1979), chapter 3; refer also to the entry *fiction and truth*. A detailed application to literary theory is Mary Louise Pratt's *Toward a Speech Act Theory of Literary Discourse* (1977). For views of the limitations of speech-act theory when applied in literary criticism, see Stanley Fish, "How to Do Things with Austin and Searle: Speech-Act Theory and Literary Criticism," in *Is There a Text in This Class?* (1980); and Joseph Margolis, "Literature and Speech Acts," *Philosophy and Literature*, Vol. 3 (1979). For Jacques Derrida's deconstructive analysis of Austin's views, and John Searle's reply, see under *deconstruction*. For references to *speech-act theory* in other entries, see pages *81, 115, 117, 315*.

**Spenserian sonnet: 336**.

**Spenserian stanza: 342**.

**spiritual autobiography: 26**; *56*.

**spirituals** (African-American): **149**.

**spondaic** (spŏndā′ ĭk): **196**; *198*.

**sprezzatura** (sprēts′ ătoo″ rǎ): **308**.

**sprung rhythm: 198**.

**stable irony: 166**.

**stanza:** A stanza (Italian for "stopping place") is a grouping of the verse lines in a poem, often set off by a space in the printed text. Usually the stanzas of a given poem are marked by a recurrent pattern of rhyme and are also uniform in the number and lengths of the component lines. Some unrhymed poems, however, are divided into stanzaic units (for example, William Collins' "Ode to Evening,"

1747), and some rhymed poems are composed of stanzas that vary in their component lines (for example, the *irregular ode*).

Of the great diversity of English stanza forms, many have no special names and must be described by specifying the number of lines, the type and number of metric *feet* in each line, and the pattern of the *rhyme*. Certain stanzas, however, are used so often that they have been given the convenience of a name. Some literary scholars apply the term "stanza" only to divisions of four or more lines. This entry, however, follows a widespread application of the term also to divisions of two and three lines.

A **couplet** is a pair of rhymed lines that are equal in length. The **octosyllabic couplet** has lines of eight syllables, usually consisting of four iambic feet, as in Andrew Marvell's "To His Coy Mistress" (1681):

> The grave's a fine and private place,
> But none, I think, do there embrace.

*Iambic pentameter* lines rhyming in pairs are called **decasyllabic** ("ten-syllable") **couplets** or "heroic couplets." (For examples, see the entry *heroic couplet*.)

The **tercet**, or **triplet**, is a stanza of three lines, usually with a single rhyme. The lines may be the same length (as in Robert Herrick's "Upon Julia's Clothes," 1648, written in tercets of iambic tetrameter), or else of varying lengths. In Richard Crashaw's "Wishes to His Supposed Mistress" (1646), the lines of each tercet are successively in *iambic dimeter, trimeter*, and *tetrameter*:

> Who e'er she be
> That not impossible she
> That shall command my heart and me.

**Terza rima** is composed of tercets which are interlinked, in that each is joined to the one following by a common rhyme: *aba, bcb, cdc*, and so on. Dante composed his *Divine Comedy* (early fourteenth century) in terza rima; but although Sir Thomas Wyatt introduced the form early in the sixteenth century, it has not been a common meter in English, in which rhymes are much harder to find than in Italian. Shelley, however, used it brilliantly in "Ode to the West Wind" (1820), and it occurs also in the poetry of Milton, Browning, and T. S. Eliot.

The **quatrain**, or four-line stanza, is the most common in English versification, and is employed with various meters and rhyme schemes. The *ballad stanza* (in alternating four- and three-foot lines rhyming *abcb*, or less frequently *abab*) is one common quatrain; when this same stanza occurs in *hymns*, it is called **common measure**. Emily Dickinson is the most subtle, varied, and persistent of all users of this type of quatrain; her frequent resort to *partial rhyme* prevents monotony:

> Purple—is fashionable twice—
> This season of the year,
> And when a soul perceives itself
> To be an Emperor.

The **heroic quatrain**, in iambic pentameter rhyming *abab*, is the stanza of Gray's "Elegy Written in a Country Churchyard" (1751):

> The curfew tolls the knell of parting day,
>     The lowing herd winds slowly o'er the lea,
> The plowman homeward plods his weary way,
>     And leaves the world to darkness, and to me.

**Rime royal** was introduced by Chaucer in *Troilus and Criseyde* (the latter 1380s) and other narrative poems; it is believed to take its name, however, from its later use by "the Scottish Chaucerian," King James I of Scotland, in his poem *The Kingis Quair* ("The King's Book"), written about 1424. It is a seven-line, iambic pentameter stanza rhyming *ababbcc*. This form was quite widely used by Elizabethan poets, including by Shakespeare in "A Lover's Complaint" and *The Rape of Lucrece*, which begins:

> From the besieged Ardea all in post,
> Borne by the trustless wings of false desire,
> Lust-breathèd Tarquin leaves the Roman host
> And to Collatium bears the lightless fire
> Which, in pale embers hid, lurks to aspire
>     And girdle with embracing flames the waist
>     Of Collatine's fair love, Lucrece the chaste.

**Ottava rima**, as the Italian name indicates, has eight lines; it rhymes *abababcc*. Like terza rima and the sonnet, it was brought from Italian into English by Sir Thomas Wyatt in the first half of the sixteenth century. Although employed by a number of earlier poets, it is notable especially as the stanza which helped Byron discover what he was born to write, the satiric poem *Don Juan* (1819–24). Note the comic effect of the *forced rhyme* in the concluding couplet:

> Juan was taught from out the best edition,
> Expurgated by learned men, who place,
> Judiciously, from out the schoolboy's vision,
> The grosser parts; but, fearful to deface
> Too much their modest bard by this omission,
> And pitying sore his mutilated case,
> They only add them all in an appendix,
> Which saves, in fact, the trouble of an index.

**Spenserian stanza** is a still longer form devised by Edmund Spenser for *The Faerie Queene* (1590–96)—nine lines, in which the first eight lines are iambic pentameter and the last iambic hexameter (an *Alexandrine*), rhyming *ababbcbcc*. Enchanted by Spenser's gracious movement and music, many poets have attempted this stanza in spite of its difficulties. Its greatest successes have been in poems which, like *The Faerie Queene*, evolve in a leisurely way, with ample time for unrolling the richly textured stanzas; for example, James Thomson's "The Castle of Indolence" (1748), John Keats' "The Eve of St. Agnes" (1820), Percy Bysshe Shelley's "Adonais" (1821), and the narrative section of Alfred, Lord

Tennyson's "The Lotos-Eaters" (1832). The following is a stanza from Spenser's *Faerie Queene* 1.1.41:

> And more, to lulle him in his slumber soft,
>> A trickling streame from high rocke tumbling downe
>> And ever-drizling raine upon the loft
>> Mixt with a murmuring winde, much like the sowne
>> Of swarming Bees, did cast him in a swowne:
>> No other noyse, nor peoples troublous cryes,
>> As still are wont t'annoy the wallèd towne,
>> Might there be heard: but carelesse Quiet lyes,
> Wrapt in eternall silence farre from enemyes.

There are also various elaborate stanza forms imported from France, such as the rondeau, the villanelle, and the triolet, containing intricate repetitions, at set intervals, both of rhymes and of entire lines; these stanzas have been used mainly, but not exclusively, for *light verse*. Their revival by W. H. Auden, William Empson, and other mid-twentieth-century poets was a sign of renewed interest in high metrical artifice. Dylan Thomas' "Do not go gentle into that good night" is a **villanelle**; that is, it consists of five *tercets* and a *quatrain*, all on two rhymes, and with systematic later repetitions of lines 1 and 3 of the first tercet.

One of the most intricate of poetic forms is the **sestina**: a poem of six six-line stanzas in which the end words in the lines of the first stanza are repeated, in a set order of variation, as the end words of the stanzas that follow. The sestina concludes with a three-line envoy which incorporates, in the middle and at the end of the lines, all six of these end words. (An **envoy**, or "send-off," is a short formal stanza which is appended to a poem by way of conclusion.) This form, introduced in the twelfth century, was cultivated by Italian, Spanish, and French poets. Despite its extreme difficulty, the sestina has also been managed with success by the Elizabethan Sir Philip Sidney, the Victorian Algernon Swinburne, and the modern poets W. H. Auden and John Ashbery.

See *meter*. Poetic stanzas and nonstanzaic forms of verse discussed elsewhere in the *Glossary* are *ballad stanza, blank verse, free verse, heroic couplet, limerick,* and *sonnet.* The pattern and history of the various stanzas are described and exemplified in R. M. Alden, *English Verse* (1903), and in Paul Fussell, *Poetic Meter and Poetic Form* (rev. 1979). For references to *stanza* in other entries, see page *318*.

**stock characters:** Stock characters are types of persons that occur repeatedly in a particular literary genre, and so are recognizable as part of the *conventions* of the form. The *Old Comedy* of the Greeks had three stock characters whose interactions constituted the standard plot: the **alazon**, or impostor and self-deceiving braggart; the **eiron**, or self-derogatory and understating character, whose contest with the alazon is central to the comic plot; and the **bomolochos**, or buffoon, whose antics add an extra comic element. (See Lane Cooper, *An Aristotelian Theory of Comedy*, 1922.) In his *Anatomy of Criticism* (1957), Northrop Frye revived these old terms, added a fourth, the **agroikos**—the rustic or easily deceived character—and identified the persistence of these types (very broadly defined) in comic plots up to our own time. The Italian commedia dell'arte revolved around such stock characters as Pulcinella and Pantaloon; see *commedia dell'arte*.

The plot of an Elizabethan *romantic comedy*, such as Shakespeare's *As You Like It* and *Twelfth Night*, often turned on a heroine disguised as a handsome young man; and a stock figure in the Elizabethan comedy of intrigue was the clever servant who, like Mosca in Ben Jonson's *Volpone*, connives with his master to fleece another stock character, the stupid **gull**. Nineteenth-century comedy, on stage and in fiction, exploited the stock Englishman with a monocle, an exaggerated Oxford accent, and a defective sense of humor. Western stories and films generated the tight-lipped sheriff who lets his gun do the talking; while a familiar figure in the fiction of the recent past was the stoical Hemingway hero, unillusioned but faithful to his primal code of honor and loyalty in a civilization grown effete and corrupt. The *Beat* or hipster or alienated protagonist who, with or without the help of drugs, has opted out of the Establishment is an even more recent stock character.

In some literary forms, such as the *morality play* and Ben Jonson's *comedy of humours*, the artistic aim does not require more than type characters. (See also *flat character*, under *character and characterization*.) But even in realistic literary forms, the artistic success of a protagonist does not depend on whether or not an author incorporates an established type, but on how well the type is re-created as a convincing individual who fulfills his or her function in the overall plot. Two of Shakespeare's greatest characters are patently conventional. Falstaff is in part a re-rendering of the *Vice*, the comic tempter of the medieval morality play, and in part of the familiar braggart soldier, or **miles gloriosus**, of Roman and Renaissance comedy, whose ancestry goes back to the Greek *alazon*; and Hamlet combines some stock attributes of the hero of Elizabethan *revenge tragedies* with those of the Elizabethan melancholic man. Jane Austen's delightful Elizabeth Bennet in *Pride and Prejudice* (1813) can be traced back through Restoration comedy to the type of intelligent, witty, and dauntless heroines that enliven Shakespeare's romantic comedies.

For references to *stock character* in other entries, see page *52*.

**stock response:** A derogatory term for a reader's reaction that is considered to be habitual and stereotyped, in place of one which is genuinely and aptly responsive to a given literary passage or text. The term is sometimes applied to the response of authors themselves to characters, situations, or topics that they set forth in a work; usually, however, it is used to describe standard and inadequate responses of the readers of the work. I. A. Richards, in his *Practical Criticism* (1929), chapter 5, gave currency to this term by citing and analyzing stock responses by students and other respondents who wrote critiques of unidentified poems presented for their interpretation and evaluation.

**stock situations:** Stock situations are the counterparts to *stock characters*; that is, they are recurrent types of incidents or of sequences of actions in a drama or narrative. Instances range from single situations or events—the eavesdropper who is hidden behind a bush or in a closet, or the suddenly discovered will or birthmark—to the overall pattern of a plot. The Horatio Alger books for boys, in mid-nineteenth-century America, were all variations on the stock plot of rags-to-riches-by-pluck-and-luck, and we recognize the standard boy–meets–girl incident in the opening episode of much popular fiction and in many motion pictures.

Some recent critics distinguish certain recurrent character types and elements of plot, such as the sexually irresistible but fatal enchantress, the sacrificial scapegoat, and the underground journey, as "archetypal" components which are held to recur, not simply because they are functional literary conventions, but because, like dreams and myths, they express and appeal to universal human impulses, anxieties, and needs. See *archetype*, and for structuralist analyses of recurrent plot types, *narrative and narratology*.

**story: 209**.

**stream of consciousness:** Stream of consciousness was a phrase used by William James in his *Principles of Psychology* (1890) to describe the unbroken flow of perceptions, memories, thoughts, and feelings in the waking mind; it has since been adopted to describe a narrative method in modern fiction. Long passages of **introspection**, in which the narrator records in detail what passes through a character's awareness, are found in novelists from Samuel Richardson, through William James' brother Henry James, to many novelists of the present era. The long chapter 42 of James' *Portrait of a Lady*, for example, is entirely given over to the narrator's description of the sustained process of Isabel's memories, thoughts, and varying feelings. As early as 1888 a minor French writer, Edouard Dujardin, wrote a short novel *Les Lauriers sont coupés* ("The Laurels Have Been Cut") which undertakes to represent the scenes and events of the story solely as they impinge upon the consciousness of the central character. As it has been refined since the 1920s, "stream of consciousness" is the name applied specifically to a mode of narration that undertakes to reproduce the full spectrum and continuous flow of a character's mental process, in which sense perceptions mingle with conscious and half-conscious thoughts, memories, expectations, feelings, and random associations.

Some critics use "stream of consciousness" interchangeably with the term **interior monologue**. It is useful, however, to follow the usage of critics who use the former as the inclusive term, denoting all the diverse means employed by authors to communicate the total state and process of consciousness in a character. "Interior monologue" is then reserved for that species of stream of consciousness which undertakes to present to the reader the course and rhythm of consciousness precisely as it occurs in a character's mind. In interior monologue the author does not intervene, or at any rate intervenes minimally, as describer, guide, or commentator, and does not tidy the vagaries of the mental process into grammatical sentences or into a logical or coherent order. The interior monologue, in its radical form, is sometimes described as the exact presentation of the process of consciousness; but because sense perceptions, mental images, feelings, and some aspects of thought itself are nonverbal, it is clear that the author can present these elements only by converting them into some sort of verbal equivalent. Much of this conversion is a matter of narrative *conventions* rather than of unedited, point-for-point reproduction, and each author puts his or her own imprint on the interior monologues that are attributed to characters in the narrative. (For the linguistic techniques that have been used to render the states and flow of consciousness, see Dorrit Cohn, *Transparent Minds: Narrative Modes for Presenting Consciousness in Fiction*, 1978.)

James Joyce developed a variety of devices for stream-of-consciousness narrative in *Ulysses* (1922). Here is a passage of interior monologue from the "Lestrygonians" episode, in which Leopold Bloom saunters through Dublin, observing and musing:

> Pineapple rock, lemon platt, butter scotch. A sugar-sticky girl shoveling scoopfuls of creams for a christian brother. Some school treat. Bad for their tummies. Lozenge and comfit manufacturer to His Majesty the King. God. Save. Our. Sitting on his throne, sucking red jujubes white.

Dorothy Richardson sustains a stream-of-consciousness mode of narrative, focused exclusively on the mind and perceptions of her heroine, throughout the twelve volumes of her novel *Pilgrimage* (1915–38); Virginia Woolf employs the procedure as a prominent, although not exclusive, narrative mode in several novels, including *Mrs. Dalloway* (1925) and *To the Lighthouse* (1927); and William Faulkner exploits it in the first three of the four parts of *The Sound and the Fury* (1929).

Refer to *narratology* and *point of view*, and see Leon Edel, *The Modern Psychological Novel* (1955, rev. 1964); Robert Humphrey, *Stream of Consciousness in the Modern Novel* (1954); Melvin Friedman, *Stream of Consciousness: A Study in Literary Method* (1955). For a review of early and more recent scientific writings on the stream of consciousness, see Oliver Sachs, "In the River of Consciousness," *New York Review of Books*, 15 Jan. 2004.

**stress** (in linguistics): **175**.

**stress** (in meter): **194**.

**strong–stress meter: 198**; *10*.

**strophe** (strō′ fē): **235**.

**structural irony: 166**.

**structuralism: 347**; *128, 175, 209, 262, 279*.

**structuralist criticism:** Almost all literary theorists beginning with Aristotle have emphasized the importance of *structure*, conceived in diverse ways, in analyzing a work of literature. (See *form and structure*.) "Structuralist criticism," however, now designates the practice of critics who analyze literature on the explicit model of structuralist linguistics. The class includes a number of *Russian formalists*, especially Roman Jakobson, but consists most prominently of a group of writers, with their headquarters in Paris, who applied to literature the concepts and analytic distinctions developed by Ferdinand de Saussure in his *Course in General Linguistics* (1915). This mode of criticism is part of a larger movement, French **structuralism**, inaugurated in the 1950s by the cultural anthropologist Claude Lévi-Strauss, who analyzed, on the model of Saussure's linguistics, such cultural phenomena as mythology, kinship relations, and modes of preparing food. (See *linguistics in literary criticism*.)

In its early form, as employed by Lévi-Strauss and other writers in the 1950s and 1960s, structuralism cuts across the traditional disciplinary areas within and between the humanities and social sciences by undertaking to provide an objective account of all social and cultural practices, in a range that includes mythical narratives, literary texts, advertisements, fashions in clothes, and patterns of social decorum. It views these practices as combinations of *signs* that have a set significance for the members of a particular culture, and undertakes to make explicit the rules and procedures by which the practices have achieved their cultural significance, and to specify what that significance is, by reference to an underlying system (analogous to Saussure's *langue*, the implicit system of a particular language) of the relationships among signifying elements and their rules of combination. The elementary cultural phenomena, like the elements of language in Saussure's exposition, are not objective facts identifiable by their inherent properties, but purely "relational" entities; that is, their identity as signs is given to them by their relationships of differences from, and binary oppositions to, other elements within the cultural system. This system of internal relationships, and of "codes" that determine significant combinations, has been mastered by each person competent within a given culture, although he or she remains largely unaware of its nature and operations. The primary interest of the structuralist, like that of Saussure, is not in the cultural *parole* but in the *langue*; that is, not in any particular cultural phenomenon or event except as it provides access to the structure, features, and rules of the general system that engenders its significance.

As applied in literary studies, **structuralist criticism** conceives *literature* to be a second-order signifying system that uses the first-order structural system of language as its medium, and is itself to be analyzed primarily on the model of linguistic theory. Structuralist critics often apply a variety of linguistic concepts to the analysis of a literary text, such as the distinction between *phonemic* and *morphemic* levels of organization, or between *paradigmatic* and *syntagmatic* relationships; and some critics analyze the structure of a literary text on the model of the *syntax* in a well-formed sentence. The undertaking of a thoroughgoing literary structuralism, however, is to explain how it is that a competent reader is able to make sense of a particular literary text by specifying the underlying system of literary conventions and rules of combination that has been unconsciously mastered by such a reader. The aim of classic literary structuralism, accordingly, is not (as in *New Criticism*) to provide the interpretation of single texts, but to make explicit, in a quasi-scientific way, the tacit *grammar* (the system of rules and codes) that governs the forms and meanings of all literary productions. As Jonathan Culler put it in his lucid exposition, the aim of structuralist criticism is "to construct a poetics which stands to literature as linguistics stands to language" (*Structuralist Poetics*, 1975, p. 257).

Roland Barthes, Gérard Genette, Julia Kristeva, and Tzvetan Todorov were, at least in some part of their careers, prominent structuralist critics of literature.

Structuralism is in explicit opposition to *mimetic criticism* (the view that literature is primarily an imitation of reality), to *expressive criticism* (the view that literature primarily expresses the feelings or temperament or creative imagination of its author), and to any form of the view that literature is a mode of communication between author and readers. More generally, in its attempt to develop a science of literature and in many of its salient concepts, the radical forms of structuralism depart from the assumptions and ruling ideas of traditional humanistic criticism. (See *humanism*.) For example:

1. In the structuralist view, what had been called a literary "work" becomes a *text*; that is, a mode of writing constituted by a play of internal elements according to specifically literary conventions and codes. These factors may generate an illusion of reality, but have no truth-value, nor even any reference to a reality existing outside the literary system itself.

2. The individual author, or *subject*, is not assigned any initiative, expressive intentions, or design as the "origin" or producer of a work. Instead the conscious "self" is declared to be a construct that is itself the product of the workings of the linguistic system, and the mind of an author is described as an imputed "space" within which the impersonal, "always-already" existing system of literary language, conventions, codes, and rules of combination gets precipitated into a particular text. Roland Barthes expressed, dramatically, this subversion of the traditional humanistic view, "As institution, the author is dead" ("The Death of the Author," in *Image-Music-Text*, trans. 1977). See *author and authorship* and the *subject*, under *poststructuralism*.

3. Structuralism replaces the author with the reader as the central agency in criticism; but the traditional reader, as a conscious, purposeful, and feeling individual, is replaced by the impersonal activity of "reading," and what is read is not a work imbued with meanings, but *écriture*, writing. The focus of structuralist criticism, accordingly, is not on the sensibility of the reader, but on the impersonal process of reading which, by bringing into play the requisite conventions, codes, and expectations, makes literary sense of the sequence of words, phrases, and sentences that constitute a text. See *text and writing (écriture)*.

In the late 1960s, the structuralist enterprise, in its rigorous form and inclusive pretensions, ceded its central position to deconstruction and other modes of poststructural theories, which subverted the scientific claims of structuralism and its view that literary meanings are made determinate by a system of invariant conventions and codes. (See *poststructuralism*.) This shift in the prevailing point of view is exemplified by the changing emphases in the lively and influential writings of the French critic and man of letters, Roland Barthes (1915–80). His early work developed the structuralist theory that was based on the linguistics of Saussure—a theory that Barthes applied not only to literature but to decoding, by reference to an underlying signifying system, many aspects of popular culture. (See Barthes' *Mythologies*, 1957, trans. 1972, and refer to *cultural studies*.) In his later writings, Barthes abandoned the scientific aspiration of structuralism, and distinguished between the "readerly" text such as the realistic novel that tries to "close" interpretation by insisting on specific meanings, and the "writerly" text that aims at the ideal of "a galaxy of signifiers," and so encourages the reader to be a producer of his or her own meanings according not to one code but to a multiplicity of codes. And in *The Pleasure of the Text* (1973) Barthes lauds, in contrast to the comfortable pleasure offered by a traditional text that accords with cultural codes and conventions, the "jouissance" (or orgasmic bliss) evoked by a text that incites a hedonistic abandon to the uncontrolled play of its signifiers. See Roland Barthes, in the entry *text and writing (écriture)*.

Structuralist premises and procedures, however, continue to be deployed in a number of current enterprises, and especially in the semiotic analysis of cultural phenomena, in stylistics, and in the investigation of the formal structures that, in their combinations and variations, constitute the plots in novels. See *semiotics, cultural studies, stylistics*, and *narrative and narratology*.

A clear and comprehensive survey of the program and accomplishments of structuralist literary criticism, in poetry as well as narrative prose, is Jonathan Culler, *Structuralist Poetics* (1975); also Robert Scholes, *Structuralism in Literature: An Introduction* (1974). For an introduction to the general movement of structuralism see Peter Caws, *Structuralism: The Art of the Intelligible* (1960); Philip Pettit, *The Concept of Structuralism: A Critical Analysis* (1975); and Terence Hawkes, *Structuralism and Semiotics* (1977). For critical views of structuralism see Gerald Graff, *Literature Against Itself* (1979); Frank Lentricchia, *After the New Criticism* (1980), chapters 4–5; J. G. Merquior, *From Prague to Paris: A Critique of Structuralist and Post-Structuralist Thought* (1986); Leonard Jackson, *The Poverty of Structuralism: Literature and Structuralist Theory* (1991). Some collections of structuralist writings: Richard T. De George and M. Fernande, eds., *The Structuralists: From Marx to Lévi-Strauss* (1972); David Robey, ed., *Structuralism: An Introduction* (1973); see also Richard Macksey and Eugenio Donato, eds., *The Structuralist Controversy: The Languages of Criticism and the Sciences of Man* (1970). Among the books of structuralist literary criticism available in English translations are Roland Barthes, *Critical Essays* (1964); Stephen Heath, *The Nouveau Roman: A Study in the Practice of Writing* (1972); Tzvetan Todorov, *The Poetics of Prose* (trans. 1977) and *Introduction to Poetics* (trans. 1981); Gérard Genette, *Figures of Literary Discourse* (trans. 1984). Structuralist treatments of cinema are Peter Wollen, *Signs and Meaning in the Cinema* (1969), and Christian Metz, *Language of Film* (1973).

For references to *structuralist criticism* in other entries, see pages *18, 44, 63, 126, 135, 173, 206, 268, 303, 325, 326, 346, 352, 364*.

**structure: 126**. See also *structuralism*.

**style:** Style has traditionally been defined as the manner of linguistic expression in prose or verse—as *how* speakers or writers say whatever it is that they say. The style specific to a particular work or writer, or else distinctive of a type of writings, has been analyzed in such terms as the rhetorical situation and aim (see *rhetoric*); the characteristic *diction*, or choice of words; the type of sentence structure and syntax; and the density and kinds of *figurative language*.

In standard theories based on Cicero and other classical rhetoricians, styles were usually classified into three main levels: the **high** (or "grand"), the **middle** (or "mean"), and the **low** (or "plain") **style**. The doctrine of *decorum*, which was influential through the eighteenth century, required that the level of style in a work be appropriate to the social class of the speaker, to the occasion on which it is spoken, and to the dignity of its literary genre (see *poetic diction*). The critic Northrop Frye introduced a variant of this long-persisting analysis of stylistic levels in literature. He made a primary differentiation between the **demotic style** (which is modeled on the language, rhythms, and associations of ordinary speech) and the **hieratic style** (which employs a variety of formal elaborations that separate the literary language from ordinary speech). Frye then proceeded to distinguish a high, middle, and low level in each of these classes. See *The Well-Tempered Critic* (1963), chapter 2.

In analyzing style, two types of sentence structure are often distinguished:

The **periodic sentence** is one in which the component parts, or "members," are so composed that the close of its syntactic structure remains suspended until the end of the sentence; the effect tends to be formal or oratorical. An example is the eloquent opening sentence of James Boswell's *Life of Samuel Johnson* (1791), in which the structure of the syntax is not concluded until we reach the final noun, "task":

> To write the life of him who excelled all mankind in writing the lives
> of others, and who, whether we consider his extraordinary endow-
> ments, or his various works, has been equaled by few in any age, is an
> arduous, and may be reckoned in me a presumptuous task.

In the **nonperiodic** (or **loose**) **sentence**—more relaxed and conversational in its effect—the component members are continuous, but so loosely joined that the sentence would have been syntactically complete if a period had been inserted at one or more places before the actual close. So the two sentences in Joseph Addison's *Spectator 105*, describing the limited topics in the conversation of a "man-about-town," or dilettante, could each have closed at several points in the sequence of their component clauses:

> He will tell you the names of the principal favourites, repeat the
> shrewd sayings of a man of quality, whisper an intrigue that is not yet
> blown upon by common fame; or, if the sphere of his observations is a
> little larger than ordinary, will perhaps enter into all the incidents,
> turns, and revolutions in a game of ombre. When he has gone thus far
> he has shown you the whole circle of his accomplishments, his parts
> are drained, and he is disabled from any farther conversation.

Another distinction often made in discussing prose style is that between parataxis and hypotaxis:

A **paratactic style** is one in which the members within a sentence, or else a sequence of complete sentences, are put one after the other without any expression of their connection or relations except (at most) the noncommittal connective "and." An example is the passage just quoted from Addison's *Spectator*. Ernest Hemingway's style is characteristically paratactic. The members in this sentence from his novel *The Sun Also Rises* (1926) are joined merely by "ands": "It was dim and dark and the pillars went high up, and there were people praying, and it smelt of incense, and there were some wonderful big buildings." The curt paratactic sentences in his short story "Indian Camp" omit all connectives: "The sun was coming over the hills. A bass jumped, making a circle in the water. Nick trailed his hand in the water. It felt warm in the sharp chill of the morning."

A **hypotactic style** is one in which the temporal, causal, logical, and syntactic relations between members and sentences are specified by words (such as "when," "then," "because," "therefore") or by phrases (such as "in order to," "as a result") or by the use of subordinate phrases and clauses. The style in this *Glossary* is mainly hypotactic.

A very large number of loosely descriptive terms have been used to characterize kinds of style, such as "pure," "ornate," "florid," "gay," "sober," "simple," "elaborate," and so on. Styles are also classified according to a literary period or tradition ("the *metaphysical* style," "Restoration prose style"); according to an influential text ("biblical style," *euphuism*); according to an institutional use ("a scientific style," "journalese"); or according to the distinctive practice of an individual author (the "Shakespearean" or "Miltonic style"; "Johnsonese"). Historians of English prose style, especially in the seventeenth and eighteenth centuries, have distinguished between the vogue of the "Ciceronian style" (named after the characteristic practice of the Roman writer Cicero), which is elaborately constructed, highly periodic, and typically builds to a climax, and the opposing vogue of the clipped, concise, pointed, and uniformly stressed sentences in the "Attic" or "Senecan" styles (named after the practice of the Roman Seneca). See J. M. Patrick and others, eds., *Style, Rhetoric, and Rhythm: Essays by Morris W. Croll* (1966), and George Williamson, *The Senecan Amble: A Study in Prose Form from Bacon to Collier* (1951).

Francis-Noël Thomas and Mark Turner, in *Clear and Simple as the Truth* (1994), claim that standard treatments of style such as those described above deal only with the surface features of writing. They propose instead a basic analysis of style in terms of a set of fundamental decisions or assumptions by an author concerning "a series of relationships: What can be known? What can be put into words? What is the relationship between thought and language? Who is the writer addressing and why? What is the implied relationship between writer and reader? What are the implied conditions of discourse?" An analysis based on all these elements yields an indefinite number of types, or "families," of styles, each with its own criteria of excellence. The authors focus on what they call "the classic style" exemplified in writings like René Descartes' *Discourse on Method* (1637) or Thomas Jefferson's "Declaration of Independence" (1776), but identify and discuss briefly a number of other styles such as "plain style," "practical style," "contemplative style," and "prophetic style."

For some recent developments in the analysis of style based on modern linguistic theory and philosophy of language, see *stylistics* and *discourse analysis*. Among the more traditional theorists and analysts of style are Herbert Read,

*English Prose Style* (1928); Bonamy Dobree, *Modern Prose Style* (1934); W. K. Wimsatt, *The Prose Style of Samuel Johnson* (1941); P. F. Baum, *The Other Harmony of Prose* (1952); Erich Auerbach, *Mimesis: The Representation of Reality in Western Literature* (trans. 1953, reissued 2003); Josephine Miles, *Eras and Modes in English Poetry* (1957); Louis T. Milic, ed., *Stylists on Style: A Handbook with Selections for Analysis* (1969).

For references to *style* in other entries, see pages *269, 311, 352, 353*. See also *connotation and denotation; decorum; stream of consciousness.* For features of style, see *ambiguity; antithesis; archaism; bathos and anticlimax; bombast; cliché; conceit; concrete and abstract; epithet; euphemism; euphony and cacophony; euphuism; figurative language; grand style; imagery; purple patch.*

**stylistics:** Since the 1950s the term **stylistics** has been applied to critical procedures which undertake to replace what is claimed to be the subjectivity and impressionism of standard analyses with an "objective" or "scientific" analysis of the style of literary texts. Much of the impetus toward these analytic methods, as well as models for their practical application, was provided by the writings of Roman Jakobson and other *Russian formalists*, as well as by European *structuralists*.

We can distinguish two main modes of stylistics, which differ both in conception and in the scope of their application:

1. In the narrower mode of formal stylistics, style is identified, in the traditional way, by the distinction between what is said and how it is said, or between the content and the form of a text. (See *style*.) The content is now often denoted, however, by terms such as "information," "message," or "propositional meaning," while the style is defined as variations in the presentation of this information that serve to alter its "aesthetic quality" or the reader's emotional response. The concepts of modern *linguistics* are used to identify the stylistic features, or "formal properties," which are held to be distinctive of a particular work, or else of an author, or a literary tradition, or an era. These stylistic features may be phonological (patterns of speech sounds, meter, or rhyme), or syntactic (types of sentence structure), or lexical (*abstract* vs. *concrete* words, the relative frequency of nouns, verbs, adjectives), or rhetorical (the characteristic use of *figurative language, imagery*, and so on). A basic problem, acknowledged by a number of stylisticians, is to distinguish between the innumerable features and patterns of a text which can be isolated by linguistic analysis, and those features which are functionally stylistic—that is, features which make an actual difference in the aesthetic and other effects on a competent reader. See, for example, Michael Riffaterre's objection to the elaborate stylistic analysis of Charles Baudelaire's sonnet "Les Chats" (The Cats) by Roman Jakobson and Claude Lévi-Strauss, in *Structuralism*, ed. Jacques Ehrmann (1966).

   Stylisticians who aim either to replace or supplement the qualitative judgments of literary scholars by objectively determinable methods of research exploit the ever-increasing technological resources of computers in the service of what has come to be called **stylometry**: the quantitative measurement of the features of an individual writer's style. *Literary and Linguistic Computing* is a journal devoted to the use of computers in literary studies. See also B. H. Rudall and T. N. Corns, *Computers and Literature: A Practical Guide* (1987). Other analysts of style who use nonquantitative methods adopt concepts derived from language theory, such as the distinction between *paradigmatic* and *syntagmatic* relations, or the distinction between surface structure and deep structure in *transformational linguistics*, or the distinction between the propositional content and the *illocutionary force* of an utterance in *speech-act theory*. For a stylistic analysis of the ways a character's speech and thought are represented in narratives, refer to *free indirect discourse*, under *point of view*.

Sometimes the stylistic enterprise stops with the qualitative or quantitative determination, or "fingerprinting," of the style of a single text or class of texts. Often, however, the analyst tries also to relate distinctive stylistic features to traits in an author's psyche; or to an author's characteristic ways of perceiving the world and organizing experience (see Leo Spitzer, *Linguistics and Literary History*, 1948); or to the typical conceptual frame and the attitude toward reality in an historical era [Erich Auerbach, *Mimesis: The Representation of Reality in Western Literature* (reissued 2003); or else to semantic, aesthetic, and emotional functions and effects in a particular literary text (Michael Riffaterre and others)].

Stanley Fish wrote a sharp critique of the scientific pretensions of formal stylistics; he proposed that since, in his view, the meaning of a text consists of a reader's total response to it, there is no valid way to make a distinction in this spectrum of response between style and content ("What Is Stylistics and Why Are They Saying Such Terrible Things About It?" in *Is There a Text in This Class?* 1980; see also *reader-response criticism*). For extended critiques both of traditional analyses of style, and of modern stylistics, based on the thesis that style is not a separable feature of language, see Bennison Gray, *Style: The Problem and Its Solution* (1969), and "Stylistics: The End of a Tradition," *Journal of Aesthetics and Art Criticism*, Vol. 31 (1973). In *Clear and Simple as the Truth* (1994), Francis-Nöel Thomas and Mark Turner claim that standard stylistic analyses concern merely the surface features of writing, and propose a set of more basic features by which to define styles of writing; see under *style*. On the other side, the validity of distinguishing between style and propositional meaning—not absolutely, but on an appropriate level of analysis—is defended by E. D. Hirsch, "Stylistics and Synonymity," in *The Aims of Interpretation* (1976).

2. In the second mode of stylistics, which has been prominent since the mid-1960s, proponents greatly expand the conception and scope of their inquiry by defining stylistics as, in the words of one theorist, "the study of the use of language in literature," involving the entire range of the "general characteristics of language . . . as a medium of literary expression." (Geoffrey N. Leech, *A Linguistic Guide to English Poetry*, 1969; see also Mick Short, "Literature and Language," in *Encyclopedia of Literature and Criticism*, ed. Martin Coyle and others, 1990.) By this definition, stylistics is expanded so as to incorporate most of the concerns of both traditional literary *criticism* and traditional *rhetoric*; its distinction from these earlier pursuits is that it insists on the need to be objective by focusing sharply on the text itself and by setting out to discover the

"rules" governing the process by which linguistic elements and patterns in a text accomplish their meanings and literary effects. The historian of criticism René Wellek has described this tendency of stylistic analysis to enlarge its territorial domain as "the imperialism of modern stylistics."

A comprehensive anthology is *The Stylistics Reader from Roman Jakobson to the Present*, ed. Jean Jacques Weber (1996). On formal stylistics see Thomas A. Sebeok, ed., *Style in Language* (1960); Seymour Chatman, ed., *Literary Style: A Symposium* (1971); Howard S. Babb, ed., *Essays in Stylistic Analysis* (1972); Richard Bradford, *Stylistics* (1997). For an exhaustive stylistic analysis of a twelve-line poem, see Roman Jakobson and Stephen Rudy, *Yeats's "Sorrow of Love" Through the Years* (1977).

In the practice of some critics, stylistics includes the area of study known as *discourse analysis*, which is treated in a separate entry in this *Glossary*. For inclusive views of the realm of stylistics, see M. A. K. Halliday, *Explorations in the Functions of Language* (1973); G. N. Leech and M. H. Short, *Style in Fiction* (1981); Roger Fowler, *Linguistic Criticism* (1986); Ronald Carter and Paul Simpson, eds., *Language, Discourse and Literature: An Introductory Reader in Discourse Stylistics* (1989). For references to *stylistics* in other entries, see pages *82, 128, 351*.

**stylometry** (stīlŏ' mĕtrē): **352**.

**subaltern: 277**.

**subject, the** (in poststructural criticism): **280**; *146, 161, 219, 221, 277, 348*.

**subjective: 233**.

**sublimate: 291**.

**sublime:** The concept was introduced into the criticism of literature and art by a Greek treatise *Peri hupsous* ("On the sublime"), attributed in the manuscript to Longinus and probably written in the first century AD. As defined by Longinus, the sublime is a quality that can occur in any type of discourse, whether poetry or prose. Whereas the effect of *rhetoric* on the hearer or reader of a discourse is persuasion, the effect of the sublime is "transport" *(ekstasis)*—it is that quality of a passage which "shatters the hearer's composure," exercises irresistible "domination" over him, and "scatters the subjects like a bolt of lightning." The source of the sublime lies in the capabilities of the speaker or writer. Three of these—the use of figurative language, nobility of expression, and elevated composition—are matters of art that can be acquired by practice; but two other, and more important, capabilities, are largely innate: "loftiness of thought" and "strong and inspired passion." The ability to achieve sublimity is in itself enough to prove the transcendent genius of a writer, and expresses the nobility of the writer's character: "sublimity is the ring of greatness in the soul." Longinus' examples of sublime passages in poems range from the epics of Homer through the tragedies of Aeschylus to a love lyric by Sappho; his examples in prose are taken from the writings of the philosopher Plato, the orator Demosthenes, and the historian Herodotus. Especially notable is his quotation, as a prime instance of sublimity, of the passage in the Book of Genesis written by "the lawgiver of the Jews": "And God said, 'Let there be light,' and there was light, 'Let there be land,' and there was land."

Longinus' innovative treatise exerted a strong and persistent effect on literary criticism after it became widely known by way of a French translation by Boileau in 1674; eventually, it helped establish both the *expressive* theory of poetry and the critical method of *impressionism* (see under *criticism*). In the eighteenth century an important tendency in critical theory was to shift the application of the term, "the sublime," from a quality of linguistic discourse that originates in the powers of a writer's mind, to a quality inherent in external objects, and above all in the scenes and occurrences of the natural world. Thus Edmund Burke's highly influential *Philosophical Enquiry into the Origin of Our Ideas of the Sublime and Beautiful*, published in 1757, attributes the source of the sublime to those things which are "in any sort terrible"—that is, to whatever is "fitted in any sort to excite the ideas of pain, and danger"—provided that the observer is in a situation of safety from danger, and so is able to experience what would otherwise be a painful terror as a "delightful horror." (Compare *distance and involvement*.) The features of objects which evoke sublime horror that Burke stresses are obscurity, immense power, and vastness in dimension or quantity. Burke's examples of the sublime include vast architectural structures, Milton's description of Satan in *Paradise Lost*, the description of the king's army in Shakespeare's *1 Henry IV*, and natural phenomena; a sublime passion may be produced by "the noise of vast cataracts, raging storms, thunder or artillery," all of which evoke "a great and awful sensation in the mind."

During the eighteenth century, tourists and landscape painters traveled to the English Lake Country and to the Alps in search of sublime scenery that was thrillingly vast, dark, wild, stormy, and ominous. Writers of what was called "the sublime ode," such as Thomas Gray and William Collins, sought to achieve effects of wildness and obscurity in their descriptive style and abrupt transitions, as well as to render the wildness, vastness, and obscurity of the sublime objects they described. (See *ode*.) Authors of *Gothic novels* exploited the sublimity of delightful horror both in the natural and architectural settings of their narratives and in the actions and events that they narrated. Samuel H. Monk, a pioneer historian of the concept of the sublime in the eighteenth century, cites as the "apotheosis" of the natural sublime the description of Simplon Pass in Wordsworth's *The Prelude* (1805), 4.554ff.:

> The immeasurable height
> Of woods decaying, never to be decayed,
> The stationary blasts of waterfalls,
> And everywhere along the hollow rent
> Winds thwarting winds, bewildered and forlorn,
> The torrents shooting from the clear blue sky,
> The rocks that muttered close upon our ears—
> Black drizzling crags that spake by the wayside

> As if a voice were in them—the sick sight
> And giddy prospect of the raving stream,
> Tumult and peace, the darkness and the light. . . .

(Samuel H. Monk, *The Sublime: A Study of Critical Theories in Eighteenth-Century England*, 1935)

In an extended analysis of the sublime in his *Critique of Judgment* (1790), the German philosopher Immanuel Kant divided the sublime objects specified by Burke and other earlier theorists into two kinds: (1) the "mathematical sublime" encompasses the sublime of magnitude—of vastness in size or seeming limitlessness or infinitude in number. (2) The "dynamic sublime" encompasses the objects conducive to terror at our seeming helplessness before the overwhelming power of nature, provided that the terror is rendered pleasurable by the safe situation of the observer. All of Kant's examples of sublimity are scenes and events in the natural world: "the immeasurable host" of starry systems such as the Milky Way, "shapeless mountain masses towering one above the other in wild disorder," "volcanoes in all their violence of destruction, hurricanes leaving desolation in their track, the boundless ocean rising with rebellious force, the high waterfall of some mighty river." Kant maintains, however, that the sublimity resides "not in the Object of nature" itself, but "only in the mind of the judging Subject" who contemplates the object. In a noted passage he describes the experience of sublimity as a rapid sequence of painful blockage and pleasurable release—"the feeling of a momentary check to the vital forces followed at once by a discharge all the more powerful." In the mathematical sublime, the mind is checked by its inadequacy to comprehend as a totality the boundlessness or seeming infinity of natural magnitudes, and in the dynamic sublime, it is checked by its helplessness before the seeming irresistibility of natural powers. But the mind then goes on to feel exultation at the recognition of its inherent capacity to think a totality in a way that transcends "every standard of sense," or else at its discovery within itself of a capacity for resistance which "gives us courage to be able to measure ourselves against the seeming omnipotence of nature." In Kant's view, the experience of the sublime manifests on the one hand the limitations and weakness of finite humanity, but on the other hand its "pre-eminence over nature," even when confronted by the "immeasurability" of nature's magnitude and the "irresistibility" of its might.

In *The Romantic Sublime: Studies in the Structure and Psychology of Transcendence* (1976), Thomas Weiskel undertook to translate Kant's theory of the sublime, and especially his analysis of blockage and release, into terms both of recent *semiotic* theory and of the *psychoanalytic* theory of the Oedipus complex. See also the development of Kant's views by Neil Hertz, *The End of the Line: Essays on Psychoanalysis and the Sublime* (1985). Slavoj Žižek applied the concept of the sublime to a Lacanian interpretation of *ideology* (see under *Marxist criticism*) in *The Sublime Object of Ideology* (1989). For the argument that eighteenth-century debates about the sublime illuminate some debates in recent literary theory, see Frances Ferguson, *Solitude and the Sublime: Romanticism and the Aesthetics of Individuation* (1992).

Refer to Elder Olson, "The Argument of Longinus' *On the Sublime*," in *Critics and Criticism, Ancient and Modern*, ed. R. S. Crane (1952); W. J. Hipple, *The Beautiful, the Sublime, and the Picturesque in Eighteenth-Century British Aesthetic Theory* (1957); Marjorie Nicholson, *Mountain Gloom and Mountain Glory* (1959); Steven Knapp, *Personification and the Sublime: Milton to Coleridge* (1985).

**subplot: 266**.

**subtext: 283**; *186, 222*.

**subversion-containment dialectic: 223**.

**superego: 291**.

**suprasegmental** (in linguistics): **175**.

**surface structure** (in linguistics): **177**.

**surfiction: 232**.

**surprise** (in a plot): **266**.

**surrealism** ("superrealism"): Surrealism was launched as a concerted artistic movement in France by André Breton's *Manifesto on Surrealism* (1924). It was a successor to the brief movement known as **Dadaism**, which emerged in 1916 out of disgust with the brutality and destructiveness of the First World War, and set out, according to its manifestos, to engender a negative art and literature that would shock and bewilder observers and serve to destroy the false values of modern bourgeois society, including its rationality and the kind of art and literature that rationality had fostered. Among the exponents of Dadaism were, for a time, artists and writers such as Tristan Tzara, Marcel Duchamp, Man Ray, and Max Ernst.

The expressed aim of surrealism was a revolt against all restraints on free creativity, including logical reason, standard morality, social and artistic conventions and norms, and all control over the artistic process by forethought and intention. To ensure the unhampered operation of the "deep mind," which they regarded as the only source of valid knowledge as well as art, surrealists turned to *automatic writing* (writing delivered over to the promptings of the unconscious mind), and to exploiting the material of dreams, of states of mind between sleep and waking, and of natural or drug-induced hallucinations.

Surrealism was a revolutionary movement in painting, sculpture, and the other arts, as well as literature; and it often joined forces, although briefly, with one or another revolutionary movement in the political and social realm. The effects of surrealism extended far beyond the small group of its professed adherents such as André Breton, Louis Aragon, and the painter Salvador Dali. The influence, direct or indirect, of surrealist innovations can be found in many modern writers of prose and verse who have broken with conventional modes of artistic organization to experiment with free association, a broken syntax, nonlogical and nonchronological order, dreamlike and nightmarish sequences, and the juxtaposition of bizarre, shocking, or seemingly unrelated images. In England and America such effects can be found in a wide range of writings, from the poetry of Dylan Thomas to the flights of fantasy, hallucinative writing, startling inconsequences, and *black humor* in the novels of Henry Miller, William Burroughs, and Thomas Pynchon.

For a precursor of some aspects of surrealism, see *decadence*; for later developments that continued some of the surrealist innovations, see literature of the *absurd, antinovel, magic realism*, and *postmodernism*. Refer to David Gascoyne, *A Short Survey of Surrealism* (1935); A. E. Balakian, *Literary Origins of Surrealism* (1947); Maurice Nadeau, *History of Surrealism* (trans. 1989); Mary Ann Caws, *The Poetry of Dada and Surrealism* (1970); Mary Ann Caws, ed., *Surrealist Painters and Poets: An Anthology* (2001); and Paul C. Ray, *The Surrealist Movement in England* (1971). In *Dada Turns Red* (1990), Helena Lewis explores the relations between Surrealists and Communists from the 1920s to the 1950s. In *Automatic Woman: The Representation of Women in Surrealism* (1996), Katharine Conley writes a *feminist* analysis of the obsessive and complex concern of male surrealists with the female body, which they often represented in a distorted or dissected form; she also discusses the work of two female surrealists, Unica Zürn and Leonora Carrington.

**suspense** (in a plot): **266**.

**syllabic meter: 194**.

**symbol:** In the broadest sense a symbol is anything which signifies something else; in this sense all words are symbols. In discussing literature, however, the term "symbol" is applied only to a word or phrase that signifies an object or event which in its turn signifies something, or suggests a range of reference, beyond itself. Some symbols are "conventional" or "public": thus "the Cross," "the Red, White, and Blue," and "the Good Shepherd" are terms that refer to symbolic objects of which the further significance is determinate within a particular culture. Poets, like all of us, use such conventional symbols; many poets, however, also use "private" or "personal symbols." Often they do so by exploiting widely shared associations between an object or event or action and a particular concept; for example, the general association of a peacock with pride and of an eagle with heroic endeavor, or the rising sun with birth and the setting sun with death, or climbing with effort or progress and descent with surrender or failure. Some poets, however, repeatedly use symbols whose significance they largely generate themselves, and these pose a more difficult problem in interpretation.

Take as an example the word "rose," which in its literal use signifies a species of flower. In Robert Burns' line "O my love's like a red, red rose," the word "rose" is used as a *simile*; and in the lines by Winthrop Mackworth Praed (1802–39),

> She was our queen, our rose, our star;
> And then she danced—O Heaven, her dancing!

the word "rose" is used as a *metaphor*. In *The Romance of the Rose*, a long medieval *dream vision*, we read about a half-opened rose to which the dreamer's access is aided by a character called "Fair Welcome," but impeded or forbidden by other characters called "Reason," "Shame," and "Jealousy." We readily recognize that the whole narrative is a sustained *allegory* about an elaborate courtship, in which most of the agents are personified abstractions and the rose itself functions as an allegorical **emblem** (that is, an object whose significance is made determinate by its qualities and by the role it plays in the narrative) which represents both the lady's love and her lovely body. Then we read William Blake's poem "The Sick Rose."

> O Rose, thou art sick.
> The invisible worm
> That flies in the night
> In the howling storm
> Has found out thy bed
> Of crimson joy,
> And his dark secret love
> Does thy life destroy.

This rose is not the *vehicle* for a simile or metaphor, because it lacks the paired subject—"my love," or the girl referred to as "she," in the examples just cited—which is an identifying feature of these figures. And it is not an allegorical rose, since, unlike the flower in *The Romance of the Rose*, it is not part of an obvious double order of correlated references, one literal and the second allegorical, in which the allegorical or emblematic reference of the rose is made determinate by its role within the literal narrative. Blake's rose *is* a rose—yet it is patently also something more than a rose: words such as "bed," "joy," "love," which do not comport literally with an actual flower, together with the sinister tone, and the intensity of the lyric speaker's feeling, press the reader to infer that the described object has a further range of suggested but unspecified reference which makes it a symbol. But Blake's rose is a personal symbol and not—like the symbolic rose in the closing cantos of Dante's fourteenth-century *Paradiso* and other Christian poems—an element in a set of conventional and widely known (hence "public") religious symbols, in which concrete objects of this passing world are used to signify, in a relatively determinate way, the objects and truths of a higher and eternal realm. (See Barbara Seward, *The Symbolic Rose*, 1960.) Only from the implicit suggestions in Blake's poem itself—the sexual connotations, in the realm of human experience, of "bed" and "love," especially in conjunction with "joy" and "worm"—supplemented by our knowledge of similar elements and topics in his other poems, are we led to infer that Blake's lament for a crimson rose which has been entered and sickened unto death by a dark and secret worm symbolizes, in the human realm, the destruction wrought by furtiveness, deceit, and hypocrisy in what should be a frank and joyous relationship of physical love. Various critics of the poem, however, have proposed alternative interpretations of its symbolic significance. It is an attribute of many private symbols—the White Whale in Melville's *Moby-Dick* (1851) is another famed example—as well as a reason why they are an irreplaceable literary device, that they suggest a direction or a broad area of significance rather than, like an emblem in an allegorical narrative, a relatively determinate reference.

In the copious modern literature on the nature of the literary symbol, reference is often made to two seminal passages, written early in the nineteenth century by Coleridge in England and Goethe in Germany, concerning the difference between an allegory and a symbol. Coleridge is in fact describing what he believes to be the uniquely symbolic nature of the Bible as a sacred text, but later commentators have assumed that he intended his comment to apply also to the symbol in secular literature:

> Now an allegory is but a translation of abstract notions into a picture-language, which is itself nothing but an abstraction from objects of the senses. . . . On the other hand a symbol . . . is characterized by a translucence of the special [i.e., of the species] in the individual, or of the general [i.e., of the genus] in the special, or of the universal in the general; above all by the translucence of the eternal through and in the temporal. It always partakes of the reality which it renders intelligible; and while it enunciates the whole, abides itself as a living part in that unity of which it is the representative. [Allegories] are but empty echoes which the fancy arbitrarily associates with apparitions of matter. . . .

(Coleridge, *The Statesman's Manual*, 1816)

Goethe had been meditating about the nature of the literary symbol in secular writings since the 1790s, but gave his concept its most specific formulation in 1824:

> There is a great difference, whether the poet seeks the particular for the sake of the general or sees the general in the particular. From the former procedure there ensues allegory, in which the particular serves only as illustration, as example of the general. The latter procedure, however, is genuinely the nature of poetry; it expresses something particular, without thinking of the general or pointing to it.
>
> Allegory transforms the phenomenon into a concept, the concept into an image, but in such a way that the concept always remains bounded in the image, and is entirely to be kept and held in it, and to be expressed by it.
>
> Symbolism [however] transforms the phenomenon into idea, the idea into an image, and in such a way that the idea remains always infinitely active and unapproachable in the image, and even if expressed in all languages, still would remain inexpressible.

(Goethe, *Maxims and Reflections*, Nos. 279, 1112, 1113)

It will be noted that, whatever the differences between these cryptic passages, both Coleridge and Goethe stress that an allegory presents a pair of subjects (an image and a concept) but a symbol only one (the image alone); that the allegory is relatively specific in its reference, while the symbol remains indefinite, but richly —even boundlessly—suggestive in its significance; and also that for this very reason, a symbol is the higher mode of expression. To these claims, characteristic in the *Romantic Period*, critics until the recent past have for the most part agreed. In express opposition to romantic theory, however, Paul de Man has elevated allegory over symbol because, he claims, it is less "mystified" (confused and deceived) about its status as a purely rhetorical device. See de Man, "The Rhetoric of Temporality," in *Interpretation: Theory and Practice*, ed. C. S. Singleton (1969), and *Allegories of Reading* (1979).

See also W. B. Yeats, "The Symbolism of Poetry" (1900), in *Essays and Introductions* (1961); H. Flanders Dunbar, *Symbolism in Medieval Thought* (1929); C. S. Lewis, *The Allegory of Love: A Study in Medieval Tradition* (1936); Elder Olson, "A Dialogue on Symbolism," in R. S. Crane, ed., *Critics and Criticism* (1952); W. Y. Tindall, *The Literary Symbol* (1955); Harry Levin, "Symbolism and Fiction," in *Contexts of Criticism* (1957); Isabel C. Hungerland, *Poetic Discourse* (1958), chapter 5; Maurice Beebe, ed., *Literary Symbolism* (1960); Michael Ferber, *A Dictionary of Literary Symbols* (1999). For references to a literary *symbol* in other entries, see page *361*.

**symbol** (in semiotics): **324**.

**symbolic** (in Lacanian criticism): **294**.

**symbolism: 361**; *213, 248*.

**Symbolist Movement:** Various poets of the *Romantic Period*, including Novalis and Hölderlin in Germany and Shelley in England, often used private symbols in their poetry (see *symbol*). Shelley, for example, repeatedly made symbolic use of objects such as the morning and evening star, a boat moving upstream, winding caves, and the conflict between a serpent and an eagle. William Blake, however, exceeded all his romantic contemporaries in his recourse to a persistent and sustained **symbolism**—that is, a coherent system composed of a number of symbolic elements—both in his lyric poems and his long "prophetic," or epic poems. (See, for example, Northrop Frye, *Fearful Symmetry: A Study of William Blake*, 1947.) In nineteenth-century America, a symbolist procedure was a prominent element in the novels of Nathaniel Hawthorne and Herman Melville, the prose of Emerson and Thoreau, and the poetic theory and practice of Poe. (See Charles Feidelson, Jr., *Symbolism and American Literature*, 1953.) These writers derived the mode in large part from the native Puritan tradition of typology (see *interpretation: typological and allegorical*), and also from the theory of "correspondences" of the Swedish theologian Emanuel Swedenborg (1688–1772).

In the usage of literary historians, however, **Symbolist Movement** designates specifically a group of French writers beginning with Charles Baudelaire (*Fleurs du mal*, 1857) and including such later poets as Arthur Rimbaud, Paul Verlaine, Stéphane Mallarmé, and Paul Valéry. Baudelaire based the symbolic mode of his poems in part on the example of the American Edgar Allan Poe, but especially on the ancient belief in **correspondences**—the doctrine that there exist inherent and systematic analogies between the human mind and the outer world, and also between the material and the spiritual worlds. As Baudelaire put this doctrine: "Everything, form, movement, number, color, perfume, in the *spiritual* as in the *natural* world, is significative, reciprocal, converse, *correspondent*." The techniques of the French **Symbolists**, who exploited an order of private symbols in a poetry of rich suggestiveness rather than explicit signification, had an immense influence throughout Europe, and (especially in the 1890s and later) in England and America on poets such as Arthur Symons and Ernest Dowson (see *Decadence*) as well as W. B. Yeats, Ezra Pound, Dylan Thomas, Hart Crane, e. e. cummings, and Wallace Stevens. Major symbolist poets in Germany are Stefan George and Rainer Maria Rilke.

The *Modern Period*, in the decades after World War I, was a notable era of symbolism in literature. Many of the major writers of the period exploit symbols which are in part drawn from religious and esoteric traditions and in part invented. Some of the works of the age are symbolist in their settings, their agents, and their actions, as well as in the objects they refer to. Instances of a persistently symbolic procedure occur in lyrics (Yeats' "Byzantium" poems, Dylan Thomas' series of sonnets *Altarwise by Owl-light*), in longer poems (Hart Crane's *The Bridge*, T. S. Eliot's *The Waste Land*, Wallace Stevens' "The Comedian as the Letter C"), and in novels (James Joyce's *Finnegans Wake*, William Faulkner's *The Sound and the Fury*).

See Arthur Symons, *The Symbolist Movement in Literature* (1899, reprinted 1958); Edmund Wilson, *Axel's Castle* (1936); C. M. Bowra, *The Heritage of Symbolism* (1943); Edward Engelberg, ed., *The Symbolist Poem* (1967); Anna Balakian, ed., *The Symbolist Movement in the Literature of European Languages* (1982); and René Taupin, *The Influence of French Symbolism on Modern American Poetry* (1920, trans. 1985).

**Symbolists: 362**; *129, 231.*

**sympathy: 94**.

**synchronic** (sīnkrŏn′ ĭk): **172**.

**synecdoche** (sīněk′ dōkē): **120**; *121*.

**synesthesia:** Synesthesia, in psychology, signifies the experience of two or more modes of sensation when only one sense is being stimulated. In literature the term is applied to descriptions of one mode of sensation in terms of another; color is attributed to sounds, odor to colors, sound to odors, and so on. We often, for example, speak of loud colors, bright sounds, and sweet music. A complex literary instance of synesthesia (which is sometimes also called "sense transference" or "sense analogy") is this passage from Shelley's "The Sensitive Plant" (1820):

> And the hyacinth purple, and white, and blue,
> Which flung from its bells a sweet peal anew
> Of music so delicate, soft, and intense,
> It was felt like an odor within the sense.

The varicolored, bell-shaped flowers of the hyacinth send out a peal of music which effects a sensation as though it were (what in fact it is) the scent of the flowers. Keats, in the "Ode to a Nightingale" (1819), calls for a draught of wine

> Tasting of Flora and the country green,
> Dance, and Provençal song, and sunburnt mirth;

that is, he calls for a drink tasting of sight, color, motion, sound, and heat.

Occasional uses of synesthetic imagery have been made by poets ever since Homer. Such imagery became much more frequent in the *Romantic Period*, and was especially exploited by the French *Symbolists* of the middle and later nineteenth century; see Baudelaire's sonnet "Correspondences," and Rimbaud's sonnet on the color of vowel sounds "A black, E white, I red, U green, O blue."

Refer to the detailed analyses of literary synesthesia in Richard H. Fogel, *The Imagery of Keats and Shelley* (1949), chapter 3; also Simon Baron-Cohen, *Synaesthesia: Classic and Contemporary Readings* (1996); and John E. Harrison, *Synaesthesia: The Strangest Thing* (2001).

**syntagmatic** (sĭn′ tăgmăt″ ĭk): **176**.

**syntax: 174**.

**syuzhet** (in Russian formalism): **209**.

**tale: 331**.

**tall tale: 149**.

**telling** (in narrative): **43**.

**tenor** (of a metaphor): **119**; *190*.

**tension:** Tension became a common descriptive and evaluative word in the criticism of the 1930s and later, especially after Allen Tate, one of the *New Critics*, proposed it as a term to be made by "lopping the prefixes off the logical terms *ex*tension and *in*tension." In technical logic the "intension" of a word is the set of abstract attributes which must be possessed by any object to which the word can be literally applied, and the "extension" of a word is the class of concrete objects to which the word applies. The meaning of good poetry, according to Tate, "is its 'tension,' the full organized body of all the extension and intension that we can find in it." ("Tension in Poetry," 1938, in *On the Limits of Poetry*, 1948.) It would seem that by this statement Tate meant that a good poem incorporates both the abstract and the concrete, the general idea and the particular image, in an integral whole. (See *concrete and abstract*.)

Other critics use "tension" to characterize poetry that manifests an equilibrium of the serious and the ironic, or "a pattern of resolved stresses," or a harmony of opponent tendencies, or any other mode of that stability-in-opposition which was the favorite way in the *New Criticism* for conceiving the organization of a good poem. And some critics, dubious perhaps about the validity of Tate's logical derivation of the term, simply apply "tension" to any poem in which the elements seem tightly rather than loosely interrelated.

**tercet** (tŭr′ sĕt): **341**.

**terza rima** (tĕr′ tsă rē″ mă): **341**.

**tetrameter** (tĕtrăm′ ĕtĕr): **196**.

**text and writing (écriture):** Traditional critics conceived the object of their critical concern to be a literary "work"; that is, a human product whose form is achieved by its author's design and its meanings by the author's intentional uses of the verbal medium. French *structuralist* critics, on the other hand, depersonalized a literary product by conceiving it to be not a "work," but an impersonal **text**, a manifestation of the social institution called **écriture** (writing). The author is regarded as no more than an intermediary in whom the action of writing precipitates the elements and codes of the pre-existing linguistic and literary system into a particular text. The interpretation of this writing is effected by "lecture" (in French, the process of reading) which, by bringing to bear expectations formed by earlier exposure to the functioning of the linguistic system, invests the marks on the page with what merely seem to be their inherent meanings and references to an outer world. Structuralists differ about the degree to which the activity of reading a text is constrained by the literary conventions and codes that went into the writing; many *deconstructive critics*, however, propose that all writing, by the internal play of opposing forces, necessarily disseminates into an indefinite array of diverse and opposed meanings.

   The system of linguistic and literary conventions that constitute a literary text are said by structuralist and *poststructuralist* critics to be "naturalized" in the activity of reading, in that the artifices of a nonreferential "textuality" are made to seem **vraisemblable** (credible)—that is, made to give the illusion of referring to reality —by being brought into accord with modes of discourse and cultural stereotypes that are so familiar and habitual as to seem natural. **Naturalization** (an alternative term is **recuperation**) takes place through such habitual procedures in reading as assigning the text to a specific *genre*, or taking a fictional text to be the speech of a credibly human narrator, or interpreting its artifices as signifying characters, actions, and values that represent, or accord with, those in an extratextual world. To a thoroughgoing structuralist or poststructuralist critic, however, not only is the text's representation of the world no more than an illusory "effect" generated by the process of reading, but the world is itself held to be in its turn a text; that is, simply a structure of *signs* whose significance is constituted by the cultural conventions, codes, and *ideology* that happen to be shared by members of a cultural community. The term **intertextuality**, popularized especially by Julia Kristeva, is used to signify the multiple ways in which any one literary text is in fact made up of other texts, by means of its open or covert citations and *allusions*, its repetitions and transformations of the formal and substantive features of earlier texts, or simply its unavoidable participation in the common stock of linguistic and literary conventions and procedures that are "always-already" in place and constitute the discourses into which we are born. In Kristeva's formulation, accordingly, any text is in fact an "intertext"—the site of an intersection of numberless other texts, and existing only through its relations to other texts.

Roland Barthes in *S/Z* (1970) proposed a distinction between a text which is "lisible" (readable) and one which, although "scriptible" (writable) is "illisible" (unreadable). Readable texts are traditional or "classical" ones—such as the realistic novels by Honoré Balzac and other nineteenth-century authors—which for the most part conform to the prevailing codes and conventions, literary and social, and so are readily and comfortably interpretable and naturalizable in the process of reading. An "unreadable" text (such as James Joyce's *Finnegans Wake*, or the French *new novel*, or a poem by a highly experimental poet) is one which largely violates, parodies, or innovates upon prevailing conventions, and thus persistently shocks, baffles, and frustrates standard expectations. In Barthes' view an unreadable text, by drawing attention in this way to the pure conventionality and artifice of literature, laudably destroys any illusion that it represents reality. In *The Pleasure of the Text* (published 1973), Barthes assigns to the readable text the response of mere "plaisir" (quasi-erotic pleasure), but to the unreadable text the response of "jouissance" (orgasmic ecstasy); as Jonathan Culler has put Barthes' view, jouissance is "a rapture of dislocation produced by ruptures or violations of intelligibility" (*Structuralist Poetics*, p. 192).

For related matters and relevant bibliographic references, see *structuralist criticism, poststructuralism,* and *semiotics.*

**textual criticism:** Textual criticism expounds the principles and procedures that will establish and validate the text of a literary or other work that an editor prepares and publishes. The theory and practice of textual criticism goes back many centuries. It was applied at first to biblical and classical texts, of which all the surviving manuscripts had been written (and often altered, deliberately or inadvertently) by scribes long after the death of the original writers. Later, textual criticism was adapted to apply to the early era of the printed book, then to later times when editors had access to diverse *editions* of a printed text, and sometimes to differing manuscripts written by the authors themselves, as well as differing transcripts of such manuscripts by various people. (See *book editions* and *book format.*) Until recently the ruling principle, whether explicit or tacit, was that the invariable task of a scholarly editor is to establish, from all the available evidences in manuscript and print, the text that as nearly as possible conforms to the text originally composed by its author.

In the mid-twentieth century, most scholarly editors subscribed to the principles of the **copy-text**, as propounded in a highly influential paper by the English bibliographer W. W. Greg. Greg formulated his views mainly with reference to editing Shakespeare and other Renaissance authors, but the principles he proposed were soon expanded and modified by Fredson Bowers and others to apply al theory later authors and modes of publication and transmission. The Greg-Bowh a single (as it is often called) proposed, as the goal of a scholarly edition, to ntentions" of gle "authoritative" or "definitive" text that represented the "g and revising a the author at the conclusion of his or her process of co isting texts judged work. Editors choose, as the "copy-text," that one rite; usually the copy- to be closest to what the author wrote or inten cases, the author's written text is the earliest printed edition of a work ( e closest to the author's own manuscript of a work), since this is con intentions. This base-text is emended by the editor to eliminate what are judged to be inadvertent errors made by the author in writing out his composition, and also to delete intrusive "substantive" changes (changes in wording) that are judged to have been introduced by other people without the author's "authorization." (Such nonauthorial intrusions and changes in the words of a text, by copy editors, printers, and others, are often labeled "corruptions" or "contaminations" of the original text.) The copy-text is further emended to include any later deletions or additions that the editor judges, from the available evidence, to have been introduced or authorized by the author himself or herself, and that therefore may be assumed to embody the author's "final intentions." The resulting published document (often with copious editorial footnotes and other materials to identify all these emendations and to record the textual "variants" that the editor has rejected) is known as an **eclectic text**, in that it accords with no single existing model, but is constructed by fitting together materials from a variety of texts—materials that are sometimes supplemented by the editor's own conjectures.

Beginning in the late 1920s, two developments helped to bring the copy-text theory under increasing scrutiny and objection. One was the appearance of scholarly publications that made available a multitude of diverse forms of a single literary work, in drafts, manuscripts, transcriptions (sometimes with changes and insertions) by family and friends, and corrected proof sheets, even before the poem was originally published. The many volumes of the *Cornell Wordsworth*, for example, begun in 1975 under the general editorship of Stephen Parrish, record all such variants; for a number of Wordsworth's writings, they also print "reading copies" of the full text at sequential stages in the author's composition and revision of a single work. There are being printed also a number of texts from manuscripts that are versions of works by novelists that were rejected by the author, or radically revised before the final text was published. An early example was *Stephen Hero*, published in 1944, part of the first draft of *A Portrait of the Artist*, which Joyce had published thirty years earlier; other examples are uncut versions from manuscript of F. Scott Fitzgerald's *The Great Gatsby*, Thomas Wolfe's *Look Homeward, Angel*, and Richard Wright's *Native Son*. Another development was the poststructural climate of critical opinion, which brought into radical question the centrality of the "subject," or author, and denied the validity of appealing to the intention of a writer as determinative of text or meaning. A number of poststructural theorists also stressed the role of social factors in "constructing" the meanings of a text, or emphasized the variability in the reception and interpretation of a text over time. (See *author and authorship, poststructuralism,* and *reception theory*.)

Scholarly endeavors at a single, eclectic, and definitive text of a literary work are now often derogated as resulting in an "ideal" text that never in fact existed, the aim to incorporate the inclinations of the editor, labeled as the intentions of McGann. In a *Critique of Modern Textual Criticism* (1983, reissued 1992), Jerome extended his **social theory of textual criticism**, in which he attributes "textual authority" to the cumulative social history of the work, including the contributions not only of the author, but also of the editor, publisher, printer, and all others who operated in bringing into being and producing a book that is made available to the public; all these components, in McGann's view, are valid determinants of a text and its meanings, considered as social constructions. (See *social constructs*, under *new historicism*, and *book history studies*.) In later writings, McGann has stressed also the material features of a book—including its typography, paper, format, and even pricing and advertising—as cooperative with its verbal element in generating its total cultural significance. (See McGann, *The Textual Condition*, 1991; refer also to D. F. McKenzie, *Bibliography and Sociology of Texts*, 1986.) Attempts to edit by reference to an author's final intentions have been brought into further question by the view that most published works are in fact products of **multiple authorship**. See Jack Stillinger's *Multiple Authorship and the Myth of Solitary Genius* (1991), which demonstrates by many examples that the printed text of a work is typically the joint product of a number of participants, including friends, family members, transcribers, literary agents, editors, and printers, in addition to the person who is ordinarily considered to be its sole author.

Despite such critiques, the Greg-Bowers copy-text theory has continued to be defended and applied, although with various modifications, by a number of scholars, most prominently by G. Thomas Tanselle (see his *A Rationale of Textual Criticism*, 1989). Many editors now subscribe to some form of a theory of textual **versions**, of which an early exponent was James Thorpe in *Principles of Textual Criticism* (1972). The growing consensus is that the composition of a literary work is a continuous process without a fixed terminus or perfected state, and that each existing stage, or "version," of the process, whether in manuscript or print, has an equal right to be regarded as a product intended by the author at its particular time. A scholarly editor ought, therefore, to give up the hopeless aim to achieve a single definitive master text of a literary work. Instead, the editor should select and edit that textual "version" of a work that accords with the circumstances of the particular case, and also according to whether the editor's purpose is to approximate what the author wrote, or else to reproduce the printed text, however it came about, as it existed for its readers when it was first published.

For a concise survey of the history of textual theory and criticism, see D. C. Greetham, *Textual Scholarship: An Introduction* (1992). Greetham has also edited, for the Modern Language Association of America, *Scholarly Editing: A Guide to Research* (1995), which includes a survey, written by specialists, of the history and types of scholarly editing applied to classical literature, the Bible, and a number of foreign literatures, as well as to the various periods of English literature. See also, in addition to works cited above: W. W. Greg, "The Rationale for Copy-Text," reprinted in his *Collected Papers*, ed. J. C. Maxwell (1966); Fredson Bowers, *Bibliography and Textual Criticism* (1964); and for subsequent developments, Gary Taylor and Michael Warren, eds., *The Division of the Kingdoms: Shakespeare's Two Versions of "King Lear"* (1983); Donald H. Reiman, *Romantic Texts and Contexts* (1982); George Bornstein and Ralph G. Williams, eds., *Palimpsest: Editorial Theory in the Humanities* (1993). Walter Gabler describes briefly current modes of German and French textual theory and procedures in *The Johns Hopkins Guide to Literary Theory and Criticism*, ed. Michael Groden and Martin Kreiswirth.

For references to *textual criticism* in other entries, see page *63*.

**theater in the round: 58**.

**theater of the absurd: 108**.

**theme: 205**; *79, 117, 152*.

**theodicy** (thē·ŏd′ ĭ·sē): **140**.

**theoretical criticism: 61**.

**theories and movements in recent criticism:** The entry in this *Glossary* on *criticism* describes traditional types of literary theory and of applied criticism from Aristotle through the early twentieth century. Since World War I, and especially since the 1960s, there have appeared a large number of innovative literary theories and methods of critical analysis, including revised and amplified versions of the earlier forms of *Marxist criticism* and *psychoanalytic criticism*. An entry on each of these recent critical modes is included in the *Glossary*, according to the alphabetic order of its title. Following is a table of the approximate time when these modes became prominent in literary criticism:

| | |
|---|---|
| 1920s–1930s | *Russian Formalism* |
| 1930s–1940s | *archetypal criticism* |
| 1940s–1950s | *New Criticism; phenomenological criticism* |
| 1960s | modern forms of *feminist criticism; structuralist criticism; stylistics* |
| 1970s | theory of the *anxiety of influence; deconstruction; discourse analysis*; various forms of *reader-response criticism; reception theory; semiotics; speech-act theory* |
| 1980s | *cultural studies; dialogic criticism; gender criticism; new historicism; queer theory* |
| 1990s | *Darwinian literary studies; ecocriticism; postcolonial studies* |

See the entry *poststructuralism* for current uses of the term "theory," as well as for a description of some critical perspectives and practices shared by a number of the theories that have appeared after the 1960s.

**theory** (in poststructuralism): **280**.

**theory** (in traditional criticism): **61**.

**thesis** (of a literary work): **117**.

**thick descriptions: 219**.

**third-person narrative: 272**.

**three unities:** In the sixteenth and seventeenth centuries, critics of the drama in Italy and France added to Aristotle's *unity of action*, which he describes in his

*Poetics*, two other unities, to constitute one of the so-called *rules* of drama known as "the three unities." On the assumption that **verisimilitude**—the achievement of an illusion of reality in the audience of a stage play—requires that the action represented by a play approximate the actual conditions of the staging of the play, these critics imposed the requirement of the "unity of place" (that the action represented be limited to a single location) and the requirement of the "unity of time" (that the time represented be limited to the two or three hours it takes to act the play, or at most to a single day of either twelve or twenty-four hours). In large part because of the potent example of Shakespeare, many of whose plays represent frequent changes of place and the passage of many years, the unities of place and time never dominated English *neoclassicism* as they did criticism in Italy and France. A final blow was the famous attack against them, and against the principle of dramatic verisimilitude on which they were based, in Samuel Johnson's "Preface to Shakespeare" (1765). Since then in England, the unities of place and time (as distinguished from the unity of action) have been regarded as optional devices, available as needed by the playwright to achieve special effects of dramatic concentration.

See René Wellek, *A History of Modern Criticism*, Vol. 1, *The Later Eighteenth Century* (1955); Bernard Weinberg, *A History of Literary Criticism in the Italian Renaissance* (1961). For references to the *three unities* in other entries, see page *212*.

**threnody** (thrĕn′ ŏdē): **92**.

**tone: 258**.

**topographical poetry:** Topographical poetry, also called **local poetry**, combines the description of a specific natural scene with historical, political, or moral reflections that are associated with the scene or are suggested by its details. Samuel Johnson, in his "Life of John Denham" (1779), attributed its origin to Denham's fine poem *Cooper's Hill*, first written in 1642; as Johnson defines the *genre*, "local poetry" is a species "of which the fundamental subject is some particular landscape to be poetically described, with the addition of such embellishments as may be supplied by historical retrospection or incidental meditation." (See the analysis of a passage from *Cooper's Hill*, under *heroic couplet*.)

This poetic type had an enormous vogue through the eighteenth century; Robert Aubin, in *Topographical Poetry in XVIII-Century England* (1936), lists some two thousand examples. Many of these, like "Cooper's Hill," are **prospect poems** that describe the landscape that is visible from a high point of vantage; notable examples are John Dyer's "Grongar Hill" (1726) and Thomas Gray's "Ode on a Distant Prospect of Eton College" (1747). Local poems were later developed into a major Romantic form, the **descriptive-meditative lyric**, which is characterized by a sustained flow of consciousness; a subtle interweaving of perceptions, thoughts, and feelings; and an integrated design. Early examples are Coleridge's "The Eolian Harp" (1796) and "Frost at Midnight" (1798), and Wordsworth's "Tintern Abbey" (1798); formal variants of the mode include

Coleridge's "Dejection: An Ode" (1802) and Wordsworth's "Ode: Intimations of Immortality" (1807). (See M. H. Abrams, "Structure and Style in the Greater Romantic Lyric," in *The Correspondent Breeze: Essays on English Romanticism*, 1984.)

Related to the topographical poem is the **country house poem**, which had a brief vogue in the seventeenth century. This form describes and praises a rural estate and its grounds, and uses the occasion, by sometimes ingenious connections, to extol also its owner and the owner's family and family history. It was inaugurated by Aemilia Lanyer's "The Description of Cooke-ham" (1611) and Ben Jonson's "To Penshurst" (1616). Andrew Marvell's "Upon Appleton House" (1651) is the longest (776 lines), the most intricately wrought, and the wittiest of the country house poems.

**topos** (tŏp′ ŏs): **205**.

**touchstone:** A touchstone is a hard stone used to determine, by the streak left on it when rubbed by a piece of gold, whether the metal is pure gold, and if not, the degree to which it contains an alloy. The word was introduced into literary criticism by Matthew Arnold in "The Study of Poetry" (1880) to denote short but distinctive passages, selected from the writings of the greatest poets, which he used to determine the relative value of passages or poems which are compared to them. Arnold proposed this method of evaluation as a corrective for what he called the "fallacious" estimates of poems according to their "historic" importance in the development of literature, or else according to their "personal" appeal to an individual critic. As Arnold put it:

> There can be no more useful help for discovering what poetry belongs
> to the class of the truly excellent . . . than to have always in one's
> mind lines and expressions of the great masters, and to apply them as a
> touchstone to other poetry. . . . If we have any tact we shall find them
> . . . an infallible touchstone for detecting the presence or absence of
> high poetic quality, and also the degree of this quality, in all other
> poetry which we may place beside them.

The touchstones he proposed are passages from Homer, Dante, Shakespeare, and Milton, ranging in length from one to four lines. Two of his best-known touchstones are also the shortest: Dante's "In la sua volontade è nostra pace" ("In His will is our peace"; *Paradiso*, III. 85), and the close of Milton's description in *Paradise Lost*, IV, 271–2, of the loss to Ceres of her daughter Proserpine, ". . . which cost Ceres all that pain/To seek her through the world."

**trace** (in deconstruction): **71**.

**traditional ballad: 21**.

**tragedy:** The term is broadly applied to literary, and especially to dramatic, representations of serious actions which eventuate in a disastrous conclusion for the *pro-*

*tagonist* (the chief character). More precise and detailed discussions of the tragic form properly begin—although they should not end—with Aristotle's classic analysis in the *Poetics* (fourth century BC). Aristotle based his theory on induction from the only examples available to him, the tragedies of Greek dramatists such as Aeschylus, Sophocles, and Euripides. In the subsequent two thousand years and more, various new types of serious plots ending in a catastrophe have been developed—types that Aristotle had no way of foreseeing. The many attempts to stretch Aristotle's analysis to apply to later tragic forms serve merely to blur his critical categories and to obscure important differences among a diversity of plays, all of which have proved to be dramatically effective. When flexibly managed, however, Aristotle's discussions apply in some part to many tragic plots, and his analytic concepts serve as a suggestive starting point for identifying the differentiae of various non–Aristotelian modes of tragic construction.

Aristotle defined tragedy as "the imitation of an action that is serious and also, as having magnitude, complete in itself," in the medium of poetic language and in the manner of dramatic rather than of narrative presentation, involving "incidents arousing pity and fear, wherewith to accomplish the catharsis of such emotions." (See *imitation*; and for an enlightening discussion of the emotions, "pity and fear," refer to Martha C. Nussbaum, "Tragedy and Self-Sufficiency: Plato and Aristotle on Fear and Pity," *Oxford Studies in Ancient Philosophy*, Vol. 10, 1992, 107–59.) Precisely how to interpret Aristotle's **catharsis**—which in Greek signifies "purgation," or "purification," or both—is much disputed. On two matters, however, many commentators agree. Aristotle in the first place sets out to account for the undeniable, though remarkable, fact that many tragic representations of suffering and defeat leave an audience feeling not depressed, but relieved, or even exalted. In the second place, Aristotle uses this distinctive effect on the reader, which he calls "the pleasure of pity and fear," as the basic way to distinguish the tragic from comic or other forms, and he regards the dramatist's aim to produce this effect in the highest degree as the principle that determines the choice and moral qualities of the tragic protagonist and the organization of the tragic plot.

Accordingly, Aristotle says that the **tragic hero** will most effectively evoke both our pity and terror if he is neither thoroughly good nor thoroughly bad but a mixture of both; and also that this tragic effect will be stronger if the hero is "better than we are," in the sense that he is of higher than ordinary moral worth. Such a man is exhibited as suffering a change in fortune from happiness to misery because of his mistaken choice of an action, to which he is led by his **hamartia**—his "error" or "mistake of judgment" or, as it is often, although misleadingly and less literally translated, his **tragic flaw**. (One common form of hamartia in Greek tragedies was **hubris**, that "pride" or overweening self-confidence which leads a protagonist to disregard a divine warning or to violate an important moral law.) The tragic hero, like Oedipus in Sophocles' *Oedipus the King*, moves us to pity because, since he is not an evil man, his misfortune is greater than he deserves; but he moves us also to fear, because we recognize similar possibilities of error in our own lesser and fallible selves. Aristotle grounds his analysis of "the very structure and incidents of the play" on the same principle; the plot, he says, which will most effectively evoke "tragic pity and fear" is one in which the events develop through complication to a *catastrophe* in which there occurs (often by an *anagnorisis*, or discovery of facts hitherto unknown to the hero) a sudden *peripeteia*, or reversal in his fortune from happiness to disaster. (See *plot*.)

Authors in the Middle Ages lacked direct knowledge either of classical tragedies or of Aristotle's *Poetics*. **Medieval tragedies** are simply the story of a person of high status who, whether deservedly or not, is brought from prosperity to wretchedness by an unpredictable turn of the wheel of fortune. The short narratives in "The Monk's Tale" of *The Canterbury Tales* (late fourteenth century) are all, in Chaucer's own term, "tragedies" of this kind. With the Elizabethan era came both the beginning and the acme of dramatic tragedy in England. The tragedies of this period owed much to the native religious drama, the *miracle* and *morality plays*, which had developed independently of classical influence, but with a crucial contribution from the Roman writer Seneca (first century), whose dramas got to be widely known earlier than those of the Greek tragedians.

**Senecan tragedy** was written to be recited rather than acted; but to English playwrights, who thought that these tragedies had been intended for the stage, they provided the model for an organized five-act play with a complex plot and an elaborately formal style of dialogue. Senecan drama, in the Elizabethan Age, had two main lines of development. One of these consisted of academic tragedies written in close imitation of the Senecan model, including the use of a *chorus*, and usually constructed according to the rules of the *three unities*, which had been elaborated by Italian critics of the sixteenth century; the earliest English example was Thomas Sackville and Thomas Norton's *Gorboduc* (1562). The other and much more important development was written for the popular stage, and is called the **revenge tragedy**, or (in its most sensational form) the **tragedy of blood**. This type of play derived from Seneca's favorite materials of murder, revenge, ghosts, mutilation, and carnage, but while Seneca had relegated such matters to long reports of offstage actions by messengers, Elizabethan dramatists usually represented them on stage to satisfy the appetite of the contemporary audience for violence and horror. Thomas Kyd's *The Spanish Tragedy* (1586) established this popular form; its subject is a murder and the quest for vengeance, and it includes a ghost, insanity, suicide, a play-within-a-play, sensational incidents, and a gruesomely bloody ending. Christopher Marlowe's *The Jew of Malta* (c. 1592) and Shakespeare's early play *Titus Andronicus* (c. 1590) are in this mode; and from this lively but unlikely prototype came one of the greatest of tragedies, *Hamlet*, as well as John Webster's fine horror plays of 1612–13, *The Duchess of Malfi* and *The White Devil*.

Many major tragedies in the brief flowering time between 1585 and 1625, by Marlowe, Shakespeare, George Chapman, Webster, Sir Francis Beaumont and John Fletcher, and Philip Massinger, deviate radically from the Aristotelian norm. Shakespeare's *Othello* is one of the few plays which accords closely with Aristotle's basic concepts of the tragic hero and plot. The hero of *Macbeth*, however, is not a good man who commits a tragic error, but an ambitious man who knowingly turns great gifts to evil purposes and therefore, although he retains something of our sympathy by his courage and self-insight, deserves his destruction at the hands of his morally superior antagonists. Shakespeare's *Richard III* presents first the success, then the ruin, of a protagonist who is thoroughly malign, yet arouses in us a reluctant admiration by his intelligence and imaginative power and by the shameless candor with which he glories in his ambition and malice. Most Shakespearean tragedies, like Elizabethan tragedies generally, also depart radically from Aristotle's paradigm by introducing humorous characters, incidents, or scenes, called *comic relief*, which were in various ways and degrees made relevant to the tragic plot and conducive to enriching the tragic effect. There developed also in this age the mixed mode called *tragicomedy*, a popular non-Aristotelian form which produced a number of artistic successes. And later in the seventeenth century the Restoration Period produced the curious genre, a cross between epic and tragedy, called *heroic tragedy*.

Until the close of the seventeenth century almost all tragedies were written in verse and had as protagonists men of high rank whose fate affected the fortunes of a state. A few minor Elizabethan tragedies, such as *A Yorkshire Tragedy* (of uncertain authorship), had as the chief character a man of the lower class, but it remained for eighteenth-century writers to popularize the **bourgeois** or **domestic tragedy**, which was written in prose and presented a protagonist from the middle or lower social ranks who suffers a commonplace or domestic disaster. George Lillo's *The London Merchant: or, The History of George Barnwell* (1731), about a merchant's apprentice who succumbs to a heartless courtesan and comes to a bad end by robbing his employer and murdering his uncle, is still read, at least in college courses.

Since that time most of the successful tragedies have been in prose and represent middle-class, or occasionally even working-class, heroes and heroines. The great and highly influential Norwegian playwright, Henrik Ibsen, wrote in the latter part of the nineteenth century tragedies in prose, many of which (such as *A Doll's House, Ghosts, An Enemy of the People*) revolve around an issue of general social or political significance. (See *problem play*.) One of the more notable modern tragedies, Arthur Miller's *Death of a Salesman* (1949), relies for its tragic seriousness on the degree to which Willy Loman, in his bewildered defeat by life, is representative of the ordinary man whose aspirations reflect the false values of a commercial society; the effect on the audience is one of compassionate understanding rather than of tragic pity and terror. The protagonists of some recent tragedies are not heroic but antiheroic, in that they manifest a character that is at an extreme from the dignity and courage of the protagonists in traditional dramas (see *antihero*); while in some recent works, tragic effects involve elements that were once specific to the genre of farce (see literature of the *absurd* and *black comedy*).

Tragedy since World War I has also been innovative in other ways, including experimentation with new versions of ancient tragic forms. Eugene O'Neill's *Mourning Becomes Electra* (1931), for example, is an adaptation of Aeschylus' *Oresteia*, with the locale shifted from Greece to New England, the poetry altered to what is for the most part rather flat prose, and the tragedy of fate converted into a tragedy of the psychological compulsions of a family trapped in a tangle of Freudian complexes (see *psychoanalysis*). T. S. Eliot's *Murder in the Cathedral* (1935) is a tragic drama which, like Greek tragedy, is written in verse and has a chorus, but also incorporates elements of two early Christian forms, the medieval *miracle play* (dealing with the martyrdom of a saint) and the medieval *morality play*. A recent tendency, especially in some critics associated with *new historicism*, has been to interpret traditional tragedies primarily in political terms, as incorporating in the problems and catastrophe of the tragic individual an indirect representation of contemporary social or ideological dilemmas and crises. See Froma I. Zeitlin and John J. Winkler, eds., *Nothing to Do with Dionysos? Athenian Drama in Its Social Context* (1990) and Linda Kintz, *The Subject's Tragedy: Political Poetics, Feminist Theory, and Drama* (1992).

See *genre*, and refer to A. C. Bradley, *Shakespearean Tragedy* (1904); H. D. F. Kitto, *Greek Tragedy* (rev. 1954); Elder Olson, *Tragedy and the Theory of Drama* (1961); George Steiner, *The Death of Tragedy* (1961); R. B. Sewall, ed., *Tragedy: Modern Essays in Criticism* (1963). For recent theoretical treatments of tragedy, see Linda Bamber, *Comic Women, Tragic Men: A Study of Gender and Genre in Shakespeare* (1982); and Catherine Belsey, *The Subject of Tragedy: Identity and Difference in Renaissance Drama* (1985). Richard H. Palmer, *Tragedy and Tragic Theory: An Analytical Guide* (1992), is a useful survey of contested issues in the theory and criticism of tragedy, with many quotations by theorists from the ancient Greeks to the present. For references to *tragedy* in other entries, see pages *14, 304, 374*. See also *heroic drama; tragic irony; tragicomedy.*

**tragedy of blood: 372**.

**tragic flaw: 371**; *270*.

**tragic hero: 371**.

**tragic irony: 167**.

**tragicomedy:** A type of *Elizabethan* and *Jacobean* drama which intermingled the standard characters and subject matter and the typical plot forms of *tragedy* and *comedy*. Thus, the important agents in tragicomedy included both people of high degree and people of low degree, even though, according to the reigning critical theory of that time, only upper-class characters were appropriate to tragedy, while members of the middle and lower classes were the proper subject solely of comedy; see *decorum*. Also, tragicomedy represented a serious action which threatened a tragic disaster to the protagonist, yet, by an abrupt reversal of circumstance, turned out happily. As John Fletcher wrote in his preface to *The Faithful Shepherdess* (c. 1610), tragicomedy "wants [that is, lacks] deaths, which is enough to make it no tragedy, yet brings some near it, which is enough to make it no comedy, which must be a representation of familiar people. . . . A god is as lawful in [tragicomedy] as in a tragedy, and mean [that is, middle-class] people as in a comedy." (See *comedy* and *tragedy*.)

Shakespeare's *Merchant of Venice* is by these criteria a tragicomedy, because it mingles people of the aristocracy with lower-class characters (such as the Jewish merchant Shylock and the clown Launcelot Gobbo), and also because the developing threat of death to Antonio is suddenly reversed at the end by Portia's ingenious casuistry in the trial scene. Francis Beaumont and John Fletcher in *Philaster*, and numerous other plays on which they collaborated from about 1606 to 1613, inaugurated a mode of tragicomedy that employs a romantic and fast-moving plot of love, jealousy, treachery, intrigue, and disguises, and ends in a melodramatic reversal of fortune for the protagonists, who had hitherto seemed headed for a tragic *catastrophe*. Shakespeare wrote his late plays *Cymbeline* and *The Winter's Tale*, between 1609 and 1611, in this very popular mode of the tragicomic *romance*. The name "tragicomedy" is sometimes also applied more loosely to plays with double plots, one serious and the other comic; see *double plots*, under *plot*.

Refer to E. M. Waith, *The Pattern of Tragicomedy in Beaumont and Fletcher* (1952); M. T. Herrick, *Tragicomedy* (1955). Gordon McMullan and Jonathan Hope have edited a collection of recent essays on *The Politics of Tragicomedy: Shakespeare and After* (1992).

**Transcendental Club: 375**.

**transcendental signified: 71**.

**Transcendentalism in America:** A philosophical and literary movement, centered in Concord and Boston, which was prominent in the intellectual and cultural life of New England from 1836 until just before the Civil War. It was inaugurated in 1836 by a Unitarian discussion group that came to be called the **Transcendental Club**. In the seven years or so that the group met at various houses, it included at one time or another Ralph Waldo Emerson, Bronson Alcott, Frederick Henry Hedge, W. E. Channing and W. H. Channing, Theodore Parker, Margaret Fuller, Elizabeth Peabody, George Ripley, Nathaniel Hawthorne, Henry Thoreau, and Jones Very. A quarterly periodical *The Dial* (1840–44) printed many of the early essays, poems, and reviews by the Transcendentalists.

Transcendentalism was neither a systematic nor a sharply definable philosophy, but rather an intellectual mode and emotional mood that was expressed by diverse, and in some instances rather eccentric, voices. Modern historians of the movement tend to take as its central exponents Emerson (especially in *Nature*, "The American Scholar," the Divinity School Address, "The Over-Soul," and "Self Reliance") and Thoreau (especially in *Walden* and his journals). The term "transcendental," as Emerson pointed out in his lecture "The Transcendentalist" (1841), was taken from the writings of the German philosopher Immanuel Kant (1724–1804). Kant had confined the expression "transcendental knowledge" to the cognizance of those forms and categories—such as space, time, quantity, causality—which, in his view, are imposed on whatever we perceive by the constitution of the human mind. Emerson and others, however, extended the concept of transcendental knowledge, in a way whose validity Kant had specifically denied, to include an intuitive cognizance of moral and other truths that transcend the limits of sense experience. The intellectual antecedents of American Transcendentalism, in addition to Kant, were many and diverse, and included post-Kantian German Idealists, the English thinkers Samuel Taylor Coleridge and Thomas Carlyle (themselves exponents of forms of German Idealism), Plato and Neoplatonists, the occult Swedish theologian Emanuel Swedenborg, and some varieties of Asian philosophy.

What the various Transcendentalists had in common was less what they proposed than what they were reacting against. By and large, they were opposed to rigid rationalism; to eighteenth-century empirical philosophy of the school of John Locke, which derived all knowledge from sense impressions; to highly formalized religion, especially the Calvinist orthodoxy of New England; and to the social conformity, materialism, and commercialism that they found increasingly dominant in American life. Among the counterviews that were affirmed by Transcendentalists, especially Emerson, were confidence in the validity of a mode of knowledge that is grounded in feeling and intuition, and a consequent tendency to accept what, to logical reasoning, might seem contradictions; an ethics of individualism that stressed self-trust, self-reliance, and self-sufficiency; a turn away from modern society, with its getting and spending, to the scenes and objects of the natural world, which were regarded both as physical entities and as correspondences to aspects of the human spirit (see *correspondences*); and, in place of a formal or doctrinal religion, a faith in a divine "Principle," or "Spirit," or "Soul" (Emerson's "Over-Soul") in which both humanity and the cosmos participate. This omnipresent Spirit, Emerson said, constitutes the "Unity within which every man's particular being is contained and made one with all other"; it manifests itself to human consciousness as influxes of inspired insights; and it is the source of the profoundest truths and the necessary condition of all moral and spiritual development.

*Walden* (1854) records how Thoreau tested his distinctive and radically individualist version of Transcendental values by withdrawing from societal complexities and distractions to a life of solitude and self-reliance in a natural setting at Walden Pond. He simplified his material wants to those he could satisfy by the bounty of the woods and lake or could provide by his own labor, attended minutely to natural objects both for their inherent interest and as correlatives to the mind of the observer, and devoted his leisure to reading, meditation, and writing. In his nonconformity to any social and legal requirements that violated his moral sense, he chose a day in jail rather than pay his poll tax to a government that supported the Mexican War and slavery. Brook Farm, on the other hand, was a short-lived experiment (1841–47) by more community-oriented Transcendentalists who established a commune on the professed principle of the equal sharing of work, pay, and cultural benefits. Hawthorne, who lived there for a while, later wrote about Brook Farm, with considerable skepticism about both its goals and practices, in *The Blithedale Romance* (1852).

The Transcendental movement, with its optimism about the indwelling divinity, self-sufficiency, and high potentialities of human nature, did not survive the crisis of the Civil War and its aftermath; and Herman Melville, like Nathaniel Hawthorne, satirized aspects of Transcendentalism in his fiction. Some of its basic concepts and values, however, were assimilated by Walt Whitman, were later echoed in writings by Henry James and other major American authors, and continue to re-emerge, in both liberal and radical modes, in latter-day

America. The voice of Thoreau, for example, however distorted, can be recognized still in some doctrines of the *counterculture* of the 1960s and later.

See *periods of American literature*, and refer to F. O. Matthiessen, *American Renaissance* (1941); the anthology edited, together with commentary, by Perry Miller, *The Transcendentalists* (1950); Joel Porte, *Emerson and Thoreau: Transcendentalists in Conflict* (1966); Lawrence Buell, *Literary Transcendentalism: Style and Vision in the American Renaissance* (1973). For a collection of writings on transcendentalism, see Perry Miller, ed., *Transcendentalists: An Anthology* (1971), and Joel Myerson, ed., *Transcendentalism: A Reader* (2000). See also *Encyclopedia of Transcendentalism*, ed. Wesley T. Mott (1996).

**transformational-generative grammar: 176**.

**transformational linguistics: 176**.

**travesty: 37**.

**trickster: 9**.

**trimeter** (trĭm′ ĕter): **196**.

**triple rhyme: 317**.

**triplet: 341**.

**trochaic** (trōkā′ ĭk): **195**.

**trope** (figurative) (trōp): **118**; *149, 312*.

**trope** (liturgical): **200**.

**troubadour: 60**.

**truth** (in fiction): **117**.

**type** (in biblical interpretation): **162**.

**type** (in characters): **43**.

**typological interpretation: 162**.

**ubi sunt motif** (oo′ bē sŭnt mōtēf″): **205**.

**understatement: 149**.

**unintrusive** (narrator): **273**.

**unities, three: 329**.

**unity of action: 266**.

**unreliable narrator: 276**.

**unstable irony: 166**.

**utopias and dystopias:** The term **utopia** designates the class of fictional writings that represent an ideal, nonexistent political and social way of life. It derives from *Utopia* (1515–16), a book written in Latin by the Renaissance humanist Sir Thomas More which describes a perfect commonwealth; More formed his title by conflating the Greek words "eutopia" (good place) and "outopia" (no place). The first and greatest instance of the literary type was Plato's *Republic* (later fourth century BC), which sets forth, in dialogue, the eternal Idea, or Form, of a perfect commonwealth that can at best be merely approximated by political organizations in the actual world. Most of the later utopias, like that of Sir Thomas More, represent their ideal state in the fiction of a distant country reached by a venturesome traveler. There have been many utopias written since More gave impetus to the genre, some as mere Arcadian dreams, others intended as blueprints for social and technological improvements in the actual world. They include Tommaso Campanella's *City of the Sun* (1623), Francis Bacon's *New Atlantis* (1627), Edward Bellamy's *Looking Backward* (1888), William Morris' *News from Nowhere* (1891), Charlotte Perkins Gilman's *Herland* (1915), and James Hilton's *Lost Horizon* (1934).

The utopia can be distinguished from literary representations of imaginary places which, either because they are inordinately superior to the present world or manifest exaggerated versions of some of its unsavory aspects, serve primarily as vehicles for *satire* on contemporary human life and society; notable examples are the fourth book of Swift's *Gulliver's Travels* (1726) and Samuel Butler's *Erewhon* (1872). Samuel Johnson's *Rasselas* (1759) presents the "Happy Valley," which functions as a gentle satire on humanity's stubborn but hopeless dream of a utopia. Not only does Rasselas discover that no mode of life available in this world guarantees happiness; he also realizes that the utopian satisfaction of all human wishes in the Happy Valley merely replaces the unhappiness of frustrated desires with the unhappiness of boredom; see chapters 1–3.

The term **dystopia** ("bad place") has recently come to be applied to works of fiction, including science fiction, that represent a very unpleasant imaginary world in which ominous tendencies of our present social, political, and technological order are projected into a disastrous future culmination. Examples are Aldous Huxley's *Brave New World* (1932), George Orwell's *Nineteen Eighty-Four* (1949), and Margaret Atwood's *The Handmaid's Tale* (1986). Cormac McCarthy's *The Road* (2006), set in a bleak, postnuclear landscape, represents a dystopian extreme. Ursula K. Le Guin's *The Dispossessed: An Ambiguous Utopia* (1974) contains both utopian and dystopian scenarios.

For utopias and dystopias based on future developments in science and technology, see *science fiction*. Refer to Karl Mannheim, *Ideology and Utopia* (1934); Chad Walsh, *From Utopia to Nightmare* (1962); Nell Eurich, *Science in Utopia* (1967); Frank E. Manuel and Fritzie P. Manuel, *Utopian Thought in the Western World* (1979). For collections of Utopian writings, see *Utopian Literature: A Selection*, ed. J. W. Johnson (1968), and *The Utopia Reader*, ed. Gregory Claeys and Lyman Tower Sargent (1999). Francis Bartkowski has analyzed *Feminist Utopias* (1989), from Charlotte Perkins Gilman's *Herland* (1915) to the present.

**variorum edition** (văr ēor′ ŭm): **32**.

**Varronian satire** (vărō′ nian): **321**.

**vehicle** (of a metaphor): **119**; *190*.

**verbal irony: 165**.

**verbal meaning: 160**.

**vellum: 30**.

**verisimilitude** (věr′ ĭsĭmĭl″ ĭtood): **369**.

**vers de société** (věr′ dě sōsyātā″): **171**.

**vers libre** (věr lē′ br): **129**.

**verse: 194**.

**verse paragraph: 29**.

**versification: 289**; *84*.

**versions** (of a text): **367**.

**verso** (vŭr′ sō): **32**.

**Vice** (the character): **201**.

**Victorian and Victorianism:** In its value-neutral use, "Victorian" simply identifies the historical era in England roughly coincident with the reign of Queen Victoria, 1837–1901. (See *Victorian period*, under *periods of English literature*.) It was a time of rapid and wrenching economic and social changes that had no parallel in earlier history—changes that made small-scale England, in the course of the nineteenth century, the leading industrial power, with an empire that occupied more than a quarter of the earth's surface. The pace and depth of such developments, while they fostered a mood of nationalist pride and optimism about future progress, also produced social stresses, class conflicts, and widespread anxiety about the ability of the nation and the individual to cope, socially, politically, and psychologically, with the cumulative problems of the age.

England was the first nation to exploit the technological possibilities of steam power and steel, but its unregulated industrialization, while it produced great wealth for an expanding middle class, led also to the deterioration of rural England, a mushroom growth of often shoddy urbanization, and massive poverty concentrated in slum neighborhoods. Charles Darwin's theory of evolution (*On the Origin of Species* was published in 1859), together with the extension into all intellectual areas of **positivism** (the view that all valid knowledge must be based on the methods of empirical investigation established by the natural sciences), engendered sectarian controversy, doubts about the truth of religious beliefs, and in some instances, a reversion to strict biblical fundamentalism. Contributing to the social and political unrest was what was labeled "the woman question"; that is, the early *feminist* agitation for equal status and rights.

The Victorian age, for all its conflicts and anxieties, was one of immense, variegated, and often self-critical intellectual and literary activities. In our time, the term "Victorian," and still more **Victorianism**, is frequently used in a derogatory way, to connote narrow-mindedness, sexual priggishness, the determination to maintain feminine "innocence" (that is, sexual ignorance), and an emphasis on social respectability. Such views have a valid basis in attitudes and values expressed (and sometimes exemplified) by many members of the expanding middle class, with its roots in Puritanism and its insecurity about its newly won status. Later criticism of such Victorian attitudes, however, merely echo the vigorous attacks and devastating ridicule mounted against prevailing beliefs and attitudes by a number of thinkers and literary authors in the Victorian age itself.

Refer to G. M. Young, *Victorian England: Portrait of an Age* (republished 1977); David Thomson, *England in the Nineteenth Century* (1950); Jerome Buckley, *The Victorian Temper* (1951); W. E. Houghton, *The Victorian Frame of Mind* (1957). On Victorian attitudes to love and sexuality see Peter Gay, *The Bourgeois Experience, Victoria to Freud* (Vol. 1, *Education of the Senses*, 1984; Vol. 2, *The Tender Passion*, 1986); and on the undercover aspect of Victorian sexual life, Steven Marcus, *The Other Victorians* (republished 1974).

**Victorian Period: 255**; *169, 188, 379.*

**Victorianism: 380**.

**villain** (in a plot): **265**.

**villanelle** (vĭl′ ănĕl″): **343**; *171*.

**voice** (in a literary work): **259**; *262*.

**vraisemblable** (vrā′ sŏmblä″ bl): **364**.

**wilderness romance: 89**.

**wit, humor, and the comic:** At present both "wit" and "humor" designate species of the **comic**; that is, any element in a work of literature, whether a character, event, or utterance, which is designed to amuse or to excite mirth in the reader or audience. The words "wit" and "humor," however, had a variety of meanings in earlier literary criticism, and a brief comment on their history will help to clarify the differences between them in present usage.

The term "wit" once signified the human faculty of intelligence, inventiveness, and mental acuity, a sense it still retains in the term "half-wit." In the sixteenth and seventeenth centuries it came to be used also for ingenuity in literary invention, and especially for the ability to develop brilliant, surprising, and paradoxical figures of speech; hence "wit" was often applied to the figurative language in what we now call *metaphysical poetry*. And in the eighteenth century there were attempts to distinguish the **false wit** of Abraham Cowley and other metaphysical stylists, who were said to aim at a merely superficial dazzlement, and "true wit," regarded as the apt rephrasing of truths whose enduring validity is attested by the fact that they are universal commonplaces. Thus Alexander Pope defined "true wit" in his *Essay on Criticism* (1711) as "What oft was thought, but ne'er so well expressed." (See *neoclassic*.)

The most common present use of the term derives from its seventeenth-century application to a brilliant and paradoxical style. **Wit**, that is, now denotes a kind of verbal expression which is brief, deft, and intentionally contrived to produce a shock of comic surprise; a typical form is that of the *epigram*. The surprise is usually the result of a connection or distinction between words or concepts which frustrates the listener's expectation, only to satisfy it in an unexpected way. Philip Guedalla wittily said: "History repeats itself. Historians repeat each other." Thus the trite comment about history turns out to be unexpectedly appropriate, with an unlooked-for turn of meaning, to the writers of history as well. The film actress Mae West once remarked: "Too much of a good thing can be—*wonderful*." The resulting laughter, in a famous phrase of the German philosopher Immanuel Kant, arises "from the sudden transformation of a strained expectation into nothing"; it might be more precise to say, however, "from the sudden satisfaction of an expectation, but in a way we did not expect."

Mae West's remark is what the *psychoanalyst* Sigmund Freud called "harmless wit," which evokes a laugh or smile that is without malice. What Freud distinguished as "tendency wit," on the other hand, is aggressive: it is a derisive and derogatory turn of phrase, directing the laugh at a particular person or butt. "Mr. James Payn," in Oscar Wilde's barbed comment on a novelist of the 1890s, "hunts down the obvious with the enthusiasm of a short-sighted detective. As one turns over the pages, the suspense of the author becomes almost unbearable."

**Repartee** is a term taken from fencing to signify a contest of wit, in which each person tries to cap the remark of the other, or to turn it to his or her own advantage. Attacking his opponent Disraeli in Parliament, Gladstone remarked that "the honorable gentleman will either end on the gallows or die of some loathsome disease." To which Disraeli rejoined: "That depends on whether I embrace the honorable gentleman's principles or his mistresses." *Restoration comedies* often included episodes of sustained repartee; a classic example is the give and take in the discussion of their coming marriage by the witty lovers Mirabel and Millamant in William Congreve's *The Way of the World* (1700), Act IV.

"Humor" is a term that goes back to the ancient theory that the particular mixture of the *four humours* determines each type of personality, and from the derivative application of the term "humorous" to one of the comically eccentric characters in the Elizabethan *comedy of humours*. As we now use the word, **humor** may be ascribed either to a comic utterance or to a comic appearance or mode of behavior. In a useful distinction between the two terms, a humorous utterance may be said to differ from a witty utterance in one or both of two ways: (1) wit, as we saw, is always intended by the speaker to be comic, but many utterances that we find comically humorous are intended by the speakers themselves to be serious; and (2) a humorous saying is not cast in the neatly epigrammatic form of a witty saying. For example, the chatter of the old Nurse in Shakespeare's *Romeo and Juliet* is verbose, and humorous to the audience, but not to the speaker; similarly, the discussion of the mode of life of the goldfish in Central Park by the inarticulate and irascible taxi driver in J. D. Salinger's *The Catcher in the Rye* (1951) is unintentionally but richly humorous, and is not cast in the form of a witty turn of phrase.

More important still is the difference that wit refers only to the spoken or written word, while humor has a much broader range of reference. We find humor, for example, in the way Charlie Chaplin looks, dresses, and acts, and also in the sometimes wordless cartoons in *The New Yorker*. In a thoroughly humorous situation, the sources of the fun may be complex. In Act III, Scene iv of Shakespeare's *Twelfth Night*, Malvolio's appearance and actions, and his utterances as well, are humorous, but all despite his own very solemn intentions; and our comic enjoyment is increased by our knowledge of the suppressed hilarity of the plotters who are hidden auditors onstage. The greatness of a comic creation like Shakespeare's Falstaff is that he exploits the full gamut of comic possibilities. Falstaff is humorous in the way he looks and in what he does; what he says is sometimes witty, and at most other times humorous; while his actions and speech are sometimes unintentionally humorous, sometimes intentionally humorous, and not infrequently—as in his whimsical account to his skeptical auditors of how heroically he bore himself in the highway robbery, in the second act of *1 Henry IV* —they are humorous even beyond his intention.

One other point should be made about humor and the comic. In normal use, the term "humor" refers to what is purely comic: it evokes, as it is sometimes said, sympathetic laughter, or else laughter which is an end in itself. If we extend Freud's distinction between harmless and tendency wit, we can say that humor is a "harmless" form of the comic. There is, however, another mode of the comic that might be called "tendency comedy," in which we are made to laugh at a person not merely because he is ridiculous, but because he is being ridiculed— the laughter is derisive, with some element of contempt or malice, and serves as a weapon against its subject. Tendency comedy and tendency wit, rather than humor, are among the devices that a writer most exploits in *satire*, the literary art of derogating by deriding a subject.

On the alternative use of the term "comic" to define the formal features of a type of dramatic or narrative plot, see *comedy*; on the form of humor-in-horror in some present-day literature, see *black humor*. For diverse theories of wit, humor, and the comic, together with copious examples, refer to Sigmund Freud, *Wit and Its Relation to the Unconscious* (1916); Max Eastman, *Enjoyment of Laughter* (1936); D. H. Monro, *The Argument of Laughter* (1951); Louis Kronenberger, *The Thread of Laughter* (1952); Stuart M. Tave, *The Amiable Humorist* (1960); Jerry Palmer, *Taking Humor Seriously* (1994).

# Index of Authors

This Index lists significant references to authors; it does not include passing references or the authors listed for supplementary reading. Following each name are the page numbers of general references and then, in alphabetic sequence, the page numbers of references to works written by the author.